KU-369-838

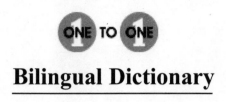

Bilingual Dictionary

English-Chinese (Mandarin) Chinese (Mandarin)-English Dictionary

Compiled by
Yinghong Shang & Ruihua Yao

STAR Foreign Language BOOKS
55, Warren Street, LONDON W1T 5NW (UK)

Buckinghamshire County Council	
06 663 278 2	
Askews & Holts	Feb-2012
R495.1321	£17.95

© Publishers

All rights reserved with the Publishers. No part of this publication may be reproduced or transmitted in any form or by any means, electronic, mechanical, photocopying, recording or otherwise, without the prior written permission of the Publishers.

First Edition: 2011

Published
STAR Foreign Language BOOKS
55, Warren Street, LONDON W1T 5NW (UK)
E-mail : starbooksuk@aol.com
www.foreignlanguagebooks.co.uk

Printed in India at
Star Print-O-Bind, New Delhi-110020

About this Dictionary

Developments in science and technology today have narrowed down distances between countries, and have made the world a small place. A person living thousands of miles away can learn and understand the culture and lifestyle of another country with ease and without travelling to that country. Languages play an important role as facilitators of communocation in this respect.

To promote such an understanding, **STAR Foreign Language BOOKS** *has planned to bring out a series of bilingual dictionaries in which important English words have been translated into other languages, with Roman transliteration in case of languages that have different scripts. This is a humble attempt to bring people of the word closer through the medium of language, thus making communication esay and convenient.*

These dictionaries have been compiled and edited by teachers and scholars of relative languages.

Bilingual Dictionaries in this Series

English-Amharic / Amharic-English	Aschalew Mekonnen Bekele
English-Arabic / Arabic-English	Rania-al-Qass
English-Bengali / Bengali-English	Amit Majumdar
English-Bosnian / Bosnian-English	Boris Kazanegra
English-Cantonese / Cantonese-English	Nisa Yang
English-Chinese (Mandarin) / Chinese (Mandarin)-Eng	Y. Shang & R. Yao
English-Croatian / Croatin-English	Vesna Kazanegra
English-Dari / Dari-English	Amir Khan
English-Estonian / Estonian-English	Lana Haleta
English-Farsi / Farsi-English	Maryam Zaman Khani
English-Gujarati / Gujarati-English	Sujata Basaria
English-Hindi / Hindi-English	Sudhakar Chaturvedi
English-Hungarian / Hungarian-English	Lucy Mallows
English-Latvian / Latvian-English	Julija Baranovska
English-Lithuanian / Lithuanian-English	Regina Kazakeviciute
English-Marathi / Marathi-English	Sahard Thackerey
English-Nepali / Nepali-English	Anil Mandal
English-Pashto / Pashto-English	Amir Khan
English-Polish / Polish-English	Magdalena Herok
English-Punjabi / Punjabi-English	Teja Singh Chatwal
English-Romanian / Romanian-English	Georgeta Laura Dutulescu
English-Serbian / Serbian-English	Vesna Kazanegra
English-Slovak / Slovak-English	Zozana Horvathova
English-Somali / Somali-English	Ali Mohamud Omer
English-Tamil / Tamil-English	Sandhya Mahadevan
English-Thai / Thai-English	Suwan Kaewkongpan
English-Turkish / Turkish-English	Nagme Yazgin
English-Urdu / Urdu-English	S. A. Rahman
English-Vietnamese / Vietnamese-English	Hoa Hoang

More languages in print

STAR Foreign Language BOOKS
55, Warren Street, LONDON W1T 5NW (UK)

ENGLISH-CHINESE (MANDARIN)

A

a *a.* 一 yī
aback *adv.* 向后 xiàng hòu
abaction *n* 强抢 qiáng qiǎng
abactor *n* 强抢者 qiáng qiǎng zhě
abandon *v.t.* 遗弃 yí qì
abase *v.t.* 屈从 qū cóng
abasement *n* 屈从 qū cóng
abash *v.t.* 使羞愧 shǐ xiū kuì
abate *v.t.* 减轻 jiǎn qīng
abatement *n.* 减轻 jiǎn qīng
abbey *n.* 修道院 xiū dào yuàn
abbreviate *v.t.* 缩写 suō xiě
abbreviation *n* 缩写 suō xiě
abdicate *v.t,* 放弃 fàng qì
abdication *n* 放弃 fàng qì
abdomen *n* 腹部 fù bù
abdominal *a.* 腹部的 fù bù de
abduct *v.t.* 诱拐 yòu guǎi
abduction *n* 诱拐 yòu guǎi
abed *adv.* 在床上 zài chuáng shàng
aberrance *n.* 反常 fǎn cháng
abet *v.t.* 教唆 jiào suō
abetment *n.* 教唆 jiào suō
abeyance *n.* 搁置 gē zhì
abhor *v.t.* 恨 hèn
abhorrence *n.* 恨 hèn
abide *v.i* 容忍 róng rěn
abiding *a* 永恒的 yǒng héng de
ability *n* 能力 néng lì
abject *a.* 卑微 bēi wēi
ablactate *v.t* 戒奶 jiè nǎi
ablactation *n* 戒奶 jiè nǎi
ablaze *adv.* 着火 zháo huǒ
able *a* 可以 ké yǐ
ablepsy *n* 失明 shī míng
ablush *adv* 脸红 liǎn hóng
ablution *n* 洗澡 xí zǎo
abnegate *v.t* 否认 fǒu rèn
abnegation *n* 否认 fǒu rèn
abnormal *a* 不正常 bú zhèng cháng
aboard *adv.* 上车 shàng chē

abode *n* 住所 zhù suǒ
abolish *v.t.* 废除 fèi chú
abolition *v* 废除 fèi chú
abominable *a* 讨厌 tǎo yàn
aboriginal *a* 本地 běn dì
aborigines *n. pl* 原住民 yuán zhù mín
abort *v.i* 终止 zhōng zhǐ
abortion *n* 堕胎 duò tāi
abortive *adj* 失败的 shī bài de
abound *v.i.* 充足 chōng zú
about *adv* 大概 dà gài
about *prep* 关于 guān yú
above *adv* 以上 yǐ shàng
above *prep.* 上面 shàng mian
abreast *adv* 并肩 bìng jiān
abridge *v.t* 删节 shān jié
abridgement *n* 摘要 zhāi yào
abroad *adv* 出国 chū guó
abrogate *v.t.* 废除 fèi chú
abrupt *a* 突然的 tū rán de
abruption *n* 中断 zhōng duàn
abscess *n* 脓肿 nóng zhǒng
absonant *adj* 不一致 bù yí zhì
abscond *v.i* 逃走 táo zǒu
absence *n* 缺席 quē xí
absent *a* 缺席 quē xí
absent *v.t* 缺席 quē xí
absolute *a* 绝对 jué duì
absolutely *adv* 绝对 jué duì
absolve *v.t* 解除 jiě chú
absorb *v.t* 吸收 xī shōu
abstain *v.i.* 戒 jiè
abstract *a* 抽象 chōu xiàng
abstract *n* 摘要 zhāi yào
abstract *v.t* 抽出 chōu chū
abstraction *n.* 抽象的概念 chōu xiàng de gài niàn
absurd *a* 荒谬 huāng miù
absurdity *n* 荒谬 huāng miù
abundance *n* 充足 chōng zú
abundant *a* 充足的 chōng zú de
abuse *v.t.* 虐待 nüè dài
abuse *n* 滥用 làn yòng
abusive *a* 侮辱的 wú rǔ de
abutted *v* 紧靠 jǐn kào
abyss *n* 深处 shēn chù

academic *a* 学术的 xué shù
de

academy *n* 学院 xué yuàn

acarpous *adj.* 无果的植物
wú guǒ de zhí wù

accede *v.t.* 同意 tóng yì

accelerate *v.t* 加速 jiā sù

acceleration *n* 加速 jiā sù

accent *n* 口音 kǒu yīn

accent *v.t* 强调 qiáng diào

accept *v* 接受 jiē shòu

acceptable *a* 可以接受的
ké yǐ jiē shòu de

acceptance *n* 接受 jiē shòu

access *n* 用 yòng

accession *n* 就任 jiù rèn

accessory *n* 饰物 shì wù

accident *n* 意外 yì wài

accidental *a* 不小心 bù xiǎo
xīn

acclaim *v.t* 称赞 chēng zàn

acclaim *n* 称赞 chēng zàn

acclamation *n* 欢呼 huān hū

acclimatise *v.t* 适应 shì yìng

accommodate *v.t* 容纳 róng
nà

accommodation *n.* 住宿
zhù sù

accompaniment *n* 伴奏 bàn
zòu

accompany *v.t.* 陪伴 péi bàn

accomplice *n* 帮凶 bāng
xiōng

accomplish *v.t.* 完成 wán
chéng

accomplished *a* 完成了的
wán chéng le de

accomplishment *n.* 成就
chéng jiù

accord *v.t.* 符合 fú hé

accordingly *adv.* 按照 àn zhào

account *n.* 账号 zhàng hào

account *v.t.* 说明 shuō míng

accountable *a* 有责任 yǒu
zé rèn

accountancy *n.* 会计学 kuài
jì xué

accountant *n.* 会计 kuài jì

accredit *v.t.* 委任 wěi rèn

accrementition *n* 增长 zēng
zhǎng

accrete *v.t.* 增加 zēng jiā

accrue *v.i.* 增值 zēng zhí

accumulate *v.t.* 积累 jī lěi

accumulation *n* 积累 jī lěi

accuracy *n.* 准确性 zhǔn què
xìng

accurate *a.* 准确的 zhǔn què
de

accursed *a.* 被诅咒的 bèi zǔ
zhòu de

accusation *n* 控告 kòng gào

accuse *v.t.* 控告 kòng gào

accused *n.* 被告 bèi gào

accustom *v.t.* 使习惯 shǐ xí
guàn

accustomed *a.* 习惯于 xí
guàn yú

ace *n* 高手 gāo shǒu

acentric *adj* 不正常 bú zhèng
cháng

acephalous *adj.* 没有头的
méi yǒu tóu de

acephalus *n.* 无头怪胎 wú
tóu guài tāi

acetify *v.* 醋化 cù huà

ache *n.* 疼痛 téng tòng

ache *v.i.* 疼痛 téng tòng

achieve *v.t.* 实现 shí xiàn

achievement *n.* 成就 chéng
jiù

achromatic *adj* 无色的 wú sè de
acid *a* 酸的 suān de
acid *n* 酸 suān
acidity *n.* 酸性 suān xìng
acknowledge *v.* 承认 chéng rèn
acknowledgement *n.* 承认 chéng rèn
acne *n* 粉刺 fěn cì
acorn *n.* 橡子 xiàng zǐ
acoustic *a* 声音的 shēng yīn de
acoustics *n.* 音响效果 yīn xiǎng xiào guǒ
acquaint *v.t.* 熟悉 shú xī
acquaintance *n.* 熟人 shú rén
acquest *n* 取得 qǔ dé
acquiesce *v.i.* 默认 mò rèn
acquiescence *n.* 默认 mò rèn
acquire *v.t.* 获得 huò dé
acquirement *n.* 才能 cái néng
acquisition *n.* 获得 huò dé
acquit *v.t.* 宣判无罪 xuān pàn wú zuì
acquittal *n.* 无罪的判决 wú zuì de pàn jué
acre *n.* 英亩 yīng mǔ
acreage *n.* 英亩数 yīng mǔ shù
acrimony *n* 尖刻 jiān kè
acrobat *n.* 杂技演员 zá jì yǎn yuán
across *adv.* 穿过 chuān guò
across *prep.* 对面 duì miàn
act *n.* 行为 xíng wéi
act *v.i.* 演 yǎn
acting *n.* 演出 yǎn chū
action *n.* 动作 dòng zuò
activate *v.t.* 使活化 shǐ huó huà
active *a.* 活跃的 huó yuè de
activity *n.* 活动 huó dòng
activity *n.* 活动 huó dòng
actor *n.* 演员 yǎn yuán
actress *n.* 女演员 nǔ yǎnyuán

actual *a.* 真实的 zhēn shí de
actually *adv.* 实际上 shí jì shàng
acumen *n.* 敏锐 mǐn ruì
acute *a.* 尖锐的 jiān ruì de
adage *n.* 谚语 yàn yǔ
adamant *a.* 坚决的 jiān jué de
adamant *n.* 坚决 jiān jué
adapt *v.t.* 适应 shì yìng
adaptation *n.* 改写本 gái xiě běn
adays *adv* 白天 bái tiān
add *v.t.* 加 jiā
addict *v.t.* 上瘾 shàng yǐn
addict *n.* 上瘾者 shàng yǐn zhě
addiction *n.* 瘾 yǐn
addition *n.* 添加 tiān jiā
additional *a.* 额外的 é wài de
addle *adj* 糊涂的 hú tu de
address *v.t.* 称呼 chēng hu
address *n.* 地址 dì zhǐ
addressee *n.* 收件人 shōu jiàn rén
adduce *v.t.* 举例 jǔ lì
adept *n.* 擅长 shàn cháng
adept *a.* 内行的 nèi háng de
adequacy *n.* 恰当 qià dàng
adequate *a.* 适当的 shì dàng de
adhere *v.i.* 遵守 zūn shǒu
adherence *n.* 遵守 zūn shǒu
adhesion *n.* 粘住 zhān zhù
adhesive *n.* 粘合剂 zhān hé jì
adhesive *a.* 粘合的 zhān hé de
adhibit *v.t.* 引入 yǐn rù
adieu *n.* 辞别 cí bié
adieu *interj.* 辞别 cí bié
adjacent *a.* 邻近的 lín jìn de
adjective *n.* 形容词 xíng róng cí
adjoin *v.t.* 紧挨 jǐn āi
adjourn *v.t.* 延后 yán hòu
adjournment *n.* 延期 yán qī
adjudge *v.t.* 判决 pàn jué
adjunct *n.* 附属物 fù shǔ wù
adjure *v.t.* 严令 yán lìng
adjure *v.t.* 严令 yán lìng
adjuration *n* 恳求 kěn qiú

adjust *v.t.* 调整 tiáo zhěng
adjustment *n.* 调整 tiáo zhěng
administer *v.t.* 管理 guán lǐ
administration *n.* 行政 xíng zhèng
administrative *a.* 行政的 xíng zhèng de
administrator *n.* 行政人员 xíng zhèng rén yuán
admirable *a.* 可钦佩的 kě qīn pèi de
admiral *n.* 海军上将 hǎi jūn shàng jiāng
admiration *n.* 欣赏 xīn shǎng
admire *v.t.* 欣赏 xīn shǎng
admissible *a.* 可以接受的 ké yǐ jiē shòu de
admission *n.* 入场费 rù chǎng fèi
admit *v.t.* 承认 chéng rèn
admittance *n.* 进入权 jìn rù quán
admonish *v.t.* 告诫 gào jiè
admonition *n.* 警告 jǐng gào
adnascent *adj.* 寄生的 jì shēng de
ado *n.* 麻烦 má fan
adobe *n.* 粘土 nián tǔ
adolescence *n.* 青春期 qīng chūn qī
adolescent *a.* 青少年的 qīng shào nián de
adopt *v.t.* 领养 lǐng yǎng
adoption *n* 领养 lǐng yǎng
adorable *a.* 可爱的 kě ài de
adoration *n.* 爱慕 ài mù
adore *v.t.* 崇拜 chóng bài
adorn *v.t.* 装扮 zhuāng bàn

adscititious *adj* 外加的 wài jiā de
adscript *adj.* 写在后边的 xiě zài hòu bian de
adulation *n* 奉承 fèng cheng
adult *a* 成年的 chéng nián de
adult *n.* 成年人 chéng nián rén
adulterate *v.t.* 掺杂 chān zá
adulteration *n.* 掺假 chān jiǎ
adultery *n.* 奸淫 jiān yín
advance *v.t.* 促进 cù jìn
advance *n.* 进展 jìn zhǎn
advancement *n.* 晋升 jìn shēng
advantage *n.* 好处 hǎo chu
advantage *v.t.* 有助于 yǒu zhù yú
advantageous *a.* 有利的 yǒu lì de
advent *n.* 出现 chū xiàn
adventure *n* 冒险 mào xiǎn
adventurous *a.* 大胆 dà dǎn
adverb *n.* 副词 fù cí
adverbial *a.* 副词的 fù cí de
adversary *n.* 对手 duì shǒu
adverse *a* 不利的 bú lì de
adversity *n.* 困境 kùn jìng
advert *v.* 广告 guǎng gào
advertise *v.t.* 宣传 xuān chuán
advertisement *n* 广告 guǎng gào
advice *n* 建议 jiàn yì
advisable *a.* 适当的 shì dàng de
advisability *n* 适当性 shì dàng xìng
advise *v.t.* 劝告 quàn gào
advocacy *n.* 辩护 biàn hù
advocate *n* 辩方律师 biàn fāng lù shī
advocate *v.t.* 拥护 yōng hù

aerial *a.* 空中的 kōng zhōng dì

aerial *n.* 天线 tiān xiàn

aeriform *adj.* 无形的 wú xíng de

aerify *v.t.* 气体化 qì tǐ huà

aerodrome *n* 机场 jī chǎng

aeronautics *n.pl.* 航空学 háng kōng xué

aeroplane *n.* 飞机 fēi jī

aesthetic *a.* 美学的 měi xué de

aesthetics *n.pl.* 美感 méi gǎn

aestival *adj* 夏季的 xià jì de

afar *adv.* 远 yuǎn

affable *a.* 和蔼可亲的 hé ǎi kě qīn de

affair *n.* 婚外情 hūn wài qíng

affect *v.t.* 影响 yíng xiǎng

affectation *n* 假装 jiǎ zhuāng

affection *n.* 感情 gǎn qíng

affectionate *a.* 深情的 shēn qíng de

affidavit *n* 宣誓书 xuān shì shū

affiliation *n.* 加入 jiā rù

affinity *n* 密切的关系 mì qiè de guān xì

affirm *v.t.* 肯定 kěn dìng

affirmation *n* 证实 zhèng shí

affirmative *a* 肯定的 kěn dìng de

affix *v.t.* 贴上 tiē shàng

afflict *v.t.* 折磨 zhé mó

affliction *n.* 痛苦 tòng kǔ

affluence *n.* 富裕 fù yù

affluent *a.* 富足的 fù zú de

afford *v.t.* 花费得起 huā fèi dé qǐ

afforest *v.t.* 绿化 lǜ huà

affray *n* 闹事 nào shì

affront *v.t.* 侮辱 wú rǔ

affront *n* 侮辱 wú rǔ

afield *adv.* 太远 tài yuǎn

aflame *adv.* 烧着 shāo zháo

afloat *adv.* 漂浮 piāo fú

afoot *adv.* 进行中 jìn xíng

afore *prep.* 之前 zhī qián

afraid *a.* 惊 jīng

afresh *adv.* 重新 chóng xīn

after *prep.* 之后 zhī hòu

after *adv* 后来 hòu lái

after *conj.* 以后 yǐ hòu

after *a* 后 hòu

afterwards *adv.* 之后 zhī hòu

again *adv.* 再 zài

against *prep.* 反对 fǎn duì

agamist *n* 未婚人士 wèi hūn rén shì

agape "*adv.,*" 目瞪口呆 mù dèng kǒu dāi

agaze *adv* 注视 zhù shì

age *n.* 年龄 nián líng

aged *a.* 老年的 lǎo nián de

agency *n.* 代理 dài lǐ

agenda *n.* 议程表 yì chéng biǎo

agent *n* 经纪人 jīng jì rén

aggravate *v.t.* 加重 jiā zhòng

aggravation *n.* 恶化 è huà

aggregate *v.t.* 集合 jí hé

aggression *n.* 攻击性 gōng jī xìng

aggressive *a.* 攻击性的 gōng jī xìng de

aggressor *n.* 侵略者 qīn lüè zhě

aggrieve *v.t.* 使悲伤 shǐ bēi shāng

aghast *a.* 吓呆的 xià dāi de

agile *a.* 敏捷 mǐn jié

agility *n.* 轻快 qīng kuài

agitate *v.t.* 激动 jī dòng

agitation *n* 焦虑 jiāo lǜ

agist *v.t.* 代人放牧 dài rén fàng mù

aglow *adv.* 兴奋 xīng fèn

ago *adv.* 之前 zhī qián

agog *adj.* 渴望 kě wàng

agonist *n* 兴奋剂 xīng fèn jì

agonize *v.t.* 苦闷 kǔ mèn

agony *n.* 痛苦 tòng kǔ

agronomy *n.* 农学 nóng xué

agoraphobia *n.* 旷野恐怖症 kuàng yě kǒng bù zhèng

agrarian *a.* 农业的 nóng yè de

agree *v.i.* 同意 tóng yì

agreeable *a.* 可以接受的 ké yǐ jiē shòu de

agreement *n.* 协议书 xié yì shū

agricultural *a* 农业的 nóng yè de

agriculture *n* 农业 nóng yè

agriculturist *n.* 农业家 nóng yè jiā

ague *n* 疟疾 nuè ji

ahead *adv.* 前面 qián mian

aheap *adv* 堆积的 duī jī de

aid *n* 援助 yuán zhù

aid *v.t* 帮助 bāng zhù

aigrette *n* 白鹭 bái lù

ail *v.t.* 困扰 kùn rǎo

ailment *n.* 小病 xiǎo bìng

aim *n.* 目标 mù biāo

aim *v.i.* 瞄准 miáo zhǔn

air *n* 空气 kōng qì

aircraft *n.* 飞艇 fēi tǐng

airy *a.* 空气的 kōng qì de

ajar *adv.* 半开 bàn kāi

akin *a.* 类似的 lèi shì de

alacrious *adj* 兴奋的 xīng fèn de

alacrity *n.* 乐意 lè yì

alamort *adj.* 去死 qù sǐ

alarm *n* 警报 jǐng bào

alarm *v.t* 惊动 jīng dòng

alas *interj.* 唉 āi

albeit *conj.* 虽然 suī rán

albion *n* 英格兰 yīng gé lán

album *n.* 专辑 zhuān jí

albumen *n* 蛋白 dàn bái

alchemy *n.* 炼金术 liàn jīn shù

alcohol *n* 酒精 jiǔ jīng

ale *n* 浓啤酒 nóng pí jiǔ

alegar *n* 啤酒醋 pí jiǔ cù

alert *a.* 警觉的 jǐng jué de

alertness *n.* 警觉性 jǐng jué xìng

algebra *n.* 代数 dài shù

alias *n.* 化名 huà míng

alias *adv.* 别名 bié míng

alibi *n.* 不在场证据 bú zài chǎng zhèng jù

alien *a.* 外国人 wài guó rén

alienate *v.t.* 疏远 shū yuǎn

aliferous *adj.* 有翼的 yǒu yì de

alight *v.i.* 照亮的 zhào liàng de

align *v.t.* 对齐 duì qí

alignment *n.* 列队 liè duì

alike *a.* 相同 xiāng tóng

alike *adv* 相似 xiāng sì

aliment *n.* 营养 yíng yǎng

alimony *n.* 赡养费 shàn yǎng fèi

aliquot *n.* 徐得尽的 xú dé jìn de

alive *a* 活着的 huó zhe de

alkali *n* 碱 jiǎn

all *a.* 全部 quán bù

all *n* 一切 yì qiè

all *adv* 完全 wán quán

all *pron* 所有 suó yǒu

allay *v.t.* 减轻 jiǎn qīng

allegation *n.* 断言 duàn yán

allege *v.t.* 声称 shēng chēng

allegiance *n.* 忠诚 zhōng chéng

allegorical *a.* 比喻的 bǐ yù de

allegory *n.* 寓意 yù yì

allergy *n.* 过敏 guò mǐn

alleviate *v.t.* 减轻 jiǎn qīng

alleviation *n.* 减轻 jiǎn qīng

alley *n.* 小巷 xiǎo xiàng

alliance *n.* 联盟 lián méng
alligator *n* 钝吻鳄 dùn wěn è
alliterate *v.* 押头韵 yā tóu yùn
alliteration *n.* 押头韵 yā tóu yùn
allocate *v.t.* 分配 fēn pèi
allocation *n.* 配给 pèi jǐ
allot *v.t.* 分配 fēn pèi
allotment *n.* 份 fèn
allow *v.t.* 允许 yún xǔ
allowance *n.* 津贴 jīn tiē
alloy *n.* 合金 hé jīn
allude *v.i.* 暗示 àn shì
allure *v.t.* 诱惑 yòu huò
allurement *n* 诱惑 yòu huò
allusion *n* 暗示 àn shì
allusive *a.* 暗指的 àn zhǐ de
ally *v.t.* 结盟 jié méng
ally *n.* 盟国 méng guó
almanac *n.* 年鉴 nián jiàn
almighty *a.* 全能的 quán néng de
almond *n.* 杏仁 xìng rén
almost *adv.* 几乎 jī hū
alms *n.* 救济品 jiù jì pǐn
aloft *adv.* 在上面 zài shàng mian
alone *a.* 独自 dú zì
along *adv.* 一齐 yì qí
along *prep.* 沿着 yán zhe
aloof *adv.* 避开 bì kāi
aloud *adv.* 大声 dà shēng
alp *n.* 高山 gāo shān
alpha *n* 阿尔法 ā ěr fǎ
alphabet *n.* 字母 zì mǔ
alphabetical *a.* 字母顺序 zì mǔ shùn xù
alpinist *n* 登山家 dēng shān jiā
already *adv.* 已经 yǐ jīng
also *adv.* 而且 ér qiě
altar *n.* 祭坛 jì tán
alter *v.t.* 改变 gǎi biàn
alteration *n* 修改 xiū gǎi
altercation *n.* 争论 zhēng lùn
alternate *a.* 轮流的 lún liú de
alternate *v.t.* 轮流 lún liú

alternative *n.* 代替品 dài tì pǐn
alternative *a.* 代替的 dài tì de
although *conj.* 虽然 suī rán
altimeter *n* 测高计 cè gāo jì
altitude *n.* 高度 gāo dù
alto *n* 女低音 nǚ dī yīn
altogether *adv.* 一齐 yì qí
aluminate *n.* 铝酸盐 lǚ suān yán
aluminium *n.* 铝 lǚ
alumna *n* 女校友 nǚ xiào yǒu
always *adv.* 总是 zǒng shì
alveary *n* 蜂窝 fēng wō
alvine *adj.* 腹部的 fù bù de
am 是 shì
amalgam *n* 混合物 hùn hé wù
amalgamate *v.t.* 合并 hé bìng
amalgamation *n* 合并 hé bìng
amass *v.t.* 累积 lěi jī
amateur *n.* 业余爱好者 yè yú ài hào zhě
amatory *adj* 恋爱的 liàn ài de
amaurosis *n* 青光眼 qīng guāng yǎn
amaze *v.t.* 惊奇 jīng qí
amazement *n.* 惊奇 jīng qí
ambassador *n.* 大使 dà shǐ
amberite *n.* 琥珀炸药 hǔ pò zhà yào
ambient *adj.* 周围的 zhōu wéi de
ambiguity *n.* 模糊 mó hú
ambiguous *a.* 模糊的 mó hú de
ambition *n.* 抱负 bào fù
ambitious *a.* 野心勃勃的 yě xīn bó bó de
ambry *n.* 橱柜 chú guì
ambulance *n.* 救护车 jiù hù chē
ambulant *adj* 移动的 yí dòng de
ambulate *v.t.* 步行 bù xíng
ambush *n.* 埋伏 mái fú
ameliorate *v.t.* 改良 gǎi liáng
amelioration *n.* 改良 gǎi liáng
amen *interj.* 阿门 ā mén

amend *v.t.* 修改 xiū gǎi

amendment *n.* 修改 xiū gǎi

amends *n.pl.* 修改 xiū gǎi

amenorrhoea *n* 月经不调 yuè jīng bú diào

amiability *n.* 亲切 qīn qiè

amiable *a.* 亲切的 qīn qiè de

amicable *adj.* 和蔼的 hé ǎi de

amid *prep.* 在中间 zài zhōng jiān

amiss *adv.* 差错 chā cuò

amity *n.* 友好 yóu hǎo

ammunition *n.* 弹药 dàn yào

amnesia *n* 失忆 shī yì

amnesty *n.* 大赦 dà shè

among *prep.* 之中 zhī zhōng

amongst *prep.* 之中 zhī zhōng

amoral *a.* 不遵守道德的 bù zūn shǒu dào dé de

amount *n* 数量 shù liàng

amount *v.i* 总计 zǒng jì

amount *v.* 等于 děng yú

amorous *a.* 好色的 hǎo sè de

amour *n* 私通 sī tōng

ampere *n* 安(培) ān (péi)

amphibious *adj* 水陆两栖的 shuǐ lù liǎng qī de

amphitheatre *n* 古罗马剧场 gǔ luó mǎ jù chǎng

ample *a.* 足够 zú gòu

amplification *n* 扩大 kuò dà

amplifier *n* 扩音器 kuò yīn qì

amplify *v.t.* 放大 fàng dà

amuck *adv.* 狂怒 kuáng nù

amulet *n.* 护身符 hù shēn fú

amuse *v.t.* 娱乐 yú lè

amusement *n* 娱乐 yú lè

an *art* 一 yī

anabaptism *n* 再洗礼 zà ixǐ lǐ

anachronism *n* 时代错误 shí dài cuò wù

anaclisis *n* 依赖 yī lài

anadem *n* 花冠 huā guàn

anaemia *n* 贫血 pín xuè

anaesthesia *n* 麻醉 má zuì

anaesthetic *n.* 麻醉药 má zuì yào

anal *adj.* 肛门的 gāng mén de

analogous *a.* 相似的 xiāng sì de

analogy *n.* 类比 lèi bǐ

analyse *v.t.* 分析 fēn xi

analysis *n.* 分析 fēn xi

analyst *n* 分析员 fēn xi yuán

analytical *a* 分析的 fēn xi de

anamnesis *n* 回想 huí xiǎng

anamorphous *adj* 再次形成 zài cì xíng chéng

anarchism *n.* 无政府主义 wú zhèng fǔ zhǔ yì

anarchist *n* 无政府主义者 wú zhèng fǔ zhǔ yì zhě

anarchy *n* 无政府 wú zhèng fǔ

anatomy *n.* 解剖学 jiě pōu xué

ancestor *n.* 祖先 zǔ xiān

ancestral *a.* 祖先的 zǔ xiān de

ancestry *n.* 祖先 zǔ xiān

anchor *n.* 锚 máo

anchorage *n* 抛锚 pāo máo

ancient *a.* 古老的 gú lǎo de

ancon *n* 肘 zhǒu

and *conj.* 和 hé

androphagi *n.* 食人族 shí rén zú

anecdote *n.* 轶事 yì shì

anemometer *n* 风速计 fēng sù jì

anew *adv.* 重新 chóng xīn

anfractuous *adj* 迂回的 yū huí de

angel *n* 天使 tiān shǐ

anger *n.* 怒火 nù huǒ

angina *n* 心绞痛 xīn jiǎo tòng

angle *n.* 角度 jiǎo dù

angle *n* 观点 guān diǎn

angry *a.* 愤怒的 fèn nù de

anguish *n.* 苦恼 kú nǎo

angular *a.* 有角的 yǒu jiǎo de

anigh *adv.* 近 jìn

animal *n.* 动物 dòng wù

animate *v.t.* 制成动画 zhì chéng dòng huà

animate *a.* 有生气的 yǒu shēng qì de

animation *n* 动画 dòng huà

animosity *n* 仇恨 chóu hèn

animus *n* 敌意 dí yì

aniseed *n* 八角 bā jiǎo

ankle *n.* 脚踝 jiǎo huái

anklet *n* 脚镯 jiǎo zhuó

annalist *n.* 史官 shǐ guān

annals *n.pl.* 编年史 biān nián shǐ

annectant *adj.* 连接着 lián jiē zhe

annex *v.t.* 附加 fù jiā

annexation *n* 附加 fù jiā

annihilate *v.t.* 毁灭 huǐ miè

annihilation *n* 毁灭 huǐ miè

anniversary *n.* 纪念日 jì niàn rì

announce *v.t.* 宣布 xuān bù

announcement *n.* 宣布 xuān bù

annoy *v.t.* 使烦恼 shǐ fán nǎo

annoyance *n.* 烦恼 fán nǎo

annual *a.* 一年一次的 yì nián yí cì de

annuitant *n* 领养老金人 lǐng yáng lǎo jīn rén

annuity *n.* 养老金 yáng lǎo jīn

annul *v.t.* 废除 fèi chú

annulet *n* 小环 xiǎo huán

anoint *v.t.* 涂油 tú yóu de

anomalous *a* 异常的 yì cháng de

anomaly *n* 异常 yì cháng

anon *adv.* 立即 lì jí

anonymity *n.* 匿名 nì míng

anonymous *a.* 匿名的 nì míng de

another *a* 另外 lìng wài

answer *n* 答案 dá àn

answer *v.t* 回答 huí dá

answerable *a.* 应负责的 yīng fù zé de

ant *n* 蚂蚁 má yǐ

antacid *adj.* 中和酸的 zhōng hé suān de

antagonism *n* 敌意 dí yì

antagonist *n.* 敌人 dí rén

antagonize *v.t.* 对抗 duì kàng

antarctic *a.* 南极 nán jí

antecede *v.t.* 在之前 zài zhī qián

antecedent *n.* 先例 xiān lì

antecedent *a.* 先前的 xiān qián de

antedate *n* 预期 yù qī

antelope *n.* 羚羊 líng yáng

antenatal *adj.* 产前的 chǎn qián de

antennae *n.* 触角 chù jiǎo

antenuptial *adj.* 结婚前的 jié hūn qián de

anthem *n* 国歌 guó gē

anthology *n* 选集 xuǎn jí

anthropoid *adj.* 类人猿 lèi rén yuán

anti *pref.* 反 fǎn

anti-aircraft *a.* 防空 fáng kōng

antic *n* 滑稽的 huá jī de

anticardium *n* 腹上部 fù shàng bù

anticipate *v.t.* 预料 yù liào

anticipation *n.* 预计 yù jì

antidote *n.* 解药 jiě yào

antinomy *n.* 矛盾 máo dùn

antipathy *n.* 反感 fǎn gǎn

antiphony *n.* 轮唱 lún chàng

antipodes *n.* 相反 xiāng fǎn

antiquarian *a.* 古文物的 gǔ wén wù de

antiquarian *n* 古物收藏家 gǔ wù shōu cáng jiā

antiquary *n.* 古物收藏家 gǔ wù shōu cáng jiā

antiquated *a.* 陈旧的 chén jiù de

antique *a.* 古董 gú dǒng

antiquity *n.* 古旧 gǔ jiù

antiseptic *n.* 防腐剂 fáng fú jì

antiseptic *a.* 消过毒的 xiāo guò dú de

antithesis *n.* 对立 duì lì

antitheist *n* 无神论者 wú shén lùn zhě

antler *n.* 鹿角 lù jiǎo

antonym *n.* 反义词 fǎn yì cí

anus *n.* 肛门 gāng mén

anvil *n.* 砧 zhēn

anxiety *a* 忧虑 yōu lù

anxious *a.* 忧虑的 yōu lù de

any *a.* 任何 rèn hé

any *adv.* 任何 rèn hé

anyhow *adv.* 无论如何 wú lùn rú hé

apace *adv.* 迅速的 xùn sù de

apart *adv.* 分开 fēn kāi

apartment *n.* 公寓 gōng yù

apathy *n.* 冷漠 lěng mò

ape *n* 猿 yuán

ape *v.t.* 模仿 mó páng

aperture *n.* 孔 kǒng

apex *n.* 顶点 díng diǎn

aphorism *n* 格言 gé yán

apiary *n.* 养蜂场 yǎng fēng chǎng

apiculture *n.* 养蜂业 yǎng fēng yè

apish *a.* 傻气的 shǎ qì de

apnoea *n* 窒息 zhì xī

apologize *v.i.* 道歉 dào qiàn

apnoea *n* 窒息 zhì xī

apologize *v.i.* 道歉 dào qiàn

apologue *n* 寓言 yù yán

apology *n.* 道歉 dào qiàn

apostle *n.* 信徒 xìn tú

apostrophe *n.* 撇号 piě hào

apotheosis *n.* 崇拜 chóng bài

apparatus *n.* 仪器 yí qì

apparel *n.* 服装 fú zhuāng

apparel *v.t.* 装饰 zhuāng shì

apparent *a.* 明显 míng xiǎn

appeal *n.* 上诉 shàng sù

appeal *v.t.* 吸引 xī yǐn

appear *v.i.* 出现 chū xiàn

appearance *n* 外表 wài biǎo

appease *v.t.* 安抚 ān fú

appellant *n.* 上诉人 shàng sù rén

append *v.t.* 附加 fù jiā

appendage *n.* 附属物 fù shǔ wù

appendicitis *n.* 阑尾炎 lán wěi yán

appendix *n.* 阑尾 lán wěi

appendix *n.* 附录 fù lù

appetence *n.* 欲望 yù wàng

appetent *adj.* 渴望的 kě wàng de

appetite *n.* 胃口 wèi kǒu

appetite *n.* 欲望 yù wàng

appetizer *n* 头盘 tóu pán

applaud *v.t.* 鼓掌 gú zhǎng

applause *n.* 掌声 zhǎng shēng

apple *n.* 苹果 píng guǒ

appliance *n.* 器具 qì jù

applicable *a.* 适合 shì hé

applicant *n.* 申请人 shēn qǐng rén

application *n.* 申请 shēn qǐng

apply *v.t.* 申请 shēn qǐng

appoint *v.t.* 委任 wěi rèn

apportion *v.t.* 分配 fēn pèi

apposite *adj* 适合的 shì hé de

apposite *a.* 恰当的 qià dàng de

appositely *adv* 贴切 tiē qiē

approbate *v.t.* 批准 pī zhǔn

appraise *v.t.* 评价 píng jià

appreciable *a.* 可觉察的 kě jué chá de

appreciate *v.t.* 欣赏 xīn shǎng

appreciation *n.* 感谢 gǎn xiè

apprehend *v.t.* 理解 lí jiě

apprehension *n.* 理解 lí jiě

apprehensive *a.* 担心的 dān xīn de

apprentice *n.* 徒弟 tú dì

apprise *v.t.* 报告 bào gào

approach *v.t.* 接近 jiē jìn

approach *n.* 方式 fāng shì

approbation *n.* 嘉奖 jiā jiǎng

appropriate *v.t.* 盗用 dào yòng

appropriate *a.* 适当的 shì dàng de

appropriation *n.* 挪用 nuó yòng

approval *n.* 批准 pī zhǔn

approve *v.t.* 批准 pī zhǔn

approximate *a.* 大概 dà gài

apricot *n.* 杏 xìng

appurtenance *n* 附属物 fù shǔ wù

apron *n.* 围裙 wéi qún

apt *a.* 有可能的 yǒu kě néng de

aptitude *n.* 天赋 tiān fù

aquarium *n.* 水族馆 shuǐ zú guǎn

aquarius *n.* 宝瓶座 bǎo píng zuò

aqueduct *n* 输水管 shū shuǐ guǎn

arable *adj* 适合耕种的 shì hé gēng zhòng de

arbiter *n.* 裁判 cái pàn

arbitrary *a.* 任意的 rèn yì de

arbitrate *v.t.* 仲裁 zhòng cái

arbitration *n.* 仲裁 zhòng cái

arbitrator *n.* 仲裁人 zhòng cái rén

arc *n.* 弧 hú

arcade *n* 拱廊 gǒng láng

arch *n.* 拱顶 gǒng dǐng

arch *v.t.* 弓着 gōng zhe

arch *a* 调皮的 tiáo pí de

archaic *a.* 古代的 gǔ dài de

archangel *n* 天使长 tiān shǐ cháng

archbishop *n.* 大主教 dà zhǔ jiāo

archer *n* 弓箭手 gōng jiàn shǒu

architect *n.* 建筑师 jiàn zhù shī

architecture *n.* 建筑学 jiàn zhù xué

archives *n.pl.* 档案 dàng àn

Arctic *n* 北极 běi jí

ardent *a.* 热心的 rè xīn de

ardour *n.* 热情 rè qíng

arduous *a.* 艰难 jiān nán

area *n* 地方 dì fang

areca *n* 槟榔树 bīng lang shù

arefaction *n* 干燥 gān zào

arena *n.* 竞技场 jìng jì chǎng

argil *n* 陶土 táo tǔ

argue *v.t.* 争辩 zhēng biàn

argument *n.* 辩论 biàn lùn

argute *adj* 尖锐的 jiān ruì de

arid *adj.* 贫瘠的 pín jí de

aries *n* 白羊座 bái yáng zuò

aright *adv* 正确 zhèng què

aright *v.* 纠正 jiū zhèng

arise *v.i.* 出现 chū xiàn

aristocracy *n.* 贵族 guì zú

aristocrat *n.* 一个贵族 yí gè guì zú

aristophanic *adj* 讽刺喜剧的 fěng cì xǐ jù de

arithmetic *n.* 算术 suàn shù

arithmetical *a.* 算术的 suàn shù de

ark *n* 方舟 fāng zhōu

arm *n.* 手臂 shǒu bì

arm *v.t.* 装备 zhuāng bèi

armada *n.* 舰队 jiàn duì

armament *n.* 军备 jūn bèi

armature *n.* 转子 zhuǎn zǐ

armistice *n.* 休战 xiū zhàn

armlet *a* 臂饰 bì shì

armour *n.* 盔甲 kuī jiǎ

armoury *n.* 军械库 jūn xiè kù

army *n.* 军队 jūn duì

around *prep.* 周围 zhōu wéi

around *adv* 到处 dào chù

arouse *v.t.* 激起 jī qǐ

arraign *v.* 提审 tí shěn

arrange *v.t.* 安排 ān pái

arrangement *n.* 安排 ān pái

arrant *n.* 十足的 shí zú de

array *v.t.* 召集 zhào jí

array *n.* 排列 pái liè

arrears *n.pl.* 债 zhài

arrest *v.t.* 逮捕 dài bǔ

arrest *n.* 拘留 jū liú

arrival *n.* 到达 dào dá

arrive *v.i.* 到达 dào dá

arrogance *n.* 自大 zì dà

arrogant *a.* 嚣张的 xiāo zhāng de

arrow *n* 箭 jiàn

arrowroot *n.* 竹芋 zhú yù

arsenal *n.* 武器 wǔ qì

arsenic *n* 砒霜 pī shuāng

arson *n* 纵火罪 zòng huǒ zuì

art *n.* 艺术 yì shù

artery *n.* 动脉 dòng mài

artful *a.* 巧妙的 qiǎo miào de

arthritis *n* 关节炎 guān jié yán

artichoke *n.* 朝鲜蓟 cháo xiān jì

article *n* 文章 wén zhāng

articulate *a.* 明了的 míng liǎo de

artifice *n.* 技巧 jì qiǎo

artificial *a.* 人造的 rén zào de

artillery *n.* 大炮 dà pào

artisan *n.* 工匠 gōng jian

artist *n.* 艺术家 yì shù jiā

artistic *a.* 艺术的 yì shù de

artless *a.* 天真 tiān zhēn

as *adv.* 同...一样 tóng... yí yàng

as *conj.* 因为 yīn wèi

as *prep..* 做 zuò

asafoetida *n.* 阿魏树脂 ā wèi shù zhī

asbestos *n.* 石棉 shí mián

ascend *v.t.* 上升 shàng shēng

ascent *n.* 上升 shàng shēng

ascertain *v.t.* 查明 chá míng

ascetic *n.* 禁欲 jìn yù

ascetic *a.* 禁欲的 jìn yù de

ascribe *v.t.* 归因于 guī yīn yú

ash *n.* 灰 huī

ashamed *a.* 惭愧的 cán kuì de

ashore *adv.* 上岸 shàng àn

aside *adv.* 一边 yì biān

aside *n.* 旁边 páng biān

asinine *adj.* 固执的 gù zhí de

ask *v.t.* 问 wèn

asleep *adv.* 睡着 shuì zháo

aspect *n.* 方面 fāng miàn

asperse *v.* 诽谤 fěi bàng

aspirant *n.* 有志者 yǒu zhì zhě

aspiration *n.* 志向 zhì xiàng

aspire *v.t.* 立志做 lì zhì zuò

ass *n.* 驴 lú

assail *v.* 攻击 gōng jī

assassin *n.* 刺客 cì kè

assassinate *v.t.* 行刺 xíng cì

assassination *n* 刺杀 cì shā

assault *n.* 袭击 xí jī

assault *v.t.* 殴打 ōu dǎ

assemble *v.t.* 招集 zhāo jí

assembly *n.* 集会 jí huì

assent *v.i.* 赞成 zàn chéng

assent *n.* 同意 tóng yì

assert *v.t.* 肯定 kěn dìng

assess *v.t.* 评估 píng gū

assessment *n.* 评价 píng jià

asset *n.* 资产 zī chǎn

assibilate *v.* 齿音化 chǐ yīn huà

assign *v.t.* 指派 zhǐ pài

assignee *n.* 代理人 dài lǐ rén

assimilate *v.* 同化 tóng huà

assimilation *n* 同化 tóng huà
assist *v.t.* 帮助 bāng zhù
assistance *n.* 帮助 bāng zhù
assistant *n.* 助手 zhù shǒu
associate *v.t.* 交往 jiāo wǎng
associate *a.* 有关系的 yǒu guān xi de
associate *n.* 同事 tóng shì
association *n.* 协会 xié huì
assoil *v.t.* 赦免 shè miǎn
assort *v.t.* 分类 fēn lèi
assuage *v.t.* 缓和 huǎn hé
assume *v.t.* 假设 jiǎ shè
assumption *n.* 假设 jiǎ shè
assurance *n.* 保证 bǎo zhèng
assure *v.t.* 保证 bǎo zhèng
astatic *adj.* 不安定的 bù ān dìng de
asterisk *n.* 星号 xīng hào
asterism *n.* 星群 xīng qún
asteroid *adj.* 星状的 xīng zhuàng de
asthma *n.* 哮喘 xiāo chuǎn
astir *adv.* 哄动 hōng dòng
astonish *v.t.* 惊讶 jīng yà
astonishment *n.* 惊讶 jīng yà
astound *v.t* 使震惊 shǐ zhèn jīng
astray "*adv.,*" 迷路 mí lù
astrologer *n.* 占星学家 zhàn xīng xué jiā
astrology *n.* 占星学 zhàn xīng xué
astronaut *n.* 太空人 tài kōng rén
astronomer *n.* 天文学家 tiān wén xué jiā
astronomy *n.* 天文学 tiān wén xué
asunder *adv.* 折断 zhé duàn
asylum *n* 庇护 bì hù
at *prep.* 在 zài
athirst *adj.* 渴望的 kě wàng de
athlete *n.* 运动员 yùn dòng yuán
athletic *a.* 运动的 yùn dòng de

athletics *n.* 田径运动 tián jīng yùn dòng
athwart *adv.* 横过 héng guò
atlas *n.* 地图集 dì tú jí
atmosphere *n.* 气氛 qì fēn
atoll *n.* 环状珊瑚岛 huán zhuàng shān hú dǎo
atom *n.* 原子 yuán zǐ
atomic *a.* 原子的 yuán zǐ de
atone *v.i.* 赎罪 shú zuì
atonement *n.* 赎罪 shú zuì
atrocious *a.* 残忍的 cán rěn de
atrocity *n* 残忍 cán rěn
attach *v.t.* 附加 fù jiā
attache *n.* 使馆馆员 shǐ guǎn guǎn yuán
attachment *n.* 附件 fù jiàn
attack *n.* 袭击 xí jī
attack *v.t.* 袭击 xí jī
attain *v.t.* 获得 huò dé
attainment *n.* 成就 chéng jiù
attaint *v.t.* 污辱 wū rǔ
attempt *v.t.* 尝试 cháng shì
attempt *n.* 尝试 cháng shì
attend *v.t.* 出席 chū xí
attendance *n.* 出勤率 chū qín lù
attendant *a.* 随行的 suí háng de
attendant *n.* 服务员 fú wù yuán
attention *n.* 注意 zhù yì
attentive *a.* 留心 liú xīn
attest *v.t.* 证实 zhèng shí
attire *n.* 服装 fú zhuāng
attire *v.t.* 打扮 dǎ bàn
attitude *n.* 态度 tài dù
attorney *n.* 辩护律师 biàn hù lù shī
attract *v.t.* 吸引 xī yǐn
attraction *n.* 吸引 xī yǐn
attractive *a.* 吸引人的 xī yǐn rén de
attribute *v.t.* 归因于 guī yīn yú
attribute *n.* 属性 shǔ xìng
auction *n* 拍卖 pāi mài
auction *v.t.* 拍卖 pāi mài
audible *a* 听到的 tīng dào de

audience *n.* 观众 guān zhòng
audit *n.* 审查 shěn chá
audit *v.t.* 审计 shěn jì
auditive *adj.* 听觉的 tīng jué de
auditor *n.* 审计员 shěn jì yuán
auditorium *n.* 观众席 guān zhòng xí
auger *n.* 钻孔器 zuān kǒng qì
aught *n.* 任何事物 rèn hé shì wù
augment *v.t.* 增加 zēng jiā
augmentation *n.* 增加 zēng jiā
August *n.* 八月 bá yuè
august *a.* 威严的 wēi yán de
aunt *n.* 姨 yí
auriform *adj.* 耳形的 ěr xíng de
aurilave *n.* 洗耳器 xǐ ěr qì
aurora *n* 曙光 shǔ guāng
auspicate *v.t.* 开张 kāi zhāng
auspice *n.* 预兆 yù zhào
auspicious *a.* 吉利的 jí lì de
austere *a.* 严肃的 yán sù de
authentic *a.* 真正的 zhēn zhèng de
author *n.* 作者 zuò zhě
authoritative *a.* 有权威的 yǒu quán wēi de
authority *n.* 权力 quán lì
authorize *v.t.* 批准 pī zhǔn
autobiography *n.* 自传 zì zhuàn
autocracy *n* 独裁政治 dú cái zhèng zhì
autocrat *n* 独裁者 dú cái zhě
autocratic *a* 专横的 zhuān hèng de
autograph *n.* 签名 qiān míng
automatic *a.* 自动的 zì dòng de
automobile *n.* 汽车 qì chē
autonomous *a* 自治的 zì zhì de
autumn *n.* 秋天 qiū tiān
auxiliary *a.* 辅助的 fǔ zhù de
auxiliary *n.* 辅助人员 fǔ zhù rén yuán
avale *v.t.* 下降 xià jiàng

avail *v.t.* 有益于 yǒu yì yú
available *a* 可用的 kě yòng de
avarice *n.* 贪钱 tān qián
avenge *v.t.* 报仇 bào chóu
avenue *n.* 街道 jiē dào
average *n.* 平均数 píng jūn shù
average *a.* 平均的 píng jūn de
average *v.t.* 平均为 píng jūn wéi
averse *a.* 反对的 fǎn duì de
aversion *n.* 反感 fǎn gǎn
avert *v.t.* 避免 bì miǎn
aviary *n.* 鸟舍 niǎo shě
aviation *n.* 航空 háng kōng
aviator *n.* 飞行员 fēi háng yuán
avid *adj.* 热爱 rè ài
avidity *adv.* 热情 rè qíng
avidly *adv* 渴望的 kě wàng de
avoid *v.t.* 避免 bì miǎn
avoidance *n.* 避免 bì miǎn
avow *v.t.* 声明 shēng míng
avulsion *n.* 撕开 sī kāi
await *v.t.* 等待 děng dài
awake *v.t.* 叫醒 jiào xǐng
awake *a* 醒 xǐng
award *v.t.* 颁奖 bān jiǎng
award *n.* 奖 jiǎng
aware *a.* 知道 zhī dào
away *adv.* 离开 lí kāi
awe *n.* 敬畏 jìng wèi
awful *a.* 可怕的 kě pà de
awhile *adv.* 片刻 piàn kè
awkward *a.* 为难的 wéi nán de
axe *n.* 斧头 fǔ tou
axis *n.* 轴 zhóu
axle *n.* 车轴 chē zhóu

B

babble *n.* 胡言乱语 hú yán luàn yǔ
babble *v.i.* 胡言乱语 hú yán luàn yǔ
babe *n.* 宝贝 bǎo bèi
babel *n* 喧哗 xuān huá

baboon *n.* 狒狒 fèi fèi
baby *n.* 宝宝 bǎo bao
bachelor *n.* 学士 xué shì
bachelor *n.* 单身汉 dān shēn hàn
back *n.* 背面 bèi miàn
back *a.* 后面的 hòu mian de
back *adv.* 向后 xiàng hòu
backbite *v.t.* 中伤 zhòng shāng
backbone *n.* 脊骨 jǐ gǔ
background *n.* 背景 bèi jǐng
backhand *n.* 反手 fǎn shǒu
backslide *v.i.* 退步 tuì bù
backward *a.* 反向的 fǎn xiàng de
backward *adv.* 相反地 xiāng fǎn dì
bacon *n.* 熏肉 xūn ròu
bacteria *n.* 细菌 xì jūn
bad *a.* 差 chà
badge *n.* 奖章 jiǎng zhāng
badger *n.* 獾 huān
badly *adv.* 坏地 huài dì
badminton *n.* 羽毛球 yǔ máo qiú
baffle *v. t.* 困扰 kùn rǎo
bag *n.* 包 bāo
bag *v. i.* 装入包里 zhuāng rù bāo lǐ
baggage *n.* 行李 xíng li
bagpipe *n.* 风笛 fēng dí
bail *n.* 保释 bǎo shì
bail *v. t.* 保释 bǎo shì
bailable *a.* 可保释的 kě bǎo shì de
bailiff *n.* 执达员 zhí dá yuán
bait *n* 诱饵 yòu ěr
bait *v.t.* 放饵 fàng ěr
bake *v.t.* 烤 kǎo
bait *v.t.* 放饵 fàng ěr
bake *v.t.* 烤 kǎo
baker *n.* 面包师 miàn bāo shī
bakery *n* 面包店 miàn bāo diàn
balance *n.* 余额 yú é
balance *n.* 平衡 píng héng
balcony *n.* 阳台 yáng tái
bald *a.* 光头 guāng tóu
bale *n.* 大包 dà bāo

bale *v.t.* 打成大包 dǎ chéng dà bāo
baleful *a.* 恶意的 è yì de
baleen *n.* 鲸须 jīng xū
ball *n.* 球 qiú
ballad *n.* 民歌 mín gē
ballet *sn.* 芭蕾舞 bā lěi wǔ
balloon *n.* 气球 qì qiú
ballot *n* 选票 xuǎn piào
ballot *v.i.* 投票 tóu piào
balm *n.* 香脂油 xiāng zhī yóu
balsam *n.* 香脂树 xiāng zhī shù
bam *n.* 嘭 pēng
bamboo *n.* 竹子 zhú zi
ban *v.* 禁止 jìn zhǐ
ban *n* 禁令 jìn lìng
banal *a.* 平凡的 píng fán de
banana *n.* 香蕉 xiāng jiāo
band *n.* 乐团 yuè tuán
bandage *n.* 绷带 bēng dài
bandage *v.t* 包扎 bāo zā
bandit *n.* 强盗 qiáng dào
bang *v.t.* 撞 zhuàng
bang *n.* 巨响 jù xiǎng
bangle *n.* 手镯 shǒu zhuó
banish *v.t.* 放走 fàng zǒu
banishment *n.* 放走 fàng zǒu
banjo *n.* 班卓琴 bān zhuó qín
bank *n.* 银行 yín háng
bank *v.t.* 存钱 cún qián
banker *n.* 银行家 yín háng jia
bankrupt *a.* 破产 pò chǎn
bankruptcy *n.* 破产 pò chǎn
banner *n.* 旗 qí
banquet *n.* 宴会 yàn huì
banquet *v.t.* 宴请 yàn qǐng
bantam *n.* 矮脚鸡 ǎi jiǎo jī
banter *v.t.* 开玩笑 kāi wán xiào
banter *n.* 玩笑 wán xiào
bantling *n.* 婴孩 yīng hái
banyan *n.* 榕树 róng shù
baptism *n.* 洗礼 xǐ lǐ
baptize *v.t.* 受洗 shòu xǐ
bar *n.* 酒吧 jiǔ bā
bar *v.t* 禁止 jìn zhǐ
barb *n.* 倒钩 dǎo gōu
barbarian *a.* 野蛮 yě mán

barbarian *n.* 野蛮人 yě mán rén

barbarism *n.* 野蛮 yě mán

barbarity *n* 残忍 cán rěn

barbarous *a.* 残酷 cán kù

barbed *a.* 有刺的 yǒu cì de

barber *n.* 理发师 lǐ fà shī

bard *n.* 诗人 shī rén

bare *a.* 秃的 tū de

bare *a.* 空的 kōng de

bare *v.t.* 揭开 jiē kāi

barely *adv.* 仅仅 jín jǐn

bargain *n.* 便宜货 pián yi huò

bargain *v.t.* 讲价 jiǎng jià

barge *n.* 驳船 bó chuán

bark *n.* 树皮 shù pí

bark *v.t.* 狗叫声 gǒu jiào shēng

barley *n.* 大麦 dà mài

barn *n.* 谷仓 gǔ cāng

barnacles *n* 藤壶 téng hú

barometer *n* 气压计 qì yā jì

barouche *n.* 马车 mǎ chē

barrack *n.* 兵营 bīng yíng

barrage *n.* 弹幕射击 dàn mù shè jī

barrator *ns.* 教唆犯 jiào suō fàn

barrel *n.* 桶 tǒng

barren *n* 不育 bú yù

barricade *n.* 路障 lù zhàng

barrier *n.* 障碍 zhàng ài

barrister *n.* 大律师 dà lǜ shī

barter *v.t.* 以物换物 yǐ wù

barter *v.t.* 交换 jiāo huàn

barton *n.* 农场 nóng chǎng

basal *adj.* 基础的 jī chǔ de

base *n.* 根基 gēn jī

base *a.* 卑鄙的 bēi bǐ de

base *v.t.* 设在 shè zài

baseless *a.* 无低的 wú dī de

basement *n.* 地下室 dì xià shì

bashful *a.* 害羞的 hài xiū de

basic *a.* 基本的 jī běn de

basil *n.* 罗勒 luó lè

basin *n.* 盆 pén

basis *n.* 基础 jī chǔ

bask *v.i.* 晒太阳 shài tài yáng

basket *n.* 篮 lán

baslard *n.* 刀 dāo

bass *n.* 电吉他 diàn jí tā

bass *n.* 男低音 nán dī yīn

bastard *n.* 私生子 sī shēng zǐ

bastard *a* 坏蛋 huài dàn

bat *n* 蝙蝠 biān fú

bat *n* 球拍 qiú pāi

bat *v.i* 拍 pāi

batch *n* 批 pī

bath *n* 浴缸 yù gāng

bathe *v.t* 洗澡 xí zǎo

baton *n* 接力棒 jiē lì bàng

batsman *n.* 击球手 jī qiú shǒu

battalion *n* 军队 jūn duì

battery *n* 电池 diàn chí

battle *n* 战斗 zhàn dòu

battle *v.i.* 搏斗 bó dòu

bawd *n.* 妓女 jì nǚ

bawl *n.i.* 大喊 dà hǎn

bawn *n.* 围墙 wéi qiáng

bay *n* 海湾 hǎi wān

bayard *n.* 骑士 qí shì

bayonet *n* 刺刀 cì dāo

be *v.t.* 存在 cún zài

be *v.* 是 shì

beach *n* 沙滩 shā tān

beacon *n* 灯塔 dēng tǎ

bead *n* 珠子 zhū zi

beadle *n.* 仪仗官 yí zhàng guān

beak *n* 鸟嘴 niǎo zuǐ

beaker *n* 烧杯 shāo bēi

beam *n* 光线 guāng xiàn

beam *v.i* 容光焕发 róng guāng huàn fā

bean *n.* 豆 dòu

bear *n* 熊 xióng

bear *v.t* 承受 chéng shòu

beard *n* 胡须 hú xū

bearing *n* 方位 fāng wèi

beast *n* 野兽 yě shòu

beastly *a* 野兽一样的 yě shòu yí yàng de

beat *v.t.* 打 dǎ

beat *n* 拍子 pāi zi

beautiful *a* 漂亮 piào liang

beautify *v.t* 美化 měi huà

beauty *n* 美丽 měi lì
beaver *n* 海狸 hǎi lí
because *conj.* 因为 yīn wèi
beck *n.* 小溪 xiǎo xī
beckon *v.t.* 吸引 xī yǐn
beckon *v. t* 招手 zhāo shǒu
become *v. i* 变成 biàn chéng
becoming *a* 相称的 xiāng chèn de
bed *n* 床 chuáng
bedevil *v. t* 折磨 zhé mó
bedding *n.* 床上用品 chuáng shàng yòng pǐn
bedight *v.t.* 装饰 zhuāng shì
bed-time *n.* 睡觉时间 shuì jiào shí jiān
bee *n.* 蜜蜂 mì fēng
beech *n.* 山毛榉 shān máo jǔ
beef *n* 牛肉 niú ròu
beehive *n.* 蜂房 fēng fáng
beer *n* 啤酒 pí jiǔ
beet *n* 甜菜 tián cài
beetle *n* 甲虫 jiǎ chóng
befall *v. t* 降临到 jiàng lín dào
before *prep* 之前 zhī qián
before *adv.* 以前 yǐ qián
before *conj* 之前 zhī qián
beforehand *adv.* 事先 shì xiān
befriend *v. t.* 做朋友 zuò péng you
beg *v. t.* 求 qiú
beget *v. t* 引起 yǐn qǐ
beggar *n* 乞丐 qǐ gài
begin *n* 开始 kāi shǐ
beginning *n.* 开始 kāi shǐ
begird *v.t.* 围绕 wéi rǎo
beguile *v. t* 骗 piàn
behalf *n* 代表 dài biǎo
behave *v. i.* 表现 biǎo xiàn
behaviour *n* 行为 xíng wéi
behead *v. t.* 砍头 kǎn tóu
behind *adv* 后面 hòu mian
behind *prep* 后面 hòu mian
behold *v. t* 注视 zhù shì
being *n* 生命 shēng mìng
belabour *v. t* 痛骂 tòng mà

belated *adj.* 迟到的 chí dào de
belch *v. t* 打嗝 dǎ gé
belch *n* 打嗝声 dǎ gé shēng
belief *n* 信仰 xìn yǎng
believe *v. t* 相信 xiāng xìn
bell *n* 铃 líng
belle *n* 美女 měi nǚ
bellicose *a* 好斗的 hǎo dòu de
belligerency *n* 交战 jiāo zhàn
belligerent *a* 好斗的 hǎo dòu de
belligerent *n* 交战国 jiāo zhàn guó
bellow *v. i* 咆哮 páo xiāo
bellows *n.* 叫声 jiào shēng
belly *n* 肚 dù
belong *v. i* 属于 shǔ yú
belongings *n.* 财物 cái wù
beloved *a* 深爱的 shēn ài de
beloved *n* 心爱的人 xīn ài de rén
below *adv* 下面 xià mian
below *prep* 少于 shǎo yú
belt *n* 皮带 pí dài
belvedere *n* 瞭望塔 liào wàng tǎ
bemask *v. t* 隐藏 yǐn cáng
bemire *v. t* 被泥弄脏 bèi ní nòng zāng
bemuse *v. t* 使着迷 shǐ zháo mí
bench *n* 长凳 cháng dèng
bend *n* 弯 wān
bend *v. t* 弯 wān
beneath *adv* 下面 xià mian
beneath *prep* 下面 xià mian
benefaction *n.* 慈善 cí shàn
benefice *n* 圣俸 shèng fèng
beneficial *a* 有利的 yǒu lì de
benefit *n* 津贴 jīn tiē
benefit *n* 津贴 jīn tiē
benefit *v. t.* 有利于 yǒu lì yú
benevolence *n* 善心 shàn xīn
benevolent *a* 有爱心的 yǒu ài xīn de
benight *v. t* 落后 luò hòu
benign *adj* 仁慈的 rén cí de
benignly *adv* 仁慈地 rén cí dì
benison *n* 祝福 zhù fú

bent *n* 弯的 wān de
bequeath *v. t.* 遗留 yí liú
bereave *v. t.* 丧失 sàng shī
bereavement *n* 丧失亲友 sàng shī qīn yǒu
berth *n* 卧铺 wò pū
beside *prep.* 侧边 cè biān
besides *prep* 徐了 xú le
besides *adv* 而且 ér qiě
beslaver *v. t* 献媚 xiàn mèi
besiege *v. t* 围攻 wéi gōng
bestow *v. t* 赠 zèng
bestrew *v. t* 散布 sàn bù
bet *v.i* 赌 dǔ
bet *n* 预计 yù jì
betel *n* 槟榔叶 bīng lang yè
betray *v.t.* 背叛 bèi pàn
betrayal *n* 背叛 bèi pàn
betroth *v. t* 许配 xǔ pèi
betrothal *n.* 订婚 dìng hūn
better *a* 较好 jiào hǎo
better *adv.* 更好 gèng hǎo
better *v. t* 好过 hǎo guò
betterment *n* 改善 gǎi shàn
between *prep* 之间 zhī jiān
beverage *n* 饮品 yǐn pǐn
bewail *v. t* 哀悼 āi dào
beware *v.i.* 提防 dī fang
bewilder *v. t* 混乱 hùn luàn
bewitch *v.t* 迷惑 mí huò
beyond *prep.* 超出 chāo chū
beyond *adv.* 更远 gèng yuǎn
bi *pref* 双 shuāng
biangular *adj.* 双角的 shuāng jiǎo de
bias *n* 偏心 piān xīn
bias *v. t* 有偏见 yǒu piān jiàn
biaxial *adj* 双轴的 shuāngzhóu de
bibber *n* 酒鬼 jiú guǐ
bible *n* 圣经 shèng jīng
bibliography +*n* 书目 shū mù
bibliographer *n* 书目编者 shū mù biān zhě
bicentenary *adj* 二百週年 èr bǎi zhōu nián
biceps *n* 二头肌 èr tóu jī
bicker *v. t* 争吵 zhēng chǎo

bicycle *n.* 自行车 zì xíng chē
bid *v.t* 出价 chū jià
bid *n* 投标 tóu biāo
bidder *n* 投标人 tóu biāo rén
bide *v. t* 等 děng
biennial *adj* 两年一次的 liǎng nián yí cì de
bier *n* 棺材架 guān cai jià
big *a* 大 dà
bigamy *n* 重婚罪 chóng hūn zuì
bight *n* 海湾 hǎi wān
bigot *a* 顽固的 wán gù de
bigot *n* 顽固 wán gù
bigotry *n* 顽固 wán gù
bile *n* 胆汁 dǎn zhī
bilingual *a* 双语的 shuāng yǔ de
bill *n* 账单 zhàng dān
billion *n* 十亿 shí yì
billow *n* 巨浪 jù làng
billow *v.i* 大量冒出 dà liàng mào chū
biliteral *adj* 两个字母的 liǎng gè zì mǔ de
bilk *v. t.* 赖账 lài zhàng
bimensal *adj* 每两个月 měi liǎng gè yuè
bimonthly *adj.* 隔个月的 gé gè yuè de
binary *adj* 二进制 èr jìn zhì
bind *v.t* 绑 bǎng
binding *a* 有约束力的 yǒu yuē shù lì de
binocular *n.* 望远镜 wàng yuǎn jìng
biographer *n* 传记作家 zhuàn jì zuò jiā
biography *n* 传记 zhuàn jì
biologist *n* 生物学家 shēng wù xué jiā
biology *n* 生物学 shēng wù xué
bioscope *n* 放映机 fàng yìng jī
biped *n* 两足动物 liǎng zú dòng wù
birch *n.* 桦树 huà shù
bird *n* 鸟 niǎo

birdlime *n* 鸟胶 niǎo jiāo
birth *n.* 出生 chū shēng
biscuit *n* 饼干 bǐng gān
bisect *v.t* 平分 píng fēn
bisexual *adj.* 双性恋的
　shuāng xìng liàn de
bishop *n* 主教 zhǔ jiāo
bison *n* 野牛 yě niú
bisque *n* 黄褐色 huáng hè sè
bit *n* 一点儿 yì dián ér
bitch *n* 贱女人 jiàn nǚ rén
bite *v.t.* 咬 yǎo
bite *n* 一口 yì kǒu
bitter *a* 苦 kǔ
bi-weekly *adj* 两星期一次
　liǎng xīng qi yí cì
bizarre *adj* 奇怪的 qí guài de
blab *v.t.&i* 乱讲 luàn jiǎng
black *a* 黑色的 hēi sè de
blacken *v.t.* 使黑 shǐ hēi
blackmail *n* 敲诈 qiāo zhà
blackmail *v.t* 勒索 lè suǒ
blacksmith *n* 铁匠 tiě jiang
bladder *n* 膀胱 páng guāng
blade *n.* 刀片 dāo piàn
blain *n* 水泡 shuǐ pào
blame *v.t* 责怪 zé guài
blame *n* 责任 zé rèn
blanch *v.t.&i* 漂白 piǎo bái
bland *adj.* 平淡无味的 píng
　dàn wú wèi de
blank *a* 空白的 kòng bái de
blank *n* 空格 kōng gé
blanket *n* 毛毯 máo tǎn
blare *v.t* 吼 hǒu
blast *n* 爆炸 bào zhà
blast *v.i* 炸烂 zhà làn
blaze *n* 火焰 huǒ yàn
blaze *v.i* 燃烧 rán shāo
bleach *v.t* 漂白 piǎo bái
blear *v.t* 使模糊 shǐ mó hu
bleat *n* 羊叫声 yáng jiào
　shēng
bleat *v.i* 咩咩叫 miē miē jiào
bleb *n* 水泡 shuǐ pào
bleed *v.i* 流血 liú xuè
blemish *n* 瑕疵 xiá cī
blend *v.t* 混合 hùn hé
blend *n* 混合品 hùn hé pǐn

bless *v.t* 祝福 zhù fú
blether *v.i* 啰唆 luo suo
blight *n* 损害 sǔn hài
blind *a* 盲 máng
blindage *n* 掩体 yán tǐ
blindfold *v.t* 蒙住眼 méng
　zhù yǎn
blindness *n* 失明 shī míng
blink *v.t.&i* 眨眼 zhá yǎn
bliss *n* 极乐 jí lè
blister *n* 水泡 shuǐ pào
blizzard *n* 暴风雪 bào fēng
　xuě
bloc *n* 国家集团 guó jiā jí tuán
block *n* 块 kuài
block *v.t* 阻塞 zǔ sè
blockade *n* 封锁 fēng suǒ
blockhead *n* 傻瓜 shǎ guā
blood *n* 血 xuè
bloodshed *n* 伤亡 shāng
　wáng
bloody *a* 血淋淋的 xiě lín
lín de
bloom *n* 花 huā
bloom *v.i.* 开花 kāi huā
blossom *n* 花朵 huā duǒ
blossom *v.i* 开花 kāi huā
blot *n.* 污点 wū diǎn
blot *v.t* 除去 chú qù
blouse *n* 衬衫 chèn shān
blow *v.i.* 吹 chuī
blow *n* 打击 dǎ jī
blue *n* 蓝色 lán sè
blue *a* 忧郁 yōu yù
bluff *v.t* 虚张声势 xū zhāng
　shēng shì
bluff *a* 粗率的 cū shuài de
bluff *n* 峭壁 qiào bì
blunder *n* 失策 shī cè
blunder *v.i* 犯大错 fàn dà cuò
blunt *a* 钝 dùn
blur *n* 模糊 mó hú
blurt *v.t* 冲口而出 chōng kǒu
　ér chū
blush *n* 脸红 liǎn hóng
blush *v.i* 脸红 liǎn hóng
boar *n* 公猪 gōng zhū
board *n* 板 bǎn
board *v.t.* 上船 shàng chuán

boast *v.i* 自夸 zì kuā
boast *n* 自夸 zì kuā
boat *n* 船 chuán
boat *v.i* 撑船 chēng chuán
bodice *n* 紧身胸衣 jǐn shēn xiōng yi
bodily *a* 身体的 shēn tǐ de
bodily *adv.* 全身的 quán shēn de
body *n* 身 shēn
bodyguard *n.* 保镖 bǎo biāo
bog *n* 沼泽 zhǎo zé
bog *v.i* 阻止 zǔ zhǐ
bogle *n* 妖怪 yāo guài
bogus *a* 假的 jiǎ de
boil *n* 脓肿 nóng zhǒng
boil *v.i.* 沸腾 fèi téng
boiler *n* 锅炉 guō lú
bold *a.* 大胆 dà dǎn
boldness *n* 胆量 dǎn liàng
bolt *n* 门闩 mén shuān
bolt *v.t* 锁门 suǒ mén
bomb *n* 炸弹 zhà dàn
bomb *v.t* 炸 zhà
bombard *v.t* 轰炸 hōng zhà
bombardment *n* 轰炸 hōng zhà
bomber *n* 投弹手 tóu dàn shǒu
bonafide *adv* 诚实地 chéng shí dì
bonafide *a* 真正的 zhēn zhèng de
bond *n* 联结 lián jié
bondage *n* 束缚 shù fù
bone *n.* 骨 gǔ
bonfire *n* 篝火 gōu huǒ
bonnet *n* 罩子 zhào zi
bontebok *n* 南非羚羊 nán fēi líng yáng
bonus *n* 奖金 jiǎng jīn
book *n* 书 shū
book *v.t.* 订 dìng
book-keeper *n* 记帐人 jì zhàng rén
book-mark *n.* 书签 shū qiān
book-seller *n* 书商 shū shāng
book-worm *n* 书虫 shū

bookish *a* 书呆子的 shū dāi zi de
booklet *n* 小册子 xiǎo cè zǐ
boon *n* 恩惠 ēn huì
boor *n* 乡下人 xiāng xia rén
boost *n* 吹捧 chuī pěng
boost *v.t* 吹捧 chuī pěng
boot *n* 靴子 xuē zi
booth *n* 摊子 tān zi
booty *n* 赃物 zāng wù
booze *v.i* 暴饮 bào yǐn
border *n* 边界 biān jiè
border *v.t* 镶边 xiāng biān
bore *v.t* 烦 fán
bore *n* 烦人 fán rén
born *v.* 出生 chū shēng
born rich *adj.* 出生富裕的 chū shēng fù yù de
borne *adj.* 携带 xié dài
borrow *v.t* 借 jiè
bosom *n* 胸部 xiōng bù
boss *n* 老板 lǎo bǎn
botany *n* 植物学 zhí wù xué
botch *v.t* 笨手笨脚地弄坏 bèn shǒu bèn jiǎo dì nòng huài
both *a* 双方的 shuāng fāng de
both *pron* 两个 liǎng gè
both *conj* 而且 ér qiě
bother *v.t* 麻烦 má fan
botheration *n* 烦恼 fán nǎo
bottle *n* 瓶 píng
bottler *n* 装瓶机 zhuāng píng jī
bottom *n* 底部 dǐ bù
bough *n* 大树枝 dà shù zhī
boulder *n* 大石头 dà shí tou
bouncer *n* 大话 dà huà
bound *v* 限制 xiàn zhì
bound *n.* 界限 jiè xiàn
boundary *n* 边界 biān jiè
bountiful *a* 大方 dà fāng
bounty *n* 慷慨 kāng kǎi
bouquet *n* 花束 huā shù
bout *n* 一阵 yí zhèn
bow *v.t* 鞠躬 jū gōng
bow *n* 鞠躬 jū gōng
bow *n* 蝴蝶结 hú dié jié
bowel *n.* 肠 cháng
bower *n* 凉亭 liáng tíng
bowl *n* 碗 wǎn

bowl v.i 投球 tóu qiú	**brewery** n 啤酒厂 pí jiǔ chǎng
box n 箱 xiāng	**bribe** n 贿赂 huì lù
boxing n 拳击 quán jī	**bribe** v.t. 贿赂 huì lù
boy n 男孩 nán hái	**brick** n 砖 zhuān
boycott v.t. 抵制 dǐ zhì	**bride** n 新娘 xīn niáng
boycott n 抵制 dǐ zhì	**bridegroom** n. 新郎 xīn láng
boyhood n 童年 tóng nián	**bridge** n 桥 qiáo
brace n 支持物 zhī chí wù	**bridle** n 笼头 lóng tou
bracelet n 手链 shǒu liàn	**brief** a. 简单的 jiǎn dān de
brag v.i 吹牛 chuī niú	**brigade** n. 陆军 lù jūn
brag n 自大 zì dà	**brigadier** n 陆军准将 lù jūn
braille n 盲文 máng wén	zhǔn jiāng
brain n 脑 nǎo	**bright** a 亮的 liàng de
brake n 刹车 shā chē	**brighten** v.t 使发亮 shǐ fā
brake v.t 刹车 shā chē	liàng
branch n 树枝 shù zhī	**brilliance** n 光彩 guāng cǎi
brand n 牌子 pái zi	**brilliant** a 精彩的 jīng cǎi de
brandy n 白兰地 bái lán dì	**brim** n 边沿 biān yán
brangle v.t 吵架 chǎo jià	**brine** n 盐水 yán shuǐ
brass n. 黄铜 huáng tóng	**bring** v.t 带来 dài lái
brave a 勇敢的 yóng gǎn de	**brinjal** n 茄子 qié zi
bravery n 勇敢 yóng gǎn	**brink** n. 边缘 biān yuán
brawl v.i. & n 打斗 dǎ dòu	**brisk** adj 轻快的 qīng kuài de
bray n 驴叫声 lú jiào shēng	**bristle** n 短而硬的毛 duǎn ér
bray v.i 喧嚷 xuān rǎng	yìng de máo
breach n 违法 wéi fǎ	**british** adj 英国的 yīng guó de
bread n 面包 miàn bāo	**brittle** a. 脆的 cuì de
breaden v.t. & i 面包做的	**broad** a 宽阔的 kuān kuò de
miàn bāo zuò de	**broadcast** n 广播 guǎng bō
breadth n 宽度 kuān dù	**broadcast** v.t 广播 guǎng bō
break v.t 损坏 sǔn huài	**brocade** n 锦缎 jǐn duàn
break n 休息 xiū xi	**broccoli** n. 西兰花 xī lán huā
breakage n 破损 pò sǔn	**brochure** n 手册 shǒu cè
breakdown n 故障 gù zhàng	**brochure** n 小册子 xiǎo cè zǐ
breakfast n 早餐 zǎo cān	**broker** n 经纪人 jīng jì rén
breakneck a 惊险的 jīng	**brood** n 一窝 yì wō
xiǎn de	**brook** n. 小溪 xiǎo xī
breast n 胸 xiōng	**broom** n 扫帚 sào zhou
breath n 气息 qì xī	**bronze** n. & adj 青铜 qīng tóng
breathe v.i. 呼吸 hū xī	**broth** n 肉汤 ròu tāng
breeches n. 马裤 mǎ kù	**brothel** n 妓院 jì yuàn
breed v.t 交配繁殖 jiāo pèi	**brother** n 兄弟 xiōng di
fán zhí	**brotherhood** n 手足之情
breed n 品种 pín zhǒng	shǒu zú zhī qíng
breeze n 微风 wēi fēng	**brow** n 眉 méi
breviary n. 摘要 zhāi yào	**brown** a 棕色 zōng sè
brevity n 简洁 jiǎn jié	**brown** n 棕色 zōng sè
brew v.t. 冲茶 chōng chá	**browse** n 浏览 liú lǎn
	bruise n 伤痕 shāng hén

bruit *n* 传闻 chuán wén

brush *n* 刷子 shuā zi

brustle *v. t* 摩擦 mó cā

brutal *a* 残忍 cán rěn

brute *n* 禽兽 qín shòu

bubble *n* 泡泡 pào pào

bucket *n* 水桶 shuí tǒng

buckle *n* 扣住 kòu zhù

bud *n* 花蕾 huā lěi

budge *v. i. & n* 推动 tuī dòng

budget *n* 预算 yù suàn

buff *n* 淡黄色 dàn huáng sè

buffalo *n.* 水牛 shuǐ niú

buffoon *n* 小丑 xiáo chǒu

bug *n.* 昆虫 kūn chóng

bugle *n* 号角 hào jiǎo

build *v. t* 建 jiàn

build *n* 体格 tǐ gé

building *n* 建筑 jiàn zhù

bulb *n.* 灯泡 dēng pào

bulk *n* 大量 dà liàng

bulky *a* 庞大的 páng dà de

bull *n* 公牛 gōng niú

bulldog *n* 牛头犬 niú tóu quǎn

bull's eye *n* 靶心 bǎ xīn

bullet *n* 子弹 zǐ dàn

bulletin *n* 公告 gōng gào

bullock *n* 阉牛 yān niú

bully *n* 暴徒 bào tú

bully *v. t.* 欺负 qī fu

bulwark *n* 堡垒 báo lěi

bumper *n.* 减震器 jiǎn zhèn qì

bumpy *adj* 崎岖不平的 qí qū bù píng de

bunch *n* 束 shù

bundle *n* 捆 kǔn

bungalow *n* 平房 píng fáng

bungle *v. t* 搞坏 gǎo huài

bungle *n* 失误 shī wù

bunk *n* 床铺 chuáng pù

bunker *n* 地堡 dì bǎo

buoy *n* 浮标 fú biāo

buoyancy *n* 浮力 fú lì

burden *n* 包袱 bāo fu

burden *v. t* 负担 fù dān

burdensome *a* 沉重的 chén zhòng de

bureau *n.* 局 jú

Bureaucuracy *n.* 官僚主义 guān liáo zhǔ yì

bureaucrat *n* 官僚 guān liáo

burglar *n* 贼 zéi

burglary *n* 盗窃 dào qiè

burial *n* 葬礼 zàng lǐ

burk *n* 傻瓜 shǎ guā

burn *v. t* 燃烧 rán shāo

burn *n* 烧伤 shāo shāng

burrow *n* 地洞 dì dòng

burst *v. i.* 爆炸 bào zhà

burst *n* 爆破 bào pò

bury *v. t.* 埋 mái

bus *n* 公共汽车 gōng gòng qì chē

bush *n* 灌木 guàn mù

business *n* 生意 shēng yi

businessman *n* 生意人 shēng yi rén

bustle *v. t* 奔忙 bēn máng

busy *a* 忙 máng

but *prep* 但是 dàn shì

but *conj.* 不过 bú guò

butcher *n* 屠夫 tú fū

butcher *v. t* 屠杀 tú shā

butter *n* 黄油 huáng yóu

butter *v. t* 涂黄油 tú huáng yóu

butterfly *n* 蝴蝶 hú dié

buttermilk *n* 脱脂奶 tuō zhī nǎi

buttock *n* 屁股 pì gu

button *n* 纽扣 niǔ kòu

button *v. t.* 扣紧 kòu jǐn

buy *v. t.* 买 mǎi

buyer *n.* 买方 mǎi fāng

buzz *v. i* 嗡嗡叫 wēng wēng jiào

buzz *n.* 嗡嗡声 wēng wēng shēng

by *prep* 靠近 kào jìn

by *adv* 经过 jīng guò

bye-bye *interj.* 再见 zài jiàn

by-election *n* 补选 bǔ xuǎn

"bylaw, bye-law " *n* 地方法 dì fang fǎ

bypass *n* 旁路 páng lù

by-product *n* 副产品 fù chán pǐn

byre *n* 牛棚 niú péng

byword *n* 俗话 sú huà

C

cab *n.* 出租车 chū zū chē

cabaret *n.* 歌舞表演 gē wǔ biáo yǎn

cabbage *n.* 生菜 shēng cài

cabin *n.* 船舱 chuán cāng

cabinet *n.* 柜橱 guì chú

cable *n.* 电缆 diàn lǎn

cable *v. t.* 打电报 dǎ diàn bào

cache *n* 储藏物 chǔ cáng wù

cachet *n* 标志 biāo zhì

cackle *v. i* 嘎嘎笑 gā gā xiào

cactus *n.* 仙人掌 xiān rén zhǎng

cad *n* 无赖 wú lài

cadet *n.* 军校生 jūn xiào shēng

cadge *v. i* 乞讨 qí tǎo

cadmium *n* 镉 gé

cafe *n.* 咖啡店 kā fēi diàn

cage *n.* 笼子 lóng zi

cain *n* 凶手 xiōng shǒu

cake *n.* 蛋糕 dàn gāo

calamity *n* 灾难 zāi nàn

calcium *n* 钙 gài

calculate *v. t.* 计算 jì suàn

calculator *n* 计数机 jì shù jī

calculation *n.* 计算 jì suàn

calendar *n.* 日历 rì lì

calf *n.* 小牛 xiǎo niú

call *v. t.* 叫 jiào

call *n.* 电话 diàn huà

caller *n* 打电话人 dǎ diàn huà rén

calligraphy *n* 书法 shū fǎ

calling *n.* 呼召 hū zhào

callow *adj* 幼稚的 yòu zhì de

callous *a.* 冷酷无情的 lěng kù wú qíng de

calm *n.* 冷静 lěng jìng

calm *n.* 平静 píng jìng

calm *v. t.* 镇静 zhèn jìng

calmative *adj* 镇静的 zhèn jìng de

calorie *n.* 热量 rè liàng

calumniate *v. t.* 诽谤 fěi bàng

camel *n.* 骆驼 luò tuo

camera *n.* 相机 xiàng jī

camlet *n* 羽纱 yǔ shā

camp *n.* 度假营 dù jiǎ yíng

camp *v. i.* 野营 yě yíng

campaign *n.* 运动 yùn dòng

camphor *n.* 樟脑 zhāng nǎo

can *n.* 罐 guàn

can *v. t.* 可以 ké yǐ

can *v.* 装罐 zhuāng guàn

canal *n.* 运河 yùn hé

canard *n* 谣言 yáo yán

cancel *v. t.* 取消 qǔ xiāo

cancellation *n* 取消 qǔ xiāo

cancer *n.* 癌症 ái zhèng

candid *a.* 公正 gōng zhèng

candidate *n.* 候选人 hòu xuǎn rén

candle *n.* 蜡烛 là zhú

candour *n.* 坦率 tǎn shuài

candy *n.* 糖 táng

candy *v. t.* 用糖煮 yòng táng zhǔ

cane *n.* 甘蔗 gān zhe

cane *v. t.* 用藤条打 yòng téng tiáo dǎ

canister *n.* 罐 guàn

cannon *n.* 大炮 dà pào

cannonade *n. v. & t* 连续炮轰 lián xù pào hōng

canon *n* 经典 jīng diǎn

canopy *n.* 覆盖 fù gài

canteen *n.* 食堂 shí táng

canter *n* 骑马慢跑 qí mǎ màn pǎo

canton *n* 行政区 xíng zhèng qū

cantonment *n.* 兵营 bīng yíng

canvas *n.* 帆布 fān bù

canvass *v. t.* 拉票 lā piào

cap *n.* 帽子 mào zi

cap *v. t.* 盒盖 hé gài

capability *n.* 能力 néng lì

capable *a.* 有能力的 yǒu néng lì de

capacious *a.* 宽敞 kuān chǎng

capacity *n.* 容量 róng liàng

cape *n.* 披肩 pī jiān

capital *n.* 首都 shǒu dū

capital *a.* 死刑的 sǐ xíng de

capitalist *n.* 资本主义者 zī běn zhǔ yì zhě

capitulate *v. t* 投降 tóu xiáng

caprice *n.* 任性 rén xìng

capricious *a.* 善变的 shàn biàn de

Capricorn *n* 山羊座 shān yáng zuò

capsicum *n* 辣椒 là jiāo

capsize *v. i.* 翻转 fān zhuǎn

capsular *adj* 胶囊状的 jiāo náng zhuàng de

captain *n.* 队长 duì zhǎng

captaincy *n.* 队长职位 duì

caption *n.* 插图说明 chā tú shuō míng

captivate *v. t.* 迷住 mí zhù

captive *n.* 俘虏 fú lǔ

captive *a.* 被监禁的 bèi jiān jìn de

captivity *n.* 监禁 jiān jìn

capture *v. t.* 捉 zhuō

capture *n.* 捉 zhuō

car *n.* 车 chē

carat *n.* 克拉 kè lā

caravan *n.* 大篷车 dà péng chē

carbide *n.* 碳化物 tàn huà wù

carbon *n.* 碳 tàn

card *n.* 卡 kǎ

cardamom *n.* 豆蔻 dòu kòu

cardboard *n.* 硬纸板 yìng zhí bǎn

cardiacal *adjs* 心脏的 xīn zàng de

cardinal *a.* 主要的 zhǔ yào de

cardinal *n.* 枢机主教 shū jī zhǔ jiāo

care *n.* 照顾 zhào gù

care *v. i.* 关心 guān xīn

career *n.* 职业生涯 zhí yè shēng yá

careful *a* 小心 xiǎo xīn

careless *a.* 粗心的 cū xīn de

caress *v. t.* 爱抚 ài fǔ

cargo *n.* 货船 huò chuán

caricature *n.* 漫画 màn huà

carious *adj* 腐烂的 fǔ làn de

carl *n* 粗人 cū rén

carnage *n* 大屠杀 dà tú shā

carnival *n* 欢宴 huān yàn

carol *n* 颂歌 sòng gē

carpal *n.* 腕骨 wàn gǔ

carpenter *n.* 木匠 mù jiang

carpentry *n.* 木工 mù gōng

carpet *n.* 地毯 dì tǎn

carriage *n.* 车厢 chē xiāng

carrier *n.* 运输行 yùn shū xíng

carrot *n.* 红萝卜 hóng luó bo

carry *v. t.* 搬运 bān yùn

cart *n.* 马车 mǎ chē

cartage *n.* 运输费 yùn shū fèi

carton *n* 盒 hé

cartoon *n.* 动画 dòng huà

cartridge *n.* 盒 hé

carve *v. t.* 刻 kè

cascade *n.* 小瀑布 xiǎo pù bù

case *n.* 箱 xiāng

cash *n.* 现金 xiàn jīn

cash *v. t.* 兑现支票 duì xiàn zhī piào

cashier *n.* 收银员 shōu yín yuán

casing *n.* 箱 xiāng

cask *n* 木桶 mù tǒng

casket *n* 珠宝盒 zhū bǎo hé

cassette *n.* 录音带 lù yīn dài

cast *v. t.* 投射 tóu shè

cast *n.* 全体演员 quán tǐ yǎn yuán

caste *n* 社会地位 shè huì dì wèi

castigate *v. t.* 严厉批评 yán lì pī píng

casting *n* 角色分配 jué sè fēn pèi

cast-iron *n* 铸铁 zhù tiě

castle *n.* 城堡 chéng bǎo

castor oil *n.* 蓖麻油 bìmá yóu

castral *adj* 营的 yíng de

casual *a.* 平常的 píng cháng de

casualty *n.* 遇难者 yù nàn zhě

cat *n.* 猫 māo

cause *n.* 起因 qǐ yīn

cause *v.t* 引起 yǐn qǐ

causeway *n* 堤道 dī dào

caustic *a.* 碱性的 jiǎn xìng de

caution *n.* 警告 jǐng gào

caution *v.t.* 提醒 tí xǐng

cautious *a.* 谨慎的 jǐn shèn de

cavalry *n.* 骑兵 qí bīng

cave *n.* 山洞 shān dòng

cavern *n.* 大山洞 dà shān dòng

cavil *v.t* 挑剔 tiāo ti

cavity *n.* 窝 wō

caw *n.* 鸦叫声 yā jiào shēng

caw *v.i.* 鸦叫 yā jiào

cease *v.i.* 终止 zhōng zhǐ

ceaseless ~*a.* 不停的 bù tíng de

cedar *n.* 雪松 xuě sōng

ceiling *n.* 天花板 tiān huā bǎn

celebrate *v.t. & i.* 庆祝 qìng zhù

celebration *n.* 庆祝活动 qìng zhù huó dòng

celebrity *n* 名人 míng rén

celestial *adj* 天上的 tiān shàng de

celibacy *n.* 独身生活 dú shēn shēng huó

celibacy *n.* 独身 dú shēn

cell *n.* 细胞 xì bāo

cellar *n* 地窖 dì jiào

cellular *adj* 细胞的 xì bāo de

cement *n.* 水泥 shuǐ ní

cement *v.t.* 加强 jiā qiáng

cemetery *n.* 墓地 mù dì

cense *v.t* 焚香致敬 fén xiāng zhì jìng

censer *n* 香炉 xiāng lú

sor *v.t.* 审查 shěn chá

censor *n.* 审查官 shěn chá guān

censor *v.t.* 审查 shěn chá

censorious *adj* 爱挑剔的 ài tiāo ti de

censorship *n.* 审查 shěn chá

censure *n.* 批评 pī píng

censure *v.t.* 谴责 qiǎn zé

census *n.* 人口调查 rén kǒu diào chá

cent *n* 分 fēn

centenarian *n* 百岁老人 bǎi suì lǎo rén

centenary *n.* 一百週年 yì bǎi zhōu nián

centennial *adj.* 一百週年的 yì bǎi zhōu nián de

center *n* 中心 zhōng xīn

centigrade *a.* 摄氏的 shè shì de

centipede *n.* 蜈蚣 wú gōng

central *a.* 中心的 zhōng xīn de

centre *n* 中心 zhōng xīn

centrifugal *adj.* 离心的 lí xīn de

centuple *n. & adj* 百倍 bǎi bèi

century *n.* 世纪 shì jì

ceramics *n* 陶瓷 táo cí

cerated *adj.* 涂蜡的 tú là de

cereal *n.* 麦片 mài piàn

cereal *a* 谷类的 gǔ lèi de

cerebral *adj* 大脑的 dà nǎo de

ceremonial *a.* 礼仪的 lǐ yí de

ceremonious *a.* 讲究礼仪 jiǎng jiū lǐ yí

ceremony *n.* 仪式 yí shì

certain *a* 确定的 què dìng de

certainly *adv.* 当然 dāng rán

certainty *n.* 确定性 què dìng xìng

certificate *n.* 证书 zhèng shū

certify *v.t.* 证实 zhèng shí

cerumen *n* 耳垢 ěr gòu

cesspool *n.* 污水坑 wū shuǐ kēng

chain *n* 链条 liàn tiáo

chair *n.* 椅子 yǐ zi

chairman *n* 主席 zhǔ xí

chaise *n* 马车 mǎ chē

chaise *n* 躺椅 táng yǐ
challenge *n.* 挑战 tiǎo zhàn
challenge *v. t.* 挑战 tiǎo zhàn
chamber *n.* 会议厅 huì yì tīng
chamberlain *n* 管家 guǎn jiā
champion *n.* 冠军 guàn jūn
champion *v. t.* 声援 shēng yuán
chance *n.* 机会 jī huì
chancellor *n.* 大臣 dà chén
chancery *n* 档案馆 dàng àn guǎn
change *v. t.* 改变 gǎi biàn
change *n.* 改变 gǎi biàn
channel *n* 频道 pín dào
chant *n* 圣歌 shèng gē
chaos *n.* 混乱 hùn luàn
chaotic *adj.* 混乱的 hùn luàn de
chapel *n.* 小教堂 xiǎo jiào táng
chapter *n.* 章 zhāng
character *n.* 角色 jué sè
charge *v. t.* 收费 shōu fèi
charge *n.* 责任 zé rèn
chariot *n* 战车 zhàn chē
charitable *a.* 慈善的 cí shàn de
charity *n.* 慈善 cí shàn
charm1 *n.* 魅力 mèi lì
charm2 *v. t.* 吸引 xī yǐn
chart *n.* 图表 tú biǎo
charter *n* 宪章 xiàn zhāng
chase1 *v. t.* 追 zhuī
chase2 *n.* 追捕 zhuī bǔ
chaste *a.* 贞节的 zhēn jié de
chastity *n.* 贞节 zhēn jié
chat1 *n.* 聊天 liáo tiān
chat2 *v. i.* 聊天 liáo tiān
chatter *v. t.* 饶舌 ráo shé
chauffeur *n.* 司机 sī jī
cheap *a* 便宜 pián yi
cheapen *v. t.* 降价 jiàng jià

cheat *v. t.* 哄骗 hǒng piàn
cheat *n.* 骗子 piàn zi
check *v. t.* 检查 jiǎn chá
check *n* 检查 jiǎn chá
checkmate *n* 将军 jiāng jūn
cheek *n* 面颊 miàn jiá
cheep *v. i* 吱吱叫 zhī zhī jiào
cheer *n.* 欢呼声 huān hū shēng
cheer *v. t.* 喝彩 hè cǎi
cheer *v. t.* 喝彩 hè cǎi
cheerful *a.* 高兴的 gāo xìng de
cheerless *a* 阴暗的 yīn àn de
cheese *n.* 奶酪 nǎi lào
chemical *a.* 化学的 huà xué de
chemical *n.* 化学物品 huà xué wù pǐn
chemise *n* 无袖衬衫 wú xiù chèn shān
chemist *n.* 化学家 huà xué jiā
chemistry *n.* 化学 huà xué
cheque *n.* 支票 zhī piào
cherish *v. t.* 珍惜 zhēn xī
cheroot *n* 雪茄烟 xuě jiā yān
chess *n.* 国际象棋 guó jì xiàng qí
chest *n* 胸部 xiōng bù
chestnut *n.* 栗子 lì zi
chew *v. t* 咀嚼 jǔ jué
chevalier *n* 骑士 qí shì
chicken *n.* 鸡 jī
chide *v. t.* 责备 zé bèi
chief *a.* 首要的 shǒu yào de
chieftain *n.* 首领 shóu lǐng
child *n* 孩子 hái zi
childhood *n.* 童年 tóng nián
childish *n.* 幼稚 yòu zhì
chill *n.* 寒冷 hán lěng
chilli *n.* 辣椒 là jiāo
chilly *a* 寒冷的 hán lěng de
chiliad *n.* 一千 yì qiān
chimney *n.* 烟囱 yān cōng
chimpanzee *n.* 黑猩猩 hēi xīng xing
chin *n.* 下巴 xià bā
china *n.* 瓷器 cí qì
chirp *v. i.* 鸟叫 niǎo jiào

chirp *n* 鸟叫声 niǎo jiào shēng

chisel *n* 凿子 záo zi

chisel *v. t.* 雕刻 diāo kè

chit *n.* 幼芽 yòu yá

chivalrous *a.* 骑士的 qí shì de

chivalry *n.* 骑士气概 qí shì qì gài

chlorine *n* 氯气 lù qì

chloroform *n* 氯仿 lù fǎng

choice *n.* 选择 xuǎn zé

choir *n* 合唱团 hé chàng tuán

choke *v. t.* 堵塞 dǔ sài

cholera *n.* 霍乱 huò luàn

chocolate *n* 巧克力 qiǎo kè lì

choose *v. t.* 选择 xuǎn zé

chop *v. t* 切 qiē

chord *n.* 和弦 hé xián

choroid *n* 脉络膜 mài luò mó

chorus *n.* 副歌 fù gē

Christ *n.* 基督 jī dū

Christendom *n.* 基督教徒 jī dū jiào tú

Christian *n* 基督徒 jī dū tú

Christian *a.* 基督徒的 jī dū tú de

Christianity *n.* 基督教 jī dū jiào

Christmas *n* 圣诞节 shèng dàn jié

chrome *n* 铬 gè

chronic *a.* 慢性的 màn xìng de

chronicle *n.* 编年史 biān nián shǐ

chronology *n.* 年表 nián biǎo

chronograph *n* 记时器 jì shí qì

chuckle *v. i* 笑 xiào

chum *n* 密友 mì yǒu

church *n.* 教堂 jiào táng

churchyard *n.* 教堂墓地 jiào táng mù dì

churl *n* 下贱的人 xià jiàn de rén

churn *v. t. & i.* 搅拌 jiǎo bàn

churn *n.* 搅乳机 jiǎo rǔ jī

cigar *n.* 雪茄 xuě jiā

cigarette *n.* 香烟 xiāng yān

cinema *n.* 电影院 diàn yǐng yuàn

cinnabar *n* 朱砂 zhū shā

cinnamon *n* 肉桂粉 ròu guì fěn

cipher, cipher *n.* 暗号 àn hào

circle *n.* 圆圈 yuán quān

circuit *n.* 线路 xiàn lù

circuit *n.* 线路 xiàn lù

circumfluence *n.* 环流 huán liú

circumspect *adj.* 慎重的 shèn zhòng de

circular *a* 圆形 yuán xíng

circular *n.* 传单 chuán dān

circulate *v. i.* 环绕 huán rào

circulation *n* 循环 xún huán

circumference *n.* 圆周 yuán zhōu

circumstance *n* 情况 qíng kuàng

circus *n.* 马戏团 mǎ xì tuán

cist *n* 石棺 shí guān

citadel *n.* 堡垒 báo lěi

cite *v. t* 引用 yǐn yòng

citizen *n* 公民 gōng mín

citizenship *n* 公民权利 gōng mín quán lì

citric *adj.* 柠檬的 níng méng de

city *n* 城市 chéng shì

civic *a* 城市的 chéng shì de

civics *n* 公民学 gōng mín xué

civil *a* 平民的 píng mín de

civilian *n* 平民 píng mín

civilization *n.* 文明社会 wén míng shè huì

civilize *v. t* 开化 kāi huà

clack *n. & v. i* 唠叨 láo dāo

claim *n* 宣称 xuān chēng

claim *v. t* 声称 shēng chēng

claimant *n* 申请者 shēn qǐng zhě

clamber *v. i* 攀登 pān dēng

clamour *n.* 吵闹声 chǎo nào shēng

clamour *v. i.* 吵闹 chǎo nào

clamp *n* 钳子 qián zi

clandestine *adj.* 秘密的 mì mì de

clap *v. i.* 拍手 pāi shǒu

clap *n* 鼓掌 gú zhǎng

clarify *v. t* 澄清 chéng qīng

clarification *n* 澄清 chéng qīng

clarion *n.* 号角声 hào jiǎo shēng

clarity *n* 清晰 qīng xī

clarity *n* 清晰 qīng xī

clash *n.* 分歧 fēn qí

clash *v. t.* 碰撞 pèng zhuàng

clasp *n* 扣紧 kòu jǐn

class *n* 班 bān

classic *a* 典型的 diǎn xíng de

classic *n* 典范 diǎn fàn

classical *a* 古典的 gú diǎn de

classification *n* 种类 zhǒng lèi

classify *v. t* 分类 fēn lèi

clause *n* 条款 tiáo kuǎn

claw *n* 爪 zhǎo

clay *n* 泥土 ní tǔ

clean *n.* 干净的 gān jìng de

clean *v. t* 清洁 qīng jié

cleanliness *n* 干净 gān jìng

cleanse *v. t* 清洗 qīng xǐ

clear *a* 清楚的 qīng chu de

clear *v. t* 搬走 bān zǒu

clearance *n* 清除 qīng chú

clearly *adv* 明显地 míng xiǎn dì

cleft *a* 裂开的 liè kāi de

clergy *n* 牧师 mù shī

clerical *a* 职员的 zhí yuán de

clerk *n* 文员 wén yuán

clever *a.* 聪明的 cōng míng de

clew *n.* 线团 xiàn tuán

click *n.* 点击 diǎn jī

client *n..* 顾客 gù kè

cliff *n.* 悬崖 xuán yá

climate *n.* 气候 qì hòu

climax *n.* 高潮 gāo cháo

climb *n.* 攀登 pān dēng

climb *v. i* 爬 pá

cling *v. i.* 缠住 chán zhù

clinic *n.* 诊所 zhén suǒ

clink *n.* 叮当声 dīng dāng shēng

cloak *n.* 斗篷 dǒu peng

clock *n.* 钟表 zhōng biǎo

clod *n.* 泥块 ní kuài

cloister *n.* 修道院 xiū dào yuàn

close *n.* 完结 wán jié

close *a.* 近的 jìn de

close *v. t* 关 guān

closet *n.* 壁柜 bì guì

closure *n.* 停业 tíng yè

clot *n.* 聚集 jù jí

clot *v. t* 凝结 níng jié

cloth *n* 布 bù

clothe *v. t* 穿衣 chuān yī

clothes *n.* 衣服 yī fu

clothing *n* 衣服类 yī fu lèi

cloud *n.* 云 yún

cloudy *a* 多云的 duō yún de

clove *n* 丁香 dīng xiāng

clown *n* 小丑 xiáo chǒu

club *n* 俱乐部 jù lè bù

clue *n* 线索 xiàn suǒ

clumsy *a* 笨拙的 bèn zhuō de

cluster *n* 群 qún

cluster *v. i.* 聚集 jù jí

clutch *n* 掌握 zhǎng wò

clutter *v. t* 混乱 hùn luàn

coach *n* 大巴 dà bā

coachman *n* 马车夫 mǎ chē fū

coal *n* 煤 méi

coalition *n* 联盟 lián méng

coarse *a* 粗的 cū de

coast *n* 海滨 hǎi bīn

coat *n* 外衣 wài yī

coating *n* 涂层 tú céng

coax *v. t* 哄 hǒng

cobalt *n* 钴 gǔ

cobbler *n* 鞋匠 xié jiang

cobra *n* 眼睛蛇 yǎn jing shé

collision *n* 碰撞 pèng zhuàng

collusion *n* 勾结 gōu jié

cobweb *n* 蜘蛛网 zhī zhū wǎng

cocaine *n* 可卡因 kě kǎ yīn

cock *n* 公鸡 gōng jī

cocker *v. t* 娇养 jiāo yǎng

cockle *v. i* 乌蛤 niǎo há

cock-pit *n.* 驾驶舱 jià shǐ cāng

cockroach *n* 蟑螂 zhāng láng

coconut *n* 椰子 yē zi

code *n* 密码 mì mǎ

co-education *n.* 男女同校 nán nǚ tóng xiào

co-exist *v. i* 共存 gòng cún

co-existence *n* 共存 gòng cún

coffee *n* 咖啡 kā fēi

coffin *n* 棺材 guān cai

cog *n* 钝齿 dùn chǐ

cogent *adj.* 有说服力的 yǒu shuō fú lì de

cognate *adj* 同族的 tóng zú de

cognizance *n* 标记 biāo jì

cohabit *v. t* 同居 tóng jū

coherent *a* 有条理的 yǒu tiáo lǐ de

cohesive *adj* 有凝聚力的 yǒu níng jù lì de

coif *n* 白帽 bái mào

coin *n* 硬币 yìng bì

coinage *n* 货币制度 huò bì zhì dù

coincide *v. i* 巧合 qiǎo hé

coir *n* 椰壳纤维 yē ké xiān wéi

coke *v. t* 炼焦 liàn jiāo

cold *a* 冷的 lěng de

cold *n* 感冒 gǎn mào

collaborate *v. i* 合作 hé zuò

collaboration *n* 合作 hé zuò

collapse *v. i* 倒塌 dǎo tā

collar *n* 衣领 yī lǐng

colleague *n* 同事 tóng shì

collect *v. t* 收集 shōu jí

collection *n* 系列 xì liè

collective *a* 集体 jí tǐ

collector *n* 收集家 shōu jí jiā

college *n* 学院 xué yuàn

collide *v. i.* 碰撞 pèng zhuàng

collision *n* 碰撞 pèng zhuàng

collusion *n* 勾结 gōu jié

collusion *n* 勾结 gōu jié

colon *n* 冒号 mào hào

colon *n* 大肠 dà cháng

colonel *n.* 上校 shàng xiào

colonial *a* 殖民的 zhí mín de

colony *n* 殖民地 zhí mín dì

colour *n* 颜色 yán sè

colour *v. t* 上色 shàng sè

colter *n* 犁头 lí tóu

column *n* 栏 lán

coma *n.* 昏迷 hūn mí

comb *n* 梳 shū

combat *n* 搏斗 bó dòu

combat *v. t.* 防止 fáng zhǐ

combatant *n* 战士 zhàn shì

combatant *a.* 战斗 zhàn dòu

combination *n* 组合 zǔ hé

combine *v. t* 结合 jié hé

come *v. i.* 来 lái

comedian *n.* 喜剧家 xǐ jù jiā

comedy *n.* 喜剧 xǐ jù

comet *n* 彗星 huì xīng

comfit *n.* 蜜饯 mì jiàn

comfort *n.* 舒服 shū fu

comfort *v. t* 安慰 ān wèi

comfortable *a* 舒服的 shū fu de

comic *a* 戏剧的 xì jù de

comic *n* 漫画 màn huà

comical *a* 好笑的 hǎo xiào de

comma *n* 逗号 dòu hào

command *n* 命令 mìng lìng

command *v. t* 命令 mìng lìng

commandant *n* 司令 sī lìng

commander *n* 指挥官 zhǐ huī guān

commemorate *v. t.* 纪念 jì niàn

commemoration *n.* 纪念 jì niàn

commence *v. t* 开始 kāi shǐ

commence *v. t* 开始 kāi shǐ
commencement *n* 开始 kāi shǐ
commend *v. t* 表扬 biǎo yáng
commendable *a.* 值得赞美的 zhí dé zàn měi de
commendation *n* 称赞 chēng zàn
comment *v. i* 评论 píng lùn
comment *n* 评论 píng lùn
commentary *n* 评论 píng lùn
commentator *n* 评论员 píng lùn yuán
commerce *n* 贸易 mào yì
commercial *a* 商业的 shāng yè de
commiserate *v. t* 同情 tóng qíng
commission *n.* 使命 shǐ mìng
commissioner *n.* 特派员 tè pài yuán
commissure *n.* 接缝处 jiē féng chù
commit *v. t.* 做 zuò
committee *n* 委员会 wěi yuán huì
commodity *n.* 商品 shāng pǐn
common *a.* 常见 cháng jiàn
commoner *n.* 平民 píng mín
commonplace *a.* 平凡的 píng fán de
commonwealth *n.* 联邦 lián bāng
commotion *n* 骚乱 sāo luàn
commove *v. t* 搅乱 jiǎo luàn
communal *a* 公共的 gōng gòng de
commune *v. t* 交谈 jiāo tán
communicate *v. t* 沟通 gōu tōng
communication *n.* 通讯 tōng xùn
communiqué *n.* 公报 gōng bào

communism *n* 共产主义 gòng chǎn zhǔ yì
community *n.* 社区 shè qū
commute *v. t* 减刑 jiǎn xíng
compact *a.* 压缩的 yā suō de
compact *n.* 契约 qì yuē
companion *n.* 伙伴 huǒ bàn
company *n.* 公司 gōng sī
comparative *a* 比较的 bǐ jiào de
compare *v. t* 比较 bǐ jiào
comparison *n* 比较 bǐ jiào
compartment *n.* 间隔 jiàn gé
compass *n* 指南针 zhǐ nán zhēn
compassion *n* 同情 tóng qíng
compel *v. t* 强迫 qiǎng pò
compensate *v.t* 赔偿 péi cháng
compensation *n* 赔偿 péi cháng
compete *v. i* 竞争 jìng zhēng
competence *n* 能力 néng lì
competent *a.* 有能力的 yǒu néng lì de
competition *n.* 比赛 bǐ sài
competitive *a* 竞争的 jìng zhēng de
compile *v. t* 编写 biān xiě
complacent *adj.* 自满的 zì mǎn de
complain *v. i* 抱怨 bào yuàn
complaint *n* 怨言 yuàn yán
complaisance *n.* 殷勤 yīn qín
complaisant *adj.* 殷勤的 yīn qín de
complement *n* 补充物 bǔ chōng wù
complementary *a* 补充的 bǔ chōng de
complete *a* 完整的 wán zhěng de
complete *v. t* 完成 wán chéng
completion *n* 完成 wán chéng
complex *a* 复杂的 fù zá de

complex *n* 联合企业 lián hé qǐ yè

complexion *n* 气色 qì sè

compliance *n.* 顺从 shùn cóng

compliant *adj.* 顺从的 shùn cóng de

complicate *v. t* 复杂化 fù zá huà

complication *n.* 混杂 hùn zá

compliment *n.* 赞扬 zàn yáng

compliment *v. t* 赞扬 zàn yáng

comply *v. i* 应允 yīng yǔn

component *n.* 组件 zǔ jiàn

compose *v. t* 创作 chuàng zuò

composition *n* 作品 zuò pǐn

compositor *n.* 排字工人 pái zì gōng rén

compost *n* 肥料 féi liào

composure *n.* 镇静 zhèn jìng

compound *n* 化合物 huà hé wù

compound *a* 混合的 hùn hé de

compound *n* 复合词 fù hé cí

compound *v. i* 恶化 è huà

compounder *n.* 製药公司 zhì yào gōng si

comprehend *v. t* 理解 lǐ jiě

comprehension *n* 理解力 lǐ jiě lì

comprehensive *a* 全面的 quán miàn de

compress *v. t.* 压缩 yā suō

compromise *n* 妥协 tuǒ xié

compromise *v. t* 妥协 tuǒ xié

compulsion *n* 强迫 qiǎng pò

compulsory *a* 强制的 qiǎng zhì de

compunction *n.* 后悔 hòu huǐ

computation *n.* 计算 jì suàn

compute *v.t.* 计算 jì suàn

comrade *n.* 同志 tóng zhì

conation *n.* 企求 qǐ qiú

concave *adj.* 凹的 āo de

conceal *v. t* 隐瞒 yǐn mán

concede *v.t.* 承认 chéng rèn

conceit *n* 自负 zì fù

conceive *v. t* 想像 xiǎng xiàng

concentrate *v. t* 集中 jí zhōng

concentration *n.* 专心 zhuān xīn

concept *n* 概念 gài niàn

conception *n* 构思 gòu sī

concern *v. t* 关系到 guān xi dào

concern *n* 关心 guān xīn

concert *n* 演唱会 yǎn chàng huì

concert *v. t* 协商 xié shāng

concession *n* 让步 ràng bù

conch *n.* 海螺壳 hǎi luó ké

conciliate *v.t.* 安抚 ān fǔ

concise *a* 简洁的 jiǎn jié de

conclude *v. t* 结束 jié shù

conclusion *n.* 结论 jié lùn

conclusive *a* 结论性的 jié lùn xìng de

concoct *v. t* 调制 tiáo zhì

concoction *n.* 调和品 tiáo hé pǐn

concord *n.* 和谐 hé xié

concrescence *n.* 增生 zēng shēng

concrete *n* 混凝土 hùn níng tǔ

concrete *a* 确实的 què shí de

concrete *v. t* 使凝固 shǐ níng gù

concubinage *n.* 非法同居 fēi fǎ tóng jū

concubine *n* 妾 qiè

conculcate *v.t.* 踩 cǎi

condemn *v. t.* 指责 zhǐ zé

condemnation *n* 谴责 qiǎn zé

condense *v. t* 压缩 yā suō

condite *v.t.* 醃 yān

condition *n* 条件 tiáo jiàn

conditional *a* 有条件的 yǒu tiáo jiàn de

condole *v. i.* 哀悼 āi dào

condolence *n* 慰问 wèi wèn

condonation *n.* 宽恕 kuān shù

conduct *n* 行为举止 xíng wéi jú zhǐ

conduct *v. t* 安排 ān pái

conductor *n* 指挥家 zhǐ huī jiā

cone *n.* 圆锥形 yuán zhuī xíng

confectioner *n* 糖果点心店 táng guǒ diǎn xin diàn

confectionery *n* 糖果点心 táng guǒ diǎn xin

confer *v. i* 协商 xié shāng

conference *n* 会议 huì yì

confess *v. t.* 承认 chéng rèn

confession *n* 坦白 tǎn bái

confidant *n* 知己 zhī jǐ

confide *v. i* 委托 wěi tuō

confidence *n* 信心 xìn xīn

confident *a.* 有信心 yǒu xìn xīn

confidential *a.* 秘密的 mì mì de

confine *v. t* 限制 xiàn zhì

confinement *n.* 监禁 jiān jìn

confirm *v. t* 确认 què rèn

confirmation *n* 确定 què dìng

confiscate *v. t* 没收 mò shōu

confiscation *n* 没收 mò shōu

conflict *n.* 争论 zhēng lùn

conflict *v. i* 冲突 chōng tū

confluence *n* 汇流处 huì liú chù

confluent *adj.* 汇合的 huì hé de

conformity *n.* 遵从 zūn cóng

conformity *n.* 一致 yí zhì

confraternity *n.* 团体 tuán tǐ

confrontation *n.* 对质 duì zhì

confuse *v. t* 混乱 hùn luàn

confusion *n* 混乱 hùn luàn

confute *v.t.* 驳倒 bó dǎo

conge *n.* 撤职 chè zhí

congenial *a* 一致的 yí zhì de

conglutinate *v.t.* 愈合 yù hé

congratulate *v. t* 恭喜 gōng xǐ

congratulation *n* 祝贺 zhù hè

congress *n* 国会 guó huì

conjecture *n* 猜测 cāi cè

conjecture *v. t* 推测 tuī cè

conjugal *a* 婚姻上的 hūn yīn shàng de

conjugate *v.t. & i.* 动词变化 dòng cí biàn huà

conjunct *adj.* 结合的 jié hé de

conjunctiva *n.* 结膜 jié mó

conjuncture *n.* 紧要关头 jǐn yào guān tóu

conjure *v.t.* 祈求 qí qiú

conjure *v.i.* 变魔术 biàn mó shù

connect *v. t.* 连接 lián jiē

connection *n* 关连 guān lián

connivance *n.* 纵容 zòng róng

conquer *v. t* 征服 zhēng fú

conquest *n* 征服 zhēng fú

conscience *n* 良心 liáng xīn

conscious *a* 清醒的 qīng xǐng de

consecrate *v.t.* 献祭 xiàn jì

consecutive *adj.* 连续的 lián xù de

consecutively *adv* 连续地 lián xù dì

consensus *n.* 共识 gòng shí

consent *n.* 允许 yún xǔ

consent *v. i* 同意 tóng yì

consent *v.t.* 允许 yún xǔ

consequence *n* 后果 hòu guǒ

consequent *a* 后果的 hòu guǒ de

conservative *a* 保守的 báo shǒu de

conservative *n* 保守党支持者 báo shǒu dǎng zhī chí zhě
conserve *v. t* 保存 bǎo cún
consider *v. t* 考虑 kǎo lǜ
considerable *a* 相当大的 xiāng dāng dà de
considerate *a.* 体贴的 tǐ tiē de
consideration *n* 考虑 kǎo lǜ
considering *prep.* 考虑到 kǎo lǜ dào
consign *v.t.* 委托 wěi tuō
consign *v. t.* 打发 dǎ fa
consignment *n.* 委托 wěi tuō
consist *v. i* 并存 bìng cún
consistence,-cy *n.* 连贯性 lián guàn xìng
consistent *a* 一致的 yí zhì de
consolation *n* 安慰 ān wèi
console *v. t* 安慰 ān wèi
consolidate *v. t.* 加强 jiā qiáng
consolidation *n* 强化 qiáng huà
consonance *n.* 共鸣 gòng míng
consonant *a.* 调和的 tiáo hé de
consort *n.* 配偶 pèi ǒu
conspectus *n.* 大纲 dà gāng
conspicuous *a.* 显著的 xiǎn zhù de
conspiracy *n.* 阴谋 yīn móu
conspirator *n.* 共谋者 gòng móu zhě
conspire *v. i.* 密谋 mì móu
constable *n* 警察 jǐng chá
constant *a* 固定的 gù dìng de
constellation *n.* 星座 xīng zuò
constipation *n.* 便秘 biàn bì
constituency *n* 选区 xuǎn qū

constituent *n.* 选民 xuǎn mín
constituent *adj.* 组成的 zǔ chéng de
constitute *v. t* 构成 gòu chéng
constitution *n* 宪法 xiàn fǎ
constrict *v.t.* 压缩 yā suō
construct *v. t.* 构成 gòu chéng
construction *n* 结构 jié gòu
consult *v. t* 协商 xié shāng
consultation *n* 商讨会 shāng tǎo huì
consume *v. t* 消费 xiāo fèi
consumption *n* 消费量 xiāo fèi liàng
consumption *n* 消费 xiāo fèi
contact *n.* 接触 jiē chù
contact *v. t* 联系 lián xì
contagious *a* 传染的 chuán rǎn de
contain *v.t.* 含有 hán yǒu
contaminate *v.t.* 污染 wū rǎn
contemplate *v. t* 细想 xì xiǎng
contemplation *n* 沉思 chén sī
contemporary *a* 现代的 xiàn dài de
contempt *n* 轻蔑 qīng miè
contemptuous *a* 轻蔑的 qīng miè de
contend *v. i* 竞争 jìng zhēng
content *a.* 满足的 mǎn zú de
content *v. t* 知足 zhī zú
content *n* 内容 nèi róng
content *n.* 目录 mù lù
contention *n* 争论 zhēng lùn
contentment *n* 满意 mǎn yì
contest *v. t* 争辩 zhēng biàn
contest *n.* 比赛 bǐ sài
context *n* 上下文 shàng xià wén
continent *n* 洲 zhōu
continental *a* 大陆的 dà lù de
contingency *n.* 事故 shì gù
continual *adj.* 连续的 lián xù de

continuation *n.* 持续 chí xù

continue *v. i.* 继续 jì xù

continuity *n* 连续性 lián xù xìng

continuous *a* 不断的 bú duàn de

contour *n* 轮廓 lún kuò

contra *n.* 反对票 fǎn duì piào

contraception *n.* 避孕 bì yùn

contract *n* 合同 hé tong

contract *v. t* 收缩 shōu suō

contrapose *v.t.* 对照 duì zhào

contractor *n* 承包人 chéng bāo rén

contradict *v. t* 反驳 fǎn bó

contradiction *n* 矛盾 máo dùn

contrary *a* 相反的 xiāng fǎn de

contrast *v. t* 对比 duì bǐ

contrast *n* 对照 duì zhào

contribute *v. t* 捐赠 juān zèng

contribution *n* 贡献 gòng xiàn

control *n* 控制权 kòng zhì quán

control *v. t* 控制 kòng zhì

controller *n.* 遥控器 yáo kòng qì

controversy *n* 争论 zhēng lùn

contuse *v.t.* 挫伤 cuò shāng

conundrum *n.* 谜语 mí yǔ

convene *v. t* 聚集 jù jí

convener *n* 召集人 zhào jí rén

convenience *n.* 方便 fāng biàn

convenient *a* 方便 fāng biàn

convent *n* 女修道院 nǔ xiū dào yuàn

convention *n.* 集会 jí huì

conversant *a* 亲近的 qīn jìn de

conversant *adj.* 熟悉的 shú xī de

conversation *n* 会谈 huì tán

converse *v.t.* 谈话 tán huà

conversion *n* 转换 zhuǎn huàn

convert *v. t* 转化 zhuǎn huà

convert *n* 改变信仰者 gǎi biàn xìn yǎng zhě

convey *v.t.* 输送 shū sòng

conveyance *n* 运输 yùn shū

convict *v. t.* 宣判有罪 xuān pàn yǒu zuì

convict *n* 罪犯 zuì fàn

conviction *n* 有罪判决 yǒu zuì pàn jué

convince *v. t* 说服 shuō fú

convivial *adj.* 宴会的 yàn huì de

convocation *n.* 集会 jí huì

convoke *v.t.* 召集 zhào jí

convolve *v.t.* 缠绕 chán rào

coo *n* 鸽叫声 gē jiào shēng

coo *v. i* 咕咕叫 gū gū jiào

cook *v. t* 烹调 pēng tiáo

cook *n* 厨师 chú shī

cooker *n* 炉 lú

cool *a* 凉 liáng

cool *v. i.* 变凉 biàn liáng

cooler *n* 冷却器 lěng què qì

coolie *n* 苦力 kǔ lì

co-operate *v. i* 合作 hé zuò

co-operation *n* 合作 hé zuò

co-operative *a* 配合的 pèi hé de

co-ordinate *a.* 协调的 xié tiáo de

co-ordinate *v. t* 协调 xié tiáo

co-ordination *n* 协调 xié tiáo

coot *n.* 傻瓜 shǎ guā

co-partner *n* 伙伴 huǒ bàn

cope *v. i* 应付 yìng fù

coper *n.* 马贩子 mǎ fàn zi

copper *n* 铜 tóng

coppice *n.* 小树林 xiǎo shù lín

coprology *n.* 粪便学 fèn biàn xué

copulate *v.i.* 交配 jiāo pèi

copy *n* 复制品 fù zhì pǐn

copy *v. t* 复制 fù zhì
coral *n* 珊瑚 shān hú
cord *n* 绳子 shéng zi
cordial *a* 亲切的 qīn qiè de
corbel *n.* 翘托 chì tuō
cordate *adj.* 心脏形的 xīn zàng xíng de
core *n.* 果心 guǒ xīn
coriander *n.* 香菜 xiāng cài
Corinth *n.* 科林斯 kē lín sī
cork *n.* 软木塞 ruǎn mù sāi
cormorant *n.* 鸬鹚 lú cí
corn *n* 玉米 yù mǐ
cornea *n* 角膜 jiǎo mó
corner *n* 角落 jiǎo luò
cornet *n.* 短号 duǎn hào
cornicle *n.* 腹管 fù guǎn
coronation *n* 加冕典礼 jiā miǎn dián lǐ
coronet *n.* 冠冕 guàn miǎn
corporal *a* 肉体的 ròu tǐ de
corporate *adj.* 公司的 gōng sī de
corporation *n* 大公司 dà gōng sī
corps *n* 兵团 bīng tuán
corpse *n* 尸体 shī tǐ
correct *a* 正确的 zhèng què de
correct *v. t* 更改 gēng gǎi
correction *n* 改正 gǎi zhèng
correlate *v.t.* 相互关联 xiāng hù guān lián
correlation *n.* 相关 xiāng guān
correspond *v. i* 符合 fú hé
correspondence *n.* 通信 tōng xìn
correspondent *n.* 记者 jì zhě
corridor *n.* 走廊 zǒu láng
corroborate *v.t.* 证实 zhèng shí
corrosive *adj.* 腐蚀性的 fǔ shí xìng de
corrupt *v. t.* 破坏 pò huài
corrupt *a.* 腐烂的 fǔ làn de
corruption *n.* 贪污 tān wū
cosier *n.* 更舒适 gèng shū shì

cosmetic *a.* 表面的 biǎo miàn de
cosmetic *n.* 化妆品 huà zhuāng pǐn
cosmic *adj.* 宇宙的 yǔ zhòu de
cost *v.t.* 花费 huā fèi
cost *n.* 价格 jià gé
costal *adj.* 肋骨的 lèi gǔ de
cote *n.* 小屋 xiǎo wū
costly *a.* 昂贵的 áng guì de
costume *n.* 服装 fú zhuāng
cosy *a.* 舒适的 shū shì de
cot *n.* 幼儿床 yòu ér chuáng
cottage *n* 小屋 xiǎo wū
cotton *n.* 棉 mián
couch *n.* 长椅 cháng yǐ
cough *n.* 咳嗽 ké sou
cough *v. i.* 咳嗽 ké sou
council *n.* 理事会 lǐ shì huì
councillor *n.* 委员 wěi yuán
counsel *n.* 忠告 zhōng gào
counsel *v. t.* 劝导 quàn dǎo
counsellor *n.* 顾问 gù wèn
count *n.* 总数 zǒng shù
count *v. t.* 数 shù
countenance *n.* 容貌 róng mào
counter *n.* 柜台 guì tái
counter *v. t* 反驳 fǎn bó
counteract *v.t.* 抵消 dǐ xiāo
countercharge *n.* 反控 fǎn kòng
counterfeit *a.* 仿造的 fǎng zào de
counterfeiter *n.* 伪造者 wěi zào zhě
countermand *v.t.* 撤回 chè huí
counterpart *n.* 相对物 xiāng duì wù
countersign *v. t.* 副署 fù shǔ
countess *n.* 伯爵夫人 bó jué fū rén
countless *a.* 无数的 wú shù de
country *n.* 国家 guó jiā
county *n.* 县 xiàn
coup *n.* 政变 zhèng biàn

couple *n* 一对 yí duì

couple *v. t* 连接 lián jiē

couplet *n.* 对联 duì lián

coupon *n.* 优惠券 yōu huì quàn

courage *n.* 勇气 yǒng qì

courageous *a.* 勇敢的 yóng gǎn de

courier *n.* 专递公司 zhuān dì gōng sī

course *n.* 课程 kè chéng

court *n.* 法庭 fǎ tíng

court *v. t.* 求爱 qiú ài

courteous *a.* 有礼貌的 yǒu lǐ mào de

courtesan *n.* 情妇 qíng fù

courtesy *n.* 礼貌 lǐ mào

courtier *n.* 朝臣 cháo chén

courtship *n.* 求爱期 qiú ài qī

courtyard *n.* 庭院 tíng yuàn

cousin *n.* 表亲 biǎo qīn

covenant *n.* 誓约 shì yuē

cover *v. t.* 遮蔽 zhē bì

cover *n.* 封面 fēng miàn

coverlet *n.* 床单 chuáng dān

covet *v.t.* 贪求 tān qiú

cow *n.* 牛 niú

cow *v. t.* 恐吓 kǒng hè

coward *n.* 胆小鬼 dǎn xiáo guǐ

cowardice *n.* 懦弱 nuò ruò

cower *v.i.* 退缩 tuì suō

cozy *a.* 舒适的 shū shì de

crab *n* 螃蟹 páng xiè

crack *n* 裂痕 liè hén

crack *v. i* 裂开 liè kāi

cracker *n* 鞭炮 biān pào

crackle *v.t.* 噼里啪啦 pī lǐ pā lā

cradle *n* 摇篮 yáo lán

craft *n* 手艺 shǒu yì

craftsman *n* 工匠 gōng jiang

crafty *a* 狡猾的 jiǎo huá de

cram *v. t* 塞满 sāi mǎn

crambo *n.* 对韵游戏 duì yùn yóu xì

crane *n* 吊车 diào chē

crankle *v.t.* 弯曲 wān qū

crash *v. i* 撞 zhuàng

crash *n* 碰撞 pèng zhuàng

crass *adj.* 粗鲁的 cū lǔ de

crate *n.* 板条箱 bǎn tiáo xiāng

crave *v.t.* 渴望的 kě wàng de

craw *n.* 嗉囊 sù náng

crawl *v. t* 爬 pá

crawl *n* 慢速 màn sù

craze *n* 热潮 rè cháo

crazy *a* 粘线 zhān xiàn

creak *v. i* 嘎吱声 gā zī shēng

creak *n* 嘎吱声 gā zī shēng

cream *n* 奶油 nǎi yóu

crease *n* 摺痕 zhé hén

create *v. t* 整 zhěng

creation *n* 作品 zuò pǐn

creative *adj.* 创意 chuàng yì

creator *n* 创作者 chuàng zuò zhě

creature *n* 生物 shēng wù

credible *a* 可靠的 kě kào de

credit *n* 信用 xìn yòng

creditable *a* 可钦佩的 kě qīn pèi de

creditor *n* 债主 zhài zhǔ

credulity *n* 轻信 qīng xìn

creed *n.* 原则 yuán zé

creed *n* 信念 xìn niàn

creek *n.* 小溪 xiǎo xī

creep *v. i* 爬 pá

creeper *n* 攀缘植物 pān yuán zhí wù

cremate *v. t* 火化 huǒ huà

cremation *n* 火化 huǒ huà

crest *n* 徽章 huī zhāng

crevet *n.* 熔炉 róng lú

crew *n.* 工作人员 gōng zuò rén yuán

crib *n.* 幼儿床 yòu ér chuáng

cricket *n* 板球 bǎn qiú

crime *n* 犯罪 fàn zuì

crimp *v.* 起皱 qǐ zhòu

crimple *n* 皱褶 zhòu zhě

criminal *n* 罪犯 zuì fàn

criminal *a* 犯法的 fàn fǎ de

crimson *n* 深红色 shēn hóng sè

cringe v. i. 畏缩 wèi suō

cripple n 瘸子 qué zi

crisis n 危机 wēi jī

crisp a 脆的 cuì de

criterion n 标准 biāo zhǔn

critic n 批评家 pī píng jiā

critical a 危机的 wēi jī de

criticism n 批评 pī píng

criticize v. t 批评 pī píng

croak n. 青蛙声 qīng wā shēng

crockery n. 陶器 táo qì

crocodile n 鳄鱼 è yú

croesus n. 大富豪 dà fù háo

crook a 骗人的 piàn rén de

crop n 农作物 nóng zuò wù

cross v. t 穿过 chuān guò

cross n 十字架 shí zì jià

cross a 易怒的 yì nù de

crossing n. 十字路口 shí zì lù kǒu

crotchet n. 四分音符 sì fēn yīn fú

crouch v. i. 蹲着 dūn zhe

crow n 乌鸦 wū yā

crow v. i 报晓 bào xiǎo

crowd n 人群 rén qún

crown n 皇冠 huáng guàn

crown v. t 加冕 jiā miǎn

crucial adj. 决定性的 jué dìng xìng de

crude a 粗糙的 cū cāo de

cruel a 残忍的 cán rěn de

cruelty n 残酷 cán kù

cruise v. i. 巡航 xún háng

cruiser n 巡洋舰 xún yáng jiàn

crumb n 碎屑 suì xiè

crumble v. t 弄碎 nòng suì

crump v 猛打 měng dǎ

crusade n 十字军 shí zì jūn

crush v. t 呀碎 ya suì

crust n. 面包皮 miàn bāo pí

crutch n 拐杖 guǎi zhàng

cry n 叫声 jiào shēng

cry v. i 喊 hǎn

cryptography n. 密码学 mì mǎ xué

crystal n 水晶 shuǐ jīng

cub n 幼兽 yòu shòu

cube n 立方形 lì fāng xíng

cubical a 立方体的 lì fāng tǐ de

cubiform adj. 立方形的 lì fāng xíng de

cuckold n. 戴绿帽的人 dài lù mào de rén

cuckoo n 杜鹃鸟 dù juān niǎo

cucumber n 黄瓜 huáng guā

cudgel n 棍棒 gùn bàng

cue n 提示 tí shì

cuff n 手铐 shǒu kào

cuff v. t 打 dǎ

cuisine n. 菜肴 cài yáo

cullet n. 碎玻璃 suì bō li

culminate v. i. 告终 gào zhōng

culpable a 有罪的 yǒu zuì de

culprit n 罪犯 zuì fàn

cult n 邪教 xié jiāo

cultivate v. t 耕作 gēng zuò

cultrate adj. 锐利的 ruì lì de

cultural a 文化的 wén huà de

culture n 文化 wén huà

culvert n. 阴沟 yīn gōu

cunning a 狡猾的 jiǎo huá de

cunning n 狡猾 jiǎo huá

cup n. 杯 bēi

cupboard n 柜 guì

Cupid n 邱比特 qiū bǐ tè

cupidity n 贪婪 tān lán

curable a 可医治的 kě yī zhì de

curative a 有疗效的 yǒu liáo xiào de

curb n 勒马绳 lè mǎ shéng

curb v. t 束缚 shù fù

curcuma n. 郁金香 yù jīn xiāng

curd n 凝乳 níng rǔ

cure n 药 yào

cure v. t. 医好 yī hǎo

curfew n 宵禁令 xiāo jìn lìng

curiosity n 好奇心 hào qí xīn

curious a 好奇的 hào qí de

curl v 卷曲 juǎn qǔ

currant n. 提子干 tí zǐ gān

currency n 货币 huò bì

current n 水流 shuǐ liú

current *a* 流行的 liú xíng de
curriculum *n* 课程 kè chéng
curse *n* 咒 zhòu
curse *v. t* 诅咒 zǔ zhòu
cursory *a* 仓促的 cāng cù de
curt *a* 简短而无礼的 jián duǎn ér wú lǐ de
curtail *v. t* 消减 xiāo jiǎn
curtain *n* 窗帘 chuāng lián
curve *n* 曲线 qū xiàn
curve *v. t* 弄弯 nòng wān
cushion *n* 垫 diàn
cushion *v. t* 缓和撞击 huǎn hé zhuàng jī
custard *n* 乳蛋糕 rǔ dàn gāo
custodian *n* 监护人 jiān hù rén
custody *v* 监护权 jiān hù quán
custom *n.* 习俗 xí sú
customary *a* 惯例的 guàn lì de
customer *n* 客户 kè hù
cut *v. t* 切 qiē
cut *n* 伤口 shāng kǒu
cutis *n.* 表皮 biǎo pí
cuvette *n.* 小玻璃管 xiǎo bō li guǎn
cycle *n* 循环 xún huán
cyclic *a* 循环的 xún huán de
cyclist *n* 骑自行车的人 qí zì xíng chē de rén
cyclone *n.* 旋风 xuàn fēng
cyclostyle *n* 复写器 fù xiě qì
cyclostyle *v. t* 复写 fù xiě
cylinder *n* 圆柱型 yuán zhù xíng
cynic *n* 犬儒学者 quǎn rú xué zhě
cypress *n* 柏树 bǎi shù

D

dabble *v. i.* 玩水 wán shuǐ
dacoit *n.* 强盗 qiáng dào
dacoity *n.* 抢劫 qiǎng jié
dad, daddy *n* 爸爸 bà ba

daffodil *n.* 水仙花 shuǐ xiān huā
daft *adj.* 愚笨的 yú bèn de
dagger *n.* 匕首 bí shǒu
daily *a* 每日的 měi rì de
daily *adv.* 每日地 měi rì dì
daily *n.* 日报 rì bào
dainty *a.* 小巧的 xiáo qiǎo de
dainty *n.* 美味 měi wèi
dairy *n* 乳品店 rǔ pǐn diàn
dais *n.* 台 tái
daisy *n* 雏菊 chú jú
dale *n* 小谷 xiǎo gǔ
dam *n* 水坝 shuǐ bà
damage *n.* 损害 sǔn hài
damage *v. t.* 损害 sǔn hài
dame *n.* 夫人 fū rén
damn *v. t.* 诅咒 zǔ zhòu
damnation *n.* 非难 fēi nàn
damp *a* 潮湿的 cháo shī de
damp *n* 潮湿 cháo shī
damp *v. t.* 使潮湿 shǐ cháo shī
damsel *n.* 少女 shǎo nǚ
dance *n* 舞 wǔ
dance *v. t.* 跳舞 tiào wǔ
dandelion *n.* 蒲公英 pú gōng yīng
dandle *v.t.* 抱着逗弄 bào zhe dòu nong
dandruff *n* 头皮屑 tóu pí xiè
dandy *n* 花花公子 huā huā gōng zǐ
danger *n.* 危险 wēi xiǎn
dangerous *a* 危险的 wēi xiǎn de
dangle *v. t* 使摇晃地悬挂 shǐ yáo huàng dì xuán guà
dank *adj.* 阴湿的 yīn shī de
dap *v.i.* 轻点水面 qīng diǎn shuǐ miàn
dare *v. i.* 胆敢 dán gǎn
daring *n.* 胆量 dǎn liàng
daring *a* 大胆的 dà dǎn de
dark *a* 黑暗的 hēi àn de
dark *n* 黑暗 hēi àn
darkle *v.i.* 变暗 biàn àn
darling *n* 亲爱的 qīn ài de
darling *a* 可爱的 kě ài de
dart *n.* 飞镖 fēi biāo

dash *v. i.* 猛冲 měng chōng

dash *n* 冲撞 chōng zhuàng

date *n* 日期 rì qī

date *v. t* 约会 yuē huì

daub *n.* 污迹 wū jì

daub *v. t.* 涂抹 tú mǒ

daughter *n* 女儿 nǔ ér

daunt *v. t* 威吓 wēi hè

dauntless *a* 不屈不挠的 bù qū bù náo de

dawdle *v.i.* 游手好闲 yóu shǒu hǎo xián

dawn *n* 黎明 lí míng

dawn *v. i.* 破晓 pò xiǎo

day *n* 天 tiān

daze *n* 迷乱 mí luàn

daze *v. t* 凝视 níng shì

dazzle *n* 迷惑 mí huò

dazzle *v. t.* 使茫然 shǐ máng rán

deacon *n.* 执事 zhí shì

dead *a* 死的 sǐ de

deadlock *n* 僵局 jiāng jú

deadly *a* 致命的 zhì mìng de

deaf *a* 聋的 lóng de

deal *n* 交易 jiāo yì

deal *v. i* 处理 chú lǐ

dealer *n* 经销商 jīng xiāo shāng

dealing *n.* 经营行为 jīng yíng xíng wéi

dean *n.* 院长 yuàn zhǎng

dear *a* 亲爱的 qīn ài de

dearth *n* 缺乏 quē fá

death *n* 死亡 sǐ wáng

debar *v. t.* 禁止 jìn zhǐ

debase *v. t.* 降低 jiàng dī

debate *n.* 辩论 biàn lùn

debate *v. t.* 争论 zhēng lùn

debauch *v. t.* 使堕落 shǐ duò luò

debauch *n* 放荡 fàng dàng

debauchee *n* 浪荡子 làng dàng zǐ

debauchery *n* 放荡 fàng dàng

debility *n* 虚弱 xū ruò

debit *n* 借方 jiè fāng

debris *n* 残骸 cán hái

debt *n* 债务 zhài wù

debtor *n* 债务人 zhài wù rén

decade *n* 十年 shí nián

decadent *a* 衰微的 shuāi wēi de

decamp *v. i* 逃走 táo zǒu

decay *n.* 腐败 fǔ bài

decay *v. i* (使)腐败 (shǐ) fǔ bài

decease *n* 死亡 sǐ wáng

decease *v. i* 死 sǐ

deceit *n* 欺骗 qī piàn

deceive *v. t* 欺骗 qī piàn

december *n* 十二月 shí èr yuè

decency *n* 得体 dé tǐ

decennary *n.* 十周年 shí zhōu nián

decent *a* 有分寸的 yǒu fēn cùn de

deception *n* 欺骗 qī piàn

decide *v. t* 决定 jué dìng

decillion *n.* 十分之一升 shí fēn zhǐ yì shēng

decimal *a* 十进位的 shí jìn wèi de

decimate *v.t.* 大批杀害 dà pī shā hài

decision *n* 决定 jué dìng

decisive *a* 决定性的 jué dìng xìng de

deck *n* 甲板 jiá bǎn

deck *v. t* 装饰 zhuāng shì

declaration *n* 宣告 xuān gào

declare *v. t.* 宣布 xuān bù

decline *n* 下降 xià jiàng

decline *v. t.* 婉谢 wǎn xiè

declivous *adj.* 倾斜的 qīng xié de

decompose *v. t.* 分解 fēn jiě

decomposition *n.* 分解 fēn jiě

decontrol *v.t.* 解除管理 jiě chú guǎn lǐ

decorate *v. t* 装饰 zhuāng shì

decoration *n* 装饰品 zhuāng shì pǐn

decorum *n* 得体 dé tǐ

decrease *v. t* 减少 jiǎn shǎo

decrease *n* 减少 jiǎn shǎo

decree *n* 法令 fǎ lìng

decree *v. i* 发布命令 fā bù mìng lìng

decrement *n.* 渐减 jiàn jiǎn

dedicate *v. t.* 贡献 gòng xiàn

dedication *n* 奉献 fèng xiàn

deduct *v.t.* 扣除 kòu chú

deed *n* 行为 xíng wéi

deem *v.i.* 认为 rèn wéi

deep *a.* 深的 shēn de

deer *n* 鹿 lù

defamation *n* 诽谤 fěi bàng

defame *v. t.* 中伤 zhòng shāng

default *n.* 违约 wéi yuē

defeat *n* 失败 shī bài

defeat *v.t.* 击败 jī bài

defect *n* 缺点 quē diǎn

defence *n* 防卫 fáng wèi

defend *v. t* 防护 fáng hù

defendant *n* 被告 bèi gào

defensive *adv.* 自卫的 zì wèi de

deference *n* 尊重 zūn zhòng

defiance *n* 违抗 wéi kàng

deficit *n* 赤字 chì zì

deficient *adj.* 有缺陷的 yǒu quē xiàn de

defile *n.* 狭道 xiá dào

define *v.t* 定义 dìng yì

definite *a* 一定的 yí dìng de

definition *n* 定义 dìng yì

deflation *n.* 通货紧缩 tōng huò jǐn suō

deflect *v.t.* 转移 zhuǎn yí

deft *adj.* 灵巧的 líng qiǎo de

degrade *v. t* (使)降级 (shǐ) jiàng jí

degree *n* 学位 xué wèi

deice *v.t.* 防止结冰 fáng zhǐ jié bīng

deist *n.* 自然神论信仰者 zì rán shén lùn xìn yǎng zhě

deity *n.* 神 shén

deject *v. t* 使灰心 shǐ huī xīn

dejection *n* 沮丧 jǔ sàng

delay *v.t. & i.* 延迟 yán chí

deli *n* 熟食店 shú shí diàn

delegate *n* 代表 dài biǎo

delegate *v. t* 委派...为代表 wěi pài... wéi dài biǎo

delegation *n* 代表团 dài biǎo tuán

delete *v. t* 删除 shān chú

deliberate *v. i* 仔细考虑 zǐ xì kǎo lǜ

deliberate *a* 深思熟虑的 shēn sī shú lǜ de

deliberation *n* 熟虑 shú lǜ

delicate *a* 柔弱的 róu ruò de

delicious *a* 美味的 měi wèi de

delight *n* 高兴 gāo xìng

delight *v. t.* 使高兴 shǐ gāo xìng

deliver *v. t* 递送 dì sòng

delivery *n* 递送 dì sòng

delta *n* 三角洲 sān jiǎo zhōu

delude *v.t.* 迷惑 mí huò

delusion *n.* 错觉 cuò jué

demand *n* 需求 xū qiú

demand *v. t* 要求 yāo qiú

demarcation *n.* 划界 huà jiè

dement *v.t* 使发狂 shǐ fā kuáng

demerit *n* 过失 guò shī

democracy *n* 民主政治 mín zhǔ zhèng zhì

democratic *a* 民主的 mín zhǔ de

demolish *v. t.* 毁坏 huǐ huài

demon *n.* 魔鬼 mó guǐ

demonetize *v.t.* (使通货)废止使用 (shǐ tōng huò) fèi zhǐ shǐ yòng

demonstrate *v. t* 示范 shì fàn

demonstration *n.* 示范 shì fàn

demoralize *v. t.* 使道德败坏 shǐ dào dé bài huài

demur *n* 异议 yì yì

demur *v. i* 反对 fǎn duì

demurrage *n.* 滞留费 zhì liú fèi

den *n* 兽穴 shòu xué

dengue *n.* 登革热 dēng gé rè

denial *n* 否认 fǒu rèn

denote *v. t* 指示 zhǐ shì

denounce *v. t* 告发 gào fā

dense *a* 浓厚的 nóng hòu de

density *n* 密度 mì dù

dentist *n* 牙科医生 yá kē yī sheng

denude *v.t.* 使裸露 shǐ luǒ lù

denunciation *n.* 谴责 qiǎn zé

deny *v. t.* 否认 fǒu rèn

depart *v. i.* 离开 lí kāi

department *n* 部门 bù mén

departure *n* 离开 lí kāi

depauperate *v.t.* 使贫穷 shǐ pín qióng

depend *v. i.* 信赖 xìn lài

dependant *n* 受赡养人 shòu shàn yǎng rén

dependence *n* 依赖 yī lài

dependent *a* 依赖的 yī lài de

depict *v. t.* 描述 miáo shù

deplorable *a* 可叹的 kě tàn de

deploy *v.t.* 展开 zhǎn kāi

deponent *n.* 证明人 zhèng míng rén

deport *v.t.* 驱逐出境 qū zhú chū jìng

depose *v. t* 免职 miǎn zhí

deposit *n.* 定金 dìng jīn

deposit *v. t* 存放 cún fàng

depot *n* 仓库 cāng kù

depreciate *v.t.* 贬低 biǎn dī

depredate *v.t.* 掠夺 lüè duó

depress *v. t* 使沮丧 shǐ jǔ sàng

depression *n* 抑郁[症] yì yù [zhèng]

deprive *v. t* 剥夺 bō duó

depth *n* 深度 shēn dù

deputation *n* 代表团 dài biǎo tuán

depute *v. t* 指定代理人 zhǐ dìng dài lǐ rén

deputy *n* 代理人 dài lǐ rén

derail *v. t.* 使出轨 shǐ chū guǐ

derive *v. t.* 得自 dé zì

descend *v. i.* 下降 xià jiàng

descendant *n* 后裔 hòu yì

descent *n.* 降落 jiàng luò

describe *v. t* 描述 miáo shù

description *n* 描述 miáo shù

descriptive *a* 描述的 miáo shù de

desert *v. t.* 放弃 fàng qì

desert *n* 沙漠 shā mò

deserve *v. t.* 该得到 gāi dé dào

design *v. t.* 设计 shè jì

design *n.* 设计 shè jì

desirable *a* 令人想望的 lìng rén xiǎng wàng de

desire *n* 欲望 yù wàng

desire *v.t* 想要 xiǎng yào

desirous *a* 渴望的 kě wàng de

desk *n* 书桌 shū zhuō

despair *n* 绝望 jué wàng

despair *v. i* 绝望 jué wàng

desperate *a* 不顾一切的 bú gù yì qiè de

despicable *a* 可鄙的 ké bǐ de

despise *v. t* 轻视 qīng shì

despot *n* 暴君 bào jūn

destination *n* 目的地 mù dì dì

destiny *n* 命运 mìng yùn

destroy *v. t* 破坏 pò huài

destruction *n* 毁灭 huǐ miè

detach *v. t* 使分离 shǐ fēn lí

detachment *n* 分遣队 fēn qiǎn duì

detail *n* 细节 xì jié

detail *v. t* 详述 xiáng shù

detain *v. t* 扣留 kòu liú

detect *v. t* 探测 tàn cè

detective *a* 侦探的 zhēn tàn de

detective *n.* 侦探 zhēn tàn

determination *n.* 决心 jué xīn

determine *v. t* 决定 jué dìng

dethrone *v. t* 废黜 fèi chù

develop *v. t* 发展 fā zhǎn

development *n.* 发展 fā zhǎn

deviate *v. i* 偏离 piān lí

deviation *n* 背离 bèi lí

device *n* 装置 zhuāng zhì

devil *n* 魔鬼 mó guǐ

devise *v.t* 发明 fā míng

devoid *a* 全无的 quán wú de

devote *v.t* 献身 xiàn shēn

devotee *n* 爱好者 ài hào zhě

devotion *n* 热爱 rè ài

devour *v.t* 吞食 tūn shí

dew *n.* 露水 lù shuǐ

diabetes *n* 糖尿病 táng niào bìng

diagnose *v.t* 诊断 zhěn duàn

diagnosis *n* 诊断 zhěn duàn

diagram *n* 图表 tú biǎo

dial *n* 刻度盘 kè dù pán

dialect *n* 方言 fāng yán

dialogue *n* 对话 duì huà

diameter *n* 直径 zhí jìng

diamond *n* 钻石 zuàn shí

diarrhoea *n* 腹泻 fù xiè

diary *n* 日记 rì jì

dice *n.* 骰子 tóu zǐ

dice *v.i.* 掷骰子 zhì tóu zǐ

dictate *v.t* 口述 kǒu shù

dictation *n* 口述 kǒu shù

dictator *n* 独裁者 dú cái zhě

diction *n* 用语 yòng yǔ

dictionary *n* 字典 zì diǎn

dictum *n* 格言 gé yán

didactic *a* 教诲的 jiào huì de

die *v.i* 死亡 sǐ wáng

die *n* 冲模 chòng mú

diet *n* 日常饮食 rì cháng yǐn shí

differ *v.i* 不一致 bù yí zhì

difference *n* 差异 chā yì

different *a* 不同的 bù tóng de

difficult *a* 困难的 kùn nan de

difficulty *n* 难点 nán diǎn

dig *n* 挖掘 wā jué

dig *v.t.* 挖 wā

digest *v.t.* 消化 xiāo huà

digest *n.* 摘要 zhāi yào

digestion *n* 消化力 xiāo huà lì

digit *n* 数字 shù zì

dignify *v.t* 增威严 zēng wēi yán

dignity *n* 尊严 zūn yán

dilemma *n* 困境 kùn jìng

diligence *n* 勤奋 qín fèn

diligent *a* 勤勉的 qín miǎn de

dilute *v.t* 稀释 xī shì

dilute *a* 稀释的 xī shì de

dim *a* 暗淡的 àn dàn de

dim *v.t* 使暗淡 shǐ àn dàn

dimension *n* 尺寸 chǐ cùn

diminish *v.t* (使)减少 (shǐ) jiǎn shǎo

din *n* 喧嚣 xuān xiāo

dine *v.t.* 宴请 yàn qǐng

dinner *n* 晚餐 wǎn cān

dip *n.* 涉猎 shè liè

dip *v.t* 浸 jìn

diploma *n* 文凭 wén píng

diplomacy *n* 外交 wài jiāo

diplomat *n* 外交官 wài jiāo guān

diplomatic *a* 外交的 wài jiāo de

dire *a* 可怕的 kě pà de

direct *a* 直接的 zhí jiē de

direct *v.t* 指导 zhí dǎo

direction *n* 方向 fāng xiàng

director *n.* 导演 dáo yǎn

directory *n* 工商名录 gōng shāng míng lù

dirt *n* 泥土 ní tǔ

dirty *a* 肮脏的 āng zang de

disability *n* 无力 wú lì

disable *v.t* 使失去能力 shǐ shī qù néng lì

disabled *a* 残废的 cán fèi de

disadvantage *n* 不利 bú lì

disagree *v.i* 不同意 bù tóng yì

disagreeable *a.* 令人不快的 lìng rén bú kuài de

disagreement *n.* 不一致 bù yí zhì

disappear *v.i* 消失 xiāo shī

disappearance *n* 失踪 shī zōng

disappoint *v.t.* 使失望 shǐ shī wàng

disapproval *n* 不赞成 bú zàn chéng

disapprove *v. t* 不赞成 bú zàn chéng

disarm *v. t* 解除武装 jiě chú wǔ zhuāng

disarmament *n.* 裁军 cái jūn

disaster *n* 灾祸 zāi huò

disastrous *a* 损失惨重的 sǔn shī cǎn zhòng de

disc *n.* 圆盘 yuán pán

discard *v. t* 丢弃 diū qì

discharge *v. t* 卸下 xiè xià

discharge *n.* 卸货 xiè huò

disciple *n* 门徒 mén tú

discipline *n* 纪律 jì lǜ

disclose *v. t* 透露 tòu lù

discomfort *n* 不舒适 bù shū shì

disconnect *v. t* 使分离 shǐ fēn lí

discontent *n* 不满 bù mǎn

discontinue *v. t* 停止 tíng zhǐ

discord *n* 不调和 bú tiáo hé

discount *n* 折扣 zhé kòu

discourage *v. t.* 阻碍 zǔ ài

discourse *n* 谈话 tán huà

discourteous *a* 失礼的 shī lǐ de

discover *v. t* 发现 fā xiàn

discovery *n.* 发现 fā xiàn

discretion *n* 慎重 shèn zhòng

discriminate *v. t.* 区别 qū bié

discrimination *n* 歧视 qí shì

discuss *v. t.* 讨论 tǎo lùn

disdain *n* 蔑视 miè shì

disdain *v. t.* 蔑视 miè shì

disease *n* 疾病 jí bìng

disguise *n* 假装 jiǎ zhuāng

disguise *v. t* 假装 jiǎ zhuāng

dish *n* 碟 dié

dishearten *v. t* 使...沮丧 shǐ... jǔ sàng

dishonest *a* 不诚实的 bù chéng shí de

dishonesty *n.* 不诚实 bù chéng shí

dishonour *v. t* 使丧失名誉 shǐ sàng shī míng yù

dishonour *n* 耻辱 chí rǔ

dislike *v. t* 讨厌 tǎo yàn

dislike *n* 嫌恶 xián wù

disloyal *a* 不忠的 bù zhōng de

dismiss *v. t.* 解散 jiě sàn

dismissal *n* 解雇 jiě gù

disobey *v. t* 违反 wéi fǎn

disorder *n* 杂乱 zá luàn

disparity *n* 差异 chā yì

dispensary *n* 药房 yào fáng

disperse *v. t* 分散 fēn sàn

displace *v. t* 移置 yí zhì

display *v. t* 陈列 chén liè

display *n* 显示 xiǎn shì

displease *v. t* 使不愉快 shǐ bù yú kuài

displeasure *n* 不满 bù mǎn

disposal *n* 丢掉 diū diào

dispose *v. t* 处理 chú lǐ

disprove *v. t* 反驳 fǎn bó

dispute *n* 争论 zhēng lùn

dispute *v. i* 争论 zhēng lùn

disqualification *n* 取消资格 qǔ xiāo zī gé

disqualify *v. t.* 取消...资格 qǔ xiāo... zī gé

disquiet *n* 不安 bù ān

disregard *n* 忽视 hū shì

disregard *v. t* 不理 bù lǐ

disrepute *n* 丧失名誉 sàng shī míng yù

disrespect *n* 不敬 bú jìng

disrupt *v. t* 使分裂 shǐ fēn liè

dissatisfaction *n* 不满 bù mǎn

dissatisfy *v. t.* 不满足 bù mǎn zú

dissect *v. t* 解剖 jiě pōu

dissection *n* 解剖 jiě pōu

dissimilar *a* 不同的 bù tóng de

dissolve *v.t* 溶解 róng jiě

dissuade *v. t* 劝阻 quàn zǔ

distance *n* 距离 jù lí

distant *a* 远的 yuǎn de

distil *v. t* 蒸馏 zhēng liú

distillery *n* 酿酒厂 niàng jiǔ chǎng

distinct *a* 清楚的 qīng chu de

distinction *n* 区别 qū bié

distinguish *v. i* 区别 qū bié

distort *v. t* 扭曲 niǔ qǔ

distress *n* 苦恼 kú nǎo

distress *v. t* 使苦恼 shǐ kú nǎo

distribute *v. t* 分配 fēn pèi

distribution *n* 分配 fēn pèi

district *n* 区域 qū yù

distrust *n* 不信任 bú xìn rèn

distrust *v. t.* 不信任 bú xìn rèn

disturb *v. t* 扰乱 rǎo luàn

ditch *n* 沟渠 gōu qú

ditto *n.* 同上 tóng shàng

dive *v. i* 跳水 tiào shuǐ

dive *n* 潜水 qián shuǐ

diverse *a* 不同的 bù tóng de

divert *v. t* 转移 zhuǎn yí

divide *v. t* 分 fēn

divine *a* 神圣的 shén shèng de

divinity *n* 神 shén

division *n* 除法 chú fǎ

divorce *n* 离婚 lí hūn

divorce *v. t* 与...离婚 yǔ... lí hūn

divulge *v. t* 泄露 xiè lòu

do *v. t* 做 zuò

docile *a* 温顺的 wēn shùn de

dock *n.* 码头 mǎ tou

doctor *n* 医生 yī sheng

doctorate *n* 博士头衔 bó shì tóu xián

doctrine *n* 教条 jiào tiáo

document *n* 文件 wén jiàn

dodge *n* 诡计 guǐ jì

dodge *v. t* 避开 bì kāi

doe *n* 母鹿 mǔ lù

dog *n* 狗 gǒu

dog *v. t* 跟踪 gēn zōng

dogma *n* 教条 jiào tiáo

dogmatic *a* 教条的 jiào tiáo de

doll *n* 洋娃娃 yáng wá wa

dollar *n* 美元 měi yuán

domain *n* 领域 lǐng yù

dome *n* 圆顶 yuán dǐng

domestic *a* 家庭的 jiā tíng de

domestic *n* 佣人 yōng rén

domicile *n* 住所 zhù suǒ

dominant *a* 占优势的 zhàn yōu shì de

dominate *v. t* 支配 zhī pèi

domination *n* 控制 kòng zhì

dominion *n* 统治权 tǒng zhì quán

donate *v. t* 捐赠 juān zèng

donation *n.* 捐款 juān kuǎn

donkey *n* 驴子 lú zǐ

donor *n* 赠送人 zèng sòng rén

doom *n* 命运 mìng yùn

doom *v. t.* 注定 zhù dìng

door *n* 门 mén

dose *n* 一剂 yí jì

dot *n* 点 diǎn

dot *v. t* 打点于 dǎ dian yú

double *a* 两倍的 liǎng bèi de

double *v. t.* 使加倍 shǐ jiā bèi

double *n* 双倍 shuāng bèi

doubt *v. i* 怀疑 huái yí

doubt *n* 疑问 yí wèn

dough *n* 生面团 shēng miàn tuán

dove *n* 鸽 gē

down *adv* 下 xià

down *prep* 往下 wǎng xià

down *v. t* 咽下 yàn xià

downfall *n* 衰败 shuāi bài

downpour *n* 倾盆大雨 qīng pén dà yǔ

downright *adv* 彻底 chè dǐ

downright *a* 明白的 míng bai de

downward *a* 下降的 xià jiàng de

downward *adv* 向下地 xiàng xià dì

downwards *adv* 向下 xiàng xià

dowry *n* 嫁妆 jià zhuang

doze *n.* 瞌睡 kē shuì

doze *v. i* 打瞌睡 dǎ kē shuì

dozen *n* 一打 yì dá

draft *v. t* 起草 qí cǎo

draft *n* 草稿 cǎo gǎo

draftsman *n* 起草人 qí cǎo rén

drag *n* 拖累 tuō lěi

drag *v. t* 拖 tuō

dragon *n* 龙 lóng

drain *n* 排水沟 pái shuǐ gōu

drain *v. t* 排出 pái chū

drainage *n* 排水 pái shuǐ

dram *n* 少量的酒 shǎo liàng de jiǔ

drama *n* 戏剧 xì jù

dramatic *a* 戏剧的 xì jù de

dramatist *n* 剧作家 jù zuò jiā

draper *n* 绸布商 chóu bù shāng

drastic *a* 激烈的 jī liè de

draught *n* 通风 tōng fēng

draw *v. t* 拉 lā

draw *n* 牵引 qiān yǐn

drawback *n* 缺点 quē diǎn

drawer *n* 抽屉 chōu ti

drawing *n* 图画 tú huà

drawing-room *n* 客厅 kè tīng

dread *n* 恐怖 kǒng bù

dread *v. t* 担心 dān xīn

dread *a* 令人恐惧的 lìng rén kǒng jù de

dream *n* 梦 mèng

dream *v. i.* 做梦 zuò mèng

drench *v. t* 使湿透 shǐ shī tòu

dress *n* 衣服 yī fu

dress *v. t* 使穿衣 shǐ chuān yī

dressing *n* 调味品 tiáo wèi pǐn

drill *n* 演习 yǎn xí

drill *v. t.* 操练 cāo liàn

drink *n* 饮料 yǐn liào

drink *v. t* 饮 yǐn

drip *n* 滴 dī

drip *v. i* 滴 dī

drive *v. t* 驾驶 jià shǐ

drive *n* 旅程 lǚ chéng

driver *n* 司机 sī jī

drizzle *n* 细雨 xì yǔ

drizzle *v. i* 下毛毛雨 xià máo mao yǔ

drop *n* 滴 dī

drop *v. i* 跌落 diē luò

drought *n* 干旱 gān hàn

drown *v.i* 沉没 chén mò

drug *n* 毒品 dú pǐn

druggist *n* 药剂师 yào jì shī

drum *n* 鼓 gǔ

drum *v.i.* 敲鼓 qiāo gǔ

drunkard *n* 酒鬼 jiǔ guǐ

dry *a* 干的 gān de

dry *v. i.* 把…弄干 bǎ … nòng gān

dual *a* 二的 èr de

duck *n.* 鸭 yā

duck *v.i.* 忽潜忽露 hū qián hū lù

due *a* 当付的 dāng fù de

due *n* 应得物 yīng dé wù

due *adv* 正 zhèng

duel *n* 决斗 jué dòu

duel *v. i* 决斗 jué dòu

duke *n* 公爵 gōng jué

dull *a* 愚钝的 yú dùn de

dull *v. t.* 变迟钝 biàn chí dùn

duly *adv* 适当地 shì dàng dì

dumb *a* 哑的 yǎ de

dunce *n* 笨人 bèn rén

dung *n* (牛马等的)粪 (niú mǎ děng de) fèn

duplicate *a* 双份的 shuāng fèn de

duplicate *n* 副本 fù běn

duplicate *v. t* 使加倍 shǐ jiā bèi

duplicity *n* 口是心非 kǒu shì xīn fēi

durable *a* 耐用的 nài yòng de

duration *n* 期间 qī jiān

during *prep* 在…的期间 zài … de qī jiān

dusk *n* 黄昏 huáng hūn

dust *n* 尘 chén

dust *v.t.* 掸(灰) dǎn (huī)

duster *n* 掸子 dǎn zi

dutiful *a* 孝顺的 xiào shùn de
duty *n* 责任 zé rèn
dwarf *n* 矮小的动物 ái xiǎo de dòng wù
dwell *v. i* 住 zhù
dwelling *n* 居住 jū zhù
dwindle *v. t* 使减少 shǐ jiǎn shǎo
dye *v. t* 染 rǎn
dye *n* 染料 rǎn liào
dynamic *a* 动力的 dòng lì de
dynamics *n.* 动态 dòng tài
dynamite *n* 甘油炸药 gān yóu zhà yào
dynamo *n* 发电机 fā diàn jī
dynasty *n* 朝代 cháo dài
dysentery *n* 痢疾 lì ji

E

each *a* 每 měi
each *pron.* 各自 gè zì
eager *a* 渴望 kě wàng
eagle *n* 鹰 yíng
ear *n* 耳朵 ěr duo
early *adv* 早 zǎo
early *a* 早日的 zǎo rì de
earn *v. t* 赚得 zhuàn dé
earnest *a* 认真 rèn zhēn
earth *n* 地球 dì qiú
earthen *a* 土制的 tǔ zhì de
earthly *a* 地球的 dì qiú de
earthquake *n* 地震 dì zhèn
ease *n* 快活 kuài huo
ease *v. t* 使安逸 shǐ ān yì
east *n* 东 dōng
east *adv* 向东 xiàng dōng
east *a* 东方的 dōng fāng de
easter *n* 复活节 fù huó jié
eastern *a* 东方的 dōng fāng de
easy *a* 容易的 róng yì de
eat *v. t* 吃 chī
eatable *n.* 食物 shí wù
eatable *a* 可食用的 kě shí yòng de
ebb *n* 减退 jiǎn tuì

ebb *v. i* 衰退 shuāi tuì
ebony *n* 乌木 wū mù
echo *n* 回声 huí shēng
echo *v. t* 使反响 shǐ fán xiǎng
eclipse *n* 蚀 shí
economic *a* 经济的 jīng jì de
economical *a* 经济学上的 jīng jì xué shàng de
economics *n.* 经济学 jīng jì xué
economy *n* 经济 jīng jì
edge *n* 边 biān
edible *a* 可以吃的 ké yǐ chī de
edifice *n* 大厦 dà shà
edit *v. t* 校订 jiào dìng
edition *n* 版 bǎn
editor *n* 编辑 biān jí
editorial *a* 编辑的 biān jí de
editorial *n* (期刊的)社论 (qī kān de) shè lùn
educate *v. t* 教育 jiào yù
education *n* 教育 jiào yù
efface *v. t* 消去 xiāo qù
effect *n* 效果 xiào guǒ
effect *v. t* 引起 yín qǐ
effective *a* 有效 yǒu xiào
effeminate *a* 女人似的 nǚ rén shì de
efficacy *n* 功效 gōng xiào
efficiency *n* 效率 xiào lù
efficient *a* 效率高的 xiào lù gāo de
effigy *n* 雕像 diāo xiàng
effort *n* 努力 nǔ lì
egg *n* 鸡蛋 jī dàn
ego *n* 自我 zì wǒ
egotism *n* 自我主义 zì wǒ zhǔ yì
eight *n* 八 bā
eighteen *a* 十八 shí bā
eighty *n* 八十 bā shí
either *a* 两者之一的 liǎng zhě zhǐ yī de
either *adv.* 而且还 ér qiě hái
eject *v. t* 喷出 pēn chū
elaborate *v. t* 认真做 rèn zhēn zuò
elaborate *a* 认真的 rèn zhēn de

elapse *n* 消逝 xiāo shì

elastic *a* 有弹性 yǒu tán xìng

elbow *n* 肘 zhǒu

elder *a* 年长的 nián zhǎng de

elder *n* 年长者 nián zhǎng zhě

elderly *a* 较老的 jiào lǎo de

elect *v. t* 推选 tuī xuǎn

election *n* 选举 xuǎn jǔ

electorate *n* 选举区 xuán jǔ qū

electric *a* 电的 diàn de

electricity *n* 电 diàn

electrify *v. t* 使兴奋 shǐ xīng fèn

elegance *n* 风雅 fēng yǎ

elegant *adj* 优雅的 yōu yǎ de

elegy *n* 挽歌 wǎn gē

element *n* 要素 yào sù

elementary *a* 基本的… jī běn de…

elephant *n* 象 xiàng

elevate *v. t* 抬高 tái gāo

elevation *n* 海拔 hǎi bá

eleven *n* 十一 shí yī

elf *n* 小精灵 xiǎo jīng líng

eligible *a* 有被选举资格的 yǒu bèi xuán jǔ zī gé de

eliminate *v. t* 除去 chú qù

elimination *n* 除去 chú qù

elope *v. i* 私奔 sī bēn

eloquence *n* 口才 kǒu cái

eloquent *a* 雄辩的 xióng biàn de

else *a* 不同的 bù tóng de

else *adv* 其他 qí tā

elucidate *v. t* 解释 jiě shì

elude *v. t* 闪避 shǎn bì

elusion *n* 逃避 táo bì

elusive *a* 无从捉摸的 wú cóng zhuō mō de

emancipation *n.* 解放 jiě fàng

embalm *v. t* 用防腐药物 yòng fáng fǔ yào wù

embankment *n* 筑堤 zhù dī

embark *v. t* 使上飞机 shǐ shàng fēi jī

embarrass *v. t* 使窘迫 shǐ jiǒng pò

embassy *n* 大使馆 dà shǐ guǎn

embitter *v. t* 使变苦 shǐ biàn kǔ

emblem *n* 象征 xiàng zhēng

embodiment *n* 具体化 jù tǐ huà

embody *v. t.* 使具体化 shǐ jù tǐ huà

embolden *v. t.* 给…壮胆 gěi… zhuàng dǎn

embrace *v. t.* 抱 bào

embrace *n* 接受 jiē shòu

embroidery *n* 刺绣 cì xiù

embryo *n* 胚胎 pēi tāi

emerald *n* 绿宝石 lǜ bǎo shí

emerge *v. i* 出现 chū xiàn

emergency *n* 紧急情况 jǐn jí qíng kuàng

eminance *n* 显赫 xiǎn hè

eminent *a* 杰出的 jié chū de

emissary *n* 密使 mì shǐ

emit *v. t* 放射(热等) fàng shè (rè děng)

emolument *n* 薪水 xīn shuǐ

emotion *n* 感情 gǎn qíng

emotional *a* 感情的 gǎn qíng de

emperor *n* 皇帝 huáng dì

emphasis *n* 强调 qiáng diào

emphasize *v. t* 强调 qiáng diào

emphatic *a* 强调的 qiáng diào de

empire *n* 帝国 dì guó

employ *v. t* 雇用 gù yòng

employee *n* 雇员 gù yuán

employer *n* 雇主 gù zhǔ

employment *n* 工作 gōng zuò

empower *v. t* 授权 shòu quán

empress *n* 皇后 huáng hòu

empty *a* 空的 kōng de

empty *v* 弄空 nòng kōng

emulate *v. t.* 与…竞赛[竞争] yǔ… jìng sài [jìng zhēng]

enable *v. t* 使能够 shǐ néng gòu

enact *v. t* 制定(法律) zhì dìng (fǎ lù)

enamel *n* 珐琅 fà láng

enamour *v. t* 使倾心 shǐ qīng xīn

encase *v. t* 把…装箱 bǎ … zhuāng xiāng

enchant *v. t* 使迷住 shǐ mí zhù

encircle *v. t.* 围绕 wéi rǎo

enclose *v. t* 包 bāo

enclosure *n.* 包围 bāo wéi

encompass *v. t* 包含 bāo hán

encounter *n.* 遭遇 zāo yù

encounter *v. t* 遇见 yù jiàn

encourage *v. t* 鼓励 gǔ lì

encroach *v. i* 侵佔 qīn zhàn

encumber *v. t.* 阻碍 zǔ ài

encyclopaedia *n.* 百科全书 bǎi kē quán shū

end *v. t* 使完结 shǐ wán jié

end *n.* 端 duān

endanger *v. t.* 危及 wēi jí

endear *v. t* 使受喜爱 shǐ shòu xǐ ài

endearment *n.* 亲爱 qīn ài

endeavour *n* 尽全力 jìn quán lì

endeavour *v. i* 尽力 jìn lì

endorse *v. t.* 背面签名 bèi miàn qiān míng

endow *v. t* 捐赠基金 juān zèng jī jīn

endurable *a* 可忍受的 kě rěn shòu de

endurance *n.* 耐久 nài jiǔ

endure *v. t.* 忍耐 rěn nài

enemy *n* 敌人 dí rén

energetic *a* 积极的 jī jí de

energy *n.* 能量 néng liàng

enfeeble *v. t.* 使衰弱 shǐ shuāi ruò

enforce *v. t.* 推行 tuī xíng

enfranchise *v. t.* 释放(奴隶) shì fàng (nú lì)

engage *v. t.* 使忙于 shǐ máng yú

engagement *n.* 约会 yuē huì

engine *n* 引擎 yǐn qíng

engineer *n* 工程师 gōng chéng shī

English *n* 英语 yīng yǔ

engrave *v. t* 刻上 kè shàng

engross *v. t* 使全神贯注 shǐ quán shén guàn zhù

engulf *v. t* 吞没 tūn mò

enigma *n* 谜 mí

enjoy *v. t* 享受 xiǎng shòu

enjoyment *n* 愉快 yú kuài

enlarge *v. t* 放大 fàng dà

enlighten *v. t.* 启发 qǐ fā

enlist *v. t* 使入伍 shǐ rù wǔ

enliven *v. t.* 使快活 shǐ kuài huo

enmity *n* 仇恨 chóu hèn

ennoble *v. t.* 使高贵 shǐ gāo guì

enormous *a* 巨大的 jù dà de

enough *a* 足够的 zú gòu de

enough *adv* 足够 zú gòu

enrage *v. t* 激怒 jī nù

enrapture *v. t* 使狂喜 shǐ kuáng xǐ

enrich *v. t* 使丰富 shǐ fēng fù

enrol *v. t* 使入学 shǐ rù xué

enshrine *v. t* 把…置于殿内祀奉 zhì yú diàn nèi sì fèng

enslave *v. t.* 使做奴隶 shǐ zuò nú lì

ensue *v. i* 跟着发生 gēn zhe fā shēng

ensure *v. t* 保护 bǎo hù

entangle *v. t* 使卷入 shǐ juǎn rù

enter *v. t* 入 rù

enterprise *n* 企[事]业单位 qǐ [shì] yè dān wèi

entertain *v. t* 使快乐 shǐ kuài lè

entertainment *n.* 娱乐 yú lè

enthrone *v. t* 使登基 shǐ dēng jī

enthusiasm *n* 热心 rè xīn

enthusiastic *a* 热情的 rè qíng de

entice *v. t.* 引诱 yǐn yòu

entire *a* 全部的 quán bù de
entirely *adv* 完全地 wán quán dì
entitle *v. t.* 使…有资格 shǐ … yǒu zī gé
entity *n* 实体 shí tǐ
entomology *n.* 昆虫学 kūn chóng xué
entrails *n.* 内脏 nèi zàng
entrance *n* 入场 rù chǎng
entrap *v. t.* 使陷罗网 shǐ xiàn luó wǎng
entreat *v. t.* 请求 qǐng qiú
entreaty *n.* 恳求 kěn qiú
entrust *v. t* 委托 wěi tuō
entry *n* 进入 jìn rù
enumerate *v. t.* 列举 liè jǔ
envelop *v. t* 包 bāo
envelope *n* 信封 xìn fēng
enviable *a* 令人羡慕 lìng rén xiàn mù
envious *a* 忌妒的 jì dù de
environment *n.* 环境 huán jìng
envy *v* 羡慕 xiàn mù
envy *v. t* 忌妒 jì dù
epic *n* 史诗 shǐ shī
epidemic *n* 流行病 liú xíng bìng
epigram *n* 讽刺短诗 fěng cì duǎn shī
epilepsy *n* 羊痫疯 yáng xián fēng
epilogue *n* 后记 hòu jì
episode *n* 一段情节 yí duàn qíng jié
epitaph *n* 墓志铭 mù zhì míng
epoch *n* 时代 shí dài
equal *a* 相等的 xiāng děng de
equal *v. t* 等于 děng yú
equal *n* 地位相等的人 dì wèi xiāng děng de rén
equality *n* 平等 píng děng
equalize *v. t.* 使相等 shǐ xiāng děng
equate *v. t* 使相等 shǐ xiāng děng

equation *n* 方程式 fāng chéng shì
equator *n* 赤道 chì dào
equilateral *a* 等边的 děng biān de
equip *v. t* 装备 zhuāng bèi
equipment *n* 设备 shè bèi
equitable *a* 公平的 gōng píng de
equivalent *a* 相当的 xiāng dāng de
equivocal *a* 含糊的 hán hu de
era *n* 时代 shí dài
eradicate *v. t* 根除 gēn chú
erase *v. t* 删除 shān chú
erect *v. t* 创立 chuàng lì
erect *a* 直立的 zhí lì de
erection *n* 直立 zhí lì
erode *v. t* 侵蚀 qīn shí
erosion *n* 侵蚀 qīn shí
erotic *a* 性爱的 xìng ài de
err *v. i* 犯错误 fàn cuò wù
errand *n* 差事 chāi shi
erroneous *a* 错误的 cuò wù de
error *n* 错误 cuò wù
erupt *v. i* 爆发 bào fā
eruption *n* 爆发 bào fā
escape *n* 逃避 táo bì
escape *v.i* 逃走 táo zǒu
escort *n* 护送 hù sòng
escort *v. t* 护送 hù sòng
especial *a* 特别的 tè bié de
essay *n.* 随笔 suí bǐ
essay *v. t.* 企图 qǐ tú
essayist *n* 随笔作家 suí bǐ zuò jiā
essence *n* 实质 shí zhì
essential *a* 必要的 bì yào de
establish *v. t.* 建立 jiàn lì
establishment *n* 确立 què lì
estate *n* 不动产 bú dòng chǎn
esteem *n* 尊敬 zūn jìng
esteem *v. t* 尊敬 zūn jìng
estimate *n.* 估计 gū jì
estimate *v. t* 估计 gū jì
estimation *n* 判断 pàn duàn
etcetera *adv.* 等等 děng děng

eternal *a.* 永远的 yóng yuǎn de

eternity *n* 永远 yóng yuǎn

ether *n* 醚 mí

ethical *a* 道德的 dào dé de

ethics *n.* 道德规范 dào dé gui fàn

etiquette *n* 礼节 lǐ jié

etymology *n.* 词源学 cí yuán xué

eunuch *n* 太监 tài jiàn

evacuate *v. t* 疏散 shū sàn

evacuation *n* 疏散 shū sàn

evade *v. t* 逃避 táo bì

evaluate *v. t* 评估 píng gū

evaporate *v. i* 蒸发 zhēng fā

evasion *n* 逃避 táo bì

even *a* 平坦的 píng tǎn de

even *v. t* 使平坦 shǐ píng tǎn

even *adv* 甚至 shèn zhì

evening *n* 傍晚 bàng wǎn

event *n* 事件 shì jiàn

eventually *adv.* 最后 zuì hòu

ever *adv* 曾经 céng jing

evergreen *a* 常绿的 cháng lù de

evergreen *n* 常绿树 cháng lù shù

everlasting *a.* 永恆的 yǒng héng de

every *a* 每一 měi yī

evict *v. t* 逐出 zhú chū

eviction *n* 逐出 zhú chū

evidence *n* 证据 zhèng jù

evident *a.* 显然的 xiǎn rán de

evil *n* 邪恶 xié è

evil *a* 邪恶的 xié è de

evoke *v. t* 引起 yín qǐ

evolution *n* 进化 jìn huà

evolve *v. t* 使进化 shǐ jìn huà

ewe *n* 母羊 mǔ yáng

exact *a* 准确的 zhǔn què de

exaggerate *v. t.* 夸大 kuā dà

exaggeration *n.* 夸张 kuā zhāng

exalt *v. t* 赞扬 zàn yáng

examination *n.* 考试 kǎo shì

examine *v. t* 检查 jiǎn chá

examinee *n* 应试者 yìng shì zhě

examiner *n* 主考者 zhú kǎo zhě

example *n* 例子 lì zi

excavate *v. t.* 挖空 wā kōng

excavation *n.* 挖掘 wā jué

exceed *v.t* 超越 chāo yuè

excel *v.i* 胜过其他 shèng guò qí tā

excellence *n.* 优秀 yōu xiù

excellency *n* 优点 yōu diǎn

excellent *a.* 优良的 yōu liáng de

except *v. t* 除外 chú wài

except *prep* 除了...之外 chú le... zhī wài

exception *n* 例外 lì wài

excess *n* 过度 guò dù

excess *a* 过量的 guò liàng de

exchange *n* 交换 jiāo huàn

exchange *v. t* 交换 jiāo huàn

excise *n* 消费税 xiāo fèi shuì

excite *v. t* 使兴奋 shǐ xing fèn

exclaim *v.i* 大叫 dà jiào

exclamation *n* 惊叹词 jīng tàn cí

exclude *v. t* 排除 pái chú

exclusive *a* 独占的 dú zhàn de

excommunicate *v. t.* 逐出教会 zhú chū jiào huì

excursion *n.* 远足 yuǎn zú

excuse *v.t* 原谅 yuán liàng

excuse *n* 借口 jiè kǒu

execute *v. t* 执行 zhí xíng

execution *n* 实行 shí xíng

executioner *n.* 刽子手 guì zǐ shǒu

exempt *v. t.* 使免除 shǐ miǎn chú

exempt *a.* 免除的 miǎn chú de

exercise *n.* 运动 yùn dòng

exercise *v. i* 锻炼 duàn liàn

exhaust *v. t.* 使精疲力尽 shǐ jing pí lì jìn

exhibit *n.* 展览品 zhán lǎn pǐn
exhibit *v. t* 展出 zhǎn chū
exhibition *n.* 展览 zhán lǎn
exile *n.* 流放 liú fàng
exile *v. t* 放逐 fàng zhú
exist *v.i* 存在 cún zài
existence *n* 存在 cún zài
exit *n.* 出口 chū kǒu
expand *v.t.* 使膨胀 shǐ péng zhàng
expansion *n.* 扩充 kuò chōng
ex-parte *a* 单方面的 dān fāng miàn de
ex-parte *adv* 单方 dān fāng
expect *v. t* 预期 yù qī
expectation *n.* 期待 qī dài
expedient *a* 权宜之计 quán yí zhī jì
expedite *v. t.* 加快 jiā kuài
expedition *n* 远征 yuǎn zhēng
expel *v. t.* 赶出 gǎn chū
expend *v. t* 花费 huā fèi
expenditure *n* 消费 xiāo fèi
expense *n.* 开支 kāi zhī
expensive *a* 贵的 guì de
experience *n* 经验 jīng yàn
experience *v. t.* 经历 jīng lì
experiment *n* 实验 shí yàn
expert *a* 专门的 zhuān mén de
expert *n* 专家 zhuān jiā
expire *v.i.* 过期 guò qī
expiry *n* 到期 dào qī
explain *v. t.* 解释 jiě shì
explanation *n* 解释 jiě shì
explicit *a.* 清楚的 qīng chu de
explode *v. t.* 爆炸 bào zhà
exploit *n* 功绩 gōng jì
exploit *v. t* 利用 lì yòng
exploration *n* 勘探 kān tàn
explore *v.t* 探险 tàn xiǎn
explosion *n.* 爆炸 bào zhà
explosive *n.* 炸药 zhà yào
explosive *a* 爆炸的 bào zhà de

exponent *n* 倡导者 chàng dǎo zhě
export *n* 输出品 shū chū pǐn
export *v. t.* 出口 chū kǒu
expose *v. t* 暴露 bào lù
express *v. t.* 表达 biǎo dá
express *a* 快的 kuài de
express *n* 快车 kuài chē
expression *n.* 表达 biǎo dá
expressive *a.* 表达的 biǎo dá de
expulsion *n.* 逐出 zhú chū
extend *v. t* 延伸 yán shēn
extent *n.* 范围 fàn wéi
external *a* 外面的 wài miàn de
extinct *a* 灭绝的 miè jué de
extinguish *v.t* 熄灭 xī miè
extol *v. t.* 颂扬 sòng yáng
extra *a* 额外的 é wài de
extra *adv* 额外地 é wài dì
extract *n* 榨出物 zhà chū wù
extract *v.t* 榨取 zhà qǔ
extraordinary *a.* 非常的 fēi cháng de
extravagance *n* 奢侈 shē chǐ
extravagant *a* 奢侈的 shē chǐ de
extreme *a* 偏激的 piān jī de
extreme *n* 极端 jí duān
extremist *n* 偏激份子 piān jī fèn zi
exult *v. i* 非常高兴 fēi cháng gāo xìng
eye *n* 眼睛 yǎn jing
eyeball *n* 眼球 yǎn qiú
eyelash *n* 睫毛 jié máo
eyelet *n* 孔眼 kǒng yǎn
eyewash *n* 洗眼药水 xǐ yǎn yào shuǐ

F

fable *n.* 寓言 yù yán
fabric *n* 布 bù
fabricate *v.t* 伪造 wěi zào
fabrication *n* 制造 zhì zào
fabulous *a* 传说的 chuán shuō de

facade *n* 表面 biǎo miàn
face *n* 脸 liǎn
face *v.t* 面对 miàn duì
facet *n* 方面 fāng miàn
facial *a* 脸的 liǎn de
facile *a* 容易的 róng yì de
facilitate *v.t* 帮助 bāng zhù
facility *n* 设施 shè shī
facsimile *n* 传真 chuán zhēn
fact *n* 事实 shì shí
faction *n* 小派系 xiǎo pài xì
factious *a* 好搞派系的 hǎo gǎo pài xì de
factor *n* 因素 yīn sù
factory *n* 工厂 gōng chǎng
faculty *n* [大学]院系 [dà xué] yuàn xì
fad *n* 时尚 shí shàng
fade *v.i* 褪色 tuì sè
faggot *n* 柴把 chái bǎ
fail *v.i* 失败 shī bài
failure *n* 失败 shī bài
faint *a* 微弱的 wēi ruò de
faint *v.i* 昏倒 hūn dǎo
fair *a* 公平的 gōng píng de
fair *n.* 美好的事物 méi hǎo de shì wù
fairly *adv.* 公平地 gōng píng dì
fairy *n* 仙女 xiān nǚ
faith *n* 信心 xìn xīn
faithful *a* 忠实的 zhōng shí de
falcon *n* 猎鹰 liè yīng
fall *v.i.* 下跌 xià diē
fall *n* 落下 luò xià
fallacy *n* 谬论 miù lùn
fallow *a* 休耕的 xiū gēng de
false *a* 假的 jiǎ de
falter *v.i* 支吾 zhī wú
fame *n* 名望 míng wàng
familiar *a* 熟悉的 shú xī de
family *n* 家庭 jiā tíng
famine *n* 饥荒 jī huang
famous *a* 出名的 chū míng de
fan *n* 风扇 fēng shàn
fanatic *a* 狂热的 kuáng rè de

fanatic *n* 狂热者 kuáng rè zhě
fancy *n* 幻想 huàn xiǎng
fancy *v.t* 想象 xiǎng xiàng
fantastic *a* 奇妙的 qí miào de
far *adv.* 甚远地 shèn yuǎn dì
far *a* 远的 yuǎn de
far *n* 小麦 xiǎo mài
farce *n* 闹剧 nào jù
fare *n* 费用 fèi yong
farewell *n* 辞别 cí bié
farewell *interj.* 再会 zài huì
farm *n* 农场 nóng chǎng
farmer *n* 农夫 nóng fū
fascinate *v.t* 令人入神 lìng rén rù shén
fascination *n.* 令人着迷的事物 lìng rén zháo mí de shì wù
fashion *n* 流行 liú xíng
fashionable *a* 流行的 liú xíng de
fast *a* 快速的 kuài sù de
fast *adv* 很快地 hěn kuài dì
fast *n* 绝食 jué shí
fast *v.i* 斋戒 zhāi jiè
fasten *v.t* 拴紧 shuān jǐn
fat *a* 肥的 féi de
fat *n* 脂肪 zhī fáng
fatal *a* 致命的 zhì mìng de
fate *n* 命运 mìng yùn
father *n* 父亲 fù qīn
fathom *v.t* 彻底了解 chè dǐ liáo jiě
fathom *n* 英寻 yīng xún
fatigue *n* 疲劳 pí láo
fatigue *v.t* 使心智衰弱 shǐ xīn zhì shuāi ruò
fault *n* 过错 guò cuò
faulty *a* 有过失的 yǒu guò shī de
fauna *n* 动物群 dòng wù qún
favour1 *n* 喜爱 xǐ ài
favour *v.t* 赞成 zàn chéng
favourable *a* 有用的 yǒu yòng de
favourite *a* 喜爱的 xǐ ài de
favourite *n* 喜欢的事物 xǐ huan de shì wù
fear *n* 恐怖 kǒng bù

fear *v.i* 害怕 hài pà

fearful *a.* 可怕的 kě pà de

feasible *a* 可行的 kě xíng de

feast *n* 宴会 yàn huì

feast *v.i* 尽情地吃 jìn qíng dì chī

feat *n* 功绩 gōng jì

feather *n* 羽毛 yǔ máo

feature *n* 特色 tè sè

February *n* 二月 èr yuè

federal *a* 联邦的 lián bāng de

federation *n* 联邦 lián bāng

fee *n* 小费 xiǎo fèi

feeble *a* 微弱的 wēi ruò de

feed *v.t* 喂 wèi

feed *n* 一餐 yì cān

feel *v.t* 触摸 chù mō

feeling *n* 感觉 gǎn jué

feign *v.t* 假装 jiǎ zhuāng

felicitate *v.t* 庆贺 qìng hè

felicity *n* 幸福 xìng fú

fell *v.t* 击倒 jī dǎo

fellow *n* 同事 tóng shì

female *a* 女性的 nǔ xìng de

female *n* 女性 nǔ xìng

feminine *a* 女性的 nǔ xìng de

fence *n* 围墙 wéi qiáng

fence *v.t* 用篱笆围住 yòng lí ba wéi zhù

fend *v.t* 击退 jī tuì

ferment *n* 动乱 dòng luàn

ferment *v.t* (使)动乱 (shǐ) dòng luàn

fermentation *n* 发酵 fā jiào

ferocious *a* 残忍的 cán rěn de

ferry *n* 渡船 dù chuán

ferry *v.t* 运送 yùn sòng

fertile *a* 可繁殖的 kě fán zhí de

fertility *n* 生育力 shēng yù lì

fertilize *v.t* 使受精 shǐ shòu jīng

fertilizer *n* 肥料 féi liào

fervent *a* 热的 rè de

fervour *n* 热情 rè qíng

festival *n* 节日 jié rì

festive *a* 喜庆的 xǐ qìng de

festivity *n* 节日 jié rì

festoon *n* 花彩 huā cǎi

fetch *v.t* 接来 jiē lái

fetter *n* 束缚 shù fù

fetter *v.t* 加脚镣 jiā jiǎo liào

feud *n.* 不和 bù hé

feudal *a* 封建制度的 fēng jiàn zhì dù de

fever *n* 发烧 fā shāo

few *a* 很少的 hěn shǎo de

fiasco *n* 惨败 cǎn bài

fibre *n* 纤维 xiān wéi

fickle *a* 变幻无常的 biàn huàn wú cháng de

fiction *n* 小说 xiǎo shuō

fictitious *a* 虚构的 xū gòu de

fiddle *n* 小提琴 xiǎo tí qín

fiddle *v.i* 瞎搞 xiā gǎo

fidelity *n* 忠实 zhōng shí

fie *interj* 咄 duō

field *n* 田地 tián dì

fiend *n* 魔鬼 mó guǐ

fierce *a* 凶猛的 xiōng měng de

fiery *a* 暴躁的 bào zào de

fifteen *n* 十五 shí wǔ

fifty *n.* 五十 wǔ shí

fig *n* 无花果 wú huā guǒ

fight *n* 斗志 dòu zhì

fight *v.t* 打架 dǎ jià

figment *n* 虚构的事 xū gòu de shì

figurative *a* 比喻的 bǐ yù de

figure *n* 数字 shù zì

figure *v.t* 认为 rèn wéi

file *n* 文件 wén jiàn

file *v.t* 提交 tí jiāo

file *n* 指甲锉 zhǐ jia cuò

file *v.t* 锉 cuò

file *n* 档案 dàng àn

file *v.i.* 列队行进 liè duì xíng jìn

fill *v.t* 装满 zhuāng mǎn

film *n* 电影 diàn yǐng

film *v.t* 拍摄 pāi shè

filter *n* 过滤器 guò lù qì

filter *v.t* 过滤 guò lù

filth *n* 污秽 wū huì

filthy *a* 污秽的 wū huì de

fin *n* 鳍 qí
final *a* 最后的 zuì hòu de
finance *n* 财政 cái zhèng
finance *v.t* 供给...经费 gōng jǐ... jīng fèi
financial *a* 财政的 cái zhèng de
financier *n* 金融家 jīn róng jiā
find *v.t* 发现 fā xiàn
fine *n* 罚款 fá kuǎn
fine *v.t* 罚款 fá kuǎn
fine *a* 好的 hǎo de
finger *n* 手指 shóu zhǐ
finger *v.t* 用手指拨弄 yòng shóu zhǐ bō nòng
finish *v.t* 完成 wán chéng
finish *n* 结局 jié jú
finite *a* 有限的 yǒu xiàn de
fir *n* 杉木 shā mù
fire *n* 火 huǒ
fire *v.t* 点燃 diǎn rán
firm *a* 结实的 jiē shi de
firm *n.* 公司 gōng sī
first *a* 第一的 dì yī de
first *n* 第一 dì yī
first *adv* 首先 shǒu xiān
fiscal *a* 财政的 cái zhèng de
fish *n* 鱼 yú
fish *v.i* 钓鱼 diào yú
fisherman *n* 渔夫 yú fū
fissure *n* 裂缝 liè fèng
fist *n* 拳头 quán tou
fistula *n* 瘘管 lòu guǎn
fit *v.t* 适合 shì hé
fit *a* 适宜的 shì yí de
fit *n* 发作 fā zuò
fitful *a* 断断续续的 duàn duàn xù xù de
fitter *n* 装配工 zhuāng pèi gōng
five *n* 五 wǔ
fix *v.t* 使固定 shǐ gù dìng
fix *n* 困境 kùn jìng
flabby *a* 松弛的 sōng chí de
flag *n* 旗子 qí zi
flagrant *a* 极端明显的 jí duān míng xiǎn de
flame *n* 火焰 huǒ yàn

flame *v.i* 燃烧 rán shāo
flannel *n* 法兰绒 fǎ lán róng
flare *v.i* 闪光 shǎn guāng
flare *n* 闪耀 shǎn yào
flash *n* 闪光 shǎn guāng
flash *v.t* 使闪光 shǐ shǎn guāng
flask *n* 烧瓶 shāo píng
flat *a* 平坦的 píng tǎn de
flat *n* 平地 píng dì
flatter *v.t* 奉承 fèng cheng
flattery *n* 谄媚 chǎn mèi
flavour *n* 味 wèi
flaw *n* 瑕疵 xiá cī
flea *n.* 蚤 zǎo
flee *v.i* 逃 táo
fleece *n* 羊毛 yáng máo
fleece *v.t* 诈取 zhà qǔ
fleet *n* 舰队 jiàn duì
flesh *n* 肉 ròu
flexible *a* 柔顺的 róu shùn de
flicker *n* 闪烁 shǎn shuò
flicker *v.t* 使闪烁 shǐ shǎn shuò
flight *n* 班机 bān jī
flimsy *a* 易坏的 yì huài de
fling *v.t* 投 tóu
flippancy *n* 轻率 qīng shuài
flirt *n* 卖弄风骚的人 mài nòng fēng sāo de rén
flirt *v.i* 调情 tiáo qíng
float *v.i* 浮动 fú dòng
flock *n* 兽群 shòu qún
flock *v.i* 成群而行 chéng qún ér xíng
flog *v.t* 鞭打 biān dǎ
flood *n* 洪水 hóng shuǐ
flood *v.t* 淹没 yān mò
floor *n* 地板 dì bǎn
floor *v.t* 铺地板 pū dì bǎn
flora *n* 植物群 zhí wù qún
florist *n* 花商 huā shāng
flour *n* 面粉 miàn fěn
flourish *v.i* 繁荣 fán róng
flow *n* 流动 liú dòng
flow *v.i* 流动 liú dòng
flower *n* 花 huā
flowery *a* 多花的 duō huā de
fluent *a* 流利的 liú lì de

fluid *a* 流动的 liú dòng de
fluid *n* 液体 yè tǐ
flush *v.t.* 冲洗 chōng xǐ
flush *n* 面红 miàn hóng
flute *n* 笛 dí
flute *v.i* 吹笛子 chuī dí zi
flutter *n* 摆动 bǎi dòng
flutter *v.t* 拍(翅) pāi (chì)
fly *n* 苍蝇 cāng ying
fly *v.i* 飞 fēi
foam *n* 泡沫 pào mò
foam *v.t* 使起泡沫 shǐ qǐ pào mò
focal *a* 焦点的 jiāo diǎn de
focus *n* 焦点 jiāo diǎn
focus *v.t* 使聚焦 shǐ jù jiāo
fodder *n* 饲料 sì liào
foe *n* 敌人 dí rén
fog *n* 雾 wù
foil *v.t* 阻止 zǔ zhǐ
fold *n* 折层 zhé céng
fold *v.t* 折叠 zhé dié
foliage *n* 树叶 shù yè
follow *v.t* 跟随 gēn suí
follower *n* 追补者 zhuī bǔ zhě
folly *n* 愚蠢 yú chǔn
foment *v.t* 挑唆者 tiǎo suō zhě
fond *a* 喜欢的 xǐ huan de
fondle *v.t* 爱抚 ài fǔ
food *n* 食物 shí wù
fool *n* 愚人 yú rén
foolish *a* 愚蠢的 yú chǔn de
foolscap *n* 大页纸 dà yè zhǐ
foot *n* 脚 jiǎo
for *prep* 为 wéi
for *conj.* 因为 yīn wèi
forbid *v.t* 禁止 jìn zhǐ
force *n* 力量 lì liàng
force *v.t* 强迫 qiǎng pò
forceful *a* 有力的 yǒu lì de
forcible *a* 强制的 qiǎng zhì de
forearm *n* 前臂 qián bì
forearm *v.t* 预先武装 yù xiān wǔ zhuāng
forecast *n* 预想 yù xiǎng
forecast *v.t* 预测 yù cè

forefather *n* 祖先 zǔ xiān
forefinger *n* 食指 shí zhǐ
forehead *n* 额 é
foreign *a* 外国的 wài guó de
foreigner *n* 外国人 wài guó rén
foreknowledge *n.* 预知 yù zhī
foreleg *n* 前脚 qián jiǎo
forelock *n* 额发 é fà
foreman *n* 工头 gōng tóu
foremost *a* 最重要的 zuì zhòng yào de
forenoon *n* 上午 shàng wǔ
forerunner *n* 预兆 yù zhào
foresee *v.t* 预见 yù jiàn
foresight *n* 先见之明 xiān jiàn zhī míng
forest *n* 森林 sēn lín
forestall *v.t* 预先阻止 yù xiān zǔ zhǐ
forester *n* 林务官 lín wù guān
forestry *n* 林业 lín yè
foretell *v.t* 预言 yù yán
forethought *n* 预谋 yù móu
forever *adv* 永远 yóng yuǎn
forewarn *v.t* 预先警告 yù xiān jǐng gào
foreword *n* 序 xù
forfeit *v.t* 没收 mò shōu
forfeit *n* 罚金 fá jīn
forfeiture *n* 丧失 sàng shī
forge *n* 熔炉 róng lú
forge *v.t* 伪造 wěi zào
forgery *n* 伪造品 wěi zào pǐn
forget *v.t* 忘记 wàng jì
forgetful *a* 健忘的 jiàn wàng de
forgive *v.t* 原谅 yuán liàng
forgo *v.t* 放弃 fàng qì
forlorn *a* 孤独的 gū dú de
form *n* 表格 biǎo gé
form *v.t.* 形成 xíng chéng
formal *a* 正式的 zhèng shì de
format *n* 格式 gé shì
formation *n* 编队 biān duì
former *a* 从前的 cóng qián de
former *pron* 前者 qián zhě

formerly *adv* 以前 yǐ qián

formidable *a* 可怕的 kě pà de

formula *n* 公式 gōng shì

formulate *v.t* 用公式表示 yòng gōng shì biǎo shì

forsake *v.t.* 放弃 fàng qì

forswear *v.t.* 发誓抛弃 fā shì pāo qì

fort *n.* 堡垒 báo lěi

forte *n.* 长处 cháng chu

forth *adv.* 往前 wǎng qián

forthcoming *a.* 即将来临 的 jí jiāng lái lín de

forthwith *adv.* 立刻 lì kè

fortify *v.t.* 使坚强 shǐ jiān qiáng

fortitude *n.* 不屈不挠 bù qū bù náo

fortnight *n.* 两星期 liǎng xīng qī

fortress *n.* 城堡 chéng bǎo

fortunate *a.* 幸运的 xìng yùn de

fortune *n.* 财产 cái chǎn

forty *n.* 四十 sì shí

forum *n.* 论坛 lùn tán

forward *a.* 向前的 xiàng qián de

forward *adv* 向前地 xiàng qián dì

forward *v.t* 转寄 zhuǎn jì

fossil *n.* 化石 huà shí

foster *v.t.* 养育 yǎng yù

foul *a.* 恶臭的 è chòu de

found *v.t.* 建立 jiàn lì

foundation *n.* 基础 jī chǔ

founder *n.* 创立者 chuàng lì zhě

foundry *n.* 铸造厂 zhù zào chǎng

fountain *n.* 喷水池 pēn shuǐ chí

four *n.* 四 sì

fourteen *n.* 十四 shí sì

fowl *n.* 家禽 jiā qín

fowler *n.* 捕鸟者 bǔ niǎo zhě

fox *n.* 狐狸 hú li

fraction *n.* 小部份 xiǎo bù

fracture *n.* 骨折 gǔ zhé

fracture *v.t* (使)破碎 (shǐ) pò suì

fragile *a.* 脆弱的 cuì ruò de

fragment *n.* 碎片 suì piàn

fragrance *n.* 香味 xiāng wèi

fragrant *a.* 芬香的 fēn xiāng de

frail *a.* 脆弱的 cuì ruò de

frame *v.t.* 构成 gòu chéng

frame *n* 框 kuàng

frachise *n.* 特许经营权 tè xǔ jīng yíng quán

frank *a.* 坦白的 tǎn bái de

frantic *a.* 疯狂的 fēng kuáng de

fraternal *a.* 兄弟的 xiōng di de

fraternity *n.* 友爱 yǒu ài

fratricide *n.* 兄弟杀害的行为 xiōng di shā hài de xíng wéi

fraud *n.* 骗子 piàn zi

fraudulent *a.* 欺诈的 qī zhà de

fraught *a.* 充满...的 chōng mǎn... de

fray *n* 磨损 mó sǔn

free *a.* 自由的 zì yóu de

free *v.t* 释放 shì fàng

freedom *n.* 自由 zì yóu

freeze *v.i.* 冻结 dòng jié

freight *n.* 船货 chuán huò

French *n* 法国的 fǎ guó de

French *n* 法国人 fǎ guó rén

frenzy *n.* 疯狂 fēng kuáng

frequency *n.* 频率 pín lǜ

frequent *a.* 时常发生的 shí cháng fā shēng de

fresh *a.* 新鲜的 xīn xiān de

fret *n.* 烦躁 fán zào

fret *v.t.* 使烦恼 shǐ fán nǎo

friction *n.* 摩擦 mó cā

Friday *n.* 星期五 xīng qī wǔ

fridge *n.* 电冰箱 diàn bīng xiāng

friend *n.* 朋友 péng you

fright *n.* 惊吓 jīng xià

frighten *v.t.* 使惊吓 shǐ jīng xià

frigid *a.* 冷淡的 lěng dàn de

frill *n.* 皱边 zhòu biān

fringe *n.* 边缘 biān yuán

fringe *v.t* 加穗于 jiā suì yú

frivolous *a.* 轻佻的 qīng tiāo de

frock *n.* 连衣裙 lián yī qún

frog *n.* 青蛙 qīng wā

frolic *a.* 欢乐的 huān lè de

frolic *v.i.* 嬉戏 xī xì

from *prep.* 从 cóng

front *n.* 前面 qián mian

front *v.i.* 朝向 cháo xiàng

front *v.t* 面对 miàn duì

frontier *n.* 边界 biān jiè

frost *n.* 霜 shuāng

frown *n.* 皱眉 zhòu méi

frown *v.i* 皱眉头 zhòu méi tóu

frugal *a.* 节俭的 jié jiǎn de

fruit *n.* 水果 shuí guǒ

fruitful *a.* 结果实的 jié guǒ shí de

frustrate *v.t.* 挫败 cuò bài

frustration *n.* 挫折 cuò zhé

fry *v.t.* 油炸 yóu zhà

fry *n* 鱼苗 yú miáo

fuel *n.* 燃料 rán liào

fugitive *a.* 逃亡的 táo wáng de

fugitive *n.* 逃亡者 táo wáng zhě

fulfil *v.t.* 实践 shí jiàn

fulfilment *n.* 履行 lǚ xíng

full *a.* 丰满的 fēng mǎn de

full *adv.* 完全地 wán quán dì

fullness *n.* 充满 chōng mǎn

fully *adv.* 完全地 wán quán de

fumble *v.i.* 乱摸 luàn mō

fun *n.* 乐趣 lè qù

function *n.* 功能 gōng néng

function *v.i* 运行 yùn xíng

functionary *n.* 官员 guān yuán

fund *n.* 资金 zī jīn

fundamental *a.* 基本的 jī běn de

funeral *n.* 葬礼 zàng lǐ

fungus *n.* 真菌 zhēn jūn

funny *n.* 滑稽人物 huá jī rén wù

fur *n.* 毛皮 máo pí

furious *a.* 狂怒的 kuáng nù de

furl *v.t.* 卷收 juǎn shōu

furlong *n.* 弗隆 fú lóng

furnace *n.* 火炉 huǒ lú

furnish *v.t.* 供给 gōng jǐ

furniture *n.* 家具 jiā jù

furrow *n.* 皱纹 zhòu wén

further *adv.* 更远地 gèng yuǎn dì

further *a* 更远的 gèng yuǎn de

further *v.t* 增进 zēng jìn

fury *n.* 愤怒 fèn nù

fuse *v.t.* 结合 jié hé

fuse *n* 保险丝 báo xiǎn sī

fusion *n.* 结合 jié hé

fuss *n.* 大惊小怪 dà jīng xiǎo guài

fuss *v.i* 无事自扰 wú shì zì rǎo

futile *a.* 无用的 wú yòng de

futility *n.* 无益 wú yì

future *a.* 未来的 wèi lái de

future *n* 将来 jiāng lái

G

gabble *v.i.* 七嘴八舌地说 qī zuǐ bā zuǐ dì shuō

gadfly *n.* 讨厌的人 tǎo yàn de rén

gag *v.t.* 使呕吐 shǐ ǒu tù

gag *n.* 箝口物 qián kǒu wù

gaiety *n.* 高兴 gāo xìng

gain *v.t.* 增进 zēng jin

gain *n* 增益 zēng yì

gainsay *v.t.* 否定 fǒu dìng

gait *n.* 步法 bù fǎ

galaxy *n.* 星系 xīng xì

gale *n.* 狂风 kuáng fēng

gallant *a.* 英勇的 yīng yǒng de

gallant *n* 豪侠 háo xiá

gallantry *n.* 勇敢行为 yóng gǎn xíng wéi

gallery *n.* 画廊 huà láng

gallon *n.* 加仑 jiā lún

gallop *n.* 飞奔 fēi bēn

gallop *v.t.* 使飞跑 shǐ fēi pǎo

gallows *n.* . 绞刑架 jiǎo xíng jià

galore *adv.* 丰富地 fēng fù dì

galvanize *v.t.* 通电 tōng diàn

gamble *v.i.* 孤注一掷 gū zhù yí zhì

gamble *n* 赌博 dǔ bó

gambler *n.* 赌博者 dǔ bó zhě

game *n.* 游戏 yóu xì

game *v.i* 赌博 dǔ bó

gander *n.* 雄鹅 xióng é

gang *n.* 队 duì

gangster *n.* 流氓 liú máng

gap *n* 缝隙 fèng xì

gape *v.i.* 裂开 liè kāi

garage *n.* 车库 chē kù

garb *n.* 打扮 dǎ bàn

garb *v.t* 打扮 dǎ bàn

garbage *n.* 垃圾 lā jī

garden *n.* 花园 huā yuán

gardener *n.* 园艺家 yuán yì jiā

gargle *v.i.* 漱口 shù kǒu

garland *n.* 花环 huā huán

garland *v.t.* 戴花环 dài huā huán

garlic *n.* 大蒜 dà suàn

garment *n.* 衣服 yī fu

garter *n.* 袜带 wà dài

gas *n.* 气体 qì tǐ

gasket *n.* 垫圈 diàn quān

gasp *n.* 喘气 chuǎn qì

gasp *v.i* 喘气 chuǎn qì

gassy *a.* 气体的 qì tǐ de

gastric *a.* 胃的 wèi de

gate *n.* 闸 zhá

gather *v.t.* 使聚集 shǐ jù jí

gaudy *a.* 俗丽的 sú lì de

gauge *n.* 计量器 jì liàng qì

gauntlet *n.* 铁手套 tiě shǒu tào

gay *a.* 同性恋的 tóng xìng liàn de

gaze *v.i.* 注视 zhù shì

gaze *n* 凝视 níng shì

gazette *n.* 报 bào

gear *n.* 齿轮 chǐ lún

geld *v.t.* 阉割 yān gē

gem *n* 宝石 bǎo shí

gender *n.* 性 xìng

general *a.* 普遍的 pǔ biàn de

generally *adv.* 通常 tōng cháng

generate *v.t.* 产生 chǎn shēng

generation *n.* 一代 yí dài

generator *n.* 发电器 fā diàn qì

generosity *n.* 慷慨 kāng kǎi

generous *a.* 慷慨的 kāng kǎi de

genius *n.* 天才 tiān cái

gentle *a.* 温和的 wēn hé de

gentleman *n.* 绅士 shēn shì

gentry *n.* 上等人 shàng děng rén

genuine *a.* 真正的 zhēn zhèng de

geographer *n.* 地理学家 dì lǐ xué jiā

geographical *a.* 地理的 dì lǐ de

geography *n.* 地理学 dì lǐ xué

geological *a.* 地质的 dì zhì de

geologist *n.* 地质学研究者或专家 dì zhì xué yán jiū zhě huò zhuān jiā

geology *n.* 地质学 dì zhì xué

geometrical *a.* 几何学的 jǐ hé xué de

geometry *n.* 几何学 jǐ hé xué

germ *n.* 病菌 bìng jūn

germicide *n.* 杀菌剂 shā jūn jì

germinate *v.i.* 发芽 fā yá

germination *n.* 成长 chéng zhǎng

gerund *n.* 动名词 dòng míng cí

gesture *n.* 手势 shǒu shì

get *v.t.* 得到 dé dào

ghastly *a.* 可怕的 kě pà de

ghost *n.* 鬼 guǐ

giant *n.* 巨人 jù rén

gibbon *n.* 长臂猿 cháng bì yuán

gibe *v.i.* 嘲笑 cháo xiào

gibe *n* 嘲笑 cháo xiào

giddy *a.* 眼花的 yǎn huā de

gift *n.* 礼物 lǐ wù

gifted *a.* 有天才的 yǒu tiān cái de

gigantic *a.* 巨大的 jù dà de

giggle *v.i.* 咯咯地笑 gē gē dì xiào

gild *v.t.* 镀金 dù jīn

gilt *a.* 镀金 dù jīn

ginger *n.* 姜 jiāng

giraffe *n.* 长颈鹿 cháng jǐng lù

gird *v.i.* 准备 zhǔn bèi

girder *n.* 大梁 dà liáng

girdle *n.* 腰带 yāo dài

girdle *v.t* 围绕 wéi rǎo

girl *n.* 女孩 nǚ hái

girlish *a.* 少女的 shǎo nǚ de

gist *n.* 要点 yào diǎn

give *v.t.* 给 gěi

glacier *n.* 冰川 bīng chuān

glad *a.* 高兴的 gāo xìng de

gladden *v.t.* 使喜悦 shǐ xǐ yuè

glamour *n.* 魅力 mèi lì

glance *n.* 一瞥 yì piē

glance *v.i.* 闪光 shǎn guāng

gland *n.* 腺 xiàn

glare *n.* 闪耀光 shǎn yào guāng

glare *v.i* 发眩光 fā xuàn guāng

glass *n.* 玻璃 bō li

glaucoma *n.* 青光眼 qīng guāng yǎn

glaze *v.t.* 装以玻璃 zhuāng yǐ bō li

glaze *n* 釉 yòu

glazier *n.* 装玻璃工 zhuāng bō li gōng

glee *n.* 高兴 gāo xìng

glide *v.t.* 滑动 huá dòng

glider *n.* 滑翔机 huá xiáng jī

glimpse *n.* 一瞥 yì piē

glitter *v.i.* 闪烁 shǎn shuò

glitter *n* 闪烁 shǎn shuò

global *a.* 全球的 quán qiú de

globe *n.* 球 qiú

gloom *n.* 幽暗 yōu àn

gloomy *a.* 黑暗的 hēi àn de

glorification *n.* 美化了的东西 měi huà le de dōng xi

glorify *v.t.* 赞美 zàn měi

glorious *a.* 光荣的 guāng róng de

glory *n.* 荣誉 róng yù

gloss *n.* 光泽 guāng zé

glossary *n.* 专业词典 zhuān yè cí diǎn

glossy *a.* 平滑的 píng huá de

glove *n.* 手套 shǒu tào

glow *v.i.* 发红光 fā hóng guāng

glow *n* 赤热 chì rè

glucose *n.* 葡萄糖 pú tao táng

glue *n.* 胶水 jiāo shuǐ

glut *v.t.* 过多供应 guò duō gōng yīng

glut *n* 供过于求 gōng guò yú qiú

glutton *n.* 暴食者 bào shí zhě

gluttony *n.* 暴食 bào shí

glycerine *n.* 甘油 gān yóu

go *v.i.* 去 qù

goad *n.* 激励 jī lì

goad *v.t* 激励 jī lì

goal *n.* 目标 mù biāo

goat *n.* 山羊 shān yáng

gobble *n.* 狼吞虎咽 láng tūn hǔ yàn

goblet *n.* 酒杯 jiǔ bēi

god *n.* 上帝 shàng dì

goddess *n.* 女神 nǚ shén

godhead *n.* 神性 shén xìng

godly *a.* 虔诚的 qián chéng de

godown *n.* 仓库 cāng kù

godsend *n.* 天赐 tiān cì

goggles *n.* 护目镜 hù mù jìng

gold *n.* 黄金 huáng jīn

golden *a.* 金的 jīn de

goldsmith *n.* 金匠 jīn jiàng

golf *n.* 高尔夫球 gāo ěr fū qiú

gong *n.* 铜锣 tóng luó

good *a.* 好的 hǎo de

good *n* 好处 hǎo chu

good-bye *interj.* 再见 zài jiàn

goodness *n.* 仁慈 rén cí

goodwill *n.* 善意 shàn yì

goose *n.* 鹅 é

gooseberry *n.* 醋栗 cù lì

gorgeous *a.* 华丽的 huá lì de

gorilla *n.* 大猩猩 dà xīng xing

gospel *n.* 福音 fú yīn

gossip *n.* 闲聊 xián liáo

gourd *n.* 葫芦 hú lu

gout *n.* 痛风 tòng fēng

govern *v.t.* 统治 tǒng zhì

governance *n.* 统治 tǒng zhì

governess *n.* 女家庭教师 nǚ jiā tíng jiào shī

government *n.* 政府 zhèng fǔ

governor *n.* 州长 zhōu zhǎng

gown *n.* 睡衣 shuì yī

grab *v.t.* 攫取 jué qǔ

grace *n.* 优雅 yōu yǎ

grace *v.t.* 使优美 shǐ yōu měi

gracious *a.* 慈善的 cí shàn de

gradation *n.* 阶段 jiē duàn

grade *n.* 等级 děng jí

grade *v.t* 分级 fēn jí

gradual *a.* 逐渐的 zhú jiàn de

graduate *v.i.* 毕业 bì yè

graduate *n* 毕业生 bì yè shēng

graft *n.* 嫁接 jià jiē

graft *v.t* 嫁接 jià jiē

grain *n.* 谷粒 gǔ lì

granary *n.* 谷仓 gǔ cāng

grand *a.* 庄重的 zhuāng zhòng de

grandeur *n.* 庄严 zhuāng yán

grant *v.t.* 允许 yún xǔ

grant *n* 授予 shòu yǔ

grape *n.* 葡萄 pú tao

graph *n.* 图表 tú biǎo

graphic *a.* 绘画似的 huì huà shì de

grapple *n.* 与...扭打 yǔ... niǔ dǎ

grapple *v.i.* 抓住 zhuā zhù

grasp *v.t.* 抓住 zhuā zhù

grasp *n* 把握 bǎ wò

grass *n* 草 cǎo

grate *n.* 火炉 huǒ lú

grate *v.t* 磨碎 mó suì

grateful *a.* 感激的 gǎn jī de

gratification *n.* 满足 mǎn zú

gratis *adv.* 免费地 miǎn fèi dì

gratitude *n.* 感激之情 gǎn jī zhī qíng

gratuity *n.* 小费 xiǎo fèi

grave *n.* 坟墓 fén mù

grave *a.* 严肃的 yán sù de

gravitate *v.i.* 被重力吸引 bèi zhòng lì xī yǐn

gravitation *n.* 引力 yǐn lì

gravity *n.* 地心引力 dì xīn yǐn lì

graze *v.i.* (使)吃草 (shǐ) chī cǎo

graze *n* 擦伤 cā shāng

grease *n* 脂肪 zhī fáng

grease *v.t* 涂脂于 tú zhī yú

greasy *a.* 油腻的 yóu nì de

great *a* 非常的 fēi cháng de

greed *n.* 贪慾 tān yù

greedy *a.* 贪婪的 tān lán de

Greek *n.* 希腊人 xī là rén

Greek *a* 希腊的 xī là de

green *a.* 绿色的 lǜ sè de

green *n.* 绿色 lǜ sè

greenery *n.* 绿叶 lǜ yè

greet *v.t.* 问候 wèn hòu

grenade *n.* 手榴弹 shǒu liú dàn

grey *a.* 灰色的 huī sè de

greyhound *n.* 快速船 kuài sù chuán

grief *n.* 悲痛 bēi tòng

grievance *n.* 委屈 wěi qu

grieve *v.i.* 伤心 shāng xīn

grievous *a.* 痛苦的 tòng kǔ de

grind *v.i.* 磨碎 mó suì

grinder *n.* 推磨的人 tuī mó de rén

grip *v.t.* 抓紧 zhuā jǐn

grip *n* 紧握 jǐn wò

groan *v.i.* 呻吟 shēn yín

groan *n* 呻吟 shēn yín

grocer *n.* 食品商 shí pǐn shāng

grocery *n.* 食品杂货店 shí pǐn zá huò diàn

groom *n.* 新郎 xīn láng

groom *v.t* 喂马 wèi mǎ

groove *n.* 凹槽 āo cáo

groove *v.t* 开槽于 kāi cáo yú

grope *v.t.* 摸索 mō suǒ

gross *n.* 总数 zǒng shù

gross *a* 恶劣的 è liè de

grotesque *a.* 奇怪的 qí guài de

ground *n.* 土地 tǔ dì

group *n.* 组 zǔ

group *v.t.* 成群 chéng qún

grow *v.t.* 种植 zhòng zhí

grower *n.* 栽培者 zāi péi zhě

growl *v.i.* 咆哮 páo xiāo

growl *n* 咆哮声 páo xiāo shēng

growth *n.* 生长 shēng zhǎng

grudge *v.t.* 怀恨 huái hèn

grudge *n* 怨恨 yuàn hèn

grumble *v.i.* 发牢骚 fā láo sāo

grunt *n.* 呼噜声 hū lū shēng

grunt *v.i.* 作呼噜声 zuò hū lū shēng

guarantee *n.* 担保 dān bǎo

guarantee *v.t* 担保 dān bǎo

guard *v.i.* 看守 kān shǒu

guard *n.* 护卫队 hù wèi duì

guardian *n.* 看守者 kān shǒu zhě

guess *n.* 猜测 cāi cè

guess *v.i* 猜测 cāi cè

guest *n.* 客人 kè rén

guidance *n.* 指导 zhí dǎo

guide *v.t.* 指导 zhí dǎo

guide *n.* 指南 zhǐ nán

guild *n.* 团体 tuán tǐ

guile *n.* 狡猾 jiǎo huá

guilt *n.* 内疚 nèi jiù

guilty *a.* 犯罪的 fàn zuì de

guise *n.* 外观 wài guān

guitar *n.* 吉他 jí tā

gulf *n.* 海湾 hǎi wān

gull *n.* 鸥 ōu

gull *n* 易受骗之人 yì shòu piàn zhī rén

gull *v.t* 骗 piàn

gulp *n.* 吞咽 tūn yàn

gum *n.* 牙床 yá chuáng

gun *n.* 枪 qiāng

gust *n.* 突然一阵 tū rán yí zhèn

gutter *n.* 排水沟 pái shuǐ gōu

guttural *a.* 喉咙的 hóu lóng de

gymnasium *n.* 体育馆 tǐ yù guǎn

gymnast *n.* 体操运动员 tǐ cāo yùn dòng yuán

gymnastic *a.* 体操的 tǐ cāo de

gymnastics *n.* 体操 tǐ cāo

H

habeas corpus *n.* 人身保护权 rén shēn bǎo hù quán

habit *n.* 习惯 xí guàn

habitable *a.* 适于居住的 shì yú jū zhù de

habitat *n.* 栖息地 qī xī dì

habitation *n.* 居住 jū zhù

habituate *v.t.* 使习惯于 shǐ xí guàn yú

hack *v.t.* 劈 pī

hag *n.* 丑老太婆 chǒu lǎo tài pó

haggard *a.* 憔悴的 qiáo cuì de

haggle *v.i.* 杀价 shā jià

hair *n.* 头发 tóu fa

hale *a.* 强壮的 qiáng zhuàng de

half *n.* 一半 yí bàn

half *a* 一半的 yí bàn de

hall *n.* 会堂 huì táng

hallmark *n.* 品质证明 pǐn zhì zhèng míng

hallow *v.t.* 使...神圣 shǐ... shén shèng

halt *v. t.* 使停止 shǐ tíng zhǐ

halt *n* 停止 tíng zhǐ

halve *v.t.* 二等分 èr děng fēn

hamlet *n.* 小村 xiǎo cūn

hammer *n.* 锤 chuí

hammer *v.t* 锤打 chuí dǎ

hand *n* 手 shǒu

hand *v.t* 交给 jiāo gěi

handbill *n.* 传单 chuán dān

handbook *n.* 手册 shǒu cè

handcuff *n.* 手铐 shǒu kào

handcuff *v.t* 给...戴上手铐 gěi... dài shàng shǒu kào

handful *n.* 少数 shǎo shù

handicap *v.t.* 妨碍 fáng ài

handicap *n* 障碍 zhàng ài

handicraft *n.* 手工艺 shǒu gōng yì

handiwork *n.* 手工 shǒu gōng

handkerchief *n.* 手帕 shǒu pà

handle *n.* 柄 bǐng

handle *v.t* 处理 chú lǐ

handsome *a.* 英俊的 yīng jùn de

handy *a.* 便利的 biàn lì de

hang *v.t.* 悬挂 xuán guà

hanker *v.i.* 渴望 kě wàng

haphazard *a.* 无计划的 wú jì huà de

happen *v.t.* 发生 fā shēng

happening *n.* 事件 shì jiàn

happiness *n.* 快乐 kuài lè

happy *a.* 快乐的 kuài lè de

harass *v.t.* 骚扰 sāo rǎo

harassment *n.* 骚扰 sāo rǎo

harbour *n.* 港 gǎng

harbour *v.t* 藏匿 cáng nì

hard *a.* 硬的 yìng de

harden *v.t.* 使变硬 shǐ biàn yìng

hardihood *n.* 胆大无敌 dǎn dà wú dí

hardly *adv.* 几乎不 jī hū bú

hardship *n.* 艰难 jiān nán

hardy *adj.* 难的 nán de

hare *n.* 野兔 yě tù

harm *n.* 伤害 shāng hài

harm *v.t* 伤害 shāng hài

harmonious *a.* 和谐的 hé xié de

harmonium *n.* 簧风琴 huáng fēng qín

harmony *n.* 和睦 hé mù

harness *n.* 马具 mǎ jù

harness *v.t* 给...上挽具 gěi... shàng wǎn jù

harp *n.* 竖琴 shù qín

harsh *a.* 粗糙的 cū cāo de

harvest *n.* 收获 shōu huò

harvester *n.* 收割机 shōu gē jī

haste *n.* 匆忙 cōng máng

hasten *v.i.* 赶快 gǎn kuài

hasty *a.* 轻率的 qīng shuài de

hat *n.* 帽子 mào zi

hatchet *n.* 斧头 fǔ tou

hate *n.* 仇恨 chóu hèn

hate *v.t.* 憎恨 zēng hèn

haughty *a.* 傲慢的 ào màn de

haunt *v.t.* 常到 cháng dào

haunt *n* 常到的地方 cháng dào de dì fang

have *v.t.* 有 yǒu

haven *n.* 避难所 bì nàn suǒ

havoc *n.* 浩劫 hào jié

hawk *n* 鹰 yīng

hawker *n* 叫卖小贩 jiào mài xiǎo fàn

hawthorn *n.* 山楂 shān zhā

hay *n.* 干草 gān cǎo

hazard *n.* 危险 wēi xiǎn

hazard *v.t* 冒...的危险 mào... de wēi xiǎn

haze *n.* 薄雾 báo wù

hazy *a.* 朦胧的 méng lóng de

he pron. 他 tā

head *n.* 头 tóu
head *v.t* 为首 wéi shǒu
headache *n.* 头痛 tóu tòng
heading *n.* 标题 biāo tí
headlong *adv.* 用力地 yòng lì dì
headstrong *a.* 顽固的 wán gù de
heal *v.i.* 痊愈 quán yù
health *n.* 健康 jiàn kāng
healthy *a.* 健康的 jiàn kāng de
heap *n.* 堆 duī
heap *v.t* 堆积 duī jī
hear *v.t.* 听到 tīng dào
hearsay *n.* 谣言 yáo yán
heart *n.* 心 xīn
hearth *n.* 炉床 lú chuáng
heartily *adv.* 衷心地 zhōng xīn dì
heat *n.* 热 rè
heat *v.t* 加热 jiā rè
heave *v.i.* 抛出 pāo chū
heaven *n.* 天堂 tiān táng
heavenly *a.* 天上的 tiān shàng de
hedge *n.* 树篱 shù lí
hedge *v.t* 用树篱围 yòng shù lí wéi
heed *v.t.* 注意 zhù yì
heed *n* 留心 liú xīn
heel *n.* 脚后跟 jiǎo hòu gēn
hefty *a.* 重的 zhòng de
height *n.* 高度 gāo dù
heighten *v.t.* 增高 zēng gāo
heinous *a.* 可憎的 kě zēng de
heir *n.* 继承人 jì chéng rén
hell *a.* 地狱 dì yù
helm *n.* 舵 duò
helmet *n.* 盔 kuī
help *v.t.* 帮助 bāng zhù
help *n* 帮忙 bāng máng
helpful *a.* 有帮助的 yǒu bāng zhù de
helpless *a.* 无助的 wú zhù de
helpmate *n.* 伴侣 bàn lǚ
hemisphere *n.* 半球 bàn qiú

hemp *n.* 大麻 dà má
hen *n.* 母鸡 mǔ jī
hence *adv.* 因此 yīn cǐ
henceforth *adv.* 自此以后 zì cǐ yǐ hòu
henceforward *adv.* 从今以后 cóng jīn yǐ hòu
henchman *n.* 亲信 qīn xìn
henpecked *a.* 怕老婆的 pà lǎo po de
her *pron.* 她 tā
her *a* 她的 tā de
herald *n.* 使者 shí zhě
herald *v.t* 预报 yù bào
herb *n.* 药草 yào cǎo
herculean *a.* 魁梧有力的 kuí wú yǒu lì de
herd *n.* 兽群 shòu qún
herdsman *n.* 牧人 mù rén
here *adv.* 在这里 zài zhè lǐ
hereabouts *adv.* 在这里附近 zài zhè lǐ fù jìn
hereafter *adv.* 此后 cǐ hòu
hereditary *n.* 遗传的 yí chuán de
heredity *n.* 遗传 yí chuán
heritable *a.* 可遗传的 kě yí chuán de
heritage *n.* 遗产 yí chǎn
hermit *n.* 隐士 yǐn shì
hermitage *n.* 隐居处 yǐn jū chù
hernia *n.* 突出 tū chū
hero *n.* 英雄 yīng xióng
heroic *a.* 英勇的 yīng yǒng de
heroine *n.* 女主角 nǚ zhǔ jué
heroism *n.* 英勇 yīng yǒng
herring *n.* 鲱 fēi
hesitant *a.* 犹豫不定的 yóu yù bú dìng de
hesitate *v.i.* 犹豫 yóu yù
hesitation *n.* 犹豫 yóu yù
hew *v.t.* 砍 kǎn
heyday *n.* 全盛期 quán shèng qī
hibernation *n.* 冬眠 dōng mián
hiccup *n.* 打嗝 dǎ gé
hide *n.* 躲藏处 duǒ cáng chù

hideous *a.* 丑恶的 chǒu è de

hierarchy *n.* 等级制度 děng jí zhì dù

high *a.* 高的 gāo de

highly *adv.* 非常 fēi cháng

Highness *n.* 殿下 diàn xià

highway *n.* 大路 dà lù

hilarious *a.* 喜不自禁的 xǐ bú zì jìn de

hilarity *n.* 高兴 gāo xìng

hill *n.* 小山 xiǎo shān

hillock *n.* 小丘 xiǎo qiū

him *pron.* 他 tā

hinder *v.t.* 阻碍 zǔ ài

hindrance *n.* 阻碍物 zǔ ài wù

hint *n.* 提示 tí shì

hint *v.i* 暗示 àn shì

hip *n* 臀部 tún bù

hire *n.* 租用 zū yòng

hire *v.t* 出租 chū zū

hireling *n.* 雇工 gù gōng

his *pron.* 他的 tā de

hiss *n* 嘶嘶声 sī sī shēng

hiss *v.i* 发嘶嘶声 fā sī sī shēng

historian *n.* 历史学家 lì shǐ xué jiā

historic *a.* 历史性的 lì shǐ xìng de

historical *a.* 历史的 lì shǐ de

history *n.* 历史 lì shǐ

hit *v.t.* 打 dǎ

hit *n* 打击 dǎ jī

hitch *n.* 故障 gù zhàng

hither *adv.* 向这边 xiàng zhè biān

hitherto *adv.* 至今 zhì jīn

hive *n.* 蜂房 fēng fáng

hoarse *a.* 沙哑的 shā yǎ de

hoax *n.* 恶作剧 è zuò jù

hoax *v.t* 欺骗 qī piàn

hobby *n.* 嗜好 shì hào

hobby-horse *n.* 竹马 zhú mǎ

hockey *n.* 曲棍球 qū gùn qiú

hoist *v.t.* 升起 shēng qǐ

hold *n.* 控制 kòng zhì

hold *v.t* 握住 wò zhù

hole *n* 洞 dòng

hole *v.t* 挖洞 wā dòng

holiday *n.* 假日 jià rì

hollow *a.* 空的 kōng de

hollow *n.* 洞 dòng

hollow *v.t* 凹 āo

holocaust *n.* 大屠杀 dà tú shā

holy *a.* 神圣的 shén shèng de

homage *n.* 尊崇 zūn chóng

home *n.* 家 jiā

homicide *n.* 杀人者 shā rén zhě

homoeopath *n.* 采用顺势疗法的医生 cǎi yòng shùn shì liáo fǎ de yī sheng

homeopathy *n.* 顺势疗法 shùn shì liáo fǎ

homogeneous *a.* 同种的 tóng zhǒng de

honest *a.* 诚实的 chéng shí de

honesty *n.* 诚实 chéng shí

honey *n.* 蜂蜜 fēng mì

honeycomb *n.* 蜂巢 fēng cháo

honeymoon *n.* 蜜月 mì yuè

honorarium *n.* 酬金 chóu jīn

honorary *a.* 道义上的 dào yì shàng de

honour *n.* 荣誉 róng yù

honour *v.t* 尊敬 zūn jìng

honourable *a.* 高贵的 gāo guì de

hood *n.* 兜帽 dōu mào

hoodwink *v.t.* 遮眼 zhē yǎn

hoof *n.* 蹄 tí

hook *n.* 钩 gōu

hooligan *n.* 小流氓 xiǎo liú máng

hoot *n.* 叫嚣 jiào xiāo

hoot *v.i* 鸣响 míng xiǎng

hop *v.i* 单脚跳 dān jiǎo tiào

hop *n* 单脚跳 dān jiǎo tiào

hope *v.t.* 希望 xī wàng

hope *n* 希望 xī wàng

horde *n.* 群 qún

horizon *n.* 地平线 dì píng xiàn

horn *n.* 角 jiǎo

hornet *n.* 大黄峰 dài huáng fēng

horrible *a.* 可怕的 kě pà de

horrify *v.t.* 使恐惧 shǐ kǒng jù

horror *n.* 恐怖 kǒng bù

horse *n.* 马 mǎ

horticulture *n.* 园艺 yuán yì

hose *n.* 水管 shuǐ guǎn

hosiery *n.* 袜 wà

hospitable *a.* 好客的 hào kè de

hospital *n.* 医院 yī yuàn

hospitality *n.* 款待 kuǎn dài

host *n.* 节目主持人 jié mù zhǔ chí rén

hostage *n.* 人质 rén zhì

hostel *n.* 宿舍 sù shè

hostile *a.* 敌人的 dí rén de

hostility *n.* 敌意 dí yì

hot *a.* 热 rè

hotchpotch *n.* 什锦浓汤 shí jǐn nóng tāng

hotel *n.* 旅馆 lǚ guǎn

hound *n.* 猎犬 liè quǎn

hour *n.* 钟头 zhōng tóu

house *n* 房子 fáng zi

house *v.t* 给...房子住 gěi... fáng zi zhù

how *adv.* 怎样 zěn yàng

however *adv.* 无论如何 wú lùn rú hé

however *conj* 然而 rán ér

howl *v.t.* 对...吼叫 duì... hǒu jiào

howl *n* 号叫 háo jiào

hub *n.* 毂 gū

hubbub *n.* 吵闹声 chǎo nào shēng

huge *a.* 巨大的 jù dà de

hum *v.i* 发低哼声 fā dī hēng shēng

hum *n* 嗡嗡声 wēng wēng shēng

human *a.* 人类 rén lèi

humane *a.* 有人情的 yǒu rén qíng de

humanitarian *a* 人道主义的 rén dào zhǔ yì de

humanity *n.* 人类 rén lèi

humanize *v.t.* 赋予人性 fù yǔ rén xìng

humble *a.* 谦逊的 qiān xùn de

humdrum *a.* 单调的 dān diào de

humid *a.* 潮湿的 cháo shī de

humidity *n.* 湿度 shī dù

humiliate *v.t.* 使丢脸 shǐ diū liǎn

humiliation *n.* 耻辱 chí rǔ

humility *n.* 谦虚 qiān xū

humorist *n.* 幽默作家 yōu mò zuò jiā

humorous *a.* 富幽默感的 fù yōu mò gǎn de

humour *n.* 幽默 yōu mò

hunch *n.* 预感 yù gǎn

hundred *n.* 百 bǎi

hunger *n* 渴望 kě wàng

hungry *a.* 饥饿的 jī è de

hunt *v.t.* 打猎 dǎ liè

hunt *n* 狩猎 shòu liè

hunter *n.* 猎人 liè rén

huntsman *n.* 猎人 liè rén

hurdle *n.* 跳栏 tiào lán

hurdle *v.t* 越过 yuè guò

hurl *v.t.* 用力投掷 yòng lì tóu zhì

hurrah *interj.* 万岁 wàn suì

hurricane *n.* 飓风 jù fēng

hurry *v.t.* 赶快 gǎn kuài

hurry *n* 急忙 jí máng

hurt *v.t.* (使)伤心 (shǐ) shāng xīn

hurt *n* 伤害 shāng hài

husband *n* 丈夫 zhàng fu

husbandry *n.* 农事 nóng shì

hush *n* 安静 ān jìng

hush *v.t.* (使)肃静 (shǐ) sù jìng

husk *n.* 外壳 wài ké

husky *a.* 声音沙哑的 shēng yīn shā yǎ de

hut *n.* 茅舍 máo shè

hyaena *n.* 猎狗 liè gǒu

hyena *n.* 猎狗 liè gǒu
hybrid *a.* 杂种的 zá zhǒng de
hybrid *n* 杂种 zá zhǒng
hydrogen *n.* 氢 qīng
hygiene *n.* 卫生 wèi shēng
hygienic *a.* 卫生的 wèi shēng de
hymn *n.* 圣歌 shèng gē
hyperbole *n.* 夸张法 kuā zhāng fǎ
hypnotism *n.* 催眠术 cuī mián shù
hypnotize *v.t.* 催眠 cuī mián
hypocrisy *n.* 伪善 wěi shàn
hypocrite *n.* 伪君子 wěi jūn zǐ
hypocritical *a.* 伪善的 wěi shàn de
hypothesis *n.* 假设 jiǎ shè
hypothetical *a.* 假设的 jiǎ shè de
hysteria *n.* 歇斯底里症 xiē sī dǐ lǐ zhèng
hysterical *a.* 歇斯底里的 xiē sī dǐ lǐ de

I

I *pron.* 我 wǒ
ice *n.* 冰 bīng
iceberg *n.* 冰山 bīng shān
icicle *n.* 冰柱 bīng zhù
icy *a.* 冰的 bīng de
idea *n.* 主意 zhǔ yi
ideal *a.* 理想的 lí xiǎng de
ideal *n* 理想 lí xiǎng
idealism *n.* 理想主义 lí xiǎng zhǔ yì
idealist *n.* 理想主义者 lí xiǎng zhǔ yì zhě
idealistic *a.* 理想主义的 lí xiǎng zhǔ yì de
idealize *v.t.* 使理想化 shǐ lí xiǎng huà
identical *a.* 同一的 tóng yī de
indentification *n.* 身分证明 shēn fēn zhèng míng

identify *v.t.* 识别 shí bié
identity *n.* 身份 shēn fèn
idiocy *n.* 白痴 bái chī
idiom *n.* 成语 chéng yǔ
idiomatic *a.* 惯用的 guàn yòng de
idiot *n.* 白痴 bái chī
idiotic *a.* 愚蠢的 yú chǔn de
idle *a.* 懒惰的 lǎn duò de
idleness *n.* 闲散 xián sǎn
idler *n.* 游手好闲的人 yóu shǒu hǎo xián de rén
idol *n.* 偶像 ǒu xiàng
idolater *n.* 崇拜者 chóng bài zhě
if *conj.* 如果 rú guǒ
ignoble *a.* 卑贱的 bēi jiàn de
ignorance *n.* 无知 wú zhī
ignorant *a.* 无知的 wú zhī de
ignore *v.t.* 忽视 hū shì
ill *a.* 生病的 shēng bìng de
ill *adv.* 有害地 yǒu hài dì
ill *n* 疾病 jí bìng
illegal *a.* 违法的 wéi fǎ de
illegibility *n.* 模糊不清 mó hú bù qīng
illegible *a.* 难辨认的 nán biàn rèn de
illegitimate *a.* 私生的 sī shēng de
illicit *a.* 不法的 bù fǎ de
illiteracy *n.* 文盲 wén máng
illiterate *a.* 目不识丁的 mù bù shí dīng de
illness *n.* 疾病 jí bìng
illogical *a.* 不合逻辑的 bù hé luó jí de
illuminate *v.t.* 照明 zhào míng
illumination *n.* 照明 zhào míng
illusion *n.* 错觉 cuò jué
illustrate *v.t.* 举例说明 jǔ lì shuō míng
illustration *n.* 插图 chā tú
image *n.* 图像 tú xiàng
imagery *n.* 肖像 xiāo xiàng
imaginary *a.* 想像的 xiǎng xiàng de

imagination *n.* 想像力
xiǎng xiàng lì
imaginative *a.* 想像的 xiǎng
xiàng de
imagine *v.t.* 想像 xiǎng xiàng
imitate *v.t.* 模仿 mó páng
imitation *n.* 模仿 mó fǎng
imitator *n.* 模仿者 mó fǎng
zhě
immaterial *a.* 无形的 wú
xíng de
immature *a.* 不成熟的 bù
chéng shu de
immaturity *n.* 未成年 wèi
chéng nián
immeasurable *a.* 无限的
wú xiàn de
immediate *a* 立即的 lì jí de
immemorial *a.* 太古的 tài
gǔ de
immense *a.* 无边的 wú biān
de
immensity *n.* 巨物 jù wù
immerse *v.t.* 浸 jìn
immersion *n.* 浸 jìn
immigrant *n.* 移民 yí mín
immigrate *v.i.* 移入 yí rù
immigration *n.* 移民 yí mín
imminent *a.* 即将来临的 jí
jiāng lái lín de
immodest *a.* 不谦虚的 bù
qiān xū de
immodesty *n.* 不谦虚 bù
qiān xū
immoral *a.* 不道德的 bú dào
dé de
immorality *n.* 不灭的声望
bú miè de shēng wàng
immortal *a.* 不死的 bù sǐ de
immortality *n.* 不朽 bù xiǔ
immortalize *v.t.* 使不灭 shǐ
bú miè
immovable *a.* 固定的 gù
dìng de
immune *a.* 免疫的 miǎn yì
de
immunity *n.* 免疫 miǎn yì
immunize *v.t.* 使免疫 shǐ
miǎn yì

impact *n.* 影响 yíng xiǎng
impart *v.t.* 给予 jí yǔ
impartial *a.* 公平的 gōng
píng de
impartiality *n.* 公平 gōng
píng
impassable *a.* 不能通行的
bù néng tōng xíng de
impasse *n.* 死路 sǐ lù
impatience *n.* 难耐 nán nài
impatient *a.* 不耐烦的 bú nài
fán de
impeach *v.t.* 控告 kòng gào
impeachment *n.* 控告 kòng
gào
impede *v.t.* 阻止 zǔ zhǐ
impediment *n.* 障碍 zhàng ài
impenetrable *a.* 不能通过的
bù néng tōng guò de
imperative *a.* 急需的 jí xū de
imperfect *a.* 不完美的 bù
wán měi de
imperfection *n.* 疵点 cī diǎn
imperial *a.* 帝王的 dì wáng de
imperialism *n.* 帝国主义 dì
guó zhǔ yì
imperil *v.t.* 使处于危险 shǐ
chǔ yú wēi xiǎn
imperishable *a.* 不朽的 bù
xiǔ de
impersonal *a.* 客观的 kè
guān de
impersonate *v.t.* 模仿 mó
fǎng
impersonation *n.* 模仿 mó
fǎng
impertinence *n.* 无礼 wú lǐ
impertinent *a.* 不切题的 bù
qiè tí de
impetuosity *n.* 冲力 chōng lì
impetuous *a.* 轻率的 qīng
shuài de
implement *n.* 工具 gōng jù
implement *v.t.* 执行 zhí xíng
implicate *v.t.* 牵连 qiān lián
implication *n.* 牵连 qiān lián
implicit *a.* 含蓄的 hán xù de
implore *v.t.* 恳求 kěn qiú
imply *v.t.* 暗示 àn shì

impolite *a.* 无礼的 wú lǐ de

import *v.t.* 输入 shū rù

import *n.* 进口货 jìn kǒu huò

importance *n.* 重要性 zhòng yào xìng

important *a.* 重要的 zhòng yào de

impose *v.t.* 以...欺骗 yǐ... qī piàn

imposing *a.* 令人难忘的 lìng rén nán wàng de

imposition *n.* 征收 zhēng shōu

impossibility *n.* 不可能性 bù kě néng xìng

impossible *a.* 不可能的 bù kě néng de

impostor *n.* 骗子 piàn zi

imposture *n.* 冒牌 mào pái

impotence *n.* 无能力 wú néng lì

impotent *a.* 无力的 wú lì de

impoverish *v.t.* 使贫穷 shǐ pín qióng

impracticability *n.* 无法实施 wú fǎ shí shī

impracticable *a.* 不能实施的 bù néng shí shī de

impress *v.t.* 使有印象 shǐ yǒu yìn xiàng

impression *n.* 印象 yìn xiàng

impressive *a.* 给人深刻印象的 gěi rén shēn kè yìn xiàng de

imprint *v.t.* 印 yìn

imprint *n.* 印 yìn

imprison *v.t.* 拘禁 jū jìn

improper *a.* 不合适的 bù hé shì de

impropriety *n.* 不适当 bú shì dàng

improve *v.t.* 改良 gǎi liáng

improvement *n.* 进步 jìn bù

imprudence *n.* 轻率 qīng shuài

imprudent *a.* 轻率的 qīng shuài de

impulse *n.* 冲动 chōng dòng

impulsive *a.* 冲动的 chōng dòng de

impunity *n.* 免罪 miǎn zuì

impure *a.* 不纯的 bù chún de

impurity *n.* 杂质 zá zhì

impute *v.t.* 归罪 guī zuì

in *prep.* 在...期间 zài... qī jiān

inability *n.* 无能 wú néng

inaccurate *a.* 不准确的 bù zhǔn què de

inaction *n.* 不活动 bù huó dòng

inactive *a.* 不活跃的 bù huó yuè de

inadmissible *a.* 不许可的 bù xú kě de

inanimate *a.* 无生命的 wú shēng mìng de

inapplicable *a.* 不适用的 bú shì yòng de

inattentive *a.* 不注意的 bú zhù yì de

inaudible *a.* 听不见的 tīng bú jiàn de

inaugural *a.* 就任的 jiù rèn de

inauguration *n.* 就职 jiù zhí

inauspicious *a.* 不吉的 bù jí de

inborn *a.* 天生的 tiān shēng de

incalculable *a.* 无法计数的 wú fǎ jì shù de

incapable *a.* 无能力的 wú néng lì de

incapacity *n.* 无能力 wú néng lì

incarnate *a.* 实体化的 shí tǐ huà de

incarnate *v.t.* 使具体化 shǐ jù tǐ huà

incarnation *n.* 化身 huà shēn

incense *v.t.* 用香焚 yòng xiāng fén

incense *n.* 香 xiāng

incentive *n.* 鼓励 gǔ lì

inception *n.* 起初 qǐ chū

inch *n.* 英寸 yīng cùn

incident *n.* 事件 shì jiàn

incidental *a.* 非主要的 fēi zhǔ yào de

incite *v.t.* 刺激 cì jī

inclination *n.* 倾向 qīng xiàng

incline *v.i.* 倾向 qīng xiàng

include *v.t.* 包括 bāo kuò

inclusion *n.* 包含 bāo hán

inclusive *a.* 包括的 bāo kuò de

incoherent *a.* 不连贯的 bù lián guàn de

income *n.* 收入 shōu rù

incomparable *a.* 无比的 wú bǐ de

incompetent *a.* 无能力的 wú néng lì de

incomplete *a.* 未完成的 wèi wán chéng de

inconsiderate *a.* 不顾别人的 bú gù bié rén de

inconvenient *a.* 不便的 bú biàn de

incorporate *v.t.* 吸收 xī shōu

incorporate *a.* 合并的 hé bìng de

incorporation *n.* 编入 biān rù

incorrect *a.* 不正确的 bú zhèng què de

incorrigible *a.* 无药可救的 wú yào kě jiù de

incorruptible *a.* 清廉的 qīng lián de

increase *v.t.* 增加 zēng jiā

increase *n* 增加 zēng jiā

incredible *a.* 难以置信的 nán yǐ zhì xìn de

increment *n.* 增值 zēng zhí

incriminate *v.t.* 连累 lián lěi

incubate *v.i.* 孵卵 fū

inculcate *v.t.* 反复灌输 fǎn fù guàn shū

incumbent *n.* 在职者 zài zhí zhě

incumbent *a* 负有义务的 fù yǒu yì wù de

incur *v.t.* 招致 zhāo zhì

incurable *a.* 不能医治的 bù néng yī zhì de

indebted *a.* 负债的 fù zhài de

indecency *n.* 无礼 wú lǐ

indecent *a.* 下流的 xià liú de

indecision *n.* 优柔寡断 yōu róu guǎ duàn

indeed *adv.* 的确 dí què

indefensible *a.* 不能防卫的 bù néng fáng wèi de

indefinite *a.* 无限的 wú xiàn de

indemnity *n.* 保障 bǎo zhàng

independence *n.* 独立 dú lì

independent *a.* 独立的 dú lì de

indescribable *a.* 不能用语言表达的 bù néng yòng yǔ yán biǎo dá de

index *n.* 索引 suó yǐn

Indian *a.* 印度的 yìn dù de

indicate *v.t.* 指出 zhǐ chū

indication *n.* 指示 zhǐ shì

indicative *a.* 表示...的 biǎo shì... de

indicator *n.* 指示器 zhǐ shì qì

indict *v.t.* 起诉 qǐ sù

indictment *n.* 控告 kòng gào

indifference *n.* 漠不关心 mò bù guān xīn

indifferent *a.* 漠不关心的 mò bù guān xīn de

indigenous *a.* 本土的 běn tǔ de

indigestible *a.* 难消化的 nán xiāo huà de

indigestion *n.* 消化不良 xiāo huà bù liáng

indignant *a.* 愤慨的 fèn kǎi de

indignation *n.* 愤慨 fèn kǎi

indigo *n.* 靛蓝色 diàn lán sè

indirect *a.* 间接的 jiàn jiē de

indiscipline *n.* 无纪律 wú jì lù

indiscreet *a.* 欠慎重的 qiàn shèn zhòng de

indiscretion *n.* 不慎重 bú shèn zhòng

indiscriminate *a.* 无差别的 wú chā bié de

indispensable *a.* 不可缺少之物 bù kě quē shǎo zhī wù

indisposed *a.* 不舒服的 bù shū fu de

indisputable *a.* 无争论之余地的 wú zhēnglùn zhī yú dì de

indistinct *a.* 不清楚的 bù qīng chu de

individual *a.* 个别的 gè bié de

individualism *n.* 个人主义 gè rén zhǔ yì

individuality *n.* 个性 gè xìng

indivisible *a.* 不能分割的 bù néng fēn gē de

indolent *a.* 懒惰的 lǎn duò de

indomitable *a.* 不屈服的 bù qū fú de

indoor *a.* 室内的 shì nèi de

indoors *adv.* 在户内 zài hù nèi

induce *v.t.* 引诱 yǐn yòu

inducement *n.* 引诱 yǐn yòu

induct *v.t.* 使就职 shǐ jiù zhí

induction *n.* 就职 jiù zhí

indulge *v.t.* 纵情于 zòng qíng yú

indulgence *n.* 纵容 zòng róng

indulgent *a.* 纵容的 zòng róng de

industrial *a.* 工业的 gōng yè de

industrious *a.* 勤勉的 qín miǎn de

industry *n.* 工业 gōng yè

ineffective *a.* 无效的 wú xiào de

inert *a.* 惰性的 duò xìng de

inertia *n.* 惯性 guàn xìng

inevitable *a.* 不可避免的 bù kě bì miǎn de

inexact *a.* 不正确的 bú zhèng què de

inexorable *a.* 无情的 wú qíng de

inexpensive *a.* 不贵重的 bú guì zhòng de

inexperience *n.* 无经验 wú jīng yàn

inexplicable *a.* 不能解释的 bù néng jiě shì de

infallible *a.* 绝无错误的 jué wú cuò wù de

infamous *a.* 声名狼藉 shēng míng láng jí

infamy *n.* 恶行 è xíng

infancy *n.* 初期 chū qī

infant *n.* 初学者 chū xué zhě

infanticide *n.* 杀婴 shā yīng

infantile *a.* 幼稚的 yòu zhì de

infantry *n.* 步兵 bù bīng

infatuate *v.t.* 使迷恋 shǐ mí liàn

infatuation *n.* 迷恋 mí liàn

infect *v.t.* 传染 chuán rǎn

infection *n.* 感染 gǎn rǎn

infectious *a.* 传染性的 chuán rǎn xìng de

infer *v.t.* 推断 tuī duàn

inference *n.* 推论 tuī lùn

inferior *a.* 较差的 jiào chà de

inferiority *n.* 自卑 zì bēi

infernal *a.* 恶魔的 è mó de

infinite *a.* 无限的 wú xiàn de

infinity *n.* 无限 wú xiàn

infirm *a.* 弱的 ruò de

infirmity *n.* 虚弱 xū ruò

inflame *v.t.* 激起 jī qǐ

inflammable *a.* 易燃的 yì rán de

inflammation *n.* 发炎 fā yán

inflammatory *a.* 炎症性的 yán zhèng xìng de

inflation *n.* 通货膨胀 tōng huò péng zhàng

inflexible *a.* 不屈曲的 bù qū qǔ de

inflict *v.t.* 加害 jiā hài

influence *n.* 影响力 yǐng xiǎng lì

influence *v.t.* 影响 yǐng xiǎng

influential *a.* 有影响的 yǒu yíng xiǎng de

influenza *n.* 流行性感冒 liú xíng xìng gǎn mào

influx *n.* 流入 liú rù

inform *v.t.* 通知 tōng zhī

informal *a.* 日常使用的 rì cháng shǐ yòng de

information *n.* 消息 xiāo xi

informative *a.* 提供消息的 tí gōng xiāo xi de

informer *n.* 密告者 mì gào zhě

infringe *v.t.* 侵犯 qīn fàn

infringement *n.* 违犯 wéi fàn

infuriate *v.t.* 激怒 jī nù

infuse *v.t.* 注入 zhù rù

infusion *n.* 输入 shū rù

ingrained *a.* 根深蒂固的 gēn shēn dì gù de

ingratitude *n.* 忘恩负义 wàng ēn fù yì

ingredient *n.* 成分 chéng fen

inhabit *v.t.* 居住于 jū zhù yú

inhabitable *a.* 可居住的 kě jū zhù de

inhabitant *n.* 居民 jū mín

inhale *v.i.* 吸入 xī rù

inherent *a.* 固有的 gù yǒu de

inherit *v.t.* 继承 jì chéng

inheritance *n.* 遗产 yí chǎn

inhibit *v.t.* 禁止 jìn zhǐ

inhibition *n.* 禁止 jìn zhǐ

inhospitable *a.* 不适于居住的 bú shì yú jū zhù de

inhuman *a.* 残忍的 cán rěn de

inimical *a.* 有敌意的 yǒu dí yì de

inimitable *a.* 独特的 dú tè de

initial *a.* 最初的 zuì chū de

initial *n.* 首字母 shǒu zì mǔ

initial *v.t* 用姓名的首字母签名 yòng xìng míng de shǒu zì mǔ qiān míng

initiate *v.t.* 开始 kāi shǐ

initiative *n.* 主动行动 zhǔ dòng xíng dòng

inject *v.t.* 注射 zhù shè

injection *n.* 注射 zhù shè

injudicious *a.* 判决不当的 pàn jué bù dāng de

injunction *n.* 禁令 jìn lìng

injure *v.t.* 伤害 shāng hài

injurious *a.* 有害的 yǒu hài de

injury *n.* 伤害 shāng hài

injustice *n.* 不公正 bù gōng zhèng

ink *n.* 墨水 mò shuǐ

inkling *n.* 暗示 àn shì

inland *a.* 内陆的 nèi lù de

inland *n.* 内地 nèi dì

in-laws *n.* 姻亲 yīn qīn

inmate *n.* 同住者 tóng zhù zhě

inmost *a.* 内心深处的 nèi xīn shēn chù de

inn *n.* 旅馆 lǚ guǎn

innate *a.* 天生的 tiān shēng de

inner *a.* 内部的 nèi bù de

innermost *a.* 内心的 nèi xīn de

innings *n.* 局 jú

innocence *n.* 天真无邪 tiān zhēn wú xié

innocent *a.* 无罪的 wú zuì de

innovate *v.i.* 改革 gǎi gé

innovation *n.* 创新 chuàng xīn

innovator *n.* 创新者 chuàng xīn zhě

innumerable *a.* 无数的 wú shù de

inoculate *v.t.* 接种 jiē zhòng

inoculation *n.* 接种 jiē zhòng

inoperative *a.* 无效力的 wú xiào lì de

inopportune *a.* 不合时机的 bù hé shí jī de

input *n.* 输入 shū rù

inquest *n.* 审讯 shěn xùn

inquire *v.t.* 查究 chá jiū

inquiry *n.* 询问 xún wèn

inquisition *n.* 调查 diào chá

inquisitive *a.* 好追根究底的 hǎo zhuī gēn jiū dǐ de

insane *a.* 患精神病的 huàn jīng shen bìng de

insanity *n.* 精神病 jīng shen bìng

insatiable *a.* 不知足的 bù zhī zú de

inscribe *v.t.* 登记 dēng jì

inscription *n.* 题字 tí zì

insect *n.* 昆虫 kūn chóng

insecticide *n.* 杀虫剂 shā chóng jì

insecure *a.* 不安全的 bù ān quán de

insecurity *n.* 不安全 bù ān quán

insensibility *n.* 人事不省 rén shì bù xǐng

insensible *a.* 无知觉的 wú zhī jué de

inseparable *a.* 不能分的 bù néng fēn de

insert *v.t.* 插入 chā rù

insertion *n.* 插入 chā rù

inside *n.* 内部 nèi bù

inside *prep.* 在...之内 zài... zhī nèi

inside *a* 内部的 nèi bù de

inside *adv.* 在里面 zài lǐ miàn

insight *n.* 见识 jiàn shí

insignificance *n.* 无意义 wú yì yì

insignificant *a.* 无关紧要的 wú guān jǐn yào de

insincere *a.* 不诚实的 bù chéng shí de

insincerity *n.* 不诚实 bù chéng shí

insinuate *v.t.* 暗示 àn shì

insinuation *n.* 暗示 àn shì

insipid *a.* 无味的 wú wèi de

insipidity *n.* 无味 wú wèi

insist *v.t.* 坚持 jiān chí

insistence *n.* 坚持 jiān chí

insistent *a.* 坚持的 jiān chí de

insolence *n.* 无礼 wú lǐ

insolent *a.* 无礼的 wú lǐ de

insoluble *n.* 不能溶解的 bù néng róng jiě de

insolvency *n.* 破产 pò chǎn

insolvent *a.* 无力偿还的 wú lì cháng huán de

inspect *v.t.* 检查 jiǎn chá

inspection *n.* 检查 jiǎn chá

inspector *n.* 检查员 jiǎn chá yuán

inspiration *n.* 灵感 líng gǎn

inspire *v.t.* 使感动 shǐ gǎn dòng

instability *n.* 不稳定性 bù wěn dìng xìng

install *v.t.* 安装 ān zhuāng

installation *n.* 安装 ān zhuāng

instalment *n.* 分期付款 fēn qī fù kuǎn

instance *n.* 例子 lì zi

instant *n.* 立即 lì jí

instant *a.* 即时的 jí shí de

instantaneous *a.* 即时的 jí shí de

instantly *adv.* 即刻地 jí kè dì

instigate *v.t.* 煽动 shān dòng

instigation *n.* 煽动 shān dòng

instil *v.t.* 不断灌输 bú duàn guàn shū

instinct *n.* 直觉 zhí jué

instinctive *a.* 直觉的 zhí jué de

institute *n.* 学会 xué huì

institution *n.* 机构 jī gòu

instruct *v.t.* 指示 zhǐ shì

instruction *n.* 指令 zhǐ lìng

instructor *n.* 教员 jiào yuán

instrument *n.* 工具 gōng jù

instrumental *a.* 仪器的 yí qì de

instrumentalist *n.* 乐器演奏者 yuè qì yǎn zòu zhě

insubordinate *a.* 不顺从的 bú shùn cóng de

insubordination *n.* 不顺从 bú shùn cóng

insufficient *a.* 不够的 bú gòu de

insular *a.* 保守的 báo shǒu de

insularity *n.* 孤立 gū lì

insulate *v.t.* 使绝缘 shǐ jué yuán

insulation *n.* 隔离 gé lí

insulator *n.* 绝缘体 jué yuán tǐ

insult *n.* 侮辱 wú rǔ

insult *v.t.* 侮辱 wú rǔ

insupportable *a.* 忍耐不住的 rěn nài bú zhù de

insurance *n.* 保险 báo xiǎn

insure *v.i.* 投保 tóu bǎo

insurgent *a.* 谋叛的 móu pàn de

insurgent *n.* 起义者 qǐ yì zhě

insurmountable *a.* 难以克服的 nán yǐ kè fú de

insurrection *n.* 叛乱 pàn luàn

intact *a.* 完整的 wán zhěng de

intangible *a.* 难以明了的 nán yǐ míng liǎo de

integral *a.* 固有的 gù yǒu de

integrity *n.* 完整 wán zhěng

intellect *n.* 智力 zhì lì

intellectual *a.* 智力的 zhì lì de

intellectual *n.* 知识分子 zhì shí fèn zǐ

intelligence *n.* 智力 zhì lì

intelligent *a.* 聪明的 cōng míng de

intelligentsia *n.* 知识界 zhī shí jiè

intelligible *a.* 易理解的 yì lí jiě de

intend *v.t.* 打算 dǎ suan

intense *a.* 紧张的 jǐn zhāng de

intensify *v.t.* 加强 jiā qiáng

intensity *n.* 强度 qiáng dù

intensive *a.* 密集的 mì jí de

intent *n.* 目的 mù dì

intent *a.* 专心的 zhuān xīn de

intention *n.* 目的 mù dì

intentional *a.* 故意的 gù yì de

intercept *v.t.* 截取 jié qǔ

interception *n.* 拦截 lán jié

interchange *n.* 互换 hù huàn

interchange *v.* 交换 jiāo huàn

intercourse *n.* 交流 jiāo liú

interdependence *n.* 互相依赖 hù xiāng yī lài

interdependent *a.* 相互依赖的 xiāng hù yī lài de

interest *n.* 兴趣 xìng qù

interested *a.* 感兴趣的 gǎn xìng qù de

interesting *a.* 有趣的 yǒu qù de

interfere *v.i.* 干涉 gān shè

interference *n.* 干涉 gān shè

interim *n.* 间歇的 jiàn xiē de

interior *a.* 内部的 nèi bù de

interior *n.* 内部 nèi bù

interjection *n.* 感叹词 gǎn tàn cí

interlock *v.t.* (使)连结 (shǐ) lián jié

interlude *n.* 幕间 mù jiān

intermediary *n.* 中间人 zhōng jiān rén

intermediate *a.* 中间的 zhōng jiān de

interminable *a.* 冗长的 rǒng cháng de

intermingle *v.t.* 使混合 shǐ hùn hé

intern *v.t.* 扣留 kòu liú

internal *a.* 内部的 nèi bù de

international *a.* 国际的 guó jì de

interplay *n.* 互相影响 hù xiāng yíng xiǎng

interpret *v.t.* 翻译 fān yì

interpreter *n.* 解释者 jiě shì zhě

interrogate *v.t.* 审问 shěn wèn

interrogation *n.* 审问 shěn wèn

interrogative *a.* 疑问的 yí wèn de

interrogative *n* 疑问词 yí wèn cí

interrupt *v.t.* 中断 zhōng duàn

interruption *n.* 打扰 dá rǎo

intersect *v.t.* 贯穿 guàn chuān

intersection *n.* 交叉点 jiāo chā diǎn

interval *n.* 间隔 jiàn gé

intervene *v.i.* 插入 chā rù

intervention *n.* 介入 jiè rù

interview *n.* 面试 miàn shì

interview *v.t.* 接见 jiē jiàn

intestinal *a.* 肠的 cháng de

intestine *n.* 肠 cháng

intimacy *n.* 亲密 qīn mì

intimate *a.* 密切 mì qiè

intimate *v.t.* 暗示 àn shì

intimation *n.* 暗示 àn shì

intimidate *v.t.* 威胁 wēi xié

intimidation *n.* 恐吓 kǒng hè

into *prep.* 进入...之内 jìn rù... zhī nèi

intolerable *a.* 无法忍受的 wú fǎ rěn shòu de

intolerance *n.* 不宽容 bù kuān róng

intolerant *a.* 不容忍的 bù róng rěn de

intoxicant *n.* 酒类饮料 jiǔ lèi yǐn liào

intoxicate *v.t.* 使陶醉 shǐ táo zuì

intoxication *n.* 使醉 shǐ zuì

intransitive *a.* (verb) 不及物的 bù jí wù de

interpid *a.* 勇猛的 yóng měng de

intrepidity *n.* 大胆 dà dǎn

intricate *a.* 复杂的 fù zá de

intrigue *v.t.* 激起...的兴趣 jī qǐ... de xìng qù

intrigue *n* 阴谋 yīn móu

intrinsic *a.* 内在的 nèi zài de

introduce *v.t.* 介绍 jiè shào

introduction *n.* 介绍 jiè shào

introductory *a.* 介绍的 jiè shào de

introspect *v.i.* 进行反省 jìn xíng fǎn xǐng

introspection *n.* 反省 fǎn xǐng

intrude *v.t.* 硬把自己挤进 yìng bǎ zì jǐ jǐ jìn

intrusion *n.* 闯入,侵扰 chuǎng rù, qīn rǎo

intuition *n.* 直觉 zhí jué

intuitive *a.* 直觉的 zhí jué de

invade *v.t.* 侵略 qīn lüè

invalid *a.* 无效的 wú xiào de

invalid *a.* 有病的 yǒu bìng de

invalid *n* 病人 bìng rén

invalidate *v.t.* 作废 zuò fèi

invaluable *a.* 无价的 wú jià de

invasion *n.* 侵入 qīn rù

invective *n.* 臭骂 chòu mà

invent *v.t.* 发明 fā míng

invention *n.* 发明 fā míng

inventive *a.* 善于创造的 shàn yú chuàng zào de

inventor *n.* 发明家 fā míng jiā

invert *v.t.* 使转化 shǐ zhuǎn huà

invest *v.t.* 投资 tóu zī

investigate *v.t.* 调查 diào chá

investigation *n.* 调查 diào chá

investment *n.* 投资 tóu zī

invigilate *v.i.* 监考 jiān kǎo

invigilation *n.* 监考 jiān kǎo

invigilator *n.* 监考人 jiān kǎo rén

invincible *a.* 无敌的 wú dí de

inviolable *a.* 不可侵犯的 bù kě qīn fàn de

invisible *a.* 看不见的 kàn bú jiàn de

invitation *v.* 邀请 yāo qǐng

invite *v.t.* 邀请 yāo qǐng

invocation *n.* 祈祷 qí dǎo

invoice *n.* 发票 fā piào

invoke *v.t.* 祈求 qí qiú

involve *v.t.* 包括 bāo kuò

inward *a.* 向内的 xiàng nèi de

inwards *adv.* 向内 xiàng nèi

irate *a.* 发怒的 fā nù de

ire *n.* 忿怒 fèn nù

Irish *a.* 爱尔兰的 ài ěr lán de

Irish *n.* 爱尔兰人 ài ěr lán rén

irksome *a.* 令人厌烦的 lìng rén yàn fán de

iron *n.* 熨斗 yùn dǒu

iron *v.t.* 烫平 tàng píng

ironical *a.* 讽刺的 fěng cì de

irony *n.* 反语 fǎn yǔ

irradiate *v.i.* 发光 fā guāng

irrational *a.* 不合理的 bù hé lǐ de

irreconcilable *a.* 不能和解的 bù néng hé jiě de

irrecoverable *a.* 不能收回的 bù néng shōu huí de

irrefutable *a.* 不可否认的 bù kě fǒu rèn de

irregular *a.* 不规则的 bù guī zé de

irregularity *n.* 不规则 bù guī zé

irrelevant *a.* 无关的 wú guān de

irrespective *a.* 无关的 wú guān de

irresponsible *a.* 不负责任的 bú fù zé rèn de

irrigate *v.t.* 灌溉 guàn gài

irrigation *n.* 灌溉 guàn gài

irritable *a.* 易怒的 yì nù de

irritant *a.* 刺激的 cì jī de

irritant *n.* 刺激物 cì jī wù

irritate *v.t.* 激怒 jī nù

irritation *n.* 刺激 cì jī

irruption *n.* 侵入 qīn rù

island *n.* 岛 dǎo

isle *n.* 小岛 xiǎo dǎo

isobar *n.* 等压线 děng yā xiàn

isolate *v.t.* 使隔离 shǐ gé lí

isolation *n.* 隔绝 gé jué

issue *v.i.* 发行 fā xíng

issue *n.* 问题 wèn tí

it *pron.* 它 tā

Italian *a.* 意大利的 yì dà lì de

Italian *n.* 意大利人 yì dà lì rén

italic *a.* 斜体的 xié tǐ de

italics *n.* 斜体字 xié tǐ zì

itch *n.* 痒 yǎng

itch *v.i.* 发痒 fā yǎng

item *n.* 项目 xiàng mù

ivory *n.* 象牙 xiàng yá

ivy *n* 常春藤 cháng chūn téng

J

jab *v.t.* 刺 cì

jabber *v.t.* 快而含糊地说 kuài ér hán hu dì shuō

jack *n.* 千斤顶 qiān jīn dǐng

jack *v.t.* 抬起 tái qǐ

jackal *n.* 豺 chái

jacket *n.* 外套 wài tào

jade *n.* 玉 yù

jail *n.* 监牢 jiān láo

jailer *n.* 狱卒 yù zú

jam *n.* 果酱 guǒ jiàng

jam *v.t.* 使塞满 shǐ sāi mǎn

jar *n.* 广口瓶 guǎng kǒu píng

jargon *n.* 专门术语 zhuān mén shù yǔ

jasmine, jessamine *n.* 茉莉 mò lì

jaundice *n.* 黄疸 huáng da

jaundice *v.t.* 使患黄疸 shǐ huàn huáng da

javelin *n.* 标枪 biāo qiāng

jaw *n.* 颚 è

jay *n.* 鸟 niǎo

jealous *a.* 嫉妒的 jí dù de

jealousy *n.* 妒忌 dù jì

jean *n.* 牛仔裤 niú zǎi kù

jeer *v.i.* 嘲弄 cháo nòng

jelly *n.* 果冻 guǒ dòng

jeopardize *v.t.* 危害 wēi hài

jeopardy *n.* 危险 wēi xiǎn

jerk *n.* 性情古怪的人 xìng qíng gǔ guài de rén

jerkin *n.* 短上衣 duǎn shàng yī

jerky *a.* 急动的 jí dòng de

jersey *n.* 运动衫 yùn dòng shān

jest *n.* 笑话 xiào hua

jest *v.i.* 讲笑话 jiǎng xiào hua

jet *n.* 喷射流 pēn shè liú

Jew *n.* 犹太人 yóu tài rén

jewel *n.* 珠宝 zhū bǎo

jewel *v.t.* 镶以宝石 xiāng yǐ bǎo shí

jeweller *n.* 珠宝商 zhū bǎo shāng

jewellery *n.* 宝石 bǎo shí

jingle *n.* 叮当声 dīng dāng shēng

jingle *v.i.* (使)作叮当声（shǐ) zuò dīng dāng shēng

job *n.* 工作 gōng zuò

jobber *n.* 股票经纪人 gǔ piào jing jì rén

jobbery *n.* 假公济私 jiǎ gōng jì sī

jocular *a.* 诙谐的 huī xié de

jog *v.t.* 慢跑 màn pǎo

join *v.t.* 参加 cān jiā

joiner *n.* 细工木匠 xì gōng mù jiang

joint *n.* 关节 guān jié

jointly *adv.* 共同地 gòng tóng dì

joke *n.* 笑话 xiào hua

joke *v.i.* 开玩笑 kāi wán xiào

joker *n.* 诙谐者 huī xié zhě

jollity *n.* 高兴 gāo xìng

jolly *a.* 愉快的 yú kuài de

jolt *n.* 震摇 zhèn yáo

jolt *v.t.* 使颠簸 shǐ diān bǒ

jostle *n.* 推挤 tuī jǐ

jostle *v.t.* 推 tuī

jot *n.* 少量 shǎo liàng

jot *v.t.* 略记 lüè jì

journal *n.* 日记 rì jì

journalism *n.* 新闻业 xīn wén yè

journalist *n.* 新闻记者 xīn wén jì zhě

journey *n.* 旅程 lǚ chéng

journey *v.i.* 旅行 lǚ xíng

jovial *a.* 快活的 kuài huo de

joviality *n.* 快乐 kuài lè

joy *n.* 欢喜 huān xǐ

joyful, joyous *a.* 高兴的 gāo xìng de

jubilant *a.* 欢呼的 huān hū de

jubilation *n.* 欢呼 huān hū

jubilee *n.* 五十周年纪念 wǔ shí zhōu nián jì niàn

judge *n.* 法官 fǎ guān

judge *v.i.* 下判断 xià pàn duàn

judgement *n.* 判断 pàn duàn

judicature *n.* 司法 sī fǎ

judicial *a.* 司法的 sī fǎ de

judiciary *n.* 法官 fǎ guān

judicious *a.* 头脑精明的 tóu nǎo jīng míng de

jug *n.* 水壶 shuǐ hú

juggle *v.t.* 耍弄 shuǎ nòng

juggler *n.* 表演者 biáo yǎn zhě

juice *n* 汁 zhī

juicy *a.* 多汁液的 duō zhī yè de

jumble *n.* 混乱 hùn luàn

jumble *v.t.* 搞乱 gǎo luàn

jump *n.* 跳动 tiào dòng

jump *v.i* 跳跃 tiào yuè

junction *n.* 交叉点 jiāo chā diǎn

juncture *n.* 接合 jiē hé

jungle *n.* 丛林 cóng lín

junior *a.* 年少的 nián shào de

junior *n.* 年少者 nián shào zhě

junk *n.* 垃圾 lā jī

jupiter *n.* 木星 mù xīng

jurisdiction *n.* 司法权 sī fǎ quán

jurisprudence *n.* 法律学 fǎ lǜ xué

jurist *n.* 法学家 fǎ xué jiā

juror *n.* 陪审员 péi shěn yuán

jury *n.* 陪审团 péi shěn tuán

juryman *n.* 陪审员 péi shěn yuán

just *a.* 正直的 zhèng zhí de

just *adv.* 正好 zhèng hǎo

justice *n.* 正义 zhèng yì

justifiable *a.* 有理的 yóu lǐ de

justification *n.* 证明正当 zhèng míng zhèng dāng

justify *v.t.* 证明 zhèng míng

justly *adv.* 公正地 gōng zhèng dì

jute *n.* 黄麻 huáng má

juvenile *a.* 幼稚的 yòu zhì de

K

keen *a.* 热心的 rè xīn de

keenness *n.* 锐利 ruì lì

keep *v.t.* 保持 bǎo chí

keeper *n.* 保管人 báo guǎn rén

keepsake *n.* 纪念品 jì niàn pǐn

kennel *n.* 狗舍 gǒu shè

kerchief *n.* 头巾 tóu jīn

kernel *n.* 核心 hé xīn

kerosene *n.* 煤油 méi yóu

ketchup *n.* 蕃茄酱 fān qié jiàng

kettle *n.* 茶壶 chá hú

key *n.* 钥匙 yào shi

key *v.t* 调音 tiáo yīn

kick *n.* 踢 tī

kick *v.t.* 踢 tī

kid *n.* 小山羊 xiǎo shān yáng

kidnap *v.t.* 拐骗 guǎi piàn

kidney *n.* 肾 shèn

kill *v.t.* 杀 shā

kill *n.* 杀 shā

kiln *n.* 窑 yáo

kin *n.* 亲戚 qīn qi

kind *n.* 种类 zhǒng lèi

kind *a* 亲切的 qīn qiè de

kindergarten *n.* 幼稚园 yòu zhì yuán

kindle *v.t.* 点燃 diǎn rán

kindly *adv.* 温和地 wēn hé dì

king *n.* 国王 guó wáng

kingdom *n.* 王国 wáng guó

kinship *n.* 亲属关系 qīn shǔ guān xi

kiss *n.* 吻 wěn

kiss *v.t.* 吻 wěn

kit *n.* 装备 zhuāng bèi

kitchen *n.* 厨房 chú fáng

kite *n.* 风筝 fēng zheng

kith *n.* 朋友 péng you

kitten *n.* 小猫 xiǎo māo

knave *n.* 无赖 wú lài

knavery *n.* 恶棍行为 è gùn xíng wéi

knee *n.* 膝 xī

kneel *v.i.* 跪下 guì xià

knife *n.* 小刀 xiǎo dāo

knight *n.* 骑士 qí shì

knight *v.t.* 封...为爵士 fēng...wéi jué shì

knit *v.t.* 编织 biān zhī

knock *v.t.* 敲 qiāo

knot *n.* 结 jié

knot *v.t.* 打结 dǎ jié

know *v.t.* 知道 zhī dào

knowledge *n.* 知识 zhī shí

L

label *n.* 标签 biāo qiān

label *v.t.* 贴标签于 tiē biāo qiān yú

labial *a.* 唇音的 chún yīn de

laboratory *n.* 实验室 shí yàn shì

laborious *a.* 艰苦的 jiān kǔ de

labour *n.* 劳工 láo gōng

labour *v.i.* 努力 nǔ lì

laboured *a.* 吃力的 chī lì de

labourer *n.* 劳工 láo gōng

labyrinth *n.* 迷宫 mí gōng

lac, lakh *n.* 虫胶 chóng jiāo

lace *n.* 花边 huā biān

lace *v.t.* 结带子 jié dài zi

lacerate *v.t.* 划破 huá pò

lachrymose *a.* 爱哭的 ài kū de

lack *n.* 不足 bù zú

lack *v.t.* 缺乏 quē fá

lackey *n.* 仆人 pú rén

lacklustre *a.* 无光泽的 wú guāng zé de

laconic *a.* 简洁的 jiǎn jié de

lactate *v.i.* 分泌乳汁 fēn mì rǔ zhī

lactometer *n.* 检乳器 jiǎn rǔ qì

lactose *n.* 乳糖 rǔ táng

lacuna *n.* 空白 kòng bái

lacy *a.* 丝带的 sī dài de

lad *n.* 青年 qīng nián

ladder *n.* 梯 tī

lade *v.t.* 装载 zhuāng zài

ladle *n.* 勺子 sháo zi

ladle *v.t.* 以勺舀取 yǐ sháo yǎo qǔ

lady *n.* 女士 nǚ shì

lag *v.i.* 落后 luò hòu

laggard *n.* 迟钝者 chí dùn zhě

lagoon *n.* 环礁湖 huán jiāo hú

lair *n.* 兽穴 shòu xué

lake *n.* 湖 hú

lama *n.* 喇嘛 lǎ ma

lamb *n.* 羔羊 gāo yáng

lambaste *v.t.* 痛打 tòng dǎ

lame *a.* 跛足的 bǒ zú de

lame *v.t.* 使成残废 shǐ chéng cán fèi

lament *v.i.* 悔恨 huǐ hèn

lament *n* 悲叹 bēi tàn

lamentable *a.* 可悲的 kě bēi de

lamentation *n.* 悲叹 bēi tàn

lambkin *n.* 羔羊 gāo yáng

laminate *v.t.* 制成薄板 zhì chéng báo bǎn

lamp *n.* 灯 dēng

lampoon *n.* 讽刺文 fěng cì wén

lampoon *v.t.* 讽刺 fěng cì

lance *n.* 长矛 cháng máo

lance *v.t.* 以长矛攻击 yǐ cháng máo gōng jī

lancer *n.* 长矛 cháng máo

lancet *n.* 柳叶刀 liǔ yè dāo

land *n.* 地面 dì miàn

land *v.i.* 使上岸 shǐ shàng àn

landing *n.* 降落 jiàng luò

landscape *n.* 风景 fēng jǐng

lane *n.* 小路 xiǎo lù

language *n.* 语言 yǔ yán

languish *v.i.* 憔悴 qiáo cuì

lank *a.* 瘦的 shòu de

lantern *n.* 灯笼 dēng long

lap *n.* 一圈 yì quān

lapse *v.i.* 犯错 fàn cuò

lapse *n* .时间的消逝 shí jiān de xiāo shì

lard *n.* 猪油 zhū yóu

large *a.* 大的 dà de

largesse *n.* 慷慨地赏赐 kāng kǎi dì shǎng cì

lark *n.* 云雀 yún què

lascivious *a.* 淫荡的 yín dàng de

lash *v.t.* 用绳捆绑 yòng shéng kún bǎng

lash *n* 鞭打 biān dǎ

lass *n.* 少女 shǎo nǚ

last *a.* 最后的 zuì hòu de

last *adv.* 最后 zuì hòu

last *v.i.* 持续 chí xù

last *n* 最后 zuì hòu

lastly *adv.* 最后 zuì hòu

lasting *a.* 永久的 yóng jiǔ de

latch *n.* 门闩 mén shuān

late *a.* 晚的 wǎn de

late *adv.* 很迟 hěn chí

lately *adv.* 最近 zuì jìn

latent *a.* 潜伏性的 qián fú xìng de

lath *n.* 板条 bǎn tiáo

lathe *n.* 车床 chē chuáng

lather *n.* 肥皂泡 féi zào pào

latitude *n.* 纬度 wěi dù

latrine *n.* 厕所 cè suǒ

latter *a.* 后者的 hòu zhě de

lattice *n.* 格子 gé zi

laud *v.t.* 称赞 chēng zàn

laud *n* 赞美 zàn měi

laudable *a.* 值得赞赏的 zhí dé zàn shǎng de

laugh *n.* 笑 xiào

laugh *v.i* 笑 xiào

laughable *a.* 有趣的 yǒu qù de

laughter *n.* 笑声 xiào shēng

launch *v.t.* 发动 fā dòng

launch *n.* 发射 fā shè

launder *v.t.* 洗衣 xǐ yī

laundress *n.* 洗衣女工 xǐ yī nǔ gōng

laundry *n.* 洗衣店 xǐ yī diàn

laureate *n.* 桂冠诗人 guì guān shī rén

laureate *a.* 戴桂冠的 dài guì guān de

laurel *n* 月桂树 yuè guì shù

lava *n.* 熔岩 róng yán

lavatory *n.* 洗脸盆 xǐ liǎn pén

lavender *n.* 薰衣草 xūn yī cǎo

lavish *a.* 大方的 dà fāng de

lavish *v.t.* 慷慨给予 kāng kǎi jí yǔ

law *n.* 法律 fǎ lǜ

lawful *a.* 合法的 hé fǎ de

lawless *a.* 非法的 fēi fǎ de

lawn *n.* 草地 cǎo dì

lawyer *n.* 律师 lǜ shī

lax *a.* 松的 sōng de

laxative *n.* 泻药 xiè yào

laxative *a* 通便的 tōng biàn de

laxity *n.* 松弛 sōng chí

lay *v.t.* 放置 fàng zhì

lay *n.* 位置 wèi zhi

lay *a.* 外行的 wài háng de

layer *n.* 层 céng

layman *n.* 外行 wài háng

laze *v.i.* 偷懒 tōu lǎn

laziness *n.* 怠惰 dài duò

lazy *a.* 懒惰的 lǎn duò de

lea *n.* 草地 cǎo dì

leach *v.t.* 过滤 guò lǜ

lead *n.* 领先 lǐng xiān

lead *v.t.* 带领 dài lǐng

lead *n.* 铅 qiān

leaden *a.* 沉闷的 chén mèn de

leader *n.* 领导者 lǐng dǎo zhě

leadership *n.* 领导能力 lǐng dǎo néng lì

leaf *n.* 叶 yè

leaflet *n.* 传单 chuán dān

leafy *a.* 多叶的 duō yè de

league *n.* 联盟 lián méng

leak *n.* 漏洞 lòu dòng

leak *v.i.* 漏 lòu

leakage *n.* 漏 lòu

lean *n.* 瘦肉 shòu ròu

lean *v.i.* 倚靠 yǐ kào

leap *v.i.* 突然经过 tū rán jìng guò

leap *n* 跳跃 tiào yuè

learn *v.i.* 学 xué

learned *a.* 有学问的 yǒu xué wen de

learner *n.* 学习者 xué xí zhě

learning *n.* 学习 xué xí

lease *n.* 租约 zū yuē

lease *v.t.* 租出 zū chū

least *a.* 最少 zuì shǎo

least *adv.* 最小 zuì xiǎo

leather *n.* 皮革 pí gé

leave *n.* 告别 gào bié

leave *v.t.* 离开 lí kāi

lecture *n.* 演讲 yǎn jiǎng

lecture *v* 讲演 jiáng yǎn

lecturer *n.* 讲师 jiǎng shī

ledger *n.* 分类帐 fēn lèi zhàng

lee *n.* 庇护 bì hù

leech *n.* 水蛭 shuǐ zhì

leek *n.* 葱 cōng

left *a.* 左边的 zuǒ bian de

left *n.* 左 zuǒ

leftist *n* 左派 zuǒ pài

leg *n.* 腿 tuǐ

legacy *n.* 遗产 yí chǎn

legal *a.* 合法的 hé fǎ de

legality *n.* 合法 hé fǎ

legalize *v.t.* 使合法化 shǐ hé fǎ huà

legend *n.* 传奇文学 chuán qí wén xué

legendary *a.* 传说的 chuán shuō de

leghorn *n.* 来航鸡 lái háng jī

legible *a.* 清晰的 qīng xī de

legibly *adv.* 易读地 yì dú dì

legion *n.* 军团 jūn tuán

legionary *n.* 军团士兵 jūn tuán shì bīng

legislate *v.i.* 制定法律 zhì dìng fǎ lǜ

legislation *n.* 立法 lì fǎ

legislative *a.* 立法的 lì fǎ de

legislator *n.* 立法委员 lì fǎ wěi yuán

legislature *n.* 立法机关 lì fǎ jī guān

legitimacy *n.* 合法性 hé fǎ xìng

legitimate *a.* 合法的 hé fǎ de

leisure *n.* 空闲 kòng xián

leisure *a* 空闲的 kòng xián de

leisurely *a.* 悠闲的 yōu xián de

leisurely *adv.* 从容地 cōng róng dì

lemon *n.* 柠檬 níng méng

lemonade *n.* 柠檬水 níng méng shuǐ

lend *v.t.* 借 jiè

length *n.* 长度 cháng dù

lengthen *v.t.* 加长 jiā cháng

lengthy *a.* 冗长的 rǒng cháng de

lenience, leniency *n.* 宽大 kuān dà

lenient *a.* 宽大的 kuān dà de

lens *n.* 镜片 jìng piàn

lentil *n.* 小扁豆 xiǎo biǎn dòu

Leo *n.* 狮子座 shī zi zuò

leonine *a* 狮子的 shī zi de

leopard *n.* 豹 bào

leper *n.* 麻疯病患者 má fēng bìng huàn zhě

leprosy *n.* 麻疯病 má fēng bìng

leprous *a.* 麻疯病的 má fēng bìng de

less *a.* 少的 shǎo de

less *n* 较少 jiào shǎo

less *adv.* 较少 jiào shǎo

less *prep.* 减去 jiǎn qù

lessee *n.* 承租人 chéng zū rén

lessen *v.t* 减少 jiǎn shǎo

lesser *a.* 较少的 jiào shǎo de

lesson *n.* 课 kè

lest *conj.* 以免 yǐ miǎn

let *v.t.* 让 ràng

lethal *a.* 致命的 zhì mìng de

lethargic *a.* 昏睡的 hūn shuì de

lethargy *n.* 无力气 wú lì qi

letter *n* 信 xìn

level *n.* 级别 jí bié

level *a* 平坦的 píng tǎn de

level *v.t.* 弄平 nòng píng

lever *n.* 杠杆 gàng gǎn

lever *v.t.* 撬开 qiào kāi

leverage *n.* 杠杆作用 gàng gǎn zuò yòng

levity *n.* 轻率 qīng shuài

levy *v.t.* 征收 zhēng shōu

levy *n.* 税款 shuì kuǎn

lewd *a.* 淫荡的 yín dàng de

lexicography *n.* 辞典编纂 cí diǎn biān zuǎn

lexicon *n.* 词汇 cí huì

liability *n.* 责任 zé rèn

liable *a.* 有义务的 yǒu yì wù de

liaison *n.* 联络 lián luò

liar *n.* 说谎者 shuō huǎng zhě

libel *n.* 诽谤罪 fěi bàng zuì

libel *v.t.* 中伤 zhòng shāng

liberal *a.* 慷慨的 kāng kǎi de

liberalism *n.* 自由主义 zì yóu zhǔ yì

liberality *n.* 慷慨 kāng kǎi

liberate *v.t.* 解放 jiě fàng

liberation *n.* 解放 jiě fàng

liberator *n.* 解放者 jiě fàng zhě

libertine *n.* 放荡者 fàng dàng zhě

liberty *n.* 自由 zì yóu

librarian *n.* 图书馆员 tú shū guǎn yuán

library *n.* 图书馆 tú shū guǎn

licence *n.* 执照 zhí zhào

license *v.t.* 许可 xú kě

licensee *n.* 获许可的人 huò xú kě de rén

licentious *a.* 放肆的 fàng sì de

lick *v.t.* 舔 tiǎn

lick *n* 少许 sháo xǔ

lid *n.* 盖 gài

lie *v.t.* 谎骗 huǎng piàn

lie *v.i* 说谎 shuō huǎng

lie *n* 谎言 huǎng yán

lien *n.* 扣押权 kòu yā quán

lieu *n.* 场所 cháng suǒ

lieutenant *n.* 中尉 zhōng wèi

life *n* 生命 shēng mìng

lifeless *a.* 无生命的 wú shēng mìng de

lifelong *a.* 终身的 zhōng shēn de

lift *n.* 电梯 diàn tī

lift *v.t.* 升高 shēng gāo

light *n.* 光 guāng

light *a* 轻的 qīng de

light *v.t.* 点燃 diǎn rán

lighten *v.i.* 减轻 jiǎn qīng

lighter *n.* 打火机 dǎ huǒ jī

lightly *adv.* 轻轻地 qīng qīng dì

lightening *n.* 孕腹轻松 yùn fù qīng sōng

lignite *n.* 褐煤 hè méi

like *a.* 相似的 xiāng sì de

like *n.* 爱好 ài hào

like *v.t.* 喜欢 xǐ huan

like *prep* 象 xiàng

likelihood *n.* 可能性 kě néng xìng

likely *a.* 有可能的 yǒu kě néng de

liken *v.t.* 比喻 bǐ yù

likeness *n.* 相似物 xiāng sì wù

likewise *adv.* 同样地 tóng yàng dì

liking *n.* 爱好 ài hào

lilac *n.* 丁香 dīng xiāng

lily *n.* 百合花 bǎi hé huā

limb *n.* 肢 zhī

limber *v.t.* 使柔软 shǐ róu ruǎn

limber *n* 拖车 tuō chē

lime *n.* 酸橙 suān chéng

lime *v.t* 撒石灰 sā shí huī

lime *n.* 石灰 shí huī

limelight *n.* 石灰光 shí huī guāng

limit *n.* 界限 jiè xiàn

limit *v.t.* 限制 xiàn zhì

limitation *n.* 限制 xiàn zhì

limited *a.* 有限的 yǒu xiàn de

limitless *a.* 无限的 wú xiàn de

line *n.* 线 xiàn

line *v.i.* 排队 pái duì

line *v.t.* 加衬里 jiā chèn lǐ

lineage *n.* 血统 xuè tǒng

linen *n.* 亚麻布 yà má bù

linger *v.i.* 徘徊 pái huái

lingo *n.* 外国话 wài guó huà

lingua franca *n.* 混合语 hùn hé yǔ

lingual *a.* 语言的 yǔ yán de

linguist *n.* 语言学家 yǔ yán xué jiā

linguistic *a.* 语言的 yǔ yán de

linguistics *n.* 语言学 yǔ yán xué

lining *n* 衬里 chèn lǐ

link *n.* 链接 liàn jiē

link *v.t* 连结 lián jié

linseed *n.* 亚麻子 yà má zi

lintel *n.* 过梁 guò liáng

lion *n* 狮子 shī zi

lioness *n.* 雌狮 cí shī

lip *n.* 唇 chún

liquefy *v.t.* 液化 yè huà

liquid *a.* 液体的 yè tǐ de

liquidate *v.t.* 清算 qīng suàn

liquidation *n.* 偿还 cháng huán

liquor *n.* 酒 jiǔ

lisp *v.t.* 咬着舌说 yǎo zhe shé shuō

lisp *n* 口齿不清 kóu chǐ bù qīng

list *n.* 清单 qīng dān
list *v.t.* 列出 liè chū
listen *v.i.* 听 tīng
listener *n.* 收听者 shōu tīng zhě
listless *a.* 无精打采的 wú jīng dǎ cǎi de
lists *n.* 竞技场 jìng jì chǎng
literacy *n.* 读写能力 dú xiě néng lì
literal *a.* 字面上的 zì miàn shàng de
literary *a.* 文学的 wén xué de
literate *a.* 有读写能力的 yǒu dú xiě néng lì de
literature *n.* 文学 wén xué
litigant *n.* 诉讼当事人 sù sòng dāng shì rén
litigate *v.t.* 在法庭相争 zài fǎ tíng xiāng zhēng
litigation *n.* 诉讼 sù sòng
litre *n.* 公升 gōng shēng
litter *n.* 垃圾 lā jī
litter *v.t.* 乱丢(东西) luàn diū (dōng xi)
litterateur *n.* 文学家 wén xué jiā
little *a.* 小的 xiǎo de
little *adv.* 很少 hěn shǎo
little *n.* 少许 shǎo xǔ
littoral *a.* 海滨的 hǎi bīn de
liturgical *a.* 礼拜仪式的 lǐ bài yí shì de
live *v.i.* 居住 jū zhù
live *a.* 活的 huó de
livelihood *n.* 生计 shēng jì
lively *a.* 活泼的 huó po de
liver *n.* 肝 gān
livery *n.* 制服 zhì fú
living *a.* 活的 huó de
living *n* 生计 shēng jì
lizard *n.* 蜥蜴 xī yì
load *n.* 负荷 fù hè
load *v.t.* 装载 zhuāng zài
loadstar *n.* 北极星 běi jí xīng
loadstone *n.* 天然磁石 tiān rán cí shí

loaf *n.* 一条面包 yì tiáo miàn bāo
loaf *v.i.* 游手好闲 yóu shǒu hǎo xián
loafer *n.* 懒汉鞋 lǎn hàn xié
loan *n.* 贷款 dài kuǎn
loan *v.t.* 借 jiè
loath *a.* 不情愿的 bù qíng yuàn de
loathe *v.t.* 憎恶 zēng wù
loathsome *a.* 令人憎恶的 lìng rén zēng wù de
lobby *n.* 大厅 dà tīng
lobe *n.* 耳垂 ěr chuí
lobster *n.* 龙虾 lóng xiā
local *a.* 地方性的 dì fang xìng de
locale *n.* 现场 xiàn chǎng
locality *n.* 地区 dì qū
localize *v.t.* 局部化 jú bù huà
locate *v.t.* 位于 wèi yú
location *n.* 位置 wèi zhi
lock *n.* 锁 suǒ
lock *v.t* 锁 suǒ
lock *n* 一缕头发 yì lǚ tóu fa
locker *n.* 抽屉 chōu ti
locket *n.* 金属小盒 jīn shǔ xiǎo hé
locomotive *n.* 火车头 huǒ chē tóu
locus *n.* 所在地 suǒ zài dì
locust *n.* 蝗虫 huáng chóng
locution *n.* 语言风格 yǔ yán fēng gé
lodge *n.* 小屋 xiǎo wū
lodge *v.t.* 安顿 ān dùn
lodging *n.* 寄宿处 jì sù chù
loft *n.* 阁楼 gé lóu
lofty *a.* 高的 gāo de
log *n.* 圆木 yuán mù
logarithm *n.* 对数 duì shù
loggerhead *n.* 傻瓜 shǎ guā
logic *n.* 逻辑 luó jí
logical *a.* 合乎逻辑的 hé hū luó jí de
logician *n.* 逻辑学家 luó jí xué jiā
loin *n.* 腰肉 yāo ròu
loiter *v.i.* 徘徊 pái huái

logician n. 逻辑学家 luó jí xué jiā

loin n. 腰肉 yāo ròu

loiter v.i. 徘徊 pái huái

loll v.i. 懒散地闲荡 lán sǎn dì xián dàng

lollipop n. 棒棒糖 bàng bàng táng

lone a. 孤单的 gū dān de

loneliness n. 孤独 gū dú

lonely a. 孤单的 gū dān de

lonesome a. 寂寞的 jì mò de

long a. 长的 cháng de

long adv 长久 cháng jiǔ

long v.i 渴望 kě wàng

longevity n. 长命 cháng mìng

longing n. 渴望 kě wàng

longitude n. 经度 jīng dù

look v.i 看 kàn

look n. 神色 shén sè

loom n 织布机 zhī bù jī

loom v.i. 朦胧地出现 méng lóng dì chū xiàn

loop n. 圈 quān

loop-hole n. 漏洞 lòu dòng

loose a. 松的 sōng de

loose v.t. 释放 shì fàng

loosen v.t. 松开 sōng kāi

loot n. 赃物 zāng wù

loot v.i. 洗劫 xǐ jié

lop v.t. 斩 zhǎn

lop n. 砍伐 kǎn fá

lord n. 统治者 tǒng zhì zhě

lordly a. 有威严的 yǒu wēi yán de

lordship n. 贵族身分 guì zú shēn fēn

lore n. 知识 zhī shí

lorry n. 货车 huò chē

lose v.t. 输去 shū qù

loss n. 损失 sǔn shī

lot n. 全部 quán bù

lot n 一堆 yì duī

lotion n. 洗液 xǐ yè

lottery n. 彩票 cǎi piào

lotus n. 莲花 lián huā

loud a. 大声的 dà shēng de

lounge v.i. 闲混 xián hún

lounge n. 休闲室 xiū xián shì

louse n. 虱子 shī zi

lovable a. 惹人爱的 rě rén ài de

love n 爱情 ài qíng

love v.t. 爱 ài

lovely a. 可爱的 kě ài de

lover n. 爱人 ài ren

loving a. 亲爱的 qīn ài de

low a. 低的 dī de

low adv. 低 dī

low v.i. 牛叫 niú jiào

low n. 低点 dī diǎn

lower v.i. 降低 jiàng dī

lowliness n. 卑微 bēi wēi

lowly a. 地位低的 dì wèi dī de

loyal a. 忠诚的 zhōng chéng de

loyalist n. 忠诚的人 zhōng chéng de rén

loyalty n. 忠心 zhōng xīn

lubricant n. 润滑油 rùn huá yóu

lubricate v.t. 使润滑 shǐ rùn huá

lubrication n. 润滑 rùn huá

lucent a. 发亮的 fā liàng de

lucerne n. 苜蓿 mù xu

lucid a. 明晰的 míng xī de

lucidity n. 明朗 míng lǎng

luck n. 运气 yùn qi

luckily adv. 幸运地 xìng yùn dì

luckless a. 不幸的 bú xìng de

lucky a. 幸运的 xìng yùn de

lucrative a. 有利益的 yǒu lì yì de

lucre n. 收益 shōu yì

luggage n. 行李 xíng li

lukewarm a. 微温的 wēi wēn de

lull v.t. 使平静 shǐ píng jìng

lull n. 间歇 jiàn xiē

lullaby n. 摇篮曲 yáo lán qǔ

luminary n. 发光体 fā guāng tǐ

luminous a. 发光的 fā guāng de

lump *n.* 肿块 zhǒng kuài
lump *v.t.* 使成块状 shǐ chéng kuài zhuàng
lunacy *n.* 精神错乱 jīng shen cuò luàn
lunar *a.* 阴历的 yīn lì de
lunatic *n.* 疯人 fēng rén
lunatic *a.* 疯癫的 fēng diān de
lunch *n.* 午餐 wǔ cān
lunch *v.i.* 进午餐 jìn wǔ cān
lung *n* 肺 fèi
lunge *n.* 刺 cì
lunge *v.i* 突进 tū jìn
lurch *n.* 徘徊 pái huái
lurch *v.i.* 惨败 cǎn bài
lure *n.* 引诱剂 yǐn yòu jì
lure *v.t.* 诱惑 yòu huò
lurk *v.i.* 埋伏 mái fú
luscious *a.* 甘美的 gān měi de
lush *a.* 豪华的 háo huá de
lust *n.* 欲望 yù wàng
lustful *a.* 贪欲的 tān yù de
lustre *n.* 光泽 guāng zé
lustrous *a.* 有光泽的 yǒu guāng zé de
lusty *a.* 健壮的 jiàn zhuàng de
lute *n.* 鲁特诗琴 lǔ tè shī qín
luxuriance *n.* 繁茂 fán mào
luxuriant *a.* 过盛的 guò shèng de
luxurious *a.* 豪华的 háo huá de
luxury *n.* 奢侈 shē chǐ
lynch *v.t.* 私刑 sī xíng
lyre *n.* 琵琶类乐器 pí pá lèi yuè qì
lyric *a.* 抒情的 shū qíng de
lyric *n.* 歌词 gē cí
lyrical *a.* 抒情诗调的 shū qíng shī diào de
lyricist *n.* 抒情诗人 shū qíng shī rén

M

magical *a.* 魔术的 mó shù de
magician *n.* 魔术家 mó shù jiā
magisterial *a.* 有权威的 yǒu quán wēi de
magistracy *n.* 地方行政长官 dì fang xíng zhèng zhǎng guān
magistrate *n.* 地方法官 dì fang fǎ guān
magnanimity *n.* 宽宏大量 kuān hóng dà liàng
magnanimous *a.* 宽宏大量的 kuān hóng dà liàng de
magnate *n.* 权贵 quán guì
magnet *n.* 磁石 cí shí
magnetic *a.* 有磁性的 yǒu cí xìng de
magnetism *n.* 磁性 cí xìng
magnificent *a.* 宏伟的 hóng wěi de
magnify *v.t.* 放大 fàng dà
magnitude *n.* 巨大 jù dà
magpie *n.* 鹊 què
mahogany *n.* 桃花心木 táo huā xīn mù
mahout *n.* 象夫 xiàng fū
maid *n.* 女仆 nǚ pú
maiden *n.* 处女 chú nǚ
maiden *a* 未婚的 wèi hūn de
mail *n.* 邮件 yóu jiàn
mail *v.t.* 邮寄 yóu jì
mail *n* 邮递 yóu dì
main *a* 主要的 zhǔ yào de
main *n* 电源 diàn yuán
mainly *adv.* 主要地 zhǔ yào dì
mainstay *n.* 支柱 zhī zhù
maintain *v.t.* 维持 wéi chí
maintenance *n.* 维修 wéi xiū
maize *n.* 玉蜀黍 yù shǔ shǔ
majestic *a.* 庄严的 zhuāng yán de
majesty *n.* 最高权威 zuì gāo quán wēi
major *a.* 主要的 zhǔ yào de
major *n* 主修课 zhǔ xiū kè
majority *n.* 多数 duō shù
make *v.t.* 整理 zhéng lǐ
make *n* 制造 zhì zào
maker *n.* 制造者 zhì zào zhě

mal adjustment *n.* 失调 shī tiáo

mal administration *n.* 管理不善 guǎn lǐ bú shàn

malady *n.* 病 bìng

malaria *n.* 疟疾 nuè ji

maladroit *a.* 轮尽 lún jìn

malafide *a.* 不诚实 bù chéng shí

malafide *adv* 不诚实 bù chéng shí

malaise *n.* 不舒服 bù shū fu

malcontent *a.* 抱不平的 bào bù píng de

malcontent *n* 反叛者 fǎn pàn zhě

male *a.* 男性的 nán xìng de

male *n* 男性 nán xìng

malediction *n.* 诅咒 zǔ zhòu

malefactor *n.* 罪犯 zuì fàn

maleficent *a.* 作恶的 zuò è de

malice *n.* 恶意 è yì

malicious *a.* 恶毒的 è dú de

malign *v.t.* 诽谤 fěi bàng

malign *a* 有害的 yǒu hài de

malignancy *n.* 恶性 è xìng

malignant *a.* 恶性的 è xìng de

malignity *n.* 恶意 è yì

malleable *a.* 可塑的 kě sù de

malmsey *n.* 马姆齐甜酒 mǎ mǔ qí tián jiǔ

malnutrition *n.* 营养不良 yíng yǎng bù liáng

malpractice *n.* 不法行为 bù fǎ xíng wéi

malt *n.* 麦芽 mài yá

mal-treatment *n.* 虐待 nüè dài

mamma *n.* 妈妈 mā ma

mammal *n.* 哺乳类动物 bǔ rǔ lèi dòng wù

mammary *a.* 乳房的 rǔ fáng de

mammon *n.* 财富 cái fù

mammoth *n.* 毛象 máo

mammoth *a* 庞大的 páng dà de

man *n.* 男人 nán rén

man *v.t.* 操纵 cāo zòng

manage *v.t.* 管理 guán lǐ

manageable *a.* 可以处理的 ké yǐ chú lǐ de

management *n.* 管理 guán lǐ

manager *n.* 经理 jīng lǐ

managerial *a.* 经理的 jīng lǐ de

mandate *n.* 命令 mìng lìng

mandatory *a.* 规定的 guī dìng de

mane *n.* 狮鬣 shī liè

manes *n.* 鬃毛 zōng máo

manful *a.* 阴间的诸神 yīn jiān de zhū shén

manganese *n.* 锰 měng

manger *n.* 马槽 mǎ cáo

mangle *v.t.* 损坏 sǔn huài

mango *n* 芒果 máng guǒ

manhandle *v.t.* 用人力推动 yòng rén lì tuī dòng

manhole *n.* 进人孔 jìn rén kǒng

manhood *n.* 男子 nán zǐ

mania *n* 狂人 kuáng rén

maniac *n.* 颠佬 diān lǎo

manicure *n.* 修指甲 xiū zhǐ jia

manifest *a.* 明显的 míng xiǎn de

manifest *v.t.* 表明 biǎo míng

manifestation *n.* 显现 xiǎn xiàn

manifesto *n.* 宣言 xuān yán

manifold *a.* 多种的 duō zhǒng de

manipulate *v.t.* 操纵 cāo zòng

manipulation *n.* 操作 cāo zuò

mankind *n.* 人类 rén lèi

manlike *a.* 有男子气概的 yǒu nán zǐ qì gài de

manliness *n* 男子气 nán zǐ qì

manly *a.* 强壮的 qiáng zhuàng de

manna *n.* 吗哪天赐食物 ma
nǎ tiān cì shí wù

mannequin *n.* 人体模型
rén tǐ mó xíng

manner *n.* 礼貌 lǐ mào

mannerism *n.* 矫揉造作
jiǎo róu zào zuò

mannerly *a.* 客气的 kè qi de

manoeuvre *n.* 策略 cè lüè

manoeuvre *v.i.* 调动 diào
dòng

manor *n.* 庄园 zhuāng yuán

manorial *a.* 庄园的 zhuāng
yuán de

mansion *n.* 公馆 gōng guǎn

mantel *n.* 壁炉架 bì lú jià

mantle *n* 斗篷 dǒu peng

mantle *v.t* 覆盖 fù gài

manual *a.* 手的 shǒu de

manual *n* 手册 shǒu cè

manufacture *v.t.* 生产
shēng chǎn

manufacture *n* 制造业者
zhì zào yè zhě

manufacturer *n* 制造商 zhì
zào shāng

manumission *n.* 解放 jiě
fàng

manumit *v.t.* 解放奴隶 jiě
fàng nú lì

manure *n.* 肥料 féi liào

manure *v.t.* 施肥于… shī féi
yú…

manuscript *n.* 手稿 shóu
gǎo

many *a.* 许多的 xǔ duō de

map *n* 地图 dì tú

map *v.t.* 绘制…地图 huì zhì…
dì tú

mar *v.t.* 毁损 huǐ sǔn

marathon *n.* 马拉松长跑
mǎ lā sōng cháng pǎo

maraud *v.i.* 抢劫 qiǎng jié

marauder *n.* 抢劫者 qiǎng
jié zhě

marble *n.* 大理石 dà lǐ shí

march *n* 步伐 bù fá

March *n.* 三月 sān yuè

march *v.i* 进军 jìn jūn

mare *n.* 母马 mǔ mǎ

margarine *n.* 人造奶油 rén
zào nǎi yóu

margin *n.* 边缘 biān yuán

marginal *a.* 边缘的 biān yuán
de

marigold *n.* 万寿菊 wàn shòu
jú

marine *a.* 海的 hǎi de

mariner *n.* 水手 shuí shǒu

marionette *n.* 牵线木偶 qiān
xiàn mù ǒu

marital *a.* 婚姻的 hūn yīn de

maritime *a.* 海的 hǎi de

mark *n.* 痕迹 hén jì

mark *v.t* 做标记于 zuò biāo
jì yú

marker *n.* 作记号的人 zuò jì
hao de rén

market *n* 市场 shì chǎng

market *v.t* 在市场上出售 zài
shì chǎng shàng chū shòu

marketable *a.* 有销路的 yǒu
xiāo lù de

marksman *n.* 神枪手 shén
qiāng shǒu

marl *n.* 泥灰砖 ní huī zhuān

marmalade *n.* 橘子果酱 jú zi
guǒ jiàng

maroon *n.* 褐紫红色 hè zǐ
hóng sè

maroon *a* 褐紫红色的 hè zǐ
hóng sè de

maroon *v.t* 使孤立 shǐ gū lì

marriage *n.* 婚姻 hūn yīn

marriageable *a.* 可以结婚的
ké yǐ jié hūn de

marry *v.t.* 嫁 jià

Mars *n* 火星 huǒ xīng

marsh *n.* 湿地 shī dì

marshal *n* 元帅 yuán shuài

marshal *v.t* 整理 zhéng lǐ

marshy *a.* 沼地的 zhǎo dì de

marsupial *n.* 有袋动物 yǒu
dài dòng wù

mart *n.* 商业中心 shāng yè
zhōng xīn

marten *n.* 貂 diāo

martial *a.* 战争的 zhàn zhēng de

martinet *n.* 严格执行纪律的人 yán gé zhí xíng jì lù de rén

martyr *n.* 殉教者 xùn jiāo zhě

martyrdom *n.* 殉教 xùn jiāo

marvel *n.* 奇异事物 qí yì shì wù

marvel *v.i* 惊异 jīng yì

marvellous *a.* 奇异的 qí yì de

mascot *n.* 吉祥物 jí xiáng wù

masculine *a.* 有男子气的 yǒu nán zǐ qì de

mash *n.* 碎麦芽 suì mài yá

mash *v.t* 捣碎 dǎo suì

mask *n.* 假面具 jiǎ miàn jù

mask *v.t.* 掩饰 yǎn shì

mason *n.* 石匠 shí jiang

masonry *n.* 石造建筑 shí zào jiàn zhù

masquerade *n.* 掩饰 yǎn shì

mass *n.* 块 kuài

mass *v.i* 聚集 jù jí

massacre *n.* 大屠杀 dà tú shā

massacre *v.t.* 屠杀 tú shā

massage *n.* 按摩 àn mó

massage *v.t.* 按摩 àn mó

masseur *n.* 男按摩师 nán àn mó shī

massive *a.* 重的 zhòng de

massy *a.* 大而重的 dà ér zhòng de

mast *n.* 桅 wéi

master *n.* 主人 zhǔ rén

master *v.t.* 统治 tǒng zhì

masterly *a.* 巧妙的 qiǎo miào de

masterpiece *n.* 杰作 jié zuò

mastery *n.* 精通 jīng tōng

masticate *v.t.* 嚼 jiáo

masturbate *v.i.* 行手淫 xíng shǒu yín

mat *n.* 蹭鞋垫 cèng xié diàn

matador *n.* 斗牛士 dòu niú shì

match *n.* 比赛 bǐ sài

match *v.i.* 相配 xiāng pèi

match *n* 火柴 huǒ chái

matchless *a.* 无比的 wú bǐ de

mate *n.* 朋友 péng you

mate *v.t.* 交配 jiāo pèi

mate *n* 老兄 lǎo xiōng

material *a.* 物质的 wù zhì de

material *n* 材料 cái liào

materialism *n.* 唯物主义 wéi wù zhǔ yì

materialize *v.t.* 实现 shí xiàn

maternal *a.* 母亲的 mǔ qīn de

maternity *n.* 怀孕 huái yùn

mathematical *a.* 数学的 shù xué de

mathematician *n.* 数学家 shù xué jiā

mathematics *n* 数学 shù xué

matinee *n.* 白天音乐会 bái tiān yīn yuè huì

matriarch *n.* 女族长 nǚ zú zhǎng

matricidal *a.* 杀母的 shā mǔ de

matricide *n.* 杀母(罪) shā mǔ (zuì)

matriculate *v.t.* 录取 lù qǔ

matriculation *n.* 录取入学 lù qǔ rù xué

matrimonial *a.* 婚姻的 hūn yīn de

matrimony *n.* 婚姻 hūn yīn

matrix *n* 母体 mǔ tǐ

matron *n.* 护士长 hù shi zhǎng

matter *n.* 事 shì

matter *v.i.* 要紧 yào jǐn

mattock *n.* 鹤嘴锄 hè zuǐ chú

mattress *n.* (床用)垫子 (chuáng yòng) diàn zi

mature *a.* 成熟的 chéng shu de

mature *v.i* 成熟 chéng shu

maturity *n.* 成熟 chéng shu

maudlin *a* 易哭的 yì kū de

maul *n.* 大木槌 dà mù chuí

maul *v.t* 打伤 dǎ shāng

maulstick *n.* 支腕杖 zhī wàn zhàng

maunder *v.t.* 徘徊 pái huái

mausoleum *n.* 陵墓 líng mù

mawkish *a.* 叫人作呕的 jiào rén zuò ǒu de

maxilla *n.* 下颚 xià è

maxim *n.* 格言 gé yán

maximize *v.t.* 使···增加 shǐ ··· zēng jiā

maximum *a.* 最大的 zuì dà de

maximum *n* 最大限度 zuì dà xiàn dù

May *n.* 五月 wǔ yuè

may *v* 愿能 yuàn néng

mayor *n.* 市长 shì zhǎng

maze *n.* 迷宫 mí gōng

me pron. 我 wǒ

mead *n.* 蜂蜜酒 fēng mì jiǔ

meadow *n* 草地 cǎo dì

meagre *a.* 不毛的 bù máo de

meal *n.* 一餐 yì cān

mealy *a.* 粉状的 fěn zhuàng de

mean *a.* 吝啬的 lìn sè de

mean *n.* 平均数 píng jūn shù

mean *v.t* 有···的意思 yǒu ··· de yì si

meander *v.i.* 漫步 màn bù

meaning *n.* 意思 yì si

meaningful *a.* 意思 yì si

meaningless *a.* 无意义的 wú yì yì de

meanness *n.* 卑鄙 bēi bǐ

means *n* 方法 fāng fǎ

meanwhile *adv.* 其间 qí jiān

measles *n* 麻疹 má zhěn

measurable *a.* 可测量的 kě cè liáng de

measure *n.* 措施 cuò shī

measure *v.t* 计量 jì liàng

measureless *a.* 无限的 wú xiàn de

measurement *n.* 量度 liáng dù

meat *n.* 肉 ròu

mechanic *n.* 机械地工作的人 jī xiè dì gōng zuò de rén

mechanic *a* 手工的 shǒu gōng de

mechanical *a.* 机械的 jī xiè de

mechanics *n.* 机械学 jī xiè xué

mechanism *n.* 机械装置 jī xiè zhuāng zhì

medal *n.* 奖章 jiǎng zhāng

medallist *n.* 得奖章者 dé jiǎng zhāng zhě

medieval *a.* 中世纪的 zhōng shì jì de

medieval *a.* 中古的 zhōng gǔ de

median *a.* 中间的 zhōng jiān de

mediate *v.i.* 调停 tiáo tíng

mediation *n.* 调解 tiáo jiě

mediator *n.* 调解人 tiáo jiě rén

medical *a.* 医疗的 yī liáo de

medicament *n.* 药物 yào wù

medicinal *a.* 医药的 yī yào de

medicine *n.* 医药 yī yào

medico *n.* 医生 yī sheng

mediocre *a.* 普普通通的 pǔ pǔ tōng tōng de

mediocrity *n.* 普通 pǔ tōng

meditate *v.t.* 考虑 kǎo lù

meditation *n.* 冥想录 míng xiǎng lù

meditative *a.* 默想的 mò xiǎng de

medium *n* 媒介物 méi jiè wù

medium *a* 中号尺寸 zhōng hào chǐ cùn

meek *a.* 温顺的 wēn shùn de

meet *n.* 运动会 yùn dòng huì

meet *v.t.* 遇见 yù jiàn

meeting *n.* 会 huì

megalith *n.* 巨石 jù shí

megalithic *a.* 巨石的 jù shí de

megaphone n. 喇叭筒 lǎ ba tǒng

melancholia n. 忧郁病 yōu yù bìng

melancholic a. 忧郁(症)的 yōu yù (zhèng) de

melancholy n. 忧郁 yōu yù

melancholy adj 忧郁的 yōu yù de

melee n. 混战 hùn zhàn

meliorate v.t. 改善 gǎi shàn

mellow a. 甘美多汁的 gān měi duō zhī de

melodious a. 旋律的 xuán lǜ de

melodrama n. 情节剧 qíng jié jù

melodramatic a. 感情夸张的 gǎn qíng kuā zhāng de

melody n. 旋律 xuán lǜ

melon n. 甜瓜 tián guā

melt v.i. 熔化 róng huà

member n. 会员 huì yuán

membership n. 会员的资格 huì yuán de zī gé

membrane n. 膜 mó

memento n. 纪念品 jì niàn pǐn

memoir n. 回忆录 huí yì lù

memorable a. 难忘的 nán wàng de

memorandum n 备忘录 bèi wàng lù

memorial n. 纪念碑 jì niàn bēi

memorial a 纪念的 jì niàn de

memory n. 记忆 jì yì

menace n 威胁 wēi xié

menace v.t 胁迫 xié pò

mend v.t. 修补 xiū bǔ

mendacious a. 虚假的 xū jiǎ de

menial a. 卑下的 bēi xià de

menial n 奴仆 nú pú

meningitis n. 脑膜炎 nǎo mó yán

menopause n. 绝经期 jué jing qi

menses n. 月经 yuè jing

menstrual a. 月经的 yuè jing de

menstruation n. 月经期间 yuè jing qi jiān

mental a. 智慧的 zhì huì de

mentality n. 心理 xīn lǐ

mention n. 提及 tí jí

mention v.t. 提到 tí dào

mentor n. 辅导教师 fú dǎo jiào shī

menu n. 餐 cān

mercantile a. 商业的 shāng yè de

mercenary a. 被雇佣的 bèi gù yōng de

mercerize v.t. 作丝光处理 zuò sī guāng chú lǐ

merchandise n. 商品 shāng pǐn

merchant n. 商人 shāng rén

merciful a. 宽大的 kuān dà de

merciless adj. 冷酷无情的 lěng kù wú qíng de

mercurial a. 轻松的 qīng sōng de

mercury n. 水银 shuǐ yín

mercy n. 宽恕 kuān shù

mere a. 单单的 dān dān de

merge v.t. 吞没 tūn mò

merger n. 合并 hé bìng

meridian a. 子午线 zǐ wǔ xiàn

merit n. 优点 yōu diǎn

merit v.t 有…的价值 yǒu … de jià zhí

meritorious a. 值得奖励的 zhí dé jiǎng lì de

mermaid n. 美人鱼 měi rén yú

merman n. 雄人鱼 xióng rén yú

merriment n. 欢乐 huān lè

merry a 愉快的 yú kuài de

mesh n. 网状物 wǎng zhuàng wù

mesh v.t 落网 luò wǎng

mesmerism n. 催眠术 cuī mián shù

mesmerize *v.t.* 迷惑 mí huò

mess *n.* 混乱 hùn luàn

mess *v.i* 搞乱 gǎo luàn

message *n.* 通信 tōng xìn

messenger *n.* 送信人 sòng xìn rén

messiah *n.* 救世主 jiù shì zhǔ

Messrs *n.* 先生 xiān sheng

metabolism *n.* 新陈代谢 xīn chén dài xiè

metal *n.* 金属 jīn shǔ

metallic *a.* 金属的 jīn shǔ de

metallurgy *n.* 冶金学 zhì jīn xué

metamorphosis *n.* 变质 biàn zhì

metaphor *n.* 暗喻 àn yù

metaphysical *a.* 玄学的 xuán xué de

metaphysics *n.* 玄学 xuán xué

mete *v.t* 测量 cè liáng

meteor *n.* 流星 liú xīng

meteoric *a.* 流星的 liú xīng de

meteorologist *n.* 气象学家 qì xiàng xué jiā

meteorology *n.* 气象学 qì xiàng xué

meter *n.* 计量器 jì liàng qì

method *n.* 方法 fāng fǎ

methodical *a.* 有次序的 yǒu cì xù de

metre *n.* 米 mǐ

metric *a.* 公制的 gōng zhì de

metrical *a.* 格律的 gé lù de

metropolis *n.* 首都 shǒu dū

metropolitan *a.* 主要城市的 zhǔ yào chéng shì de

metropolitan *n.* 大主教 dà zhǔ jiāo

mettle *n.* 勇气 yǒng qì

mettlesome *a.* 勇敢的 yóng gǎn de

mew *v.i.* 咪咪地叫 mī mī dì jiào

mew *n.* 咪咪 mī mī

mezzanine *n.* 夹层(楼面) jiā céng (lóu miàn)

mica *n.* 云母 yún mǔ

microfilm *n.* 缩微胶卷 suō wēi jiāo juǎn

micrology *n.* 显微学 xiǎn wēi xué

micrometer *n.* 千分尺 qiān fēn chǐ

microphone *n.* 话筒 huà tǒng

microscope *n.* 显微镜 xiǎn wēi jìng

microscopic *a.* 显微镜的 xiǎn wēi jìng de

microwave *n.* 微波 wēi bō

mid *a.* 中间的 zhōng jiān de

midday *n.* 正午 zhèng wǔ

middle *a.* 中间的 zhōng jiān de

middle *n* 中间 zhōng jiān

middleman *n.* 中间人 zhōng jiān rén

middling *a.* 中等的 zhōng děng de

midget *n.* 极小者 jí xiǎo zhě

midland *n.* 中部地区 zhōng bù dì qū

midnight *n.* 午夜 wǔ yè

mid-off *n.* 投球员左侧的外场守场员 tóu qiú yuán zuǒ cè de wài cháng shǒu chǎng yuán

mid-on *n.* 投球员右侧的外场守场员 tóu qiú yuán yòu cè de wài cháng shǒu chǎng yuán

midriff *n.* 下腹部 xià fù bù

midst *n.* 中间 zhōng jiān

midsummer *n.* 仲夏 zhòng xià

midwife *n.* 助产士 zhù chǎn shì

might *n.* 力气 lì qi

mighty *a.* 强大的 qiáng dà de

migraine *n.* 周期性偏头痛 zhōu qī xìng piān tóu tòng

migrant *n.* 移民者 yí mín zhě

migrate *v.i.* 移居 yí jū

migration *n.* 移住 yí zhù

milch *a.* 有奶的 yǒu nǎi de

mild *a.* 温和的 wēn hé de
mildew *n.* 霉 méi
mile *n.* 英里 yīng lǐ
mileage *n.* 英里数 yīng lǐ shù
milestone *n.* 里程碑 lǐ chéng bēi
milieu *n.* 环境 huán jìng
militant *a.* 战斗中的 zhàn dòu zhōng dì
militant *n* 斗士 dòu shì
military *a.* 军事的 jūn shì de
military *n* 军队 jūn duì
militate *v.i.* 发生影响 fā shēng yíng xiǎng
militia *n.* 民兵 mín bīng
milk *n.* 奶 nǎi
milk *v.t.* 挤…的奶 jǐ … de nǎi
milky *a.* 像牛奶的 xiàng niú nǎi de
mill *n.* 面粉厂 miàn fěn chǎng
mill *v.t.* 磨碎 mó suì
millennium *n.* 千周年纪念 qiān zhōu nián jì niàn
miller *n.* 磨坊主 mò fáng zhǔ
millet *n.* 粟 sù
milliner *n.* 杂货商 zá huò shāng
milliner *n.* 女帽头饰商 nǚ mào tóu shì shāng
millinery *n.* 女帽类 nǚ mào lèi
million *n.* 无数 wú shù
millionaire *n.* 百万富翁 bǎi wàn fù wēng
millipede *n.* 千足虫 qiān zú chóng
mime *n.* 哑剧演员 yǎ jù yǎn yuán
mime *v.i* 作摹拟表演 zuò mó nǐ biáo yǎn
mimesis *n.* 模仿 mó páng
mimic *a.* 模仿的 mó páng de
mimic *n* 巧于模仿的人 qiǎo yú mó fǎng de rén
mimic *v.t* 学样 xué yàng

mimicry *n* 模仿 mó páng
minaret *n.* 尖塔 jiān tǎ
mince *v.t.* 绞碎 jiǎo suì
mind *n.* 心 xīn
mind *v.t.* 注意 zhù yì
mindful *a.* 注意…的 zhù yì … de
mindless *a.* 不注意的 bú zhù yì de
mine *pron.* 我的 wǒ de
mine *n* 矿 kuàng
miner *n.* 矿工 kuàng gōng
mineral *n.* 矿物 kuàng wù
mineral *a* 矿物(性)的 kuàng wù (xìng) de
mineralogist *n.* 矿物学家 kuàng wù xué jiā
mineralogy *n.* 矿物学 kuàng wù xué
mingle *v.t.* 使混合 shǐ hùn hé
miniature *n.* 微小画像 wēi xiǎo huà xiàng
miniature *a.* 小型器件 xiǎo xíng qì jiàn
minim *n.* 半音符 bàn yīn fú
minimal *a.* 最少的 zuì shǎo de
minimize *v.t.* 使减到最少 shǐ jiǎn dào zuì shǎo
minimum *n.* 最少限度 zuì shǎo xiàn dù
minimum *a* 最少的 zuì shǎo de
minion *n.* 僚属 liáo shǔ
minister *n.* 大臣 dà chén
minister *v.i.* 服侍 fú shì
ministrant *a.* 服务的 fú wù de
ministry *n.* 服务 fú wù
mink *n.* 水貂 shuǐ diāo
minor *a.* 较小的 jiào xiǎo de
minor *n* 未成年者 wèi chéng nián zhě
minority *n.* 少数 shǎo shù
minster *n.* 大教堂 dà jiào táng
mint *n.* 薄荷 bò he
mint *n* 造币厂 zào bì chǎng
mint *v.t.* 铸造 zhù zào
minus *prep.* 减(去) jiǎn (qù)

minus *a* 负 fù

minus *n* 负号 fù hào

minuscule *a.* 用小书写体的 yòng xiǎo shū xiě tǐ de

minute *a.* 细小的 xì xiǎo de

minute *n.* 分 fēn

minutely *adv.* 每分钟的 měi fēn zhōng de

minx *n.* 顽皮姑娘 wán pí gū niang

miracle *n.* 奇迹 qí jì

miraculous *a.* 奇迹般的 qí jì bān de

mirage *n.* 海市蜃楼 hǎi shì shèn lóu

mire *n.* 泥沼 ní zhǎo

mire *v.t.* 使溅满泥泞 shǐ jiàn mǎn ní nìng

mirror *n* 镜 jìng

mirror *v.t.* 反射 fǎn shè

mirth *n.* 欢笑 huān xiào

mirthful *a.* 高兴的 gāo xìng de

misadventure *n.* 意外事故 yì wài shì gù

misalliance *n.* 不适当的配合 bú shì dàng de pèi hé

misanthrope *n.* 厌世者 yàn shì zhě

misapplication *n.* 滥用 làn yòng

misapprehend *v.t.* 误解 wù jiě

misapprehension *n* 误解 wù jiě

misappropriate *v.t.* 乱用 luàn yòng

misappropriation *n.* 侵吞 qīn tūn

misbehave *v.i.* 做坏事 zuò huài shì

misbehaviour *n.* 品行不良 pǐn xíng bù liáng

misbelief *n.* 误信 wù xìn

miscalculate *v.t.* 算错 suàn cuò

miscalculation *n.* 算错 suàn cuò

miscall *v.t.* 叫错 jiào cuò

miscarriage *n.* 流产 liú chǎn

miscarry *v.i.* 早产 záo chǎn

miscellaneous *a.* 各种各样的 gè zhǒng gè yàng de

miscellany *n.* 杂记 zá jì

mischance *n.* 不幸 bú xìng

mischief *n* 损害 sǔn hài

mischievous *a.* 为害的 wéi hài de

misconceive *v.t.* 误解 wù jiě

misconception *n.* 误解 wù jiě

misconduct *n.* 行为不正 xíng wéi bú zhèng

misconstrue *v.t.* 误会 wù huì

miscreant *n.* 恶棍 è gùn

misdeed *n.* 罪行 zuì xíng

misdemeanour *n.* 不正当的行为 bú zhèng dāng de xíng wéi

misdirect *v.t.* 误导 wù dǎo

misdirection *n.* 错误指导 cuò wù zhí dǎo

miser *n.* 吝啬的人 lìn sè de rén

miserable *a.* 可怜的 kě lián de

miserly *a.* 吝啬的 lìn sè de

misery *n.* 苦难 kǔ nàn

misfire *v.i.* 不发火 bù fā huǒ

misfit *n.* 不适合 bú shì hé

misfortune *n.* 不幸 bú xìng

misgive *v.t.* 使怀疑 shǐ huái yí

misgiving *n.* 疑惑 yí huò

misguide *v.t.* 使误入歧途 shǐ wù rù qí tú

mishap *n.* 不幸的事 bú xìng de shì

misjudge *v.t.* 判断错 pàn duàn cuò

mislead *v.t.* 把…引入歧途 bǎ … yǐn rù qí tú

mismanagement *n.* 把…办错 bǎ … bàn cuò

mismatch *v.t.* 错配 cuò pèi

misnomer *n.* 用词不当 yòng cí bù dāng

misplace *v.t.* 把…放错地方 bǎ … fàng cuò dì fang

misprint *n.* 印错 yìn cuò

misrepresent *v.t.* 曲解 qū jiě

misrule *n.* 无秩序 wú zhì xù

miss *n.* 小姐 xiáo jiě

miss *v.t.* 缺席 quē xí

missile *n.* 导弹 dǎo dàn

mission *n.* 传道 chuán dào

missionary *n.* 传教士 chuán jiào shì

missis, missu *n..* …夫人 … fū rén

missive *n.* 书信 shū xìn

mist *n.* 雾 wù

mistake *n.* 错误 cuò wù

mistake *v.t.* 弄错 nòng cuò

mister *n.* 先生 xiān sheng

mistletoe *n.* 寄生 jì shēng

mistreat *v.t.* 虐待 nüè dài

mistress *n.* 女主人 nǔ zhǔ rén

mistrust *n.* 疑惑 yí huò

mistrust *v.t.* 不相信 bù xiāng xìn

misty *a.* 有薄雾的 yǒu báo wù de

misunderstand *v.t.* 误会 wù huì

misunderstanding *n.* 误会 wù huì

misuse *n.* 滥用 làn yòng

misuse *v.t.* 滥用 làn yòng

mite *n.* 螨类 mǎn lèi

mite *n* 极小的东西 jí xiǎo de dōng xi

mithridate *n.* 万应解毒药 wàn yìng jiě dú yào

mitigate *v.t.* 减轻 jiǎn qīng

mitigation *n.* 减轻 jiǎn qīng

mitre *n.* 主教冠 zhǔ jiāo guàn

mitten *n.* 两指手套 liǎng zhǐ shǒu tào

mix *v.i* 相混合 xiāng hùn hé

mixture *n.* 混合 hùn hé

moan *v.i.* 呻吟 shēn yín

moan *n.* 呻吟声 shēn yín shēng

moat *n.* 护城河 hù chéng hé

moat *v.t.* 挖壕围绕 wā háo wéi rǎo

mob *n.* 暴民 bào mín

mob *v.t.* 群众袭击 qún zhòng xí jī

mobile *a.* 活动的 huó dòng de

mobility *n.* 可动性 kě dòng xìng

mobilize *v.t.* 调动 diào dòng

mock *v.i.* 嘲笑 cháo xiào

mock *adj* 虚幻的 xū huàn de

mockery *n.* 笑柄 xiào bǐng

modality *n.* 形态 xíng tài

mode *n.* 方式 fāng shì

model *n.* 时装模特儿 shí zhuāng mó tè ér

model *v.t.* 作…的模型 zuò … de mó xíng

moderate *a.* 适度的 shì dù de

moderate *v.t.* 使和缓 shǐ hé huǎn

moderation *n.* 缓和 huǎn hé

modern *a.* 现代的 xiàn dài de

modernity *n.* 现代性 xiàn dài xìng

modernize *v.t.* 使现代化 shǐ xiàn dài huà

modest *a.* 谦虚的 qiān xū de

modesty *n* 谦虚 qiān xū

modicum *n.* 少量 shǎo liàng

modification *n.* 更改 gēng gǎi

modify *v.t.* 劳动 láo dòng

modulate *v.t.* 调整 tiáo zhěng

moil *v.i.* 劳动 láo dòng

moist *a.* 湿润的 shī rùn de

moisten *v.t.* 弄湿 nòng shī

moisture *n.* 水分 shuǐ fèn

molar *n.* 臼齿 jiù chǐ

molar *a* 臼齿的 jiù chǐ de

molasses *n* 糖浆 táng jiāng

mole *n.* 鼹鼠 yǎn shǔ

molecular *a.* 分子的 fèn zǐ de

molecule *n.* 分子 fèn zǐ

molest *v.t.* 调戏 tiáo xì

molestation *n.* 调戏 tiáo xì

molten *a.* 熔化了的 róng huà le de

moment *n.* 片刻 piàn kè

momentary *a.* 顷刻的 qǐng kè de

momentous *a.* 重大的 zhòng dà de

momentum *n.* 动力 dòng lì

monarch *n.* 帝王 dì wáng

monarchy *n.* 君主政治 jūn zhǔ zhèng zhì

monastery *n.* 寺院 sì yuàn

monasticism *n* 修道生活 xiū dào shēng huó

Monday *n.* 星期一 xing qī yī

monetary *a.* 金钱的 jin qián de

money *n.* 钱 qián

monger *n.* …商… shāng

mongoose *n.* 麝(香)猫 shè (xiāng) māo

mongrel *a* 杂种狗 zá zhǒng gǒu

monitor *n.* 监督器 jiān dū qì

monitory *a.* 警告的 jǐng gào de

monk *n.* 僧侣 sēng lǚ

monkey *n.* 猴子 hóu zi

monochromatic *a.* 单色光的 dān sè guāng de

monocle *n.* 单片眼镜 dān piàn yǎn jing

monocular *a.* 单眼的 dān yǎn de

monody *n.* 挽歌 wǎn gē

monogamy *n.* 一夫一妻制 yì fū yì qī zhì

monogram *n.* 花押字 huā yā zì

monograph *n.* 专论 zhuān lùn

monogynous *a.* 一夫一妻的 yì fū yì qī de

monolatry *n.* 一神崇拜 yì shén chóng bài

monolith *n.* 磐石 pán shí

monologue *n.* 独白 dú bái

monopolist *n.* 专利者 zhuān lì zhě

monosyllable *n.* 单音节词 dān yin jié cí

monosyllabic *a.* 单音节的 dān yin jié de

monotheism *n.* 一神教 yì shén jiāo

monotheist *n.* 一神论者 yì shén lùn zhě

monotonous *a.* 单调的 dān diào de

monotony *n* 单调 dān diào

monsoon *n.* 雨季 yǔ jì

monster *n.* 怪物 guài wu

monstrous *a.* 可怕的 kě pà de

monstrous *adv.* 非常 fēi cháng

month *n.* 月 yuè

monthly *a.* 每月的 měi yuè de

monthly *adv* 每月 měi yuè

monthly *n* 月刊 yuè kān

monument *n.* 纪念碑 jì niàn bēi

monumental *a.* 纪念碑的 jì niàn bēi de

moo *v.i* 哞 mōu

mood *n.* 心情 xīn qíng

moody *a.* 喜怒无常的 xǐ nù wú cháng de

moon *n.* 月亮 yuè liang

moor *n.* 停泊 tíng bó

moor *v.t* 使停泊 shǐ tíng bó

moorings *n.* 系泊 xì bó

moot *n.* 讨论 tǎo lùn

mop *n.* 拖把 tuō bǎ

mop *v.t.* 拿墩布拖 ná dūn bù tuō

mope *v.i.* 郁郁不乐 yù yù bú lè

moral *a.* 道德的 dào dé de

moral *n.* 寓意 yù yì

morale *n.* 士气 shì qì

moralist *n.* 道德家 dào dé jiā

morality *n.* 道德 dào dé

moralize *v.t.* 训导 xùn dǎo

morbid *a.* 病态的 bìng tài de

morbidity *n* 病状 bìng zhuàng

more *a.* 多的 duō de

more *adv* 多 duō

moreover *adv.* 况且 kuàng qiě

morganatic *a.* 不般配的 bù bān pèi de

morgue *n.* 停尸室 tíng shī shì

moribund *a.* 垂死的 chuí sǐ de

morning *n.* 早晨 zǎo chén

moron *n.* 白痴 bái chī

morose *a.* 郁闷的 yù mèn de

morphia *n.* 吗啡 ma fēi

morrow *n.* 次日 cì rì

morsel *n.* 少量 shǎo liàng

mortal *a.* 死的 sǐ de

mortal *n* 凡人 fán rén

mortality *n.* 死亡率 sǐ wáng lǜ

mortar *v.t.* 灰泥 huī ní

mortgage *n.* 抵押借款 dǐ yā jiè kuǎn

mortgage *v.t.* 抵押 dǐ yā

mortagagee *n.* 承受抵押者 chéng shòu dǐ yā zhě

mortgagor *n.* 抵押人 dǐ yā rén

mortify *v.t.* 抑制 yì zhì

mortuary *n.* 太平间 tài píng jiān

mosaic *n.* 马赛克 mǎ sài kè

mosque *n.* 清真寺 qīng zhēn sì

mosquito *n.* 蚊 wén

moss *n.* 苔藓 tái xiǎn

most *a.* 大多数的 dà duō shù de

most *adv.* 最多 zuì duō

most *n* 最多 zuì duō

mote *n.* 尘埃 chén āi

motel *n.* 旅馆 lǚ guǎn

moth *n.* 蛾 é

mother *n* 母亲 mǔ qīn

mother *v.t.* 保育 bǎo yù

motherhood *n.* 母性 mǔ xìng

motherlike *a.* 母亲似的 mǔ qīn shì de

motherly *a.* 母爱的 mǔ ài de

motif *n.* 主题 zhǔ tí

motion *n.* 运动 yùn dòng

motion *v.i.* 打手势要求 dǎ shǒu shì yāo qiú

motionless *a.* 不动的 bú dòng de

motivate *v* 激发 jī fā

motivation *n.* 动机的形成 dòng jī de xíng chéng

motive *n.* 动机 dòng jī

motley *a.* 杂色的 zá sè de

motor *n.* 马达 mǎ dá

motor *v.i.* 坐汽车 zuò qì chē

motorist *n.* 开汽车的人 kāi qì chē de rén

mottle *n.* 斑点 bān diǎn

motto *n.* 标语 biāo yǔ

mould *n.* 霉菌 méi jūn

mould *v.t.* 装饰 zhuāng shì

mould *n* 土地 tǔ dì

mould *n* 模制品 mó zhì pǐn

mouldy *a.* 发了霉的 fā le méi de

moult *v.i.* 脱换 tuō huàn

mound *n.* 土墩 tǔ dūn

mount *n.* 山 shān

mount *v.t.* 乘 chéng

mount *n* 乘骑用马 chéng qí yòng mǎ

mountain *n.* 山 shān

mountaineer *n.* 登山家 dēng shān jiā

mountainous *a.* 山多的 shān duō de

mourn *v.i.* 哀悼 āi dào

mourner *n.* 悲伤的人 bēi shāng de rén

mournful *a* 悲哀似的 bēi āi shì de

mourning *n.* 哀悼 āi dào

mouse *n.* 小鼠 xiǎo shǔ

moustache *n.* 小胡子 xiǎo hú zǐ

mouth *n.* 嘴 zuǐ

mouth *v.t.* 说出 shuō chū

mouthful *n.* 满口 mǎn kǒu

movable *a.* 可动的 kě dòng de

movables *n.* 动产 dòng chǎn

move *n.* 搬家 bān jiā

move *v.t.* 动 dòng

movement *n.* 动作 dòng zuò

mover *n.* 搬场工人 bān chǎng gōng rén

movies *n.* 电影 diàn yǐng

mow *v.t.* 收割 shōu gē

much *a* 很多的 hěn duō de

much *adv* 多 duō

mucilage *n.* 胶水 jiāo shuǐ

muck *n.* 牛马粪 niú mǎ fèn

mucous *a.* 分泌黏液的 fēn mì nián yè de

mucus *n.* 黏液 nián yè

mud *n.* 泥 ní

muddle *n.* 混乱 hùn luàn

muddle *v.t.* 使混乱 shǐ hùn luàn

muffle *v.t.* 覆 fù

muffler *n.* 围巾 wéi jīn

mug *n.* 大杯 dà bēi

muggy *a.* 闷热的 mèn rè de

mulatto *n.* 黑白混血儿 hēi bái hùn xuè ér

mulberry *n.* 桑 sāng

mule *n.* 骡 luó

mulish *a.* 骡子似的 luó zi shì de

mull *n.* 软薄布 ruǎn báo bù

mull *v.t.* 细想 xì xiǎng

mullah *n.* 毛拉 máo lā

mullion *n.* 竖框 shù kuàng

multifarious *a.* 形形色色的 xíng xíng sè sè de

multiform *a* 多种形式的 duō zhǒng xíng shì de

multilateral *a.* 多边的 duō biān de

multiparous *a.* 多胎产的 duō tāi chǎn de

multiple *a.* 多样的 duō yàng de

multiple *n* 倍数 bèi shù

multiped *n.* 多足动物 duō zú dòng wù

multiplex *a.* 多样的 duō yàng de

multiplicand *n.* 被乘数 bèi chéng shù

multiplication *n.* 乘法 chéng fǎ

multiplicity *n.* 多重性 duō zhòng xìng

multiply *v.t.* 乘 chéng

multitude *n.* 许多 xǔ duō

mum *a.* 沉默的 chén mò de

mum *n* 妈 mā

mumble *v.i.* 咕噜咕噜地说 gū lū gū lū dì shuō

mummer *n.* 哑剧演员 yǎ jù yǎn yuán

mummy *n.* 妈咪 mā mī

mummy *n* 木乃伊 mù nǎi yī

mumps *n.* 流行性腮腺炎 liú xíng xìng sāi xiàn yán

munch *v.t.* 贪馋地咀嚼 tān chán dì jǔ jué

mundane *a.* 现世的 xiàn shì de

municipal *a.* 内政的 nèi zhèng de

municipality *n.* 市自治主义 shì zì zhì zhǔ yì

munificent *a.* 慷慨给予的 kāng kǎi jí yǔ de

muniment *n.* 契据 qì jù

munitions *n.* 军火 jūn huǒ

mural *a.* 壁的 bì de

mural *n.* 壁画 bì huà

murder *n.* 凶杀 xiōng shā

murder *v.t.* 凶杀 xiōng shā

murderer *n.* 杀人犯凶手 shā rén fàn xiōng shǒu

murderous *a.* 残忍的 cán rěn de

murmur *n.* 低语声 dī yǔ shēng

murmur *v.i.* 发牢骚 fā láo sāo

muscle *n.* 肌肉 jī ròu

muscovite *n.* 莫斯科人 mò sī kē rén

muscular *a.* 强壮的 qiáng zhuàng de

muse *v.i.* 冥想 míng xiǎng

muse *n* 沉思 chén sī

museum *n.* 博物馆 bó wù guǎn

mush *n.* 软块 ruǎn kuài

mushroom *n.* 蘑菇 mó gu

music *n.* 音乐 yīn yuè

musical *a.* 音乐的 yīn yuè de

musician *n.* 音乐家 yīn yuè jiā

musk *n.* 麝香 shè xiāng

musket *n.* 火枪 huǒ qiāng

musketeer *n.* 火枪车 huǒ qiāng chē

muslin *n.* 平纹细布 píng wén xì bù

must *v.* 一定 yí dìng

must *n.* 必需的东西 bì xū de dōng xi

must *n* 必须 bì xū

mustache *n.* 胡子 hú zǐ

mustang *n.* 北美野马 běi měi yě mǎ

mustard *n.* 芥末 jiè mo

muster *v.t.* 集合 jí hé

muster *n* 群集 qún jí

musty *a.* 发霉的 fā méi de

mutation *n.* 变化 biàn huà

mutative *a.* 突变的 tū biàn de

mute *a.* 哑的 yǎ de

mute *n.* 哑巴 yǎ ba

mutilate *v.t.* 使断肢 shǐ duàn zhī

mutilation *n.* 切断者 qiē duàn zhě

mutinous *a.* 叛变的 pàn biàn de

mutiny *n.* 暴动 bào dòng

mutiny *v. i* 反抗 fǎn kàng

mutter *v.i.* 喃喃自语 nán nán zì yǔ

mutton *n.* 羊肉 yáng ròu

mutual *a.* 共同的 gòng tóng de

muzzle *n.* 口鼻 kǒu bí

muzzle *v.t* 使缄默 shǐ jiān mò

my *a.* 我的 wǒ de

myalgia *n.* 肌痛 jī tòng

myopia *n.* 近视 jìn shì

myopic *a.* 近视的 jìn shì de

myosis *n.* 缩瞳症 suō tóng zhèng

myriad *n.* 无数 wú shù

myriad *a* 无数的 wú shù de

myrrh *n.* 没药 mò yào

myrtle *n.* 番樱桃 fān yīng táo

myself *pron.* 我自己 wǒ zì jǐ

mysterious *a.* 神祕的 shén mì de

mystery *n.* 神秘 shén mì

mystic *a.* 神祕的 shén mì de

mystic *n* 神祕主义者 shén mì zhǔ yì zhě

mysticism *n.* 神秘 shén mì

mystify *v.t.* 使神秘化 shǐ shén mì huà

myth *n.* 神话 shén huà

mythical *a.* 神话的 shén huà de

mythological *a.* 神话的 shén huà de

mythology *n.* 神话学 shén huà xué

N

nab *v.t.* 逮捕 dài bǔ

nabob *n.* 对穆斯林的尊称 duì mù sī lín de zūn chēng

nadir *n.* 最低点 zuì dī diǎn

nag *n.* 马 mǎ

nag *v.t.* 不断地唠叨 bú duàn dì láo dāo

nail *n.* 钉 dìng

nail *v.t.* 用钉钉牢 yòng dìng dīng láo

naive *a.* 天真的 tiān zhēn de

naivete *n.* 天真烂漫 tiān zhēn làn màn

naivety *n.* 天真 tiān zhēn

naked *a.* 裸体的 luǒ tǐ de

name *n.* 名字 míng zi

name *v.t.* 命名 mìng míng

namely *adv.* 就是 jiù shì

namesake *n.* 同姓名的人 tóng xìng míng de rén

nap *v.i.* 打瞌睡 dǎ kē shuì

nap *n.* 绒 róng

nap *n* 小睡 xiǎo shuì
nape *n.* 颈 jǐng
napkin *n.* 餐巾 cān jīn
narcissism *n.* 自恋 zì liàn
narcissus *n* 水仙 shuǐ xiān
narcosis *n.* 麻醉 má zuì
narcotic *n.* 麻醉剂 má zuì jì
narrate *v.t.* 讲(故事) jiǎng (gù shi)
narration *n.* 叙述 xù shù
narrative *n.* 记事 jì shì
narrative *a.* 叙述的 xù shù de
narrator *n.* 讲述者 jiǎng shù zhě
narrow *a.* 窄 zhǎi
narrow *v.t.* 缩小 suō xiǎo
nasal *a.* 鼻的 bí de
nasal *n* 鼻音 bí yīn
nascent *a.* 初期的 chū qī de
nasty *a.* 下流的 xià liú de
natal *a.* 出生的 chū shēng de
natant *a.* 浮游的 fú yóu de
nation *n.* 国家 guó jiā
national *a.* 全国性的 quán guó xìng de
nationalism *n.* 国家主义 guó jiā zhǔ yì
nationalist *n.* 民族主义者 mín zú zhǔ yì zhě
nationality *n.* 国籍 guó jí
nationalization *n.* 国有化 guó yǒu huà
nationalize *v.t.* 使国家化 shǐ guó jiā huà
native *a.* 本地的 běn dì de
native *n* 土著 tǔ zhù
nativity *n.* 诞生 dàn shēng
natural *a.* 天然的 tiān rán de
naturalist *n.* 博物学家 bó wù xué jiā
naturalize *v.t.* 使入国籍 shǐ rù guó jí
naturally *adv.* 自然地 zì rán dì
nature *n.* 大自然 dà zì rán
naughty *a.* 顽皮的 wán pí de
nausea *n.* 晕船 yùn chuán

nautic(al) *a.* 航海的 háng hǎi de
naval *a.* 海军的 hǎi jūn de
nave *n.* 中殿 zhōng diàn
navigable *a.* 可通船的 kě tōng chuán de
navigate *v.i.* 航行 háng xíng
navigation *n.* 导航 dǎo háng
navigator *n.* 航行者 háng xíng zhě
navy *n.* 海军 hǎi jūn
nay *adv.* 不 bú
neap *a.* 小潮 xiǎo cháo
near *a.* 近 jìn
near *prep.* 接近 jiē jìn
near *adv.* 近的 jìn de
near *v.i.* 接近 jiē jìn
nearly *adv.* 差不多 chà bù duō
neat *a.* 整洁的 zhěng jié de
nebula *n.* 星云 xīng yún
necessary *n.* 必需品 bì xū pǐn
necessary *a* 必要的 bì yào de
necessitate *v.t.* 使成为必需 shǐ chéng wéi bì xū
necessity *n.* 必要性 bì yào xìng
neck *n.* 颈 jǐng
necklace *n.* 项圈 xiàng quān
necklet *n.* 小项圈 xiǎo xiàng quān
necromancer *n.* 巫师 wū shī
necropolis *n.* 大墓地 dà mù dì
nectar *n.* 甘露 gān lù
need *n.* 需要 xū yào
need *v.t.* 要 yào
needful *a.* 需要的 xū yào de
needle *n.* 针 zhēn
needless *a.* 不需要的 bù xū yào de
needs *adv.* 必须 bì xū
needy *a.* 贫穷的 pín qióng de
nefalon *n.* 聚酰胺纤维 jù xiān àn xiān wéi
nefarious *a.* 恶毒的 è dú de
negation *n.* 反对 fǎn duì

negative *a.* 反面的 fǎn miàn de

negative *n.* 消极性 xiāo jí xìng

negative *v.t.* 拒绝 jù jué

neglect *v.t.* 忽略 hū lüè

neglect *n* 忽略 hū lüè

negligence *n.* 疏忽 shū hu

negligent *a.* 对…玩忽 duì … wán hū

negligible *a.* 微不足道的 wēi bù zú dào de

negotiable *a.* 可协商的 kě xié shāng de

negotiate *v.t.* 议定 yì dìng

nagotiation *n.* 谈判 tán pàn

negotiator *n.* 谈判者 tán pàn zhě

negress *n.* 女黑人 nǔ hēi rén

negro *n.* 黑人 hēi rén

neigh *v.i.* (马)嘶 (mǎ) sī

neigh *n.* 嘶鸣声 sī míng shēng

neighbour *n.* 邻居 lín jū

neighbourhood *n.* 附近 fù jìn

neighbourly *a.* 邻人似的 lín rén shì de

neither *conj.* 也不 yě bú

nemesis *n.* 报应 bào yìng

neolithic *a.* 新石器时代的 xīn shí qì shí dài de

neon *n.* 氖 nǎi

nephew *n.* 侄子 zhí zi

nepotism *n.* 裙带关系 qún dài guān xi

Neptune *n.* 海王星 hǎi wáng xīng

nerve *n.* 神经 shén jīng

nerveless *a.* 无力的 wú lì de

nervous *a.* 紧张不安的 jǐn zhāng bù ān de

nescience *n.* 无知 wú zhī

nest *n.* 巢 cháo

nest *v.t.* 筑巢 zhù cháo

nether *a.* 下面的 xià mian de

nestle *v.i.* 造窝 zào wō

nestling *n.* 未离巢的雏 wèi lí cháo de chú

net *n.* 网 wǎng

net *v.t.* 净的 jìng de

net *a* 淨低的 jìng dī de

net *v.t.* 撒网 sā wǎng

nettle *n.* 荨麻 xún má

nettle *v.t.* 拿荨麻打 ná xún má dǎ

network *n.* 网眼织物 wǎng yǎn zhī wù

neurologist *n.* 神经病专科医生 shén jīng bìng zhuān kē yī sheng

neurology *n.* 神经病学 shén jīng bìng xué

neurosis *n.* 神经病 shén jīng bìng

neuter *a.* 中性的 zhōng xìng de

neuter *n* 无性动物 wú xìng dòng wù

neutral *a.* 中立的 zhōng lì de

neutralize *v.t.* 使中立化 shǐ zhōng lì huà

neutron *n.* 中子 zhōng zǐ

never *adv.* 永不 yǒng bú

nevertheless *conj.* 然而 rán ér

new *a.* 新的 xīn de

news *n.* 新闻 xīn wén

next *a.* 其次的 qí cì de

next *adv.* 下次 xià cì

nib *n.* 笔尖 bǐ jiān

nibble *v.t.* 啃 kěn

nibble *n* 啃 kěn

nice *a.* 好的 hǎo de

nicety *n.* 美好 měi hǎo

niche *n.* 适当地位 shì dàng dì wèi

nick *n.* 刻痕 kè hén

nickel *n.* 镍 niè

nickname *n.* 爱称 ài chēng

nickname *v.t.* 给…起绰号 gěi … qí chuò hào

nicotine *n.* 尼古丁 ní gǔ dīng

niece *n.* 侄女 zhí nǔ

niggard *n.* 小气鬼 xiǎo qi guǐ

niggardly *a.* 小气的 xiǎo qi de

nigger *n.* 黑人 hēi rén

nigh *adv.* 差不多 chà bù duō

nigh *prep.* 近 jìn

night *n.* 夜晚 yè wǎn

nightingale *n.* 夜莺 yè yīng

nightly *adv.* 每夜的 měi yè de

nightmare *n.* 恶梦 è mèng

nightie *n.* 小睡衣 xiǎo shuì yī

nihilism *n.* 虚无主义 xū wú zhǔ yì

nil *n.* 零 líng

nimble *a.* 敏捷的 mǐn jié de

nimbus *n.* 雨云 yǔ yún

nine *n.* 九 jiǔ

nineteen *n.* 十九 shí jiǔ

nineteenth *a.* 第十九 dì shí jiǔ

ninetieth *a.* 第九十 dì jiǔ shí

ninth *a.* 第九 dì jiǔ

ninety *n.* 九十 jiǔ shí

nip *v.t* 夹 jiá

nipple *n.* 奶头 nǎi tóu

nitrogen *n.* 氮气 dàn qì

no *a.* 不是 bú shì

no *adv.* 不 bú

no *n* 不 bú

nobility *n.* 贵族 guì zú

noble *a.* 高贵的 gāo guì de

noble *n.* 贵族 guì zú

nobleman *n.* 贵族 guì zú

nobody *pron.* 无人 wú rén

nocturnal *a.* 夜间的 yè jiān de

nod *v.i.* 点头 diǎn tóu

node *n.* 节 jié

noise *n.* 声音 shēng yīn

noisy *a.* 嘈杂 cáo zá

nomad *n.* 游牧民的一员 yóu mù mín de yì yuán

nomadic *a.* 游牧的 yóu mù de

nomenclature *n.* 命名法 mìng míng fǎ

nominal *a.* 名义上的 míng yì shàng de

nominate *v.t.* 推荐 tuī jiàn

nomination *n.* 推荐 tuī jiàn

nominee *n* 被提名者 bèi tí míng zhě

non-alignment *n.* 不结盟 bù jié méng

nonchalance *n.* 不关心 bù guān xīn

nonchalant *a.* 冷淡的 lěng dàn de

none *pron.* 并无一个 bìng wú yí gè

none *adv.* 一点也不 yì diǎn yě bú

nonentity *n.* 不存在的东西 bù cún zài de dōng xi

nonetheless *adv.* 尽管如此 jín guǎn rú cǐ

nonpareil *a.* 无比的 wú bǐ de

nonpareil *n.* 无比的人[东西] wú bǐ de rén [dōng xi]

nonplus *v.t.* 使为难 shǐ wéi nán

nonsense *n.* 废话 fèi huà

nonsensical *a.* 没有意义的 méi yǒu yì yì de

nook *n.* 角落 jiǎo luò

noon *n.* 正午 zhèng wǔ

noose *n.* 绞索 jiǎo suǒ

noose *v.t.* 用套索捕捉 yòng tào suǒ bǔ zhuō

nor *conj* …也不 … yě bú

norm *n.* 基准 jī zhǔn

norm *n.* 标准 biāo zhǔn

normal *a.* 正常的 zhèng cháng de

normalcy *n.* 正常状态 zhèng cháng zhuàng tài

normalize *v.t.* 使正常化 shǐ zhèng cháng huà

north *n.* 北 běi

north *a* 北方的 běi fāng de

north *adv.* 向北方 xiàng běi fāng

northerly *a.* 自北(的) zì běi (de)

northerly *n.* 北风 běi fēng

northern *a.* 北方的 běi fāng de

nose *n.* 鼻 bí

nose *v.t* 闻 wén
nosegay *n.* 花束 huā shù
nosey *a.* 大鼻子的 dà bí zi de
nosy *a.* 好管闲事的 hǎo guǎn xián shì de
nostalgia *n.* 乡愁 xiāng chóu
nostril *n.* 鼻孔 bí kǒng
nostrum *n.* 秘方 mì fāng
not *adv.* 不 bú
notability *n.* 显要人物 xiǎn yào rén wù
notable *a.* 值得注意的 zhí děi zhù yì de
notary *n.* 公证人 gōng zhèng rén
notation *n.* 符号 fú hào
notch *n.* 缺口 quē kǒu
note *n.* 备忘录 bèi wàng lù
note *v.t.* 笔录 bǐ lù
noteworthy *a.* 值得注意的 zhí děi zhù yì de
nothing *n.* 没有 méi yǒu
nothing *adv.* 毫不 háo bú
notice *n.* 通知 tōng zhī
notice *v.t.* 注意 zhù yì
notification *n.* 通知 tōng zhī
notify *v.t.* 通知 tōng zhī
notion *n.* 意见 yì jiàn
notional *a.* 纯理论的 chún lǐ lùn de
notoriety *n.* 臭名昭著 chòu míng zhāo zhù
notorious *a.* 声名狼藉的 shēng míng láng jiè de
notwithstanding *prep.* 虽然 suī rán
notwithstanding *adv.* 虽然 suī rán
notwithstanding *conj.* 尽管 jín guǎn
nought *n.* 零 líng
noun *n.* 名词 míng cí
nourish *v.t.* 滋养 zī yǎng
nourishment *n.* 营养 yíng yǎng
novel *a.* 新颖的 xīn yǐng de
novel *n* 小说 xiǎo shuō

novelette *n.* 中篇小说 zhōng piān xiǎo shuō
novelist *n.* 小说家 xiǎo shuō jiā
novelty *n.* 新奇 xīn qí
November *n.* 十一月 shí yí yuè
novice *n.* 新手 xīn shǒu
now *adv.* 立刻 lì kè
now *conj.* 既然 jì rán
nowhere *adv.* 什么地方都不到 shén me dì fang dōu bú dào
noxious *a.* 有害的 yǒu hài de
nozzle *n.* 管嘴 guǎn zuǐ
nuance *n.* 细微差别 xì wēi chā bié
nubile *a.* 已到结婚年龄的 yǐ dào jié hūn nián líng de
nuclear *a.* 原子核的 yuán zǐ hé de
nucleus *n.* 原子核 yuán zǐ hé
nude *a.* 赤裸裸的 chì luǒ luǒ de
nude *n* 裸体者 luǒ tǐ zhě
nudity *n.* 裸体 luǒ tǐ
nudge *v.t.* 轻推 qīng tuī
nugget *n.* 块金 kuài jīn
nuisance *n.* 麻烦事情 má fan shì qíng
null *a.* 无效的 wú xiào de
nullification *n.* 无效 wú xiào
nullify *v.t.* 使无效 shǐ wú xiào
numb *a.* 麻木的 má mù de
number *n.* 号码 hào mǎ
number *v.t.* 给…编号 gěi … biān hào
numberless *a.* 无数的 wú shù de
numeral *a.* 数的 shù de
numerator *n.* 分子 fèn zǐ
numerical *a.* 数字的 shù zì de
numerous *a.* 许多的 xǔ duō de
nun *n.* 修女 xiū nǚ
nunnery *n.* 尼姑庵 ní gū ān
nuptial *a.* 婚礼的 hūn lǐ de
nuptials *n.* 婚礼 hūn lǐ
nurse *n.* 护士 hù shi

108

nurse *v.t* 照料 zhào liào
nursery *n.* 托儿所 tuō ér suǒ
nurture *n.* 给…营养 gěi… yíng yǎng
nurture *v.t.* 养育 yǎng yù
nut *n* 坚果果仁 jiān guǒ guǒ rén
nutrition *n.* 营养 yíng yǎng
nutritious *a.* 有营养的 yǒu yíng yǎng de
nutritive *a.* 营养的 yíng yǎng de
nuzzle *v.* 将鼻突入 jiāng bí tū rù
nylon *n.* 尼龙 ní lóng
nymph *n.* 美少女 měi shǎo nǚ

O

oak *n.* 橡树 xiàng shù
oar *n.* 桨 jiǎng
oarsman *n.* 划手 huá shǒu
oasis *n.* 沙漠的绿洲 shā mò de lǜ zhōu
oat *n.* 燕麦 yàn mài
oath *n.* 誓言 shì yán
obduracy *n.* 顽固 wán gù
obdurate *a.* 顽固的 wán gù de
obedience *n.* 服从 fú cóng
obedient *a.* 服从的 fú cóng de
obeisance *n.* 敬礼 jìng lǐ
obesity *n.* 肥胖 féi pàng
obey *v.t.* 服从 fú cóng
obituary *a.* 讣告 fù gào
object *n.* 物体 wù tǐ
object *v.i.* 反对 fǎn duì
objection *n.* 反对 fǎn duì
objectionable *a.* 令人讨厌的 lìng rén tǎo yàn de
objective *n.* 目的 mù dì
objective *a.* 客观的 kè guān de
oblation *n.* 祭品 jì pǐn
obligation *n.* 责任 zé rèn
obligatory *a.* 义务的 yì wù de

oblige *v.t.* 迫使 pò shǐ
oblique *a.* 倾斜的 qīng xié de
obliterate *v.t.* 消灭…的痕迹 xiāo miè…de hén jì
obliteration *n.* 消灭 xiāo miè
oblivion *n.* 易忘 yì wàng
oblivious *a.* 易忘的 yì wàng de
oblong *a.* 长方形的 cháng fāng xíng de
oblong *n.* 长方形 cháng fāng xíng
obnoxious *a.* 可憎的 kě zēng de
obscene *a.* 猥亵的 wěi xiè de
obscenity *n.* 猥亵 wěi xiè
obscure *a.* 不清楚的 bù qīng chu de
obscure *v.t.* 遮蔽 zhē bì
obscurity *n.* 含糊 hán hu
observance *n.* (宗教)典礼 (zōng jiào) dián lǐ
observant *a.* 观察力敏锐的 guān chá lì mǐn ruì de
observation *n.* 观察 guān chá
observatory *n.* 天文台 tiān wén tái
observe *v.t.* 观察 guān chá
obsess *v.t.* 迷住 mí zhù
obsession *n.* 着魔 zháo mó
obsolete *a.* 已废弃的 yǐ fèi qì de
obstacle *n.* 障碍物 zhàng ài wù
obstinacy *n.* 固执 gù zhí
obstinate *a.* 顽固的 wán gù de
obstruct *v.t.* 堵塞 dǔ sāi
obstruction *n.* 堵塞 dǔ sè
obstructive *a.* 阻碍的 zǔ ài de
obtain *v.t.* 得到 dé dào
obtainable *a.* 能得到的 néng dé dào de
obtuse *a.* 钝的 dùn de
obvious *a.* 明显的 míng xiǎn de
occasion *n.* 场合 chǎng hé

occasion v.t 惹起 rě qǐ

occasional a. 非经常的 fēi jīng cháng de

occasionally adv. 非经常地 fēi jīng cháng dì

occident n. 西方 xī fāng

occidental a. 西方的 xī fāng de

occult a. 神秘的 shén mì de

occupancy n. 占有 zhàn yǒu

occupant n. 占有人 zhàn yǒu rén

occupation n. 职业 zhí yè

occupier n. 占用者 zhàn yòng zhě

occupy v.t. 占用 zhàn yòng

occur v.i. 发生 fā shēng

occurrence n. 出现 chū xiàn

ocean n. 洋 yáng

oceanic a. 大洋的 dà yáng de

octagon n. 八边形 bā biān xíng

octagonal a. 八边形的 bā biān xíng de

octave n. 八音度 bā yīn dù

October n. 十月 shí yuè

octogenarian a. 八十岁的(人) bā shí suì de (rén)

octroi n. 入市税 rù shì shuì

ocular a. 眼睛的 yǎn jing de

oculist n. 眼科医生 yǎn kē yī sheng

odd a. 古怪的 gǔ guài de

oddity n. 古怪 gǔ guài

odds n. 不平等 bù píng děng

ode n. 颂歌 sòng gē

odious a. 讨厌的 tǎo yàn de

odium n. 反感 fǎn gǎn

odorous a. 有味的 yǒu wèi de

odour n. 臭气 chòu qì

offence n. 罪 zuì

offend v.t. 得罪 dé zuì

offender n. 犯人 fàn rén

offensive a. 讨厌的 tǎo yàn de

offer v.t. 提供 tí gōng

offer n 提议 tí yì

offering n. 祭品 jì pǐn

office n. 公司 gōng sī

officer n. 官员 guān yuán

official a. 正式的 zhèng shì de

official n 官制 guān zhì

officially adv. 以职员身分 yǐ zhí yuán shēn fēn

officiate v.i. 主持 zhǔ chí

officious a. 爱管闲事的 ài guǎn xián shì de

offing n. 不远的将来 bù yuǎn de jiāng lái

offset v.t. 抵销 dǐ xiāo

offset n 抵销 dǐ xiāo

offshoot n. 分枝 fēn zhī

offspring n. 子女 zí nǚ

oft adv. 经常 jīng cháng

often adv. 常常 cháng cháng

ogle v.t. 送秋波 sòng qiū bō

ogle n 秋波 qiū bō

oil n. 油 yóu

oil v.t 上油 shàng yóu

oily a. 油的 yóu de

ointment n. 药膏 yào gāo

old a. 旧的 jiù de

oligarchy n. 寡头政治 guǎ tóu zhèng zhì

olive n. 橄榄树 gǎn lǎn shù

olympiad n. 奥林匹克运动会 ào lín pǐ kè yùn dòng huì

omega n. 最后一个 zuì hòu yí gè

omelette n. 煎蛋饼 jiān dàn bǐng

omen n. 预兆 yù zhào

ominous a. 不吉的 bù jí de

omission n. 遗漏 yí lòu

omit v.t. 省去 shěng qù

omnipotence n. 全能 quán néng

omnipotent a. 全能的 quán néng de

omnipresence n. 无所不在 wú suǒ bú zài

omnipresent a. 无所不在的 wú suǒ bú zài de

omniscience *n.* 全知 quán zhī

omniscient *a.* 无所不知的 wú suǒ bù zhī de

on *prep.* 在…上 zài … shàng

on *adv.* 上去 shàng qù

once *adv.* 一次 yí cì

one *a.* 一 yī

one *pron.* 一 yī

oneness *n.* 一致 yí zhì

onerous *a.* 繁重的 fán zhòng de

onion *n.* 洋葱 yáng cōng

on-looker *n.* 旁观者 páng guān zhě

only *a.* 唯一的 wéi yī de

only *adv.* 仅仅 jǐn jǐn

only *conj.* 但是 dàn shì

onomatopoeia *n.* 象声词 xiàng shēng cí

onrush *n.* 突击 tū jī

onset *n.* 开始 kāi shǐ

onslaught *n.* 猛攻 měng gōng

onus *n.* 责任 zé rèn

onward *a.* 向前的 xiàng qián de

onwards *adv.* 向前 xiàng qián

ooze *n.* 渗漏 shèn lòu

ooze *v.i.* 渗出 shèn chū

opacity *n.* 不透明部 bú tòu míng bù

opal *n.* 蛋白石 dàn bái shí

opaque *a.* 不透明的 bú tòu míng de

open *a.* 开着的 kāi zhe de

open *v.t.* 打开 dǎ kāi

opening *n.* 开头 kāi tóu

openly *adv.* 公开地 gōng kāi dì

opera *n.* 歌剧 gē jù

operate *v.t.* 操纵 cāo zòng

operation *n.* 动作 dòng zuò

operative *a.* 工作着的 gōng zuò zhe de

operator *n.* 操作者 cāo zuò zhě

opine *v.t.* 认为 rèn wéi

opinion *n.* 意见 yì jiàn

opium *n.* 鸦片 yā piàn

opponent *n.* 对手 duì shǒu

opportune *a.* 及时的 jí shí de

opportunism *n.* 机会主义 jī huì zhǔ yì

opportunity *n.* 机会 jī huì

oppose *v.t.* 反对 fǎn duì

opposite *a.* 相对的 xiāng duì de

opposition *n.* 对立 duì lì

oppress *v.t.* 压制 yā zhì

oppression *n.* 压制 yā zhì

oppressive *a.* 压制的 yā zhì de

oppressor *n.* 压迫者 yā pò zhě

opt *v.i.* 选择 xuǎn zé

optic *a.* 眼的 yǎn de

optician *n.* 眼镜商 yǎn jìng shāng

optimism *n.* 乐观 lè guān

optimist *n.* 乐观者 lè guān zhě

optimistic *a.* 乐观的 lè guān de

optimum *n.* 最适条件 zuì shì tiáo jiàn

optimum *a* 最适宜的 zuì shì yí de

option *n.* 选择 xuǎn zé

optional *a.* 可自由选择的 kě zì yóu xuǎn zé de

opulence *n.* 丰富 fēng fù

opulent *a.* 富裕的 fù yù de

oracle *n.* 先知 xiān zhi

oracular *a.* 天启的 tiān qǐ de

oral *a.* 口头的 kǒu tóu de

orally *adv.* 口述 kǒu shù

orange *n.* 橙 chéng

orange *a* 橙色的 chéng sè de

oration *n.* 演讲 yán jiǎng

orator *n.* 演讲者 yán jiǎng zhě

oratorical *a.* 演说(家)的 yǎn shuō (jiā) de

oratory *n.* 演讲术 yán jiǎng shù

orb *n.* 球 qiú

orbit *n.* 轨道 guǐ dào

orchard *n.* 果园 guǒ yuán

orchestra *n.* 管弦乐队 guǎn xián yuè duì

orchestral *a.* 管弦乐的 guǎn xián yuè de

ordeal *n.* 折磨 zhé mó

order *n.* 次序 cì xù

order *v.t* 命令 mìng lìng

orderly *a.* 有秩序的 yǒu zhì xù de

orderly *n.* 护理员 hù lǐ yuán

ordinance *n.* 法令 fǎ lìng

ordinarily *adv.* 平凡 píng fán

ordinary *a.* 普通的 pǔ tōng de

ordnance *n.* 军用品 jūn yòng pǐn

ore *n.* 矿石 kuàng shí

organ *n.* 器官 qì guān

organic *a.* 有机的 yǒu jī de

organism *n.* 生物 shēng wù

organization *n.* 组织 zǔ zhī

organize *v.t.* 组织 zǔ zhī

orient *n.* 东方 dōng fāng

orient *v.t.* 使适应(新环境) shǐ shì yìng (xīn huán jìng)

oriental *a.* 东方的 dōng fāng de

oriental *n* 东方人 dōng fāng rén

orientate *v.t.* 定…的方位 dìng … de fāng wèi

origin *n.* 根源 gēn yuán

original *a.* 原始的 yuán shǐ de

original *n* 原物 yuán wù

originality *n.* 独创性 dú chuàng xìng

originate *v.t.* 发起 fā qǐ

originator *n.* 创作者 chuàng zuò zhě

ornament *n.* 装饰品 zhuāng shì pǐn

ornament *v.t.* 装饰 zhuāng shì

ornamental *a.* 装饰的 zhuāng shì de

ornamentation *n.* 装饰 zhuāng shì

orphan *n.* 孤儿 gū ér

orphan *v.t* 使成孤儿 shǐ chéng gū ér

orphanage *n.* 孤儿院 gū ér yuàn

orthodox *a.* 正统派的 zhèng tǒng pài de

orthodoxy *n.* 正统派的观念 zhèng tǒng pài de guān niàn

oscillate *v.i.* 动摇 dòng yáo

oscillation *n.* 摆动 bǎi dòng

ossify *v.t.* 使僵化 shǐ jiāng huà

ostracize *v.t.* 排斥 pái chì

ostrich *n.* 鸵鸟 tuó niǎo

other *a.* 其次的 qí cì de

other *pron.* 别的东西 bié de dōng xi

otherwise *adv.* 不那样 bú nà yàng

otherwise *conj.* 否则 fǒu zé

otter *n.* 水獭 shuǐ tǎ

ottoman *n.* 椅子 yǐ zi

ounce *n.* 盎司 àng sī

our *pron.* 我们的 wǒ men de

oust *v.t.* 逐出 zhú chū

out *adv.* 出去 chū qu

out-balance *v.t.* 逐出 zhú chū

outbid *v.t.* 出价高过(别人) chū jià gāo guò (bié rén)

outbreak *n.* 爆发 bào fā

outburst *n.* 爆发 bào fā

outcast *n.* 被驱逐的人 bèi qū zhú de rén

outcast *a* 被排斥的 bèi pái chì de

outcome *n.* 结果 jié guǒ

outcry *a.* 强烈抗议 qiáng liè kàng yì

outdated *a.* 过时 guò shí

outdo *v.t.* 胜过 shèng guò

outdoor *a.* 户外的 hù wài de

outer *a.* 外的 wài de

outfit *n.* 准备 zhǔn bèi

outfit *v.t* 装备 zhuāng bèi

outgrow *v.t.* 长得比…快 zhǎng dé bǐ … kuài

outhouse *n.* 屋外厕所 wū wài cè suǒ

outing *n.* 出游 chū yóu

outlandish *a.* 外国气派的 wài guó qì pài de

outlaw *n.* 逃犯 táo fàn

outlaw *v.t* 剥夺…的法律保护 bō duó … de fǎ lǜ bǎo hù

outline *n.* 外形 wài xíng

outline *v.t.* 画轮廓 huà lún kuò

outlive *v.t.* 比…长寿 bǐ … cháng shòu

outlook *n.* 景色 jǐng sè

outmoded *a.* 过时的 guò shí de

outnumber *v.t.* 数量上胜过 shù liàng shàng shèng guò

outpatient *n.* 门诊病人 mén zhěn bìng rén

outpost *n.* 前哨 qián shào

output *n.* 产量 chǎn liàng

outrage *n.* 义愤 yì fèn

outrage *v.t.* 伤害 shāng hài

outright *adv.* 彻底 chè dǐ

outright *a* 彻底的 chè dǐ de

outrun *v.t.* 超过 chāo guò

outset *n.* 开头 kāi tóu

outshine *v.t.* 胜过 shèng guò

outside *a.* 出边的 chū biān de

outside *n* 外面的 wài miàn de

outside *adv* 在外面 zài wài miàn

outside *prep* 在…之上 zài … zhī shàng

outsider *n.* 外来者 wài lái zhě

outsize *a.* 特别大的 tè bié dà de

outskirts *n.pl.* 郊外 jiāo wài

outspoken *a.* 直率的人 zhí shuài de rén

outstanding *a.* 杰出的 jié chū de

outward *a.* 向外的 xiàng wài de

outward *adv* 外观 wài guān

outwards *adv* 向外 xiàng wài

outwardly *adv.* 外表上 wài biǎo shàng

outweigh *v.t.* 比…重 bǐ … zhòng

outwit *v.t.* 哄骗 hǒng piàn

oval *a.* 卵形的 luǎn xíng de

oval *n* 卵形 luǎn xíng

ovary *n.* 卵巢 luǎn cháo

ovation *n.* 热烈欢迎 rè liè huān yíng

oven *n.* 炉 lú

over *prep.* 越过… yuè guò …

over *adv* 越过 yuè guò

over *n* 连续投球比赛 lián xù tóu qiú bǐ sài

overact *v.t.* 夸张表演 kuā zhāng biáo yǎn

overall *n.* 罩衫 zhào shān

overall *a* 全部的 quán bù de

overawe *v.t.* 威慑 wēi shè

overboard *adv.* 在船外 zài chuán wài

overburden *v.t.* 负担过多 fù dān guò duō

overcast *a.* 多云的 duō yún de

overcharge *v.t.* 讨价过高 tǎo jià guò gāo

overcharge *n* 超载 chāo zài

overcoat *n.* 大衣 dà yī

overcome *v.t.* 克服 kè fú

overdo *v.t.* 过于… guò yú …

overdose *n.* 适量用药 shì liàng yòng yào

overdose *v.t.* 使…服药过量 shǐ … fú yào guò liàng

overdraft *n.* 透支 tòu zhī

overdraw *v.t.* 透支 tòu zhī

overdue *a.* 过期 guò qī

overhaul *v.t.* 翻查 fān chá

overhaul *n.* 检查 jiǎn chá

overhear *v.t.* 无意中听到 wú yì zhōng tīng dào

overjoyed *a* 非常高兴的 fēi cháng gāo xìng de

overlap *v.t.* 叠盖 dié gài

overlap *n* 重叠 chóng dié

overleaf *adv.* 次页 cì yè

overload *v.t.* 装载过重 zhuāng zài guò zhòng

overload *n* 过重装载 guò zhòng zhuāng zài

overlook *v.t.* 忽略 hū lüè

overnight *adv.* 一夜工夫 yí yè gōng fu

overnight *a* 昨晚的 zuó wǎn de

overpower *v.t.* 压服 yā fú

overrate *v.t.* 高估 gāo gū

overrule *v.t.* 驳回 bó huí

overrun *v.t* 超出 chāo chū

oversee *v.t.* 监督 jiān dū

overseer *n.* 监工 jiān gōng

overshadow *v.t.* 遮阴 zhē yīn

oversight *n.* 疏忽 shū hu

overt *a.* 公开的 gōng kāi de

overtake *v.t.* 追上 zhuī shàng

overthrow *v.t.* 推翻 tuī fān

overthrow *n* 倾覆 qīng fù

overtime *adv.* 在规定时间之外 zài guī dìng shí jiān zhī wài

overtime *n* 加班 jiā bān

overture *n.* 前奏曲 qián zòu qǔ

overwhelm *v.t.* 压倒 yā dǎo

overwork *v.i.* 工作过度 gōng zuò guò dù

overwork *n.* 过度的劳动 guò dù de láo dòng

owe *v.t* 对…负有 duì…fù yǒu

owl *n.* 猫头鹰 māo tóu yīng

own *a.* 自己的 zì jǐ de

own *v.t.* 拥有 yōng yǒu

owner *n.* 物主 wù zhǔ

ownership *n.* 所有权 suó yǒu quán

ox *n.* 牛 niú

oxygen *n.* 氧气 yǎng qì

oyster *n.* 蚝 háo

P

pace *n* 速度 sù dù

pace *v.i.* 慢慢地走 màn màn de zǒu

pacific *a.* 和平的 hé píng de

pacify *v.t.* 平息 píng xī

pack *n.* 包 bāo

pack *v.t.* 拉拢 lā lǒng

package *n.* 包裹 bāo guǒ

packet *n.* 包裹 bāo guǒ

packing *n.* 包装 bāo zhuāng

pact *n.* 合同 hé tong

pad *n.* 衬垫 chèn diàn

pad *v.t.* 装填 zhuāng tián

padding *n.* 垫充 diàn chōng

paddle *v.i.* 划桨 huá jiǎng

paddle *n* 桨 jiǎng

paddy *n.* 水稻田 shuǐ dào tián

page *n.* 页 yè

page *v.t.* 给…标页数 gěi…biāo yè shù

pageant *n.* 赛会 sài huì

pageantry *n.* 盛观 shèng guān

pagoda *n.* 塔 tǎ

pail *n.* 桶 tǒng

pain *n.* 痛 tòng

pain *v.t.* 使疼痛 shǐ téng tòng

painful *a.* 疼痛的 téng tòng de

painstaking *a.* 劳苦的 láo kǔ de

paint *n.* 油漆 yóu qī

paint *v.t.* 给…上油漆 gěi…shàng yóu qī

painter *n.* 画家 huà jiā

painting *n.* 绘画 huì huà

pair *n.* 一对 yí duì

pair *v.t.* 使成对 shǐ chéng duì

pal *n.* 好朋友 hǎo péng you

palace *n.* 宫 gōng

palanquin *n.* 四[六]人大轿 sì [liù] rén dà jiào

palatable *a.* 好吃的 hǎo chī de

palatal *a.* 腭的 è de

palate *n.* 腭 è

palatial *a.* 宏伟的 hóng wěi de

pale *n.* 桩 zhuāng

pale *a* 灰白的 huī bái de

pale *v.i.* 使变苍白 shǐ biàn cāng bái

palette *n.* 调色板 tiáo sè bǎn

palm *n.* 手掌 shóu zhǎng

palm *v.t.* 用手掌抚摩 yòng shóu zhǎng fǔ mó

palm *n.* 棕榈树 zōng lú shù

palmist *n.* 手相术 shǒu xiàng shù

palmistry *n.* 手相术 shǒu xiàng shù

palpable *a.* 明显的 míng xiǎn de

palpitate *v.i.* 跳动 tiào dòng

palpitation *n.* 心悸 xīn jì

palsy *n.* 麻痹 má bì

paltry *a.* 不足取的 bù zú qǔ de

pamper *v.t.* 纵容 zòng róng

pamphlet *n.* 小册子 xiǎo cè zǐ

pamphleteer *n.* 小册子作者 xiǎo cè zǐ zuò zhě

panacea *n.* 万应药 wàn yīng yào

pandemonium *n.* 群魔殿 qún mó diàn

pane *n.* 窗格玻璃 chuāng gé bō li

panegyric *n.* 颂词 sòng cí

panel *n.* 镶板 xiāng bǎn

panel *v.t.* 在…上嵌板子 zài … shàng qiàn bǎn zi

pang *n.* 一阵剧痛 yí zhèn jù tòng

panic *n.* 恐慌 kǒng huāng

panorama *n.* 全景 quán jǐng

pant *v.i.* 喘息 chuǎn xī

pant *n.* 喘息 chuǎn xī

pantaloon *n.* 老丑角 lǎo chǒu jué

pantheism *n.* 泛神论 fàn shén lùn

pantheist *n.* 泛神论者 fàn shén lùn zhě

panther *n.* 黑豹 hēi bào

pantomime *n.* 童话剧 tóng huà jù

pantry *n.* 食品储存室 shí pǐn chǔ cún shì

papacy *n.* 教皇制度 jiào huáng zhì dù

papal *a.* 天主教的 tiān zhǔ jiāo de

paper *n.* 纸 zhǐ

par *n.* 标准打数 biāo zhǔn dǎ shù

parable *n.* 寓言 yù yán

parachute *n.* 降落伞 jiàng luò sǎn

parachutist *n.* 跳伞者 tiào sǎn zhě

parade *n.* 游行 yóu xíng

parade *v.t.* 游行 yóu xíng

paradise *n.* 天堂 tiān táng

paradox *n.* 自相矛盾的话 zì xiāng máo dùn de huà

paradoxical *a.* 自相矛盾的 zì xiāng máo dùn de

paraffin *n.* 石蜡 shí là

paragon *n.* 模范 mó fàn

paragraph *n.* 段 duàn

parallel *a.* 平行的 píng xíng de

parallel *v.t.* 使成平行 shǐ chéng píng xíng

parallelism *n.* 类似 lèi sì

parallelogram *n.* 平行四边形 píng xíng sì biān xíng

paralyse *v.t.* 使麻痹 shǐ má bì

paralysis *n.* 麻痹 má bì

paralytic *a.* 麻痹的 má bì de

paramount *a.* 最高的 zuì gāo de

paramour *n.* 情人 qíng rén

paraphernalia *n. pl* 随身用具 suí shēn yòng jù

paraphrase *n.* 意译 yì yì

paraphrase *v.t.* 释义 shì yì

parasite *n.* 寄生虫 jì shēng chóng

parcel *n.* 包裹 bāo guǒ

parcel *v.t.* 把…作成包裹 bǎ … zuò chéng bāo guǒ

parch *v.t.* 烘 hōng

pardon *v.t.* 赦免 shè miǎn

pardon *n.* 特赦 tè shè

pardonable *a.* 可以原谅的 ké yǐ yuán liàng de
parent *n.* 父母 fù mǔ
parentage *n.* 出身 chū shēn
parental *a.* 父母的 fù mǔ de
parenthesis *n.* 插入语 chā rù yǔ
parish *n.* 教区 jiào qū
parity *n.* 平等 píng děng
park *n.* 公园 gōng yuán
park *v.i.* 停车 tíng chē
parlance *n.* 说法 shuō fǎ
parley *n.* 会谈 huì tán
parley *v.i* 谈判 tán pàn
parliament *n.* 国会 guó huì
parliamentarian *n.* 国会议员 guó huì yì yuán
parliamentary *a.* 国会的 guó huì de
parlour *n.* 客厅 kè tīng
parody *n.* 拙劣的模仿 zhuō liè de mó fǎng
parody *v.t.* 拙劣地模仿 zhuō liè dì mó fǎng
parole *n.* 释放宣誓 shì fàng xuān shì
parole *v.t.* 使宣誓后释放 shǐ xuān shì hòu shì fàng
parricide *n.* 叛逆罪 pàn nì zuì
parrot *n.* 鹦鹉 yīng wǔ
parry *v.t.* 挡开 dǎng kāi
parry *n.* 挡开 dǎng kāi
parson *n.* 牧师 mù shī
part *n.* 部分 bù fen
part *v.t.* 使分开 shǐ fēn kāi
partake *v.i.* 参与 cān yù
partial *a.* 一部分的 yí bù fen de
partiality *n.* 偏心 piān xīn
participate *v.i.* 参与 cān yù
participant *n.* 参加者 cān jiā zhě
participation *n.* 参与 cān yù
particle *n.* 微粒 wēi lì
particular *a.* 特别的 tè bié de
particular *n.* 详细情节 xiáng xì qíng jié

partisan *n.* 游击队员 yóu jī duì yuán
partisan *a.* 有偏袒的 yǒu piān tǎn de
partition *n.* 区分 qū fēn
partition *v.t.* 分割 fēn gē
partner *n.* 搭档 dā dàng
partnership *n.* 合伙 hé huǒ
party *n.* 聚会 jù huì
pass *v.i.* 通过 tōng guò
pass *n* 通行 tōng xíng
passage *n.* 通行 tōng xíng
passenger *n.* 乘客 chéng kè
passion *n.* 热情 rè qíng
passionate *a.* 热烈的 rè liè de
passive *a.* 被动的 bèi dòng de
passport *n.* 护照 hù zhào
past *a.* 过去的 guò qù de
past *n.* 过去 guò qù
past *prep.* 过… guò…
paste *n.* 酱 jiàng
paste *v.t.* 狠狠地打 hěn hěn dì dǎ
pastel *n.* 彩色笔 cǎi sè fěn bǐ
pastime *n.* 消遣 xiāo qiǎn
pastoral *a.* 牧人的 mù rén de
pasture *n.* 牧场 mù chǎng
pasture *v.t.* 放牧 fàng mù
pat *v.t.* 轻拍 qīng pāi
pat *n* 拍 pāi
pat *adv* 适当 shì dàng
patch *v.t.* 修补 xiū bǔ
patch *n* 补钉 bǔ dìng
patent *a.* 专利的 zhuān lì de
patent *n* 专利权 zhuān lì quán
patent *v.t.* 批准给予…专利 pī zhǔn jí yǔ…zhuān lì
paternal *a.* 父亲的 fù qīn de
path *n.* 小路 xiǎo lù
pathetic *a.* 可怜的 kě lián de
pathos *n.* 感伤力 gǎn shāng lì
patience *n.* 耐性 nài xìng
patient *a.* 有耐性的 yǒu nài xìng de
patient *n* 病人 bìng rén
patricide *n.* 杀父者 shā fù zhě

patrimony n. 遗产 yí chǎn

patriot n. 爱国者 ài guó zhě

patriotic a. 爱国的 ài guó de

partiotism n. 爱国精神 ài guó jīng shen

patrol v.i. 巡逻 xún luó

patrol n 巡逻 xún luó

patron n. 赞助人 zàn zhù rén

patronage n. 赞助 zàn zhù

patronize v.t. 保护 bǎo hù

pattern n. 模范 mó fàn

paucity n. 少量 shǎo liàng

pauper n. 穷人 qióng rén

pause n. 暂停 zàn tíng

pause v.i. 暂停 zàn tíng

pave v.t. 铺设 pū shè

pavement n. 人行道 rén xíng dào

pavilion n. 楼阁 lóu gé

paw n. 爪 zhǎo

paw v.t. 以蹄扒地 yǐ tí bā dì

pay v.t. 支付 zhī fù

pay n 薪资 xīn zī

payable a. 可付的 kě fù de

payee n. 收款人 shōu kuǎn rén

payment n. 付款 fù kuǎn

pea n. 豌豆 wān dòu

peace n. 和平 hé píng

peaceable a. 和平的 hé píng de

peaceful a. 平静的 píng jìng de

peach n. 桃子 táo zi

peacock n. 孔雀 kǒng què

peahen n. 雌孔雀 cí kǒng què

peak n. 山峰 shān fēng

pear n. 梨子 lí zǐ

pearl n. 珍珠 zhēn zhū

peasant n. 农夫 nóng fū

peasantry n. 农民 nóng mín

pebble n. 小鹅卵石 xiǎo é luǎn shí

peck n. 啄痕 zhuó hén

peck v.i. 啄 zhuó

peculiar a. 奇特的 qí tè de

peculiarity n. 怪癖 guài pǐ

pecuniary a. 金钱的 jīn qián de

pedagogue n. 小学教师 xiǎo xué jiào shī

pedagogy n. 教育学 jiào yù xué

pedal n. 踏板 tà bǎn

pedal v.t. 用脚踏动 yòng jiǎo tà dòng

pedant n. 书呆子 shū dāi zi

pedantic a. 学究式的 xué jiū shì de

pedantry n. 迂腐 yū fǔ

pedestal n. 基座 jī zuò

pedestrian n. 行人 xíng rén

pedigree n. 家谱 jiā pǔ

peel v.t. 削...皮 xuē... pí

peel n. 皮 pí

peep v.i. 窥视 kuī shì

peep n 偷看 tōu kàn

peer n. 同等的人 tóng děng de rén

peerless a. 无比的 wú bǐ de

peg n. 钉 dìng

peg v.t. 钉木钉 dìng mù dìng

pelf n. 不义之财 bú yì zhī cái

pell-mell adv. 乱七八糟地 luàn qī bā zāo dì

pen n. 笔 bǐ

pen v.t. 写 xiě

penal a. 刑罚的 xíng fá de

penalize v.t. 处刑 chǔ xíng

penalty n. 处罚 chǔ fá

pencil n. 铅笔 qiān bǐ

pencil v.t. 用铅笔写或涂 yòng qiān bǐ xiě huò tú

pending prep. 在等待...之际 zài děng dài... zhī jì

pending a 未决定的 wèi jué dìng de

pendulum n. 钟摆 zhōng bǎi

penetrate v.t. 进入 jìn rù

penetration n. 浸透 jìn tòu

penis n. 阴茎 yīn jīng

penniless a. 赤贫的 chì pín de

penny n. 便士 biàn shì

pension n. 退休金 tuì xiū jīn

pension *v.t.* 发给退休金 fā gěi tuì xiū jīn

pensioner *n.* 领取抚恤金者 líng qǔ fǔ xù jīn zhě

pensive *a.* 沉思的 chén sī de

pentagon *n.* 五角形 wǔ jiǎo xíng

peon *n.* 劳工 láo gōng

people *n.* 人 rén

people *v.t.* 住满人 zhù mǎn rén

pepper *n.* 胡椒粉 hú jiāo fěn

pepper *v.t.* 加胡椒粉于 jiā hú jiāo fěn yú

per *prep.* 每 měi

perambulator *n.* 摇篮车 yáo lán chē

perceive *v.t.* 感觉 gǎn jué

perceptible *adj* 可察觉的 kě chá jué de

per cent *n.* 百分比 bǎi fēn bǐ

percentage *n.* 感知 gǎn zhī

perception *n.* 知觉 zhī jué

perceptive *a.* 知觉的 zhī jué de

perch *n.* 栖木 qī mù

perch *v.i.* 就位 jiù wèi

perennial *a.* 常年的 cháng nián de

perennial *n.* 多年生的 duō nián shēng de

perfect *a.* 完美的 wán měi de

perfect *v.t.* 使完美 shǐ wán měi

perfection *n.* 完美 wán měi

perfidy *n.* 背信弃义 bèi xìn qì yì

perforate *v.t.* 穿孔于 chuān kǒng yú

perforce *adv.* 必然地 bì rán dì

perform *v.t.* 表演 biǎo yǎn

performance *n.* 演出 yǎn chū

performer *n.* 表演者 biǎo yǎn zhě

perfume *n.* 香水 xiāng shuǐ

perfume *v.t.* 洒香水于 sǎ xiāng shuǐ yú

perhaps *adv.* 也许 yé xǔ

peril *n.* 危险 wēi xiǎn

peril *v.t.* 置...于险境 zhì... yú xiǎn jìng

perilous *a.* 危险的 wēi xiǎn de

period *n.* 时期 shí qī

periodical *n.* 期刊 qī kān

periodical *a.* 定期的 dìng qī de

periphery *n.* 周围 zhōu wéi

perish *v.i.* 死亡 sǐ wáng

perishable *a.* 易腐坏的 yì fǔ huài de

perjure *v.t.* 使发伪誓 shǐ fā wěi shì

perjury *n.* 伪誓 wěi shì

permanence *n.* 永久 yóng jiǔ

permanent *a.* 永久的 yóng jiǔ de

permissible *a.* 可允许的 kě yún xǔ de

permission *n.* 许可 xú kě

permit *v.t.* 允许 yún xǔ

permit *n.* 许可证 xú kě zhèng

permutation *n.* 排列 pái liè

pernicious *a.* 有害的 yǒu hài de

perpendicular *a.* 垂直的 chuí zhí de

perpendicular *n.* 垂直线 chuí zhí xiàn

perpetual *a.* 不断的 bú duàn de

perpetuate *v.t.* 使困惑 shǐ kùn huò

perplex *v.t.* 困扰 kùn rǎo

perplexity *n.* 困惑 kùn huò

persecute *v.t.* 迫害 pò hài

persecution *n.* 迫害 pò hài

perseverance *n.* 毅力 yì lì

persevere *v.i.* 坚持 jiān chí

persist *v.i.* 坚持 jiān chí

persistence *n.* 固执 gù zhí

persistent *a.* 固执的 gù zhí de

person *n.* 人 rén

personage n. 名士 míng shì

personal a. 私人的 sī rén de

personality n. 个性 gè xìng

personification n. 人格化 rén gé huà

personify v.t. 看做人 kàn zuò rén

personnel n. 人事部门 rén shì bù mén

perspective n. 远景 yuán jǐng

perspiration n. 汗 hàn

perspire v.i. 出汗 chū hàn

persuade v.t. 说服 shuō fú

persuasion n. 说服力 shuō fú lì

pertain v.i. 关于 guān yú

pertinent a. 有关的 yǒu guān de

perturb v.t. 使心绪不宁 shǐ xīn xù bù níng

perusal n. 熟读 shú dú

peruse v.t. 熟读 shú dú

pervade v.t. 遍及 biàn jí

perverse a. 乖张的 guāi zhāng de

perversion n. 变态 biàn tài

perversity n. 倔强 jué jiàng

pervert v.t. 使堕落 shǐ duò luò

pessimism n. 悲观 bēi guān

pessimist n. 悲观者 bēi guān zhě

pessimistic a. 悲观的 bēi guān de

pest n. 害虫 hài chóng

pesticide n. 杀虫剂 shā chóng jì

pestilence n. 瘟疫 wēn yì

pet n. 宠物 chǒng wù

pet v.t. 宠爱 chǒng ài

petal n. 花瓣 huā bàn

petition n. 请愿 qǐng yuàn

petition v.t. 请愿 qǐng yuàn

petitioner n. 请愿人 qǐng yuàn rén

petrol n. 汽油 qì yóu

petroleum n. 石油 shí yóu

petticoat n. 衬裙 chèn qún

petty a. 琐碎的 suǒ suì de

petulance n. 坏脾气 huài pí qi

petulant a. 任性的 rén xìng de

phantom n. 幻影 huàn yǐng

pharmacy n. 药房 yào fáng

phase n. 阶段 jiē duàn

phenomenal a. 现象的 xiàn xiàng de

phenomenon n. 现象 xiàn xiàng

phial n. 管形瓶 guǎn xíng píng

philanthropic a. 慈善的 cí shàn de

philanthropist n. 慈善家 cí shàn jiā

philanthropy n. 慈善 cí shàn

philological a. 语文学的 yǔ wén xué de

philologist n. 语文学者 yǔ wén xué zhě

philology n. 语文学 yǔ wén xué

philosopher n. 哲学家 zhé xué jiā

philosophical a. 哲学的 zhé xué de

philosophy n. 哲学 zhé xué

phone n. 电话 diàn huà

phonetic a. 语音的 yǔ yīn de

phonetics n. 语音学 yǔ yīn xué

phosphate n. 磷酸盐 lín suān yán

phosphorus n. 磷 lín

photo n 相片 xiàng piàn

photograph v.t. 照相 zhào xiàng

photograph n 相片 xiàng piàn

photographer n. 摄影师 shè yǐng shī

photographic a. 摄影用的 shè yǐng yòng de

photography n. 摄影 shè yǐng

phrase n. 成语 chéng yǔ

phrase v.t. 表达 biǎo dá

phraseology *n.* 措辞 cuò cí

physic *n.* 药品 yào pǐn

physic *v.t.* 给...服药 gěi... fú yào

physical *a.* 身体的 shēn tǐ de

physician *n.* 医师 yī shī

physicist *n.* 物理学家 wù lǐ xué jiā

physics *n.* 物理学 wù lǐ xué

physiognomy *n.* 外貌 wài mào

physique *n.* 体格 tǐ gé

pianist *n.* 钢琴家 gāng qín jiā

piano *n.* 钢琴 gāng qín

pick *v.t.* 摘 zhāi

pick *n.* 选择 xuǎn zé

picket *n.* 纠察队 jiū chá duì

picket *v.t.* 围住 wéi zhù

pickle *n.* 泡菜 pào cài

pickle *v.t* 腌制 yān zhì

picnic *n.* 野餐 yě cān

picnic *v.i.* 去野餐 qù yě cān

pictorical *a.* 绘画的 huì huà de

picture *n.* 图画 tú huà

picture *v.t.* 想像 xiǎng xiàng

picturesque *a.* 生动的 shēng dòng de

piece *n.* 块 kuài

piece *v.t.* 修补 xiū bǔ

pierce *v.t.* 穿透 chuān tòu

piety *n.* 虔诚 qián chéng

pig *n.* 猪 zhū

pigeon *n.* 鸽子 gē zi

pigmy *n.* 微不足道的 wēi bù zú dào de

pile *n.* 堆 duī

pile *v.t.* 堆于 duī yú

piles *n.* 痔 zhì

pilfer *v.t.* 盗取 dào qǔ

pilgrim *n.* 朝圣者 cháo shèng zhě

pilgrimage *n.* 朝圣 cháo shèng

pill *n.* 药丸 yào wán

pillar *n.* 柱子 zhù zi

pillow *n* 枕头 zhěn tou

pillow *v.t.* 作...的枕头 zuò... de zhěn tou

pilot *n.* 飞行员 fēi háng yuán

pilot *v.t.* 领航 lǐng háng

pimple *n.* 丘疹 qiū zhěn

pin *n.* 针 zhēn

pin *v.t.* 钉住 dìng zhù

pinch *v.t.* 捏 niē

pinch *n.* 捏 niē

pine *n.* 松树 sōng shù

pine *v.i.* 消瘦 xiāo shòu

pineapple *n.* 菠萝 bō luó

pink *n.* 粉红色 fěn hóng sè

pink *a* 粉红的 fěn hóng de

pinkish *a.* 略带桃色的 lüè dài táo sè de

pinnacle *n.* 小尖塔 xiǎo jiān tǎ

pioneer *n.* 拓荒者 tuò huāng zhě

pioneer *v.t.* 倡导 chàng dǎo

pious *a.* 虔诚的 qián chéng de

pipe *n.* 管 guǎn

pipe *v.i* 吹笛 chuī dí

piquant *a.* 开胃的 kāi wèi de

piracy *n.* 海盗行为 hǎi dào xíng wéi

pirate *n.* 海盗 hǎi dào

pirate *v.t* 盗印 dào yìn

pistol *n.* 手枪 shǒu qiāng

piston *n.* 活塞 huó sāi

pit *n.* 深坑 shēn kēng

pit *v.t.* 窖藏 jiào cáng

pitch *n.* 程度 chéng dù

pitch *v.t.* 投 tóu

pitcher *n.* 投手 tóu shǒu

piteous *a.* 可怜的 kě lián de

pitfall *n.* 陷阱 xiàn jǐng

pitiable *a.* 引人怜悯的 yǐn rén lián mǐn de

pitiful *a.* 可怜的 kě lián de

pitiless *a.* 无情的 wú qíng de

pitman *n.* 矿工 kuàng gōng

pittance *n.* 少量津贴 shǎo liàng jīn tiē

pity *n.* 同情 tóng qíng

pity *v.t.* 可怜 kě lián

pivot *n.* 中枢 zhōng shū

pivot *v.t.* 旋转 xuán zhuǎn

placard *n.* 公告 gōng gào

place *n.* 地方 dì fang

place *v.t.* 摆 bǎi

placid *a.* 温和的 wēn hé de

plague *n.* 瘟疫 wēn yì

plague *v.t.* 折磨 zhé mó

plain *a.* 简单的 jiǎn dān de

plain *n.* 平原 píng yuán

plaintiff *n.* 原告 yuán gào

plan *n.* 计划 jì huà

plan *v.t.* 计划 jì huà

plane *n.* 飞机 fēi jī

plane *v.t.* 刨平 bào píng

plane *a.* 平的 píng de

plane *n* 平面 píng miàn

planet *n.* 行星 xíng xing

planetary *a.* 行星的 xíng xīng de

plank *n.* 厚木板 hòu mù bǎn

plank *v.t.* 在...上铺板 zài... shàng pù bǎn

plant *n.* 植物 zhí wù

plant *v.t.* 种植 zhòng zhí

plantain *n.* 车前草 chē qián cǎo

plantation *n.* 种植园 zhòng zhí yuán

plaster *n.* 膏药 gāo yao

plaster *v.t.* 涂以灰泥 tú yǐ huī ní

plate *n.* 碟 dié

plate *v.t.* 电镀 diàn dù

plateau *n.* 高地 gāo dì

platform *n.* 站台 zhàn tái

platonic *a.* 空谈的 kōng tán de

platoon *n.* 排 pái

play *n.* 游戏 yóu xì

play *v.i.* 玩 wán

player *n.* 竞赛者 jìng sài zhě

plea *n.* 恳求 kěn qiú

plead *v.i.* 恳求 kěn qiú

pleader *n.* 辩论者 biàn lùn zhě

pleasant *a.* 愉快的 yú kuài de

pleasantry *n.* 幽默的话 yōu mò de huà

please *v.t.* 使高兴 shǐ gāo xìng

pleasure *n.* 愉快 yú kuài

plebiscite *n.* 公民投票 gōng mín tóu piào

pledge *n.* 保证 bǎo zhèng

pledge *v.t.* 许诺 xǔ nuò

plenty *n.* 充分 chōng fēn

plight *n.* 困境 kùn jìng

plod *v.i.* 沉重地走 chén zhòng dì zǒu

plot *n.* 情节 qíng jié

plot *v.t.* 密谋 mì móu

plough *n.* 犁 lí

plough *v.t.* 耕 gēng

ploughman *n.* 庄稼汉 zhuāng jia hàn

pluck *v.t.* 猛拉 měng lā

pluck *n* 勇气 yǒng qì

plug *n.* 塞子 sāi zi

plug *v.t.* 插入 chā rù

plum *n.* 李子 lǐ zi

plumber *n.* 水管工人 shuǐ guǎn gōng rén

plunder *v.t.* 抢劫 qiǎng jié

plunder *n* 抢夺 qiǎng duó

plunge *v.t.* 使投入 shǐ tóu rù

plunge *n* 钻进 zuàn jìn

plural *a.* 复数的 fù shù de

plurality *n.* 复数 fù shù

plus *a.* 正的 zhèng de

plus *n* 正号 zhèng hào

ply *v.t.* 使用 shǐ yòng

ply *n* 板层 bǎn céng

pneumonia *n.* 肺炎 fèi yán

pocket *n.* 口袋 kǒu dai

pocket *v.t.* 装在口袋里 zhuāng zài kǒu dai lǐ

pod *n.* 豆荚 dòu jiá

poem *n.* 诗 shī

poesy *n.* 诗 shī

poet *n.* 诗人 shī rén

poetaster *n.* 冒牌诗人 mào pái shī rén

poetess *n.* 女诗人 nǚ shī rén

poetic *a.* 诗的 shī de

poetics *n.* 诗学 shī xué

poetry *n.* 诗 shī

poignancy *n.* 辛酸 xīn suān

poignant *a.* 辛酸的 xīn suān de

point *n.* 点 diǎn

point *v.t.* 指出 zhǐ chū

poise *v.t.* 使平衡 shǐ píng héng

poise *n* 平衡 píng héng

poison *n.* 毒 dú

poison *v.t.* 毒害 dú hài

poisonous *a.* 有毒的 yǒu dú de

poke *v.t.* 戳 chuō

poke *n.* 刺 cì

polar *a* 极地的 jí dì de

pole *n.* 地极 dì jí

police *n.* 警察 jǐng chá

policeman *n.* 警察 jǐng chá

policy *n.* 方针 fāng zhēn

polish *v.t.* 擦亮 cā liàng

polish *n* 上光剂 shàng guāng jì

polite *a.* 有礼貌的 yǒu lǐ mào de

politeness *n.* 有礼 yǒu lǐ

politic *a.* 明智的 míng zhì de

political *a.* 政治的 zhèng zhì de

politician *n.* 政治家 zhèng zhì jiā

politics *n.* 政治 zhèng zhì

polity *n.* 政治组织 zhèng zhì zǔ zhī

poll *n.* 投票 tóu piào

poll *v.t.* 对...进行民意测验 duì... jìn xíng mín yì cè yàn

pollen *n.* 花粉 huā fěn

pollute *v.t.* 污染 wū rǎn

pollution *n.* 污染 wū rǎn

polo *n.* 马球 mǎ qiú

polygamous *a.* 多配偶(制)的 duō pèi ǒu (zhì) de

polygamy *n.* 多配偶(制) duō pèi ǒu (zhì)

polyglot *n.* 使用多种语言的人 shǐ yòng duō zhǒng yǔ yán de rén

polyglot *a.* 多种语言的 duō zhǒng yǔ yán de

polytechnic *a.* 各种工艺的 gè zhǒng gōng yì de

polytechnic *n.* 理工专科学校 lǐ gōng zhuān kē xué xiào

polytheism *n.* 多神教 duō shén jiāo

polytheist *n.* 多神教徒 duō shén jiào tú

polytheistic *a.* 多神教的 duō shén jiāo de

pomp *n.* 壮丽 zhuàng lì

pomposity *n.* 炫耀 xuàn yào

pompous *a.* 虚夸的 xū kuā de

pond *n.* 池塘 chí táng

ponder *v.t.* 沉思 chén sī

pony *n.* 矮种马 ǎi zhǒng mǎ

poor *a.* 穷 qióng

pop *v.i.* 发出爆裂声 fā chū bào liè shēng

pop *n* 流行音乐 liú xíng yīn yuè

pope *n.* 罗马教皇 luó mǎ jiào huáng

poplar *n.* 杨树 yáng shù

poplin *n.* 毛葛 máo gě

populace *n.* 平民 píng mín

popular *a.* 受欢迎的 shòu huān yíng de

popularity *n.* 受大众欢迎 shòu dà zhòng huān yíng

popularize *v.t.* 使成通俗性 shǐ chéng tōng sú xìng

populate *v.t.* 使人口聚居在...中 shǐ rén kǒu jù jū zài... zhōng

population *n.* 人口 rén kǒu

populous *a.* 人口多的 rén kǒu duō de

porcelain *n.* 瓷器 cí qì

porch *n.* 门廊 mén láng

pore *n.* 毛孔 máo kǒng

pork *n.* 猪肉 zhū ròu

porridge *n.* 粥 zhōu

port *n.* 港口 gáng kǒu

portable *a.* 可携带的 kě xié dài de

portage *n.* 搬运 bān yùn

portal *n.* 入口 rù kǒu

portend *v.t.* 成为...的前兆 chéng wéi... de qián zhào

porter *n.* 搬运工人 bān yùn gōng rén

portfolio *n.* 文件夹 wén jiàn jiá

portico *n.* 门廊 mén láng

portion *n* 一份 yí fèn

portion *v.t.* 分配 fēn pèi

portrait *n.* 肖像 xiāo xiàng

portraiture *n.* 肖像画 xiāo xiàng huà

portray *v.t.* 描绘...的肖像 miáo huì... de xiāo xiàng

portrayal *n.* 描绘 miáo huì

pose *v.i.* 摆姿势 bǎi zī shì

pose *n.* 姿势 zī shì

position *n.* 位置 wèi zhi

position *v.t.* 放在适当位置 fàng zài shì dàng wèi zhi

positive *a.* 正的 zhèng de

possess *v.t.* 拥有 yōng yǒu

possession *n.* 财产 cái chǎn

possibility *n.* 可能性 kě néng xìng

possible *a.* 可能的 kě néng de

post *n.* 邮政 yóu zhèng

post *v.t.* 邮递 yóu dì

post *n* 职位 zhí wèi

post *v.t.* 张帖 zhāng tiē

post *adv.* 急速地 jí sù dì

postage *n.* 邮费 yóu fèi

postal *a.* 邮政的 yóu zhèng de

post-date *v.t.* 把日期填迟 bǎ rì qì tián chí

poster *n.* 海报 hǎi bào

posterity *n.* 后代 hòu dài

posthumous *a.* 死后的 sǐ hòu de

postman *n.* 邮递员 yóu dì yuán

postmaster *n.* 邮政局长 yóu zhèng jú zhǎng

post-mortem *a.* 死后 sǐ hòu

post-mortem *n.* 验尸 yàn shī

post-office *n.* 邮局 yóu jú

postpone *v.t.* 延迟 yán chí

postponement *n.* 延期 yán qī

postscript *n.* 附言 fù yán

posture *n.* 姿势 zī shì

pot *n.* 罐 guàn

pot *v.t.* 装入盆中 zhuāng rù pén zhōng

potash *n.* 碳酸钾 tàn suān jiǎ

potassium *n.* 钾 jiǎ

potato *n.* 马铃薯 mǎ líng shǔ

potency *n.* 力量 lì liàng

potent *a.* 有效的 yǒu xiào de

potential *a.* 有潜力的 yǒu qián lì de

potential *n.* 潜能 qián néng

potentiality *n.* 潜在性 qián zài xìng

potter *n.* 陶工 yáo gōng

pottery *n.* 陶器 táo qì

pouch *n.* 邮袋 yóu dài

poultry *n.* 家禽 jiā qín

pounce *v.i.* 突袭 tū xí

pounce *n* 猛扑 měng pū

pound *n.* 英镑 yīng bàng

pound *v.t.* 强烈打击 qiáng liè dǎ jī

pour *v.t.* 倒 dǎo

poverty *n.* 贫穷 pín qióng

powder *n.* 粉 fěn

powder *v.t.* 加粉 jiā fěn

power *n.* 权力 quán lì

powerful *a.* 有权力的 yǒu quán lì de

practicability *n.* 实用性 shí yòng xìng

practicable *a.* 可实行的 kě shí xíng de

practical *a.* 实际的 shí jì de

practice *n.* 实践 shí jiàn

practise *v.t.* 练习 liàn xí

practitioner *n.* 从业者 cóng yè zhě

pragmatic *a.* 忙碌的 máng lù de

pragmatism *n.* 实用主义 shí yòng zhǔ yì

praise *n.* 称赞 chēng zàn

praise *v.t.* 称赞 chēng zàn
praiseworthy *a.* 值得称赞
的 zhí dé chēng zàn de
prank *n.* 恶作剧 è zuò jù
prattle *v.i.* 闲聊 xián liáo
prattle *n.* 闲扯 xián chě
pray *v.i.* 祈祷 qí dǎo
prayer *n.* 祈祷 qí dǎo
preach *v.i.* 传道 chuán dào
preacher *n.* 牧师 mù shī
preamble *n.* 引言 yǐn yán
precaution *n.* 预防 yù fáng
precautionary *a.* 预防的 yù
fáng de
precede *v.* 先于 xiān yú
precedence *n.* 优先 yōu
xiān
precedent *n.* 先例 xiān lì
precept *n.* 规诫 guī jiè
preceptor *n.* 导师 dǎo shī
precious *a.* 珍贵的 zhēn
guì de
precis *n.* 摘要 zhāi yào
precise *a.* 准确的 zhǔn què
de
precision *n.* 精确度 jīng
què dù
precursor *n.* 先驱者 xiān
qū zhě
predecessor *n.* 前任 qián
rèn
predestination *n.* 宿命论
sù mìng lùn
predetermine *v.t.* 预先决定
yù xiān jué dìng
predicament *n.* 穷境 qióng
jìng
predicate *n.* 谓语 wèi yǔ
predict *v.t.* 预知 yù zhī
prediction *n.* 预言 yù yán
predominance *n.* 优势 yōu
shì
predominant *a.* 占主导地
位的 zhàn zhú dǎo dì wèi de
predominate *v.i.* 占优势
zhàn yōu shì
pre-eminence *n.* 杰出 jié
chū

pre-eminent *a.* 杰出的 jié
chū de
preface *n.* 序 xù
preface *v.t.* 给...作序 gěi... zuò
xù
prefect *n.* 长官 zhǎng guān
prefer *v.t.* 较喜欢 jiào xǐ huan
preference *n.* 偏爱 piān ài
preferential *a.* 优先的 yōu
xiān de
prefix *n.* 前缀 qián zhuì
prefix *v.t.* 加前缀 jiā qián zhuì
pregnancy *n.* 怀孕 huái yùn
pregnant *a.* 怀孕的 huái yùn
de
prehistoric *a.* 史前的 shǐ
qián de
prejudice *n.* 偏见 piān jiàn
prelate *n.* 高级教士 gāo jí
jiào shì
preliminary *a.* 初步的 chū
bù de
preliminary *n* 初步措施 chū
bù cuò shī
prelude *n.* 前奏 qián zòu
prelude *v.t.* 作为...的开头
zuò wéi... de kāi tóu
premarital *a.* 婚前的 hūn
qián de
premature *a.* 早产的 záo
chǎn de
premeditate *v.t.* 预先考虑 yù
xiān kǎo lù
premeditation *n.* 预谋 yù
móu
premier *a.* 首位的 shǒu wèi
de
premier *n* 首相 shǒu xiàng
premiere *n.* 初次的演出 chū
cì de yǎn chū
premium *n.* 保险费 báo xiǎn
fèi
premonition *n.* 预感 yù gǎn
preoccupation *n.* 抢先占据
qiǎng xiān zhàn jù
preoccupy *v.t.* 使全神贯注
shǐ quán shén guàn zhù
preparation *n.* 准备 zhǔn bèi

preparatory *a.* 准备性的
zhǔn bèi xìng de
prepare *v.t.* 准备 zhǔn bèi
preponderance *n.* 优势
yōu shì
preponderate *v.i.* 占优势
zhàn yōu shì
preposition *n.* 介词 jiè cí
prerequisite *a.* 必要的 bì
yào de
prerequisite *n* 先决条件
xiān jué tiáo jiàn
prerogative *n.* 特权 tè quán
prescience *n.* 预知 yù zhī
prescribe *v.t.* 开处方 kāi
chǔ fāng
prescription *n.* 药方 yào
fāng
presence *n.* 出现 chū xiàn
present *a.* 现在的 xiàn zài
de
present *n.* 礼品 lí pǐn
present *v.t.* 介绍 jiè shào
presentation *n.* 描述 miáo
shù
presently *adv.* 目前 mù
qián
preservation *n.* 保护 bǎo
hù
preservative *n.* 防腐剂
fáng fǔ jì
preservative *a.* 有助于保存
的 yǒu zhù yú bǎo cún de
preserve *v.t.* 保存 bǎo cún
preserve *n.* 加工成的食品
jiā gōng chéng de shí pǐn
preside *v.i.* 主持 zhǔ chí
president *n.* 总统 zóng tǒng
presidential *a.* 总统的 zóng
tǒng de
press *v.t.* 压 yā
press *n* 出版社 chū bǎn shè
pressure *n.* 压力 yā lì
pressurize *v.t.* 迫使 pò shǐ
prestige *n.* 威信 wēi xìn
prestigious *a.* 享有声望的
xiáng yǒu shēng wàng de
presume *v.t.* 推测 tuī cè

presumption *n.* 假定 jiǎ dìng
presuppose *v.t.* 预料 yù liào
presupposition *n.* 假定 jiǎ
dìng
pretence *n.* 虚伪 xū wěi
pretend *v.t.* 假装 jiǎ zhuāng
pretension *n.* 自负 zì fù
pretentious *a.* 自命不凡的
zì mìng bù fán de
pretext *n* 借口 jiè kǒu
prettiness *n.* 漂亮 piào liang
pretty *a* 漂亮的 piào liang de
pretty *adv.* 相当 xiāng dāng
prevail *v.i.* 盛行 shèng xíng
prevalence *n.* 普遍 pǔ biàn
prevalent *a.* 普遍的 pǔ biàn
de
prevent *v.t.* 防止 fáng zhǐ
prevention *n.* 预防 yù fáng
preventive *a.* 预防的 yù fáng
de
previous *a.* 生前的 shēng
qián de
prey *n.* 被掠食者 bèi lüè shí
zhě
prey *v.i.* 捕食 bǔ shí
price *n.* 价钱 jià qián
price *v.t.* 定价 dìng jià
prick *n.* 一刺 yí cì
prick *v.t.* 刺痛 cì tòng
pride *n.* 骄傲 jiāo ào
pride *v.t.* 以...自豪 yǐ... zì háo
priest *n.* 神父 shén fù
priestess *n.* 女祭司 nǔ jì sī
priesthood *n.* 神职人员 shén
zhí rén yuán
prima facie *adv.* 初步的 chū
bù de
primarily *adv.* 主要地 zhǔ
yào dì
primary *a.* 最重要的 zuì
zhòng yào de
prime *a.* 主要的 zhǔ yào de
prime *n.* 全盛期 quán shèng
qī
primer *n.* 初级读本 chū jí dú
běn
primeval *a.* 原始的 yuán shǐ
de

primitive *a.* 落后的 luò hòu de

prince *n.* 王子 wáng zǐ

princely *a.* 王子的 wáng zǐ de

princess *n.* 公主 gōng zhǔ

principal *n.* 校长 xiào zhǎng

principal *a* 最重要的 zuì zhòng yào de

principle *n.* 原则 yuán zé

print *v.t.* 打印 dǎ yìn

print *n* 打印 dǎ yìn

printer *n.* 打印机 dǎ yìn jī

prior *a.* 在先的 zài xiān de

prior *n* 隐修院院长 xiǎo yǐn xiū yuàn yuàn zhǎng

prioress *n.* 女修道院院长 xiǎo nǚ xiū dào yuàn yuàn zhǎng

priority *n.* 优先权 yōu xiān quán

prison *n.* 监狱 jiān yù

prisoner *n.* 囚犯 qiú fàn

privacy *n.* 隐私 yǐn sī

private *a.* 私人的 sī rén de

privation *n.* 穷困 qióng kùn

privilege *n.* 特权 tè quán

prize *n.* 奖品 jiáng pǐn

prize *v.t.* 珍视 zhēn shì

probability *n.* 可能性 kě néng xìng

probable *a.* 很可能的 hěn kě néng de

probably *adv.* 大概 dà gài

probation *n.* 试用 shì yòng

probationer *n.* 见习生 jiàn xí shēng

probe *v.t.* 调查 diào chá

probe *n* 探索 tàn suǒ

problem *n.* 问题 wèn tí

problematic *a.* 成问题的 chéng wèn tí de

procedure *n.* 程序 chéng xù

proceed *v.i.* 继续进行 jì xù jìn xíng

proceeding *n.* 程序 chéng xù

proceeds *n.* 收入 shōu rù

process *n.* 程序 chéng xù

procession *n.* 队伍 duì wu

proclaim *v.t.* 宣布 xuān bù

proclamation *n.* 宣言 xuān yán

proclivity *n.* 癖性 pǐ xìng

procrastinate *v.i.* 延迟 yán chí

procrastination *n.* 拖延 tuō yán

proctor *n.* 监考人 jiān kǎo rén

procure *v.t.* 获得 huò dé

procurement *n.* 采购 cǎi gòu

prodigal *a.* 浪费的 làng fèi de

prodigality *n.* 浪费 làng fèi

produce *v.t.* 生产 shēng chǎn

produce *n.* 生产品 shēng chán pǐn

product *n.* 产品 chán pǐn

production *n.* 製造 zhì zào

productive *a.* 能生产的 néng shēng chǎn de

productivity *n.* 产品 chán pǐn

profane *a.* 亵渎的 xiè dú de

profane *v.t.* 亵渎 xiè dú

profess *v.t.* 声称 shēng chēng

profession *n.* 职业 zhí yè

professional *a.* 专业的 zhuān yè de

professor *n.* 教授 jiào shòu

proficiency *n.* 精通 jīng tōng

proficient *a.* 熟练的 shú liàn de

profile *n.* 传略 zhuàn lüè

profile *v.t.* 写...的传略 xiě... de zhuàn lüè

profit *n.* 利润 lì rùn

profit *v.t.* 有益于 yǒu yì yú

profitable *a.* 有利润的 yǒu lì rùn de

profiteer *n.* 奸商 jiān shāng

profiteer *v.i.* 获暴利 huò bào lì

profligacy *n.* 浪费 làng fèi

profligate *a.* 放荡的 fàng dàng de

profound *a.* 极深的 jí shēn de

profundity *n.* 深度 shēn dù

profuse *a.* 丰富的 fēng fù de

profusion *n.* 大量 dà liàng

progeny *n.* 子孙 zǐ sūn

programme *n.* 节目 jié mù

programme *v.t.* 拟...计划 nǐ... jì huà

progress *n.* 进步 jìn bù

progress *v.i.* 进步 jìn bù

progressive *a.* 进步的 jìn bù de

prohibit *v.t.* 禁止 jìn zhǐ

prohibition *n.* 禁令 jìn lìng

prohibitive *a.* 禁止的 jìn zhǐ de

prohibitory *a.* 意在禁止的 yì zài jìn zhǐ de

project *n.* 计划 jì huà

project *v.t.* 放映 fàng yìng

projectile *n.* 抛射物 pāo shè wù

projectile *a* 发射的 fā shè de

projection *n.* 投影 tóu yǐng

projector *n.* 放映机 fàng yìng jī

proliferate *v.i.* 激增 jī zēng

proliferation *n.* 激增 jī zēng

prolific *a.* 多产的 duō chǎn de

prologue *n.* 序言 xù yán

prolong *v.t.* 延长 yán cháng

prolongation *n.* 延长 yán cháng

prominence *n.* 突出 tū chū

prominent *a.* 突出的 tū chū de

promise *n* 诺言 nuò yán

promise *v.t* 允诺 yǔn nuò

promising *a.* 有希望的 yǒu xī wàng de

promissory *a.* 约好的 yuē hǎo de

promote *v.t.* 晋升 jìn shēng

promotion *n.* 晋级 jìn jí

prompt *a.* 立刻的 lì kè de

prompt *v.t.* 提示 tí shì

prompter *n.* 提词员 tí cí yuán

prone *a.* 俯伏的 fǔ fú de

pronoun *n.* 代词 dài cí

pronounce *v.t.* 发音 fā yīn

pronunciation *n.* 发音 fā yīn

proof *n.* 证据 zhèng jù

proof *a* 不能透入的 bù néng tòu rù de

prop *n.* 道具 dào jù

prop *v.t.* 支撑 zhī chēng

propaganda *n.* 宣传 xuān chuán

propagandist *n.* 宣传者 xuān chuán zhě

propagate *v.t.* 传播 chuán bō

propagation *n.* 宣传 xuān chuán

propel *v.t.* 推进 tuī jìn

proper *a.* 适当的 shì dàng de

property *n.* 财产 cái chǎn

prophecy *n.* 预言 yù yán

prophesy *v.t.* 预言 yù yán

prophet *n.* 预言者 yù yán zhě

prophetic *a.* 预言的 yù yán de

proportion *n.* 比例 bǐ lì

proportion *v.t.* 使成比例 shǐ chéng bǐ lì

proportional *a.* 比例的 bǐ lì de

proportionate *a.* 成比例的 chéng bǐ lì de

proposal *n.* 计划 jì huà

propose *v.t.* 求婚 qiú hūn

proposition *n.* 建议 jiàn yì

propound *v.t.* 提出供考虑 tí chū gòng kǎo lù

proprietary *a.* 专有的 zhuān yǒu de

proprietor *n.* 所有者 suó yǒu zhě

propriety *n.* 礼貌 lǐ mào

prorogue *v.t.* 休会 xiū huì

prosaic *a.* 散文的 sǎn wén de

prose *n.* 散文 sǎn wén

prosecute *v.t.* 起诉 qǐ sù

prosecution *n.* 执行 zhí xíng

prosecutor *n.* 实行者 shí xíng zhě

prosody *n.* 韵律学 yùn lù xué

prospect *n.* 展望 zhǎn wàng

prospective *a.* 预期的 yù qī de

prospectus *n.* 内容简介 nèi róng jiǎn jiè

prosper *v.i.* 兴隆 xīng lóng

prosperity *n.* 繁荣 fán róng

prosperous *a.* 繁荣的 fán róng de

prostitute *n.* 妓女 jì nǚ

prostitute *v.t.* 卖淫 mài yín

prostitution *n.* 卖淫 mài yín

prostrate *a.* 俯卧的 fǔ wò de

prostrate *v.t.* 使俯伏 shǐ fǔ fú

prostration *n.* 衰竭 shuāi jié

protagonist *n.* 领导者 líng dǎo zhě

protect *v.t.* 保护 bǎo hù

protection *n.* 保护 bǎo hù

protective *a.* 保护的 bǎo hù de

protector *n.* 保护者 bǎo hù zhě

protein *n.* 蛋白质 dàn bái zhì

protest *n.* 抗议 kàng yì

protest *v.i.* 反对 fǎn duì

protestation *n.* 声明 shēng míng

prototype *n.* 原型 yuán xíng

proud *a.* 骄傲的 jiāo ào de

prove *v.t.* 证明 zhèng míng

proverb *n.* 格言 gé yán

proverbial *a.* 谚语的 yàn yǔ de

provide *v.i.* 提供 tí gōng

providence *n.* 天命 tiān mìng

provident *a.* 有先见之明的 yǒu xiān jiàn zhī míng de

providential *a.* 天意的 tiān yì de

province *n.* 省 shěng

provincial *a.* 省的 shěng de

provincialism *n.* 乡下习气 xiāng xia xí qì

provision *n.* 供应品 gōng yīng pǐn

provisional *a.* 暂时的 zàn shí de

provisonality *n.* 暂时性 zàn shí xìng

provocation *n.* 刺激 cì jī

provocative *a.* 挑拨的 tiǎo bō de

provoke *v.t.* 惹起 rě qǐ

prowess *n.* 英勇 yīng yǒng

proximate *a.* 最近的 zuì jìn de

proximity *n.* 接近 jiē jìn

proxy *n.* 代理 dài lǐ

prude *n.* 故作正经的人 gù zuò zhèng jìng de rén

prudence *n.* 审慎 shěn shèn

prudent *a.* 审慎的 shěn shèn de

prudential *a.* 审慎的 shěn shèn de

prune *v.t.* 修剪 xiū jiǎn

pry *v.i.* 打听 dǎ ting

psalm *n.* 圣诗 shèng shī

pseudonym *n.* 笔名 bǐ míng

psyche *n.* 心灵 xīn líng

psychiatrist *n.* 精神科医生 jīng shen kē yī sheng

psychiatry *n.* 精神病学 jīng shen bìng xué

psychic *a.* 灵魂的 líng hún de

psychological *a.* 心灵的 xīn líng de

psychologist *n.* 心理学家 xīn lǐ xué jiā

psychology *n.* 心理学 xīn lǐ xué

psychopath *n.* 精神病患者 jīng shen bìng huàn zhě

psychosis *n.* 精神病 jīng shen bìng

psychotherapy *n.* 心理疗法 xīn lǐ liáo fǎ

puberty *n.* 青春期 qīng chūn qī

public *a.* 公众的 gōng zhòng de

public *n.* 公众 gōng zhòng

publication *n.* 出版 chū bǎn

publicity *n.* 宣传 xuān chuán

publicize *v.t.* 宣传 xuān chuán

publish *v.t.* 出版 chū bǎn

publisher *n.* 出版者 chū bǎn zhě

pudding *n.* 布丁 bù dīng

puddle *n.* 水坑 shuǐ kēng

puddle *v.t.* 搅浊 jiǎo zhuó

puerile *a.* 幼稚的 yòu zhì de

puff *n.* 一阵喷烟 yí zhèn pēn yān

puff *v.i.* 喷出 pēn chū

pull *v.t.* 拉 lā

pull *n.* 拉 lā

pulley *n.* 滑轮 huá lún

pullover *n.* 套衫 tào shān

pulp *n.* 纸浆 zhǐ jiāng

pulp *v.t.* 使化成纸浆 shǐ huà chéng zhǐ jiāng

pulpit *a.* 讲道坛 jiǎng dào tán

pulpy *a.* 纸浆状的 zhǐ jiāng zhuàng de

pulsate *v.i.* 搏动 bó dòng

pulsation *n.* 震动 zhèn dòng

pulse *n.* 脉搏 mài bó

pulse *v.i.* 跳动 tiào dòng

pulse *n* 拍子 pāi zi

pump *n.* 泵 bèng

pump *v.t.* 打气 dǎ qì

pumpkin *n.* 南瓜 nán guā

pun *n.* 双关语 shuāng guān yǔ

pun *v.i.* 说双关语 shuō shuāng guān yǔ

punch *n.* 打洞器 dǎ dòng qì

punch *v.t.* 以拳重击 yǐ quán zhòng jī

punctual *a.* 准时的 zhǔn shí de

punctuality *n.* 严守时间 yán shǒu shí jiān

punctuate *v.t.* 加标点符号 jiā biāo diǎn fú hào

punctuation *n.* 标点符号 biāo diǎn fú hào

puncture *n.* 刺痕 cì hén

puncture *v.t.* 刺穿 cì chuān

pungency *n.* 辛辣 xīn là

pungent *a.* 刺激性的 cì jī xìng de

punish *v.t.* 处罚 chǔ fá

punishment *n.* 惩罚 chéng fá

punitive *a.* 惩罚性的 chéng fá xìng de

puny *a.* 微小的 wēi xiǎo de

pupil *n.* 学生 xué sheng

puppet *n.* 木偶 mù ǒu

puppy *n.* 小狗 xiǎo gǒu

purblind *a.* 半盲的 bàn máng de

purchase *n.* 购买 gòu mǎi

purchase *v.t.* 买 mǎi

pure *a* 纯的 chún de

purgation *n.* 净化 jìng huà

purgative *n.* 泻剂 xiè jì

purgative *a* 净化的 jìng huà de

purgatory *n.* 涤罪 dí zuì

purge *v.t.* 清除 qīng chú

purification *n.* 净化 jìng huà

purify *v.t.* 净化 jìng huà

purist *n.* 纯粹主义者 chún cuì zhǔ yì zhě

puritan *n.* 清教徒 qīng jiào tú

puritanical *a.* 清教徒的 qīng jiào tú de

purity *n.* 纯净 chún jìng

purple *adj./n.* 紫色 zǐ sè

purport *n.* 意义 yì yì

purport *v.t.* 声称 shēng chēng

purpose *n.* 目的 mù dì

purpose *v.t.* 意欲 yì yù

purposely *adv.* 故意地 gù yì dì

purr *n.* 呼噜呼噜声 hū lū hū lū shēng

purr *v.i.* 呼噜呼噜叫 hū lū hū lū jiào

purse *n.* 钱包 qián bāo

purse *v.t.* 缩拢 suō lǒng

pursuance *n.* 追赶 zhuī gǎn

pursue *v.t.* 追求 zhuī qiú

pursuit *n.* 追求 zhuī qiú

purview *n.* 范围 fàn wéi

pus *n.* 脓 nóng

push *v.t.* 推 tuī

push *n.* 推 tuī
put *v.t.* 摆 bǎi
puzzle *n.* 迷惑 mí huò
puzzle *v.t.* 使困惑 shǐ kùn huò
pygmy *n.* 侏儒 zhū rú
pyorrhoea *n.* 脓溢 nóng yì
pyramid *n.* 金字塔 jīn zì tǎ
pyre *n.* 柴堆 chái duī
python *n.* 大蟒 dà mǎng

Q

quack *v.i.* 嘎嘎叫 gā gā jiào
quack *n* 鸭叫声 yā jiào shēng
quackery *n.* 江湖医术 jiāng hú yī shù
quadrangle *n.* 四方院 sì fāng yuàn
quadrangular *a.* 像四边形 的 xiàng sì biān xíng de
quadrilateral *a. & n.* 四边形 的 sì biān xíng de
quadruped *n.* 四足动物 sì zú dòng wù
quadruple *a.* 四倍的 sì bèi de
quadruple *v.t.* 使成四倍 shǐ chéng sì bèi
quail *n.* 鹌鹑 ān chun
quaint *a.* 古雅的 gǔ yǎ de
quake *v.i.* 颤抖 chàn dǒu
quake *n* 地震 dì zhèn
qualification *n.* 学位 xué wèi
qualify *v.i.* 有资格 yǒu zī gé
qualitative *a.* 性质的 xìng zhì de
quality *n.* 质量 zhì liàng
quandary *n.* 困惑 kùn huò
quantitative *a.* 数量的 shù liàng de
quantity *n.* 数量 shù liàng
quantum *n.* 量子 liàng zǐ
quarrel *n.* 怨言 yuàn yán
quarrel *v.i.* 吵架 chǎo jià
quarrelsome *a.* 喜欢吵架的 xǐ huan chǎo jià de

quarry *n.* 采石场 cǎi shí chǎng
quarry *v.i.* 费力地找 fèi lì dì zhǎo
quarter *n.* 四分之一 sì fēn zhī yī
quarter *v.t.* 四等分 sì děng fēn
quarterly *a.* 季度的 jì dù de
queen *n.* 女王 nǚ wáng
queer *a.* 奇怪的 qí guài de
quell *v.t.* 压制 yā zhì
quench *v.t.* 熄灭 xī miè
query *n.* 疑问 yí wèn
query *v.t* 询问 xún wèn
quest *n.* 探索 tàn suǒ
quest *v.t.* 寻找 xún zhǎo
question *n.* 问题 wèn tí
question *v.t.* 怀疑 huái yí
questionable *a.* 可疑的 kě yí de
questionnaire *n.* 问卷 wèn juàn
queue *n.* 一队 yí duì
quibble *n.* 遁词 dùn cí
quibble *v.i.* 吹毛求疵 chuī máo qiú cī
quick *a.* 快的 kuài de
quick *n* 新长出的肉 xīn zhǎng chū de ròu
quicksand *n.* 流沙 liú shā
quicksilver *n.* 水银 shuǐ yín
quiet *a.* 静止的 jìng zhǐ de
quiet *n.* 安静 ān jìng
quiet *v.t.* 平静 píng jìng
quilt *n.* 棉被 mián bèi
quinine *n.* 奎宁 kuí níng
quintessence *n.* 典范 diǎn fàn
quit *v.t.* 离开 lí kāi
quite *adv.* 相当 xiāng dāng
quiver *n.* 震动 zhèn dòng
quiver *v.i.* 颤抖 chàn dǒu
quixotic *a.* 理想而不实际的 lǐ xiǎng ér bù shí jì de
quiz *n.* 智力测验 zhì lì cè yàn
quiz *v.t.* 考查 kǎo chá
quorum *n.* 法定人数 fǎ dìng rén shù

quota *n.* 配额 pèi é
quotation *n.* 报价 bào jià
quote *v.t.* 引用 yǐn yòng
quotient *n.* 商 shāng

R

rabbit *n.* 兔子 tù zi
rabies *n.* 狂犬病 kuáng quǎn bìng
race *n.* 比赛 bǐ sài
race *v.i* 赛跑 sài pǎo
racial *a.* 种族的 zhǒng zú de
racialism *n.* 种族主义 zhǒng zú zhǔ yì
rack *v.t.* 使痛苦 shǐ tòng kǔ
rack *n.* 架 jià
racket *n.* 喧闹 xuān nào
radiance *n.* 容光焕发的 róng guāng huàn fā de
radiant *a.* 光芒四射 guāng máng sì shè
radiate *v.t.* 散发 sàn fā
radiation *n.* 辐射 fú shè
radical *a.* 激进的 jī jìn de
radio *n.* 收音机 shōu yin jī
radio *v.t.* 用无线电发送 yòng wú xiàn diàn fā sòng
radish *n.* 小萝卜 xiǎo luó bo
radium *n.* 镭 léi
radius *n.* 半径 bàn jìng
rag *n.* 碎布 suì bù
rag *v.t.* 戏弄 xì nòng
rage *n.* 愤怒 fēn nù
rage *v.i.* 大怒 dà nù
raid *n.* 突袭 tū xí
raid *v.t.* 搜查 sōu chá
rail *n.* 栏杆 lán gān
rail *v.t.* 以横木围栏 yǐ héng mù wéi lán
railing *n.* 扶手 fú shou
raillery *n.* 戏谑 xì xuè
railway *n.* 铁路 tiě lù
rain *v.i.* 下雨 xià yǔ
rain *n* 雨 yǔ
rainy *a.* 多雨的 duō yǔ de
raise *v.t.* 提高 tí gāo
raisin *n.* 葡萄干 pú tao gān

rally *v.t.* 集合 jí hé
rally *n* 集合 jí hé
ram *n.* 公羊 gōng yáng
ram *v.i.* 撞 zhuàng
ramble *v.t.* 闲逛于 xián guàng yú
ramble *n* 漫步 màn bù
rampage *v.i.* 狂暴 kuáng bào
rampage *n.* 乱闹 luàn nào
rampant *a.* 猖獗的 chāng jué de
rampart *n.* 防御土墙 fáng yù tǔ qiáng
rancour *n.* 敌意 dí yì
random *a.* 任意的 rèn yì de
range *v.t.* 排列 pái liè
range *n.* 行列 háng liè
ranger *n.* 王室守林人 wáng shì shǒu lín rén
rank *n.* 等级 děng jí
rank *v.t.* 把...分等 bǎ... fēn děng
rank *a* 恶臭的 è chòu de
ransack *v.t.* 洗劫 xǐ jié
ransom *n.* 赎金 shú jīn
ransom *v.t.* 勒索赎金 lè suǒ shú jīn
rape *n.* 强奸 qiáng jiān
rape *v.t.* 强奸 qiáng jiān
rapid *a.* 飞快的 fēi kuài de
rapidity *n.* 迅速 xùn sù
rapier *n.* 双刃长剑 shuāng rèn cháng jiàn
rapport *n.* 关系 guān xi
rapt *a.* 全神贯注的 quán shén guàn zhù de
rapture *n.* 欢天喜地 huān tiān xǐ dì
rare *a.* 罕有的 hǎn yǒu de
rascal *n.* 无赖 wú lài
rash *a.* 皮疹 pí zhěn
rat *n.* 鼠 shǔ
rate *v.t.* 估价 gū jià
rate *n.* 率 lù
rather *adv.* 宁可 nìng kě
ratify *v.t.* 批准 pī zhǔn
ratio *n.* 比率 bǐ lù
ration *n.* 配给 pèi jǐ
rational *a.* 理性的 lǐ xìng de

rationale *n.* 原理 yuán lǐ

rationality *n.* 合理性 hé lǐ xìng

rationalize *v.t.* 使合理 shǐ hé lǐ

rattle *v.i.* 喋喋不休 dié dié bù xiū

rattle *n* 格格声 gé gé shēng

ravage *n.* 破坏 pò huài

ravage *v.t.* 毁坏 huǐ huài

rave *v.i.* 愤怒地说 fèn nù dì shuō

raven *n.* 渡鸦 dù yā

ravine *n.* 峡谷 xiá gǔ

raw *a.* 生的 shēng de

ray *n.* 光线 guāng xiàn

raze *v.t.* 把...夷为平地 bǎ... yí wéi píng dì

razor *n.* 剃刀 tì dāo

reach *v.t.* 到达 dào dá

react *v.i.* 起反应 qǐ fǎn yìng

reaction *n.* 反应 fǎn yìng

reactinary *a.* 保守的 bǎo shǒu de

read *v.i.* 读 dú

reader *n.* 读者 dú zhě

readily *adv.* 乐意地 lè yì dì

readiness *n.* 准备 zhǔn bèi

ready *a.* 准备好的 zhǔn bèi hǎo de

real *a.* 真的 zhēn de

realism *n.* 写实主义 xiě shí zhǔ yì

realist *n.* 现实主义者 xiàn shí zhǔ yì zhě

realistic *a.* 逼真的 bī zhēn de

reality *n.* 实在 shí zai

realization *n.* 领悟 lǐng wù

realize *v.t.* 了解 liáo jiě

really *adv.* 真实地 zhēn shí dì

realm *a.* 领域 lǐng yù

ream *n.* 令 lìng

reap *v.t.* 收割 shōu gē

reaper *n.* 收割机 shōu gē jī

rear *n.* 后面 hòu mian

rear *v.t.* 养育 yǎng yù

reason *n.* 原因 yuán yīn

reason *v.i.* 推论 tuī lùn

reasonable *a.* 合理的 hé lǐ de

reassure *v.t.* 重新保证 chóng xīn bǎo zhèng

rabate *n.* 部分退款 bù fen tuì kuǎn

rebel *v.i.* 造反 zào fǎn

rebel *n.* 叛徒 pàn tú

rebellion *n.* 谋反 móu fǎn

rebellious *a.* 反抗的 fǎn kàng de

rebirth *n.* 再生 zài shēng

rebound *v.i.* 弹回 tán huí

rebound *n.* 反弹 fǎn tán

rebuff *n.* 断然拒绝 duàn rán jù jué

rebuff *v.t.* 严厉拒绝 yán lì jù jué

rebuke *v.t.* 斥责 chì zé

rebuke *n.* 指责 zhǐ zé

recall *v.t.* 回想 huí xiǎng

recall *n.* 回忆 huí yì

recede *v.i.* 减弱 jiǎn ruò

receipt *n.* 收据 shōu jù

receive *v.t.* 收到 shōu dào

receiver *n.* 接受者 jiē shòu zhě

recent *a.* 最近的 zuì jìn de

recently *adv.* 最近 zuì jìn

reception *n.* 接待 jiē dài

receptive *a.* 能接纳的 néng jiē nà de

recess *n.* 休会 xiū huì

recession *n.* 经济衰退 jīng jì shuāi tuì

recipe *n.* 食谱 shí pǔ

recipient *n.* 领受者 lǐng shòu zhě

reciprocal *a.* 互惠的 hù huì de

reciprocate *v.t.* 回报 huí bào

recital *n.* 背诵 bèi sòng

recitation *n.* 吟诵 yín sòng

recite *v.t.* 朗读 lǎng dú

reckless *a.* 不介意的 bú jiè yì de

reckon *v.t.* 认为 rèn wéi

reclaim *v.t.* 回收 huí shōu

reclamation *n* 开垦 kāi kěn

recluse *n.* 隐遁者 yín dùn zhě

recognition *n.* 认可 rèn kě

recognize *v.t.* 认出 rèn chū

recoil *v.i.* 退却 tuì què

recoil *n.* 畏缩 wèi suō

recollect *v.t.* 回忆 huí yì

recollection *n.* 记忆 jì yì

recommend *v.t.* 推荐 tuī jiàn

recommendation *n.* 推荐 tuī jiàn

recompense *v.t.* 赔偿 péi cháng

recompense *n.* 赔偿 péi cháng

reconcile *v.t.* 使和解 shǐ hé jiě

reconciliation *n.* 和解 hé jiě

record *v.t.* 记录 jì lù

record *n.* 记录 jì lù

recorder *n.* 录音机 lù yīn jī

recount *v.t.* 详述 xiáng shù

recoup *v.t.* 偿还 cháng huán

recourse *n.* 求援 qiú yuán

recover *v.t.* 恢复 huī fù

recovery *n.* 恢复 huī fù

recreation *n.* 消遣 xiāo qiǎn

recruit *n.* 新兵 xīn bīng

recruit *v.t.* 征募 zhēng mù

rectangle *n.* 长方形 cháng fāng xíng

rectangular *a.* 矩形的 jǔ xíng de

rectification *n.* 改正 gǎi zhèng

rectify *v.t.* 矫正 jiǎo zhèng

rectum *n.* 直肠 zhí cháng

recur *v.i.* 复发 fù fā

recurrence *n.* 再现 zài xiàn

recurrent *a.* 循环的 xún huán de

red *a.* 红色的 hóng sè de

red *n.* 红色 hóng sè

redden *v.t.* 变红 biàn hóng

reddish *a.* 微红的 wēi hóng de

redeem *v.t.* 挽回 wǎn huí

redemption *n.* 赎回 shú huí

redouble *v.t.* 加倍 jiā bèi

redress *v.t.* 纠正 jiū zhèng

redress *n* 赔偿 péi cháng

reduce *v.t.* 减少 jiǎn shǎo

reduction *n.* 减少 jiǎn shǎo

redundance *n.* 过多 guò duō

redundant *a.* 多余的 duō yú de

reel *n.* 卷轴 juàn zhóu

reel *v.i.* 蹒跚地走 pán shān dì zǒu

refer *v.t.* 把...提交 bǎ... tí jiāo

referee *n.* 裁判员 cái pàn yuán

reference *n.* 参考 cān kǎo

referendum *n.* 公民复决 gōng mín fù jué

refine *v.t.* 精炼 jīng liàn

refinement *n.* 精致 jīng zhì

refinery *n.* 精炼厂 jīng liàn chǎng

reflect *v.t.* 反映 fǎn yìng

reflection *n.* 反映 fǎn yìng

reflective *a.* 反射的 fǎn shè de

reflector *n.* 反射器 fǎn shè qì

reflex *n.* 反射 fǎn shè

reflex *a* 反射的 fǎn shè de

reflexive *a* 反射的 fǎn shè de

reform *v.t.* 改革 gǎi gé

reform *n.* 改革 gǎi gé

reformation *n.* 改革 gǎi gé

reformatory *n.* 教养院 jiào yǎng yuàn

reformatory *a* 改革的 gǎi gé de

reformer *n.* 改革家 gǎi gé jiā

refrain *v.i.* 克制 kè zhì

refrain *n* 副歌 fù gē

refresh *v.t.* 使清新 shǐ qīng xīn

refreshment *n.* 点心 diǎn xīn

refrigerate *v.t.* 使冷却 shǐ lěng què

refrigeration *n.* 冷冻 lěng dòng

refrigerator *n.* 电冰箱 diàn bīng xiāng

refuge *n.* 避难 bì nàn

refugee *n.* 难民 nàn mín

refulgence *n.* 辉煌 huī huáng

refulgent *a.* 灿烂的 càn làn de

refund *v.t.* 付还 fù hái

refund *n.* 偿还 cháng huán

refusal *n.* 拒绝 jù jué

refuse *v.t.* 拒绝 jù jué

refuse *n.* 废物 fèi wù

refutation *n.* 反驳 fǎn bó

refute *v.t.* 反驳 fǎn bó

regal *a.* 帝王的 dì wáng de

regard *v.t.* 关心 guān xīn

regard *n.* 问候 wèn hòu

regenerate *v.t.* 使再生 shǐ zài shēng

regeneration *n.* 重建 chóng jiàn

regicide *n.* 弑君 shì jūn

regime *n.* 当权期间 dāng quán qī jiān

regiment *n.* 团 tuán

regiment *v.t.* 把...编成团 bǎ... biān chéng tuán

region *n.* 地区 dì qū

regional *a.* 地方的 dì fang de

register *n.* 登记簿 dēng jì bù

register *v.i.* 登记 dēng jì

registrar *n.* 登记官员 dēng jì guān yuán

registration *n.* 登记 dēng jì

registry *n.* 登记处 dēng jì chù

regret *v.i.* 感到抱歉 gǎn dào bào qiàn

regret *n* 遗憾 yí hàn

regular *a.* 规则的 guī zé de

regularity *n.* 规律性 guī lù xìng

regulate *v.t.* 控制 kòng zhì

regulation *n.* 规则 guī zé

regulator *n.* 调节器 tiáo jié qì

rehabilitate *v.t.* 恢复原状 huī fù yuán zhuàng

rehabilitation *n.* 复原 fù yuán

rehearsal *n.* 预演 yù yǎn

rehearse *v.t.* 排演 pái yǎn

reign *v.i.* 当政 dāng zhèng

reign *n* 统治 tǒng zhì

reimburse *v.t.* 偿还 cháng huán

rein *n.* 缰绳 jiāng shéng

rein *v.t.* 驾驭 jià yù

reinforce *v.t.* 加强 jiā qiáng

reinforcement *n.* 加强 jiā qiáng

reinstate *v.t.* 使复原 shǐ fù yuán

reinstatement *n.* 恢复 huī fù

reiterate *v.t.* 反复地说 fǎn fù dì shuō

reiteration *n.* 重复 chóng fù

reject *v.t.* 拒绝 jù jué

rejection *n.* 拒绝 jù jué

rejoice *v.i.* 高兴 gāo xìng

rejoin *v.t.* 使再结合 shǐ zài jié hé

rejoinder *n.* 反驳 fǎn bó

rejuvenate *v.t.* 使年轻 shǐ nián qīng

rejuvenation *n.* 返老还童 fǎn lǎo hái tóng

relapse *v.i.* 复发 fù fā

relapse *n.* 故态复萌 gù tài fù méng

relate *v.t.* 叙述 xù shù

relation *n.* 关系 guān xi

relative *a.* 有关系的 yǒu guān xi de

relative *n.* 亲戚 qīn qi

relax *v.t.* 使松弛 shǐ sōng chí

relaxation *n.* 松弛 sōng chí

relay *n.* 驿马 yì mǎ

relay *v.t.* 分程传递 fēn chéng chuán dì

release *v.t.* 释放 shì fàng

release *n* 发行 fā xíng

relent *v.i.* 变宽厚 biàn kuān hòu

relentless *a.* 无情的 wú qíng de

relevance *n.* 有关 yǒu guān

relevant *a.* 有关联的 yǒu guān lián de

reliable *a.* 可靠的 kě kào de
reliance *n.* 信任 xìn rèn
relic *n.* 遗迹 yí jì
relief *n.* 解除 jiě chú
relieve *v.t.* 减轻 jiǎn qīng
religion *n.* 宗教 zōng jiào
religious *a.* 虔诚的 qián chéng de
relinquish *v.t.* 放弃 fàng qì
relish *v.t.* 调味 tiáo wèi
relish *n* 滋味 zī wèi
reluctance *n.* 勉强 mián qiǎng
reluctant *a.* 勉强的 mián qiǎng de
rely *v.i.* 依赖 yī lài
remain *v.i.* 保持 bǎo chí
remainder *n.* 剩余物 shèng yú wù
remains *n.* 剩余物 shèng yú wù
remand *v.t.* 还押候审 hái yā hòu shěn
remand *n* 还押 hái yā
remark *n.* 评论 píng lùn
remark *v.t.* 评论 píng lùn
remarkable *a.* 值得注意的 zhí děi zhù yì de
remedial *a.* 补救的 bǔ jiù de
remedy *n.* 药物 yào wù
remedy *v.t* 治疗 zhì liáo
remember *v.t.* 记得 jì dé
remembrance *n.* 记忆 jì yì
remind *v.t.* 提醒 tí xǐng
reminder *n.* 提醒的人 tí xǐng de rén
reminiscence *n.* 回忆 huí yì
reminiscent *a.* 回忆的 huí yì de
remission *n.* 宽恕 kuān shù
remit *v.t.* 汇出 huì chū
remittance *n.* 汇款 huì kuǎn
remorse *n.* 自责 zì zé
remote *a.* 偏僻的 piān pì de
removable *a.* 可移去的 kě yí qù de
removal *n.* 切除 qiē chú
remove *v.t.* 移动 yí dòng

remunerate *v.t.* 给与报酬 gěi yǔ bào chóu
remuneration *n.* 酬劳 chóu láo
remunerative *a.* 有报酬的 yǒu bào chóu de
renaissance *n.* 复兴 fù xīng
render *v.t.* 回报 huí bào
rendezvous *n.* 约会 yuē huì
renew *v.t.* 使更新 shǐ gēng xīn
renewal *n.* 更新 gēng xīn
renounce *v.t.* 拒绝 jù jué
renovate *v.t.* 更新 gēng xīn
renovation *n.* 革新 gé xīn
renown *n.* 名声 míng shēng
renowned *a.* 有名的 yǒu míng de
rent *n.* 租金 zū jīn
rent *v.t.* 租用 zū yòng
renunciation *n.* 放弃 fàng qì
repair *v.t.* 补偿 bǔ cháng
repair *n.* 修理 xiū lǐ
raparable *a.* 可赔偿的 kě péi cháng de
repartee *n.* 机敏巧妙的回答 jī mǐn qiǎo miào de huí dá
repatriate *v.t.* 把...遣返 bǎ... qiǎn fǎn
repatriate *n* 被遣返回国者 bèi qiǎn fǎn huí guó zhě
repatriation *n.* 遣送回国 qiǎn sòng huí guó
repay *v.t.* 偿还 cháng huán
repayment *n.* 偿还 cháng huán
repeal *v.t.* 废止 fèi zhǐ
repeal *n* 废止 fèi zhǐ
repeat *v.t.* 重复 chóng fù
repel *v.t.* 逐退 zhú tuì
repellent *a.* 令人讨厌的 lìng rén tǎo yàn de
repellent *n* 驱避剂 qū bì jì
repent *v.i.* 后悔 hòu huǐ
repentance *n.* 后悔 hòu huǐ
repentant *a.* 后悔的 hòu huǐ de
repercussion *n.* 弹回 tán huí
repetition *n.* 重复 chóng fù

replace *v.t.* 代替 dài tì
replacement *n.* 代替者 dài tì zhě
replenish *v.t.* 把...重新补足 bǎ... chóng xīn bǔ zú
replete *a.* 充满的 chōng mǎn de
replica *n.* 复制品 fù zhì pǐn
reply *v.i.* 回答 huí dá
reply *n* 回答 huí dá
report *v.t.* 报告 bào gào
report *n.* 报告 bào gào
reporter *n.* 记者 jì zhě
repose *n.* 休息 xiū xi
repose *v.i.* 休息 xiū xi
repository *n.* 仓库 cāng kù
represent *v.t.* 代表 dài biǎo
representation *n.* 代表 dài biǎo
representative *n.* 代表 dài biǎo
representative *a.* 代表的 dài biǎo de
repress *v.t.* 镇压 zhèn yā
repression *n.* 压制 yā zhì
reprimand *n.* 谴责 qiǎn zé
reprimand *v.t.* 谴责 qiǎn zé
reprint *v.t.* 再版 zài bǎn
reprint *n.* 重印 chóng yìn
reproach *v.t.* 责备 zé bèi
reproach *n.* 责备 zé bèi
reproduce *v.t.* 再生 zài shēng
reproduction *n* 繁殖 fán zhí
reproductive *a.* 生殖的 shēng zhí de
reproof *n.* 责备 zé bèi
reptile *n.* 爬行动物 pá xíng dòng wù
republic *n.* 共和国 gòng hé guó
republican *a.* 共和政体的 gòng hé zhèng tǐ de
republican *n* 共和主义者 gòng hé zhǔ yì zhě
repudiate *v.t.* 拒绝 jù jué
repudiation *n.* 抛弃 pāo qì
repugnance *n.* 反感 fán gǎn

repugnant *a.* 讨厌的 tǎo yàn de
repulse *v.t.* 击退 jī tuì
repulse *n.* 拒绝 jù jué
repulsion *n.* 反感 fán gǎn
repulsive *a.* 排斥的 pái chì de
reputation *n.* 名誉 míng yù
repute *v.t.* 认为 rèn wéi
repute *n.* 名气 míng qì
request *v.t.* 要求 yāo qiú
request *n* 请求 qǐng qiú
requiem *n.* 安魂曲 ān hún qǔ
require *v.t.* 需要 xū yào
requirement *n.* 需求 xū qiú
requisite *a.* 必要的 bì yào de
requisite *n* 必需品 bì xū pǐn
requisition *n.* 正式请求 zhèng shì qǐng qiú
requisition *v.t.* 征用 zhēng yòng
requite *v.t.* 报答 bào dá
rescue *v.t.* 援救 yuán jiù
rescue *n* 援救 yuán jiù
research *v.i.* 研究 yán jiū
research *n* 调查 diào chá
resemblance *n.* 相似处 xiāng sì chù
resemble *v.t.* 相似 xiāng sì
resent *v.t.* 愤恨 fèn hèn
resentment *n.* 怨恨 yuàn hèn
reservation *n.* 预定 yù dìng
reserve *v.t.* 预订 yù dìng
reservoir *n.* 水库 shuǐ kù
reside *v.i.* 住 zhù
residence *n.* 住宅 zhù zhái
resident *a.* 居留的 jū liú de
resident *n* 居民 jū mín
residual *a.* 残渣的 cán zhā de
residue *n.* 残渣 cán zhā
resign *v.t.* 辞职 cí zhí
resignation *n.* 辞职 cí zhí
resist *v.t.* 反抗 fǎn kàng
resistance *n.* 抵抗力 dǐ kàng lì
resistant *a.* 抵抗的 dǐ kàng de
resolute *a.* 坚决的 jiān jué de
resolution *n.* 解析 jiě xī

resolve *v.t.* 解决 jiě jué

resonance *n.* 共鸣 gòng míng

resonant *a.* 共鸣的 gòng míng de

resort *v.i.* 诉诸 sù zhū

resort *n* 度假胜地 dù jiǎ shèng dì

resound *v.i.* 回响 huí xiǎng

resource *n.* 资源 zī yuán

resourceful *a.* 资源丰富的 zī yuán fēng fù de

respect *v.t.* 尊敬 zūn jìng

respect *n.* 尊重 zūn zhòng

respectful *a.* 表示尊敬的 biǎo shì zūn jìng de

respective *a.* 分别的 fēn bié de

respiration *n.* 呼吸 hū xī

respire *v.i.* 呼吸 hū xī

resplendent *a.* 辉煌的 huī huáng de

respond *v.i.* 回答 huí dá

respondent *n.* 应答者 yìng dá zhě

response *n.* 回答 huí dá

responsibility *n.* 责任 zé rèn

responsible *a.* 有责任的 yǒu zé rèn de

rest *v.i.* 休息 xiū xi

rest *n* 剩余部分 shèng yú bù fen

restaurant *n.* 餐馆 cān guǎn

restive *a.* 不愿向前走的 bú yuàn xiàng qián zǒu de

restoration *n.* 复位 fù wèi

restore *v.t.* 恢复 huī fù

restrain *v.t.* 抑制 yì zhì

restrict *v.t.* 限制 xiàn zhì

restriction *n.* 限制 xiàn zhì

restrictive *a.* 约束的 yuē shù de

result *v.i.* 产生 chǎn shēng

result *n.* 结果 jié guǒ

resume *v.t.* 重新开始 chóng xīn kāi shǐ

resume *n.* 个人简历 gè rén jiǎn lì

resumption *n.* 恢复 huī fù

resurgence *n.* 复活 fù huó

resurgent *a.* 复生的 fù shēng de

retail *v.t.* 零售 líng shòu

retail *n.* 零售 líng shòu

retail *adv.* 以零售方式 yǐ líng shòu fāng shì

retail *a* 零售的 líng shòu de

retailer *n.* 零售商 líng shòu shāng

retain *v.t.* 保持 bǎo chí

retaliate *v.i.* 报复 bào fù

retaliation *n.* 报复 bào fù

retard *v.t.* 妨碍 fáng ài

retardation *n.* 迟延 chí yán

retention *n.* 保持 bǎo chí

retentive *a.* 记性好的 jì xing hǎo de

reticence *n.* 沉默 chén mò

reticent *a.* 沉默的 chén mò de

retina *n.* 视网膜 shì wǎng mó

retinue *n.* 随行人员 suí háng rén yuán

retire *v.i.* 隐居 yǐn jū

retirement *n.* 退休 tuì xiū

retort *v.t.* 反驳 fǎn bó

retort *n.* 反驳 fǎn bó

retouch *v.t.* 润饰 rùn shì

retrace *v.t.* 追溯 zhuī sù

retread *v.t.* 翻新 fān xīn

retread *n.* 新胎面 xīn tāi miàn

retreat *v.i.* 撤退 chè tuì

retrench *v.t.* 紧缩 jǐn suō

retrenchment *n.* 节省 jié shěng

retrieve *v.t.* 取回 qǔ huí

retrospect *n.* 回顾 huí gù

retrospection *n.* 追忆 zhuī yì

retrospective *a.* 回顾的, huí gù de

return *v.i.* 返回 fǎn huí

return *n.* 回来 huí lái

revel *v.i.* 狂欢作乐 kuáng huān zuò lè

revel *n.* 狂欢 kuáng huān

revelation *n.* 揭露 jiē lù

reveller *n.* 欢宴者 huān yàn zhě

revelry *n.* 狂欢 kuáng huān

revenge *v.t.* 报仇 bào chóu

revenge *n.* 报仇 bào chóu

revengeful *a.* 报复的 bào fù de

revenue *n.* 税收 shuì shōu

revere *v.t.* 尊敬 zūn jìng

reverence *n.* 尊敬 zūn jìng

reverend *a.* 应受尊敬的 yīng shòu zūn jìng de

reverent *a.* 尊敬的 zūn jìng de

reverential *a.* 充满崇敬心的 chōng mǎn chóng jìng xīn de

reverie *n.* 幻想 huàn xiǎng

reversal *n.* 翻转 fān zhuǎn

reverse *a.* 相反的 xiāng fǎn de

reverse *n* 相反 xiāng fǎn

reverse *v.t.* 倒转 dào zhuǎn

reversible *a.* 可逆的 kě nì de

revert *v.i.* 回复 huí fù

review *v.t.* 温习 wēn xí

review *n* 评论 píng lùn

revise *v.t.* 校订 jiào dìng

revision *n.* 校订 jiào dìng

revival *n.* 复苏 fù sū

revive *v.i.* 苏醒 sū xǐng

revocable *a.* 可废止的 kě fèi zhǐ de

revocation *n.* 废止 fèi zhǐ

revoke *v.t.* 撤回 chè huí

revolt *v.i.* 反抗 fǎn kàng

revolt *n.* 反抗 fǎn kàng

revolution *n.* 革命 gé mìng

revolutionary *a.* 革命的 gé mìng de

revolutionary *n* 革命者 gé mìng zhě

revolve *v.i.* (使)旋转 (shǐ) xuán zhuǎn

revolver *n.* 左轮手枪 zuǒ lún shǒu qiāng

reward *n.* 报酬 bào chóu

reward *v.t.* 奖赏 jiáng shǎng

rhetoric *n.* 修辞 xiū cí

rhetorical *a.* 修辞学的 xiū cí xué de

rheumatic *a.* 风湿病的 fēng shī bìng de

rheumatism *n.* 风湿病的 fēng shī bìng de

rhinoceros *n.* 犀牛 xī niú

rhyme *n.* 押韵 yā yùn

rhyme *v.i.* 押韵 yā yùn

rhymester *n.* 作打油诗的人 zuò dǎ yóu shī de rén

rhythm *n* 节奏 jié zòu

rhythmic *a.* 有节奏的 yǒu jié zòu de

rib *n.* 肋骨 lèi gǔ

ribbon *n.* 缎带 duàn dài

rice *n.* 米 mǐ

rich *a.* 富裕的 fù yù de

riches *n.* 财富 cái fù

richness *a.* 富裕 fù yù

rick *n.* 草堆 cǎo duī

rickets *n.* 佝偻病 gōu lóu bìng

rickety *a.* 患佝偻病的 huàn gōu lóu bìng de

rickshaw *n.* 人力车 rén lì chē

rid *v.t.* 免除 miǎn chú

riddle *n.* 谜语 mí yǔ

riddle *v.i.* 出谜 chū mí

ride *v.t.* 骑 qí

ride *n* 骑马 qí mǎ

rider *n.* 骑手 qí shǒu

ridge *n.* 脊 jí

ridicule *v.t.* 嘲笑 cháo xiào

ridicule *n.* 嘲笑 cháo xiào

ridiculous *a.* 荒谬的 huāng miù de

rifle *v.t.* 用步枪射击 yòng bù qiāng shè jī

rifle *n* 来复枪 lái fù qiāng

rift *n.* 裂口 liè kǒu

right *a.* 正确的 zhèng què de

right *adv* 向右 xiàng yòu

right *n* 权利 quán lì

right *v.t.* 纠正 jiū zhèng

righteous *a.* 正当的 zhèng dāng de

rigid *a.* 坚硬的 jiān yìng de

rigorous *a.* 严格的 yán gé de

rigour *n.* 严厉 yán lì

rim *n.* 边 biān

ring *n.* 戒指 jiè zhi

ring *v.t.* 包围 bāo wéi

ringlet *n.* 长鬈发 cháng quán fā

ringworm *n.* 癣 xuǎn

rinse *v.t.* 以清水冲洗 yǐ qīng shuǐ chōng xǐ

riot *n.* 暴动 bào dòng

riot *v.t.* 浪费 làng fèi

rip *v.t.* 撕 sī

ripe *a* 成熟的 chéng shu de

ripen *v.i.* 成熟 chéng shu

ripple *n.* 涟波 lián bō

ripple *v.t.* 使起涟漪 shǐ qǐ lián yī

rise *v.* 升起 shēng qǐ

rise *n.* 增加 zēng jiā

risk *v.t.* 冒...的危险 mào... de wēi xiǎn

risk *n.* 冒险 mào xiǎn

risky *a.* 危险的 wēi xiǎn de

rite *n.* 仪式 yí shì

ritual *n.* 仪式 yí shì

ritual *a.* 仪式的 yí shì de

rival *n.* 竞争者 jìng zhēng zhě

rival *a.* 竞争的 jìng zhēng de

rivalry *n.* 竞争 jìng zhēng

river *n.* 河 hé

rivet *n.* 铆钉 mǎo dīng

rivet *v.t.* 吸引住 xī yǐn zhù

rivulet *n.* 小河 xiǎo hé

road *n.* 路 lù

roam *v.i.* 漫游 màn yóu

roar *n.* 吼 hǒu

roar *v.i.* 吼 hǒu

roast *v.t.* 烤 kǎo

roast *a* 烘烤的 hōng kǎo de

roast *n* 烤肉 kǎo ròu

rob *v.t.* 抢夺 qiǎng duó

robber *n.* 强盗 qiáng dào

robbery *n.* 抢劫 qiǎng jié

robe *n.* 宽松长袍 kuān sōng cháng páo

robe *v.t.* 穿长袍 chuān cháng páo

robot *n.* 机械人 jī xiè rén

robust *a.* 健康的 jiàn kāng de

rock *v.t.* 摇动 yáo dòng

rock *n.* 石头 shí tou

rocket *n.* 火箭 huǒ jiàn

rod *n.* 杆 gǎn

rodent *n.* 啮齿动物 niè chǐ dòng wù

roe *n.* 鱼子 yú zǐ

rogue *n.* 恶棍 è gùn

roguery *n.* 恶作剧 è zuò jù

roguish *a.* 流氓的 liú máng de

role *n.* 角色 jué sè

roll *n.* 卷 juǎn

roll *v.i.* 滚 gǔn

roll-call *n.* 点名 diǎn míng

roller *n.* 滚筒 gún tǒng

romance *n.* 浪漫史 làng màn shǐ

romantic *a.* 浪漫的 làng màn de

romp *v.i.* 喧闹玩耍 xuān nào wán shuǎ

romp *n.* 喧闹游玩 xuān nào yóu wán

rood *n.* 十字架 shí zì jià

roof *n.* 屋顶 wū dǐng

roof *v.t.* 给...盖屋顶 gěi... gài wū dǐng

rook *n.* 骗子 piàn zi

rook *v.t.* 骗 piàn

room *n.* 房 fáng

roomy *a.* 宽敞的 kuān chǎng de

roost *n.* 休息所 xiū xi suǒ

roost *v.i.* 栖息 qī xī

root *n.* 根 gēn

root *v.i.* 生根 shēng gēn

rope *n.* 绳 shéng

rope *v.t.* 绑 bǎng

rosary *n.* 玫瑰园 méi gui yuán

rose *n.* 玫瑰 méi gui

roseate *a.* 玫瑰色的 méi gui sè de

rostrum *n.* 讲坛 jiǎng tán

rosy *a.* 蔷薇色的 qiáng wēi sè de

rot *n.* 腐烂 fǔ làn

rot *v.i.* 腐烂 fǔ làn

rotary *a.* 旋转的 xuán zhuǎn de

rotate *v.i.* 旋转 xuán zhuǎn

rotation *n.* 旋转 xuán zhuǎn

rote *n.* 死记硬背 sǐ jì yìng bèi

rouble *n.* 卢布 lú bù

rough *a.* 粗糙的 cū cāo de

round *a.* 圆形的 yuán xíng de

round *adv.* 环绕 huán rào

round *n.* 局 jú

round *v.t.* 绕过 rào guò

rouse *v.i.* 醒来 xíng lái

rout *v.t.* 使溃败 shǐ kuì bài

rout *n* 大败 dà bài

route *n.* 路线 lù xiàn

routine *n.* 日常工作 rì cháng gōng zuò

routine *a* 日常的 rì cháng de

rove *v.i.* 流浪 liú làng

rover *n.* 流浪者 liú làng zhě

row *n.* 一行 yì xíng

row *v.t.* 划 huá

row *v.i.* 争吵 zhēng chǎo

row *n.* 排 pái

rowdy *a.* 吵闹的 chǎo nào de

royal *a.* 王室的 wáng shì de
royalist *n.* 保皇党员 bǎo huáng dǎng yuán

royalty *n.* 王室成员 wáng shì chéng yuán

rub *v.t.* 擦 cā

rub *n* 困难 kùn nan

rubber *n.* 橡胶 xiàng jiāo

rubbish *n.* 垃圾 lā jī

rubble *n.* 碎砖 suì zhuān

ruby *n.* 红宝石 hóng bǎo shí

rude *a.* 粗鲁无礼的 cū lǔ wú lǐ de

rudiment *n.* 基础 jī chǔ

rudimentary *a.* 基本的 jī běn de

rue *v.t.* 后悔 hòu huǐ

rueful *a.* 后悔的 hòu huǐ de

ruffian *n.* 恶棍 è gùn

ruffle *v.t.* 弄皱 nòng zhòu

rug *n.* 小块地毯 xiǎo kuài dì tǎn

rugged *a.* 崎岖的 qí qū de

ruin *n.* 废墟 fèi xū

ruin *v.t.* 毁坏 huǐ huài

rule *n.* 规则 guī zé

rule *v.t.* 统治 tǒng zhì

ruler *n.* 直尺 zhí chǐ

ruling *n.* 裁决 cái jué

rum *n.* 朗姆酒 lǎng mǔ jiǔ

rum *a* 古怪的 gǔ guài de

rumble *v.i.* 发隆隆声 fā lóng lóng shēng

rumble *n.* 隆隆声 lóng lóng shēng

ruminant *a.* 反刍类的 fǎn chú lèi de

ruminant *n.* 反刍动物 fǎn chú dòng wù

ruminate *v.i.* 沉思 chén sī

rumination *n.* 沉思 chén sī

rummage *v.i.* 仔细翻寻 zǐ xì fān xún

rummage *n* 仔细翻找 zǐ xì fān zhǎo

rummy *n.* 拉米纸牌戏 lā mǐ zhǐ pái xì

rumour *n.* 谣言 yáo yán

rumour *v.t.* 谣传 yáo chuán

run *v.i.* 跑 pǎo

run *n.* 跑步 pǎo bù

rung *n.* 踏步 tà bù

runner *n.* 跑步者 pǎo bù zhě

rupee *n.* 卢比 lú bǐ

rupture *n.* 破裂 pò liè

rupture *v.t.* 破裂 pò liè

rural *a.* 乡下的 xiāng xia de

ruse *n.* 诡计 guǐ jì

rush *n.* 匆促 cōng cù

rush *v.t.* 匆忙地做 cōng máng dì zuò

rush *n* 冲进 chōng jìn

rust *n.* 锈 xiù

rust *v.i* 生锈 shēng xiù

rustic *a.* 乡村的 xiāng cūn de

rustic *n* 乡下人 xiāng xia rén

rusticate *v.t.* 过乡村生活 guò xiāng cūn shēng huó

rustication *n.* 田园生活 tián yuán shēng huó

rusticity *n.* 朴素 pǔ sù

rusty *a.* 生锈的 shēng xiù de
rut *n.* 辙迹 zhé jì
ruthless *a.* 毫不留情的 háo bù liú qíng de
rye *n.* 黑麦 hēi mài

S

sabbath *n.* 安息日 ān xī rì
sabotage *n.* 破坏活动 pò huài huó dòng
sabotage *v.t.* 妨害 fáng hài
sabre *n.* 军刀 jūn dāo
sabre *v.t.* 用马刀砍 yòng mǎ dāo kǎn
saccharin *n.* 糖精 táng jīng
saccharine *a.* 极甜的 jí tián de
sack *n.* 麻布袋 má bù dài
sack *v.t.* 把...装入袋 bǎ... zhuāng rù dài
sacrament *n.* 圣礼 shèng lǐ
sacred *a.* 神圣的 shén shèng de
sacrifice *n.* 祭品 jì pǐn
sacrifice *v.t.* 牺牲 xī shēng
sacrificial *a.* 牺牲的 xī shēng de
sacrilege *n.* 亵渎圣物 xiè dú shèng wù
sacrilegious *a.* 冒渎的 mào dú de
sacrosanct *a.* 极神圣的 jí shén shèng de
sad *a.* 忧愁的 yōu chóu de
sadden *v.t.* 使忧愁 shǐ yōu chóu
saddle *n.* 马鞍 mǎ ān
saddle *v.t.* 装以马鞍 zhuāng yǐ mǎ ān
sadism *n.* 虐待狂 nüè dài kuáng
sadist *n.* 虐待狂者 nüè dài kuáng zhě
safe *a.* 安全的 ān quán de
safe *n.* 保险箱 báo xiǎn xiāng
safeguard *n.* 保护措施 bǎo hù cuò shī

safety *n.* 安全 ān quán
saffron *n.* 藏红花 zàng hóng huā
saffron *a* 橙黄色 chéng huáng sè
sagacious *a.* 聪明的 cōng míng de
sagacity *n.* 睿智 ruì zhì
sage *n.* 圣人 shèng rén
sage *a.* 贤明的 xián míng de
sail *n.* 帆 fān
sail *v.i.* 航行 háng xíng
sailor *n.* 船员 chuán yuán
saint *n.* 圣人 shèng rén
saintly *a.* 圣洁的 shèng jié de
sake *n.* 目的 mù dì
salable *a.* 适销的 shì xiāo de
salad *n.* 色拉 sè lā
salary *n.* 薪水 xīn shuǐ
sale *n.* 廉价出售 lián jià chū shòu
salesman *n.* 售货员 shòu huò yuán
salient *a.* 显著的 xiǎn zhù de
saline *a.* 盐的 yán de
salinity *n.* 盐性 yán xìng
saliva *n.* 唾液 tuò yè
sally *n.* 突击 tū jī
sally *v.i.* 突击 tū jī
saloon *n.* 酒吧 jiǔ bā
salt *n.* 盐 yán
salt *v.t* 加盐于 jiā yán yú
salty *a.* 咸味浓的 xián wèi nóng de
salutary *a.* 有益的 yǒu yì de
salutation *n.* 问候 wèn hòu
salute *v.t.* 向...致意 xiàng... zhì yì
salute *n* 敬礼 jìng lǐ
salvage *n.* 抢救 qiǎng jiù
salvage *v.t.* 抢救 qiǎng jiù
salvation *n.* 拯救 zhěng jiù
same *a.* 相同的 xiāng tóng de
sample *n.* 样本 yàng běn
sample *v.t.* 试下 shì xià
sanatorium *n.* 疗养院 liáo yǎng yuàn
sanctification *n.* 神圣化 shén shèng huà

sanctify *v.t.* 使神圣 shǐ shén shèng

sanction *n.* 制裁 zhì cái

sanction *v.t.* 制定制裁规则 zhì dìng zhì cái guī zé

sanctity *n.* 神圣 shén shèng

sanctuary *n.* 庇护所 bì hù suǒ

sand *n.* 沙 shā

sandal *n.* 凉鞋 liáng xié

sandalwood *n.* 檀香木 tán xiāng mù

sandwich *n.* 三明治 sān míng zhì

sandwich *v.t.* 把...制成三明治 bǎ... zhì chéng sān míng zhì

sandy *a.* 沙的 shā de

sane *a.* 精神健全的 jīng shen jiàn quán de

sanguine *a.* 乐观的 lè guān de

sanitary *a.* 卫生的 wèi shēng de

sanity *n.* 神智健全 shén zhì jiàn quán

sap *n.* 树液 shù yè

sap *v.t.* 使排出体液 shǐ pái chū tǐ yè

sapling *n.* 小树 xiǎo shù

sapphire *n.* 蓝宝石 lán bǎo shí

sarcasm *n.* 讽刺 fěng cì

sarcastic *a.* 讽刺的 fěng cì de

sardonic *a.* 嘲笑的 cháo xiào de

satan *n.* 魔鬼 mó guǐ

satchel *n.* 书包 shū bāo

satellite *n.* 人造卫星 rén zào wèi xīng

satiable *a.* 可满足的 kě mǎn zú de

satiate *v.t.* 使厌腻 shǐ yàn nì

satiety *n.* 满足 mǎn zú

satire *n.* 讽刺 fěng cì

satirical *a.* 讽刺的 fěng cì de

satirist *n.* 讽刺作者 fěng cì zuò zhě

satirize *v.t.* 讽刺 fěng cì

satisfaction *n.* 满意 mǎn yì

satisfactory *a.* 满意的 mǎn yì de

satisfy *v.t.* 满足 mǎn zú

saturate *v.t.* 使渗透 shǐ shèn tòu

saturation *n.* 饱和度 bǎo hé dù

Saturday *n.* 星期六 xīng qī liù

sauce *n.* 酱油 jiàng yóu

saucer *n.* 茶碟 chá dié

saunter *v.i.* 漫步 màn bù

savage *a.* 未开化的 wèi kāi huà de

savage *n* 原始人 yuán shǐ rén

savagery *n.* 兽性 shòu xìng

save *v.t.* 解救 jiě jiù

save *prep* 除...之外 chú... zhī wài

saviour *n.* 救星 jiù xīng

savour *n.* 滋味 zī wèi

savour *v.t.* 品味 pǐn wèi

saw *n.* 锯子 jù zǐ

saw *v.t.* 锯开 jù kāi

say *v.t.* 讲 jiǎng

say *n.* 发言权 fā yán quán

scabbard *n.* 鞘 qiào

scabies *n.* 疥疮 jiè chuāng

scaffold *n.* 脚手架 jiǎo shǒu jià

scale *n.* 规模 guī mó

scale *v.i.* 攀登 pān dēng

scalp *n* 头皮 tóu pí

scamper *v.i* 蹦跳 bèng tiào

scamper *n* 奔跑 bēn pǎo

scan *v.t.* 扫描 sǎo miáo

scandal *n* 丑闻 chǒu wén

scandalize *v.t.* 使生反感 shǐ shēng fǎn gǎn

scant *a.* 不充分的 bù chōng fēn de

scanty *a.* 缺乏的 quē fá de

scapegoat *n.* 替罪羔羊 tì zuì gāo yáng

scar *n* 疤痕 bā hén

scar *v.t.* 使有伤痕 shǐ yǒu shāng hén

scarce *a.* 稀罕的 xī han de

scarcely *adv.* 简直不 jiǎn zhí bú

scarcity *n.* 缺乏 quē fá

scare *n.* 惊吓 jīng xià

scare *v.t.* 惊吓 jīng xià

scarf *n.* 围巾 wéi jīn

scatter *v.t.* 使消散 shǐ xiāo sàn

scavenger *n.* 食腐动物 shí fǔ dòng wù

scene *n.* 镜头 jìng tóu

scenery *n.* 风景 fēng jǐng

scenic *a.* 风景好的 fēng jǐng hǎo de

scent *n.* 气味 qì wèi

scent *v.t.* 闻出 wén chū

sceptic *n.* 怀疑论者 huái yí lùn zhě

sceptical *a.* 怀疑的 huái yí de

scepticism *n.* 怀疑主义 huái yí zhǔ yì

sceptre *n.* 节杖 jié zhàng

schedule *n.* 时间表 shí jiān biǎo

schedule *v.t.* 安排 ān pái

scheme *n.* 方案 fāng àn

scheme *v.i.* 计划 jì huà

schism *n.* 分裂 fēn liè

scholar *n.* 学者 xué zhě

scholarly *a.* 有学问的 yǒu xué wen de

scholarship *n.* 奖学金 jiǎng xué jīn

scholastic *a.* 学校的 xué xiào de

school *n.* 学校 xué xiào

science *n.* 科学 kē xué

scientific *a.* 科学的 kē xué de

scientist *n.* 科学家 kē xué jiā

scintillate *v.i.* 发出火花 fā chū huǒ huā

scintillation *n.* 闪烁 shǎn shuò

scissors *n.* 剪刀 jiǎn dāo

scoff *n.* 嘲笑 cháo xiào

scoff *v.i.* 狼吞虎咽地吃 láng tūn hǔ yān dì chī

scold *v.t.* 责骂 zé mà

scooter *n.* 小型摩托车 xiǎo xíng mó tuō chē

scope *n.* 机会 jī huì

scorch *v.t.* 烧焦 shāo jiāo

score *n.* 得分 dé fēn

score *v.i.* 得分 dé fēn

scorer *n.* 记录员 jì lù yuán

scorn *n.* 藐视 miǎo shì

scorn *v.t.* 嘲笑 cháo xiào

scorpion *n.* 蝎子 xiē zi

Scot *n.* 苏格兰人 sū gé lán rén

scotch *a.* 苏格兰的 sū gé lán de

scotch *n.* 苏格兰威士忌 sū gé lán wēi shì jì

scot-free *a.* 不受处罚的 bú shòu chǔ fá de

scoundrel *n.* 恶棍 è gùn

scourge *n.* 苦难根源 kǔ nàn gēn yuán

scourge *v.t.* 鞭打 biān dǎ

scout *n* 侦察员 zhēn chá yuán

scout *v.i* 守候 shǒu hòu

scowl *v.i.* 怒视 nù shì

scowl *n.* 愁容 chóu róng

scramble *v.i.* 攀缘 pān yuán

scramble *n* 爬行 pá xíng

scrap *n.* 碎片 suì piàn

scratch *n.* 抓 zhuā

scratch *v.t.* 抓 zhuā

scrawl *v.t.* 乱写 luàn xiě

scrawl *n* 潦草的笔迹 liáo cǎo de bǐ jì

scream *v.i.* 尖叫 jiān jiào

scream *n* 尖叫声 jiān jiào shēng

screen *n.* 银幕 yín mù

screen *v.t.* 掩蔽 yǎn bì

screw *n.* 螺旋 luó xuán

screw *v.t.* 调节 tiáo jié

scribble *v.t.* 乱写 luàn xiě

scribble *n.* 潦草的字 liáo cǎo de zì

script *n.* 手稿 shóu gǎo

scripture *n.* 圣经 shèng jīng

scroll *n.* 画卷 huà juàn

scrutinize *v.t.* 仔细检查 zǐ xì jiǎn chá

scrutiny *n.* 仔细检查 zǐ xì jiǎn chá

scuffle *n.* 扭打 niǔ dǎ

scuffle *v.i.* 扭打 niǔ dǎ

sculptor *n.* 凋刻家 diāo kè jiā

sculptural *a.* 凋刻的 diāo kè de

sculpture *n.* 凋刻 diāo kè

scythe *n.* 长柄大镰刀 cháng bǐng dà lián dāo

scythe *v.t.* 用大镰刀割 yòng dà lián dāo gē

sea *n.* 海 hǎi

seal *n.* 海豹 hǎi bào

seal *n.* 印章 yìn zhāng

seal *v.t.* 封闭 fēng bì

seam *n.* 缝合线 féng hé xiàn

seam *v.t.* 缝合 féng hé

seamy *a.* 露出线缝的 lòu chū xiàn féng de

search *n.* 搜寻 sōu xún

search *v.t.* 搜寻 sōu xún

season *n.* 季节 jì jié

season *v.t.* 给...调味 gěi... tiáo wèi

seasonable *a.* 适合于季节的 shì hé yú jì jié de

seasonal *a.* 季节的 jì jié de

seat *n.* 座位 zuò wèi

seat *v.t.* 使坐下 shǐ zuò xià

secede *v.i.* 正式脱离 zhèng shì tuō lí

secession *n.* 脱离 tuō lí

secessionist *n.* 脱离主义者 tuō lí zhǔ yì zhě

seclude *v.t.* 使隔离 shǐ gé lí

secluded *a.* 隐退的 yǐn tuì de

seclusion *n.* 隐退 yǐn tuì

second *a.* 第二的 dì èr de

second *n* 秒 miǎo

second *v.t.* 支持 zhī chí

secondary *a.* 次要的 cì yào de

seconder *n.* 赞成人 zàn chéng rén

secrecy *n.* 保密 bǎo mì

secret *a.* 秘密的 mì mì de

secret *n.* 秘密 mì mì

secretariat (e) *n.* 秘书处 mì shū chù

secretary *n.* 秘书 mì shū

secrete *v.t.* 分泌 fēn mì

secretion *n.* 分泌 fēn mì

secretive *a.* 秘密的 mì mì de

sect *n.* 教派 jiào pài

sectarian *a.* 宗派的 zōng pài de

section *n.* 部分 bù fen

sector *n.* 部门 bù mén

secure *a.* 安全的 ān quán de

secure *v.t.* 固定 gù dìng

security *n.* 安全 ān quán

sedan *n.* 轿车 jiào chē

sedate *a.* 沉着的 chén zhuó de

sedate *v.t.* 给...服镇静剂 gěi... fú zhèn jìng jì

sedative *a.* 使安静的 shǐ ān jìng de

sedative *n* 镇静剂 zhèn jìng jì

sedentary *a.* 久坐的 jiǔ zuò de

sediment *n.* 沉淀物 chén diàn wù

sedition *n.* 煽动骚乱 shān dòng sāo luàn

seditious *a.* 煽动性的 shān dòng xìng de

seduce *v* 诱惑 yòu huò

seduction *n.* 教唆 jiào suō

seductive *a.* 诱惑的 yòu huò de

see *v.t.* 看见 kàn jiàn

seed *n.* 种子 zhǒng zi

seed *v.t.* 在...播种 zài... bō zhǒng

seek *v.t.* 寻求 xún qiú

seem *v.i.* 象是 xiàng shì

seemly *a.* 适当的 shì dàng de

seep *v.i.* 渗出 shèn chū

seer *n.* 预言者 yù yán zhě

seethe *v.i.* 冒泡 mào pào

segment *n.* 部分 bù fen
segment *v.t.* 分割 fēn gē
segregate *v.t.* 使分离 shǐ fēn lí
segregation *n.* 隔离 gé lí
seismic *a.* 地震的 dì zhèn de
seize *v.t.* 抓住 zhuā zhù
seizure *n.* 捕获 bǔ huò
seldom *adv.* 很少 hěn shǎo
select *v.t.* 选择 xuǎn zé
select *a* 挑选出来的 tiāo xuǎn chū lái de
selection *n.* 选择 xuǎn zé
selective *a.* 选择的 xuǎn zé de
self *n.* 自己 zì jǐ
selfish *a.* 自私的 zì sī de
selfless *a.* 无私的 wú sī de
sell *v.t.* 卖 mài
seller *n.* 销售者 xiāo shòu zhě
semblance *n.* 假象 jiǎ xiàng
semen *n.* 精液 jīng yè
semester *n.* 学期 xué qī
seminal *a.* 精液的 jīng yè de
seminar *n.* 专题讨论会 zhuān tí tǎo lùn huì
senate *n.* 参议院 cān yì yuàn
senator *n.* 参议员 cān yì yuán
senatorial *a.* 参议员的 cān yì yuán de
senatorial *a* 参议院的 cān yì yuàn de
send *v.t.* 发送 fā sòng
senile *a.* 高龄的 gāo líng de
senility *n.* 高龄 gāo líng
senior *a.* 年长的 nián zhǎng de
senior *n.* 年长者 nián zháng zhě
seniority *n.* 长辈 zhǎng bèi
sensation *n.* 感觉 gǎn jué
sensational *a.* 使人感动的 shǐ rén gǎn dòng de
sense *n.* 感应 gǎn yìng
sense *v.t.* 感觉 gǎn jué

senseless *a.* 无意识的 wú yì shí de
sensibility *n.* 敏感性 mín gǎn xìng
sensible *a.* 明智的 míng zhì de
sensitive *a.* 敏感的 mín gǎn de
sensual *a.* 感觉的 gǎn jué de
sensualist *n.* 好色者 hǎo sè zhě
sensuality *n.* 耽于声色 dān yú shēng sè
sensuous *a.* 感觉上的 gǎn jué shàng de
sentence *n.* 句子 jù zi
sentence *v.t.* 判决 pàn jué
sentience *n.* 有感觉性 yǒu gǎn jué xìng
sentient *a.* 有感觉力的 yǒu gǎn jué lì de
sentiment *n.* 情绪 qíng xù
sentimental *a.* 感情用事的 gǎn qíng yòng shì de
sentinel *n.* 哨兵 shào bīng
sentry *n.* 哨兵 shào bīng
separable *a.* 可分离的 kě fēn lí de
separate *v.t.* 使分开 shǐ fēn kāi
separate *a.* 分开的 fēn kāi de
separation *n.* 分离 fēn lí
sepsis *n.* 脓毒病 nóng dú bìng
September *n.* 九月 jiǔ yuè
septic *a.* 脓毒性的 nóng dú xìng de
sepulchre *n.* 坟墓 fén mù
sepulture *n.* 坟墓 fén mù
sequel *n.* 续集 xù jí
sequence *n.* 序列 xù liè
sequester *v.t.* 隔离 gé lí
serene *a.* 宁静的 níng jìng de
serenity *n.* 宁静 níng jìng
serf *n.* 农奴 nóng nú
serge *n.* 哔叽 bì jī
sergeant *n.* 警察小队长 jǐng chá xiǎo duì zhǎng

serial *a.* 连续的 lián xù de

serial *n.* 连载小说 lián zǎi xiǎo shuō

series *n.* 系列 xì liè

serious *a* 严重的 yán zhòng de

sermon *n.* 讲道 jiǎng dào

sermonize *v.i.* 说教 shuō jiào

serpent *n.* 蛇 shé

serpentine *a.* 层层卷绕的 céng céng juǎn rào de

servant *n.* 仆人 pú rén

serve *v.t.* 招待 zhāo dài

serve *n.* 发球 fā qiú

service *n.* 服务 fú wù

service *v.t* 保养 báo yǎng

serviceable *a.* 有用的 yǒu yòng de

servile *a.* 奴隶的 nú lì de

servility *n.* 卑屈 bēi qū

session *n.* 期间 qī jiān

set *v.t* 安置 ān zhì

set *a* 固定的 gù dìng de

set *n* 日落 rì luò

settle *v.i.* 解决 jiě jué

settlement *n.* 安顿 ān dùn

settler *n.* 移民者 yí mín zhě

seven *n.* 七 qī

seven *a* 七 qī

seventeen *n.* 十七 shí qī

seventeenth *a.* 第十七 dì shí qī

seventh *a.* 第七 dì qī

seventieth *a.* 第七十 dì qī shí

seventy *n.* 七十 qī shí

sever *v.t.* 切断 qiē duàn

several *a* 几个的 jǐ gè de

severance *n.* 断绝 duàn jué

severe *a.* 严重的 yán zhòng de

severity *n.* 严格 yán gé

sew *v.t.* 缝纫 féng rèn

sewage *n.* 污水 wū shuǐ

sewer *n* 污水道 wū shuǐ dào

sewerage *n.* 排水系统 pái shuǐ xì tǒng

sex *n.* 性 xìng

sexual *a.* 性的 xìng de

sexuality *n.* 性别 xìng bié

sexy *n.* 有性感的 yǒu xìng gǎn de

shabby *a.* 破旧的 pò jiù de

shackle *n.* 桎梏 zhì gù

shackle *v.t.* 束缚 shù fù

shade *n.* 阴处 yīn chù

shade *v.t.* 遮 zhē

shadow *n.* 影 yǐng

shadow *v.t* 遮住 zhē zhù

shadowy *a.* 阴暗的 yīn àn de

shaft *n.* 箭杆 jiàn gǎn

shake *v.i.* 动摇 dòng yáo

shake *n* 摇动 yáo dòng

shaky *a.* 震动的 zhèn dòng de

shallow *a.* 浅的 qiǎn de

sham *v.i.* 冒充 mào chōng

sham *n* 假冒 jiǎ mào

sham *a* 假的 jiǎ de

shame *n.* 羞耻 xiū chǐ

shame *v.t.* 使羞愧 shǐ xiū kuì

shameful *a.* 可耻的 ké chǐ de

shameless *a.* 无耻的 wú chǐ de

shampoo *n.* 洗头剂 xǐ tóu jì

shampoo *v.t.* 洗头发 xǐ tóu fa

shanty *a.* 棚屋 péng wū

shape *n.* 形状 xíng zhuàng

shape *v.t* 塑造 sù zào

shapely *a.* 有样子的 yǒu yàng zi de

share *n.* 股份 gǔ fèn

share *v.t.* 均分 jūn fèn

share *n* 一份 yí fèn

shark *n.* 鲨鱼 shā yú

sharp *a.* 锐利的 ruì lì de

sharp *adv.* 尖锐地 jiān ruì dì

sharpen *v.t.* 磨尖 mó jiān

sharpener *n.* 磨的人 mó de rén

sharper *n.* 骗子 piàn zi

shatter *v.t.* 使粉碎 shǐ fěn suì

shave *v.t.* 剃 tì

shave *n* 剃刀 tì dāo

shawl *n.* 披肩 pī jiān

she *pron.* 她 tā

sheaf *n.* 束 shù

shear *v.t.* 剪 jiǎn

shears *n. pl.* 大剪刀 dà jiǎn dāo

shed *v.t.* 落下 luò xià

shed *n* 脱落物 tuō luò wù

sheep *n.* 羊 yáng

sheepish *a.* 羞怯的 xiū qiè de

sheer *a.* 纯粹的 chún cuì de

sheet *n.* 被单 bèi dān

sheet *v.t.* 盖上被单 gài shàng bèi dān

shelf *n.* 架子 jià zi

shell *n.* 壳 ké

shell *v.t.* 去壳 qù ké

shelter *n.* 庇护所 bì hù suǒ

shelter *v.t.* 保护 bǎo hù

shelve *v.t.* 放置架子上 fàng zhì jià zi shàng

shepherd *n.* 牧羊人 mù yáng rén

shield *n.* 盾 dùn

shield *v.t.* 保护 bǎo hù

shift *v.t.* 转移 zhuǎn yí

shift *n* 班 bān

shifty *a.* 不稳定的 bù wěn dìng de

shilling *n.* 先令 xiān lìng

shilly-shally *v.i.* 优柔寡断 yōu róu guǎ duàn

shilly-shally *n.* 磨蹭 mó cèng

shin *n.* 胫 jìng

shine *v.i.* 发光 fā guāng

shine *n* 光泽 guāng zé

shiny *a.* 发光的 fā guāng de

ship *n.* 船 chuán

ship *v.t.* 装上船 zhuāng shàng chuán

shipment *n.* 装货 zhuāng huò

shire *n.* 郡 jùn

shirk *v.i.* 逃避 táo bì

shirker *n.* 逃避者 táo bì zhě

shirt *n.* 衬衫 chèn shān

shiver *v.i.* 使发抖 shǐ fā dǒu

shoal *n.* 鱼群 yú qún

shoal *n* 浅滩 qiǎn tān

shock *n.* 震动 zhèn dòng

shock *v.t.* 使震动 shǐ zhèn dòng

shoe *n.* 鞋 xié

shoe *v.t.* 为马钉蹄铁 wéi mǎ dìng tí tiě

shoot *v.t.* 发射 fā shè

shoot *n* 苗 miáo

shop *n.* 店铺 diàn pù

shop *v.i.* 买东西 mǎi dōng xi

shore *n.* 海岸 hǎi àn

short *a.* 短的 duǎn de

short *adv.* 简短的 jiǎn duǎn de

shortage *n.* 短少 duǎn shǎo

shortcoming *n.* 短处 duǎn chu

shorten *v.t.* 弄短 nòng duǎn

shortly *adv.* 不久 bù jiǔ

shorts *n. pl.* 短裤 duǎn kù

shot *n.* 射击 shè jī

shoulder *n.* 肩膀 jiān bǎng

shoulder *v.t.* 负担 fù dān

shout *n.* 呼喊 hū hǎn

shout *v.i.* 叫喊 jiào hǎn

shove *v.t.* 推 tuī

shove *n.* 推 tuī

shovel *n.* 铁铲 tiě chǎn

shovel *v.t.* 铲 chǎn

show *v.t.* 表明 biǎo míng

show *n.* 演出 yǎn chū

shower *n.* 淋浴 lín yù

shower *v.t.* 淋湿 lín shī

shrew *n.* 泼妇 pō fù

shrewd *a.* 精明的 jīng míng de

shriek *n.* 尖锐的喊声 jiān ruì de hǎn shēng

shriek *v.i.* 尖声叫喊 jiān shēng jiào hǎn

shrill *a.* 尖声的 jiān shēng de

shrine *n.* 圣地 shèng dì

shrink *v.i* 缩短 suō duǎn

shrinkage *n.* 缩水 suō shuǐ

shroud *n.* 裹尸布 guǒ shī bù

shroud *v.t.* 覆盖 fù gài

shrub *n.* 灌木 guàn mù

shrug *v.t.* 耸 sǒng

shrug *n* 耸肩 sǒng jiān

shudder *v.i.* 发抖 fā dǒu

shudder *n* 战栗 zhàn lì

shuffle *v.i.* 拖曳 tuō yè

shuffle *n.* 洗纸牌 xǐ zhǐ pái

shun *v.t.* 避开 bì kāi

shunt *v.t.* 逃避 táo bì

shut *v.t.* 关闭 guān bì

shutter *n.* 百叶窗 bǎi yè chuāng

shuttle *n.* 梭 suō

shuttle *v.t.* 来回运动 lái huí yùn dòng

shuttlecock *n.* 羽毛球 yǔ máo qiú

shy *n.* 惊退 jīng tuì

shy *v.i.* 惊退 jīng tuì

sick *a.* 病的 bìng de

sickle *n.* 镰刀 lián dāo

sickly *a.* 有病的 yǒu bìng de

sickness *n.* 疾病 jí bìng

side *n.* 侧面 cè miàn

side *v.i.* 支持 zhī chí

siege *n.* 包围 bāo wéi

siesta *n.* 午睡 wǔ shuì

sieve *n.* 筛 shāi

sieve *v.t.* 筛 shāi

sift *v.t.* 筛 shāi

sigh *n.* 叹气 tàn qì

sigh *v.i.* 叹气 tàn qì

sight *n.* 视力 shì lì

sight *v.t.* 看见 kàn jiàn

sightly *a.* 好看的 hǎo kàn de

sign *n.* 记号 jì hao

sign *v.t.* 签名于 qiān míng yú

signal *n.* 信号 xìn hào

signal *a.* 暗号的 àn hào de

signal *v.t.* 发信号 fā xìn hào

signatory *n.* 签字人 qiān zì rén

signature *n.* 签名 qiān míng

significance *n.* 有意义 yǒu yì yì

significant *a.* 重要的 zhòng yào de

signification *n.* 意义 yì yì

signify *v.t.* 表示 biǎo shì

silence *n.* 无声 wú shēng

silence *v.t.* 使安静 shǐ ān jìng

silencer *n.* 消音器 xiāo yīn qì

silent *a.* 无声的 wú shēng de

silhouette *n.* 侧面影像 cè miàn yǐng xiàng

silk *n.* 丝 sī

silken *a.* 丝的 sī de

silky *a.* 丝一样的 sī yí yàng de

silly *a.* 傻的 shǎ de

silt *n.* 泥沙 ní shā

silt *v.t.* 淤积 yū jī

silver *n.* 银 yín

silver *a* 银的 yín de

silver *v.t.* 镀银 dù yín

similar *a.* 近似的 jìn shì de

similarity *n.* 相似 xiāng sì

simile *n.* 明喻 míng yù

similitude *n.* 相似 xiāng sì

simmer *v.i.* 炖 dùn

simple *a.* 简单的 jiǎn dān de

simpleton *n.* 傻子 shǎ zi

simplicity *n.* 简单 jiǎn dān

simplification *n.* 简单化 jiǎn dān huà

simplify *v.t.* 简化 jiǎn huà

simultaneous *a.* 同时发生的 tóng shí fā shēng de

sin *n.* 罪恶 zuì è

sin *v.i.* 犯罪 fàn zuì

since *prep.* 自从 zì cóng

since *conj.* …以来 … yǐ lái

since *adv.* 以后 yǐ hòu

sincere *a.* 真挚的 zhēn zhì de

sincerity *n.* 真实 zhēn shí

sinful *a.* 邪恶的 xié è de

sing *v.i.* 歌唱 gē chàng

singe *v.t.* 燎毛 liáo máo

singe *n* 烧焦 shāo jiāo

singer *n.* 歌手 gē shǒu

single *a.* 单身的 dān shēn de

single *n.* 单程票 dān chéng piào

single *v.t.* 选出 xuǎn chū

singular *a.* 单数的 dān shù de

singularity *n.* 奇特 qí tè

singularly *adv.* 异常 yì cháng

sinister *a.* 险恶的 xiǎn è de

sink *v.i.* 下沉 xià chén

sink *n* 污水槽 wū shuǐ cáo

sinner *n.* 罪人 zuì rén

sinuous *a.* 弯曲的 wān qū de

sip *v.t.* 啜 chuò
sip *n.* 啜饮 chuò yǐn
sir *n.* 先生 xiān sheng
siren *n.* 警报器 jǐng bào qì
sister *n.* 姊，妹 zǐ，mèi
sisterhood *n.* 姊妹之谊 zǐ mèi zhī yì
sisterly *a.* 姊妹一般的 zǐ mèi yì bān de
sit *v.i.* 坐 zuò
site *n.* 现场 xiàn chǎng
situation *n.* 情况 qíng kuàng
six *n.* 六 liù
sixteen *n.* 十六 shí liù
sixteenth *a.* 第十六 dì shí liù
sixth *a.* 第六 dì liù
sixtieth *a.* 第六十 dì liù shí
sixty *n.* 六十 liù shí
sizable *a.* 相当大的 xiāng dāng dà de
size *n.* 大小 dà xiǎo
size *v.t.* 依大小排列 yī dà xiǎo pái liè
sizzle *v.i.* 嗞嗞响 zī zī xiǎng
sizzle *n.* 嗞嗞响 zī zī xiǎng
skate *n.* 冰鞋 bīng xié
skate *v.i.* 溜冰 liū bīng
skein *n.* 一束 yí shù
skeleton *n.* 骨骼 gǔ gé
sketch *n.* 草图 cǎo tú
sketch *v.t.* 给...绘草图 gěi...huì cǎo tú
sketchy *a.* 粗略的 cū lüè de
skid *v.i.* 煞着车滑行 shà zhe chē huá xíng
skid *n* 制动器 zhì dòng qì
skilful *a.* 灵巧的 líng qiǎo de
skill *n.* 技能 jì néng
skin *n.* 皮肤 pí fū
skin *v.t* 剥···的皮 bāo···de pí
skip *v.i.* 跳绳 tiào shéng
skip *n* 轻跳 qīng tiào
skipper *n.* 船长 chuán zhǎng
skirmish *n.* 小争论 xiǎo zhēng lùn
skirmish *v.i.* 争论 zhēng lùn
skirt *n.* 女裙 nǚ qún

skirt *v.t.* 用裙子覆盖 yòng qún zi fù gài
skit *n.* 滑稽短剧 huá jī duǎn jù
skull *n.* 头骨 tóu gǔ
sky *n.* 天 tiān
sky *v.t.* 打大飞球 dǎ dà fēi qiú
slab *n.* 厚片 hòu piàn
slack *a.* 宽松的 kuān sōng de
slacken *v.t.* 放慢 fàng màn
slacks *n.* 宽松的裤子 kuān sōng de kù zi
slake *v.t.* 解渴 jié kě
slam *v.t.* 砰地关上 pēng dì guān shàng
slam *n* 砰的声音 pēng de shēng yīn
slander *n.* 诋毁 dí huǐ
slander *v.t.* 讲坏话 jiǎng huài huà
slanderous *a.* 毁谤的 huǐ bàng de
slang *n.* 俚语 lǐ yǔ
slant *v.t.* 使倾斜 shǐ qīng xié
slant *n* 斜坡 xié pō
slap *n.* 一巴掌 yì bā zhang
slap *v.t.* 打 dǎ
slash *v.t.* 深深砍入 shēn shēn kǎn rù
slash *n* 深砍 shēn kǎn
slate *n.* 板石 bǎn shí
slattern *n.* 邋遢女人 lā tā nǚ rén
slatternly *a.* 不整洁的 bù zhěng jié de
slaughter *n.* 屠杀 tú shā
slaughter *v.t.* 屠宰 tú zǎi
slave *n.* 奴隶 nú lì
slave *v.i.* 拼命工作 pīn mìng gōng zuò
slavery *n.* 奴隶身分 nú lì shēn fēn
slavish *a.* 盲从的 máng cóng de
slay *v.t.* 杀死 shā sǐ
sleek *a.* 光滑的 guāng huá de
sleep *v.i.* 睡 shuì
sleep *n.* 睡眠 shuì mián
sleeper *n.* 睡眠者 shuì mián zhě

sleepy *a.* 想睡的 xiǎng shuì de

sleeve *n* 袖子 xiù zi

sleight *n.* 技巧 jì qiǎo

slender *a.* 苗条的 miáo tiao de

slice *n.* 一片 yí piàn

slice *v.t.* 切下 qiē xià

slick *a* 光滑的 guāng huá de

slide *v.i.* 滑 huá

slide *n* 滑动 huá dòng

slight *a.* 轻微的 qīng wēi de

slight *n.* 轻蔑 qīng miè

slight *v.t.* 轻视 qīng shì

slim *a.* 苗条的 miáo tiao de

slim *v.i.* 减肥 jiǎn féi

slime *n.* 黏土 nián tǔ

slimy *a.* 黏糊糊的 nián hu hú de

sling *n.* 投石器 tóu shí qì

slip *v.i.* 跌跤 diē jiāo

slip *n.* 滑动 huá dòng

slipper *n.* 拖鞋 tuō xié

slippery *a.* 滑 huá

slipshod *a.* 不齐整的 bù qí zhěng de

slit *n.* 裂缝 liè fèng

slit *v.t.* 切开 qiē kāi

slogan *n.* 口号 kǒu hào

slope *n.* 斜坡 xié pō

slope *v.i.* 倾斜 qīng xié

sloth *n.* 懒惰 lǎn duò

slothful *n.* 懒惰的 lǎn duò de

slough *n.* 蜕下的皮 tuì xià de pí

slough *n.* 泥沼 ní zhǎo

slough *v.t.* 使陷入泥沼 shǐ xiàn rù ní zhǎo

slovenly *a.* 邋遢的 lā tā de

slow *a* 慢 màn

slow *v.i.* 放慢 fàng màn

slowly *adv.* 慢慢 màn màn

slowness *n.* 慢度 màn dù

sluggard *n.* 懒人 lǎn rén

sluggish *a.* 偷懒的 tōu lǎn de

sluice *n.* 水闸 shuǐ zhá

slum *n.* 贫民窟 pín mín kū

slumber *v.i.* 睡眠 shuì mián

slumber *n.* 微睡 wēi shuì

slump *n.* 陷入 xiàn rù

slump *v.i.* 掉下 diào xià

slur *n.* 污点 wū diǎn

slush *n.* 雪水 xuě shuǐ

slushy *a.* 泥泞的 ní nìng de

slut *n.* 放荡的女人 fàng dàng de nǚ rén

sly *a.* 狡猾的 jiǎo huá de

smack *n.* 海洛因 hǎi luò yīn

smack *v.i.* 有味 yǒu wèi

smack *n* 渔船 yú chuán

smack *n.* 味 wèi

smack *v.t.* 咂嘴 zā zuǐ

small *a.* 细小的 xì xiǎo de

small *n* 腰部 yāo bù

smallness *n.* 小 xiǎo

smallpox *n.* 天花 tiān huā

smart *a.* 聪明的 cōng míng de

smart *v.i* 刺痛 cì tòng

smart *a.* 灵敏的 líng mǐn de

smash *v.t.* 打碎 dǎ suì

smash *n* 破碎 pò suì

smear *v.t.* 搽上 chá shàng

smear *n.* 油迹 yóu jì

smell *n.* 气味 qì wèi

smell *v.t.* 闻 wén

smelt *v.t.* 熔炼 róng liàn

smile *n.* 微笑 wēi xiào

smile *v.i.* 微笑 wēi xiào

smith *n.* 铁匠 tiě jiang

smock *n.* 罩衫 zhào shān

smog *n.* 烟雾 yān wù

smoke *n.* 烟尘 yān chén

smoke *v.i.* 烟 yān

smoky *a.* 冒烟的 mào yān de

smooth *a.* 滑溜的 huá liū de

smooth *v.t.* 烫平 tàng píng

smother *v.t.* 使透不过气来 shǐ tòu bú guò qì lái

smoulder *v.i.* 慢燃 màn rán

smug *a.* 整洁的 zhěng jié de

smuggle *v.t.* 走私 zǒu sī

smuggler *n.* 走私者 zǒu sī zhě

snack *n.* 快餐 kuài cān

snag *n.* 残干 cán gān

snail *n.* 蜗牛 wō niú

snake *n.* 蛇 shé

snake *v.i.* 弯曲的 wān qū de

snap *v.t.* 猛地咬住 měng de yǎo zhù

snap *n* 猛咬 měng yǎo

snap *a* 突然的 tū rán de

snare *n.* 陷阱 xiàn jǐng

snare *v.t.* 安圈套 ān quān tào

snarl *n.* 噪叫 háo jiào

snarl *v.i.* 噪叫 háo jiào

snatch *v.t.* 抢 qiǎng

snatch *n.* 抢夺 qiǎng duó

sneak *v.i.* 偷偷逃走 tōu tōu táo zǒu

sneak *n* 鬼鬼祟祟的人 guǐ guǐ suì suì de rén

sneer *v.i* 嘲笑 cháo xiào

sneer *n* 嘲笑 cháo xiào

sneeze *v.i.* 打喷嚏 dǎ pēn tì

sneeze *n* 打喷嚏 dǎ pēn tì

sniff *v.i.* 嗅 xiù

sniff *n* 闻 wén

snob *n.* 假绅士 jiǎ shēn shì

snobbery *n.* 势利 shì lì

snobbish *v* 势利的 shì lì de

snore *v.i.* 打呼噜 dǎ hū lū

snore *n* 鼾声 hān shēng

snort *v.i.* 喷响鼻子 pēn xiǎng bí zi

snort *n.* 鼻息 bí xī

snout *n.* 猪鼻子 zhū bí zi

snow *n.* 雪 xuě

snow *v.i.* 下雪 xià xuě

snowy *a.* 多雪的 duō xuě de

snub *v.t.* 故意冷落 gù yì lěng luò

snub *n.* 故意怠慢 gù yì dài màn

snuff *n.* 烛花 zhú huā

snug *a.* 舒适的 shū shì de

so *adv.* 如此 rú cǐ

so *conj.* 所以 suó yǐ

soak *v.t.* 浸 jìn

soak *n.* 浸 jìn

soap *n.* 肥皂 féi zào

soap *v.t.* 以肥皂洗 yǐ féi zào xǐ

soapy *a.* 肥皂的 féi zào de

soar *v.i.* 高飞 gāo fēi

sob *v.i.* 啜泣 chuò qì

sob *n* 畜牲 chù shēng

sober *a.* 清醒的 qīng xǐng de

sobriety *n.* 节酒 jié jiǔ

sociability *n.* 爱交际 ài jiāo jì

sociable *a.* 爱交际的 ài jiāo jì de

social *n.* 社会的 shè huì de

socialism *n* 社会主义 shè huì zhǔ yì

socialist *n* 社会主义者 shè huì zhǔ yì zhě

society *n.* 社会 shè huì

sociology *n.* 社会学 shè huì xué

sock *n.* 短袜 duǎn wà

socket *n.* 孔 kǒng

sod *n.* 草皮 cǎo pí

sodomite *n.* 鸡奸者 jī jiān zhě

sodomy *n.* 鸡奸 jī jiān

sofa *n.* 沙发 shā fā

soft *n.* 柔软 róu ruǎn

soften *v.t.* 使软化 shǐ ruǎn huà

soil *n.* 泥土 ní tǔ

soil *v.t.* 弄脏 nòng zāng

sojourn *v.i.* 逗留 dòu liú

sojourn *n* 逗留 dòu liú

solace *v.t.* 安慰 ān wèi

solace *n.* 安慰 ān wèi

solar *a.* 太阳的 tài yáng de

solder *n.* 焊药 hàn yào

solder *v.t.* 焊接 hàn jiē

soldier *n.* 士兵 shì bīng

soldier *v.i.* 当兵 dāng bīng

sole *n.* 鞋底 xié dǐ

sole *v.t* 装鞋底 zhuāng xié dǐ

sole *a* 唯一的 wéi yī de

solemn *a.* 严肃的 yán sù de

solemnity *n.* 严肃 yán sù

solemnize *v.t.* 举行典礼 jǔ xíng de diǎn lǐ

solicit *v.t.* 恳求 kěn qiú

solicitation *n.* 恳请 kén qǐng

solicitor *n.* 初级律师 chū jí lù shī

solicitous *a.* 热切要求 rè qiè yāo qiú

solicitude *n.* 挂念 guà niàn

solid *a.* 固体的 gù tǐ de

solid *n* 固体 gù tǐ

solidarity *n.* 团结一致 tuán jié yí zhì

soliloquy *n.* 独白 dú bái

solitary *a.* 独个儿的 dú gè ér de

solitude *n.* 孤独 gū dú

solo *n* 独唱 dú chàng

solo *a.* 单独的 dān dú de

solo *adv.* 独 dú

soloist *n.* 独唱者 dú chàng zhě

solubility *n.* 溶解度 róng jiě dù

soluble *a.* 可溶的 kě róng de

solution *n.* 解决 jiě jué

solve *v.t.* 解释 jiě shì

solvency *n.* 偿付能力 cháng fù néng lì

solvent *a.* 有溶解力的 yǒu róng jiě lì de

solvent *n* 溶剂 róng jì

sombre *a.* 昏暗的 hūn àn de

some *adv.* 几分 jǐ fēn

some *pron.* 有些人 yǒu xiē rén

somebody *pron.* 有人 yǒu rén

somebody *n.* 有相当身分的人 yǒu xiāng dāng shēn fēn de rén

somehow *adv.* 设法 shè fǎ

someone *pron.* 有人 yǒu rén

somersault *n.* 筋斗 jīn dòu

somersault *v.i.* 翻筋斗 fān jīn dòu

something *pron.* 某物 mǒu wù

something *adv.* 有点 yóu diǎn

sometime *adv.* 改天 gǎi tiān

sometimes *adv.* 有时 yǒu shí

somewhat *adv.* 一点儿 yì dián ér

somewhere *adv.* 某处 mǒu chù

somnambulism *n.* 梦游症 mèng yóu zhèng

somnambulist *n.* 梦游者 mèng yóu zhě

somnolence *n.* 思睡 sī shuì

somnolent *a.* 瞌睡的 kē shuì de

son *n.* 儿子 ér zi

song *n.* 歌 gē

songster *n.* 歌手 gē shǒu

sonic *a.* 声音的 shēng yīn de

sonnet *n.* 十四行诗 shí sì háng shī

sonority *n.* 洪亮 hóng liàng

soon *adv.* 立刻 lì kè

soot *n.* 煤烟弄脏 méi yān nòng zāng

soot *v.t.* 煤烟弄脏 méi yān nòng zāng

soothe *v.t.* 安慰 ān wèi

sophism *n.* 诡辩 guǐ biàn

sophist *n.* 智者 zhì zhě

sophisticate *v.t.* 用诡辩欺骗 yòng guǐ biàn qī piàn

sophisticated *a.* 非自然状态的 fēi zì rán zhuàng tài de

sophistication *n.* 玩弄诡辩 wán nòng guǐ biàn

sorcerer *n.* 术士 shù shì

sorcery *n.* 巫术 wū shù

sordid *a.* 卑鄙的 bēi bǐ de

sore *a.* 痛的 tòng de

sore *n* 痛处 tòng chù

sorrow *n.* 悲哀 bēi āi

sorrow *v.i.* 悲痛 bēi tòng

sorry *a.* 对不住 duì bú zhù

sort *n.* 种类 zhǒng lèi

sort *v.t* 整理 zhéng lǐ

soul *n.* 心灵 xīn líng

sound *a.* 合理的 hé lǐ de

sound *v.i.* 响 xiǎng

sound *n* 声音的 shēng yīn de

soup *n.* 汤 tāng

sour *a.* 酸的 suān de

sour *v.t.* 弄酸 nòng suān

source *n.* 来源 lái yuán

south *n.* 南 nán

south *a.* 南方的 nán fāng de

south *adv* 向南方 xiàng nán fāng

southerly *a.* 南 nán

southern *a.* 南方的 nán fāng de

souvenir *n.* 回忆 huí yì

sovereign *n.* 君主 jūn zhǔ

sovereign *a* 独立自主的 dú lì zì zhǔ de

sovereignty *n.* 主权 zhǔ quán

sow *v.t.* 种 zhǒng

sow *n.* 母猪 mǔ zhū

space *n.* 空间 kōng jiān

space *v.t.* 留间隔 liú jiàn gé

spacious *a.* 宽敞的 kuān chǎng de

spade *n.* 铲 chǎn

spade *v.t.* 拿铲子铲 ná chǎn zi chǎn

span *n.* 一对共轭牛 yí duì gòng è niú

span *v.t.* 观测 guān cè

Spaniard *n.* 西班牙人 xī bān yá rén

spaniel *n.* 长毛垂耳狗 zhǎng máo chuí ěr gǒu

Spanish *a.* 西班牙的 xī bān yá de

Spanish *n.* 西班牙人 xī bān yá rén

spanner *n.* 用指距测量的人 yòng zhǐ jù cè liáng de rén

spare *v.t.* 抽出 chōu chū

spare *a* 多余的 duō yú de

spare *n.* 节省 jié shěng

spark *n.* 愉快的年轻人 yú kuài de nián qīng rén

spark *v.i.* 讨好女人 táo hǎo nǚ rén

spark *n.* 火花 huǒ huā

sparkle *v.i.* 闪亮 shǎn liàng

sparkle *n.* 闪光 shǎn guāng

sparrow *n.* 麻雀 má què

sparse *a.* 稀疏的 xī shū de

spasm *n.* 抽搐 chōu chù

spasmodic *a.* 痉挛的 jìng luán de

spate *n.* 洪水 hóng shuǐ

spatial *a.* 空间的 kōng jiān de

spawn *n.* 卵 luǎn

spawn *v.i.* 产卵 chǎn luǎn

speak *v.i.* 讲 jiǎng

speaker *n.* 喇叭 lǎ ba

spear *n.* 矛 máo

spear *v.t.* 用标枪戳 yòng biāo qiāng chuō

spearhead *n.* 先锋 xiān fēng

spearhead *v.t.* 带头 dài tóu

special *a.* 特别的 tè bié de

specialist *n.* 专家 zhuān jiā

speciality *n.* 专长 zhuān cháng

specialization *n.* 专门化 zhuān mén huà

specialize *v.i.* 专攻 zhuān gōng

species *n.* 种类 zhǒng lèi

specific *a.* 特定的 tè dìng de

specification *n.* 规范 guī fàn

specify *v.t.* 详细说明 xiáng xì shuō míng

specimen *n.* 样本 yàng běn

speck *n.* 斑点 bān diǎn

spectacle *n.* 观览物 guān lǎn wù

spectacular *a.* 壮观 zhuàng guān

spectator *n.* 观众 guān zhòng

spectre *n.* 幽灵 yōu líng

speculate *v.i.* 推测 tuī cè

speculation *n.* 推测 tuī cè

speech *n.* 言语 yán yǔ

speed *n.* 速度 sù dù

speed *v.i.* 迅速前进 xùn sù qián jìn

speedily *adv.* 快 kuài

speedy *a.* 快的 kuài de

spell *n.* 符咒 fú zhòu

spell *v.t.* 拼写 pīn xiě

spell *n* 魅力 mèi lì

spend *v.t.* 花费 huā fèi

spendthrift *n.* 乱花钱的人 luàn huā qián de rén

sperm *n.* 精子 jīng zǐ

sphere *n.* 球 qiú

spherical *a.* 球的 qiú de

spice *n.* 香料 xiāng liào

spice *v.t.* 给...加香料 gěi... jiā xiāng liào

spicy *a.* 辛辣的 xīn là de

spider *n.* 蜘蛛 zhī zhū

spike *n.* 长钉 cháng dìng

spike *v.t.* 打上桩子 dǎ shàng zhuāng zi

spill *v.i.* 泻出 xiè chū

spill *n* 溢出 yì chū

spin *v.i.* 纺纱工人 fǎng shā gōng rén

spin *n.* 自转 zì zhuàn

spinach *n.* 菠菜 bō cài

spinal *a.* 针的 zhēn de

spindle *n.* 锭子 dìng zǐ

spine *n.* 脊骨 jǐ gǔ

spinner *n.* 纺纱工人 fǎng shā gōng rén

spinster *n.* 老处女 lǎo chú nǚ

spiral *n.* 螺旋形物 luó xuán xíng wù

spiral *a.* 螺旋形的 luó xuán xíng de

spirit *n.* 精神 jīng shen

spirited *a.* 精神饱满的 jīng shen báo mǎn de

spiritual *a.* 心灵的 xīn líng de

spiritualism *n.* 招魂术 zhāo hún shù

spiritualist *n.* 迷信招魂者 mí xìn zhāo hún zhě

spirituality *n.* 精神性 jīng shen xìng

spit *v.i.* 吐 tǔ

spit *n* 唾液 tuò yè

spite *n.* 怨恨 yuàn hèn

spittle *n* 唾沫 tuò mo

spittoon *n.* 痰盂 tán yú

splash *v.i.* 溅泼 jiàn pō

splash *n* 溅 jiàn

spleen *n.* 脾 pí

splendid *a.* 发亮的 fā liàng de

splendour *n.* 光辉 guāng huī

splinter *n.* 碎片 suì piàn

splinter *v.t.* 劈成碎片 pī chéng suì piàn

split *v.i.* 分开 fēn kāi

split *n* 劈开 pī kāi

spoil *v.t.* 损坏 sǔn huài

spoil *n* 抢劫 qiǎng jié

spoke *n.* 辐条 fú tiáo

spokesman *n.* 发言人 fā yán rén

sponge *n.* 海绵 hǎi mián

sponge *v.t.* 用海绵擦 yòng hǎi mián cā

sponsor *n.* 赞助者 zàn zhù zhě

sponsor *v.t.* 赞助 zàn zhù

spontaneity *n.* 自生 zì shēng

spontaneous *a.* 自发的 zì fā de

spoon *n.* 匙 chí

spoon *v.t.* 以匙舀起 yǐ chí yǎo qǐ

spoonful *n.* 调羹 tiáo gēng

sporadic *a.* 分散的 fēn sàn de

sport *n.* 运动 yùn dòng

sport *v.i.* 运动 yùn dòng

sportive *a.* 运动的 yùn dòng de

sportsman *n.* 运动员 yùn dòng yuán

spot *n.* 斑点 bān diǎn

spot *v.t.* 弄上斑点 nòng shàng bān diǎn

spotless *a.* 纯洁的 chún jié de

spousal *n.* 婚礼 hūn lǐ

spouse *n.* 配偶 pèi ǒu

spout *n.* 喷管 pēn guǎn

spout *v.i.* 喷出 pēn chū

sprain *n.* 扭伤 niǔ shāng

sprain *v.t.* 扭 niǔ

spray *v.t.* 喷 pēn

spray *n* 水花 shuǐ huā

spray *v.t.* 喷 pēn

spread *v.i.* 传开 chuán kāi

spread *n.* 传播 chuán bō

spree *n.* 欢闹 huān nào

sprig *n.* 小枝 xiǎo zhī

sprightly *a.* 活泼的 huó po de

spring *v.i.* 跳 tiào

spring *n* 春天 chūn tiān

sprinkle *v.t.* 洒 sǎ

sprint *v.i.* 全速奔跑 quán sù bēn pǎo

sprint *n* 短距离赛跑 duǎn jù lí sài pǎo

sprout *v.i.* 发芽 fā yá

sprout *n* 幼芽 yòu yá

spur *n.* 踢马刺 tī mǎ cì

spur *v.t.* 鞭策 biān cè

spurious *a.* 伪造的 wěi zào de

spurn *v.t.* 践踏 jiàn tà

spurt *v.i.* 喷出 pēn chū

spurt *n* 突然喷出 tū rán pēn chū

sputnik *n.* 人造卫星 rén zào wèi xīng

sputum *n.* 痰 tán

spy *n.* 间谍 jiàn dié

spy *v.i.* 侦察 zhēn chá

squad *n.* 小队 xiǎo duì

squadron *n.* 骑兵中队 qí bīng zhōng duì

squalid *a.* 邋遢的 lā tā de

squalor *n.* 邋遢 lā tā

squander *v.t.* 挥霍 huī huò

square *n.* 正方形 zhèng fāng xíng

square *a* 正方形的 zhèng fāng xíng de

square *v.t.* 使方正 shǐ fāng zhèng

squash *v.t.* 压扁 yā biǎn

squash *n* 扁片 biǎn piàn

squat *v.i.* 蹲 dūn

squeak *v.i.* 叽叽的叫 jī jī de jiào

squeak *n* 叽叽声 jī jī shēng

squeeze *v.t.* 挤 jǐ

squint *v.i.* 斜着眼看 xié zhuó yǎn kàn

squint *n* 斜视 xié shì

squire *n.* 乡绅 xiāng shēn

squirrel *n.* 松鼠 sōng shǔ

stab *v.t.* 刺 cì

stab *n.* 刺 cì

stability *n.* 稳定性 wěn dìng xìng

stabilization *n.* 稳定 wěn dìng

stabilize *v.t.* 使稳定 shǐ wěn dìng

stable *a.* 稳定的 wěn dìng de

stable *n* 马厩 mǎ jiù

stable *v.t.* 关进马厩里 guān jìn mǎ jiù lǐ

stadium *n.* 体育场 tǐ yù chǎng

staff *n.* 工作人员 gōng zuò rén yuán

staff *n.* 职员 zhí yuán

stag *n.* 牡鹿 mǔ lù

stage *n.* 舞台 wǔ tái

stage *v.t.* 上演 shàng yǎn

stagger *v.i.* 摇摇摆摆 yáo yáo bǎi bǎi

stagger *n.* 摇晃 yáo huàng

stagnant *a.* 停滞的 tíng zhì de

stagnate *v.i.* 停滞不流 tíng zhì bù liú

stagnation *n.* 停滞 tíng zhì

staid *a.* 不动的 bú dòng de

stain *n.* 污点 wū diǎn

stain *v.t.* 弄脏 nòng zāng

stainless *a.* 无瑕疵的 wú xiá cī de

stair *n.* 楼梯 lóu tī

stake *n* 支柱 zhī zhù

stake *v.t.* 用桩撑持 yòng zhuāng chēng chí

stale *a.* 不新鲜的 bù xīn xiān de

stale *v.t.* 使陈旧 shǐ chén jiù

stalemate *n.* 僵局 jiāng jú

stalk *n.* 梗 gěng

stalk *v.i.* 追踪 zhuī zōng

stalk *n* 柄 bǐng

stall *n.* 售货摊 shòu huò tān

stall *v.t.* 把...关进马房 bǎ... guān jìn mǎ fáng

stallion *n.* 种马 zhǒng mǎ

stalwart *a.* 绝对忠实的 jué duì zhōng shí de

stalwart *n* 忠实的成员 zhōng shí de chéng yuán

stamina n. 毅力 yì lì
stammer v.i. 口吃 kǒu chī
stammer n 口吃 kǒu chī
stamp n. 邮票 yóu piào
stamp v.i. 在…上 zài…
shàng
stampede n. 惊跑 jīng pǎo
stampede v.i 使惊逃 shǐ jīng
táo
stand v.i. 站立 zhàn lì
stand n. 货摊 huò tān
standard n. 标准 biāo zhǔn
standard a 普通的 pǔ tōng
de
standardization n. 标准化
biāo zhǔn huà
standardize v.t. 使统一 shǐ
tǒng yī
standing n. 站立 zhàn lì
standpoint n. 立场 lì chǎng
standstill n. 停止 tíng zhǐ
stanza n. 节 jié
staple n. 钉书钉 dìng shū
dìng
staple a 主要的 zhǔ yào de
star n. 星星 xīng xing
star v.t. 使演主角 shǐ yǎn
zhǔ jué
starch n. 淀粉 diàn fěn
starch v.t. 浆硬 jiāng yìng
stare v.i. 瞪眼看 dèng yǎn
kàn
stare n. 凝视 níng shì
stark a. 严格的 yán gé de
stark adv. 完全地 wán quán
dì
starry a. 多星的 duō xīng de
start v.t. 开始 kāi shǐ
start n 开始 kāi shǐ
startle v.t. 吓一跳 xià yí tiào
starvation n. 饥饿 jī è
starve v.i. 饥饿 jī è
state n. 状况 zhuàng kuàng
state v.t 讲 jiǎng
stateliness n. 庄严 zhuāng
yán
stately a. 庄严的 zhuāng
yán de

statement n. 银行报告单 yín
háng bào gào dān
statesman n. 政治家 zhèng
zhì jiā
static n. 静电干扰 jìng diàn
gān rǎo
statics n. 静力学 jìng lì xué
station n. 车站 chē zhàn
station v.t. 驻扎 zhù zhā
stationary a. 不动的 bú dòng
de
stationer n. 文具商 wén jù
shāng
stationery n. 文具 wén jù
statistical a. 统计的 tǒng jì
de
statistician n. 统计学家 tǒng
jì xué jiā
statistics n. 统计学家 tǒng
jì xué jiā
statue n. 雕像 diāo xiàng
stature n. 身长 shēn cháng
status n. 地位 dì wèi
statute n. 法令 fǎ lìng
statutory a. 法定的 fǎ dìng
de
staunch a. 坚定的 jiān dìng
de
stay v.i. 停留 tíng liú
stay n 逗留者 dòu liú zhě
steadfast a. 坚定的 jiān dìng
de
steadiness n. 稳固的 wěn
gù de
steady a. 稳固的 wěn gù de
steady v.t. 使稳固 shǐ wěn gù
steal v.i. 偷 tōu
stealthily adv. 暗地里 àn dì lǐ
steam n 蒸汽 zhēng qì
steam v.i. 蒸发 zhēng fā
steamer n. 蒸笼 zhēng lóng
steed n. 骏马 jùn mǎ
steel n. 钢 gāng
steep a. 险峻的 xiǎn jùn de
steep v.t. 浸透 jìn tòu
steeple n. 尖塔 jiān tǎ
steer v.t. 筹划 chóu huà
stellar a. 恒星的 héng xīng de
stem n. 茎 jìng

stem *v.i.* 堵住 dǔ zhù

stench *n.* 恶臭 è chòu

stencil *n.* 模板 mú bǎn

stencil *v.i.* 用模板刷印 yòng mú bǎn shuā yìn

stenographer *n.* 速记员 sù jì yuán

stenography *n.* 速记 sù jì

step *n.* 脚步 jiǎo bù

step *v.i.* 行 xíng

steppe *n.* 干草原 gān cǎo yuán

stereotype *n.* 陈规老套 chén guī lǎo tào

stereotype *v.t.* 用铅版印刷 yòng qiān bǎn yìn shuā

stereotyped *a.* 定型的 dìng xíng de

sterile *a.* 无菌的 wú jūn de

sterility *n.* 不孕 bú yùn

sterilization *n.* 消毒 xiāo dú

sterilize *v.t.* 消毒 xiāo dú

sterling *a.* 英国货币的 yīng guó huò bì de

sterling *n.* 英国货币 yīng guó huò bì

stern *a.* 严厉的 yán lì de

stern *n.* 尾部 wěi bù

stethoscope *n.* 听筒 tīng tǒng

stew *n.* 炖 dùn

stew *v.t.* 焖 mèn

steward *n.* 服务员 fú wù yuán

stick *n.* 棍 gùn

stick *v.t.* 钉住 dīng zhù

sticker *n.* 张粘物 zhāng zhān wù

stickler *n.* 固执己见的人 gù zhí jǐ jiàn de rén

sticky *a.* 黏的 nián de

stiff *n.* 死尸 sǐ shī

stiffen *v.t.* 使僵硬 shǐ jiāng yìng

stifle *v.t.* 镇压 zhèn yā

stigma *n.* 耻辱 chí rǔ

still *a.* 静止的 jìng zhǐ de

still *adv.* 还 hái

still *v.t.* 静止 jìng zhǐ

still *n.* 普通照片 pǔ tōng zhào piàn

stillness *n.* 静止 jìng zhǐ

stilt *n.* 高跷 gāo qiāo

stimulant *n.* 兴奋剂 xīng fèn jì

stimulate *v.t.* 激励 jī lì

stimulus *n.* 刺激 cì jī

sting *v.t.* 刺 cì

sting *n.* 叮 dīng

stingy *a.* 小气的 xiǎo qi de

stink *v.i.* 恶臭 è chòu

stink *n* 恶臭的人 è chòu de rén

stipend *n.* 定期津贴 dìng qī jīn tiē

stipulate *v.t.* 规定 guī dìng

stipulation *n.* 规定 guī dìng

stir *v.i.* 动 dòng

stirrup *n.* 马镫 mǎ dèng

stitch *n.* 针脚 zhēn jiǎo

stitch *v.t.* 缝 féng

stock *n.* 库存 kù cún

stock *v.t.* 进货 jìn huò

stock *a.* 存货的 cún huò de

stocking *n.* 长袜 cháng wà

stoic *n.* 禁欲主义者 jìn yù zhǔ yì zhě

stoke *v.t.* 给烧火 gěi shāo huǒ

stoker *n.* 司炉 sī lú

stomach *n.* 肚子 dù zi

stomach *v.t.* 消化 xiāo huà

stone *n.* 石头 shí tou

stone *v.t.* 扔石头 rēng shí tou

stony *a.* 石头的 shí tou de

stool *n.* 凳子 dèng zi

stoop *v.i.* 弯腰 wān yāo

stoop *n* 驼背 tuó bèi

stop *v.t.* 停止 tíng zhǐ

stop *n* 停车 tíng chē

stoppage *n* 罢工 bà gōng

storage *n.* 存储 cún chǔ

store *n.* 仓库 cāng kù

store *v.t.* 供应 gōng yìng

storey *n.* 层 céng

stork *n.* 鹳 guàn

storm *n.* 暴风雨 bào fēng yǔ

storm *v.i.* 冲击 chōng jī

stormy *a.* 暴风雨的 bào fēng yǔ de

story *n.* 故事 gù shi

stout *a.* 结实的 jiē shi de

stove *n.* 火炉 huǒ lú

stow *v.t.* 装进 zhuāng jìn

straggle *v.i.* 散开 sàn kāi

straggler *n.* 迷路者 mí lù zhě

straight *a.* 直挺的 zhí tǐng de

straight *adv.* 直 zhí

straighten *v.t.* 整顿 zhěng dùn

straightforward *a.* 真正的 zhēn zhèng de

straightway *adv.* 立刻 lì kè

strain *v.t.* 使紧张 shǐ jǐn zhāng

strain *n* 拉紧 lā jǐn

strait *n.* 海峡 hǎi xiá

straiten *v.t.* 把…弄窄 bǎ… nòng zhǎi

strand *v.i.* 处于困境 chǔ yú kùn jìng

strand *n* 滨 bīn

strange *a.* 古怪的 gǔ guài de

stranger *n.* 陌生人 mò shēng rén

strangle *v.t.* 勒死 lēi sǐ

strangulation *n.* 窒息 zhì xī

strap *n.* 带 dài

strap *v.t.* 用带子捆扎 yòng dài zi kǔn zā

stratagem *n.* 策略 cè lüè

strategic *a.* 战略的 zhàn lüè de

strategist *n.* 军事家 jūn shì jiā

strategy *n.* 策略 cè lüè

stratum *n.* 层 céng

straw *n.* 草帽 cǎo mào

strawberry *n.* 草莓 cǎo méi

stray *v.i.* 迷路 mí lù

stray *a* 走失了的 zǒu shi le de

stray *n* 迷路者 mí lù zhě

stream *n.* 小溪 xiǎo xī

stream *v.i.* 使流 shǐ liú

streamer *n.* 测风带 cè fēng dài

streamlet *n.* 小溪 xiǎo xī

street *n.* 街 jiē

strength *n.* 力量 lì liàng

strengthen *v.t.* 加强 jiā qiáng

strenuous *a.* 勤奋的 qín fèn de

stress *n.* 压力 yā lì

stress *v.t* 强调 qiáng diào

stretch *v.t.* 拉长 lā cháng

stretch *n* 伸 shēn

stretcher *n.* 担架 dān jià

strew *v.t.* 散播 sàn bō

strict *a.* 严格的 yán gé de

stricture *n.* 限制 xiàn zhì

stride *v.i.* 大踏步走 dà tà bù zǒu

stride *n* 大步 dà bù

strident *a.* 刺耳的 cì ěr de

strife *n.* 竞争 jìng zhēng

strike *v.t.* 罢工 bà gōng

strike *n* 打击 dǎ jī

striker *n.* 打击者 dǎ jī zhě

string *n.* 绳子 shéng zi

string *v.t.* 一串 yí chuàn

stringency *n.* 紧急 jǐn jí

stringent *a.* 严厉的 yán lì de

strip *n.* 条带 tiáo dài

strip *v.t.* 除去 chú qù

stripe *n.* 条纹 tiáo wén

stripe *v.t.* 使…成条纹状 shǐ… chéng tiáo wén zhuàng

strive *v.i.* 斗争 dòu zhēng

stroke *n.* 一抹 yì mǒ

stroke *v.t.* 勾消 gōu xiāo

stroke *n* 一击 yì jī

stroll *v.i.* 散步 sàn bù

stroll *n* 散步 sàn bù

strong *a.* 有力的 yǒu lì de

stronghold *n.* 要塞 yào sài

structural *a.* 结构上的 jié gòu shàng de

structure *n.* 结构 jié gòu

struggle *v.i.* 挣扎 zhēng zhá

struggle *n* 奋斗 fèn dòu

strumpet *n.* 妓女 jì nǚ

strut *v.i.* 肿胀 zhǒng zhàng

strut *n* 高视阔步 gāo shì kuòbù

stub n. 烟蒂 yān dì

stubble n. 谷茬 gǔ chá

stubborn a. 顽固的 wán gù de

stud n. 大头钉 dà tóu dìng

stud v.t. 加饰钉 jiā shì dìng

student n. 学生 xué sheng

studio n. 播音室 bō yīn shì

studious a. 好学的 hào xué de

study v.i. 学习 xué xí

study n. 书房 shū fáng

stuff n. 材料 cái liào

stuff v.t. 塞满 sāi mǎn

stuffy a. 闷热的 mèn rè de

stumble v.i. 摔倒 shuāi dǎo

stumble n. 绊倒 bàn dǎo

stump n. 树桩 shù zhuāng

stump v.t 绊倒 bàn dǎo

stun v.t. 打昏过去 dǎ hūn guò qù

stunt v.t. 阻碍生长 zǔ ài shēng zhǎng

stunt n 特技 tè jì

stupefy v.t. 使发呆 shǐ fā dāi

stupendous a. 了不起的 liǎo bù qǐ de

stupid a 愚蠢的 yú chǔn de

stupidity n. 愚笨 yú bèn

sturdy a. 健壮的 jiàn zhuàng de

sty n. 猪圈 zhū juàn

stye n. 麦粒肿 mài lì zhǒng

style n. 风格 fēng gé

subdue v.t. 征服 zhēng fú

subject n. 主题 zhǔ tí

subject a 受支配的 shòu zhī pèi de

subject v.t. 使服从 shǐ fú cóng

subjection n. 屈从 qū cóng

subjective a. 主观的 zhǔ guān de

subjudice n. 尚未决定 shàng wèi jué dìng

subjugate v.t. 征服 zhēng fú

subjugation n. 征服 zhēng fú

sublet v.t. 转租 zhuǎn zū

sublimate v.t. 使升华 shǐ shēng huá

sublime a. 崇高的 chóng gāo de

sublime n 崇高 chóng gāo

sublimity n. 崇高 chóng gāo

submarine n. 潜艇 qián tǐng

submarine a 海底的 hái dǐ de

submerge v.i. 潜水 qián shuǐ

submission n. 屈服 qū fú

submissive a. 顺从的 shùn cóng de

submit v.t. 使服从 shǐ fú cóng

subordinate a. 从属的 cóng shǔ de

subordinate n 部属 bù shǔ

subordinate v.t. 使从属 shǐ cóng shǔ

subordination n. 服从 fú cóng

subscribe v.t. 捐助 juān zhù

subscription n. 订阅 dìng yuè

subsequent a. 其后的 qí hòu de

subservience n. 从属性 cóng shǔ xìng

subservient a. 从属的 cóng shǔ de

subside v.i. 减退 jiǎn tuì

subsidiary a. 辅助的 fǔ zhù de

subsidize v.t. 给…补助金 gěi … bǔ zhù jīn

subsidy n. 津贴 jīn tiē

subsist v.i. 维持生活 wéi chí shēng huó

subsistence n. 生存 shēng cún

substance n. 物质 wù zhì

substantial a. 实质的 shí zhì de

substantially adv. 实体上 shí tǐ shàng

substantiate v.t. 证实 zhèng shí

substantiation n. 证实 zhèng shí

substitute n. 代替人 dài tì rén

substitute v.t. 代替 dài tì

substitution n. 代替 dài tì

subterranean a. 地下的 dì xià de

subtle a. 精细的 jīng xì de

subtlety n. 巧妙 qiǎo miào

subtract v.t. 减去 jiǎn qù

subtraction n. 减去 jiǎn qù

suburb n. 郊区 jiāo qū

suburban a. 郊区的 jiāo qū de

subversion n. 颠覆活动 diān fù huó dòng

subversive a. 破坏的 pò huài de

subvert v.t. 推翻 tuī fān

succeed v.i. 成功 chéng gōng

success n. 成就 chéng jiù

successful a. 成功的 chéng gōng de

succession n. 继承 jì chéng

successive a. 连续的 lián xù de

successor n. 继承人 jì chéng rén

succour n. 援助 yuán zhù

succour v.t. 帮助 bāng zhù

succumb v.i. 屈服 qū fú

such a. 这样的 zhè yàng de

such pron. 这样的人 zhè yàng de rén

suck v.t. 咂 zā

suck n. 吸入 xī rù

suckle v.t. 吮吸 shǔn xī

sudden n. 突然 tū rán

suddenly adv. 突然间 tū rán jiān

sue v.t. 控告 kòng gào

suffer v.t. 受苦 shòu kǔ

suffice v.i. 足够 zú gòu

sufficiency n. 充足 chōng zú

sufficient a. 足够的 zú gòu de

suffix n. 词尾 cí wěi

suffix v.t. 加后缀 jiā hòu zhuì

suffocate v.t 使窒息 shǐ zhì xī

suffocation n. 窒息 zhì xī

suffrage n. 投票权 tóu piào quán

sugar n. 糖 táng

sugar v.t. 加糖于 jiā táng yú

suggest v.t. 提议 tí yì

suggestion n. 提议 tí yì

suggestive a. 暗示...的 àn shì... de

suicidal a. 自杀性的 zì shā xìng de

suicide n. 自杀 zì shā

suit n. 一套衣服 yí tào yī fu

suit v.t. 给一套衣服 jǐ yí tào yī fu

suitability n. 适合 shì hé

suitable a. 适合的 shì hé de

suite n. 一套 yí tào

suitor n. 请愿者 qǐng yuàn zhě

sullen a. 不高兴的 bù gāo xìng de

sulphur n. 硫磺 liú huáng

sulphuric a. 硫的 liú de

sultry a. 闷热的 mèn rè de

sum n. 总数 zǒng shù

sum v.t. 总结 zǒng jié

summarily adv. 概括地 gài kuò dì

summarize v.t. 总结 zǒng jié

summary n. 总结 zǒng jié

summary a 概括的 gài kuò de

summer n. 夏天 xià tiān

summit n. 顶 dǐng

summon v.t. 传唤 chuán huàn

summons n. 传票 chuán piào

sumptuous a. 奢侈的 shē chǐ de

sun n. 太阳 tài yáng

sun v.t. 晒 shài

Sunday n. 星期日 xīng qī rì

sunder v.t. 分开 fēn kāi

sundry a. 杂多的 zá duō de

sunny a. 太阳般的 tài yáng bān de

sup v.i. 啜 zhuì

superabundance n. 过度 guò dù

superabundant *a.* 过多的 guò duō de

superb *a.* 宏伟的 hóng wěi de

superficial *a.* 肤浅的 fū qiǎn de

superficiality *n.* 表面现象 biǎo miàn xiàn xiàng

superfine *a.* 特级的 tè jí de

superfluity *n.* 奢侈品 shē chǐ pǐn

superfluous *a.* 过多的 guò duō de

superhuman *a.* 超过常人的 chāo guò cháng rén de

superintend *v.t.* 管理 guǎn lǐ

superintendence *n.* 监督 jiān dū

superintendent *n.* 监督人 jiān dū rén

superior *a.* 优秀的 yōu xiù de

superiority *n.* 优越 yōu yuè

superlative *a.* 最上的 zuì shàng de

superlative *n.* 最高级 zuì gāo jí

superman *n.* 超人 chāo rén

supernatural *a.* 超自然的 chāo zì rán de

supersede *v.t.* 代替 dài tì

supersonic *a.* 超音波的 chāo yīn bō de

superstition *n.* 迷信 mí xìn

superstitious *a.* 迷信上的 mí xìn shàng de

supertax *n.* 附加税 fù jiā shuì

supervise *v.t.* 监督 jiān dū

supervision *n.* 监督 jiān dū

supervisor *n.* 监督人 jiān dū rén

supper *n.* 宵夜 xiāo yè

supple *a.* 柔软的 róu ruǎn de

supplement *n.* 增补 zēng bǔ

supplement *v.t.* 补足 bǔ zú

supplementary *a.* 增补的 zēng bǔ de

supplier *n.* 供应者 gōng yìng zhě

supply *v.t.* 供应 gōng yìng

supply *n* 供应品 gōng yìng pǐn

support *v.t.* 支持 zhī chí

support *n.* 支持 zhī chí

suppose *v.t.* 推测 tuī cè

supposition *n.* 推测 tuī cè

suppress *v.t.* 镇压 zhèn yā

suppression *n.* 镇压 zhèn yā

supremacy *n.* 最高地位 zuì gāo dì wèi

supreme *a.* 最高的 zuì gāo de

surcharge *n.* 附加费 fù jiā fèi

surcharge *v.t.* 收取附加费 shōu qǔ fù jiā fèi

sure *a.* 肯定 kěn dìng

surely *adv.* 未必 wèi bì

surety *n.* 担保人 dān bǎo rén

surf *n.* 迎头碎浪 yíng tóu suì làng

surface *n.* 表面 biǎo miàn

surface *v.i* 浮出水面 fú chū shuǐ miàn

surfeit *n.* 过量 guò liàng

surge *n.* 波涛汹涌的大海 bō tāo xiōng yǒng de dà hǎi

surge *v.i.* 起大浪 qǐ dà làng

surgeon *n.* 外科医生 wài kē yī sheng

surgery *n.* 外科手术 wài kē shǒu shù

surmise *n.* 推测 tuī cè

surmise *v.t.* 推测 tuī cè

surmount *v.t.* 克服 kè fú

surname *n.* 姓 xing

surpass *v.t.* 超过 chāo guò

surplus *n.* 剩余 shèng yú

surprise *n.* 惊奇 jīng qí

surprise *v.t.* 使惊奇 shǐ jīng qí

surrender *v.t.* 放弃 fàng qì

surrender *n* 投降 tóu xiáng

surround *v.t.* 围住 wéi zhù

surroundings *n.* 周围的事物 zhōu wéi de shì wù

surtax *n.* 附加税 fù jiā shuì

surveillance *n.* 监视 jiān shì

survey *n.* 调查表 diào chá biǎo

survey *v.t.* 调查 diào chá

survival *n.* 生存 shēng cún

survive *v.i.* 残存 cán cún

suspect *v.t.* 怀疑 huái yí

suspect *a.* 可疑的 kě yí de

suspect *n* 嫌疑犯 xián yí fàn

suspend *v.t.* 暂时停止 zàn shí tíng zhǐ

suspense *n.* 悬挂 xuán guà

suspension *n.* 停职 tíng zhí

suspicion *n.* 嫌疑 xián yí

suspicious *a.* 可疑的 kě yí de

sustain *v.t.* 支撑 zhī chēng

sustenance *n.* 食物 shí wù

swagger *v.i.* 大摇大摆地走 dà yáo dà bǎi dì zǒu

swagger *n* 昂首阔步 áng shǒu kuò bù

swallow *v.t.* 吞 tūn

swallow *n.* 吞咽 tūn yàn

swallow *n.* 燕子 yàn zi

swamp *n.* 沼地 zhǎo dì

swamp *v.t.* 使浸在水中 shǐ jìn zài shuǐ zhōng

swan *n.* 天鹅 tiān é

swarm *n.* 大群 dà qún

swarm *v.i.* 蜂拥成群 fēng yōng chéng qún

swarthy *a.* 黑黝黝的 hēi yǒu yǒu de

sway *v.i.* 摇摆 yáo bǎi

sway *n* 摇动 yáo dòng

swear *v.t.* 发誓 fā shì

sweat *n.* 汗 hàn

sweat *v.i.* 出汗 chū hàn

sweater *n.* 毛衣 máo yī

sweep *v.i.* 扫 sǎo

sweep *n.* 打扫 dá sǎo

sweeper *n.* 清扫工人 qīng sǎo gōng rén

sweet *a.* 甜 tián

sweet *n* 糖 táng

sweeten *v.t.* 弄甜 nòng tián

sweetmeat *n.* 糖 táng

sweetness *n.* 甜味 tián wèi

swell *v.i.* 肿大 zhǒng dà

swell *n* 肿胀 zhǒng zhàng

swift *a.* 迅速的 xùn sù de

swim *v.i.* 游水 yóu shuǐ

swim *n* 游泳 yóu yǒng

swimmer *n.* 游泳者 yóu yǒng zhě

swindle *v.t.* 诈取 zhà qǔ

swindle *n.* 欺骗 qī piàn

swindler *n.* 骗取 piàn qǔ

swine *n.* 猪 zhū

swing *v.i.* 摇摆 yáo bǎi

swing *n* 秋千 qiū qiān

Swiss *n.* 瑞士人 ruì shì rén

Swiss *a* 瑞士的 ruì shì de

switch *n.* 电闸 diàn zhá

switch *v.t.* 转变 zhuǎn biàn

swoon *n.* 晕厥 yūn jué

swoon *v.i* 着迷 zháo mí

swoop *v.i.* 向下猛冲 xiàng xià měng chōng

swoop *n* 突袭 tū xí

sword *n.* 剑 jiàn

sycamore *n.* 西克莫 xī kè mò

sycophancy *n.* 谄媚 chǎn mèi

sycophant *n.* 谄媚者 chǎn mèi zhě

syllabic *a.* 音节的 yīn jié de

syllable *n.* 音节 yīn jié

syllabus *n.* 教学大纲 jiào xué dà gāng

sylph *n.* 窈窕的淑女 yáo tiǎo de shū nǚ

sylvan *a.* 森林的 sēn lín de

symbol *n.* 符号 fú hào

symbolic *a.* 象征的 xiàng zhēng de

symbolism *n.* 象征手法 xiàng zhēng shóu fǎ

symbolize *v.t.* 象征 xiàng zhēng

symmetrical *a.* 对称的 duì chèn de

symmetry *n.* 对称 duì chèn

sympathetic *a.* 同情的 tóng qíng de

sympathize *v.i.* 表示同情 biǎo shì tóng qíng

sympathy *n.* 同情心 tóng qíng xīn

symphony *n.* 交响曲 jiāo xiǎng qǔ

symposium *n.* 专题讨论会 zhuān tí tǎo lùn huì

symptom *n.* 症状 zhèng zhuàng

symptomatic *a.* 有症状的 yǒu zhèng zhuàng de

synonym *n.* 同义词 tóng yì cí

synonymous *a.* 同义的 tóng yì de

synopsis *n.* 概要 gài yào

syntax *n.* 句法 jù fǎ

synthesis *n.* 综合 zōng hé

synthetic *a.* 人造的 rén zào de

synthetic *n* 化学合成物 huà xué hé chéng wù

syringe *n.* 注射器 zhù shè qì

syringe *v.t.* 用注射器灌溉 yòng zhù shè qì guàn gài

syrup *n.* 糖浆 táng jiāng

system *n.* 系统 xì tǒng

systematic *a.* 有系统的 yǒu xì tǒng de

systematize *v.t.* 使体统化 shǐ tí tǒng huà

T

table *n.* 桌子 zhuō zi

table *v.t.* 搁置 gē zhì

tablet *n.* 药片 yào piàn

taboo *n.* 禁忌 jìn jì

taboo *a* 禁忌的 jìn jì de

taboo *v.t.* 禁止 jìn zhǐ

tabular *a.* 表格的 biǎo gé de

tabulate *v.t.* 制成表格 zhì chéng biǎo gé

tabulation *n.* 制表人 zhì biǎo rén

tabulator *n.* 制表人 zhì biǎo rén

tacit *a.* 缄默的 jiān mò de

taciturn *a.* 沉默寡言的 chén mò guǎ yán de

tackle *v.t.* 应付 yìng fù

tackle *n.* 滑车 huá chē

tact *n.* 得体 dé tǐ

tactful *a.* 机智的 jī zhì de

tactician *n.* 谋士 móu shì

tactics *n.* 策略 cè lüè

tactile *a.* 触觉的 chù jué de

tag *n.* 标记 biāo jì

tag *v.t.* 标签 biāo qiān

tail *n.* 尾巴 wěi ba

tailor *n.* 裁缝 cái feng

tailor *v.t.* 缝制 féng zhì

taint *n.* 污点 wū diǎn

taint *v.t.* 污染 wū rǎn

take *v.t* 捕捉 bǔ

tale *n.* 故事 gù shi

talent *n.* 才能 cái néng

talisman *n.* 护身符 hù shēn fú

talk *v.i.* 讲 jiǎng

talk *n* 演讲 yán jiǎng

talkative *a.* 健谈的 jiàn tán de

tall *a.* 高的 gāo de

tallow *n.* 动物油脂 dòng wù yóu zhi

tally *v.t.* 记录 jì lù

tally *v.i.* 吻合 wěn hé

tamarind *n.* 罗望子树 luó wàng zǐ shù

tame *a.* 温顺的 wēn shùn de

tame *v.t.* 驯服 xùn fú

tamper *v.i.* 损害 sǔn hài

tan *v.i.* 晒黑 shài hēi

tan *n.* 棕黄色 zōng huáng sè

tangent *n.* 切线 qiē xiàn

tangible *a.* 实在的 shí zai de

tangle *n.* 纠结 jiū jié

tangle *v.t.* 使缠结 shǐ chán jié

tank *n.* 罐 guàn

tanker *n.* 油槽车 yóu cáo chē

tanner *n.* 制革工人 zhì gé gōng rén

tannery *n.* 制革厂 zhì gé chǎng

tantalize *v.t.* 逗引 dòu yǐn

tantamount *a.* 同等的 tóng děng de

tap *n.* 水龙头 shuǐ lóng tou

tap *v.t.* 轻打 qīng dǎ

tape *n.* 录音带 lù yīn dài

tape *v.t* 录音 lù yīn

taper *v.i.* 渐小 jiàn xiǎo

taper *n* 带子操作工 dài zi cāo zuò gōng

tapestry *n.* 织花罩毯 zhī huā zhào tǎn

tar *n.* 沥青 lì qīng

tar *v.t.* 用沥青铺 yòng lì qīng pū

target *n.* 目标 mù biāo

tariff *n.* 收费表 shōu fèi biǎo

tarnish *v.t.* 使丧失光泽 shǐ sàng shī guāng zé

task *n.* 任务 rèn wù

task *v.t.* 派给工作 pài gěi gōng zuò

taste *n.* 尝味 cháng wèi

taste *v.t.* 尝 cháng

tasteful *a.* 雅致大方的 yǎ zhì dà fāng de

tasty *a.* 好吃的 hǎo chī de

tatter *n.* 碎布 suì bù

tatter *v.t* 撕碎 sī suì

tattoo *n.* 纹身 wén shēn

tattoo *v.i.* 纹身 wén shēn

taunt *v.t.* 辱骂 rǔ mà

taunt *n* 嘲弄 cháo nòng

tavern *n.* 酒馆 jiǔ guǎn

tax *n.* 税 shuì

tax *v.t.* 征税 zhēng shuì

taxable *a.* 应纳税的 yīng nà shuì de

taxation *n.* 征税 zhēng shuì

taxi *n.* 出租汽车 chū zū qì chē

taxi *v.i.* 滑行 huá xíng

tea *n* 茶 chá

teach *v.t.* 教 jiāo

teacher *n.* 老师 lǎo shī

teak *n.* 柚木 yóu mù

team *n.* 队 duì

tear *v.t.* 撕开 sī kāi

tear *n.* 裂缝 liè fèng

tear *n.* 泪 lèi

tearful *a.* 流泪的 liú lèi de

tease *v.t.* 戏弄 xì nòng

teat *n.* 乳头 rǔ tóu

technical *a.* 技术性的 jì shù xìng de

technicality *n.* 技术性 jì shù xìng

technician *n.* 技师 jì shī

technique *n.* 技巧 jì qiǎo

technological *a.* 技术学的 jì shù xué de

technologist *n.* 工程技术专家 gōng chéng jì shù zhuān jiā

technology *n.* 技术 jì shù

tedious *a.* 冗长乏味的 rǒng cháng fá wèi de

tedium *n.* 冗长乏味 rǒng cháng fá wèi

teem *v.i.* 充满 chōng mǎn

teenager *n.* 青少年 qīng shào nián

teens *n. pl.* 十多岁 shí duō suì

teethe *v.i.* 生牙 shēng yá

teetotal *a.* 滴酒不沾 dī jiǔ bù zhān

teetotaller *n.* 绝对戒酒主义 jué duì jiè jiǔ zhǔ yì

telecast *n.* 电视广播 diàn shì guǎng bō

telecast *v.t.* 用电视广播 yòng diàn shì guǎng bō

telecommunications *n.* 电信技术 diàn xìn jì shù

telegram *n.* 电报 diàn bào

telegraph *n.* 电报 diàn bào

telegraph *v.t.* 打电报 dǎ diàn bào

telegraphic *a.* 电报的 diàn bào de

telegraphist *n.* 电信技术 diàn xìn jì shù

telegraphy *n.* 电报学 diàn bào xué

telepathic *a.* 心灵感应的 xīn líng gǎn yìng de

telepathist *n.* 心灵感应者 xīn líng gǎn yìng zhě

telepathy *n.* 心灵感应 xīn líng gǎn yìng

telephone *n.* 电话 diàn huà

telephone *v.t.* 打电话给某人 dǎ diàn huà gěi mǒu rén

telescope *n.* 望远镜 wàng yuǎn jìng

telescopic *a.* 远视的 yuǎn shì de

televise *v.t.* 电视播送 diàn shì bō sòng

television *n.* 电视 diàn shì

tell *v.t.* 讲 jiǎng

teller *n.* 出纳员 chū nà yuán

temper *n.* 脾气 pí qi

temper *v.t.* 使缓和 shǐ huǎn hé

temperament *n.* 气质 qì zhì

temperamental *a.* 性情暴躁 xìng qíng bào zào

temperance *n.* 戒酒 jiè jiǔ

temperate *a.* 温和的 wēn hé de

temperature *n.* 温度 wēn dù

tempest *n.* 暴风雨 bào fēng yǔ

tempestuous *a.* 骚动的 sāo dòng de

temple *n.* 太阳穴 tài yáng xué

temple *n* 庙 miào

temporal *a.* 世俗的 shì sú de

temporary *a.* 暂时的 zàn shí de

tempt *v.t.* 诱惑 yòu huò

temptation *n.* 诱惑 yòu huò

tempter *n.* 诱惑者 yòu huò zhě

ten *n.* 十 shí

tenable *a.* 站得住的 zhàn dé zhù de

tenacious *a.* 固持的 gù chí de

tenacity *n.* 固执 gù zhí

tenancy *n.* 租期 zū qī

tenant *n.* 租户 zū hù

tend *v.i.* 招待 zhāo dài

tendency *n.* 倾向 qīng xiàng

tender *n* 供应船 gōng yìng chuán

tender *v.t.* 提出 tí chū

tender *n* 投标 tóu biāo

tender *a* 温柔的 wēn róu de

tenet *n.* 原则 yuán zé

tennis *n.* 网球 wǎng qiú

tense *n.* 时态 shí tài

tense *a.* 使紧张 shǐ jǐn zhāng

tension *n.* 拉紧 lā jǐn

tent *n.* 帐篷 zhàng peng

tentative *a.* 不确定的 bú què dìng de

tenure *n.* 占有 zhàn yǒu

term *n.* 学期 xué qī

term *v.t.* 把...叫做 bǎ... jiào zuò

terminable *a.* 可终止的 kě zhōng zhǐ de

terminal *a.* 末期的 mò qī de

terminal *n* 机场 jī chǎng

terminate *v.t.* 使终止 shǐ zhōng zhǐ

termination *n.* 终止 zhōng zhǐ

terminological *a.* 术语的 shù yǔ de

terminology *n.* 术语 shù yǔ

terminus *n.* 终点站 zhōng diǎn zhàn

terrace *n.* 排屋 pái wū

terrible *a.* 可怕 kě pà

terrier *n.* 灵敏的小猎狗 líng mǐn de xiǎo liè gǒu

terrific *a.* 极好的 jí hǎo de

terrify *v.t.* 吓唬 xià hu

territorial *a.* 土地的 tǔ dì de

territory *n.* 领土 líng tǔ

terror *n.* 恐怖 kǒng bù

terrorism *n.* 恐怖主义 kǒng bù zhǔ yì

terrorist *n.* 恐怖分子 kǒng bù fēn zǐ

terrorize *v.t.* 恐怖 kǒng bù

terse *a.* 简短的 jián duǎn de

test *v.t.* 试验 shì yàn

test *n* 测验 cè yàn

testament *n.* 契约 qì yuē

testicle *n.* 睾丸 gāo wán
testify *v.i.* 证实 zhèng shí
testimonial *n.* 推荐书 tuī jiàn shū
testimony *n.* 证据 zhèng jù
tete-a-tete *n.* 面对面 miàn duì miàn
tether *n.* 系绳 xì shéng
tether *v.t.* 拴系 shuān xì
text *n.* 正文 zhèng wén
textile *a.* 纺织品的 fǎng zhī pǐn de
textile *n* 纺织品 fǎng zhī pǐn
textual *n.* 原文的 yuán wén de
texture *n.* 质地 zhì dì
thank *v.t.* 感谢 gǎn xiè
thanks *n.* 多谢 duō xiè
thankful *a.* 感谢的 gǎn xiè de
thankless *a.* 不讨好的 bù táo hǎo de
that *a.* 那个 nà gè
that *dem. pron.* 那个 nà gè
that *rel. pron.* 那个 nà gè
that *adv.* 那样 nà yàng
that *conj.* 以致 yǐ zhì
thatch *n.* 草屋顶 cǎo wū dǐng
thatch *v.t.* 盖屋顶 gài wū dǐng
thaw *v.i* 解冻 jiě dòng
thaw *n* 融雪 róng xuě
theatre *n.* 剧院 jù yuàn
theatrical *a.* 戏剧的 xì jù de
theft *n.* 偷窃 tōu qiè
their *a.* 他们的东西 tā men de dōng xi
theirs *pron.* 他们的东西 tā men de dōng xi
theism *n.* 有神论 yǒu shén lùn
theist *n.* 有神论者 yǒu shén lùn zhě
them *pron.* 他们 tā men
thematic *a.* 主题的 zhǔ tí de
theme *n.* 主题 zhǔ tí
then *adv.* 然后 rán hòu
then *a* 当时 dāng shí

thence *adv.* 因此 yīn cǐ
theocracy *n.* 神权政治 shén quán zhèng zhì
theologian *n.* 神学家 shén xué jiā
theological *a.* 神学上的 shén xué shàng de
theology *n.* 神学 shén xué
theorem *n.* 定理 dìng lǐ
theoretical *a.* 理论上 lǐ lùn shàng
theorist *n.* 理论家 lǐ lùn jiā
theorize *v.i.* 理论化 lǐ lùn huà
theory *n.* 理论 lǐ lùn
therapy *n.* 疗法 liáo fǎ
there *adv.* 在那里 zài nà lǐ
thereabouts *adv.* 附近 fù jìn
thereafter *adv.* 此后 cǐ hòu
thereby *adv.* 因此 yīn cǐ
therefore *adv.* 所以 suó yǐ
thermal *a.* 温热的 wēn rè de
thermometer *n.* 体温表 tǐ wēn biǎo
thermos (flask) *n.* 热水瓶 rè shuǐ píng
thesis *n.* 论文 lùn wén
thick *a.* 厚 hòu
thick *n.* 最厚的部分 zuì hòu de bù fen
thick *adv.* 厚的 hòu de
thicken *v.i.* 使厚 shǐ hòu
thicket *n.* 灌木丛 guàn mù cóng
thief *n.* 贼 zéi
thigh *n.* 大腿骨 dà tuǐ gǔ
thimble *n.* 顶针 dǐng zhēn
thin *a.* 瘦的 shòu de
thin *v.t.* 稀疏 xī shū
thing *n.* 东西 dōng xi
think *v.t.* 想 xiǎng
thinker *n.* 思想家 sī xiǎng jiā
third *a.* 第三 dì sān
third *n.* 第三 dì sān
thirdly *adv.* 第三 dì sān
thirst *n.* 渴 kě
thirst *v.i.* 渴望 kě wàng
thirsty *a.* 口渴的 kǒu kě de
thirteen *n.* 十三 shí sān
thirteen *a* 十三 shí sān

thirteenth *a.* 第十三 dì shí
sān

thirtieth *a.* 第三十 dì sān
shí

thirtieth *n* 第三十 dì sān shí

thirty *n.* 三十的记号 sān shí
de jì hao

thirty *a* 三十 sān shí

thistle *n.* 蓟 jì

thither *adv.* 到那里 dào nà lǐ

thorn *n.* 刺 cì

thorny *a.* 多刺的 duō cì de

thorough *a* 严密的 yán mì
de

thoroughfare *n.* 大街 dà jiē

though *conj.* 虽然 suī rán

though *adv.* 不过还是 bú
guò hái shì

thought *n* 思想 sī xiǎng

thoughtful *a.* 体贴人的 tǐ
tiē rén de

thousand *n.* 一千个 yì qiān
gè

thousand *a* 千 qiān

thrall *n.* 奴隶 nú lì

thralldom *n.* 奴役 nú yì

thrash *v.t.* 反复进行 fǎn fù
jìn xíng

thread *n.* 线 xiàn

thread *v.t* 穿过 chuān guò

threadbare *a.* 破旧的 pò
jiù de

threat *n.* 威胁 wēi xié

threaten *v.t.* 恐吓 kǒng hè

three *n.* 三个人 sān gè rén

three *a* 三 sān

thresh *v.t.* 脱粒 tuō lì

thresher *n.* 打谷场 dǎ gǔ
chǎng

threshold *n.* 门口 mén kǒu

thrice *adv.* 三次 sān cì

thrift *n.* 节约的 jié yuē de

thrifty *a.* 节约的 jié yuē de

thrill *n.* 发抖 fā dǒu

thrill *v.t.* 使激动 shǐ jī dòng

thrive *v.i.* 兴旺 xīng wàng

throat *n.* 喉咙 hóu lóng

throaty *a.* 沙哑的 shā yǎ de

throb *v.i.* 抽动 chōu dòng

throb *n.* 跳动 tiào dòng

throe *n.* 剧痛 jù tòng

throne *n.* 王位 wáng wèi

throne *v.t.* 即位 jí wèi

throng *n.* 一大群人 yí dà qún
rén

throng *v.t.* 群集 qún jí

throttle *n.* 开足马力 kāi zú
mǎ lì

throttle *v.t.* 缢死 yì sǐ

through *prep.* 穿过 chuān
guò

through *adv.* 通过 tōng guò

through *a* 全程的 quán chéng
de

throughout *adv.* 全部 quán
bù

throughout *prep.* 由始至终
yóu shǐ zhì zhōng

throw *v.t.* 扔 rēng

throw *n.* 扔 rēng

thrust *v.t.* 猛推 měng tuī

thrust *n* 推荐信 tuī jiàn xìn

thud *n.* 砰的一声 pēng de yì
shēng

thud *v.i.* 砰的一声重击 pēng
de yì shēng zhòng jī

thug *n.* 凶手 xiōng shǒu

thumb *n.* 拇指 mú zhǐ

thumb *v.t.* 笨手笨脚地做 bèn
shǒu bèn jiǎo dì zuò

thump *n.* 重击 zhòng jī

thump *v.t.* 重击 zhòng jī

thunder *n.* 雷 léi

thunder *v.i.* 打雷 dǎ léi

thunderous *a.* 雷鸣似的 léi
míng shì de

Thursday *n.* 星期四 xīng qī sì

thus *adv.* 所以 suó yǐ

thwart *v.t.* 阻挠 zǔ náo

tiara *n.* 皇冠 huáng guàn

tick *n.* 嘀嗒 dī dā

tick *v.i.* 一步一步推移 yí bù yi
bù tuī yí

ticket *n.* 票 piào

tickle *v.t.* 搔触 sāo chù

ticklish *a.* 怕痒的 pà yǎng de

tidal *a.* 潮汐的 cháo xī de

tide *n.* 潮 cháo

tidings *n. pl.* 消息 xiāo xi
tidiness *n.* 整齐 zhěng qí
tidy *a.* 整齐的 zhěng qí de
tidy *v.t.* 收拾 shōu shi
tie *v.t.* 绑 bǎng
tie *n* 结扎 jié zā
tier *n.* 等级 děng jí
tiger *n.* 老虎 láo hǔ
tight *a.* 紧的 jǐn de
tighten *v.t.* 收紧 shōu jǐn
tigress *n.* 母老虎 mǔ láo hǔ
tile *n.* 瓷砖 cí zhuān
tile *v.t.* 砌瓷砖 qì cí zhuān
till *prep.* 直到…为止 zhí dào … wéi zhǐ
till *n. conj.* 直到…为止 zhí dào … wéi zhǐ
till *v.t.* 耕种 gēng zhòng
tilt *v.i.* 倾斜 qīng xié
tilt *n.* 倾斜 qīng xié
timber *n.* 木 mù
time *n.* 时间 shí jiān
time *v.t.* 测定时间 cè dìng shí jiān
timely *a.* 及时 jí shí
timid *a.* 胆小的 dǎn xiǎo de
timidity *n.* 羞怯 xiū qiè
timorous *a.* 胆小 dǎn xiǎo
tin *n.* 罐 guàn
tin *v.t.* 做成罐头食品 zuò chéng guàn tóu shí pǐn
tincture *n.* 药酒 yào jiǔ
tincture *v.t.* 染 rǎn
tinge *n.* 少许 sháo xǔ
tinge *v.t.* 较淡的色彩 jiào dàn de sè cǎi
tinker *n.* 修补匠 xiū bǔ jiàng
tinsel *n.* 金属丝 jīn shǔ sī
tint *n.* 色彩 sè cǎi
tint *v.t.* 给…着染色 gěi… zhe rǎn sè
tiny *a.* 极小的 jí xiǎo de
tip *n.* 妙法 miào fǎ
tip *v.t.* 小费 xiǎo fèi
tip *n.* 垃圾弃置场 lā jī qì zhì chǎng
tip *v.t.* 倒出 dǎo chū
tip *n.* 尖 jiān
tip *v.t.* 轻击 qīng jī

tipsy *a.* 微醉的 wēi zuì de
tirade *n.* 长篇议论 cháng piān yì lùn
tire *v.t.* 疲倦 pí juàn
tiresome *a.* 令人厌倦的 lìng rén yàn juàn de
tissue *n.* 纸巾 zhǐ jīn
Titanic *a.* 铁达尼号 tiě dá ní hào
tithe *n.* 捐税 juān shuì
title *n.* 题目 tí mù
titular *a.* 挂名的 guà míng de
toad *n.* 蟾蜍 chán chú
toast *n.* 烤面包片 kǎo miàn bāo piàn
toast *v.t.* 烘烤 hōng kǎo
tobacco *n.* 烟草 yān cǎo
today *adv.* 今天 jīn tiān
today *n.* 今天 jīn tiān
toe *n.* 脚趾 jiǎo zhǐ
toe *v.t.* 用脚趾踩 yòng jiǎo zhǐ cǎi
toffee *n.* 太妃糖 tài fēi táng
toga *n.* 宽大长袍 kuān dà cháng páo
together *adv.* 一齐 yì qí
toil *n.* 苦工 kǔ gōng
toil *v.i.* 辛苦工作 xīn kǔ gōng zuò
toilet *n.* 厕所 cè suǒ
toils *n. pl.* 圈套 quān tào
token *n.* 代币 dài bì
tolerable *a.* 可忍受的 kě rěn shòu de
tolerance *n.* 耐力 nài lì
tolerant *a.* 宽容的 kuān róng de
tolerate *v.t.* 容许 róng xǔ
toleration *n.* 宽容 kuān róng
toll *n.* 通行费 tōng xíng fèi
toll *n* 钟声 zhōng shēng
toll *v.t.* 征收 zhēng shōu
tomato *n.* 番茄 fān qié
tomb *n.* 坟墓 fén mù
tomboy *n.* 假小子 jiǎ xiǎo zi
tomcat *n.* 雄猫 xióng māo
tome *n.* 大本书 dà běn shū
tomorrow *n.* 明天 míng tiān
tomorrow *adv.* 明天 míng tiān

ton *n.* 吨 dūn

tone *n.* 语气 yǔ qì

tone *v.t.* 给...定色调 gěi... dìng sè diào

tongs *n. pl.* 钳 qián

tongue *n.* 舌 shé

tonic *a.* 滋补的 zī bǔ de

tonic *n.* 补药 bǔ yào

tonight *n.* 今晚 jīn wǎn

tonight *adv.* 今晚 jīn wǎn

tonne *n.* 吨 dūn

tonsil *n.* 扁桃体 biǎn táo tǐ

tonsure *n.* 剃发 tì fā

too *adv.* 太 tài

tool *n.* 工具 gōng jù

tooth *n.* 牙齿 yá chǐ

toothache *n.* 牙痛 yá tòng

toothsome *a.* 美味的 měi wèi de

top *n.* 顶部 dǐng bù

top *v.t.* 超越 chāo yuè

top *n.* 上面 shàng mian

topaz *n.* 黄玉 huáng yù

topic *n.* 主题 zhǔ tí

topical *a.* 论题的 lùn tí de

topographer *n.* 地志学者 dì zhì xué zhě

topographical *a.* 地形的 dì xíng de

topography *n.* 地形学 dì xíng xué

topple *v.i.* 倒塌 dǎo tā

topsy turvy *a.* 乱七八糟的 luàn qī bā zāo de

topsy turvy *adv* 颠倒地 diān dǎo dì

torch *n.* 火把 huǒ bǎ

torment *n.* 折磨者 zhé mó zhě

torment *v.t.* 折磨 zhé mó

tornado *n.* 龙卷风 lóng juǎn fēng

torpedo *n.* 鱼雷 yú léi

torpedo *v.t.* 用鱼雷袭击 yòng yú léi xí jī

torrent *n.* 奔流 bēn liú

torrential *a.* 奔流的 bēn liú de

torrid *a.* 炎热的 yán rè de

tortoise *n.* 龟 guī

tortuous *a.* 扭曲的 niǔ qǔ de

torture *n.* 苦闷 kǔ mèn

torture *v.t.* 拷问 kǎo wèn

toss *v.t.* 投掷 tóu zhì

toss *n* 掷钱币决定 zhì qián bì jué dìng

total *a.* 总的 zǒng de

total *n.* 总数 zǒng shù

total *v.t.* 共计为 gòng jì wéi

totality *n.* 全体 quán tǐ

touch *v.t.* 接触 jiē chù

touch *n* 触觉 chù jué

touchy *a.* 易怒的 yì nù de

tough *a.* 艰苦的 jiān kǔ de

toughen *v.t.* 变坚韧 biàn jiān rèn

tour *n.* 旅行 lǚ xíng

tour *v.i.* 旅行 lǚ xíng

tourism *n.* 旅游业 lǚ yóu yè

tourist *n.* 旅行者 lǚ xíng zhě

tournament *n.* 锦标赛 jǐn biāo sài

towards *prep.* 向 xiàng

towel *n.* 毛巾 máo jīn

towel *v.t.* 擦干身子 cā gān shēn zi

tower *n.* 塔 tǎ

tower *v.i.* 高耸 gāo sǒng

town *n.* 市 shì

township *a.* 镇区 zhèn qū

toy *n.* 玩具 wán jù

toy *v.i.* 玩弄 wán nòng

trace *n.* 痕迹 hén jì

trace *v.t.* 跟踪 gēn zōng

traceable *a.* 可追溯的 kě zhuī sù de

track *n.* 轨道 guǐ dào

track *v.t.* 追踪 zhuī zōng

tract *n.* 大片土地 dà piàn tǔ dì

tract *n* 小册子 xiǎo cè zǐ

traction *n.* 牵引 qiān yǐn

tractor *n.* 拖拉机 tuō lā jī

trade *n.* 贸易 mào yì

trade *v.i* 进行交易 jìn xíng jiāo yì

trader *n.* 商人 shāng rén

tradesman *n.* 商人 shāng rén

tradition *n.* 传统 chuán tǒng

traditional *a.* 传统的 chuán tǒng de

traffic *n.* 交通 jiāo tōng

traffic *v.i.* 做买卖 zuò mǎi mai

tragedian *n.* 悲剧作家 bēi jù zuò jiā

tragedy *n.* 悲剧 bēi jù

tragic *a.* 悲惨的 bēi cǎn de

trail *n.* 痕迹 hén jì

trail *v.t.* 拉 lā

trailer *n.* 拖车 tuō chē

train *n.* 火车 huǒ chē

train *v.t.* 训练 xùn liàn

trainee *n.* 实习生 shí xí shēng

training *n.* 训练 xùn liàn

trait *n.* 特征 tè zhēng

traitor *n.* 叛逆者 pàn nì zhě

tram *n.* 电车轨道 diàn chē guǐ dào

trample *v.t.* 践踏 jiàn tà

trance *n.* 昏睡状态 hūn shuì zhuàng tài

tranquil *a.* 安静的 ān jìng de

tranquility *n.* 宁静 níng jìng

tranquillize *v.t.* (使)平静 (shǐ) píng jìng

transact *v.t.* 办理 bàn lǐ

transaction *n.* 交易 jiāo yì

transcend *v.t.* 超越 chāo yuè

transcendent *a.* 卓越的 zhuó yuè de

transcribe *v.t.* 抄写 chāo xiě

transcription *n.* 抄写 chāo xiě

transfer *n.* 迁移 qiān yí

transfer *v.t.* 转让 zhuǎn ràng

transferable *a.* 可转移的 kě zhuǎn yí de

transfiguration *n.* 变形 biàn xíng

transfigure *v.t.* 使变形 shǐ biàn xíng

transform *v.* 改变 gǎi biàn

transformation *n.* 变化 biàn huà

transgress *v.t.* 越界 yuè jiè

transgression *n.* 违反 wéi fǎn

transit *n.* 运输 yùn shū

transition *n.* 转变 zhuǎn biàn

transitive *n.* 及物动词 jí wù dòng cí

transitory *a.* 暂时的 zàn shí de

translate *v.t.* 翻译 fān yì

translation *n.* 翻译 fān yì

transmigration *n.* 移居 yí jū

transmission *n.* 传输 chuán shū

transmit *v.t.* 传送 chuán sòng

transmitter *n.* 传送者 chuán sòng zhě

transparent *a.* 透明的 tòu míng de

transplant *v.t.* 移植 yí zhí

transport *v.t.* 运输 yùn shū

transport *n.* 运输工具 yùn shū gōng jù

transportation *n.* 交通车辆 jiāo tōng chē liàng

trap *n.* 陷阱 xiàn jǐng

trap *v.t.* 诱捕 yòu bǔ

trash *n.* 垃圾 lā jī

travel *v.i.* 旅行 lǚ xíng

travel *n* 旅行 lǚ xíng

traveller *n.* 旅行者 lǚ xíng zhě

tray *n.* 盘 pán

treacherous *a.* 奸诈的 jiān zhà de

treachery *n.* 背叛 bèi pàn

tread *v.t.* 践踏 jiàn tà

tread *n* 步态 bù tài

treason *n.* 叛国罪 pàn guó zuì

treasure *n.* 宝物 bǎo wù

treasure *v.t.* 珍爱 zhēn ài

treasurer *n.* 财务主任 cái wù zhǔ rèn

treasury *n.* 财政部 cái zhèng bù

treat *v.t.* 对待 duì dài

treat *n* 款待 kuǎn dài

treatise *n.* 论文 lùn wén

treatment *n.* 治疗 zhì liáo

treaty *n.* 协定 xié dìng

tree *n.* 树 shù

trek *v.i.* 艰苦跋涉 jiān kǔ bá shè

trek *n.* 艰苦跋涉 jiān kǔ bá shè

tremble *v.i.* 战栗 zhàn lì

tremendous *a.* 巨大的 jù dà de

tremor *n.* 震动 zhèn dòng

trench *n.* 渠 qú

trench *v.t.* 在...开沟 zài... kāi gōu

trend *n.* 趋势 qū shì

trespass *v.i.* 侵入 qīn rù

trespass *n.* 非法侵入 fēi fǎ qīn rù

trial *n.* 审判 shěn pàn

triangle *n.* 三角形 sān jiǎo xíng

triangular *a.* 三角形的 sān jiǎo xíng de

tribal *a.* 部落的 bù luò de

tribe *n.* 族 zú

tribulation *n.* 苦难 kǔ nàn

tribunal *n.* 法庭 fǎ tíng

tributary *n.* 支流 zhī liú

tributary *a.* 支流的 zhī liú de

trick *n* 诡计 guǐ jì

trick *v.t.* 愚弄 yú nòng

trickery *n.* 欺骗 qī piàn

trickle *v.i.* 滴 dī

trickster *n.* 骗子 piàn zi

tricky *a.* 狡猾的 jiǎo huá de

tricolour *a.* 三色的 sān sè de

tricolour *n* 三色旗 sān sè qí

tricycle *n.* 三轮车 sān lún chē

trifle *n.* 琐事 suǒ shì

trifle *v.i* 开玩笑 kāi wán xiào

trigger *n.* 板机 bǎn jī

trim *a.* 苗条 miáo tiao

trim *n* 修剪 xiū jiǎn

trim *v.t.* 修剪 xiū jiǎn

trinity *n.* 三位一体 sān wèi yì tǐ

trio *n.* 三重唱 sān chóng chàng

trip *v.t.* 绊倒 bàn dǎo

trip *n.* 旅行 lǚ xíng

tripartite *a.* 分成三部的 fēn chéng sān bù de

triple *a.* 三部分的 sān bù fen de

triple *v.i.* 增至三倍 zēng zhì sān bèi

triplicate *a.* 三倍的 sān bèi de

triplicate *n* 三份中之一 sān fèn zhōng zhī yī

triplicate *v.t.* 使成三倍 shǐ chéng sān bèi

triplication *n.* 作三份 zuò sān fèn

tripod *n.* 三脚架 sān jiǎo jià

triumph *n.* 凯旋式 kǎi xuán shì

triumph *v.i.* 欢庆胜利 huān qìng shèng lì

triumphal *a.* 凯旋的 kǎi xuán de

triumphant *a.* 得到胜利的 dé dào shèng lì de

trivial *a.* 琐细的 suǒ xì de

troop *n.* 骑兵连 qí bīng lián

troop *v.i* 排着队前进 pái zhe duì qián jìn

trooper *n.* 骑兵 qí bīng

trophy *n.* 战利品 zhàn lì pǐn

tropic *n.* 热带 rè dài

tropical *a.* 热带 rè dài

trot *v.i.* 急匆匆地走 jí cōng cōng dì zǒu

trot *n* 小跑 xiáo pǎo

trouble *n.* 苦恼 kú nǎo

trouble *v.t.* 使烦恼 shǐ fán nǎo

troublesome *a.* 讨厌的 tǎo yàn de

troupe *n.* 马戏团 mǎ xì tuán

trousers *n. pl* 裤子 kù zi

trowel *n.* 泥铲 ní chǎn

truce *n.* 停战 tíng zhàn

truck *n.* 卡车 kǎ chē

true *a.* 真实的 zhēn shí de

trump *n.* 王牌 wáng pái

trump *v.t.* 打出王牌赢 dǎ chū wáng pái yíng

trumpet *n.* 喇叭 lǎ ba
trumpet *v.t.* 到处宣扬 dào chù xuān yáng
trunk *n.* 树干 shù gàn
trust *n.* 责任 zé rèn
trust *v.t* 信任 xìn rèn
trustee *n.* 受托人 shòu tuō rén
trustful *a.* 信任的 xìn rèn de
trustworthy *a.* 可靠的 kě kào de
trusty *n.* 可信任的人 kě xìn rèn de rén
truth *n.* 真相 zhēn xiàng
truthful *a.* 诚实的 chéng shí de
try *v.i.* 试 shì
try *n* 尝试 cháng shì
trying *a.* 难受的 nán shòu de
tryst *n.* 幽会 yōu huì
tub *n.* 桶 tǒng
tube *n.* 管 guǎn
tuberculosis *n.* 结核病 jié hé bìng
tubular *a.* 管状的 guǎn zhuàng de
tug *v.t.* 拉 lā
tuition *n.* 教诲 jiào huì
tumble *v.i.* 跌倒 diē dǎo
tumble *n.* 翻滚 fān gǔn
tumbler *n.* 玻璃酒杯 bō li jiǔ bēi
tumour *n.* 肿瘤 zhǒng liú
tumult *n.* 骚动 sāo dòng
tumultuous *a.* 吵闹的 chǎo nào de
tune *n.* 曲调 qǔ diào
tune *v.t.* 音调 yīn diào
tunnel *n.* 隧道 suì dào
tunnel *v.i.* 凿隧道 záo suì dào
turban *n.* 缠头巾 chán tóu jīn
turbine *n.* 涡轮机 wō lún jī
turbulence *n.* 乱流 luàn liú
turbulent *a.* 骚乱的 sāo luàn de
turf *n.* 草皮 cǎo pí
turkey *n.* 火鸡 huǒ jī

turmeric *n.* 郁金根粉 yù jīn gēn fěn
turmoil *n.* 骚动 sāo dòng
turn *v.i.* 转动 zhuǎn dòng
turn *n* 转弯 zhuǎn wān
turner *n.* 车工 chē gōng
turnip *n.* 萝卜 luó bo
turpentine *n.* 松节油 sōng jié yóu
turtle *n.* 龟 guī
tusk *n.* 长牙 zhǎng yá
tussle *n.* 争斗 zhēng dòu
tussle *v.i.* 打斗 dǎ dòu
tutor *n.* 私人教师 sī rén jiào shī
tutorial *a.* 导师的 dǎo shī de
tutorial *n.* 个人辅导时间 gè rén fú dǎo shí jiān
twelfth *num.* 第十二 dì shí èr
twelfth *n.* 十二日 shí èr rì
twelve *n.* 十二 shí èr
twelve *num.* 十二 shí èr
twentieth *num.* 第二十 dì èr shí
twentieth *n* 二十日 èr shí rì
twenty *num.* 二十 èr shí
twenty *n* 二十 èr shí
twice *adv.* 两次 liǎng cì
twig *n.* 细枝 xì zhī
twilight *n* 黄昏 huáng hūn
twin *n.* 双胞胎 shuāng bāo tāi
twin *a* 孪生的 luán shēng de
twinkle *v.i.* 闪烁 shǎn shuò
twinkle *n.* 闪光 shǎn guāng
twist *v.t.* 扭 niǔ
twist *n.* 扭转 niú zhuàn
twitter *n.* 吃吃笑声 chī chī xiào shēng
twitter *v.i.* 喊喊喳喳地叫 qī qī chā chā dì jiào
two *n.* 二 èr
two *a.* 两 liǎng
twofold *a.* 两个部分的 liǎng gè bù fen de
type *n.* 类型 lèi xíng
type *v.i.* 打字 dǎ zì
typhoid *n.* 伤寒 shāng hán
typhoon *n.* 台风 tái fēng

typhus *n.* 斑疹伤寒 bān zhěn shāng hán

typical *a.* 典型的 diǎn xíng de

typify *v.t.* 成为...的典范 chéng wéi... de diǎn fàn

typist *n.* 打字员 dǎ zì yuán

tyranny *n.* 苛政 kē zhèng

tyrant *n.* 暴君 bào jūn

tyre *n.* 轮胎 lún tāi

U

udder *n.* 乳房 rǔ fáng

uglify *v.t.* 丑化 chǒu huà

ugliness *n.* 丑陋的人 chǒu lòu de rén

ugly *a.* 丑的 chǒu de

ulcer *n.* 溃疡 kuì yáng

ulcerous *a.* 溃疡的 kuì yáng de

ulterior *a.* 不可告人的 bù kě gào rén de

ultimate *a.* 终极 zhōng jí

ultimately *adv.* 最后 zuì hòu

ultimatum *n.* 最后通牒 zuì hòu tōng dié

umbrella *n.* 伞 sǎn

umpire *n.* 裁判员 cái pàn yuán

umpire *v.t.* 裁判 cái pàn

unable *a.* 不能 bù néng

unanimity *n.* 无异议 wú yì yì

unanimous *a.* 一致同意的 yí zhì tóng yì de

unaware *a.* 不知道的 bù zhī dào de

unawares *adv.* 没想到 méi xiǎng dào

unburden *v.t.* 使卸除负荷 shǐ xiè chú fù hè

uncanny *a.* 可怕的 kě pà de

uncertain *a.* 不定的 bú dìng de

uncle *n.* 叔伯 shū bai

uncouth *a.* 粗鲁的 cū lǔ de

under *prep.* 在…下 zài…xià

under *adv.* 在下 zài xià

under *a.* 下面的 xià mian de

undercurrent *n.* 暗流 àn liú

underdog *n.* 失败者 shī bài zhě

undergo *v.t.* 经历 jīng lì

undergraduate *n.* 大学生 dà xué sheng

underhand *a.* 秘密的 mì mì de

underline *v.t.* 划线于下面 huá xiàn yú xià mian

undermine *v.t.* 掘下面 jué xià mian

underneath *adv.* 在下面 zài xià mian

underneath *prep.* 在下面 zài xià mian

understand *v.t.* 明白 míng bai

undertake *v.t.* 承担 chéng dān

undertone *n.* 低音 dī yīn

underwear *n.* 内衣 nèi yī

underworld *n.* 地狱 dì yù

undo *v.t.* 解开 jiě kāi

undue *a.* 过分的 guò fèn de

undulate *v.i.* 起伏 qǐ fú

undulation *n.* 波动 bō dòng

unearth *v.t.* 掘出 jué chū

uneasy *a.* 担心的 dān xīn de

unfair *a.* 不公平 bù gōng píng

unfold *v.t.* 打开 dǎ kāi

unfortunate *a.* 不幸的 bú xìng de

ungainly *a.* 笨拙的 bèn zhuō de

unhappy *a.* 不快乐的 bú kuài lè de

unification *n.* 统一 tǒng yī

union *n.* 协会 xié huì

unionist *n.* 联合主义者 lián hé zhǔ yì zhě

unique *a.* 独特的 dú tè de

unison *n.* 一齐 yì qí

unit *n.* 单位 dān wèi

unite *v.i.* 团结 tuán jié

unity *n.* 统一体 tǒng yī tǐ

universal *a.* 全世界的 quán shì jiè de

universality *n.* 普遍性 pǔ biàn xìng

universe *n.* 宇宙 yǔ zhòu

university *n.* 大学 dà xué

unjust *a.* 不公平的 bù gōng píng de

unless *conj.* 徐非 xú fēi

unlike *a* 不同的 bù tóng de

unlike *prep* 不像 bú xiàng

unlikely *a.* 未必有的 wèi bì yǒu de

unmanned *a.* 无人操作的 wú rén cāo zuò de

unmannerly *a* 没礼貌的 méi lǐ mào de

unprincipled *a.* 不道德的 bú dào dé de

unreliable *a.* 不能信任的 bù néng xìn rèn de

unrest *n* 骚乱 sāo luàn

unruly *a.* 不受拘束的 bú shòu jū shù de

unsettle *v.t.* 搅乱 jiǎo luàn

unsheathe *v.t.* 拔出鞘 bá chū qiào

until *prep.* 到… dào…

until *conj* 直到…为止 zhí dào … wéi zhǐ

untoward *a.* 不顺利的 bú shùn lì de

unwell *a.* 不舒服的 bù shū fu de

unwittingly *adv.* 无意的 wú yì de

up *adv.* 向上 xiàng shàng

up *prep.* 顺着 shùn zhe

upbraid *v.t* 责备 zé bèi

upheaval *n.* 剧变 jù biàn

uphold *v.t* 支持 zhī chí

upkeep *n* 保养 bǎo yǎng

uplift *v.t.* 打起精神 dǎ qǐ jīng shen

uplift *n* 举起 jǔ qǐ

upon *prep* 上 shàng

upper *a.* 上面的 shàng mian de

upright *a.* 笔直的 bǐ zhí de

uprising *n.* 起义 qǐ yì

uproar *n.* 骚嚷 sāo rǎng

uproarious *a.* 喧闹的 xuān nào de

uproot *v.t.* 连根拔起 lián gēn bá qǐ

upset *v.t.* 不舒服 bù shū fu

upshot *n.* 结果 jié guǒ

upstart *n.* 暴发户 bào fā hù

up-to-date *a.* 最新的 zuì xīn de

upward *a.* 向上的 xiàng shàng de

upwards *adv.* 在上面 zài shàng mian

urban *a.* 城市的 chéng shì de

urbane *a.* 有礼貌的 yǒu lǐ mào de

urbanity *n.* 文雅 wén yǎ

urchin *n.* 顽童 wán tóng

urge *v.t* 催促 cuī cù

urge *n* 冲动 chōng dòng

urgency *n.* 紧急 jǐn jí

urgent *a.* 紧急的 jǐn jí de

urinal *n.* 尿壶 niào hú

urinary *a.* 尿的 niào de

urinate *v.i.* (使)小便 (shǐ) xiǎo biàn

urination *n.* 小便 xiǎo biàn

urine *n.* 尿 niào

urn *n* 骨灰瓮 gǔ huī wèng

usage *n.* 用法 yòng fǎ

use *n.* 使用 shǐ yòng

use *v.t.* 用 yòng

useful *a.* 有用的 yǒu yòng de

usher *n.* 门房 mén fáng

usher *v.t.* 引导 yín dǎo

usual *a.* 平时的 píng shí de

usually *adv.* 通常 tōng cháng

usurer *n.* 高利贷者 gāo lì dài zhě

usurp *v.t.* 侵占 qīn zhàn

usurpation *n.* 篡夺 cuàn duó

usury *n.* 高利贷 gāo lì dài

utensil *n.* 用具 yòng jù

uterus *n.* 子宫 zǐ gōng

utilitarian *a.* 有效用的 yǒu xiào yòng de

utility *n.* 效用 xiào yòng

utilization n. 利用 lì yòng

utilize v.t. 利用 lì yòng

utmost a. 极度的 jí dù de

utmost n 最大限度 zuì dà xiàn dù

utopia n. 理想国 lí xiǎng guó

utopian a. 乌托邦的 wū tuō bāng de

utter v.t. 发出声音 fā chū shēng yin

utter a 全然的 quán rán de

utterance n. 言辞 yán cí

utterly adv. 完全地 wán quán de

V

vacancy n. 空缺 kòng quē

vacant a. 空的 kōng de

vacate v.t. 搬出 bān chū

vacation n. 假期 jià qī

vaccinate v.t. 预防接种 yù fáng jiē zhòng

vaccination n. 接种 jiē zhòng

vaccinator n. 接种员 jiē zhòng yuán

vaccine n. 疫苗 yì miáo

vacillate v.i. 游移不定 yóu yí bú dìng

vacuum n. 真空 zhēn kōng

vagabond n. 流浪者 liú làng zhě

vagabond a 流浪的 liú làng de

vagary n. 狂想 kuáng xiǎng

vagina n. 阴道 yīn dào

vague a. 含糊的 hán hu de

vagueness n. 含糊 hán hu

vain a. 自负的 zì fù de

vainglorious a. 自负的 zì fù de

vainglory n. 极度的虚荣 jí dù de xū róng

vainly adv. 枉然地 wǎng rán dì

vale n. 谷 gǔ

valiant a. 英勇的 yīngyǒng de

valid a. 有效的 yǒu xiào de

validate v.t. 证实 zhèng shí

validity n. 有效性 yǒu xiào xìng

valley n. 山谷 shān gǔ

valour n. 英勇 yīng yǒng

valuable a. 有价值的 yǒu jià zhí de

valuation n. 估价 gū jià

value n. 价值 jià zhí

value v.t. 重视 zhòng shì

valve n. 活门 huó mén

van n. 货车 huò chē

vanish v.i. 消失 xiāo shī

vanity n. 自负 zì fù

vanquish v.t. 打败 dǎ bài

vaporize v.t. 蒸发 zhēng fā

vaporous a. 蒸气的 zhēng qì de

vapour n. 蒸气 zhēng qì

variable a. 可变的 kě biàn de

variance n. 不一致 bù yí zhì

variation n. 变化 biàn huà

varied a. 不同的 bù tóng de

variety n. 种类 zhǒng lèi

various a. 不同的 bù tóng de

varnish n. 清漆 qīng qī

varnish v.t. 涂清漆于 tú qīng qī yú

vary v.i. 有不同 yǒu bù tóng

vasectomy n. 输精管切除手术 shū jīng guǎn qiē chú shǒushù

vaseline n. 凡士林 fán shì lín

vast a. 巨大的 jù dà de

vault n. 保管库 báo guǎn kù

vault n. 窖 jiào

vault v.i. 跳跃 tiào yuè

vegetable n. 蔬菜 shū cài

vegetable a. 蔬菜的 shū cài de

vegetarian n. 素食者 sù shí zhě

vegetarian a 素食的 sù shí de

vegetation n. 植物 zhí wù

vehemence n. 热烈 rè liè

vehement a. 热烈的 rè liè de

vehicle n. 交通工具 jiāo tōng gōng jù

vehicular a. 车的 chē de

veil *n.* 面纱 miàn shā
veil *v.t.* 遮蔽 zhē bì
vein *n.* 静脉 jìng mài
velocity *n.* 速度 sù dù
velvet *n.* 天鹅绒 tiān é róng
velvety *a.* 像天鹅绒的 xiàng tiān é róng de
venal *a.* 可收买的 kě shōu mǎi de
venality *n.* 唯利是图 wéi lì shì tú
vendor *n.* 小贩 xiǎo fàn
venerable *a.* 值得尊敬的 zhí dé zūn jìng de
venerate *n.* 崇敬 chóng jìng
veneration *n.* 尊敬 zūn jìng
vengeance *n.* 报仇 bào chóu
venial *a.* 可宽恕的 kě kuān shù de
venom *n.* 毒液 dú yè
venomous *a.* 有毒的 yǒu dú de
vent *n.* 排气口 pái qì kǒu
ventilate *v.t.* 使空气流通 shǐ kōng qì liú tōng
ventilation *n.* 通风 tōng fēng
ventilator *n.* 通风设备 tōng fēng shè bèi
venture *n.* 冒险 mào xiǎn
venture *v.t.* 冒...的危险 mào... de wēi xiǎn
venturesome *a.* 冒险的 mào xiǎn de
venturous *a.* 大胆的 dà dǎn de
venue *n.* 犯罪地点 fàn zuì dì diǎn
veracity *n.* 诚实 chéng shí
veranda *n.* 阳台 yáng tái
verb *n.* 动词 dòng cí
verbal *a.* 口头的 kǒu tóu de
verbally *adv.* 口头地 kǒu tóu dì
verbatim *a.* 逐字的 zhú zì de
verbatim *adv.* 逐字地 zhú zì dì

verbose *a.* 冗长的 rǒng cháng de
verbosity *n.* 唠叨 láo dāo
verdant *a.* 碧绿的 bì lǜ de
verdict *n.* 裁决 cái jué
verge *n.* 边缘 biān yuán
verification *n.* 证实 zhèng shí
verify *v.t.* 证实 zhèng shí
verisimilitude *n.* 逼真 bī zhēn
veritable *a.* 名副其实的 míng fù qí shí de
vermillion *n.* 朱红色 zhū hóng sè
vermillion *a.* 朱红色的 zhū hóng sè de
vernacular *n.* 本地话 běn dì huà
vernacular *a.* 地方的 dì fang de
vernal *a.* 春天的 chūn tiān de
versatile *a.* 多才多艺的 duō cái duō yì de
versatility *n.* 多用途 duō yòng tú
verse *n.* 诗 shī
versed *a.* 熟练的 shú liàn de
versification *n.* 诗律 shī lǜ
versify *v.t.* 短诗 duǎn shī
version *n.* 版本 bǎn běn
versus *prep.* 对 duì
vertical *a.* 垂直的 chuí zhí de
verve *n.* 热情 rè qíng
very *a.* 非常 fēi cháng
vessel *n.* 船 chuán
vest *n.* 背心 bèi xīn
vest *v.t.* 使穿衣服 shǐ chuān yī fu
vestige *n.* 遗迹 yí jì
vestment *n.* 祭服 jì fú
veteran *n.* 退伍军人 tuì wǔ jūn rén
veteran *a.* 经验丰富的 jīng yàn fēng fù de
veterinary *a.* 兽医的 shòu yī de
veto *n.* 否决权 fǒu jué quán
veto *v.t.* 否决 fǒu jué
vex *v.t.* 使烦恼 shǐ fán nǎo

vexation *n* 烦恼 fán nǎo
via *prep.* 经过 jīng guò
viable *a.* 能养活的 néng yǎng huó de
vial *n.* 小瓶 xiǎo píng
vibrate *v.i.* 振动 zhèn dòng
vibration *n.* 震动 zhèn dòng
vicar *n.* 教区牧师 jiào qū mù shī
vicarious *a.* 替代的 tì dài de
vice *n.* 恶习 è xí
viceroy *n.* 总督 zǒng dū
vice-versa *adv.* 反之亦然 fǎn zhī yì rán
vicinity *n.* 附近 fù jìn
vicious *a.* 邪恶的 xié è de
vicissitude *n.* 变迁 biàn qiān
victim *n.* 受害人 shòu hài rén
victimize *v.t.* 使受害 shǐ shòu hài
victor *n.* 胜利者 shèng lì zhě
victorious *a.* 胜利的 shèng lì de
victory *n.* 胜利 shèng lì
victuals *n.pl* 饮料 yǐn liào
vie *v.i.* 争 zhēng
view *n.* 风景 fēng jǐng
view *v.t.* 看 kàn
vigil *n.* 守夜 shǒu yè
vigilance *n.* 警戒 jǐng jiè
vigilant *a.* 警觉的 jǐng jué de
vigorous *a.* 精力充沛的 jīng lì chōng pèi de
vile *a.* 恶劣的 è liè de
vilify *v.t.* 中伤 zhòng shāng
villa *n.* 别墅 bié shù
village *n.* 村庄 cūn zhuāng
villager *n.* 村民 cūn mín
villain *n.* 坏人 huài rén
vindicate *v.t.* 辩护 biàn hù
vindication *n.* 证明无辜 zhèng míng wú gū
vine *n.* 藤本植物 téng běn zhí wù
vinegar *n.* 醋 cù
vintage *n.* 葡萄收获 pú tao shōu huò

violate *v.t.* 违反 wéi fǎn
violation *n.* 违反 wéi fǎn
violence *n.* 暴力 bào lì
violent *a.* 暴力的 bào lì de
violet *n.* 紫罗兰 zǐ luó lán
violin *n.* 小提琴 xiǎo tí qín
violinist *n.* 小提琴家 xiǎo tí qín jiā
virgin *a.* 处女的 chú nǚ de
virgin *n* 处女 chú nǚ
virginity *n.* 处女贞洁 chú nǚ zhēn jié
virile *a.* 男性的 nán xìng de
virility *n.* 成年 chéng nián
virtual *a* 虚拟 xū nǐ
virtue *n.* 美德 měi dé
virtuous *a.* 品德高尚的 pǐn dé gāo shàng de
virulence *n.* 毒性 dú xìng
virulent *a.* 剧毒的 jù dú de
virus *n.* 病毒 bìng dú
visage *n.* 面貌 miàn mào
visibility *n.* 能见度 néng jiàn dù
visible *a.* 看得见的 kàn dé jiàn de
vision *n.* 视力 shì lì
visionary *a.* 梦想的 mèng xiǎng de
visionary *n.* 有眼力的人 yǒu yǎn lì de rén
visit *n.* 参观 cān guān
visit *v.t.* 探 tàn
visitor *n.* 参观者 cān guān zhě
vista *n.* 远景 yuán jǐng
visual *a.* 视觉的 shì jué de
visualize *v.t.* 想像 xiǎng xiàng
vital *a.* 重要的 zhòng yào de
vitality *n.* 活力 huó lì
vitalize *v.t.* 赋予生命 fù yǔ shēng mìng
vitamin *n.* 维生素 wéi shēng sù
vitiate *v.t.* 使变质 shǐ biàn zhì
vivacious *a.* 活泼的 huó po de
vivacity *n.* 活泼 huó po
viva-voce *adv.* 口头上的 kǒu tóu shàng de

viva-voce *a* 口头的 kǒu tóu de

viva-voce *n* 口试 kǒu shì

vivid *a.* 清晰的 qīng xī de

vixen *n.* 雌狐 cí hú

vocabulary *n.* 词汇表 cí huì biǎo

vocal *a.* 声音的 shēng yīn de

vocalist *n.* 歌手 gē shǒu

vocation *n.* 职业 zhí yè

vogue *n.* 流行 liú xíng

voice *n.* 声音 shēng yīn

voice *v.t.* 表达 biǎo dá

void *v.* 无效的 wú xiào de

void *a.* 空的 kōng de

void *n.* 空间 kōng jiān

volcanic *a.* 火山的 huǒ shān de

volcano *n.* 火山 huǒ shān

volition *n.* 意志力 yì zhì lì

volley *n.* 群射 qún shè

volley *v.t* 群射 qún shè

volt *n.* 伏特 fú tè

voltage *n.* 电压 diàn yā

volume *n.* 音量 yīn liàng

voluminous *a.* 卷数多的 juǎn shù duō de

voluntarily *adv.* 自愿地 zì yuàn dì

voluntary *a.* 自愿的 zì yuàn de

volunteer *n.* 志愿者 zhì yuàn zhě

volunteer *v.t.* 自愿 zì yuàn

voluptuary *n.* 贪恋酒色的 tān liàn jiǔ sè de

voluptuous *a.* 骄奢淫逸的 jiāo shē yín yì de

vomit *v.t.* 呕吐 ǒu tù

vomit *n* 呕吐 ǒu tù

voracious *a.* 贪吃的 tān chī de

votary *n.* 信徒 xìn tú

vote *n.* 选举 xuán jǔ

vote *v.i.* 投票 tóu piào

voter *n.* 投票人 tóu piào rén

vouch *v.i.* 担保 dān bǎo

voucher *n.* 凭单 píng dān

vouchsafe *v.t.* 允许 yún xǔ

vow *n.* 誓约 shì yuē

vow *v.t.* 郑重地宣布 zhèng zhòng dì xuān bù

vowel *n.* 元音 yuán yīn

voyage *n.* 航行 háng xíng

voyage *v.i.* 航海 háng hǎi

voyager *n.* 航行者 háng xíng zhě

vulgar *a.* 粗俗的 cū sú de

vulgarity *n.* 粗俗 cū sú

vulnerable *a.* 脆弱的 cuì ruò de

vulture *n.* 秃鹫 tū jiù

W

wade *v.i.* 跋涉 bá shè

waddle *v.i.* 摇摇摆摆地走 yáo yáo bǎi bǎi dì zǒu

waft *v.t.* 飘荡 piāo dàng

waft *n* 吹拂 chuī fú

wag *v.i.* 摆动 bǎi dòng

wag *n* 摇摆 yáo bǎi

wage *v.t.* 开展 kāi zhǎn

wage *n.* 工资 gōng zī

wager *n.* 打赌 dá dǔ

wager *v.i.* 打赌 dá dǔ

wagon *n.* 马车 mǎ chē

wail *v.i.* 恸哭 tòng kū

wail *n* 恸哭 tòng kū

wain *n.* 四轮运货马车 sì lún yùn huò mǎ chē

waist *n.* 腰 yāo

waistband *n.* 腰带 yāo dài

waistcoat *n.* 西装背心 xī zhuāng bèi xīn

wait *v.i.* 等候 děng hòu

wait *n.* 等候 děng hòu

waiter *n.* 侍者 shì zhě

waitress *n.* 女侍者 nǔ shì zhě

waive *v.t.* 放弃 fàng qì

wake *v.t.* 叫醒 jiào xǐng

wake *n* 守灵 shǒu líng

wake *n* 船迹 chuán jì

wakeful *a.* 失眠的 shī mián de

walk *v.i.* 步行 bù xíng

walk *n* 散步 sàn bù

wall *n.* 墙 qiáng

wall *v.t.* 用墙围住 yòng qiáng wéi zhù	**wary** *a.* 谨慎的 jǐn shèn de
wallet *n.* 皮夹 pí jiā	**wash** *v.t.* 洗 xǐ
wallop *v.t.* 猛击 měng jī	**wash** *n* 洗 xǐ
wallow *v.i.* 打滚 dá gǔn	**washable** *a.* 可洗的 kě xǐ de
walnut *n.* 胡桃 hú táo	**washer** *n.* 洗衣机 xǐ yī jī
walrus *n.* 海象 hǎi xiàng	**wasp** *n.* 黄蜂 huáng fēng
wan *a.* 苍白的 cāng bái de	**waspish** *a.* 易怒的 yì nù de
wand *n.* 棒 bàng	**wassail** *n.* 宴会 yàn huì
wander *v.i.* 游荡 yóu dàng	**wastage** *n.* 损耗 sǔn hào
wane *v.i.* 变小 biàn xiǎo	**waste** *a.* 无用的 wú yòng de
wane *n* 减少 jián shǎo	**waste** *n.* 废品 fèi pǐn
want *v.t.* 想要 xiǎng yào	**waste** *v.t.* 浪费 làng fèi
want *n* 需要 xū yào	**wasteful** *a.* 浪费的 làng fèi de
wanton *a.* 恶意的 è yì de	**watch** *v.t.* 注视 zhù shì
war *n.* 战争 zhàn zhēng	**watch** *n.* 表 biǎo
war *v.i.* 作战 zuò zhàn	**watchful** *a.* 注意的 zhù yì de
warble *v.i.* 鸟鸣 niǎo míng	**watchword** *n.* 口号 kǒu hào
warble *n* 鸟啭 niǎo zhuàn	**water** *n.* 水 shuǐ
warbler *n.* 苔莺 tái yīng	**water** *v.t.* 注水于 zhù shuǐ yú
ward *n.* 病房 bìng fáng	**waterfall** *n.* 瀑布 pù bù
ward *v.t.* 保护 bǎo hù	**water-melon** *n.* 西瓜 xī guā
warden *n.* 管理员 guán lǐ yuán	**waterproof** *a.* 防水的 fáng shuǐ de
warder *n.* 看守 kān shǒu	**waterproof** *n* 防水物 fáng shuǐ wù
wardrobe *n.* 衣橱 yī chú	**waterproof** *v.t.* 使防水 shǐ fáng shuǐ
wardship *n.* 监护 jiān hù	**watertight** *a.* 不透水的 bú tòu shuǐ de
ware *n.* 物品 wù pǐn	**watery** *a.* 水的 shuǐ de
warehouse *v.t* 存入仓库 cún rù cāng kù	**watt** *n.* 瓦特 wǎ tè
warfare *n.* 战争 zhàn zhēng	**wave** *n.* 波浪 bō làng
warlike *a.* 好战的 hǎo zhàn de	**wave** *v.t.* 挥 huī
warm *a.* 暖和的 nuǎn huo de	**waver** *v.i.* 动摇 dòng yáo
warm *v.t.* 使暖 shǐ nuǎn	**wax** *n.* 蜡 là
warmth *n.* 温暖 wēn nuǎn	**wax** *v.t.* 涂蜡于 tú là yú
warn *v.t.* 警告 jǐng gào	**way** *n.* 路 lù
warning *n.* 警告 jǐng gào	**wayfarer** *n.* 旅客 lǚ kè
warrant *n.* 执照 zhí zhào	**waylay** *v.t.* 埋伏等候 mái fú děng hòu
warrant *v.t.* 保证 bǎo zhèng	**wayward** *a.* 任性的 rén xìng de
warrantee *n.* 被保证人 bèi bǎo zhèng rén	**weak** *a.* 柔弱的 róu ruò de
warrantor *n.* 保证人 bǎo zhèng rén	**weaken** *v.t. & i* 削弱 xuē ruò
warranty *n.* 保证 bǎo zhèng	**weakling** *n.* 虚弱的(人) xū ruò de (rén)
warren *n.* 养兔场 yǎng tù chǎng	**weakness** *n.* 弱 ruò
warrior *n.* 武士 wǔ shì	**weal** *n.* 福利 fú lì
wart *n.* 疣 yóu	**wealth** *n.* 富裕 fù yù

wealthy *a.* 财产多的 cái chǎn duō de

wean *v.t.* 使断奶 shǐ duàn nǎi

weapon *n.* 武器 wǔ qì

wear *v.t.* 穿着 chuān zhuó

weary *a.* 困乏的 kùn fá de

weary *v.t. & i* 疲倦 pí juàn

weary *a.* 疲倦的 pí juàn de

weary *v.t.* 使疲倦 shǐ pí juàn

weather *n* 天气 tiān qì

weather *v.t.* 吹干 chuī gān

weave *v.t.* 织 zhī

weaver *n.* 织工 zhī gōng

web *n.* 蜘蛛网 zhī zhū wǎng

webby *a.* 丝网(性，状)的 sī wǎng (xìng , zhuàng) de

wed *v.t.* 与…结婚 yǔ … jié hūn

wedding *n.* 婚礼 hūn lǐ

wedge *n.* 楔子 xiē zi

wedge *v.t.* 楔住 xiē zhù

wedlock *n.* 婚姻 hūn yīn

Wednesday *n.* 星期三 xīng qī sān

weed *n.* 杂草 zá cǎo

weed *v.t.* 除草 chú cǎo

week *n.* 星期 xīng qī

weekly *a.* 一周一次的 yì zhōu yí cì de

weekly *adv.* 每周 měi zhōu

weekly *n.* 周刊 zhōu kān

weep *v.i.* 流泪 liú lèi

weevil *n.* 象鼻虫 xiàng bí chóng

weigh *v.t.* 压迫 yā pò

weight *n.* 体重 tǐ zhòng

weightage *n.* 权重 quán zhòng

weighty *a.* 重的 zhòng de

weir *n.* 坝 bà

weird *a.* 超自然的 chāo zì rán de

welcome *a.* 受欢迎的 shòu huān yíng de

welcome *n* 欢迎 huān yíng

welcome *v.t* 欢迎 huān yíng

weld *v.t.* 焊接 hàn jiē

weld *n* 焊接点 hàn jiē diǎn

welfare *n.* 福利 fú lì

well *a.* 健康的 jiàn kāng de

well *adv.* 很好地 hěn hǎo dì

well *n.* 井 jǐng

well *v.i.* 涌出 yǒng chū

wellington *n.* 惠灵顿长靴 huì líng dùn cháng xuē

well-known *a.* 著名的 zhù míng de

well-read *a.* 博学的 bó xué de

well-timed *a.* 时机正好的 shí jī zhèng hǎo de

well-to-do *a.* 富有的 fù yǒu de

welt *n.* 殴打 ōu dǎ

welter *n.* 翻滚 fān gǔn

wen *n.* 粉瘤 fěn liú

wench *n.* 少妇 shǎo fù

west *n.* 西方 xī fāng

west *a.* 西方的 xī fāng de

west *adv.* 向西 xiàng xī

westerly *a.* 向西的 xiàng xī de

westerly *adv.* 向西 xiàng xī

western *a.* 西方的 xī fāng de

wet *a.* 湿的 shī de

wet *v.t.* 使...湿 shǐ... shī

wetness *n.* 湿润 shī rùn

whack *v.t.* 猛击 měng jī

whale *n.* 鲸 jīng

wharfage *n.* 码头费 mǎ tou fèi

what *a.* 什么的 shén me de

what *pron.* 什么 shén me

what *interj.* 怎么 zěn me

whatever *pron.* 无论什么 wú lùn shén me

wheat *n.* 小麦 xiǎo mài

wheedle *v.t.* 以甜言蜜语诱惑 yǐ tián yán mì yǔ yòu huò

wheel *n.* 轮 lún

wheel *v.t.* 使旋转 shǐ xuán zhuǎn

whelm *v.t.* 淹没 yān mò

whelp *n.* 小狗 xiǎo gǒu

when *adv.* 何时 hé shí

when *conj.* 当...的时候 dāng... de shí hou

whence *adv.* 从何处 cóng hé chù

whenever *adv.* conj 不论何时 bú lùn hé shí

where *adv.* 在哪里 zài nǎ lǐ

where *pron.* 哪里 nǎ lǐ

whereabouts *adv.* 在何处 zài hé chù

whereas *conj.* 而 ér

whereat *ad.* 在那里 zài nà lǐ

wherein *adv.* 在哪方面 zài nǎ fāng miàn

whereupon *conj.* 于是 yú shì

wherever *adv.* 无论哪里 wú lùn nǎ lǐ

whet *v.t.* 刺激 cì jī

whether *conj.* 不论 bú lùn

which *pron.* 那一个 nà yí gè

which *a* 哪一个 nǎ yí gè

whichever *pron* 无论那一个 wú lùn nà yí gè

whiff *n.* 一吹 yì chuī

while *n.* 一会儿 yí huì ér

while *conj.* 当...的时候 dāng... de shí hou

while *v.t.* 消磨 xiāo mó

whim *n.* 一时的兴致 yì shí de xìng zhì

whimper *v.i.* 呜咽 wū yè

whimsical *a.* 异想天开的 yì xiǎng tiān kāi de

whine *v.i.* 哭诉 kū sù

whine *n* 哀叫声 āi jiào shēng

whip *v.t.* 鞭打 biān dǎ

whip *n.* 鞭 biān

whipcord *n.* 鞭绳 biān shéng

whir *n.* 呼呼声 hū hū shēng

whirl *v.i.* 回旋 huí xuán

whirl *n* 旋转 xuán zhuǎn

whirligig *n.* 旋转木马 xuán zhuǎn mù mǎ

whirlpool *n.* 旋涡 xuán wō

whirlwind *n.* 旋风 xuàn fēng

whisk *v.t.* 掸 dǎn

whisk *n* 搅拌器 jiǎo bàn qì

whisker *n.* 胡须 hú xū

whisky *n.* 威士忌酒 wēi shì jì jiǔ

whisper *v.t.* 低声说 dī shēng shuō

whisper *n* 耳语 ér yǔ

whistle *v.i.* 吹口哨 chuī kǒu shào

whistle *n* 口哨 kǒu shào

white *a.* 白色的 bái sè de

white *n* 白色 bái sè

whiten *v.t.* 使白 shǐ bái

whitewash *n.* 白色涂料 bái sè tú liào

whitewash *v.t.* 掩饰 yǎn shì

whither *adv.* 到哪里 dào nǎ lǐ

whitish *a.* 发白的 fā bái de

whittle *v.t.* 逐渐削薄 zhú jiàn xuē báo

whiz *v.i.* (使)飕飕作声 (shǐ) sōu sōu zuò shēng

who *pron.* 谁 shuí

whoever *pron.* 无论谁 wú lùn shuí

whole *a.* 全部 quán bù

whole *n* 整体 zhěng tǐ

whole-hearted *a.* 全心全意的 quán xīn quán yì de

wholesale *n.* 批发 pī fā

wholesale *a* 批发的 pī fā de

wholesale *adv.* 照批发 zhào pī fā

wholesaler *n.* 批发商 pī fā shāng

wholesome *a.* 有益的 yǒu yì de

wholly *adv.* 完全地 wán quán dì

whom *pron.* 谁 shuí

whore *n.* 娼妓 chāng jì

whose *pron.* 谁的 shuí de

why *adv.* 为什么 wèi shén me

wick *n.* 灯芯 dēng xīn

wicked *a.* 邪恶的 xié è de

wicker *n.* 柳条 liǔ tiáo

wicket *n.* 小门 xiǎo mén

wide *a.* 宽的 kuān de

wide *adv.* 广阔地 guǎng kuò dì

widen *v.t.* 弄宽 nòng kuān

widespread *a.* 普及的 pǔ jí de

widow *n.* 寡妇 guǎ fu

widow *v.t.* 使成寡妇 shǐ chéng guǎ fu

widower *n.* 鳏夫 guān fū

width *n.* 广阔 guǎng kuò

wield *v.t.* 运用 yùn yòng

wife *n.* 妻 qī

wig *n.* 假发 jiǎ fā

wight *n.* 活物 huó wù

wigwam *n.* 活动棚屋 huó dòng péng wū

wild *a.* 野生的 yě shēng de

wilderness *n.* 荒野 huāng yě

wile *n.* 诡计 guǐ jì

will *n.* 遗嘱 yí zhǔ

will *v.t.* 愿意 yuàn yì

willing *a.* 乐意的 lè yì de

willingness *n.* 乐意 lè yì

willow *n.* 柳 liǔ

wily *a.* 狡猾的 jiǎo huá de

wimble *n.* 锥 zhuī

wimple *n.* 修女头巾 xiū nǔ tóu jīn

win *v.t.* 赢得 yíng dé

win *n* 赢 yíng

wince *v.i.* 畏缩 wèi suō

winch *n.* 绞车 jiǎo chē

wind *n.* 风 fēng

wind *v.i.* 嗅出猎物 xiù chū liè wù

wind *v.t.* 使通风 shǐ tōng fēng

windbag *n.* 满口空话的人 mǎn kǒu kōng huà de rén

winder *n.* 开发条的钥匙 kāi fā tiáo de yào shi

windlass *v.t.* 用绞车吊起 yòng jiǎo chē diào qǐ

windmill *n.* 风车 fēng chē

window *n.* 窗 chuāng

windy *a.* 有风的 yǒu fēng de

wine *n.* 酒 jiǔ

wing *n.* 翼 yì

wink *v.i.* 眨眼 zhá yǎn

wink *n* 使眼色 shǐ yǎn sè

winner *n.* 胜利者 shèng lì zhě

winnow *v.t.* 筛掉 shāi diào

winsome *a.* 赢得人注意的 yíng dé rén zhù yì de

winter *n.* 冬季 dōng jì

winter *v.i* 过冬 guò dōng

wintry *a.* 寒冷的 hán lěng de

wipe *v.t.* 擦 cā

wipe *n.* 擦拭 cā shì

wire *n.* 电线 diàn xiàn

wire *v.t.* 拍电报 pāi diàn bào

wireless *a.* 无线的 wú xiàn de

wireless *n* 无线电 wú xiàn diàn

wiring *n.* 线路 xiàn lù

wisdom *n.* 智慧 zhì huì

wisdom-tooth *n.* 智齿 zhì chǐ

wise *a.* 明智的 míng zhì de

wish *n.* 愿望 yuàn wàng

wish *v.t.* 愿 yuàn

wishful *a.* 渴望 kě wàng

wisp *n.* 小把 xiǎo bǎ

wistful *a.* 渴望的 kě wàng de

wit *n.* 智力 zhì lì

witch *n.* 女巫 nǔ wū

witchcraft *n.* 妖术 yāo shù

witchery *n.* 巫术 wū shù

with *prep.* 由于 yóu yú

withal *adv.* 而且 ér qiě

withdraw *v.t.* 撤回 chè huí

withdrawal *n.* 提款 tí kuǎn

withe *n.* 枝条 zhī tiáo

wither *v.i.* 凋残 diāo cán

withhold *v.t.* 在···内 zài···nèi

within *prep.* 在···内 zài···nèi

within *adv.* 在内 zài nèi

within *n.* 内部 nèi bù

without *prep.* 没有 méi yǒu

without *adv.* 在外部 zài wài bù

without *n* 外面 wài miàn

withstand *v.t.* 顶住 dǐng zhù

witless *a.* 无才智的 wú cái zhì de

witness *n.* 目击者 mù jī zhě

witness *v.i.* 目击 mù jī

witticism *n.* 妙语 miào yǔ

witty *a.* 机智的 jī zhì de

wizard *n.* 男巫 nán wū
wobble *v.i* 摇晃 yáo huàng
woe *n.* 苦恼 kú nǎo
woebegone *a.* 悲哀的 bēi āi de
woeful *a.* 悲伤的 bēi shāng de
wolf *n.* 狼 láng
woman *n.* 女人 nǚ rén
womanhood *n.* 女性 nǚ xìng
womanish *n.* 女子气的 nú zǐ qì de
womanise *v.t.* 使带女子气 shǐ dài nú zǐ qì
womb *n.* 子宫 zǐ gōng
wonder *n* 惊奇 jīng qí
wonder *v.i.* 惊讶 jīng yà
wonderful *a.* 极好的 jí hǎo de
wondrous *a.* 奇异的 qí yì de
wont *a.* 惯常的 guàn cháng de
wont *n* 习惯 xí guàn
wonted *a.* 习惯的 xí guàn de
woo *v.t.* 追求 zhuī qiú
wood *n.* 木材 mù cái
woods *n.* 森林 sēn lín
wooden *a.* 木制的 mù zhì de
woodland *n.* 林区 lín qū
woof *n.* 低吠声 dī fèi shēng
wool *n.* 羊毛 yáng máo
woollen *a.* 羊毛的 yáng máo de
woollen *n* 毛织品 máo zhī pǐn
word *n.* 单词 dān cí
word *v.t* 用言辞表达 yòng yán cí biǎo dá
wordy *a.* 话多的 huà duō de
work *n.* 工作 gōng zuò
work *v.t.* 使工作 shǐ gōng zuò
workable *a.* 可经营的 kě jīng yíng de
workaday *a.* 普通的 pǔ tōng de
worker *n.* 工人 gōng rén

workman *n.* 工匠 gōng jiang
workmanship *n.* 手艺 shǒu yì
workshop *n.* 工场 gōng chǎng
world *n.* 世界 shì jiè
worldling *n.* 俗人 sú rén
worldly *a.* 世间的 shì jiān de
worm *n.* 蠕虫 rú chóng
wormwood *n.* 苦艾 kǔ ài
worn *a.* 陈腐的 chén fǔ de
worry *n.* 担忧 dān yōu
worry *v.i.* 焦虑 jiāo lù
worsen *v.t.* 使更坏 shǐ gèng huài
worship *n.* 礼拜 lǐ bài
worship *v.t.* 崇拜 chóng bài
worshipper *n.* 崇拜者 chóng bài zhě
worst *n.* 最坏的事情 zuì huài de shì qíng
worst *a* 最坏的 zuì huài de
worst *v.t.* 战胜 zhàn shèng
worsted *n.* 精纺绒 jīng fǎng róng
worth *n.* 价值 jià zhí
worth *a* 值得… zhí dé …
worthless *a.* 没有价值的 méi yǒu jià zhí de
worthy *a.* 值得的 zhí dé de
would-be *a.* 自称的 zì chēng de
wound *n.* 伤 shāng
wound *v.t.* 伤害 shāng hài
wrack *n.* 破坏 pò huài
wraith *n.* 鬼魂 guǐ hún
wrangle *v.i.* 争吵 zhēng chǎo
wrangle *n.* 争论 zhēng lùn
wrap *v.t.* 包裹 bāo guǒ
wrap *n* 包装纸 bāo zhuāng zhǐ
wrapper *n.* 包装者 bāo zhuāng zhě
wrath *n.* 愤怒 fèn nù
wreath *n.* 花圈 huā quān
wreathe *v.t.* 盘绕 pán rào
wreck *n.* 失事 shī shì
wreck *v.t.* 破坏 pò huài
wreckage *n.* 失事 shī shì

wrecker *n.* 寻觅失事船只者 xún mì shī shì chuán zhǐ zhě

wren *n.* 鹪鹩 jiāo liáo

wrench *n.* 扭转 niú zhuǎn

wrench *v.t.* 扭伤 niú shāng

wrest *v.t.* 抢去 qiǎng qù

wrestle *v.i.* 摔跤 shuāi jiāo

wrestler *n.* 摔跤运动员 shuāi jiāo yùn dòng yuán

wretch *n.* 不幸的人 bú xìng de rén

wretched *a.* 不幸的 bú xìng de

wrick *n* 扭筋 niǔ jīn

wriggle *v.i.* 蠕动着前进 rú dòng zhe qián jìn

wriggle *n* 扭动 niǔ dòng

wring *v.t* 拧 nǐng

wrinkle *n.* 皱纹 zhòu wén

wrinkle *v.t.* (使)皱起 (shǐ) zhòu qǐ

wrist *n.* 腕 wàn

writ *n.* 命令 mìng lìng

write *v.t.* 写 xiě

writer *n.* 作者 zuò zhě

writhe *v.i.* 蠕动 rú dòng

wrong *a.* 错误的 cuò wù de

wrong *adv.* 错误 cuò wù

wrong *v.t.* 不公正地对待 bù gōng zhèng dì duì dài

wrongful *a.* 不正当的 bú zhèng dāng de

wry *a.* 讽刺的 fěng cì de

X

xerox *n.* 复印机 fù yìn jī

xerox *v.t.* 静电复印 jìng diàn fù yìn

Xmas *n.* 圣诞节 shèng dàn jié

x-ray *n.* X光 X guāng

x-ray *a.* X(射)线的 X(shè) xiàn de

x-ray *v.t.* 用X光检查 yòng X guāng jiǎn chá

xylophagous *a.* 蚀木的 shí mù de

xylophilous *a.* 蛀木的 zhù mù de

xylophone *n.* 木琴 mù qín

Y

yacht *n.* 游艇 yóu tǐng

yacht *v.i* 乘快艇 chéng kuài tǐng

yak *n.* 牦牛 máo niú

yap *v.i.* 吵嚷 cháo rǎng

yap *n* 狂吠 kuáng fèi

yard *n.* 围场 wéi chǎng

yarn *n.* 纱线 shā xiàn

yawn *v.i.* 打哈欠 dǎ hā qian

yawn *n.* 哈欠 hā qian

year *n.* 年 nián

yearly *a.* 每年的 měi nián de

yearly *adv.* 一年一次 yì nián yí cì

yearn *v.i.* 渴望 kě wàng

yearning *n.* 渴望 kě wàng

yeast *n.* 酵母菌 jiào mǔ jūn

yell *v.i.* 叫喊 jiào hǎn

yell *n* 大声叫喊声 dà shēng jiào hǎn shēng

yellow *a.* 黄色的 huáng sè de

yellow *n* 黄色 huáng sè

yellow *v.t.* 弄成黄色 nòng chéng huáng sè

yellowish *a.* 淡黄色的 dàn huáng sè de

Yen *n.* 日元 rì yuán

yeoman *n.* 自由民 zì yóu mín

yes *adv.* 是 shì

yesterday *n.* 昨日 zuó rì

yesterday *adv.* 昨天 zuó tiān

yet *adv.* 还 hái

yet *conj.* 虽然…但是 suī rán …dàn shì

yield *v.i.* 屈服 qū fú

yield *n* 生产量 shēng chǎn liàng

yoke *n.* 轭 è

yoke *v.t.* 给…上轭 gěi… shàng è

yolk *n.* 蛋黄 dàn huáng

yonder *a.* 那边的 nà bian de

yonder *adv.* 在那边 zài nà bian

young *a.* 年轻的 nián qīng de

young *n* 青年们 qīng nián men

youngster *n.* 年轻人 nián qīng rén

youth *n.* 少年 shào nián

youthful *a.* 青年的 qīng nián de

Z

zany *a.* 荒唐可笑的 huāng táng kě xiào de

zeal *n.* 热情 rè qíng

zealot *n.* 热心者 rè xīn zhě

zealous *a.* 热心的 rè xīn de

zebra *n.* 斑马 bān mǎ

zenith *n.* 顶点 dǐng diǎn

zephyr *n.* 微风 wēi fēng

zero *n.* 零 líng

zest *n.* 热情 rè qíng

zigzag *n.* 曲折线条 qū zhé xiàn tiáo

zigzag *a.* 锯齿形的 jù chǐ xíng de

zigzag *v.i.* 成之字形 chéng zhī zì xíng

zinc *n.* 锌 xīn

zip *n.* 拉链 lā liàn

zip *v.t.* 拉 lā

zodiac *n* 黄道带 huáng dào dài

zonal *a.* 区域性的 qū yù xìng de

zone *n.* 地区 dì qū

zoo *n.* 动物园 dòng wù yuán

zoological *a.* 动物学的 dòng wù xué de

zoologist *n.* 动物学家 dòng wù xué jiā

zoology *n.* 动物学 dòng wù xué

zoom *n.* 急速上升 jí sù shàng shēng

zoom *v.i.* 猛增 měng zēng

CHINESE (MANDARIN)-ENGLISH

A

ā ěr fǎ　阿尔法　n　alpha
ā mén　阿门　interj.　amen
ā wèi shù zhī　阿魏树脂　n.
　asafoetida
ài　爱　v.t.　love
ài chēng　爱称　n.　nickname
ài ěr lán de　爱尔兰的　a.　Irish
ài ěr lán rén　爱尔兰人　n.　Irish
ài fǔ　爱抚　v. t.　caress
ài fǔ　爱抚　v.t　fondle
ài guǎn xián shì de　爱管闲事的
　a.　officious
ài guó de　爱国的　a.　patriotic
ài guó jīng shen　爱国精神　n.
　partiotism
ài guó zhě　爱国者　n.　patriot
ài hào　爱好　n.　like
ài hào　爱好　n.　liking
ài hào zhě　爱好者　n　devotee
ài jiāo jì　爱交际　n.　sociability
ài jiāo jì de　爱交际的　a.
　sociable
ài kū de　爱哭的　a.
　lachrymose
ài mù　爱慕　n.　adoration
ài qíng　爱情　n　love
ài ren　爱人　n.　lover
ài tiāo ti de　爱挑剔的　adj
　censorious
āi　唉　interj.　alas
āi dào　哀悼　v. t　bewail
āi dào　哀悼　v. i.　condole
āi dào　哀悼　v.i.　mourn
āi dào　哀悼　n.　mourning
āi jiào shēng　哀叫声　n　whine
ǎi jiǎo jī　矮脚鸡　n.　bantam
ái xiǎo de dòng wù　矮小的动
　物　n　dwarf
ǎi zhǒng mǎ　矮种马　n.　pony
ái zhèng　癌症　n.　cancer
ān (péi)　安(培)　n　ampere
ān dùn　安顿　v.t.　lodge
ān dùn　安顿　n.　settlement
ān fǔ　安抚　v.t.　appease
ān fǔ　安抚　v.t.　conciliate

ān jìng　安静　n　hush
ān jìng　安静　n.　quiet
ān jìng de　安静的　a.　tranquil
ān hún qǔ　安魂曲　n.　requiem
ān pái　安排　n.　arrangement
ān pái　安排　v. t　conduct
ān pái　安排　v.t.　schedule
ān quán　安全　n.　safety
ān quán　安全　n.　security
ān quán de　安全的　a.　safe
ān quán de　安全的　a.　secure
ān quān tào　安圈套　v.t.　snare
ān wèi　安慰　v. t　comfort
ān wèi　安慰　n　consolation
ān wèi　安慰　v. t　console
ān wèi　安慰　v.t.　solace
ān wèi　安慰　n.　solace
ān wèi　安慰　v.t.　soothe
ān xī rì　安息日　n.　sabbath
ān zhì　安置　v.t　set
ān zhuāng　安装　v.t.　install
ān zhuāng　安装　n.　installation
ān chun　鹌鹑　n.　quail
àn dàn de　暗淡的　a　dim
àn dì lǐ　暗地里　adv.　stealthily
àn hào　暗号　n.　cipher, cipher
àn hào de　暗号的　a.　signal
àn liú　暗流　n.　undercurrent
àn shì　暗示　v.i.　allude
àn shì　暗示　n　allusion
àn shì　暗示　v.i　hint
àn shì　暗示　v.t.　imply
àn shì　暗示　n.　inkling
àn shì　暗示　v.t.　insinuate
àn shì　暗示　n.　insinuation
àn shì　暗示　v.t.　intimate
àn shì　暗示　n.　intimation
àn shìde　暗示的　a.　suggestive
àn yù　暗喻　n.　metaphor
àn zhǐ de　暗指的　a.　allusive
àn mó　按摩　n.　massage
àn mó　按摩　v.t.　massage
ān pái　安排　v.t.　arrange
àn zhào　按照　adv.　accordingly
áng guì de　昂贵的　a.　costly
áng shǒu kuò bù　昂首阔步　n
　swagger
àng sī　盎司　n.　ounce
āng zang de　肮脏的　a　dirty

āo 凹 *v.t* hollow
āo cáo 凹槽 *n.* groove
āo de 凹的 *adj.* concave
ào lín pǐ kè yùn dòng huì 奥林匹克运动会 *n.* olympiad
ào màn de 傲慢的 *a.* haughty

B

bā 八 *n* eight
bā biān xíng 八边形 *n.* octagon
bā biān xíng de 八边形的 *a.* octagonal
bā jiǎo 八角 *n* aniseed
bā shí 八十 *n* eighty
bā shí suì de 八十岁的 *a.* octogenarian
bā yīn dù 八音度 *n.* octave
bá yuè 八月 *n.* August
bā hén 疤痕 *n* scar
bā lěi wǔ 芭蕾舞 *n.* ballet
bá shè 跋涉 *v.i.* wade
bǎ rì qī tián chí 把日期填迟 *v.t.* post-date
bǎ wò 把握 *n* grasp
bǎ xīn 靶心 *n* bull's eye
bà ba 爸爸 *n* "dad, daddy"
bà 坝 *n.* weir
bá chū qiào 拔出鞘 *v.t.* unsheathe
bà gōng 罢工 *n* stoppage
bà gōng 罢工 *v.t.* strike
bái chī 白痴 *n.* idiocy
bái chī 白痴 *n.* idiot
bái chī 白痴 *n.* moron
bái lán dì 白兰地 *n* brandy
bái lù 白鹭 *n* aigrette
bái mào 白帽 *n* coif
bái sè 白色 *n* white
bái sè de 白色的 *a.* white
bái sè tú liào 白色涂料 *n.* whitewash
bái tiān 白天 *adv* adays
bái tiān yīn yuè huì 白天音乐会 *n.* matinee

bái yáng zuò 白羊座 *n* aries
bǎi 百 *n.* hundred
bǎi bèi 百倍 *n. & adj* centuple
bǎi fēn bǐ 百分比 *n.* per cent
bǎi hé huā 百合花 *n.* lily
bǎi kē quán shū 百科全书 *n.* encyclopaedia
bǎi suì lǎo rén 百岁老人 *n* centenarian
bǎi wàn fù wēng 百万富翁 *n.* millionaire
bǎi yè chuāng 百叶窗 *n.* shutter
bǎi 摆 *v.t.* place
bǎi 摆 *v.t.* put
bǎi dòng 摆动 *n* flutter
bǎi dòng 摆动 *n.* oscillation
bǎi dòng 摆动 *v.i.* wag
bǎi zī shì 摆姿势 *v.i.* pose
bǎi shù 柏树 *n* cypress
bān 班 *n* class
bān 班 *n* shift
bān jī 班机 *n* flight
bān zhuó qín 班卓琴 *n.* banjo
bān diǎn 斑点 *n.* mottle
bān diǎn 斑点 *n.* speck
bān diǎn 斑点 *n.* spot
bān mǎ 斑马 *n.* zebra
bān zhěn shāng hán 斑疹伤寒 *n.* typhus
bān chǎng gōng rén 搬场工人 *n.* mover
bān chū 搬出 *v.t.* vacate
bān jiā 搬家 *n.* move
bān yùn 搬运 *v. t.* carry
bān yùn 搬运 *n.* portage
bān yùn gōng rén 搬运工人 *n.* porter
bān zǒu 搬走 *v. t* clear
bān jiǎng 颁奖 *v.t.* award
bǎn 板 *n* board
bǎn 版 *n* edition
bǎn qiú 板球 *n* cricket
bǎn shí 板石 *n.* slate
bǎn tiáo 板条 *n.* lath
bǎn tiáo xiāng 板条箱 *n.* crate
bǎn jī 板机 *n.* trigger
bán běn 版本 *n.* version

bǎn céng 板层 n ply
bàn cuò 办错 n.
　mismanagement
bàn lǐ 办理 v.t. transact
bàn dǎo 绊倒 n. stumble
bàn dǎo 绊倒 v.t stump bàn
dǎo 绊倒 v.t. trip
bàn jìng 半径 n. radius
bàn kāi 半开 adv. ajar
bàn máng de 半盲的 a.
　purblind
bàn qiú 半球 n. hemisphere
bàn yīn fú 半音符 n. minim
bàn lǚ 伴侣 n. helpmate
bàn zòu 伴奏 n
　accompaniment
bāng xiōng 帮凶 n accomplice
bāng zhù 帮助 v.t aid
bāng zhù 帮助 v.t. assist
bāng zhù 帮助 n. assistance
bāng zhù 帮助 v.t facilitate
bāng zhù 帮助 v.t. help
bāng zhù 帮助 v.t. succour
bāng máng 帮忙 n help
bǎng 绑 v.t bind
bǎng 绑 v.t. rope
bǎng 绑 v.t. tie
bàng 棒 n. wand
bàng bàng táng 棒棒糖 n.
　lollipop
bàng wǎn 傍晚 n evening
bāo 包 n. bag
bāo 包 v.t enclose
bāo 包 v.t envelop
bāo 包 n. pack
bāo fu 包袱 n burden
bāo guǒ 包裹 n. package
bāo guǒ 包裹 n. packet
bāo guǒ 包裹 n. parcel
bāo guǒ 包裹 v.t. wrap
bāo hán 包含 v.t encompass
bāo hán 包含 n. inclusion
bāo kuò 包括 v.t. include
bāo kuò 包括 v.t. involve
bāo kuò de 包括的 a.
　inclusive
bāo wéi 包围 n. enclosure
bāo wéi 包围 v.t. ring
bāo wéi 包围 n. siege

bāo zā 包扎 v.t bandage
bāo zhuāng 包装 n. packing
bāo zhuāng zhě 包装者 n.
　wrapper
bāo zhuāng zhǐ 包装纸 n
　wrap
bāo … de pí 剥…的皮 v.t skin
báo wù 薄雾 n. haze
bǎo bao 宝宝 n. baby
bǎo bèi 宝贝 n. babe
bǎo píng zuò 宝瓶座 n.
　aquarius
bǎo shí 宝石 n gem
bǎo shí 宝石 n. jewellery
bǎo wù 宝物 n. treasure
bǎo biāo 保镖 n. bodyguard
bǎo chí 保持 v.t. keep
bǎo chí 保持 v.i. remain
bǎo chí 保持 v.t. retain
bǎo chí 保持 n. retention
bǎo cún 保存 v.t conserve
bǎo cún 保存 v.t. preserve
bǎo guǎn kù 保管库 n. vault
bǎo guǎn rén 保管人 n. keeper
bǎo hù 保护 v.t ensure
bǎo hù 保护 v.t. patronize
bǎo hù 保护 n. preservation
bǎo hù 保护 v.t. protect
bǎo hù 保护 n. protection
bǎo hù 保护 v.t. shelter
bǎo hù 保护 v.t. shield
bǎo hù 保护 v.t. ward
bǎo hù cuò shī 保护措施 n.
safeguard
bǎo hù de 保护的 a. protective
bǎo hù zhě 保护者 n.
　protector
bǎo huáng dǎng yuán
　保皇党员 n. royalist
bǎo mì 保密 n. secrecy
bǎo shì 保释 n. bail
bǎo shì 保释 v.t. bail
bǎo shǒu dǎng zhī chí zhě
　保守党支持者 n conservative
bǎo shǒu de 保守的 a
　conservative
bǎo shǒu de 保守的 a. insular
bǎo shǒu de 保守的 a.
　reactinary

báo xiǎn 保险 *n.* insurance
báo xiǎn fèi 保险费 *n.*
  premium
báo xiǎn sī 保险丝 *n* fuse
báo xiǎn xiāng 保险箱 *n.* safe
báo yǎng 保养 *v.t* service
báo yǎng 保养 *n* upkeep
bǎo zhèng 保证 *n.* assurance
bǎo zhèng 保证 *v.t.* assure
bǎo zhèng 保证 *n.* pledge
bǎo zhèng 保证 *v.t.* warrant
bǎo zhèng (shū) 保证(书) *n.*
  warranty
bǎo zhèng rén 保证人 *n.*
  warrantor
bǎo yù 保育 *v.t.* mother
bǎo zhàng 保障 *n.* indemnity
báo lěi 堡垒 *n* bulwark
báo lěi 堡垒 *n.* citadel
báo lěi 堡垒 *n.* fort
bǎo hé dù 饱和度 *n.*
  saturation
bào 抱 *v. t.* embrace
bào bù píng de 抱不平的 *a.*
  malcontent
bào fù 抱负 *n.* ambition
bào yuàn 抱怨 *v. i* complain
bào zhe dòu nong 抱着逗弄
  v.t. dandle
bào yìng 报应 *n.* nemesis
bào chóu 报仇 *v.t.* avenge
bào chóu 报仇 *v.t.* revenge
bào chóu 报仇 *n.* revenge
bào chóu 报酬 *n.* reward
bào chóu 报仇 *n.* vengeance
bào dá 报答 *v.t.* requite
bào fù 报复 *v.i.* retaliate
bào fù 报复 *n.* retaliation
bào fù de 报复的 *a.*
  revengeful
bào gào 报告 *v.t.* apprise
bào gào 报告 *v.t.* report
bào gào 报告 *n.* report
bào jià 报价 *n.* quotation
bào xiǎo 报晓 *v. i* crow
bào 豹 *n.* leopard
bào dòng 暴动 *n.* mutiny
bào dòng 暴动 *n.* riot

bào fā hù 暴发户 *n.* upstart
bào fēng xuě 暴风雪 *n*
  blizzard
bào fēng yǔ 暴风雨 *n.* storm
bào fēng yǔ 暴风雨 *n.*
  tempest
bào fēng yǔ de 暴风雨的 *a.*
  stormy
bào jūn 暴君 *n* despot
bào jūn 暴君 *n.* tyrant
bào lì 暴力 *n.* violence
bào lì de 暴力的 *a.* violent
bào lù 暴露 *v. t* expose
bào mín 暴民 *n.* mob
bào zào de 暴躁的 *a* fiery
bào shí 暴食 *n.* gluttony
bào shí zhě 暴食者 *n.* glutton
bào tú 暴徒 *n* bully
bào yǐn 暴饮 *v. i* booze
bào fā 爆发 *v. i* erupt
bào fā 爆发 *n* eruption
bào fā 爆发 *n.* outbreak
bào pò 爆破 *n* burst
bào zhà 爆炸 *n* blast
bào zhà 爆炸 *v. i.* burst
bào zhà 爆炸 *v. t.* explode
bào zhà 爆炸 *n.* explosion
bào zhà de 爆炸的 *a* explosive
bēi 杯 *n.* cup
bēi bǐ 卑鄙 *n.* meanness
bēi bǐ de 卑鄙的 *a.* base
bēi bǐ de 卑鄙的 *a.* sordid
bēi jiàn de 卑贱的 *a.* ignoble
bēi qū 卑屈 *n.* servility
bēi wēi 卑微 *a.* abject
bēi wēi 卑微 *n.* lowliness
bēi xià de 卑下的 *a.* menial
bēi āi 悲哀 *n.* sorrow
bēi āi de 悲哀的 *a.* woebegone
bēi āi shì de 悲哀似的 *a*
  mournful
bēi cǎn de 悲惨的 *a.* tragic
bēi guān 悲观 *n.* pessimism
bēi guān de 悲观的 *a.*
  pessimistic
bēi guān zhě 悲观者 *n.*
  pessimist
bēi jù 悲剧 *n.* tragedy

bēi jù zuò jiā　悲剧作家　*n.* tragedian

bēi shāng de　悲伤的　*a.* woeful

bēi shāng de rén　悲伤的人　*n.* mourner

bēi tàn　悲叹　*n* lament

bēi tàn　悲叹　*n.* lamentation

bēi tòng　悲痛　*n.* grief

bēi tòng　悲痛　*v.i.* sorrow

běi　北　*n.* north

běi fāng de　北方的　*a* north

běi fēng　北风　*n.* northerly

běi jí　北极　*n* Arctic

běi jí xīng　北极星　*n.* loadstar

běi měi yě mǎ　北美野马　*n.* mustang

bèi bǎo zhèng rén　被保证人　*n.* warrantee

bèi chéng shù　被乘数　*n.* multiplicand

bèi dān　被单　*n.* sheet

bèi dòng de　被动的　*a.* passive

bèi gào　被告　*n.* accused

bèi gào　被告　*n* defendant

bèi gù yōng de　被雇佣的　*a.* mercenary

bèi jiān jìn de　被监禁的　*a.* captive

bèi lüè shí zhě　被掠食者　*n.* prey

bèi ní nòng zāng　被泥弄脏　*v.t* bemire

bèi pái chì de　被排斥的　*a* outcast

bèi qiǎn fǎn huí guó zhě　被遣返回国者　*n* repatriate

bèi qū zhú de rén　被驱逐的人　*n.* outcast

bèi tí míng zhě　被提名者　*n* nominee

bèi zhòng lì xī yǐn　被重力吸引　*v.i.* gravitate

bèi zǔ zhòu de　被诅咒的　*a.* accursed

bèi jǐng　背景　*n.* background

bèi lí　背离　*n* deviation

bèi miàn　背面　*n.* back

bèi miàn qiān míng　背面签名　*v.t.* endorse

bèi pàn　背叛　*v.t.* betray

bèi pàn　背叛　*n* betrayal

bèi pàn　背叛　*n.* treachery

bèi sòng　背诵　*n.* recital

bèi xīn　背心　*n.* vest

bèi xìn qì yì　背信弃义　*n.* perfidy

bèi shù　倍数　*n* multiple

bèi wàng lù　备忘录　*n* memorandum

bèi wàng lù　备忘录　*n.* note

bēn liú　奔流　*n.* torrent

bēn liú de　奔流的　*a.* torrential

bēn máng　奔忙　*v.t* bustle

bēn pǎo　奔跑　*n* scamper

běn dì　本地　*a* aboriginal

běn dì de　本地的　*a.* native

běn dì huà　本地话　*n.* vernacular

bèn rén　笨人　*n* dunce

bèn shǒu bèn jiǎo dì nòng huài　笨手笨脚地弄坏　*v.t* botch

bèn shǒu bèn jiǎo dì zuò　笨手笨脚地做　*v.t.* thumb

bén tǔ de　本土的　*a.* indigenous

bèn zhuō de　笨拙的　*a* clumsy

bèn zhuō de　笨拙的　*a.* ungainly

bēng dài　绷带　*n.* bandage

bèng　泵　*n.* pump

bèng tiào　蹦跳　*v.i* scamper

bī zhēn　逼真　*n.* verisimilitude

bī zhēn de　逼真的　*a.* realistic

bí　鼻　*n.* nose

bí de　鼻的　*a.* nasal

bí kǒng　鼻孔　*n.* nostril

bí xī　鼻息　*n.* snort

bí yīn　鼻音　*n* nasal

bǐ shǒu　匕首　*n.* dagger

bǐ … cháng shòu　比…长寿　*v.t.* outlive

bǐ … zhòng　比…重　*v.t.* outweigh

bǐ jiào　比较　*v.t* compare

bǐ jiào　比较　*n* comparison

bǐ jiào de　比较的　*a* comparative

bǐ lì　比例　*n.* proportion

bǐ lì de　比例的　*a.* proportional

bǐ lǜ　比率　*n.* ratio

bǐ sài　比赛　*n.* competition

bǐ sài　比赛　*n.* contest

bǐ sài　比赛　*n.* match

bǐ sài　比赛　*n.* race

bǐ yù　比喻　*v.t.* liken

bǐ yù de　比喻的　*a.* allegorical

bǐ yù de　比喻的　*a* figurative

bǐ　笔　*n.* pen

bǐ jiān　笔尖　*n.* nib

bǐ lù　笔录　*v.t.* note

bǐ míng　笔名　*n.* pseudonym

bǐ zhí de　笔直的　*a.* upright

bì rán dì　必然地　*adv.* perforce

bì xū　必须　*n* must

bì xū　必须　*adv.* needs

bì xū de dōng xi　必需的东西　*n.* must

bì xū pǐn　必需品　*n.* necessary

bì xū pǐn　必需品　*n* requisite

bì yào de　必要的　*a* essential

bì yào de　必要的　*a* necessary

bì yào de　必要的　*a.* prerequisite

bì yào de　必要的　*a.* requisite

bì yào xìng　必要性　*n.* necessity

bì yè　毕业　*v.i.* graduate

bì yè shēng　毕业生　*n* graduate

bì hù　庇护　*n* asylum

bì hù　庇护　*n.* lee

bì hù suǒ　庇护所　*n.* sanctuary

bì hù suǒ　庇护所　*n.* shelter

bì jī　哔叽　*n.* serge

bì de　壁的　*a.* mural

bì guì　壁柜　*n.* closet

bì huà　壁画　*n.* mural

bì lú jià　壁炉架　*n.* mantel

bì kāi　避开　*adv.* aloof

bì kāi　避开　*v.t* dodge

bì kāi　避开　*v.t.* shun

bì miǎn　避免　*v.t.* avert

bì miǎn　避免　*v.t.* avoid

bì miǎn　避免　*n.* avoidance

bì nàn　避难　*n.* refuge

bì nàn suǒ　避难所　*n.* haven

bì yùn　避孕　*n.* contraception

bì lǜ de　碧绿的　*a.* verdant

bì má yóu　蓖麻油　*n.* castor oil

bì shì　臂饰　*a* armlet

biān　边　*n* edge

biān　边　*n.* rim

biān jiè　边界　*n* border

biān jiè　边界　*n* boundary

biān jiè　边界　*n.* frontier

biān yán　边沿　*n* brim

biān yuán　边缘　*n.* brink

biān yuán　边缘　*n.* fringe

biān yuán　边缘　*n.* margin

biān yuán　边缘　*n.* verge

biān yuán de　边缘的　*a.* marginal

biān chéng tuán　编成团　*v.t.* regiment

biān duì　编队　*n* formation

biān hào　编号　*v.t.* number

biān jí　编辑　*n* editor

biān jí de　编辑的　*a* editorial

biān nián shǐ　编年史　*n.pl.* annals

biān nián shǐ　编年史　*n.* chronicle

biān rù　编入　*n.* incorporation

biān xiě　编写　*v.t* compile

biān zhī　编织　*v.t.* knit

biān fú　蝙蝠　*n* bat

biān　鞭　*n.* whip

biān dǎ　鞭打　*v.t* flog

biān dǎ　鞭打　*n* lash

biān dǎ　鞭打　*v.t.* scourge

biān dǎ　鞭打　*v.t.* whip

biān cè　鞭策　*v.t.* spur

biān pào　鞭炮　*n* cracker

biān shéng　鞭绳　*n.* whipcord

biān piàn　扁片　*n* squash

biǎn táo tǐ　扁桃体　*n.* tonsil

biǎn dī　贬低　*v.t.* depreciate

biàn àn　变暗　*v.i.* darkle

biàn chéng　变成　*v.i* become

biàn hóng　变红　*v.t.* redden

biàn chí dùn　变迟钝　*v.t.* dull

biàn huà　变化　*n.* mutation

biàn huà　变化　*n.* transformation

biàn huà　变化　*n.* variation

biàn huàn wú cháng de　变幻无常的　*a* fickle

biàn jiān rèn　变坚韧　v.t.
toughen

biàn kuān hòu　变宽厚　v.i.
relent

biàn liáng　变凉　v. i. cool

biàn mó shù　变魔术　v.i. conjure

biàn qiān　变迁　n. vicissitude

biàn tài　变态　n. perversion

biàn xiǎo　变小　v.i. wane

biàn xíng　变形　n.
transfiguration

biàn zhì　变质　n.
metamorphosis

biàn bì　便秘　n. constipation

biàn lì de　便利的　a. handy

biàn shì　便士　n. penny

biàn jí　遍及　v.t. pervade

biàn fāng lǜ shī　辩方律师　n.
advocate

biàn hù　辩护　n. advocacy

biàn hù　辩护　v.t. vindicate

biàn hù lǜ shī　辩护律师　n.
attorney

biàn lùn　辩论　n. argument

biàn lùn　辩论　n. debate

biàn lùn zhě　辩论者　n. pleader

biāo diǎn fú hào　标点符号　n.
punctuation

biāo jì　标记　n cognizance

biāo jì　标记　n. tag

biāo qiān　标签　n. label

biāo qiān　标签　v.t. tag

biāo qiāng　标枪　n. javelin

biāo tí　标题　n. heading

biāo yè shù　标页数　v.t. page

biāo yǔ　标语　n. motto

biāo zhì　标志　n cachet

biāo zhǔn　标准　n criterion

biāo zhǔn　标准　n. norm

biāo zhǔn　标准　n. standard

biāo zhǔn dǎ shù　标准打数
n. par

biāo zhǔn huà　标准化　n.
standardization

biǎo　表　n. watch

biǎo dá　表达　v. t. express

biǎo dá　表达　n. expression

biǎo dá　表达　v.t. phrase

biǎo dá　表达　v.t. voice

biǎo dá de　表达的　a.
expressive

biǎo gé　表格　n form

biǎo gé de　表格的　a. tabular

biǎo miàn　表面　n facade

biǎo miàn　表面　n. surface

biǎo miàn de　表面的　a.
cosmetic

biǎo miàn xiàn xiàng　表面现象
n. superficiality

biǎo míng　表明　v.t. manifest

biǎo míng　表明　v.t. show

biǎo pí　表皮　n. cutis

biǎo qīn　表亲　n. cousin

biǎo shì　表示　v.t. signify

biǎo shì tóng qíng　表示同情　v.i.
sympathize

biǎo shì zūn jìng de　表示尊敬的
a. respectful

biǎo shì... de　表示的　a.
indicative

biǎo xiàn　表现　v. i. behave

biáo yǎn　表演　v.t. perform

biáo yǎn zhě　表演者　n. juggler

biáo yǎn zhě　表演者　n.
performer

biǎo yáng　表扬　v. t commend

bié de dōng xi　别的东西　pron.
other

bié míng　别名　adv. alias

bié shù　别墅　n. villa

bīn　滨　n strand

bīng tuán　兵团　n corps

bīng yíng　兵营　n. cantonment

bīng yíng　兵营　n. barrack

bīng　冰　n. ice

bīng báo　冰雹　n. hail

bīng chuān　冰川　n. glacier

bīng de　冰的　a. icy

bīng shān　冰山　n. iceberg

bīng xié　冰鞋　n. skate

bīng zhù　冰柱　n. icicle

bīng lang shù　槟榔树　n areca

bīng lang yè　槟榔叶　n betel

bǐng gān　饼干　n biscuit

bǐng　柄　n. handle

bǐng　柄　n stalk

bìng cún　并存　v. i consist

bìng jiān　并肩　*adv*　abreast
bìng　病　*n.*　malady
bìng de　病的　*a.*　sick
bìng dú　病毒　*n.*　virus
bìng fáng　病房　*n.*　ward
bìng jūn　病菌　*n.*　germ
bìng rén　病人　*n*　invalid
bìng rén　病人　*n*　patient
bìng tài de　病态的　*a.*　morbid
bìng zhuàng　病状　*n*　morbidity
bō dòng　波动　*n.*　undulation
bō tāo xiōng yǒng de dà hǎi　波涛汹涌的大海　*n.*　surge
bō làng　波浪　*n.*　wave
bō li　玻璃　*n.*　glass
bō li jiǔ bēi　玻璃酒杯　*n.*　tumbler
bō duó　剥夺　*v. t*　deprive
bō duó fǎ lù bǎo hù　剥夺法律保护　*v.t*　outlaw
bō yīn shì　播音室　*n.*　studio
bō zhǒng　播种　*v.t.*　seed
bō cài　菠菜　*n.*　spinach
bō luó　菠萝　*n.*　pineapple
bó jué fū rén　伯爵夫人　*n.*　countess
bó chuán　驳船　*n.*　barge
bó dǎo　驳倒　*v.t.*　confute
bó huí　驳回　*v.t.*　overrule
bó shì tóu xián　博士头衔　*n*　doctorate
bó wù guǎn　博物馆　*n.*　museum
bó wù xué jiā　博物学家　*n.*　naturalist
bó xué de　博学的　*a.*　well-read
bó dòng　搏动　*v.i.*　pulsate
bó dòu　搏斗　*v. i.*　battle
bǒ zú de　跛足的　*a.*　lame
bó dòu　搏斗　*n*　combat
bò he　薄荷　*n.*　mint
bǔ cháng　补偿　*v.t.*　repair
bǔ chōng de　补充的　*a*　complementary
bǔ chōng wù　补充物　*n*　complement
bǔ dìng　补钉　*n*　patch
bǔ jiù de　补救的　*a.*　remedial
bǔ xuǎn　补选　*n*　by-election

bǔ yào　补药　*n.*　tonic
bǔ zhù jīn　补助金　*v.t.*　subsidize
bǔ zú　补足　*v.t.*　supplement
bǔ　捕　*v.t*　take
bǔ huò　捕获　*n.*　seizure
bǔ niǎo zhě　捕鸟者　*n.*　fowler
bǔ shí　捕食　*v.i.*　prey
bǔ rǔ lèi dòng wù　哺乳类动物　*n.*　mammal
bù　不　*adv.*　nay
bù　不　*n*　no
bù　不　*adv.*　not
bù ān　不安　*n*　disquiet
bù ān dìng de　不安定的　*adj.*　astatic
bù ān quán　不安全　*n.*　insecurity
bù ān quán de　不安全的　*a.*　insecure
bú biàn de　不便的　*a.*　inconvenient
bù chéng shí　不诚实　*n.*　dishonesty
bù chéng shí　不诚实　*n.*　insincerity
bù chéng shí　不诚实　*a.*　malafide
bù chéng shí　不诚实　*adv*　malafide
bù chéng shí de　不诚实的　*a*　dishonest
bù chéng shí de　不诚实的　*a.*　insincere
bù chéng shu de　不成熟的　*a.*　immature
bù chōng fēn de　不充分的　*a.*　scant
bù chún de　不纯的　*a.*　impure
bù cún zài de dōng xi　不存在的东西　*n.*　nonentity
bú dào dé de　不道德的　*a.*　immoral
bú dào dé de　不道德的　*a.*　unprincipled
bú dìng de　不定的　*a.*　uncertain
bú dòng chǎn　不动产　*n*　estate
bú dòng de　不动的　*a.*　motionless

bú dòng de　不动的　*a.*　staid

bú dòng de　不动的　*a.*
stationary

bú duàn de　不断的　*a*
continuous

bú duàn de　不断的　*a.*
perpetual

bú duàn dì láo dāo　不断地唠
叨　*v.t.*　nag

bú duàn guàn shū　不断灌输
v.t.　instil

bù fǎ de　不法的　*a.*　illicit

bù fā huǒ　不发火　*v.i.*　misfire

bù fǎ xíng wéi　不法行为　*n.*
malpractice

bú fù zé rèn de　不负责任的　*a.*
irresponsible

bù gāo xìng de　不高兴的　*a.*
sullen

bù gōng píng　不公平　*a*　unfair

bù gōng píng de　不公平的　*a.*
unjust

bù gōng zhèng　不公正　*n.*
injustice

bù gōng zhèng dì duì dài　不公
正地对待　*v.t.*　wrong

bú gòu de　不够的　*a.*
insufficient

bú gù bié rén de　不顾别人的
a.　inconsiderate

bú gù yì qiè de　不顾一切的　*a*
desperate

bù guān xīn　不关心　*n.*
nonchalance

bù guī zé　不规则　*n.*
irregularity

bù guī zé de　不规则的　*a.*
irregular

bú guì zhòng de　不贵重的　*a.*
inexpensive

bú guò　不过　*conj.*　but

bú guò hái shì　不过还是　*adv.*
though

bù hé　不和　*n.*　feud

bù hé lǐ de　不合理的　*a.*　ir
rational

bù hé luó jí de　不合逻辑的　*a.*
illogical

bù hé shì de　不合适的　*a.*
improper

bù hé shí jī de　不合时机的　*a.*
inopportune

bù huó dòng　不活动　*n.*
inaction

bù huó yuè de　不活跃的　*a.*
inactive

bù jí de　不吉的　*a.*　inauspicious

bù jí wù de　不及物的　*a. (verb)*
intransitive

bù jié méng　不结盟　*n.*
non-alignment

bú jiè yì de　不介意的　*a.*
reckless

bù jìng　不敬　*n*　disrespect

bù jiǔ　不久　*adv.*　shortly

bù kě bì miǎn de　不可避免的　*a.*
inevitable

bù kě fǒu rèn de　不可否认的　*a.*
irrefutable

bù kě gào rén de　不可告人的　*a.*
ulterior

bù kě néng de　不可能的　*a.*
impossible

bù kě néng xìng　不可能性　*n.*
impossibility

bù kě qīn fàn de　不可侵犯的　*a.*
inviolable

bù kě quē shǎo zhī wù　不可缺少
之物　*a.*　indispensable

bú kuài lè de　不快乐的　*a.*
unhappy

bù kuān róng　不宽容　*n.*
intolerance

bú lì　不利　*n*　disadvantage

bù lǐ　不理　*v. t*　disregard

bú lì de　不利的　*a*　adverse

bù lián guàn de　不连贯的　*a.*
incoherent

bú lùn　不论　*conj.*　whether

bú lùn hé shí　不论何时　*adv.*
conj　whenever

bù mǎn　不满　*n*　discontent

bù mǎn　不满　*n*　displeasure

bù mǎn　不满　*n*　dissatisfaction

bù mǎn zú　不满足　*v. t.*
dissatisfy

bù máo de 不毛的 *a.* meagre

bú miè de shēng wàng 不灭的 声望 *n.* immorality

bú nà yàng 不那样 *adv.* otherwise

bú nài fán de 不耐烦的 *a.* impatient

bù néng 不能 *a.* unable

bù néng fáng wèi de 不能防卫 的 *a.* indefensible

bù néng fēn de 不能分的 *a.* inseparable

bù néng fēn gē de 不能分割的 *a.* indivisible

bù néng hé jiě de 不能和解的 *a.* irreconcilable

bù néng jiě shì de 不能解释的 *a.* inexplicable

bù néng róng jiě de 不能溶解 的 *n.* insoluble

bù néng shí shī de 不能实施的 *a.* impracticable

bù néng shōu huí de 不能收回 的 *a.* irrecoverable

bù néng tōng guò de 不能通过 的 *a.* impenetrable

bù néng tōng xíng de 不能通 行的 *a.* impassable

bù néng tòu rù de 不能透入的 *a* proof

bù néng xìn rèn de 不能信任 的 *a.* unreliable

bù néng yī zhì de 不能医治的 *a.* incurable

bù néng yòng yǔ yán biǎo dá de 不能用语言表达的 *a.* indescribable

bù píng děng 不平等 *n.* odds

bù qí zhěng de 不齐整的 *a.* slipshod

bù qiān xū 不谦虚 *n.* immodesty

bù qiān xū de 不谦虚的 *a.* immodest

bù qiè tí de 不切题的 *a.* impertinent

bù qīng chu de 不清楚的 *a.* indistinct

bù qīng chu de 不清楚的 *a.* obscure

bù qíng yuàn de 不情愿的 *a.* loath

bù qū bù náo 不屈不挠 *n.* fortitude

bù qū bù náo de 不屈不挠的 *a* dauntless

bù qū fú de 不屈服的 *a.* indomitable

bù qū qǔ de 不屈曲的 *a.* inflexible

bú què dìng de 不确定的 *a.* tentative

bù róng rěn de 不容忍的 *a.* intolerant

bú shèn zhòng 不慎重 *n.* indiscretion

bú shì 不是 *a.* no

bú shì dàng 不适当 *n.* impropriety

bú shì dàng de pèi hé 不适当的 配合 *n.* misalliance

bú shì hé 不适合 *n.* misfit

bú shì yòng de 不适用的 *a.* inapplicable

bú shì yú jū zhù de 不适于居住 的 *a.* inhospitable

bú shòu chǔ fá de 不受处罚的 *a.* scot-free

bú shòu jū shù de 不受拘束的 *a.* unruly

bù shū fu 不舒服 *n.* malaise

bù shū fu 不舒服 *v.t.* upset

bù shū fu de 不舒服的 *a.* indisposed

bù shū fu de 不舒服的 *a.* unwell

bù shū shì 不舒适 *n* discomfort

bú shùn cóng 不顺从 *n.* insubordination

bú shùn cóng de 不顺从的 *a.* insubordinate

bú shùn lì de 不顺利的 *a.* untoward

bù sǐ de 不死的 *a.* immortal

bù tǎo hǎo de 不讨好的 *a.* thankless

bú tiáo hé　不调和　n discord
bù tíng de　不停的　a. ceaseless
bù tóng de　不同的　a different
bù tóng de　不同的　a dissimilar
bù tóng de　不同的　a diverse
bù tóng de　不同的　a else
bù tóng de　不同的　a. varied
bù tóng de　不同的　a. various
bù tóng yì　不同意　v. i disagree
bú tòu míng bù　不透明部　n. opacity
bú tòu míng de　不透明的　a. opaque
bú tòu shuǐ de　不透水的　a. watertight
bù wán měi de　不完美的　a. imperfect
bù wěn dìng de　不稳定的　a. shifty
bù wěn dìng xìng　不稳定性　n. instability
bú xiàng …　不像…　prep unlike
bù xiāng xìn　不相信　v.t. mistrust
bù xiǎo xīn　不小心　a accidental
bú xìn rèn　不信任　n distrust
bú xìn rèn　不信任　v. t. distrust
bù xīn xiān de　不新鲜的　a. stale
bú xìng　不幸　n. mischance
bú xìng　不幸　n. misfortune
bú xìng de　不幸的　a. luckless
bú xìng de　不幸的　a. unfortunate
bú xìng de　不幸的　a. wretched
bú xìng de rén　不幸的人　n. wretch
bú xìng de shì　不幸的事　n. mishap
bù xiǔ　不朽　n. immortality
bù xiǔ de　不朽的　a. imperishable
bù xú kě de　不许可的　a. inadmissible

bù xū yào de　不需要的　a. needless
bù yí zhì　不一致　adj absonant
bù yí zhì　不一致　v. i differ
bù yí zhì　不一致　n. disagreement
bù yí zhì　不一致　n. variance
bú yì zhī cái　不义之财　n. pelf
bú yù　不育　n barren
bù yuǎn de jiāng lái　不远的将来　n. offing
bú yuàn xiàng qián zǒu de　不愿向前走的　a. restive
bú yùn　不孕　n. sterility
bú zài chǎng zhèng jù　不在场证据　n. alibi
bú zàn chéng　不赞成　n disapproval
bú zàn chéng　不赞成　v. t disapprove
bú zhèng cháng　不正常　a abnormal
bú zhèng cháng　不正常　adj acentric
bú zhèng dāng de　不正当的　a. wrongful
bú zhèng dāng de xíng wéi　不正当的行为　n. misdemeanour
bù zhěng jié de　不整洁的　a. slatternly
bú zhèng què de　不正确的　a. incorrect
bú zhèng què de　不正确的　a. inexact
bù zhī dào de　不知道的　a. unaware
bù zhī zú de　不知足的　a. insatiable
bù zhōng de　不忠的　a disloyal
bú zhù yì de　不注意的　a. inattentive
bú zhù yì de　不注意的　a. mindless
bù zhǔn què de　不准确的　a. inaccurate
bù zú　不足　n. lack
bù zú qǔ de　不足取的　a. paltry
bù zūn shǒu dào dé de　不遵守道德的　a. amoral

bù 布 *n* cloth
bù 布 *n* fabric
bù dīng 布丁 *n.* pudding
bù bīng 步兵 *n.* infantry
bù fá 步伐 *n* march
bù fǎ 步法 *n.* gait
bù tài 步态 *n* tread
bù xíng 步行 *v.t* ambulate
bù xíng 步行 *v.i.* walk
bù fen 部分 *n.* part
bù fen 部分 *n.* section
bù fen 部分 *n.* segment
bù fen tuì kuǎn 部分退款 *n.*
　rabate
bù luò de 部落的 *a.* tribal
bù mén 部门 *n* department
bù mén 部门 *n.* sector
bù shǔ 部属 *n* subordinate

C

cā 擦 *v.t.* rub
cā 擦 *v.t.* wipe
cā gān shēn zi 擦干身子 *v.t.*
　towel
cā liàng 擦亮 *v.t.* polish
cā shāng 擦伤 *n* graze
cā shì 擦拭 *n.* wipe
cāi cè 猜测 *n* conjecture
cāi cè 猜测 *n.* guess
cāi cè 猜测 *v.i* guess
cái néng 才能 *n.* acquirement
cái néng 才能 *n.* talent
cái chǎn 财产 *n.* fortune
cái chǎn 财产 *n.* property
cái chǎn duō de 财产多的 *a.*
　wealthy
cái fù 财富 *n.* mammon
cái fù 财富 *n.* riches
cái wù 财物 *n.* belongings
cái wù zhǔ rèn 财务主任 *n.*
　treasurer
cái zhèng 财政 *n* finance
cái zhèng bù 财政部 *n.*
　treasury
cái zhèng de 财政的 *a*
　financial

cái zhèng de 财政的 *a* fiscal
cái liào 材料 *n* material
cái liào 材料 *n.* stuff
cái feng 裁缝 *n.* tailor
cái jué 裁决 *n.* ruling
cái jué 裁决 *n.* verdict
cái jūn 裁军 *n.* disarmament
cái pàn 裁判 *n.* arbiter
cái pàn 裁判 *v.t.* umpire
cái pàn yuán 裁判员 *n.*
　referee
cái pàn yuán 裁判员 *n.*
　umpire
cǎi gòu 采购 *n.* procurement
cǎi shí chǎng 采石场 *n.* quarry
cǎi piào 彩票 *n.* lottery
cǎi sè bǐ 彩色笔 *n.* pastel
cǎi 踩 *v.t.* conculcate
cài huā 菜花 *n.* cauliflower
cài yáo 菜肴 *n.* cuisine
cān guān 参观 *n.* visit
cān guān zhě 参观者 *n.* visitor
cān jiā 参加 *v.t.* join
cān jiā zhě 参加者 *n.*
　participant
cān kǎo 参考 *n.* reference
cān yì yuán 参议员 *n.* senator
cān yì yuàn 参议院 *n.* senate
cān yì yuán de 参议员的 *a.*
　senatorial
cān yì yuàn de 参议院的 *a*
　senatorial
cān yù 参与 *v.i.* partake
cān yù 参与 *v.i.* participate
cān yù 参与 *n.* participation
cān 餐 *n.* menu
cān guǎn 餐馆 *n.* restaurant
cān jīn 餐巾 *n.* napkin
cán cún 残存 *v.i.* survive
cán fèi de 残废的 *a* disabled
cán gān 残干 *n.* snag
cán hái 残骸 *n* debris
cán kù 残酷 *a.* barbarous
cán kù 残酷 *n* cruelty
cán rěn 残忍 *n* atrocity
cán rěn 残忍 *n* barbarity
cán rěn 残忍 *a* brutal
cán rěn de 残忍的 *a.* atrocious

cán rěn de 残忍的 *a* cruel
cán rěn de 残忍的 *a* ferocious
cán rěn de 残忍的 *a.* inhuman
cán rěn de 残忍的 *a.* murderous
cán zhā 残渣 *n.* residue
cán zhā de 残渣的 *a.* residual
cán kuì de 惭愧的 *a.* ashamed
cǎn bài 惨败 *n* fiasco
cǎn bài 惨败 *v.i.* lurch
càn làn de 灿烂的 *a.* refulgent
cāng cù de 仓促的 *a* cursory
cāng kù 仓库 *n* depot
cāng kù 仓库 *n.* godown
cāng kù 仓库 *n.* repository
cāng kù 仓库 *n.* store
cāng bái de 苍白的 *a.* wan
cāng ying 苍蝇 *n* fly
cáng 藏 *v.t* hide
cáng nì 藏匿 *v.t* harbour
cáo zá 嘈杂 *a.* noisy
cāo liàn 操练 *v. t.* drill
cāo zòng 操纵 *v.t.* manipulate
cāo zòng 操纵 *v.t.* operate
cāo zuò 操作 *n.* manipulation
cāo zuò zhě 操作者 *n.* operator
cǎo 草 *n* grass
cǎo dì 草地 *n.* lawn
cǎo dì 草地 *n.* meadow
cǎo duī 草堆 *n.* rick
cáo gǎo 草稿 *n* draft
cǎo mào 草帽 *n.* straw
cǎo méi 草莓 *n.* strawberry
cǎo pí 草皮 *n.* sod
cǎo pí 草皮 *n.* turf
cǎo tú 草图 *n.* sketch
cǎo wū dǐng 草屋顶 *n.* thatch
cè biān 侧边 *prep.* beside
cè miàn 侧面 *n.* side
cè miàn yǐng xiàng 侧面影像 *n.* silhouette
cè dìng shí jiān 测定时间 *v.t.* time
cè fēng dài 测风带 *n.* streamer

cè gāo jì 测高计 *n* altimeter
cè liáng 测量 *v.t* mete
cè yàn 测验 *n* test
cè suǒ 厕所 *n.* latrine
cè suǒ 厕所 *n.* toilet
cè lüè 策略 *n.* strategy
cè lüè 策略 *n.* tactics
céng 层 *n.* layer
céng 层 *n.* storey
céng 层 *n.* stratum
céng céng juǎn rào de 层层卷绕的 *a.* serpentine
céng jīng 曾经 *adv* ever
cèng xié diàn 蹭鞋垫 *n.* mat
chà 差 *a.* bad
chà bù duō 差不多 *adv.* nearly
chà bù duō 差不多 *adv.* nigh
chā cuò 差错 *adv.* amiss
chā yì 差异 *n* difference
chā yì 差异 *n* disparity
chā rù 插入 *v.t.* insert
chā rù 插入 *n.* insertion
chā rù 插入 *v.i.* intervene
chā rù 插入 *v.t.* plug
chā rù yǔ 插入语 *n.* parenthesis
chā tú 插图 *n.* illustration
chā tú shuō míng 插图说明 *n.* caption
chá shàng 搽上 *v.t.* smear
chá 茶 *n* tea
chá dié 茶碟 *n.* saucer
chá hú 茶壶 *n.* kettle
chá jiū 查究 *v.t.* inquire
chá míng 查明 *v.t.* ascertain
chāi shì 差事 *n* errand
chái bǎ 柴把 *n* faggot
chái duī 柴堆 *n.* pyre
chái 豺 *n.* jackal
chǎn 铲 *v.t.* shovel
chǎn 铲 *n.* spade
chān jiǎ 掺假 *n.* adulteration
chān zá 掺杂 *v.t.* adulterate
chán rào 缠绕 *v.t.* convolve
chán tóu jīn 缠头巾 *n.* turban
chán chú 蟾蜍 *n.* toad
chǎn liàng 产量 *n.* output
chán pǐn 产品 *n.* product

chán pǐn 产品 *n.* productivity

chǎn qián de 产前的 *adj.* antenatal

chǎn shēng 产生 *v.t.* generate

chǎn shēng 产生 *v.i.* result

chǎn mèi 谄媚 *n* flattery

chǎn mèi 谄媚 *n.* sycophancy

chǎn mèi zhě 谄媚者 *n.* sycophant

chán zhù 缠住 *v. i.* cling

chàn dǒu 颤抖 *v.i.* quake

chàn dǒu 颤抖 *v.i.* quiver

chāng jì 娼妓 *n.* whore

chāng jué de 猖獗的 *a.* rampant

cháng bì yuán 长臂猿 *n.* gibbon

cháng bǐng dà lián dāo 长柄大镰刀 *n.* scythe

cháng chu 长处 *n.* forte

cháng de 长的 *a.* long

cháng dèng 长凳 *n* bench

cháng dìng 长钉 *n.* spike

cháng dù 长度 *n.* length

cháng fāng xíng 长方形 *n.* oblong

cháng fāng xíng 长方形 *n.* rectangle

cháng fāng xíng de 长方形的 *a.* oblong

cháng jǐng lù 长颈鹿 *n.* giraffe

cháng jiǔ 长久 *adv* long

cháng máo 长矛 *n.* lance

cháng máo 长矛 *n.* lancer

cháng mìng 长命 *n.* longevity

cháng piān yì lùn 长篇议论 *n.* tirade

cháng quán fā 长鬈发 *n.* ringlet

cháng wà 长袜 *n.* stocking

cháng yǐ 长椅 *n.* couch

cháng 尝 *v.t.* taste

cháng shì 尝试 *v.t.* attempt

cháng shì 尝试 *n.* attempt

cháng shì 尝试 *n* try

cháng wèi 尝味 *n.* taste

cháng huán 偿还 *n.* liquidation

cháng huán 偿还 *v.t.* recoup

cháng huán 偿还 *n.* refund

cháng huán 偿还 *v.t.* reimburse

cháng huán 偿还 *v.t.* repay

cháng huán 偿还 *n.* repayment

cháng fù néng lì 偿付能力 *n.* solvency

cháng 肠 *n.* bowel

cháng 肠 *n.* intestine

cháng de 肠的 *a.* intestinal

cháng cháng 常常 *adv.* often

cháng chūn téng 常春藤 *n* ivy

cháng dào 常到 *v.t.* haunt

cháng dào de dì fang 常到的地方 *n* haunt

cháng jiàn 常见 *a.* common

cháng lù de 常绿的 *a* evergreen

cháng lù shù 常绿树 *n* evergreen

cháng nián de 常年的 *a.* perennial

chǎng hé 场合 *n.* occasion

chǎng suǒ 场所 *n.* lieu

chàng dǎo 倡导 *v.t.* pioneer

chàng dǎo zhě 倡导者 *n* exponent

chāo xiě 抄写 *v.t.* transcribe

chāo xiě 抄写 *n.* transcription

chāo chū 超出 *prep.* beyond

chāo chū 超出 *v.t* overrun

chāo guò 超过 *v.t.* outrun

chāo guò 超过 *v.t.* surpass

chāo guò cháng rén de 超过常人的 *a.* superhuman

chāo rén 超人 *n.* superman

chāo yīn bō de 超音波的 *a.* supersonic

chāo yuè 超越 *v.t* exceed

chāo yuè 超越 *v.t.* top

chāo yuè 超越 *v.t.* transcend

chāo zài 超载 *n* overcharge

chāo zì rán de 超自然的 *a.* supernatural

chāo zì rán de 超自然的 *a.* weird

cháo chén 朝臣 *n.* courtier

cháo dài 朝代 *n* dynasty

cháo shèng 朝圣 *n.* pilgrim-age

cháo shèng zhě 朝圣者 *n.* pilgrim

cháo xiān jì 朝鲜蓟 *n.* artichoke

cháo xiàng 朝向 *v.i.* front

cháo 巢 *n.* nest

cháo 潮 *n.* tide

cháo shī 潮湿 *n* damp

cháo shī de 潮湿的 *a* damp

cháo shī de 潮湿的 *a.* humid

cháo xī de 潮汐的 *a.* tidal

cháo nòng 嘲弄 *v.i.* jeer

cháo nòng 嘲弄 *n* taunt

cháo xiào 嘲笑 *v.t.* ridicule

cháo xiào 嘲笑 *n.* ridicule

cháo xiào 嘲笑 *v.i.* gibe

cháo xiào 嘲笑 *n* gibe

cháo xiào 嘲笑 *v.i.* mock

cháo xiào 嘲笑 *n.* scoff

cháo xiào 嘲笑 *v.i* sneer

cháo xiào 嘲笑 *n* sneer

cháo xiào de 嘲笑的 *a.* sardonic

chǎo jià 吵架 *v.t* brangle

chǎo jià 吵架 *v.i.* quarrel

chǎo nào 吵闹 *v. i.* clamour

chǎo nào de 吵闹的 *a.* rowdy

chǎo nào de 吵闹的 *a.* tumultuous

chǎo nào shēng 吵闹声 *n* clamour

chǎo nào shēng 吵闹声 *n.* hubbub

cháo rǎng 吵嚷 *v.i.* yap

chē 车 *n.* car

chē chuáng 车床 *n.* lathe

chē de 车的 *a.* vehicular

chē gōng 车工 *n.* turner

chē kù 车库 *n.* garage

chē qián cǎo 车前草 *n.* plantain

chē xiāng 车厢 *n.* carriage

chē zhàn 车站 *n.* station

chē zhóu 车轴 *n.* axle

chè dǐ 彻底 *adv* downright

chè dǐ 彻底 *adv.* outright

chè dǐ de 彻底的 *a* outright

chè dǐ liáo jiě 彻底了解 *v.t* fathom

chè huí 撤回 *v.t.* countermand

chè huí 撤回 *v.t.* revoke

chè huí 撤回 *v.t.* withdraw

chè tuì 撤退 *v.i.* retreat

chè zhí 撤职 *n.* conge

chén 尘 *n* dust

chén āi 尘埃 *n.* mote

chén diàn wù 沉淀物 *n.* sediment

chén mèn de 沉闷的 *a.* leaden

chén mò 沉没 *v.i* drown

chén mò 沉默 *n.* reticence

chén mò de 沉默的 *a.* mum

chén mò de 沉默的 *a.* reticent

chén mò guǎ yán de 沉默寡言的 *a.* taciturn

chén sī 沉思 *n* contemplation

chén sī 沉思 *n* muse

chén sī 沉思 *v.t.* ponder

chén sī 沉思 *v.i.* ruminate

chén sī 沉思 *n.* rumination

chén sī de 沉思的 *a.* pensive

chén zhòng de 沉重的 *a* burdensome

chén zhòng dì zǒu 沉重地走 *v.i.* plod

chén zhuó de 沉着的 *a.* sedate

chén fǔ de 陈腐的 *a.* worn

chén guī lǎo tào 陈规老套 *n.* stereotype

chén jiù de 陈旧的 *a.* antiquated

chén liè 陈列 *v.t* display

chèn diàn 衬垫 *n.* pad

chèn lǐ 衬里 *n* lining

chèn qún 衬裙 *n.* petticoat

chèn shān 衬衫 *n* blouse

chèn shān 衬衫 *n.* shirt

chēng hu 称呼 *v.t.* address

chēng zàn 称赞 *v.t* acclaim

chēng zàn 称赞 *n* acclaim

chēng zàn 称赞 *n* commendation

chēng zàn 称赞 *v.t.* laud

chēng zàn 称赞 *n.* praise

chēng zàn 称赞 *v.t.* praise

chēng chuán 撑船 *v.i* boat

chéng bǐ lì de 成比例的 *a.* proportionate

chéng fen 成分 *n.* ingredient

chéng gōng 成功 *v.i.* succeed

chéng gōng de 成功的 *a* successful

chéng huáng sè 成黄色 *v.t.* yellow

chéng jiù 成就 *n.* accomplishment

chéng jiù 成就 *n.* achievement

chéng jiù 成就 *n.* attainment

chéng jiù 成就 *n.* success

chéng nián 成年 *n.* virility

chéng nián de 成年的 *a* adult

chéng nián rén 成年人 *n.* adult

chéng qún 成群 *v.t.* group

chéng qún ér xíng 成群而行 *v.i* flock

chéng shu 成熟 *v.i* mature

chéng shu 成熟 *n.* maturity

chéng shu 成熟 *v.i.* ripen

chéng shu de 成熟的 *a.* mature

chéng shu de 成熟的 *a* ripe

chéng tiáo wén zhuàng 成条纹状 *v.t.* stripe

chéng wéi diǎn fàn 成为典范 *v.t.* typify

chéng wéi qián zhào 成为前兆 *v.t.* portend

chéng wèn tí de 成问题的 *a.* problematic

chéng yǔ 成语 *n.* idiom

chéng yǔ 成语 *n.* phrase

chéng zhǎng 成长 *n.* germination

chéng zhī zì xíng 成之字形 *v.i.* zigzag

chéng bāo rén 承包人 *n* contractor

chéng dān 承担 *v.t.* undertake

chéng rèn 承认 *v.* acknowledge

chéng rèn 承认 *n.* acknowledgement

chéng rèn 承认 *v.t.* admit

chéng rèn 承认 *v.t.* concede

chéng rèn 承认 *v. t.* confess

chéng shòu 承受 *v.t* bear

chéng shòu dǐ yā zhě 承受抵押者 *n.* mortagagee

chéng zū rén 承租人 *n.* lessee

chéng dù 程度 *n.* pitch

chéng xù 程序 *n.* procedure

chéng xù 程序 *n.* proceeding

chéng xù 程序 *n.* process

chéng shí 诚实 *n.* honesty

chéng shí 诚实 *n.* veracity

chéng shí de 诚实的 *a.* honest

chéng shí de 诚实的 *a.* truthful

chéng shí dì 诚实地 *adv* bonafide

chéng bǎo 城堡 *n.* castle

chéng bǎo 城堡 *n.* fortress

chéng shì 城市 *n* city

chéng shì de 城市的 *a* civic

chéng shì de 城市的 *a.* urban

chéng 乘 *v.t.* mount

chéng 乘 *v.t.* multiply

chéng fǎ 乘法 *n.* multiplication

chéng kè 乘客 *n.* passenger

chéng kuài tǐng 乘快艇 *v.i* yacht

chéng qí yòng mǎ 乘骑用马 *n* mount

chéng fá 惩罚 *n.* punishment

chéng fá xìng de 惩罚性的 *a.* punitive

chéng qīng 澄清 *v. t* clarify

chéng qīng 澄清 *n* clarification

chéng 橙 *n.* orange

chéng huáng sè 橙黄色 *a* saffron

chéng sè de 橙色的 *a* orange

chī 吃 *v. t* eat

chī cǎo 吃草 *v.i.* graze

chī chī xiào shēng 吃吃笑声 *n.* twitter

chī lì de 吃力的 *a.* laboured

chí dào de 迟到的 *adj.* belated

chí dùn zhě 迟钝者 *n.* laggard

chí yán 迟延 *n.* retardation

chí táng 池塘 *n.* pond

chí xù 持续 *n.* continuation
chí xù 持续 *v.i.* last
chí rǔ 耻辱 *n* dishonour
chí rǔ 耻辱 *n.* humiliation
chí rǔ 耻辱 *n.* stigma
chí 匙 *n.* spoon
chǐ cùn 尺寸 *n* dimension
chǐ lún 齿轮 *n.* gear
chǐ yīn huà 齿音化 *v.* assibilate
chì zé 斥责 *v.t.* rebuke
chì dào 赤道 *n* equator
chì luǒ luǒ de 赤裸裸的 *a.* nude
chì pín de 赤贫的 *a.* penniless
chì rè 赤热 *n* glow
chì zì 赤字 *n* deficit
chì tuō 翅托 *n.* corbel
chōng fēn 充分 *n.* plenty
chōng mǎn 充满 *n.* fullness
chōng mǎn 充满 *v.i.* teem
chōng mǎn chóng jìng xin de 充满崇敬心的 *a.* reverential
chōng mǎn de 充满的 *a.* replete
chōng mǎn... de 充满的 *a.* fraught
chōng zú 充足 *v.i.* abound
chōng zú 充足 *n* abundance
chōng zú 充足 *n.* sufficiency
chōng zú de 充足的 *a* abundant
chōng chá 冲茶 *v.t.* brew
chōng dòng 冲动 *n.* impulse
chōng dòng 冲动 *n* urge
chōng dòng de 冲动的 *a.* impulsive
chōng jī 冲击 *v.i.* storm
chōng jìn 冲进 *n* rush
chōng kǒu ér chū 冲口而出 *v.t* blurt
chōng lì 冲力 *n.* impetuosity
chòng mú 冲模 *n* die
chōng tū 冲突 *v.i* conflict
chōng xǐ 冲洗 *v.t.* flush
chōng zhuàng 冲撞 *n* dash
chóng jiāo 虫胶 *n* lac, lakh
chóng dié 重叠 *n* overlap
chóng fù 重复 *n.* reiteration

chóng fù 重复 *v.t.* repeat
chóng fù 重复 *n.* repetition
chóng hūn zuì 重婚罪 *n* bigamy
chóng jiàn 重建 *n.* regeneration
chóng xīn 重新 *adv.* afresh
chóng xīn 重新 *adv.* anew
chóng xīn bǎo zhèng 重新保证 *v.t.* reassure
chóng xīn bǔ zú 重新补足 *v.t.* replenish
chóng xīn kāi shǐ 重新开始 *v.t.* resume
chóng yìn 重印 *n.* reprint
chóng bài 崇拜 *v.t.* adore chóng
bài 崇拜 *n.* apotheosis
chóng bài 崇拜 *v.t.* worship
chóng bài zhě 崇拜者 *n.* idolater
chóng bài zhě 崇拜者 *n.* worshipper
chóng gāo 崇高 *n* sublime
chóng gāo 崇高 *n.* sublimity
chóng gāo de 崇高的 *a.* sublime
chóng jìng 崇敬 *n.* venerate
chǒng ài 宠爱 *v.t.* pet
chǒng wù 宠物 *n.* pet
chōu chù 抽搐 *n.* spasm
chōu chū 抽出 *v.t* abstract
chōu chū 抽出 *v.t.* spare
chōu dòng 抽动 *v.i.* throb
chōu ti 抽屉 *n* drawer
chōu ti 抽屉 *n.* locker
chōu xiàng 抽象 *a* abstract
chōu xiàng de gài niàn 抽象的概念 *n.* abstraction
chóu hèn 仇恨 *n* animosity
chóu hèn 仇恨 *n* enmity
chóu hèn 仇恨 *n.* hate
chóu huà 筹划 *v.t.* steer
chóu bù shāng 绸布商 *n* draper
chóu jīn 酬金 *n.* honorarium
chóu láo 酬劳 *n.* remuneration
chóu róng 愁容 *n.* scowl
chǒu de 丑的 *a.* ugly
chǒu è de 丑恶的 *a.* hideous
chǒu huà 丑化 *v.t.* uglify

chǒu lǎo tài pó 丑老太婆 *n.* hag

chǒu lòu de rén 丑陋的人 *n.* ugliness

chǒu wén 丑闻 *n* scandal

chòu mà 臭骂 *n.* invective

chòu míng zhāo zhù 臭名昭著 *n.* notoriety

chòu qì 臭气 *n.* odour

chū bǎn 出版 *n.* publication

chū bǎn 出版 *v.t.* publish

chū bǎn shè 出版社 *n* press

chū bǎn zhě 出版者 *n.* publisher

chū biān de 出边的 *a.* outside

chū guó 出国 *adv* abroad

chū hàn 出汗 *v.i.* perspire chū hàn 出汗 *v.i.* sweat

chū jià 出价 *v.t* bid

chū jià gāo guò 出价高过 *v.t.* outbid

chū kǒu 出口 *n. exit*

chū kǒu 出口 *v. t.* export

chū mí 出谜 *v.i.* riddle

chū míng de 出名的 *a* famous

chū nà yuán 出纳员 *n.* teller

chū qín lǜ 出勤率 *n.* attendance

chū qu 出去 *adv.* out

chū shēn 出身 *n.* parentage

chū shēng 出生 *n.* birth

chū shēng 出生 *v.* born

chū shēng de 出生的 *a.* natal

chū shēng fù yù de 出生富裕 的 *adj.* born rich

chū xí 出席 *v.t.* attend

chū xiàn 出现 *n.* advent

chū xiàn 出现 *v.i.* appear

chū xiàn 出现 *v.i.* arise

chū xiàn 出现 *v. i* emerge

chū xiàn 出现 *n.* occurrence

chū xiàn 出现 *n.* presence

chū yóu 出游 *n.* outing

chū zū 出租 *v.t* hire

chū zū chē 出租车 *n.* cab

chū zū qì chē 出租汽车 *n.* taxi

chū bù cuò shī 初步措施 *n* preliminary

chū bù de 初步的 *a.* preliminary

chū bù de 初步的 *adv.* prima facie

chū cì de yǎn chū 初次的演出 *n.* premiere

chū jí dú běn 初级读本 *n.* primer

chū jí lǜ shī 初级律师 *n.* solicitor

chū qī 初期 *n.* infancy

chū qī de 初期的 *a.* nascent

chū xué zhě 初学者 *n.* infant

chú fǎ 除法 *n* division

chú le... zhī wài 除了...之外 *prep* except

chú qù 除去 *v. t* blot

chú qù 除去 *v. t* eliminate

chú qù 除去 *n* elimination

chú qù 除去 *v.t.* strip

chú wài 除外 *v. t* except

chú... de cǎo 除草 *v.t.* weed

chú fáng 厨房 *n.* kitchen

chú shī 厨师 *n* cook

chú jú 雏菊 *n* daisy

chú guì 橱柜 *n.* ambry

chǔ fá 处罚 *n.* penalty

chǔ fá 处罚 *v.t.* punish

chú lǐ 处理 *v. i* deal

chú lǐ 处理 *v. t* dispose

chú lǐ 处理 *v.t* handle

chú nǚ 处女 *n.* maiden

chú nǚ 处女 *n* virgin

chú nǚ de 处女的 *a.* virgin

chú nǚ zhēn jié 处女贞洁 *n.* virginity

chǔ xíng 处刑 *v.t.* penalize

chǔ yú kùn jìng 处于困境 *v.i.* strand

chǔ cáng wù 储藏物 *n* cache

chù jiǎo 触角 *n.* antennae

chù jué 触觉 *n* touch

chù jué de 触觉的 *a.* tactile

chù mō 触摸 *v.t* feel

chù shēng 畜牲 *n* sob

chuān cháng páo 穿长袍 *v.t.* robe

chuān guò 穿过 *adv.* across

chuān guò 穿过 *v. t* cross

chuān guò 穿过 *v.t* thread
chuān guò 穿过 *prep.* through
chuān kǒng yú 穿孔于 *v.t.* perforate
chuān tòu 穿透 *v.t.* pierce
chuān zhuó 穿着 *v.t.* wear
chuān yī 穿衣 *v. t* clothe
chuán bō 传播 *v.t.* propagate
chuán bō 传播 *n.* spread
chuán dān 传单 *n.* circular
chuán dān 传单 *n.* handbill
chuán dān 传单 *n.* leaflet
chuán dào 传道 *n.* mission
chuán dào 传道 *v.i.* preach
chuán huàn 传唤 *v.t.* summon
chuán jiào shì 传教士 *n.* missionary
chuán kāi 传开 *v.i.* spread
chuán piào 传票 *n.* summons
chuán qí wén xué 传奇文学 *n.* legend
chuán rǎn 传染 *v.t.* infect
chuán rǎn de 传染的 *a* contagious
chuán rǎn xìng de 传染性的 *a.* infectious
chuán shū 传输 *n.* transmission
chuán shuō de 传说的 *a* fabulous
chuán shuō de 传说的 *a.* legendary
chuán sòng 传送 *v.t.* transmit
chuán sòng zhě 传送者 *n.* transmitter
chuán tǒng 传统 *n.* tradition
chuán tǒng de 传统的 *a.* traditional
chuán wén 传闻 *n* bruit
chuán zhēn 传真 *n* facsimile
chuán 船 *n* boat
chuán 船 *n.* ship
chuán 船 *n.* vessel
chuán cāng 船舱 *n.* cabin
chuán huò 船货 *n.* freight
chuán jì 船迹 *n* wake
chuán yuán 船员 *n.* sailor
chuán zhǎng 船长 *n.* skipper
chuǎn qì 喘气 *n.* gasp

chuǎn qì 喘气 *v.i* gasp
chuǎn xī 喘息 *v.i.* pant
chuǎn xī 喘息 *n.* pant
chuāng 窗 *n.* window
chuāng gé bō li 窗格玻璃 *n.* pane
chuāng lián 窗帘 *n* curtain
chuáng 床 *n* bed
chuáng pù 床铺 *n* bunk
chuáng dān 床单 *n.* coverlet
chuáng shàng yòng pǐn 床上用品 *n.* bedding
chuǎng rù, qīn rǎo 闯入, 侵扰 *n.* intrusion
chuàng lì 创立 *v. t* erect
chuàng lì zhě 创立者 *n.* founder
chuàng xīn 创新 *n.* innovation
chuàng xīn zhě 创新者 *n.* innovator
chuàng yì 创意 *adj.* creative
chuàng zuò 创作 *v. t* compose
chuàng zuò zhě 创作者 *n* creator
chuàng zuò zhě 创作者 *n.* originator
chuī 吹 *v.i.* blow
chuī dí 吹笛 *v.i* pipe
chuī dí zi 吹笛子 *v.i* flute
chuī fú 吹拂 *n* waft
chuī gān 吹干 *v.t.* weather
chuī kǒu shào 吹口哨 *v.i.* whistle
chuī máo qiú cī 吹毛求疵 *v.i.* quibble
chuī niú 吹牛 *v. i* brag
chuī pěng 吹捧 *n* boost
chuī pěng 吹捧 *v. t* boost
chuí 锤 *n.* hammer
chuí dǎ 锤打 *v.t* hammer
chuí sí de 垂死的 *a.* moribund
chuí zhí de 垂直的 *a.* perpendicular
chuí zhí de 垂直的 *a.* vertical
chuí zhí xiàn 垂直线 *n.* perpendicular
chūn tiān 春天 *n* spring
chūn tiān de 春天的 *a.* vernal
chún cuì de 纯粹的 *a.* sheer

chún cuì zhǔ yì zhě 纯粹主义者 *n.* purist
chún de 纯的 *a* pure
chún jié de 纯洁的 *a.* spotless
chún jìng 纯净 *n.* purity
chún lǐ lùn de 纯理论的 *a.* notional
chún 唇 *n.* lip
chún yīn de 唇音的 *a.* labial
chuō 戳 *v.t.* poke
chuò 啜 *v.t.* sip
chuò qì 啜泣 *v.i.* sob
chuò yǐn 啜饮 *n.* sip
cī diǎn 疵点 *n.* imperfection
cí huì 词汇 *n.* lexicon
cí huì biǎo 词汇表 *n.* vocabulary
cí wěi 词尾 *n.* suffix
cí yuán xué 词源学 *n.* etymology
cí bié 辞别 *n.* adieu
cí bié 辞别 *interj.* adieu
cí bié 辞别 *n* farewell
cí diǎn biān zuǎn 辞典编纂 *n.* lexicography
cí zhí 辞职 *v.t.* resign
cí zhí 辞职 *n.* resignation
cí shí 磁石 *n.* magnet
cí xìng 磁性 *n.* magnetism
cí hú 雌狐 *n.* vixen
cí kǒng què 雌孔雀 *n.* peahen
cí shī 雌狮 *n.* lioness
cí qì 瓷器 *n.* porcelain
cí shàn 慈善 *n.* benefaction
cí shàn 慈善 *n.* charity
cí shàn 慈善 *n.* philanthropy
cí shàn de 慈善的 *a.* charitable
cí shàn de 慈善的 *a.* gracious
cí shàn de 慈善的 *a.* philanthropic
cí shàn jiā 慈善家 *n.* philanthropist
cǐ hòu 此后 *adv.* hereafter
cǐ hòu 此后 *adv.* thereafter
cì rì 次日 *n.* morrow
cì xù 次序 *n.* order
cì yào de 次要的 *a.* secondary

cì yè 次页 *adv.* overleaf
cì 刺 *v.t.* jab
cì 刺 *n.* lunge
cì 刺 *n.* poke
cì 刺 *v.t.* stab
cì 刺 *n.* stab
cì 刺 *v.t.* sting
cì 刺 *n.* thorn
cì chuān 刺穿 *v.t.* puncture
cì dāo 刺刀 *n* bayonet
cì ěr de 刺耳的 *a.* strident
cì hén 刺痕 *n.* puncture
cì jī 刺激 *v.t.* incite
cì jī 刺激 *n.* irritation
cì jī 刺激 *n.* provocation
cì jī 刺激 *n.* stimulus
cì jī 刺激 *v.t.* whet
cì jī de 刺激的 *a.* irritant
cì jī wù 刺激物 *n.* irritant
cì jī xìng de 刺激性的 *a.* pungent
cì kè 刺客 *n.* assassin
cì shā 刺杀 *n* assassination
cì tòng 刺痛 *v.t.* prick
cì tòng 刺痛 *v.i* smart
cì xiù 刺绣 *n* embroidery
cí zhuān 瓷砖 *n.* tile
cōng cù 匆促 *n.* rush
cōng máng 匆忙 *n.* haste
cōng máng dì zuò 匆忙地做 *v.t.* rush
cōng míng de 聪明的 *a.* clever
cōng míng de 聪明的 *a.* intelligent
cōng míng de 聪明的 *a.* sagacious
cōng míng de 聪明的 *a.* smart
jiǔ 葱 *n.* leek
cóng 从 *prep.* from
cóng hé chù 从何处 *adv.* whence
cóng jīn yǐ hòu 从今以后 *adv.* henceforward
cóng qián de 从前的 *a* former
cōng róng dì 从容地 *adv.* leisurely
cóng shǔ de 从属的 *a.* subordinate

cóng shǔ de 从属的 *a.* subservient

cóng yè zhě 从业者 *n.* practitioner

cóng lín 丛林 *n.* jungle

cù jìn 促进 *v.t.* advance

cū cāo de 粗糙的 *a* crude

cū cāo de 粗糙的 *a.* harsh

cū cāo de 粗糙的 *a.* rough

cū de 粗的 *a* coarse

cū lǔ de 粗鲁的 *adj.* crass

cū lǔ de 粗鲁的 *a.* uncouth

cū lǔ wú lǐ de 粗鲁无礼的 *a.* rude

cū lüè de 粗略的 *a.* sketchy

cū rén 粗人 *n* carl

cū shuài de 粗率的 *a* bluff

cū sú 粗俗 *n.* vulgarity

cū sú de 粗俗的 *a.* vulgar

cū xīn de 粗心的 *a.* careless

cù 醋 *n.* vinegar

cù huà 醋化 *v.* acetify

cù lì 醋栗 *n.* gooseberry

cuàn duó 篡夺 *n.* usurpation

cuī cù 催促 *v.t* urge

cuī mián 催眠 *v.t.* hypnotize

cuī mián shù 催眠术 *n.* hypnotism

cuī mián shù 催眠术 *n.* mesmerism

cuì de 脆的 *a.* brittle

cuì de 脆的 *a* crisp

cuì ruò de 脆弱的 *a.* fragile

cuì ruò de 脆弱的 *a.* vulnerable

cūn mín 村民 *n.* villager

cūn zhuāng 村庄 *n.* village

cún chǔ 存储 *n.* storage

cún fàng 存放 *v.t* deposit

cún huò de 存货的 *a.* stock

cún qián 存钱 *v.t.* bank

cún rù cāng kù 存入仓库 *v.t* warehouse

cún zài 存在 *v.t.* be

cún zài 存在 *v.i* exist

cún zài 存在 *n* existence

cuò bài 挫败 *v.t.* frustrate

cuò zhé 挫折 *n.* frustration

cuò shāng 挫伤 *v.t.* contuse

cuò cí 措辞 *n.* phraseology

cuò shī 措施 *n.* measure

cuò jué 错觉 *n.* delusion

cuò jué 错觉 *n.* illusion

cuò pèi 错配 *v.t.* mismatch

cuò wù 错误 *n* error

cuò wù 错误 *n.* mistake

cuò wù 错误 *adv.* wrong

cuò wù de 错误的 *a* erroneous

cuò wù de 错误的 *a.* wrong

cuò wù zhí dǎo 错误指导 *n.* misdirection

cuò 锉 *v.t* file

D

dā dàng 搭档 *n.* partner

dá àn 答案 *n* answer

dǎ 打 *v.t.* beat

dǎ 打 *v.t* cuff

dǎ 打 *v.t.* hit

dǎ 打 *v.t.* slap

dǎ bài 打败 *v.t.* vanquish

dǎ bàn 打扮 *v.t.* attire

dǎ bàn 打扮 *n.* garb

dǎ bàn 打扮 *v.t* garb

dǎ chéng dà bāo 打成大包 *v.t.* bale

dǎ chū wáng pái yíng 打出王牌赢 *v.t.* trump

dǎ dà fēi qiú 打大飞球 *v.t.* sky

dǎ diàn bào 打电报 *v.t* cable

dǎ diàn bào 打电报 *v.t.* telegraph

dǎ diàn huà gěi mǒu rén 打电话给某人 *v.t.* telephone

dǎ diàn huà rén 打电话人 *n* caller

dǎ diǎn yú 打点于 *v.t* dot

dǎ dòng qì 打洞器 *n.* punch

dǎ dòu 打斗 *v.i. & n* brawl

dǎ dòu 打斗 *v.i.* tussle

dá dǔ 打赌 *n.* wager

dá dǔ 打赌 *v.i.* wager

dǎ fā 打发 *v.t.* consign

dǎ gé 打嗝 *v. t* belch

dǎ gǔ chǎng 打谷场 *n.* thresher

dá gǔn 打滚 *v.i.* wallow

dǎ hā qian 打哈欠 *v.i.* yawn

dǎ hū lū 打呼噜 *v.i.* snore

dǎ hūn guò qù 打昏过去 *v.t.* stun

dǎ huǒ jī 打火机 *n.* lighter

dǎ jī 打击 *n* blow

dǎ jī 打击 *n* strike

dǎ jī zhě 打击者 *n.* striker

dǎ jià 打架 *v.t* fight

dǎ jié 打结 *v.t.* knot

dǎ kāi 打开 *v.t.* open

dǎ kē shuì 打瞌睡 *v. i* doze

dǎ kē shuì 打瞌睡 *v.i.* nap

dǎ léi 打雷 *v.i.* thunder

dǎ liè 打猎 *v.t.* hunt

dǎ pēn tì 打喷嚏 *v.i.* sneeze

dǎ pēn tì 打喷嚏 *n* sneeze

dá rǎo 打扰 *n.* interruption

dá sǎo 打扫 *n.* sweep

dǎ shāng 打伤 *v.t* maul

dǎ shàng zhuāng zi 打上桩子 *v.t.* spike

dǎ qì 打气 *v.t.* pump

dǎ qǐ jīng shen 打起精神 *v.t.* uplift

dǎ suan 打算 *v.t.* intend

dǎ suì 打碎 *v.t.* smash

dǎ ting 打听 *v.i.* pry

dǎ zì 打字 *v.i.* type

dǎ yìn 打印 *v.t.* print

dǎ yìn 打印 *n* print

dǎ yìn jī 打印机 *n.* printer

dǎ zì yuán 打字员 *n.* typist

dà 大 *a* big

dà bā 大巴 *n* coach

dà bài 大败 *n* rout

dà bāo 大包 *n.* bale

dà bēi 大杯 *n.* mug

dà běn shū 大本书 *n.* tome

dà bí zi de 大鼻子的 *a.* nosey

dà bù 大步 *n* stride

dà cháng 大肠 *n* colon

dà chén 大臣 *n.* chancellor

dà chén 大臣 *n.* minister

dà dǎn 大胆 *a.* adventurous

dà dǎn 大胆 *a.* bold

dà dǎn 大胆 *n.* intrepidity

dà dǎn de 大胆的 *a* daring

dà dǎn de 大胆的 *a.* venturous

dà de 大的 *a.* large

dà duō shù de 大多数的 *a.* most

dà ér zhòng de 大而重的 *a.* massy

dà fāng 大方 *a* bountiful

dà fāng de 大方的 *a.* lavish

dà fù háo 大富豪 *n.* croesus

dà gài 大概 *adv* about

dà gài 大概 *a.* approximate

dà gài 大概 *adv* probably

dà gāng 大纲 *n.* conspectus

dà gōng sī 大公司 *n* corporation

dà hǎn 大喊 *v.i.* bawl

dà huà 大话 *n* bouncer

dà jiǎn dāo 大剪刀 *n.pl.* shears

dà jiào 大叫 *v.i* exclaim

dà jiào táng 大教堂 *n.* cathedral

dà jiào táng 大教堂 *n.* minster

dà jiē 大街 *n.* thoroughfare

dà jīng xiǎo guài 大惊小怪 *n.* fuss

dà huáng fēng 大黄峰 *n.* hornet

dà lǐ shí 大理石 *n.* marble

dà liáng 大梁 *n.* girder

dà liàng 大量 *n* bulk

dà liàng 大量 *n.* profusion

dà liàng mào chū 大量冒出 *v.i* billow

dà lù 大路 *n.* highway

dà lù de 大陆的 *a* continental

dà lǜ shī 大律师 *n.* barrister

dà má 大麻 *n.* hemp

dà mài 大麦 *n.* barley

dà mǎng 大蟒 *n.* python

dà mù chuí 大木槌 *n.* maul

dà mù dì 大墓地 *n.* necropolis

dà nǎo de 大脑的 *adj* cerebral

dà nù 大怒 *v.i.* rage

dà pào 大炮 *n.* artillery

dà pào 大炮 *n.* cannon

dà péng chē 大篷车 *n.* caravan

dà pī shā hài 大批杀害 v.t. decimate

dà piàn tǔ dì 大片土地 n. tract

dà pù bù 大瀑布 n. cataract

dà qún 大群 n. swarm

dà shà 大厦 n edifice

dà shān dòng 大山洞 n. cavern

dà shè 大赦 n. amnesty

dà shēng 大声 adv. aloud

dà shēng de 大声的 a. loud

dà shēng jiào hǎn shēng 大声叫喊声 n yell

dà shǐ 大使 n. ambassador

dà shí guǎn 大使馆 n embassy

dà shí tou 大石头 n boulder

dǎ shǒu shì yāo qiú 打手势要求 v.i. motion

dà shù zhī 大树枝 n bough

dà suàn 大蒜 n. garlic

dà tà bù zǒu 大踏步走 v.i. stride

dà tīng 大厅 n. lobby

dà tóu dìng 大头钉 n. stud

dà tú shā 大屠杀 n carnage

dà tú shā 大屠杀 n. holocaust

dà tú shā 大屠杀 n. massacre

dà tuǐ gǔ 大腿骨 n. thigh

dà xiǎo 大小 n. size

dà xīng xing 大猩猩 n. gorilla

dà xué 大学 n. university

dà xué sheng 大学生 n. undergraduate

dà yáng de 大洋的 a. oceanic

dà yáo dà bǎi dì zǒu 大摇大摆地走 v.i. swagger

dà yè zhǐ 大页纸 n foolscap

dà yī 大衣 n. overcoat

dà zhǔ jiāo 大主教 n. archbishop

dà zhǔ jiāo 大主教 n. metropolitan

dà zì rán 大自然 n. nature

dài bǔ 逮捕 v.t. arrest

dài bǔ 逮捕 v.t. nab

dài bì 代币 n. token

dài biǎo 代表 n behalf

dài biǎo 代表 n. representative

dài biǎo de 代表的 a. representative

dài biǎo tuán 代表团 n delegation

dài biǎo tuán 代表团 n deputation

dài cí 代词 n. pronoun

dài lǐ 代理 n. agency

dài lǐ 代理 n. proxy

dài lǐ rén 代理人 n. assignee

dài lǐ rén 代理人 n deputy

dài rén fàng mù 代人放牧 v.t. agist

dài shù 代数 n. algebra

dài tì 代替 v.t. replace

dài tì 代替 v.t. substitute

dài tì 代替 n. substitution

dài tì 代替 v.t. supersede

dài tì de 代替的 a. alternative

dài tì pǐn 代替品 n. alternative

dài tì rén 代替人 n. substitute

dài tì zhě 代替者 n. replacement

dài kuǎn 贷款 n. loan

dài 带 n. strap

dài lái 带来 v. t bring

dài lǐng 带领 v.t. lead

dài tóu 带头 v.t. spearhead

dài zi cāo zuò gōng 带子操作工 n taper

dài duò 怠惰 n. laziness

dài guì guān de 戴桂冠的 a. laureate

dài huā huán 戴花环 v.t. garland

dài lǜ mào de rén 戴绿帽的人 n. cuckold

dài shàng shǒu kào 戴上手铐 v.t handcuff

dān bǎo 担保 n. guarantee

dān bǎo 担保 v.t guarantee

dān bǎo 担保 v.i. vouch

dān bǎo rén 担保人 n. surety

dān jià 担架 n. stretcher

dān xīn 担心 v.t dread

dān xīn de 担心的 a. apprehensive

dān xīn de 担心的 *a.* uneasy

dān yōu 担忧 *n.* worry

dān chéng piào 单程票 *n.* single

dān cí 单词 *n.* word

dān dān de 单单的 *a.* mere

dān diào 单调 *n* monotony

dān diào de 单调的 *a.* humdrum

dān diào de 单调的 *a.* monotonous

dān dú de 单独的 *a.* solo

dān fāng 单方 *adv* ex-parte

dān fāng miàn de 单方面的 *a* ex-parte

dān jiǎo tiào 单脚跳 *v. i* hop

dān jiǎo tiào 单脚跳 *n* hop

dān piàn yǎn jìng 单片眼镜 *n.* monocle

dān sè guāng de 单色光的 *a.* monochromatic

dān shēn de 单身的 *a.* single

dān shēn hàn 单身汉 *n.* bachelor

dān shù de 单数的 *a.* singular

dān wèi 单位 *n.* unit

dān yǎn de 单眼的 *a.* monocular

dān yīn jié cí 单音节词 *n.* monosyllable

dān yīn jié de 单音节的 *a.* monosyllabic

dān yú shēng sè 耽于声色 *n.* sensuality

dǎn dà wú dí 胆大无敌 *n.* hardihood

dán gǎn 胆敢 *v. i.* dare

dǎn liàng 胆量 *n* boldness

dǎn liàng 胆量 *n.* daring

dǎn xiǎo 胆小 *a.* timorous

dǎn xiǎo de 胆小的 *a.* timid

dǎn xiáo guǐ 胆小鬼 *n.* coward

dǎn zhī 胆汁 *n* bile

dǎn 掸 *v.t.* whisk

dǎn huī 掸灰 *v.t.* dust

dǎn zi 掸子 *n* duster

dàn shì 但是 *prep* but

dàn shì 但是 *conj.* only

dàn huáng sè 淡黄色 *n* buff

dàn huáng sè de 淡黄色的 *a.* yellowish

dàn bái 蛋白 *n* albumen

dàn bái shí 蛋白石 *n.* opal

dàn bái zhì 蛋白质 *n.* protein

dàn gāo 蛋糕 *n.* cake

dàn huáng 蛋黄 *n.* yolk

dàn mù shè jī 弹幕射击 *n.* barrage

dàn yào 弹药 *n.* ammunition

dàn shēng 诞生 *n.* nativity

dàn qì 氮气 *n.* nitrogen

dāng bīng 当兵 *v.i.* soldier

dāng fù de 当付的 *a* due

dāng quán qī jiān 当权期间 *n.* regime

dāng rán 当然 *adv.* certainly

dāng shí 当时 *a* then

dāng zhèng 当政 *v.i.* reign

dāng... de shí hòu 当...的时候 *conj.* when

dāng... de shí hòu 当...的时候 *conj.* while

dàng àn 档案 *n.pl.* archives

dàng àn 档案 *n* file

dàng àn guǎn 档案馆 *n* chancery

dǎng kāi 挡开 *v.t.* parry

dǎng kāi 挡开 *n.* parry

dāo 刀 *n.* baslard

dāo piàn 刀片 *n.* blade

dǎo 岛 *n.* island

dǎo dàn 导弹 *n.* missile

dǎo háng 导航 *n.* navigation

dǎo shī 导师 *n.* preceptor

dǎo shī de 导师的 *a.* tutorial

dáo yǎn 导演 *n.* director

dǎo 倒 *v.t.* pour

dǎo chū 倒出 *v.t.* tip

dǎo gōu 倒钩 *n.* barb

dǎo tā 倒塌 *v. i* collapse

dǎo tā 倒塌 *v.i.* topple

dào zhuǎn 倒转 *v.t.* reverse

dǎo suì 捣碎 *v.t* mash

dào chù 到处 *adv* around

dào chù xuān yáng 到处宣扬 *v.t.* trumpet

dào dá 到达 *n.* arrival

dào dá 到达 *v.i.* arrive

dào nà lǐ 到那里 *adv.* thither

dào nǎ lǐ 到哪里 *adv.* whither

dào qī 到期 *n* expiry

dào... 到… *prep.* until

dào dé 道德 *n.* morality

dào dé de 道德的 *a* ethical

dào dé de 道德的 *a.* moral

dào dé guī fàn 道德规范 *n.* ethics

dào dé jiā 道德家 *n.* moralist

dào jù 道具 *n.* prop

dào qiàn 道歉 *v.i.* apologize

dào qiàn 道歉 *n.* apology

dào yì shàng de 道义上的 *a.* honorary

dào qiè 盗窃 *n* burglary

dào qǔ 盗取 *v.t.* pilfer

dào yìn 盗印 *v.t* pirate

dào yòng 盗用 *v.t.* appropriate

dé dào 得到 *v.t.* get

dé dào 得到 *v.t.* obtain

dé dào shèng lì de 得到胜利的 *a.* triumphant

dé fēn 得分 *n.* score

dé fēn 得分 *v.i.* score

dé jiǎng zhāng zhě 得奖章者 *n.* medallist

dé tǐ 得体 *n* decency

dé tǐ 得体 *n* decorum

dé tǐ 得体 *n.* tact

dé zì 得自 *v.t.* derive

dé zuì 得罪 *v.t.* offend

dēng 灯 *n.* lamp

dēng long 灯笼 *n.* lantern

dēng pào 灯泡 *n.* bulb

dēng tǎ 灯塔 *n* beacon

dēng xīn 灯芯 *n.* wick

dēng jì 登记 *v.i.* register

dēng jì 登记 *n.* registration

dēng jì bù 登记簿 *n.* register

dēng jì chù 登记处 *n.* registry

dēng jì guān yuán 登记官员 *n.* registrar

dēng shān jiā 登山家 *n.* mountaineer

děng 等 *v.t* bide

děng biān de 等边的 *a* equilateral

děng dài 等待 *v.t.* await

děng dài zhī jì 等待之际 *prep.* pending

děng děng 等等 *adv.* etcetera

děng hòu 等候 *v.i.* wait

děng hòu 等候 *n.* wait

děng jí 等级 *n.* grade

děng jí 等级 *n.* rank

děng jí 等级 *n.* tier

děng jí zhì dù 等级制度 *n.* hierarchy

děng yā xiàn 等压线 *n.* isobar

děng yú 等于 *v.* amount

děng yú 等于 *v.t* equal

dèng zi 凳子 *n.* stool

dèng yǎn kàn 瞪眼看 *v.i.* stare

dī 低 *adv.* low

dī de 低的 *a.* low

dī diǎn 低点 *n.* low

dī fèi shēng 低吠声 *n.* woof

dī shēng shuō 低声说 *v.t.* whisper

dī yīn 低音 *n.* undertone

dī yǔ shēng 低语声 *n.* murmur

dī dào 堤道 *n* causeway

dī fang 提防 *v.i.* beware

dī 滴 *n* drip

dī 滴 *v.i* drip

dī 滴 *n* drop

dī 滴 *v.i.* trickle

dī jiǔ bù zhān 滴酒不沾 *a.* teetotal

dī dā 嘀嗒 *n.* tick

dí què 的确 *adv.* indeed

dí rén 敌人 *n.* antagonist

dí rén 敌人 *n* enemy

dí rén 敌人 *n* foe

dí rén de 敌人的 *a.* hostile

dí yì 敌意 *n* animus

dí yì 敌意 *n* antagonism

dí zuì 涤罪 *n.* purgatory

dí 笛 *n* flute

dí huǐ 诋毁 *n.* slander

dǐ bù 底部 *n* bottom

dǐ kàng de 抵抗的 *a.* resistant

dǐ kàng lì 抵抗力 *n.* resistance

dǐ xiāo 抵消 *v.t.* counteract

dǐ xiāo 抵销 *v.t.* offset

dǐ xiāo　抵销　n offset dǐ yā　抵押 v.t. mortgage

dǐ yā jiè kuǎn　抵押借款　n. mortgage

dǐ yā rén　抵押人　n. mortgagor

dǐ zhì　抵制　v. t. boycott

dǐ zhì　抵制　n boycott

dì bǎn　地板　n floor

dì bǎo　地堡　n bunker

dì dòng　地洞　n burrow

dì fang　地方　n area

dì fang　地方　n. place

dì fang de　地方的　a. regional

dì fang de　地方的　a. vernacular

dì fang fǎ　地方法　n bylaw, bye-law

dì fang fǎ guān　地方法官　n. magistrate

dì fang xìng de　地方性的　a. local

dì fang xíng zhèng zhǎng guān　地方行政长官　n. magistracy

dì jí　地极　n. pole

dì jiào　地窖　n cellar

dì lǐ de　地理的　a. geographical

dì lǐ xué　地理学　n. geography

dì lǐ xué jiā　地理学家　n. geographer

dì miàn　地面　n. land

dì píng xiàn　地平线　n. horizon

dì qiú　地球　n earth

dì qiú de　地球的　a earthly

dì qū　地区　n. locality

dì qū　地区　n. region

dì qū　地区　n. zone

dì tǎn　地毯　n. carpet

dì tú　地图　n map

dì tú jí　地图集　n. atlas

dì wèi　地位　n. status

dì wèi dī de　地位低的　a. lowly

dì wèi xiāng děng de rén　地位相等的人　n equal

dì xià de　地下的　a. subterranean

dì xià shì　地下室　n. basement

dì xīn yǐn lì　地心引力　n. gravity

dì xíng de　地形的　a. topographical

dì xíng xué　地形学　n. topography

dì yù　地狱　a. hell

dì yù　地狱　n. underworld

dì zhèn　地震　n earthquake

dì zhèn　地震　n quake

dì zhèn de　地震的　a. seismic

dì zhǐ　地址　n. address

dì zhì de　地质的　a. geological

dì zhì xué　地质学　n. geology

dì zhì xué zhě　地志学者　n. topographer

dì zhì xué zhuān jiā　地质学专家　n. geologist

dì guó　帝国　n empire

dì guó zhǔ yì　帝国主义　n. imperialism

dì wáng　帝王　n. monarch

dì wáng de　帝王的　a. imperial

dì wáng de　帝王的　a. regal

dì èr de　第二的　a. second

dì èr shí　第二十　num. twentieth

dì jiǔ　第九　a. ninth

dì jiǔ shí　第九十　a. ninetieth

dì liù　第六　a. sixth

dì liù shí　第六十　a. sixtieth

dì qī　第七　a. seventh

dì qī shí　第七十　a. seventieth

dì sān　第三　a. third

dì sān　第三　n. third

dì sān　第三　adv. thirdly

dì sān shí　第三十　a. thirtieth

dì sān shí　第三十　n thirtieth

dì shí èr　第十二　num. twelfth

dì shí jiǔ　第十九　a. nineteenth

dì shí liù　第十六　a. sixteenth

dì shí qī　第十七　a. seventeenth

dì shí sān　第十三　a. thirteenth

dì yī　第一　n first

dì yī de　第一的　a first

dì sòng　递送　v. t deliver

dì sòng　递送　n delivery

diān dǎo dì　颠倒地　adv topsy turvy

diān fù huó dòng 颠覆活动 n. subversion

diān lǎo 颠佬 n. maniac

diǎn fàn 典范 n classic

diǎn fàn 典范 n. quintessence

diǎn lǐ 典礼 n. observance

diǎn xíng de 典型的 a classic

diǎn xíng de 典型的 a. typical

diǎn 点 n dot

diǎn 点 n. point

diǎn jī 点击 n. click

diǎn míng 点名 n. roll-call

diǎn rán 点燃 v.t fire

diǎn rán 点燃 v.t. kindle

diǎn rán 点燃 v.t. light

diǎn tóu 点头 v.i. nod

diǎn xin 点心 n. refreshment

diàn 电 n electricity

diàn bào 电报 n. telegram

diàn bào 电报 n. telegraph

diàn bào de 电报的 a. telegraphic

diàn bào xué 电报学 n. telegraphy

diàn bīng xiāng 电冰箱 n. fridge

diàn bīng xiāng 电冰箱 n. refrigerator

diàn chē guǐ dào 电车轨道 n. tram

diàn chí 电池 n battery

diàn de 电的 a electric

diàn dù 电镀 v.t. plate

diàn huà 电话 n. call

diàn huà 电话 n. phone

diàn huà 电话 n. telephone

diàn jí tā 电吉他 n. bass

diàn lǎn 电缆 n. cable

diàn shì 电视 n. television

diàn shì bō sòng 电视播送 v.t. televise

diàn shì guǎng bō 电视广播 n. telecast

diàn tī 电梯 n. lift

diàn xiàn 电线 n. wire

diàn xìn jì shù 电信技术 n. telecommunications

diàn xìn jì shù 电信技术 n. telegraphist

diàn yā 电压 n. voltage

diàn yǐng 电影 n film

diàn yǐng 电影 n. movies

diàn yǐng yuàn 电影院 n. cinema

diàn yuán 电源 n main

diàn zhá 电闸 n. switch

diàn pù 店铺 n. shop

diàn fěn 淀粉 n. starch

diàn 垫 n cushion

diàn chōng 垫充 n. padding

diàn quān 垫圈 n. gasket

diàn zi 垫子 n. mattress

diàn lán sè 靛蓝色 n. indigo

diàn xià 殿下 n. Highness

diāo cán 凋残 v.i. wither

diāo kè 凋刻 n. sculpture

diāo kè de 凋刻的 a. sculptural

diāo kè jiā 凋刻家 n. sculptor

diāo kè 雕刻 v. t. chisel

diāo xiàng 雕像 n effigy

diāo xiàng 雕像 n. statue

diāo 貂 n. marten

diào chē 吊车 n crane

diào chá 调查 n. inquisition

diào chá 调查 v.t. investigate

diào chá 调查 n. investigation

diào chá 调查 v.t. probe

diào chá 调查 n research

diào chá 调查 v.t. survey

diào chá biǎo 调查表 n. survey

diào dòng 调动 v.i. manoeuvre

diào dòng 调动 v.t. mobilize

diào xià 掉下 v.i. slump

diào yú 钓鱼 v.i fish

diē dǎo 跌倒 v.i. tumble

diē jiāo 跌跤 v.i. slip

diē luò 跌落 v. i drop

dié dié bù xiū 喋喋不休 v.i. rattle

dié 碟 n dish

dié 碟 n. plate

dié gài 叠盖 v.t. overlap

dīng xiāng 丁香 n clove

dīng xiāng 丁香 n. lilac

dīng 叮 n. sting

dīng dāng shēng 叮当声 n. clink

dīng dāng shēng 叮当声 *n.* jingle

dǐng 顶 *n.* summit

dǐng bù 顶部 *n.* top

díng diǎn 顶点 *n.* apex

dǐng diǎn 顶点 *n.* zenith

dǐng zhēn 顶针 *n.* thimble

dǐng zhù 顶住 *v.t.* withstand

dìng 订 *v. t.* book

dìng hūn 订婚 *n.* betrothal

dìng yuè 订阅 *n.* subscription

dìng … de fāng wèi 定…的方位 *v.t.* orientate

dìng jià 定价 *v.t.* price

dìng jīn 定金 *n.* deposit

dìng lǐ 定理 *n.* theorem

dìng qī de 定期的 *a.* periodical

dìng qī jīn tiē 定期津贴 *n.* stipend

dìng sè diào 定色调 *v.t.* tone

dìng xíng de 定型的 *a.* stereotyped

dìng yì 定义 *v. t* define

dìng yì 定义 *n* definition

dīng 钉 *n.* nail

dīng 钉 *n.* peg

dīng mù dìng 钉木钉 *v.t.* peg

dīng shū dìng 钉书钉 *n.* staple

dīng zhù 钉住 *v.t.* pin

dīng zhù 钉住 *v.t.* stick

dìng zǐ 锭子 *n.* spindle

diū diào 丢掉 *n* disposal

diū qì 丢弃 *v. t* discard

dōng 东 *n* east

dōng fāng 东方 *n.* orient

dōng fāng de 东方的 *a* eastern

dōng fāng de 东方的 *a.* oriental

dōng fāng rén 东方人 *n* oriental

dōng xi 东西 *n.* thing

dōng jì 冬季 *n.* winter

dōng mián 冬眠 *n.* hibernation

dòng 动 *v.t.* move

dòng 动 *v.i.* stir

dòng chǎn 动产 *n.* movables

dòng cí 动词 *n.* verb

dòng cí biàn huà 动词变化 *v.t. & i.* conjugate

dòng huà 动画 *n* animation

dòng huà 动画 *n.* cartoon

dòng jī 动机 *n.* motive

dòng jī de xíng chéng 动机的形成 *n.* motivation

dòng lì 动力 *n.* momentum

dòng lì de 动力的 *a* dynamic

dòng luàn 动乱 *v.t* ferment

dòng luàn 动乱 *n* ferment

dòng mài 动脉 *n.* artery

dòng jié 冻结 *v.i.* freeze

dòng míng cí 动名词 *n.* gerund

dòng tài 动态 *n.* dynamics

dòng wù 动物 *n.* animal

dòng wù qún 动物群 *n* fauna

dòng wù xué 动物学 *n.* zoology

dòng wù xué de 动物学的 *a.* zoological

dòng wù xué jiā 动物学家 *n.* zoologist

dòng wù yóu zhī 动物油脂 *n.* tallow

dòng wù yuán 动物园 *n.* zoo

dòng yáo 动摇 *v.i.* oscillate

dòng yáo 动摇 *v.i.* waver

dòng zuò 动作 *n.* action

dòng zuò 动作 *n.* movement

dòng zuò 动作 *n.* operation

dòng 洞 *n* hole

dòng 洞 *n.* hollow

dōu mào 兜帽 *n.* hood

dòu niú shì 斗牛士 *n .* matador

dǒu peng 斗篷 *n* mantle

dǒu peng 斗篷 *n.* cloak

dòu zhēng 斗争 *v.i.* strive

dòu zhì 斗志 *n* fight

dòu 豆 *n.* bean

dòu jiá 豆荚 *n.* pod

dòu kòu 豆蔻 *n.* cardamom

dòu hào 逗号 *n* comma

dòu liú 逗留 *v.i.* sojourn

dòu liú 逗留 *n* sojourn

dòu liú zhě 逗留者 *n* stay

dòu yǐn 逗引 *v.t.* tantalize

dú 独 *adv.* solo

dú bái 独白 *n.* monologue dú

cái zhě 独裁者 *n* autocrat

dú cái zhèng zhì 独裁政治 *n* autocracy

dú chàng 独唱 *n* solo

dú chàng zhě 独唱者 *n.* soloist

dú chuàng xìng 独创性 *n.* originality

dú gè ér de 独个儿的 *a.* solitary

dú lì 独立 *n.* independence

dú lì de 独立的 *a.* independent

dú lì zì zhǔ de 独立自主的 *a* sovereign

dú shēn 独身 *n.* celibacy

dú shēn shēng huó 独身生活 *n.* celibacy

dú tè de 独特的 *a.* inimitable

dú tè de 独特的 *a.* unique

dú zhàn 独占 *v.t.* monopolize

dú zhàn de 独占的 *a* exclusive

dú zì 独自 *a.* alone

dú 毒 *n.* poison

dú hài 毒害 *v.t.* poison

dú pǐn 毒品 *n* drug

dú xìng 毒性 *n.* virulence

dú yè 毒液 *n.* venom

dú 读 *v.t.* read

dú xiě néng lì 读写能力 *n.* literacy

dú zhě 读者 *n.* reader

dǔ 赌 *v.i* bet

dǔ bó 赌博 *n* gamble

dǔ bó 赌博 *v.i* game

dǔ bó zhě 赌博者 *n.* gambler

dǔ sài 堵赛 *v.t.* choke

dǔ sāi 堵塞 *v.t.* obstruct

dǔ sè 堵塞 *n.* obstruction

dǔ zhù 堵住 *v.i.* stem

dù juān niǎo 杜鹃鸟 *n* cuckoo

dù 肚 *n* belly

dù zi 肚子 *n.* stomach

dù jì 妒忌 *n.* jealousy

dù jiǎ shèng dì 度假胜地 *n* resort

dù jiǎ yíng 度假营 *n.* camp

dù jīn 镀金 *v.t.* gild

dù jīn 镀金 *a.* gilt

dù yā 渡鸦 *n.* raven

dù yín 镀银 *v.t.* silver

duān 端 *n.* end

duǎn chu 短处 *n.* shortcoming

duǎn de 短的 *a.* short

duǎn ér yìng de máo 短而硬的毛 *n* bristle

duǎn hào 短号 *n.* cornet

duǎn jù lí sài pǎo 短距离赛跑 *n* sprint

duǎn kù 短裤 *n. pl.* shorts

duǎn shàng yī 短上衣 *n.* jerkin

duán shǎo 短少 *n.* shortage

duǎn shī 短诗 *v.t.* versify

duǎn wà 短袜 *n.* sock

duàn 段 *n.* paragraph

duàn duàn xù xù de 断断续续的 *a* fitful

duàn jué 断绝 *n.* severance

duàn rán jù jué 断然拒绝 *n.* rebuff

duàn yán 断言 *n.* allegation

duàn dài 缎带 *n.* ribbon

duàn liàn 锻炼 *v. i* exercise

duī 堆 *n.* heap

duī 堆 *n.* pile

duī jī 堆积 *v.t* heap

duī jī de 堆积的 *adv* aheap

duī yú 堆于 *v.t.* pile

duì 队 *n.* gang

duì 队 *n.* team

duì zhǎng 队长 *n.* captain

duì zhǎng zhí wèi 队长职位 *n.* captaincy

duì 对 *prep.* versus

duì bǐ 对比 *v. t* contrast

duì bú zhù 对不住 *a.* sorry

duì chèn 对称 *n.* symmetry

duì chèn de 对称的 *a.* symmetrical

duì dài 对待 *v.t.* treat

duì huà 对话 *n* dialogue

duì kàng 对抗 *v.t.* antagonize

duì lì 对立 *n.* antithesis

duì lì 对立 *n.* opposition

duì lián 对联 *n.* couplet

duì miàn 对面 *prep.* across

duì qí 对齐 *v.t.* align duì shǒu
对手 *n.* adversary
duì shù 对数 *n.* logarithm
duì wu 队伍 *n.* procession
duì yùn yóu xì 对韵游戏 *n.*
    crambo
duì zhào 对照 *v.t.* contrapose
duì zhào 对照 *n* contrast
duì zhì 对质 *n.* confrontation
duì xiàn zhī piào 兑现支票
    v. t. cash
dūn 吨 *n.* tonne
dūn 蹲 *v.i.* squat
dūn zhe 蹲着 *v. i.* crouch
dùn 炖 *v.i.* simmer
dùn 炖 *n.* stew
dùn chǐ 钝齿 *n* cog
dùn de 钝的 *a.* obtuse
dùn wěn è 钝吻鳄 *n* alligator
dùn 钝 *a* blunt
dùn 盾 *n.* shield
dùn cí 遁词 *n.* quibble
duō 多 *adv* more
duō 多 *adv* much
duō biān de 多边的 *a.*
    multilateral
duō cái duō yì de 多才多艺的
    a. versatile
duō chǎn de 多产的 *a.*
    prolific
duō cì de 多刺的 *a.* thorny
duō de 多的 *a.* more
duō huā de 多花的 *a* flowery
duō nián shēng de 多年生的
    n. perennial
duō pèi ǒu 多配偶 *n.*
    polygamy
duō shén jiāo 多神教 *n.*
    polytheism
duō shén jiāo de 多神教的 *a.*
    polytheistic
duō shén jiào tú 多神教徒 *n.*
    polytheist
duō shù 多数 *n.* majority
duō tāi chǎn de 多胎产的 *a.*
    multiparous
duō xiè 多谢 *n.* thanks
duō xīng de 多星的 *a.* starry
duō xuě de 多雪的 *a.* snowy

duō yàng de 多样的 *a.*
    multiple
duō yàng de 多样的 *a.*
    multiplex
duō yè de 多叶的 *a.* leafy
duō yòng tú 多用途 *n.* versatility
duō yú de 多余的 *a.* redundant
duō yú de 多余的 *a* spare
duō yǔ de 多雨的 *a.* rainy
duō yún de 多云的 *a* cloudy
duō yún de 多云的 *a.* overcast
duō zhī yè de 多汁液的 *a.* juicy
duō zhǒng de 多种的 *a.*
    manifold
duō zhòng xìng 多重性 *n.*
    multiplicity
duō zhǒng xíng shì de 多种形式
    的 *a* multiform
duō zhǒng yǔ yán de 多种语言
    的 *a.* polyglot
duō zú dòng wù 多足动物 *n.*
    multiped
duō 咄 *interj* fie
duǒ cáng chù 躲藏处 *n.* hide
duò 舵 *n.* helm
duò xìng de 惰性的 *a.* inert
duò tāi 堕胎 *n* abortion

E

é 额 *n* forehead
é fā 额发 *n* forelock
é wài de 额外的 *a.* additional
é wài de 额外的 *a* extra
é wài dì 额外地 *adv* extra
é 鹅 *n.* goose
é 蛾 *n.* moth
è chòu 恶臭 *n.* stench
è chòu 恶臭 *v.i.* stink
è chòu de 恶臭的 *a.* foul
è chòu de 恶臭的 *a* rank
è chòu de rén 恶臭的人 *n* stink
è dú de 恶毒的 *a.* malicious
è dú de 恶毒的 *a.* nefarious
è gùn 恶棍 *n.* miscreant
è gùn 恶棍 *n.* rogue
è gùn 恶棍 *n.* ruffian

è gùn 恶棍 n. scoundrel
è gùn xíng wéi 恶棍行为 n. knavery
è huà 恶化 n. aggravation
è huà 恶化 v. i compound
è liè de 恶劣的 a gross
è liè de 恶劣的 a. vile
è mèng 恶梦 n. nightmare
è mó de 恶魔的 a. infernal
è xí 恶习 n. vice
è xíng 恶行 n. infamy
è xìng 恶性 n. malignancy
è xìng de 恶性的 a. malignant
è yì 恶意 n. malice
è yì 恶意 n. malignity
è yì de 恶意的 a. baleful
è yì de 恶意的 a. wanton
è zuò jù 恶作剧 n. hoax
è zuò jù 恶作剧 n. prank
è zuò jù 恶作剧 n. roguery
è 轭 n. yoke
è 颚 n. jaw
è 腭 n. palate
è de 腭的 a. palatal
è yú 鳄鱼 n crocodile
ēn huì 恩惠 n boon
ér zi 儿子 n. son
ér 而 conj. whereas
ér qiě 而且 adv. also
ér qiě 而且 adv besides
ér qiě 而且 conj both
ér qiě 而且 adv. withal
ér qiě hái 而且还 adv. either
ěr chuí 耳垂 n. lobe
ěr duo 耳朵 n ear
ěr gòu 耳垢 n cerumen
ěr xíng de 耳形的 adj. auriform
ér yǔ 耳语 n whisper
èr 二 n. two
èr bǎi zhōu nián 二百週年 adj bicentenary
èr de 二的 a dual
èr děng fēn 二等分 v.t. halve
èr jìn zhì 二进制 adj binary
èr shí 二十 num. twenty
èr shí rì 二十日 n twentieth
èr tóu jī 二头肌 n biceps
èr yuè 二月 n February

èr bǎi zhōu nián 二百週年 adj bicentenary
èr de 二的 a dual
èr děng fēn 二等分 v.t. halve
èr jìn zhì 二进制 adj binary
èr shí 二十 num. twenty
èr shí 二十 n twenty
èr shí rì 二十日 n twentieth
èr tóu jī 二头肌 n biceps
èr yuè 二月 n February

F

fā bái de 发白的 a. whitish
fā bù mìng lìng 发布命令 v. i decree
fā chū bào liè shēng 发出爆裂声 v.i. pop
fā chū huǒ huā 发出火花 v.i. scintillate
fā chū shēng yīn 发出声音 v.t. utter
fā dī hēng shēng 发低哼声 v. i hum
fā diàn jī 发电机 n dynamo
fā diàn qì 发电器 n. generator
fā dòng 发动 v.t. launch
fā dǒu 发抖 v.i. shudder
fā dǒu 发抖 n. thrill
fā gěi tuì xiū jīn 发给退休金 v.t. pension
fā guāng 发光 v.i. irradiate
fā guāng 发光 v.i. shine
fā guāng de 发光的 a. luminous
fā guāng de 发光的 a. shiny
fā guāng tǐ 发光体 n. luminary
fā hóng guāng 发红光 v.i. glow
fā méi de 发霉的 a. musty
fā míng 发明 v. t devise
fā míng 发明 v.t. invent
fā míng 发明 n. invention
fā míng jiā 发明家 n. inventor
fā nù de 发怒的 a. irate
fā piào 发票 n. invoice
fā qǐ 发起 v.t. originate
fā qiú 发球 n. serve

fā shāo　发烧　n fever
fā shè　发射　n.　launch
fā shè　发射　v.t.　shoot
fā shè de　发射的　a projectile
fā shēng　发生　v.t.　happen
fā shēng　发生　v.i.　occur
fā shēng xiǎo zhēng lùn　发生小争论　v.i.　skirmish
fā shēng yíng xiǎng　发生影响　v.i.　militate
fā shì　发誓　v.t.　swear
fā shì pāo qì　发誓抛弃　v.t.　forswear
fā sī sī shēng　发嘶嘶声　v.i hiss
fā sòng　发送　v.t.　send
fā xiàn　发现　v. t discover
fā xiàn　发现　n.　discovery
fā xiàn　发现　v.t find
fā xìn hào　发信号　v.t.　signal
fā xíng　发行　v.i.　issue
fā xíng　发行　n release
fā xuàn guāng　发眩光　v.i glare
fā yá　发芽　v.i.　germinate
fā yá　发芽　v.i.　sprout
fā yán　发炎　n.　inflammation
fā yán quán　发言权　n.　say
fā yán rén　发言人　n.　spokesman
fā yǎng　发痒　v.i.　itch
fā yīn　发音　v.t.　pronounce
fā yīn　发音　n.　pronunciation
fā zhǎn　发展　v. t.　develop
fā zhǎn　发展　n.　development
fā zuò　发作　n fit
fā jiào　发酵　n fermentation
fā láo sāo　发牢骚　v.i.　grumble
fā láo sāo　发牢骚　v.i.　murmur
fā le méi de　发了霉的　a.　mouldy
fā liàng de　发亮的　a.　lucent
fā liàng de　发亮的　a.　splendid
fā lóng lóng shēng　发隆隆声　v.i.　rumble
fá jīn　罚金　n forfeit
fá kuǎn　罚款　n fine
fá kuǎn　罚款　v.t fine
fǎ dìng de　法定的　a. statutory
fǎ dìng rén shù　法定人数　n.　quorum

fǎ guān　法官　n.　judge
fǎ guān　法官　n.　judiciary
fǎ guó de　法国的　a.　French
fǎ guó rén　法国人　n French
fǎ lán róng　法兰绒　n flannel
fǎ lìng　法令　n decree
fǎ lìng　法令　n.　ordinance
fǎ lìng　法令　n.　statute
fǎ lǜ　法律　n.　law
fǎ lǜ xué　法律学　n.　jurisprudence
fǎ tíng　法庭　n.　court
fǎ tíng　法庭　n.　tribunal
fǎ xué jiā　法学家　n.　jurist
fǎ láng　珐琅　n enamel
fān　帆　n.　sail
fān bù　帆布　n.　canvas
fān qié　番茄　n.　tomato
fān shí liu　番石榴　n.　guava
fān yīng táo　番樱桃　n.　myrtle
fān qié jiàng　蕃茄酱　n.　ketchup
fān chá　翻查　v.t.　overhaul
fān gǔn　翻滚　n.　tumble
fān gǔn　翻滚　n.　welter
fān jīn dòu　翻筋斗　v.i.　somersault
fān xīn　翻新　v.t.　retread
fān yì　翻译　v.t.　interpret
fān yì　翻译　v.t.　translate
fān yì　翻译　n.　translation
fān zhuǎn　翻转　v. i.　capsize
fān zhuǎn　翻转　n.　reversal
fán rén　凡人　n mortal
fán shì lín　凡士林　n.　vaseline
fán　烦　v. t bore
fán nǎo　烦恼　n.　annoyance
fán nǎo　烦恼　n botheration
fán nǎo　烦恼　n vexation
fán rén　烦人　n bore
fán zào　烦躁　n.　fret
fán mào　繁茂　n.　luxuriance
fán róng　繁荣　v.i flourish
fán róng　繁荣　n.　prosperity
fán róng de　繁荣的　a.　prosperous
fán zhí　繁殖　n reproduction
fán zhòng de　繁重的　a.　onerous

fǎn 反 *pref.* anti

fǎn bó 反驳 *v. t* contradict

fǎn bó 反驳 *n.* refutation

fǎn bó 反驳 *v.t.* refute

fǎn bó 反驳 *n.* rejoinder

fǎn bó 反驳 *n.* retort

fǎn cháng 反常 *n.* aberrance

fǎn chú dòng wù 反刍动物 *n.* ruminant

fǎn chú lèi de 反刍类的 *a.* ruminant

fǎn duì 反对 *prep.* against

fǎn duì 反对 *v. i* demur

fǎn duì 反对 *n.* negation

fǎn duì 反对 *v.i.* object

fǎn duì 反对 *n.* objection

fǎn duì 反对 *v.i.* protest

fǎn duì de 反对的 *a.* averse

fǎn duì piào 反对票 *n.* contra

fǎn fù dì shuō 反复地说 *v.t.* reiterate

fǎn fù guàn shū 反复灌输 *v.t.* inculcate

fǎn fù jìn xíng 反复进行 *v.t.* thrash

fán gǎn 反感 *n.* antipathy

fán gǎn 反感 *n.* aversion

fán gǎn 反感 *n.* odium

fán gǎn 反感 *n.* repugnance

fán gǎn 反感 *n.* repulsion

fǎn kàng 反抗 *v. i* mutiny

fǎn kàng 反抗 *v.t.* resist

fǎn kàng 反抗 *v.i.* revolt

fǎn kàng 反抗 *n.* revolt

fǎn kàng de 反抗的 *a.* rebellious

fǎn kòng 反控 *n.* countercharge

fǎn miàn de 反面的 *a.* negative

fǎn pàn zhě 反叛者 *n* malcontent

fǎn shè 反射 *v.t.* mirror

fǎn shè 反射 *n.* reflex

fǎn shè de 反射的 *a.* reflective

fǎn shè de 反射的 *a* reflexive

fǎn shè qì 反射器 *n.* reflector

fǎn shǒu 反手 *n.* backhand

fǎn tán 反弹 *n.* rebound

fǎn xiàng de 反向的 *a.* backward

fán xǐng 反省 *n.* introspection

fǎn yì cí 反义词 *n.* antonym

fǎn yìng 反应 *n.* reaction

fǎn yìng 反映 *v.t.* reflect

fǎn yìng 反映 *n.* reflection

fǎn yǔ 反语 *n.* irony

fǎn zhī yì rán 反之亦然 *adv.* vice-versa

fǎn lǎo hái tóng 返老还童 *n.* rejuvenation

fǎn huí 返回 *v.i.* return

fàn shén lùn 泛神论 *n.* pantheism

fàn cuò 犯错 *v.i.* lapse

fàn cuò wù 犯错误 *v. i* err

fàn dà cuò 犯大错 *v.i* blunder

fàn fǎ de 犯法的 *a* criminal

fàn rén 犯人 *n.* offender

fàn zuì 犯罪 *n* crime

fàn zuì 犯罪 *v.i.* sin

fàn zuì de 犯罪的 *a.* guilty

fàn zuì dì diǎn 犯罪地点 *n.* venue

fàn wéi 范围 *n.* extent

fàn wéi 范围 *n.* purview

fāng àn 方案 *n.* scheme

fāng biàn 方便 *n.* convenience

fāng biàn 方便 *a* convenient

fāng chéng shì 方程式 *n* equation

fāng fǎ 方法 *n* means

fāng fǎ 方法 *n.* method

fāng miàn 方面 *n.* aspect

fāng miàn 方面 *n* facet

fāng shì 方式 *n.* approach

fāng shì 方式 *n.* mode

fāng wèi 方位 *n* bearing

fāng xiàng 方向 *n* direction

fāng yán 方言 *n* dialect

fāng zhēn 方针 *n.* policy

fāng zhōu 方舟 *n* ark

fáng fǔ jì 防腐剂 *n.* antiseptic

fáng fǔ jì 防腐剂 *n.* preservative

fáng hù 防护 *v. t* defend

fáng kōng 防空 *a.* anti-aircraft

fáng shuǐ de 防水的 a. waterproof

fáng shuǐ wù 防水物 n waterproof

fáng wèi 防卫 n defence

fáng zhǐ 防止 v. t. combat

fáng zhǐ 防止 v.t. prevent

fáng yù tǔ qiáng 防御土墙 n. rampart

fáng zhǐ jié bīng 防止结冰 v.t. deice

fáng ài 妨碍 v.t. handicap

fáng ài 妨碍 v.t. retard

fáng hài 妨害 v.t. sabotage

fáng 房 n. room

fáng zi 房子 n house fǎng zào de 仿造的 a. counterfeit

fǎng shā gōng rén 纺纱工人 v.i. spin

fǎng shā gōng rén 纺纱工人 n. spinner

fǎng zhī pǐn 纺织品 n textile

fǎng zhī pǐn de 纺织品的 a. textile

fàng cuò dì fang 放错地方 v.t. misplace

fàng dà 放大 v.t. amplify

fàng dà 放大 v. t enlarge

fàng dà 放大 v.t. magnify

fàng dàng 放荡 n debauch

fàng dàng 放荡 n debauchery

fàng dàng de 放荡的 a. profligate

fàng dàng de nǚ rén 放荡的女人 n. slut

fàng dàng zhě 放荡者 n. libertine

fàng ěr 放饵 v.t. bait

fàng màn 放慢 v.t. slacken

fàng màn 放慢 v.i. slow

fàng mù 放牧 v.t. pasture

fàng qì 放弃 v.t abdicate

fàng qì 放弃 n abdication

fàng qì 放弃 v. t. desert

fàng qì 放弃 v.t. relinquish

fàng qì 放弃 n. renunciation

fàng qì 放弃 v.t. surrender

fàng qì 放弃 v.t. waive

fàng shè 放射 v. t emit

fàng sì de 放肆的 a. licentious

fàng yìng 放映 v.t. project

fàng yìng jī 放映机 n bioscope

fàng yìng jī 放映机 n. projector

fàng zài shì dàng wèi zhi 放在适当位置 v.t. position

fàng zhì 放置 v.t. lay

fàng zhì jià zi shàng 放置架子上 v.t. shelve

fàng zhú 放逐 v t exile

fàng zǒu 放走 v.t. banish fàng zǒu 放走 n. banishment

fēi 飞 v.i fly

fēi bēn 飞奔 n. gallop

fēi biāo 飞镖 n. dart

fēi háng yuán 飞行员 n. aviator

fēi háng yuán 飞行员 n. pilot

fēi jī 飞机 n. aeroplane

fēi jī 飞机 n. plane

fēi kuài de 飞快的 a. rapid

fēi tǐng 飞艇 n. aircraft

fēi cháng 非常 adv. highly

fēi cháng 非常 adv. monstrous

fēi cháng 非常 a. very

fēi cháng de 非常的 a. extraordinary

fēi cháng de 非常的 a great

fēi cháng gāo xìng 非常高兴 v. i exult

fēi cháng gāo xìng de 非常高兴的 a overjoyed

fēi fǎ de 非法的 a. lawless

fēi fǎ qīn rù 非法侵入 n. trespass

fēi fǎ tóng jū 非法同居 n. concubinage

fēi jīng cháng de 非经常的 a. occasional

fēi jīng cháng dì 非经常地 adv. occasionally

fēi nàn 非难 n. damnation

fēi zhǔ yào de 非主要的 a. incidental

fēi zì rán zhuàng tài de 非自然状态的 a. sophisticated

fēi 鲱 n. herring

féi de 肥的 *a* fat
féi liào 肥料 *n* compost
féi liào 肥料 *n* fertilizer
féi liào 肥料 *n.* manure
féi pàng 肥胖 *n.* obesity
féi zào 肥皂 *n.* soap
féi zào pào 肥皂泡 *n.* lather
féi zào zhuàng de 肥皂状的 *a.* soapy
fěi bàng 诽谤 *v.* asperse
fěi bàng 诽谤 *v. t.* calumniate
fěi bàng 诽谤 *n* defamation
fěi bàng 诽谤 *v.t.* malign
fěi bàng zuì 诽谤罪 *n.* libel
fèi chú 废除 *v.t* abolish
fèi chú 废除 *v* abolition
fèi chú 废除 *v. t.* abrogate
fèi chú 废除 *v.t.* annul
fèi chù 废黜 *v. t* dethrone
fèi huà 废话 *n.* nonsense
fèi pǐn 废品 *n.* waste
fèi wù 废物 *n.* refuse
fèi xū 废墟 *n.* ruin
fèi zhǐ 废止 *v.t.* repeal
fèi zhǐ 废止 *n* repeal
fèi zhǐ 废止 *n.* revocation
fèi zhǐ shǐ yòng 废止使用 *v.t.* demonetize
fèi 肺 *n* lung
fèi yán 肺炎 *n.* pneumonia
fèi téng 沸腾 *v.i.* boil
fèi fèi 狒狒 *n.* baboon
fèi lì dì zhǎo 费力地找 *v.i.* quarry
fèi yong 费用 *n* fare
fēn 分 *n* cent
fēn 分 *v. t* divide
fēn 分 *n.* minute
fēn bié de 分别的 *a.* respective
fēn chéng chuán dì 分程传递 *v.t.* relay
fēn chéng sān bù de 分成三部的 *a.* tripartite
fēn děng 分等 *v.t.* rank
fēn gē 分割 *v.t.* partition
fēn jí 分级 *v.t* grade
fēn jiě 分解 *v. t.* decompose
fēn jiě 分解 *n.* decomposition

fēn kāi 分开 *adv.* apart
fēn kāi 分开 *v.i.* split
fēn kāi 分开 *v.t.* sunder
fēn kāi de 分开的 *a.* separate
fēn lèi 分类 *v.t.* assort
fēn lèi 分类 *v. t* classify
fēn lèi zhàng 分类帐 *n.* ledger
fēn lí 分离 *n.* separation
fēn liè 分裂 *n.* schism
fēn mì 分泌 *v.t.* secrete
fēn mì 分泌 *n.* secretion
fēn mì nián yè de 分泌黏液的 *a.* mucous
fēn mì rǔ zhī 分泌乳汁 *v.i.* lactate
fēn pèi 分配 *v.t.* allocate
fēn pèi 分配 *v.t.* allot
fēn pèi 分配 *v.t.* apportion
fēn pèi 分配 *v. t* distribute
fēn pèi 分配 *n* distribution
fēn pèi 分配 *v.t.* portion
fēn qí 分歧 *n.* clash
fēn qī fù kuǎn 分期付款 *n.* instalment
fēn qiǎn duì 分遣队 *n* detachment
fēn sàn 分散 *v. t* disperse
fēn sàn de 分散的 *a.* sporadic
fēn xī 分析 *v.t.* analyse
fēn xī 分析 *n.* analysis
fēn xī de 分析的 *a* analytical
fēn xī yuán 分析员 *n* analyst
fēn zhī 分枝 *n.* offshoot
fēn zǐ 分子 *n.* molecule
fēn zǐ 分子 *n.* numerator
fēn zǐ de 分子的 *a.* molecular
fēn xiāng de 芬香的 *a.* fragrant
fén mù 坟墓 *n.* grave
fén mù 坟墓 *n.* sepulchre
fén mù 坟墓 *n.* sepulture
fén mù 坟墓 *n.* tomb
fén xiāng zhì jìng 焚香致敬 *v. t* cense
fěn 粉 *n.* powder
fěn cì 粉刺 *n* acne
fěn hóng de 粉红的 *a* pink
fěn hóng sè 粉红色 *n.* pink
fěn liú 粉瘤 *n.* wen
fěn zhuàng de 粉状的 *a.* mealy

fèn 份 *n.* allotment

fèn dòu 奋斗 *n* struggle

fèn nù 忿怒 *n.* ire

fèn hèn 愤恨 *v.t.* resent

fèn kǎi 愤慨 *n.* indignation

fèn kǎi de 愤慨的 *a.* indignant

fèn nù 愤怒 *n.* fury

fèn nù 愤怒 *n.* rage

fèn nù 愤怒 *n.* wrath

fèn nù de 愤怒的 *a.* angry

fèn nù dì shuō 愤怒地说 *v.i.* rave

fèn 粪 *n* dung

fèn biàn xué 粪便学 *n.* coprology

féng 缝 *v.t.* stitch

fēng 风 *n.* wind

fēng chē 风车 *n.* windmill

fēng dí 风笛 *n.* bagpipe

fēng gé 风格 *n.* style

fēng jǐng 风景 *n.* landscape

fēng jǐng 风景 *n.* scenery

fēng jǐng 风景 *n.* view

fēng jǐng hǎo de 风景好的 *a.* scenic

fēng shàn 风扇 *n* fan

fēng shī bìng de 风湿病的 *a.* rheumatic

fēng shī bìng de 风湿病的 *n.* rheumatism

fēng sù jì 风速计 *n* anemometer

fēng yǎ 风雅 *n* elegance

fēng zheng 风筝 *n.* kite

fēng fù 丰富 *n.* opulence

fēng fù de 丰富的 *a.* profuse

fēng fù dì 丰富地 *adv.* galore

fēng mǎn de 丰满的 *a.* full

fēng bì 封闭 *v.t.* seal

fēng jiàn zhì dù de 封建制度的 *a* feudal

fēng miàn 封面 *n.* cover

fēng suǒ 封锁 *n* blockade

fēng... wéi jué shì 封为爵士 *v.t.* knight

fēng cháo 蜂巢 *n.* honeycomb

fēng fáng 蜂房 *n.* beehive

fēng fáng 蜂房 *n.* hive

fēng mì 蜂蜜 *n.* honey

fēng mì jiǔ 蜂蜜酒 *n.* mead

fēng yōng chéng qún 蜂拥成群 *v.i.* swarm

fēng diān de 疯癫的 *a.* lunatic

fēng kuáng 疯狂 *n.* frenzy

fēng kuáng de 疯狂的 *a.* frantic

fēng rén 疯人 *n.* lunatic

féng hé 缝合 *v.t.* seam

féng hé xiàn 缝合线 *n.* seam

féng rèn 缝纫 *v.t.* sew

féng zhì 缝制 *v.t.* tailor

fēng wō 蜂窝 *n* alveary

fèng xì 缝隙 *n* gap

fěng cì 讽刺 *v.t.* lampoon

fěng cì 讽刺 *n.* sarcasm

fěng cì 讽刺 *n.* satire

fěng cì 讽刺 *v.t.* satirize

fěng cì de 讽刺的 *a.* ironical

fěng cì de 讽刺的 *a.* sarcastic

fěng cì de 讽刺的 *a.* satirical

fěng cì de 讽刺的 *a.* wry

fěng cì duǎn shī 讽刺短诗 *n* epigram

fěng cì wén 讽刺文 *n.* lampoon

fěng cì xǐ jù de 讽刺喜剧的 *adj* aristophanic

fěng cì zuò zhě 讽刺作者 *n.* satirist

fèng cheng 奉承 *n* adulation

fèng cheng 奉承 *v.t* flatter

fèng xiàn 奉献 *n* dedication

fǒu dìng 否定 *v.t.* gainsay

fǒu jué 否决 *v.t.* veto

fǒu jué quán 否决权 *n.* veto

fǒu rèn 否认 *v.t* abnegate

fǒu rèn 否认 *n* abnegation

fǒu rèn 否认 *n* denial

fǒu rèn 否认 *v.t.* deny

fǒu zé 否则 *conj.* otherwise

fū rén 夫人 *n.* dame

fū qiǎn de 肤浅的 *a.* superficial

fū 孵 *v.i.* incubate

fú lóng 弗隆 *n.* furlong

fú tè 伏特 *n.* volt

fú shou 扶手 n. railing

fú lǔ 俘虏 n. captive

fú biāo 浮标 n buoy

fú chū shuǐ miàn 浮出水面 v.i
surface

fú dòng 浮动 v.i float

fú lì 浮力 n buoyancy

fú yóu de 浮游的 a. natant

fú lì 福利 n. weal

fú lì shì yè 福利事业 n. welfare

fú cóng 服从 n. obedience

fú cóng 服从 v.t. obey

fú cóng 服从 n. subordination fú cóng de 服从的 a.
obedient

fú shì 服侍 v.i. minister

fú wù 服务 n. ministry

fú wù 服务 n. service

fú wù de 服务的 a.
ministrant

fú wù yuán 服务员 n.
attendant

fú wù yuán 服务员 n. steward

fú yào 服药 v.t. physic

fú yào guò liàng 服药过量 v.t.
overdose

fú yīn 福音 n. gospel

fú hào 符号 n. notation

fú hào 符号 n. symbol

fú hé 符合 v.t. accord

fú hé 符合 v.i correspond

fú zhòu 符咒 n. spell

fǔ fú de 俯伏的 a. prone

fǔ wò de 俯卧的 a. prostrate

fǔ dǎo jiào shī 辅导教师 n.
mentor

fú shè 辐射 n. radiation

fú tiáo 辐条 n. spoke

fǔ tou 斧头 n. axe

fǔ tou 斧头 n. hatchet

fǔ bài 腐败 v.i decay

fǔ bài 腐败 n, v.i. decay

fǔ làn 腐烂 v.i. rot

fǔ làn de 腐烂的 adj carious

fǔ làn de 腐烂的 a. corrupt

fǔ shí xìng de 腐蚀性的 adj.
corrosive

fù mǔ 父母 n. parent

fù qīn 父亲 n father

fù qīn de 父亲的 a. paternal

fù gào 讣告 a. obituary

fù hái 付还 v.t. refund

fù kuǎn 付款 n. payment

fù 负 a minus

fù dān 负担 v.t burden

fù dān 负担 v.t. shoulder

fù dān guò duō 负担过多 v.t.
overburden

fù hào 负号 n minus

fù hè 负荷 n. load

fù yǒu 负有 v.t owe

fù yǒu yì wù de 负有义务的 a
incumbent

fù zhài de 负债的 a. indebted

fù jiā 附加 v.t. annex

fù jiā 附加 n annexation

fù jiā 附加 v.t. append

fù jiā 附加 v.t. attach

fù jiā fèi 附加费 n. surcharge

fù jiā shuì 附加税 n. supertax

fù jiā shuì 附加税 n. surtax

fù jiàn 附件 n. attachment

fù jìn 附近 n. neighbourhood

fù jìn 附近 adv. thereabouts

fù jìn 附近 n. vicinity

fù lù 附录 n. appendix

fù shǔ wù 附属物 n. adjunct

fù shǔ wù 附属物 n. appendage

fù shǔ wù 附属物 n
appurtenance

fù yán 附言 n. postscript

fù fā 复发 v.i. recur

fù fā 复发 v.i. relapse

fù hé cí 复合词 n compound

fù huó 复活 n. resurgence

fù huó jié 复活节 n easter

fù shēng de 复生的 a.
resurgent

fù shù 复数 n. plurality

fù shù de 复数的 a. plural

fù sū 复苏 n. revival

fù wèi 复位 n. restoration

fù xiě 复写 v.t cyclostyle

fù xiě qì 复写器 n cyclostyle

fù xīng 复兴 n. renaissance

fù yìn jī 复印机 n. xerox

fù yuán 复原 n. rehabilitation

fù zá de 复杂的 *a* complex
fù zá de 复杂的 *a.* intricate
fù zá huà 复杂化 *v. t*
  complicate
fú zhèn jìng jì 服镇静剂 *v.t.*
  sedate
fù zhì 复制 *v. t* copy
fù zhì pǐn 复制品 *n* copy
fù zhì pǐn 复制品 *n.* replica
fù běn 副本 *n* duplicate
fù chán pǐn 副产品 *n*
  by-product
fù cí 副词 *n.* adverb
fù cí de 副词的 *a.* adverbial
fù gē 副歌 *n.* chorus
fù gē 副歌 *n* refrain
fù shǔ 副署 *v. t.* countersign
fù yǒu de 富有的 *a.*
  well-to-do
fù yōu mò gǎn de 富幽默感的
  a. humorous
fù yù 富裕 *n.* affluence
fù yù 富裕 *a.* richness
fù yù 富裕 *n.* wealth
fù yù de 富裕的 *a.* opulent
fù yù de 富裕的 *a.* rich
fù zú de 富足的 *a.* affluent
fù yǔ rén xìng 赋予人性 *v.t.*
humanize
fù yǔ shēng mìng 赋予生命
  v.t. vitalize
fù bù 腹部 *n* abdomen
fù bù de 腹部的 *a.* abdominal
fù bù de 腹部的 *adj.* alvine
fù guǎn 腹管 *n.* cornicle
fù shàng bù 腹上部 *n*
  anticardium
fù xiè 腹泻 *n* diarrhoea
fù 覆 *v.t.* muffle
fù gài 覆盖 *n.* canopy
fù gài 覆盖 *v.t* mantle
fù gài 覆盖 *v.t.* shroud
fǔ zhù de 辅助的 *a.* auxiliary
fǔ zhù de 辅助的 *a.*
  subsidiary
fǔ zhù rén yuán 辅助人员 *n.*
  auxiliary
fú zhuāng 服装 *n.* apparel
fú zhuāng 服装 *n.* attire

fú zhuāng 服装 *n.* costume

G

gā gā jiào 嘎嘎叫 *v.i.* quack
gā gā xiào 嘎嘎笑 *v. i* cackle
gā zī shēng 嘎吱声 *v. i* creak
gā zī shēng 嘎吱声 *n* creak
gāi dé dào 该得到 *v. t.* deserve
gǎi biàn 改变 *v.t.* alter
gǎi biàn 改变 *v. t.* change
gǎi biàn 改变 *n.* change
gǎi biàn 改变 *v.* transform
gǎi biàn xìn yǎng zhě 改变信仰
  者 *n* convert
gǎi gé 改革 *v.i.* innovate
gǎi gé 改革 *v.t.* reform
gǎi gé 改革 *n.* reform
gǎi gé 改革 *n.* reformation
gǎi gé de 改革的 *a* reformatory
gǎi gé jiā 改革家 *n.* reformer
gǎi liáng 改良 *v.t.* ameliorate
gǎi liáng 改良 *n.* amelioration
gǎi liáng 改良 *v.t.* improve
gǎi shàn 改善 *n* betterment
gǎi shàn 改善 *v.t.* meliorate
gǎi tiān 改天 *adv.* sometime
gái xiě běn 改写本 *n.*
  adaptation
gǎi zhèng 改正 *n* correction
gǎi zhèng 改正 *n.* rectification
gài kuò de 概括的 *a* summary
gài kuò dì 概括地 *adv.*
  summarily
gài niàn 概念 *n* concept
gài yào 概要 *n.* synopsis
gài 钙 *n* calcium
gài 盖 *n.* lid
gài shàng bèi dān 盖上被单 *v.t.*
  sheet
gài wū dǐng 盖屋顶 *v.t.* roof
gān cǎo 干草 *n.* hay
gān cǎo yuán 干草原 *n.* steppe
gān de 干的 *a* dry
gān hàn 干旱 *n* drought
gān jìng 干淨 *n* cleanliness
gān jìng de 干淨的 *n.* clean
gān shè 干涉 *v.i.* interfere

gān shè 干涉 n. interference

gān zào 干燥 n arefaction

gān lù 甘露 n. nectar

gān měi de 甘美的 a. luscious

gān měi duō zhi de 甘美多汁
的 a. mellow

gān yóu 甘油 n. glycerine

gān yóu zhà yào 甘油炸药 n
dynamite

gān zhe 甘蔗 n. cane

gān 杆 n. rod

gān 肝 n. liver

gǎn chū 赶出 v. t. expel

gǎn kuài 赶快 v.i. hasten

gǎn kuài 赶快 v.t. hurry

gǎn dào bào qiàn 感到抱歉
v.i. regret

gǎn jī de 感激的 a. grateful

gǎn jī zhī qíng 感激之情 n.
gratitude

gǎn jué 感觉 n feeling

gǎn jué 感觉 v.t. perceive

gǎn jué 感觉 n. sensation

gǎn jué 感觉 v.t. sense

gǎn jué de 感觉的 a. sensual

gǎn jué shàng de 感觉上的 a.
sensuous

gǎn mào 感冒 n cold

gǎn qíng 感情 n. affection

gǎn qíng 感情 n emotion

gǎn qíng de 感情的 a
emotional

gǎn qíng kuā zhāng de 感情夸
张的 a. melodramatic

gǎn qíng yòng shì de 感情用事
的 a. sentimental

gán rǎn 感染 n. infection

gǎn shāng lì 感伤力 n. pathos

gǎn tàn cí 感叹词 n.
interjection

gǎn xiè 感谢 n. appreciation

gǎn xiè 感谢 v.t. thank

gǎn xiè de 感谢的 a. thankful

gǎn xìng qù de 感兴趣的 a.
interested

gǎn yìng 感应 n. sense

gǎn zhī 感知 n. percentage

gǎn lǎn shù 橄榄树 n. olive

gāng mén 肛门 n. anus

gāng mén de 肛门的 adj. anal

gāng 钢 n. steel

gāng qín 钢琴 n. piano

gāng qín jiā 钢琴家 n. pianist

gǎng 港 n. harbour

gáng kǒu 港口 n. port

gàng gǎn 杠杆 n. lever

gàng gǎn zuò yòng 杠杆作用
n. leverage

gāo cháo 高潮 n. climax

gāo de 高的 a. high

gāo de 高的 a. lofty

gāo de 高的 a. tall

gāo dì 高地 n. plateau

gāo dù 高度 n. altitude

gāo dù 高度 n. height

gāo ěr fū qiú 高尔夫球 n. golf

gāo fēi 高飞 v.i. soar

gāo gū 高估 v.t. overrate

gāo guì de 高贵的 a.
honourable

gāo guì de 高贵的 a. noble

gāo jí jiào shì 高级教士 n.
prelate

gāo lì dài 高利贷 n. usury

gāo lì dài zhě 高利贷者 n.
usurer

gāo líng 高龄 n. senility

gāo líng de 高龄的 a. senile

gāo qiāo 高跷 n. stilt

gāo shān 高山 n. alp

gāo shì kuò bù 高视阔步 n
strut

gāo shǒu 高手 n ace

gāo sǒng 高耸 v.i. tower

gāo xìng 高兴 n delight

gāo xìng 高兴 n. gaiety

gāo xìng 高兴 n. glee

gāo xìng 高兴 n. hilarity

gāo xìng 高兴 n. jollity

gāo xìng 高兴 v.i. rejoice

gāo xìng de 高兴的 a. cheerful

gāo xìng de 高兴的 a. glad

gāo xìng de 高兴的 a. joyful,
joyous

gāo xìng de 高兴的 a. mirthful

gāo yáng 羔羊 n. lamb

gāo yáng 羔羊 n. lambkin

gāo yao 膏药 n. plaster

gāo wán 睾丸 *n.* testicle
gǎo huài 搞坏 *v. t* bungle
gǎo luàn 搞乱 *v.t.* jumble
gǎo luàn 搞乱 *v.i* mess
gào bié 告别 *n.* leave
gào fā 告发 *v. t* denounce
gào jiè 告诫 *v.t.* admonish
gào zhōng 告终 *v.i.* culminate
gē 歌 *n.* song
gē chàng 歌唱 *v.i.* sing
gē cí 歌词 *n.* lyric
gē jù 歌剧 *n.* opera
gē shǒu 歌手 *n.* singer
gē shǒu 歌手 *n.* songster
gē shǒu 歌手 *n.* vocalist
gē wǔ biáo yǎn 歌舞表演 *n.* cabaret
gē gē dì xiào 咯咯地笑 *v.i.* giggle
gē 鸽 *n* dove
gē jiào shēng 鸽叫声 *n* coo
gē zi 鸽子 *n.* pigeon
gē zhì 搁置 *n.* abeyance
gē zhì 搁置 *v.t.* table
gé gé shēng 格格声 *n* rattle
gé lù de 格律的 *a.* metrical
gé shì 格式 *n* format
gé yán 格言 *n* aphorism
gé yán 格言 *n* dictum
gé yán 格言 *n.* maxim
gé yán 格言 *n.* proverb
gé zi 格子 *n.* lattice
gé mìng 革命 *n.* revolution
gé mìng de 革命的 *a.* revolutionary
gé mìng zhě 革命者 *n* revolutionary
gé xīn 革新 *n.* renovation
gé lóu 阁楼 *n.* loft
gé gè yuè de 隔个月的 *adj.* bimonthly
gé jué 隔绝 *n.* isolation
gé lí 隔离 *n.* insulation
gé lí 隔离 *n.* segregation
gé lí 隔离 *v.t.* sequester
gé 镉 *n* cadmium
gè bié de 个别的 *a.* individual
gè rén fú dǎo shí jiān 个人辅导时间 *n.* tutorial

gè rén jiǎn lì 个人简历 *n.* resume
gè rén zhǔ yì 个人主义 *n.* individualism
gè xìng 个性 *n.* individuality
gè xìng 个性 *n.* personality
gè zhǒng gè yàng de 各种各样的 *a.* miscellaneous
gè zhǒng gōng yì de 各种工艺的 *a.* polytechnic
gè zì 各自 *pron.* each
gè 铬 *n* chrome
gěi 给 *v.t.* give
gěi fáng zi zhù 给房子住 *v.t* house
gěi rén shēn kè yìn xiàng de 给人深刻印象的 *a.* impressive
gěi yǔ bào chóu 给与报酬 *v.t.* remunerate
gēn 根 *n.* root
gēn chú 根除 *v. t* eradicate
gēn jī 根基 *n.* base
gēn shēn dì gù de 根深蒂固的 *a.* ingrained
gēn suí 跟随 *v.t* follow
gēn yuán 根源 *n.* origin
gēn zhe fā shēng 跟着发生 *v.i* ensue
gēn zōng 跟踪 *v. t* dog
gēn zōng 跟踪 *v.t.* trace
gēng zhòng 耕种 *v.t.* till
gēng zuò 耕作 *v. t* cultivate
gēng 耕 *v.t.* plough
gěng 梗 *n.* stalk
gēng gǎi 更改 *v. t* correct
gēng gǎi 更改 *n.* modification
gèng hǎo 更好 *adv.* better
gèng shū shì 更舒适 *n.* cosier
gēng xīn 更新 *n.* renewal
gēng xīn 更新 *v.t.* renovate
gèng yuǎn 更远 *adv.* beyond
gèng yuǎn de 更远的 *a* further
gèng yuǎn dì 更远地 *adv.* further
gōng chǎng 工厂 *n* factory
gōng chǎng 工场 *n.* workshop
gōng chéng jì shù zhuān jiā 工程技术专家 *n.* technologist

gōng chéng shī　工程师　*n* engineer

gōng jiang　工匠　*n.* artisan

gōng jiang　工匠　*n* craftsman

gōng jiang　工匠　*n.* workman

gōng jù　工具　*n.* implement

gōng jù　工具　*n.* instrument

gōng jù　工具　*n.* tool

gōng rén　工人　*n.* worker

gōng shāng míng lù　工商名录　*n* directory

gōng tóu　工头　*n* foreman

gōng yè　工业　*n.* industry

gōng yè de　工业的　*a.* industrial

gōng zī　工资　*n.* wage

gōng zuò　工作　*n* employment

gōng zuò　工作　*n.* job

gōng zuò　工作　*n.* work

gōng zuò guò dù　工作过度　*v.i.* overwork

gōng zuò rén yuán　工作人员　*n.* crew

gōng zuò rén yuán　工作人员　*n.* staff

gōng zuò zhe de　工作着的　*a.* operative

gōng jiàn shǒu　弓箭手　*n* archer

gōng zhe　弓着　*v.t.* arch

gōng bào　公报　*n.* communiqué

gōng gào　公告　*n* bulletin

gōng gào　公告　*n.* placard

gōng gòng de　公共的　*a* communal

gōng gòng qì chē　公共汽车　*n* bus

gōng guǎn　公馆　*n.* mansion

gōng jī　公鸡　*n* cock

gōng jué　公爵　*n* duke

gōng kāi de　公开的　*a.* overt

gōng kāi dì　公开地　*adv.* openly

gōng mín　公民　*n* citizen

gōng mín fù jué　公民复决　*n.* referendum

gōng mín quán lì　公民权利　*n* citizenship

gōng mín tóu piào　公民投票　*n.* plebiscite

gōng mín xué　公民学　*n* civics

gōng niú　公牛　*n* bull

gōng píng　公平　*n.* impartiality

gōng píng de　公平的　*a* equitable

gōng píng de　公平的　*a* fair

gōng píng de　公平的　*a.* impartial

gōng píng dì　公平地　*adv.* fairly

gōng shì　公式　*n* formula

gōng sī　公司　*n.* company

gōng sī　公司　*n.* firm

gōng sī　公司　*n.* office

gōng sī de　公司的　*adj.* corporate

gōng shēng　公升　*n.* litre

gōng yáng　公羊　*n.* ram

gōng yù　公寓　*n.* apartment

gōng yuán　公园　*n.* park

gōng zhèng　公正　*a.* candid

gōng zhèng dì　公正地　*adv.* justly

gōng zhèng rén　公证人　*n.* notary

gōng zhì de　公制的　*a.* metric

gōng zhòng　公众　*n.* public

gōng zhòng de　公众的　*a.* public

gōng zhǔ　公主　*n.* princess

gōng zhū　公猪　*n* boar

gōng jì　功绩　*n* exploit

gōng jì　功绩　*n* feat

gōng néng　功能　*n.* function

gōng xiào　功效　*n* efficacy

gōng jī　攻击　*v.* assail

gōng jī xìng　攻击性　*n* aggression

gōng jī xìng de　攻击性的　*a.* aggressive

gōng　宫　*n.* palace

gōng xǐ　恭喜　*v. t* congratulate

gǒng dǐng　拱顶　*n.* arch

gǒng láng　拱廊　*n* arcade

gòng chǎn zhǔ yì　共产主义　*n* communism

gòng cún 共存 *v. i* co-exist
gòng cún 共存 *n* co-existence
gòng hé guó 共和国 *n.* republic
gòng hé zhèng tǐ de 共和政体的 *a.* republican
gòng hé zhǔ yì zhě 共和主义者 *n* republican
gòng jì wéi 共计为 *v.t.* total
gòng míng 共鸣 *n.* consonance
gòng míng 共鸣 *n.* resonance
gòng míng de 共鸣的 *a.* resonant
gòng móu zhě 共谋者 *n.* conspirator
gòng shí 共识 *n.* consensus
gòng tóng de 共同的 *a.* mutual
gòng tóng dì 共同地 *adv.* jointly
gōng guò yú qiú 供过于求 *n* glut
gōng jǐ 供给 *v.t.* furnish
gōng jǐ jīng fèi 供给经费 *v.t* finance
gōng jǐ yí tào yī fu 供给一套衣服 *v.t.* suit
gōng yìng 供应 *v.t.* store
gōng yìng 供应 *v.t.* supply
gōng yìng chuán 供应船 *n* tender
gōng yìng pǐn 供应品 *n.* provision
gōng yìng pǐn 供应品 *n* supply
gōng yìng zhě 供应者 *n.* supplier
gòng xiàn 贡献 *n* contribution
gòng xiàn 贡献 *v. t.* dedicate
gōu jié 勾结 *n* collusion
gōu xiāo 勾消 *v.t.* stroke
gōu lóu bìng 佝偻病 *n.* rickets
gōu qú 沟渠 *n* ditch
gōu tōng 沟通 *v. t* communicate
gōu 钩 *n.* hook
gōu huǒ 篝火 *n* bonfire
gǒu 狗 *n* dog

gǒu jiào shēng 狗叫声 *v.t.* bark
gǒu shě 狗舍 *n.* kennel
gòu chéng 构成 *v. t* constitute
gòu chéng 构成 *v. t.* construct
gòu chéng 构成 *v.t.* frame
gòu sī 构思 *n* conception
gòu mǎi 购买 *n.* purchase
gū jì 估计 *n.* estimate
gū jì 估计 *v. t* estimate
gū jià 估价 *v.t.* rate
gū jià 估价 *n.* valuation
gū gū jiào 咕咕叫 *v. i* coo
gū lū gū lū dì shuō 咕噜咕噜地说 *v.i.* mumble
gū dān de 孤单的 *a.* lone
gū dān de 孤单的 *a.* lonely
gū dú 孤独 *n.* loneliness
gū dú 孤独 *n.* solitude
gū dú de 孤独的 *a* forlorn
gū ér 孤儿 *n.* orphan
gū ér yuàn 孤儿院 *n.* orphanage
gū lì 孤立 *n.* insularity
gū zhù yí zhì 孤注一掷 *v.i.* gamble
gū gǔ 榖 *n.* hub
gǔ dài de 古代的 *a.* archaic
gú diǎn de 古典的 *a* classical
gú dǒng 古董 *a.* antique
gǔ guài 古怪 *n.* oddity
gǔ guài de 古怪的 *a.* odd
gǔ guài de 古怪的 *a* rum
gǔ guài de 古怪的 *a.* strange
gǔ jiù 古旧 *n.* antiquity
gú lǎo de 古老的 *a.* ancient
gǔ luó mǎ jù chǎng 古罗马剧场 *n* amphitheatre
gǔ wén wù de 古文物的 *a.* antiquarian
gǔ wù shōu cáng jiā 古物收藏家 *n* antiquarian
gǔ wù shōu cáng jiā 古物收藏家 *n.* antiquary
gǔ yǎ de 古雅的 *a.* quaint
gǔ 谷 *n.* vale
gǔ cāng 谷仓 *n.* barn
gǔ cāng 谷仓 *n.* granary
gǔ chá 谷茬 *n.* stubble

gǔ lèi de 谷类的 *a* cereal

gǔ lì 谷粒 *n.* grain

gǔ fèn 股份 *n.* share

gǔ piào jīng jì rén 股票经纪人 *n.* jobber

gǔ 骨 *n.* bone

gǔ gé 骨骼 *n.* skeleton

gǔ huī wèng 骨灰瓮 *n* urn

gǔ zhé 骨折 *n.* fracture

gǔ 钴 *n* cobalt

gǔ 鼓 *n* drum

gǔ lì 鼓励 *v. t* encourage

gǔ lì 鼓励 *n.* incentive

gú zhǎng 鼓掌 *v.t.* applaud

gú zhǎng 鼓掌 *n* clap

gù shi 故事 *n.* story

gù shi 故事 *n.* tale

gù tài fù méng 故态复萌 *n.* relapse

gù yì dài màn 故意怠慢 *n.* snub

gù yì de 故意的 *a.* intentional

gù yì dì 故意地 *adv.* purposely

gù yì lěng luò 故意冷落 *v.t.* snub

gù zhàng 故障 *n* breakdown

gù zhàng 故障 *n.* hitch

gù zuò zhèng jīng de rén 故作正经的人 *n.* prude

gù chí de 固持的 *a.* tenacious

gù dìng 固定 *v.t.* secure

gù dìng de 固定的 *a* constant

gù dìng de 固定的 *a.* immovable

gù dìng de 固定的 *a* set

gù tǐ 固体 *n* solid

gù tǐ de 固体的 *a.* solid

gù yǒu de 固有的 *a.* inherent

gù yǒu de 固有的 *a.* integral

gù zhí 固执 *n.* obstinacy

gù zhí 固执 *n.* persistence

gù zhí 固执 *n.* tenacity

gù zhí de 固执的 *adj.* asinine

gù zhí de 固执的 *a.* persistent

gù zhí jǐ jiàn de rén 固执己见的人 *n.* stickler

gù kè 顾客 *n.* client

gù wèn 顾问 *n.* counsellor

gù gōng 雇工 *n.* hireling

gù yòng 雇用 *v. t* employ

gù yuán 雇员 *n* employee

gù zhǔ 雇主 *n* employer

guǎ fu 寡妇 *n.* widow

guǎ tóu zhèng zhì 寡头政治 *n.* oligarchy

guà míng de 挂名的 *a.* titular

guà niàn 挂念 *n.* solicitude

guāi zhāng de 乖张的 *a.* perverse

guǎi piàn 拐骗 *v.t.* kidnap

guǎi zhàng 拐杖 *n* crutch

guài pǐ 怪癖 *n.* peculiarity

guài wu 怪物 *n.* monster

guān 关 *v. t* close

guān bì 关闭 *v.t.* shut

guān jié 关节 *n.* joint

guān jié yán 关节炎 *n* arthritis

guān jìn mǎ fáng 关进马房 *v.t.* stall

guān jìn mǎ jiù lǐ 关进马厩里 *v.t.* stable

guān lián 关连 *n* connection

guān xi 关系 *n.* rapport

guān xi 关系 *n.* relation

guān xi dào 关系到 *v. t* concern

guān xīn 关心 *v. i.* care

guān xīn 关心 *n* concern

guān xīn 关心 *v.t.* regard

guān yú 关于 *prep* about

guān yú 关于 *v.i.* pertain

guān cè 观测 *v.t.* span

guān chá 观察 *n.* observation

guān chá 观察 *v.t.* observe

guān chá lì mǐn ruì de 观察力敏锐的 *a.* observant

guān diǎn 观点 *n* angle

guān lǎn wù 观览物 *n.* spectacle

guān zhòng 观众 *n.* audience

guān zhòng 观众 *n.* spectator

guān zhòng xí 观众席 *n.* auditorium

guān liáo 官僚 *n* bureaucrat

guān liáo zhǔ yì 官僚主义 *n.* Bureaucracy

guān yuán 官员 *n.* functionary

guān yuán 官员 *n.* officer

guān zhì 官制 *n* official
guān cai 棺材 *n* coffin
guān cai jià 棺材架 *n* bier
guān fū 鳏夫 *n.* widower
guǎn 管 *n.* pipe
guǎn 管 *n.* tube
guǎn jiā 管家 *n* chamberlain
guán lǐ 管理 *v.t.* administer
guán lǐ 管理 *v.t.* manage
guán lǐ 管理 *n.* management
guán lǐ 管理 *v.t.* superintend
guán lǐ bú shàn 管理不善 *n.* mal administration
guán lǐ yuán 管理员 *n.* warden
guǎn xián yuè de 管弦乐的 *a.* orchestral
guǎn xián yuè duì 管弦乐队 *n.* orchestra
guǎn xíng píng 管形瓶 *n.* phial
guǎn zhuàng de 管状的 *a.* tubular
guǎn zuǐ 管嘴 *n.* nozzle
guàn chuān 贯穿 *v.t.* intersect
guàn cháng de 惯常的 *a.* wont
guàn lì de 惯例的 *a* customary
guàn xìng 惯性 *n.* inertia
guàn yòng de 惯用的 *a.* idiomatic
guàn miǎn 冠冕 *n.* coronet
guàn jūn 冠军 *n.* champion
guàn gài 灌溉 *v.t.* irrigate
guàn gài 灌溉 *n.* irrigation
guàn mù 灌木 *n* bush
guàn mù 灌木 *n.* shrub
guàn mù cóng 灌木丛 *n.* thicket
guàn 罐 *n.* can
guàn 罐 *n.* canister
guàn 罐 *n.* pot
guàn 罐 *n.* tank
guàn 罐 *n.* tin
guàn 鹳 *n.* stork
guāng 光 *n.* light
guāng cǎi 光彩 *n* brilliance
guāng huá de 光滑的 *a.* sleek
guāng huá de 光滑的 *a* slick
guāng huī 光辉 *n.* splendour

guāng máng sì shè 光芒四射 *a.* radiant
guāng róng de 光荣的 *a.* glorious
guāng tóu 光头 *a.* bald
guāng xiàn 光线 *n* beam
guāng xiàn 光线 *n.* ray
guāng zé 光泽 *n.* gloss
guāng zé 光泽 *n.* lustre
guāng zé 光泽 *n* shine
guǎng bō 广播 *n* broadcast
guǎng bō 广播 *v. t* broadcast
guǎng gào 广告 *v.* advert
guǎng gào 广告 *n* advertisement
guǎng kǒu píng 广口瓶 *n.* jar
guǎng kuò 广阔 *n.* width
guǎng kuò dì 广阔地 *adv.* wide
guī yīn yú 归因于 *v.t.* ascribe
guī yīn yú 归因于 *v.t.* attribute
guī zuì 归罪 *v.t.* impute
guī 龟 *n.* tortoise
guī 龟 *n.* turtle
guī dìng 规定 *v.t.* stipulate
guī dìng 规定 *n.* stipulation
guī dìng de 规定的 *a.* mandatory
guī dìng shí jiān zhī wài 规定时间之外 *adv.* overtime
guī fàn 规范 *n.* specification
guī jiè 规诫 *n.* precept
guī lǜ xìng 规律性 *n.* regularity
guī mó 规模 *n.* scale
guī zé 规则 *n.* regulation
guī zé 规则 *n.* rule
guī zé de 规则的 *a.* regular
guǐ dào 轨道 *n.* orbit
guǐ dào 轨道 *n.* track
guǐ biàn 诡辩 *n.* sophism
guǐ jì 诡计 *n* dodge
guǐ jì 诡计 *n.* ruse
guǐ jì 诡计 *n* trick
guǐ jì 诡计 *n.* wile
guǐ 鬼 *n.* ghost
guǐ guǐ suì suì de rén 鬼鬼祟祟的人 *n* sneak
guǐ hún 鬼魂 *n.* wraith
guì guān shī rén 桂冠诗人 *n.* laureate

guì 柜 n cupboard

guì chú 柜橱 n. cabinet

guì tái 柜台 n. counter

guì zǐ shǒu 刽子手 n. executioner

guì de 贵的 a expensive

guì zú 贵族 n. aristocracy

guì zú 贵族 n. noble

guì zú 贵族 n. nobleman

guì zú (jiē céng) 贵族(阶层) n. nobility

guì zú shēn fēn 贵族身分 n. lordship

guì xià 跪下 v.i. kneel

gùn 棍 n. stick

gùn bàng 棍棒 n cudgel

gǔn 滚 v.i. roll

gún tǒng 滚筒 n. roller

guō lú 锅炉 n boiler

guó gē 国歌 n anthem

guó huì 国会 n congress

guó huì 国会 n. parliament

guó huì de 国会的 a. parliamentary

guó huì yì yuán 国会议员 n. parliamentarian

guó jí 国籍 n. nationality

guó jì de 国际的 a. international

guó jì xiàng qí 国际象棋 n. chess

guó jiā 国家 n. country

guó jiā 国家 n. nation

guó jiā jí tuán 国家集团 n bloc

guó jiā zhǔ yì 国家主义 n. nationalism

guó wáng 国王 n. king

guó yǒu huà 国有化 n. nationalization

guǒ jiàng 果酱 n. jam

guǒ dòng 果冻 n. jelly

guǒ xīn 果心 n. core

guǒ yuán 果园 n. orchard

guǒ shī bù 裹尸布 n. shroud

guò … 过… prep. past

guò cuò 过错 n fault

guò dōng 过冬 v.i winter

guò dù 过度 n excess

guò dù 过度 n. superabundance

guò dù de láo dòng 过度的劳动 n. overwork

guò duō 过多 n. redundance

guò duō de 过多的 a. superabundant

guò duō de 过多的 a. superfluous

guò duō gōng yīng 过多供应 v.t. glut

guò fèn de 过分的 a. undue

guò liáng 过梁 n. lintel

guò liàng 过量 n. surfeit

guò liàng de 过量的 a excess

guò lù 过滤 v.t filter

guò lù 过滤 v.t. leach

guò lù qì 过滤器 n filter

guò mǐn 过敏 n. allergy

guò qī 过期 v.i. expire

guò qī 过期 a. overdue

guò qù 过去 n. past

guò qù de 过去的 a. past

guò shèng de 过盛的 a. luxuriant

guò shí 过时 a. outdated

guò shí 过失 n demerit

guò shí de 过时的 a. outmoded

guò xiāng cūn shēng huó 过乡村生活 v.t. rusticate

guò yú … 过于… v.t. overdo

guò zhòng zhuāng zài 过重装载 n overload

H

hā qian 哈欠 n. yawn

hái 还 adv. still

hái 还 adv. yet

hái zi 孩子 n child

hǎi 海 n. sea

hǎi àn 海岸 n. shore

hǎi bá 海拔 n elevation

hǎi bào 海报 n. poster

hǎi bào 海豹 n. seal

hǎi bīn 海滨 n coast

hǎi bīn de　海滨的　*a.* littoral
hǎi dào　海盗　*n.* pirate
hǎi dào xíng wéi　海盗行为　*n.* piracy
hǎi de　海的　*a.* marine
hǎi de　海的　*a.* maritime
hái dǐ de　海底的　*a* submarine
hǎi jūn　海军　*n.* navy
hǎi jūn de　海军的　*a.* naval
hǎi jūn shàng jiāng　海军上将　*n.* admiral
hǎi lí　海狸　*n* beaver
hǎi luó ké　海螺壳　*n.* conch
hǎi luò yīn　海洛因　*n.* smack
hǎi mián　海绵　*n.* sponge
hǎi shì shèn lóu　海市蜃楼　*n.* mirage
hǎi wān　海湾　*n* bay
hǎi wān　海湾　*n* bight
hǎi wān　海湾　*n.* gulf
hǎi wáng xīng　海王星　*n.* Neptune
hǎi xiá　海峡　*n.* strait
hǎi xiàng　海象　*n.* walrus
hài chóng　害虫　*n.* pest
hài pà　害怕　*v.i* fear
hài xiū de　害羞的　*a.* bashful
hān shēng　鼾声　*n* snore
hán hu　含糊　*n.* obscurity
hán hu　含糊　*n.* vagueness
hán hu de　含糊的　*a* equivocal
hán hu de　含糊的　*a.* vague
hán xù de　含蓄的　*a.* implicit
hán yǒu　含有　*v.t.* contain
hán lěng　寒冷　*n.* chill
hán lěng de　寒冷的　*a* chilly
hán lěng de　寒冷的　*a.* wintry
hǎn yǒu de　罕有的　*a.* rare
hǎn　喊　*v.i* cry
hàn　汗　*n.* perspiration
hàn　汗　*n.* sweat
hàn jiē　焊接　*v.t.* solder
hàn jiē　焊接　*v.t.* weld
hàn jiē diǎn　焊接点　*n* weld
hàn yào　焊药　*n.* solder
háng liè　行列　*n.* range
háng hǎi　航海　*v.i.* voyage
háng hǎi de　航海的　*a.* nautic(al)

háng kōng　航空　*n.* aviation
háng kōng xué　航空学　*n.pl.* aeronautics
háng xíng　航行　*v.i.* navigate
háng xíng　航行　*v.i.* sail
háng xíng　航行　*n.* voyage
háng xíng zhě　航行者　*n.* navigator
háng xíng zhě　航行者　*n.* voyager
háo　蚝　*n.* oyster
háo bú　毫不　*adv.* nothing
háo bù liú qíng de　毫不留情的　*a.* ruthless
háo huá de　豪华的　*a.* lush
háo huá de　豪华的　*a.* luxurious
háo jiào　嗥叫　*n.* snarl
háo jiào　嗥叫　*v.i.* snarl
hǎo chī de　好吃的　*a.* palatable
hǎo chī de　好吃的　*a.* tasty
hǎo chu　好处　*n.* advantage
hǎo chu　好处　*n* good
hǎo de　好的　*a* fine
hǎo de　好的　*a.* good
hǎo de　好的　*a.* nice
hǎo guò　好过　*v. t* better
hǎo kàn de　好看的　*a.* sightly
hǎo péng you　好朋友　*n.* pal
háo jiào　号叫　*n* howl
hào jiǎo　号角　*n* bugle
hào jiǎo shēng　号角声　*n.* clarion
hào mǎ　号码　*n.* number
hào dòu de　好斗的　*a* bellicose
hào dòu de　好斗的　*a* belligerent
hào gǎo pài xì de　好搞派系的　*a* factious
hào guǎn xián shì de　好管闲事的　*a.* nosy
hào kè de　好客的　*a.* hospitable
hào qí de　好奇的　*a* curious
hào qí xīn　好奇心　*n* curiosity
hào sè de　好色的　*a.* amorous
hào sè zhě　好色者　*n.* sensualist
hào jié　浩劫　*n.* havoc
háo xiá　豪侠　*n* gallant

hǎo xiào de 好笑的 *a* comical
hào xué de 好学de *a.* studious
hǎo zhàn de 好战的 *a.* warlike
hǎo zhuī gēn jiū dǐ de 好追根底的 *a.* inquisitive
hé bìng 合并 *v.t.* amalgamate
hé bìng 合并 *n* amalgamation
hé bìng 合并 *n.* merger
hé bìng de 合并的 *a.* incorporate
hé chàng tuán 合唱团 *n* choir
hé fǎ 合法 *n.* legality
hé fǎ de 合法的 *a.* lawful
hé fǎ de 合法的 *a.* legal
hé fǎ de 合法的 *a.* legitimate
hé fǎ xìng 合法性 *n.* legitimacy
hé gài 盒盖 *v.t.* cap
hé hū luó jí de 合乎逻辑的 *a.* logical
hé jīn 合金 *n.* alloy
hé lǐ de 合理的 *a.* reasonable
hé lǐ de 合理的 *a.* sound
hé lǐ xìng 合理性 *n.* rationality
hé tong 合同 *n* contract
hé tong 合同 *n.* pact
hé zuò 合作 *v.i* collaborate
hé zuò 合作 *n* collaboration
hé zuò 合作 *v.i* co-operate
hé zuò 合作 *n* co-operation
hé zuò guān xi 合作关系 *n.* partnership
hé 和 *conj.* and
hé ǎi de 和蔼的 *adj.* amicable
hé ǎi kě qīn de 和蔼可亲的 *a.* affable
hé jiě 和解 *n.* reconciliation
hé mù 和睦 *n.* harmony
hé píng 和平 *n.* peace
hé píng de 和平的 *a.* pacific
hé píng de 和平的 *a.* peaceable
hé xián 和弦 *n.* chord
hé xié 和谐 *n.* concord
hé xié de 和谐的 *a.* harmonious

hé shí 何时 *adv.* when
hé 河 *n.* river
hé xīn 核心 *n.* kernel
hé 盒 *n* carton
hé 盒 *n.* cartridge
hè cǎi 喝彩 *v.t.* cheer
hè méi 褐煤 *n.* lignite
hè zǐ hóng sè 褐紫红色 *n.* maroon
hè zǐ hóng sè de 褐紫红色的 *a* maroon
hè zuǐ chú 鹤嘴锄 *n.* mattock
hēi àn 黑暗 *n* dark
hēi àn de 黑暗的 *a* dark
hēi àn de 黑暗的 *a.* gloomy
hēi bái hùn xuè ér 黑白混血儿 *n.* mulatto
hēi bào 黑豹 *n.* panther
hēi mài 黑麦 *n.* rye
hēi rén 黑人 *n.* negro
hēi rén 黑人 *n.* nigger
hēi sè de 黑色的 *a* black
hēi xīng xing 黑猩猩 *n.* chimpanzee
hēi yǒu yǒu de 黑黝黝的 *a.* swarthy
hén jì 痕迹 *n.* mark
hén jì 痕迹 *n.* trace
hén jì 痕迹 *n.* trail
hěn chí 很迟 *adv.* late
hěn duō de 很多的 *a* much
hěn hǎo dì 很好地 *adv.* well
hěn kě néng de 很可能的 *a.* probable
hěn kuài dì 很快地 *adv* fast
hěn shǎo 很少 *adv.* little
hěn shǎo 很少 *adv.* seldom
hěn shǎo de 很少的 *a* few
hěn hěn dì dǎ 狠狠地打 *v.t.* paste
hèn 恨 *v.t.* abhor
hèn 恨 *n.* abhorrence
héng xīng de 恒星的 *a.* stellar
héng guò 横过 *adv.* athwart
hóng bǎo shí 红宝石 *n.* ruby
hōng dòng 哄动 *adv.* astir
hōng 烘 *v.t.* parch
hōng kǎo 烘烤 *v.t.* toast
hōng kǎo de 烘烤的 *a* roast

hōng zhà 轰炸 *v. t* bombard

hōng zhà 轰炸 *n* bombardment

hóng luó bo 红萝卜 *n.* carrot

hóng sè 红色 *n.* red

hóng sè de 红色的 *a.* red

hóng liàng 洪亮 *n.* sonority

hóng shuǐ 洪水 *n* flood

hóng shuǐ 洪水 *n.* spate

hóng wěi de 宏伟的 *a.* magnificent

hóng wěi de 宏伟的 *a.* palatial

hóng wěi de 宏伟的 *a.* superb

hǒng 哄 *v. t* coax

hǒng piàn 哄骗 *v. t.* cheat

hǒng piàn 哄骗 *v.t.* outwit

hǒu 吼 *v. t* blare

hǒu 吼 *n.* roar

hǒu 吼 *v.i.* roar

hǒu jiào 吼叫 *v.t.* howl

hóu lóng 喉咙 *n.* throat

hóu lóng de 喉咙的 *a.* guttural

hóu zi 猴子 *n.* monkey

hòu 后 *a* after

hòu dài 后代 *n.* posterity

hòu guǒ 后果 *n* consequence

hòu guǒ de 后果的 *a* consequent

hòu huǐ 后悔 *n.* compunction

hòu huǐ 后悔 *v.i.* repent

hòu huǐ 后悔 *n.* repentance

hòu huǐ 后悔 *v.t.* rue

hòu huǐ de 后悔的 *a.* repentant

hòu huǐ de 后悔的 *a.* rueful

hòu jì 后记 *n* epilogue

hòu lái 后来 *adv* after

hòu mian 后面 *adv* behind

hòu mian 后面 *prep* behind

hòu mian 后面 *n.* rear

hòu mian de 后面的 *a.* back

hòu yì 后裔 *n* descendant

hòu zhě de 后者的 *a.* latter

hòu xuǎn rén 候选人 *n.* candidate

hòu 厚 *a.* thick

hòu de 厚的 *adv.* thick

hòu mù bǎn 厚木板 *n.* plank

hòu piàn 厚片 *n.* slab

hū hǎn 呼喊 *n.* shout

hū hū shēng 呼呼声 *n.* whir

hū lū hū lū jiào 呼噜呼噜叫 *v.i.* purr

hū lū hū lū shēng 呼噜呼噜声 *n.* purr

hū lū shēng 呼噜声 *n.* grunt

hū xī 呼吸 *v. i.* breathe

hū xī 呼吸 *n.* respiration

hū xī 呼吸 *v.i.* respire

hū zhào 呼召 *n.* calling

hū lüè 忽略 *v.t.* neglect

hū lüè 忽略 *n* neglect

hū lüè 忽略 *v.t.* overlook

hū qián hū lù 忽潜忽露 *v.i.* duck

hū shì 忽视 *n* disregard

hū shì 忽视 *v.t.* ignore

hú 弧 *n.* arc

hú li 狐狸 *n.* fox

hú jiāo fěn 胡椒粉 *n.* pepper

hú táo 胡桃 *n.* walnut

hú xū 胡须 *n* beard

hú xū 胡须 *n.* whisker

hú yán luàn yǔ 胡言乱语 *n.* babble

hú yán luàn yǔ 胡言乱语 *v.i.* babble

hú zǐ 胡子 *n.* mustache

hú 湖 *n.* lake

hú lu 葫芦 *n.* gourd

hú dié 蝴蝶 *n.* butterfly

hú dié jié 蝴蝶结 *n* bow

hú tu de 糊涂的 *adj* addle

hǔ pò zhà yào 琥珀炸药 *n.* amberite

hù wài de 户外的 *a.* outdoor

hù huàn 互换 *n.* interchange

hù huì de 互惠的 *a.* reciprocal

hù xiāng yī lài 互相依赖 *n.* interdependence

hù xiāng yíng xiǎng 互相影响 *n.* interplay

hù chéng hé 护城河 *n.* moat

hù lǐ yuán 护理员 *n.* orderly

hù mù jìng　护目镜　*n.* goggles

hù shēn fú　护身符　*n.* amulet

hù shēn fú　护身符　*n.* talisman

hù shi　护士　*n.* nurse

hù shi zhǎng　护士长　*n.* matron

hù sòng　护送　*n* escort

hù sòng　护送　*v. t* escort

hù wèi duì　护卫队　*n.* guard

hù zhào　护照　*n.* passport

huā　花　*n* bloom

huā　花　*n* flower

huā bàn　花瓣　*n.* petal

huā biān　花边　*n.* lace

huā cǎi　花彩　*n* festoon

huā duǒ　花朵　*n* blossom

huā fèi　花费　*v.t.* cost

huā fèi　花费　*v. t* expend

huā fèi　花费　*v.t.* spend

huā fèi dé qǐ　花费得起　*v.t.* afford

huā fěn　花粉　*n.* pollen

huā guàn　花冠　*n* anadem

huā quān　花圈　*n.* wreath

huā shāng　花商　*n* florist

huā shù　花束　*n* bouquet

huā shù　花束　*n.* nosegay

huā yā zì　花押字　*n.* monogram

huā yuán　花园　*n.* garden

huà hé wù　化合物　*n* compound

huā huā gōng zǐ　花花公子　*n* dandy

huā huán　花环　*n.* garland

huā lěi　花蕾　*n* bud

huá　划　*v.t.* row

huá jiǎng　划桨　*v.i.* paddle

huá pò　划破　*v.t.* lacerate

huá xiàn yú xià mian　划线于下面　*v.t.* underline

huá shǒu　划手　*n.* oarsman

huá lì de　华丽的　*a.* gorgeous

huá　滑　*v.i.* slide

huá　滑　*a.* slippery

huá chē　滑车　*n.* tackle

huá dòng　滑动　*v.t.* glide

huá dòng　滑动　*n* slide

huá dòng　滑动　*n.* slip

huá jī de　滑稽的　*n* antic

huá jī duǎn jù　滑稽短剧　*n.* skit

huá jī rén wù　滑稽人物　*n.* funny

huá liū de　滑溜的　*a.* smooth

huá lún　滑轮　*n.* pulley

huá xiáng jī　滑翔机　*n.* glider

huá xíng　滑行　*v.i.* taxi

huà míng　化名　*n.* alias

huà shēn　化身　*n.* incarnation

huà shí　化石　*n.* fossil

huà xué　化学　*n.* chemistry

huà xué de　化学的　*a.* chemical

huà xué hé chéng wù　化学合成物　*n* synthetic

huà xué jiā　化学家　*n.* chemist

huà xué wù pǐn　化学物品　*n.* chemical

huà zhuāng pǐn　化妆品　*n.* cosmetic

huà jiè　划界　*n.* demarcation

huà jiā　画家　*n.* painter

huà juàn　画卷　*n.* scroll

huà láng　画廊　*n.* gallery

huà lún kuò　画轮廓　*v.t.* outline

huà duō de　话多的　*a.* wordy

huà tǒng　话筒　*n.* microphone

huà shù　桦树　*n.* birch

huái hèn　怀恨　*v.t.* grudge

huái yí　怀疑　*v.i* doubt

huái yí　怀疑　*v.t.* question

huái yí　怀疑　*v.t.* suspect

huái yí de　怀疑的　*a.* sceptical

huái yí lùn zhě　怀疑论者　*n.* sceptic

huái yí zhǔ yì　怀疑主义　*n.* scepticism

huái yùn　怀孕　*n.* maternity

huái yùn　怀孕　*n.* pregnancy

huái yùn de　怀孕的　*a.* pregnant

huài dàn　坏蛋　*a* bastard

huài dì　坏地　*adv.* badly

huài pí qi　坏脾气　*n.* petulance

huài rén　坏人　*n.* villain

huān hū　欢呼　*n* acclamation

huān hū 欢呼 *n.* jubilation
huān hū de 欢呼的 *a.* jubilant
huān hū shēng 欢呼声 *n.*
cheer
huān lè 欢乐 *n.* merriment
huān lè de 欢乐的 *a.* frolic
huān nào 欢闹 *n.* spree
huān qìng shèng lì 欢庆胜利
v.i. triumph
huān tiān xǐ dì 欢天喜地 *n.*
rapture
huān xǐ 欢喜 *n.* joy
huān xiào 欢笑 *n.* mirth
huān yàn 欢宴 *n* carnival
huān yàn zhě 欢宴者 *n.*
reveller
huān yíng 欢迎 *n* welcome
huān yíng 欢迎 *v.t* welcome
huān 獾 *n.* badger
huán yā 还押 *n* remand
huán yā hòu shěn 还押候审
v.t. remand
huán jiāo hú 环礁湖 *n.*
lagoon
huán jìng 环境 *n.* environment
huán jìng 环境 *n.* milieu
huán liú 环流 *n.* circumfluence
huán rào 环绕 *v. i.* circulate
huán rào 环绕 *adv.* round
huán zhuàng shān hú dǎo 环状
珊瑚岛 *n.* atoll
huǎn hé 缓和 *v.t.* assuage
huǎn hé 缓和 *n.* moderation
huǎn hé zhuàng jī 缓和撞击
v. t cushion
huàn xiǎng 幻想 *n* fancy
huàn xiǎng 幻想 *n.* reverie
huàn yǐng 幻影 *n.* phantom
huàn gōu lóu bìng de 患佝偻
病的 *a.* rickety
huàn jīng shen bìng de 患精神
病的 *a.* insane
huāng miù 荒谬 *a* absurd
huāng miù 荒谬 *n* absurdity
huāng miù de 荒谬的 *a.*
ridiculous
huāng táng kě xiào de 荒唐可
笑的 *a.* zany

huāng yě 荒野 *n.* wilderness
huáng guàn 皇冠 *n* crown
huáng guàn 皇冠 *n.* tiara
huáng hòu 皇后 *n* empress
huáng dì 皇帝 *n* emperor
huáng da 黄疸 *n.* jaundice
huáng dào dài 黄道带 *n* zodiac
huáng fēng 黄蜂 *n.* wasp
huáng fēng qín 簧风琴 *n.*
harmonium
huáng guā 黄瓜 *n* cucumber
huáng hè sè 黄褐色 *n* bisque
huáng hūn 黄昏 *n* dusk
huáng hūn 黄昏 *n* twilight
huáng jīn 黄金 *n.* gold
huáng má 黄麻 *n.* jute
huáng sè 黄色 *n* yellow
huáng sè de 黄色的 *a.* yellow
huáng tóng 黄铜 *n.* brass
huáng yóu 黄油 *n* butter
huáng yù 黄玉 *n.* topaz
huáng chóng 蝗虫 *n.* locust
huǎng piàn 谎骗 *v.t.* lie
huǎng yán 谎言 *n* lie
huī 灰 *n.* ash
huī bái de 灰白的 *a* pale
huī ní 灰泥 *v.t.* mortar
huī sè de 灰色的 *a.* grey
huī xié de 诙谐的 *a.* jocular
huī xié zhě 诙谐者 *n.* joker
huī fù 恢复 *v.t.* recover
huī fù 恢复 *n.* recovery
huī fù 恢复 *n.* reinstatement
huī fù 恢复 *v.t.* restore
huī fù 恢复 *n.* resumption
huī fù yuán zhuàng 恢复原状
v.t. rehabilitate
huī 挥 *v.t.* wave
huī huò 挥霍 *v.t.* squander
huī huáng 辉煌 *n.* refulgence
huī huáng de 辉煌的 *a.*
resplendent
huī zhāng 徽章 *n* crest
huí bào 回报 *v.t.* reciprocate
huí bào 回报 *v.t.* render
huí dá 回答 *v.t* answer
huí dá 回答 *v.i.* reply
huí dá 回答 *n* reply
huí dá 回答 *v.i.* respond

huí dá　回答　*n.*　response
huí fù　回复　*v.i.*　revert
huí gù　回顾　*n.*　retrospect
huí gù de　回顾的　*a.*
　retrospective
huí lái　回来　*n.*　return
huí shēng　回声　*n*　echo
huí shōu　回收　*v.t.*　reclaim
huí xiǎng　回想　*n*　anamnesis
huí xiǎng　回想　*v.t.*　recall
huí xiǎng　回响　*v.i.*　resound
huí xuán　回旋　*v.i.*　whirl
huí yì　回忆　*n.*　recall
huí yì　回忆　*v.t.*　recollect
huí yì　回忆　*n.*　reminiscence
huí yì　回忆　*n.*　souvenir
huí yì de　回忆的　*a.*
　reminiscent
huí yì lù　回忆录　*n.*　memoir
huǐ hèn　悔恨　*v.i.*　lament
huǐ bàng de　毁谤的　*a.*
　slanderous
huǐ huài　毁坏　*v. t.*　demolish
huǐ huài　毁坏　*v.t.*　ravage
huǐ huài　毁坏　*v.t.*　ruin
huǐ miè　毁灭　*v.t.*　annihilate
huǐ miè　毁灭　*n*　annihilation
huǐ miè　毁灭　*n*　destruction
huǐ sǔn　毁损　*v.t.*　mar
huì　会　*n.*　meeting
huì tán　会谈　*n*　conversation
huì tán　会谈　*n.*　parley
huì táng　会堂　*n.*　hall
huì yì　会议　*n*　conference
huì yì tīng　会议厅　*n.*　chamber
huì yuán　会员　*n.*　member
huì yuán de zī gé　会员的资格
　n.　membership
huì hé de　汇合的　*adj.*
　confluent
huì chū　汇出　*v.t.*　remit
huì kuǎn　汇款　*n.*　remittance
huì liú chù　汇流处　*n*
　confluence
huì cǎo tú　绘草图　*v.t.*　sketch
huì huà　绘画　*n.*　painting
huì huà de　绘画的　*a.*　pictorical
huì huà shì de　绘画似的　*a.*
　graphic

huì zhì... dì tú　绘制地图　*v.t.*
　map
huì lù　贿赂　*n*　bribe
huì lù　贿赂　*v. t.*　bribe
huì xīng　彗星　*n*　comet
huì líng dùn cháng xuē　惠灵顿
　长靴　*n.*　wellington
hūn àn de　昏暗的　*a.*　sombre
hūn dǎo　昏倒　*v.i*　faint
hūn mí　昏迷　*n.*　coma
hūn shuì de　昏睡的　*a.*　lethargic
hūn shuì zhuàng tài　昏睡状态
　n.　trance
hūn lǐ　婚礼　*n.*　nuptials
hūn lǐ　婚礼　*n.*　spousal
hūn lǐ　婚礼　*n.*　wedding
hūn lǐ de　婚礼的　*a.*　nuptial
hūn qián de　婚前的　*a.*
　premarital
hūn wài qíng　婚外情　*n.*　affair
hūn yīn　婚姻　*n.*　marriage
hūn yīn　婚姻　*n.*　matrimony
hūn yīn　婚姻　*n.*　wedlock
hūn yīn de　婚姻的　*a.*　marital
hūn yīn de　婚姻的　*a.*　matrimonial
hūn yīn shàng de　婚姻上的　*a*
　conjugal
hùn hé　混合　*v. t*　blend
hùn hé　混合　*n.*　mixture
hùn hé de　混合的　*a*　compound
hùn hé pǐn　混合品　*n*　blend
hùn hé wù　混合物　*n*　amalgam
hùn hé yǔ　混合语　*n.*
　lingua franca
hùn luàn　混乱　*v. t*　bewilder
hùn luàn　混乱　*n.*　chaos
hùn luàn　混乱　*v. t*　clutter
hùn luàn　混乱　*v. t*　confuse
hùn luàn　混乱　*n*　confusion
hùn luàn　混乱　*n.*　jumble
hùn luàn　混乱　*n.*　mess
hùn luàn　混乱　*n.*　muddle
hùn luàn de　混乱的　*adj.*　chaotic
hùn níng tǔ　混凝土　*n*　concrete
hùn zá　混杂　*n.*　complication
hùn zhàn　混战　*n.*　melee
huó de　活的　*a.*　live
huó de　活的　*a.*　living

huó dòng　活动　*n.* activity

huó dòng de　活动的　*a.* mobile

huó dòng péng wū　活动棚屋　*n.* wigwam

huó lì　活力　*n.* vitality

huó mén　活门　*n.* valve

huó po　活泼　*n.* vivacity

huó po de　活泼的　*a.* lively

huó po de　活泼的　*a.* sprightly

huó po de　活泼的　*a.* vivacious

huó sāi　活塞　*n.* piston

huó wù　活物　*n.* wight

huó yuè de　活跃的　*a.* active

huó zhe de　活着的　*a* alive

huǒ　火　*n*　fire

huó bǎ　火把　*n.* torch

huǒ chē　火车　*n.* train

huǒ chē tóu　火车头　*n.* locomotive

huǒ huà　火化　*v. t* cremate

huǒ huà　火化　*n* cremation

huǒ huā　火花　*n.* spark

huǒ jī　火鸡　*n.* turkey

huǒ jiàn　火箭　*n.* rocket

huǒ chái　火柴　*n* match

huǒ lú　火炉　*n.* furnace

huǒ lú　火炉　*n.* grate

huǒ lú　火炉　*n.* stove

huǒ qiāng　火枪　*n.* musket

huǒ qiāng chē　火枪车　*n.* musketeer

huǒ shān　火山　*n.* volcano

huǒ shān de　火山的　*a.* volcanic

huǒ xīng　火星　*n* Mars

huǒ yàn　火焰　*n* blaze

huǒ yàn　火焰　*n* flame

huǒ bàn　伙伴　*n.* companion

huǒ bàn　伙伴　*n* co-partner

huò bì　货币　*n* currency

huò bì zhì dù　货币制度　*n* coinage

huò chē　货车　*n.* lorry

huò chē　货车　*n.* van

huò chuán　货船　*n.* cargo

huò tān　货摊　*n.* stand

huò bào lì　获暴利　*v.i.* profiteer

huò dé　获得　*v.t.* acquire

huò dé　获得　*n.* acquisition

huò dé　获得　*v.t.* attain

huò dé　获得　*v.t.* procure

huò xǔ kě de rén　获许可的人　*n.* licensee

huò luàn　霍乱　*n.* cholera

J

jī bài　击败　*v. t.* defeat

jī dǎo　击倒　*v.t* fell

jī qiú shǒu　击球手　*n.* batsman

jī tuì　击退　*v.t.* repulse

jī jī de jiào　叽叽的叫　*v.i.* squeak

jī jī shēng　叽叽声　*n* squeak

jī è　饥饿　*n&v.i.* starve

jī è de　饥饿的　*a.* hungry

jī huang　饥荒　*n* famine

jī chǎng　机场　*n* aerodrome

jī gòu　机构　*n.* institution

jī huì　机会　*n.* chance

jī huì　机会　*n.* opportunity

jī huì　机会　*n.* scope

jī huì zhǔ yì　机会主义　*n.* opportunism

jī mǐn qiǎo miào de huí dá　机敏巧妙的回答　*n.* repartee

jī xiè de　机械的　*a.* mechanical

jī xiè dì gōng zuò de rén　机械地工作的人　*n.* mechanic

jī xiè rén　机械人　*n.* robot

jī xiè xué　机械学　*n.* mechanics

jī xiè zhuāng zhì　机械装置　*n.* mechanism

jī zhì de　机智的　*a.* tactful

jī ròu　肌肉　*n.* muscle

jī tòng　肌痛　*n.* myalgia

jī jí de　积极的　*a* energetic

jī lěi　积累　*v.t.* accumulate

jī lěi　积累　*n* accumulation

jī　鸡　*n.* chicken

jī dàn　鸡蛋　*n* egg

jī jiān　鸡奸　*n.* sodomy

jī jiān zhě　鸡奸者　*n.* sodomite

jī běn de　基本的　*a.* basic

jī běn de 基本的 a. fundamental

jī běn de 基本的 a. rudimentary

jī běn de 基本的 a elementary

jī chǔ 基础 n. basis

jī chǔ 基础 n. foundation

jī chǔ 基础 n. rudiment

jī chǔ de 基础的 adj. basal

jī dū 基督 n. Christ

jī dū jiāo 基督教 n. Christianity

jī dū jiào tú 基督教徒 n. Christendom

jī dū tú 基督徒 n Christian

jī dū tú de 基督徒的 a. Christian

jī zhǔn 基准 n. norm

jī zuò 基座 n. pedestal

jī dòng 激动 v.t. agitate

jī fā 激发 v motivate

jī jìn de 激进的 a. radical

jī lì 激励 n. goad

jī lì 激励 v.t goad

jī lì 激励 v.t. stimulate

jī liè de 激烈的 a drastic

jī nù 激怒 v. t enrage

jī nù 激怒 v.t. infuriate

jī nù 激怒 v.t. irritate

jī qǐ 激起 v.t. arouse

jī qǐ 激起 v.t. inflame

jī qǐ de xìng qù 激起兴趣 v.t. intrigue

jī zēng 激增 v.i. proliferate

jī zēng 激增 n. proliferation

jí shí 及时 a. timely

jí shí de 及时的 a. opportune

jí wù dòng cí 及物动词 n. transitive

jí lì de 吉利的 a. auspicious

jí xiáng wù 吉祥物 n. mascot

jí tā 吉他 n. guitar

jǐ yǔ 给予 v.t. impart

jí bié 级别 n. level

jí dì de 极地的 a polar

jí dù de 极度的 a. utmost

jí dù de xū róng 极度的虚荣 n. vainglory

jí duān 极端 n extreme

jí duān míng xiǎn de 极端明显的 a flagrant

jí hǎo de 极好的 a. terrific

jí hǎo de 极好的 a. wonderful

jí lè 极乐 n bliss

jí shēn de 极深的 a. profound

jí shén shèng de 极神圣的 a. sacrosanct

jí xiǎo de 极小的 a. tiny

jí xiǎo de dōng xi 极小的东西 n mite

jí xiǎo zhě 极小者 n. midget

jí tián de 极甜的 a. saccharine

jí jiāng lái lín de 即将来临的 a. forthcoming

jí jiāng lái lín de 即将来临的 a. imminent

jí kè dì 即刻地 adv. instantly

jí shí de 即时的 a. instant

jí shí de 即时的 a. instantaneous

jí wèi 即位 v.t. throne

jí bìng 疾病 n disease

jí bìng 疾病 n ill

jí bìng 疾病 n. illness

jí bìng 疾病 n. sickness

jí cōng cōng dì zǒu 急匆匆地走 v.i. trot

jí dòng de 急动的 a. jerky

jí máng 急忙 n hurry

jí sù dì 急速地 adv. post

jí sù shàng shēng 急速上升 n. zoom

jí xū de 急需的 a. imperative

jí hé 集合 v.t. aggregate

jí hé 集合 v.t. muster

jí hé 集合 v.t. rally

jí hé 集合 n rally

jí huì 集会 n. assembly

jí huì 集会 n. convention

jí huì 集会 n. convocation

jí tǐ 集体 a collective

jí zhōng 集中 v. t concentrate

jí dù de 嫉妒的 a. jealous

jǐ fēn 几分 adv. some

jǐ gè de 几个的 a several

jǐ hé xué 几何学 n. geometry

jǐ hé xué de 几何学的 a. geometrical

jī hū 几乎 *adv.* almost
jī hū bú 几乎不 *adv.* hardly
jǐ 挤 *v.t.* squeeze
jǐ nǎi 挤奶 *v.t.* milk
jǐ 脊 *n.* ridge
jǐ gǔ 脊骨 *n.* backbone
jǐ gǔ 脊骨 *n.* spine
jì huà 计划 *n.* plan
jì huà 计划 *v.t.* plan
jì huà 计划 *n.* project
jì huà 计划 *n.* proposal
jì huà 计划 *v.i.* scheme
jì liàng 计量 *v.t* measure
jì liàng qì 计量器 *n.* gauge
jì liàng qì 计量器 *n.* meter
jì shù jī 计数机 *n* calculator
jì suàn 计算 *v. t.* calculate
jì suàn 计算 *n.* calculation
jì suàn 计算 *n.* computation
jì suàn 计算 *v.t.* compute
jì dé 记得 *v.t.* remember
jì hao 记号 *n.* sign
jì lù 记录 *v.t.* record
jì lù 记录 *n.* record
jì lù 记录 *v.t.* tally
jì lù 纪律 *n* discipline
jì lù yuán 记录员 *n.* scorer
jì rù jiè fāng 记入借方 *v. t*
   debit
jì shì 记事 *n.* narrative
jì shí qì 记时器 *n* chronograph
jì xing hǎo de 记性好的 *a.*
   retentive
jì yì 记忆 *n.* memory
jì yì 记忆 *n.* recollection
jì yì 记忆 *n.* remembrance
jì zhàng rén 记帐人 *n*
   book-keeper
jì zhě 记者 *n.* correspondent
jì zhě 记者 *n.* reporter
jì niàn 纪念 *v. t.* commemorate
jì niàn 纪念 *n.*
   commemoration
jì niàn bēi 纪念碑 *n.*
   memorial
jì niàn bēi 纪念碑 *n.*
   monument
jì niàn bēi de 纪念碑的 *a.*
   monumental

jì niàn de 纪念的 *a* memorial
jì niàn pǐn 纪念品 *n.* keepsake
jì niàn pǐn 纪念品 *n.* memento
jì niàn rì 纪念日 *n.* anniversary
jì néng 技能 *n.* skill
jì qiǎo 技巧 *n.* artifice
jì qiǎo 技巧 *n.* sleight
jì qiǎo 技巧 *n.* technique
jì shù 技术 *n.* technology
jì shù xìng 技术性 *n.*
   technicality
jì shù xìng de 技术性的 *a.*
   technical
jì shù xué de 技术学的 *a.*
   technological
jì shī 技师 *n.* technician
jì nǚ 妓女 *n.* bawd
jì nǚ 妓女 *n.* prostitute
jì nǚ 妓女 *n.* strumpet
jì yuàn 妓院 *n* brothel
jì dù de 季度的 *a.* quarterly
jì jié 季节 *n.* season
jì jié de 季节的 *a.* seasonal
jì dù de 忌妒的 *a* envious
jì dù 忌妒 *v. t* envy
jì shēng 寄生 *n.* mistletoe
jì shēng chóng 寄生虫 *n.*
   parasite
jì shēng de 寄生的 *adj.*
   adnascent
jì sù chù 寄宿处 *n.* lodging
jì rán 既然 *conj.* now
jì mò de 寂寞的 *a.* lonesome
jì chéng 继承 *v.t.* inherit
jì chéng 继承 *n.* succession
jì chéng rén 继承人 *n.* heir
jì chéng rén 继承人 *n.*
   successor
jì xù 继续 *v. i.* continue
jì xù jìn xíng 继续进行 *v.i.*
   proceed
jì fú 祭服 *n.* vestment
jì pǐn 祭品 *n.* oblation
jì pǐn 祭品 *n.* offering
jì pǐn 祭品 *n.* sacrifice
jì tán 祭坛 *n.* altar
jì 蓟 *n.* thistle
jiā zuò hòu zhuì 加作后缀 *v.t.*
   suffix

jiā 加 *v.t.* add

jiā bān 加班 *n* overtime

jiā bèi 加倍 *v.t.* redouble

jiā biāo diǎn fú hào 加标点符号 *v.t.* punctuate

jiā cháng 加长 *v.t.* lengthen

jiā chèn lǐ 加衬里 *v.t.* line

jiā fěn 加粉 *v.t.* powder

jiā gōng chéng de shí pǐn 加工成的食品 *n.* preserve

jiā hài 加害 *v.t.* inflict

jiā hú jiāo fěn yú 加胡椒粉于 *v.t.* pepper

jiā jiǎo liào 加脚镣 *v.t* fetter

jiā kuài 加快 *v. t.* expedite

jiā lún 加仑 *n.* gallon

jiā miǎn 加冕 *v. t* crown

jiā miǎn diǎn lǐ 加冕典礼 *n* coronation

jiā qián zhuì 加前缀 *v.t.* prefix

jiā qiáng 加强 *v. t.* cement

jiā qiáng 加强 *v. t.* consolidate

jiā qiáng 加强 *v.t.* intensify

jiā qiáng 加强 *v.t.* reinforce

jiā qiáng 加强 *n.* reinforcement

jiā qiáng 加强 *v.t.* strengthen

jiā rè 加热 *v.t* heat

jiā rù 加入 *n.* affiliation

jiā shì dìng 加饰钉 *v.t.* stud

jiā sù 加速 *v.t* accelerate

jiā sù 加速 *n* acceleration

jiā suì yú 加穗于 *v.t* fringe

jiā táng yú 加糖于 *v.t.* sugar

jiā xiāng liào 加香料 *v.t.* spice

jiā yán yú 加盐于 *v.t* salt

jiā zhòng 加重 *v.t.* aggravate

jiā jiǎng 嘉奖 *n.* approbation

jiā 家 *n.* home

jiā jù 家具 *n.* furniture

jiā pǔ 家谱 *n.* pedigree

jiā qín 家禽 *n.* fowl

jiā qín 家禽 *n.* poultry

jiā tíng 家庭 *n* family

jiā tíng de 家庭的 *a* domestic

jiá 夹 *v.t* nip

jiā céng 夹层 *n.* mezzanine

jiá bǎn 甲板 *n* deck

jiǎ chóng 甲虫 *n* beetle

jiǎ 钾 *n.* potassium

jiǎ de 假的 *a* bogus

jiǎ de 假的 *a* false

jiǎ de 假的 *a* sham

jiǎ dìng 假定 *n.* presumption

jiǎ dìng 假定 *n.* presupposition

jiǎ fā 假发 *n.* wig

jiǎ gōng jì sī 假公济私 *n.* jobbery

jiǎ shè 假设 *v.t.* assume

jiǎ shè 假设 *n.* assumption

jiǎ shè 假设 *n.* hypothesis

jiǎ shè de 假设的 *a.* hypothetical

jiǎ shēn shì 假绅士 *n.* snob

jiǎ xiàng 假象 *n.* semblance

jiǎ xiǎo zi 假小子 *n.* tomboy

jiǎ zhuāng 假装 *n* affectation

jiǎ zhuāng 假装 *n* disguise

jiǎ zhuāng 假装 *v. t* disguise

jiǎ zhuāng 假装 *v.t* feign

jiǎ zhuāng 假装 *v.t.* pretend

jiǎ mào 假冒 *n* sham

jiǎ miàn jù 假面具 *n.* mask

jià qī 假期 *n.* vacation

jià rì 假日 *n.* holiday

jià gé 价格 *n.* cost

jià qián 价钱 *n.* price

jià zhí 价值 *n.* value

jià zhí 价值 *n.* worth

jià zi 架子 *n.* shelf

jià 架 *n.* rack

jià shǐ 驾驶 *v. t* drive

jià shǐ cāng 驾驶舱 *n.* cock-pit

jià yù 驾驭 *v.t.* rein

jià 嫁 *v.t.* marry

jià jiē 嫁接 *n.* graft

jià jiē 嫁接 *v.t* graft

jià zhuang 嫁妆 *n* dowry

jiān 尖 *n.* tip

jiān jiào 尖叫 *v.i.* scream

jiān jiào shēng 尖叫声 *n* scream

jiān kè 尖刻 *n* acrimony

jiān ruì de 尖锐的 *a.* acute

jiān ruì de 尖锐的 *adj* argute

jiān ruì de hǎn shēng 尖锐的喊声 *n.* shriek

jiān ruì dì 尖锐地 *adv.* sharp

jiān shēng de 尖声的 *a.* shrill

jiān shēng jiào hǎn 尖声叫喊 *v.i.* shriek

jiān tǎ 尖塔 *n.* minaret

jiān tǎ 尖塔 *n.* steeple

jiān chí 坚持 *v.t.* insist

jiān chí 坚持 *n.* insistence

jiān chí 坚持 *v.i.* persevere

jiān chí 坚持 *v.i.* persist

jiān chí de 坚持的 *a.* insistent

jiān dìng de 坚定的 *a.* staunch

jiān dìng de 坚定的 *a.* steadfast

jiān guǒ guǒ rén 坚果果仁 *n* nut

jiān jué 坚决 *n.* adamant

jiān jué de 坚决的 *a.* adamant

jiān jué de 坚决的 *a.* resolute

jiān yìng de 坚硬的 *a.* rigid

jiān shāng 奸商 *n.* profiteer

jiān yín 奸淫 *n.* adultery

jiān zhà de 奸诈的 *a.* treacherous

jiān kǔ bá shè 艰苦跋涉 *v.i.* trek

jiān kǔ bá shè 艰苦跋涉 *n.* trek

jiān kǔ de 艰苦的 *a.* laborious

jiān kǔ de 艰苦的 *a.* tough

jiān nán 艰难 *a.* arduous

jiān nán 艰难 *n.* hardship

jiān dū 监督 *v.t.* oversee

jiān dū 监督 *n.* superintendence

jiān dū 监督 *v.t.* supervise

jiān dū 监督 *n.* supervision

jiān dū qì 监督器 *n.* monitor

jiān dū rén 监督人 *n.* superintendent

jiān dū rén 监督人 *n.* supervisor

jiān gōng 监工 *n.* overseer

jiān hù 监护 *n.* wardship

jiān hù quán 监护权 *v* custody

jiān hù rén 监护人 *n.* custodian

jiān jìn 监禁 *n.* captivity

jiān jìn 监禁 *n.* confinement

jiān kǎo 监考 *v.i.* invigilate

jiān kǎo 监考 *n.* invigilation

jiān kǎo rén 监考人 *n.* invigilator

jiān kǎo rén 监考人 *n.* proctor

jiān láo 监牢 *n.* jail

jiān shì 监视 *n.* surveillance

jiān yù 监狱 *n.* prison

jiān bǎng 肩膀 *n.* shoulder

jiān mò de 缄默的 *a.* tacit

jiān dàn bǐng 煎蛋饼 *n.* omelette

jiǎn chá 检查 *v. t.* check

jiǎn chá 检查 *n* check

jiǎn chá 检查 *v. t* examine

jiǎn chá 检查 *v.t.* inspect

jiǎn chá 检查 *n.* inspection

jiǎn chá 检查 *n.* overhaul

jiǎn chá yuán 检查员 *n.* inspector

jiǎn rǔ qì 检乳器 *n.* lactometer

jiǎn dān 简单 *n.* simplicity

jiǎn dān de 简单的 *a.* brief

jiǎn dān de 简单的 *a.* plain

jiǎn dān de 简单的 *a.* simple

jiǎn dān huà 简单化 *n.* simplification

jián duǎn de 简短的 *adv.* short

jiǎn duǎn de 简短的 *a.* terse

jián duǎn ér wú lǐ de 简短而无礼的 *a* curt

jiǎn huà 简化 *v.t.* simplify

jiǎn jié 简洁 *n* brevity

jiàn jiē de 间接的 *a.* indirect

jiǎn jié de 简洁的 *a* concise

jiǎn jié de 简洁的 *a.* laconic

jiǎn zhí bú 简直不 *adv.* scarcely

jiǎn (qù) 减(去) *prep.* minus

jiǎn féi 减肥 *v.i.* slim

jiǎn qīng 减轻 *v.t.* abate

jiǎn qīng 减轻 *n.* abatement

jiǎn qīng 减轻 *v.t.* allay

jiǎn qīng 减轻 *v.i.* alleviate

jiǎn qīng 减轻 *v.i.* alleviation

jiǎn qīng 减轻 *v.i.* lighten

jiǎn qīng 减轻 *v.t.* mitigate

jiǎn qīng 减轻 *n.* mitigation

jiǎn qīng 减轻 *v.t.* relieve

jiǎn qù 减去 *prep.* less

jiǎn qù 减去 v.t. subtract
jiǎn qù 减去 n. subtraction
jiǎn ruò 减弱 v.i. recede
jiǎn shǎo 减少 v. t diminish
jiǎn shǎo 减少 v. t decrease
jiǎn shǎo 减少 n decrease
jiǎn shǎo 减少 v.t lessen
jiǎn shǎo 减少 v.t. reduce
jiǎn shǎo 减少 n. reduction
jiǎn shǎo 减少 n wane
jiǎn tuì 减退 n ebb
jiǎn tuì 减退 v.i. subside
jiǎn xíng 减刑 v. t commute
jiǎn zhèn qì 减震器 n.
  bumper
jiǎn 碱 n alkali
jiǎn xìng de 碱性的 a. caustic
jiǎn 剪 v.t. shear
jiǎn dāo 剪刀 n. scissors
jiàn shí 见识 n. insight
jiàn xí shēng 见习生 n.
  probationer
jiàn dié 间谍 n. spy
jiàn gé 间隔 n. compartment
jiàn gé 间隔 n. interval
jiàn xiē 间歇 n. lull
jiàn xiē de 间歇的 n. interim
jiàn 剑 n. sword
jiàn duì 舰队 n. armada
jiàn duì 舰队 n fleet
jiàn nǚ rén 贱女人 n bitch
jiàn tà 践踏 v.t. spurn
jiàn tà 践踏 v.t. trample
jiàn tà 践踏 v.t. tread
jiàn 建 v. t build
jiàn lì 建立 v. t. establish
jiàn lì 建立 v.t. found
jiàn zhù 建筑 n building
jiàn zhù shī 建筑师 n.
  architect
jiàn zhù xué 建筑学 n.
  architecture
jiàn yì 建议 n advice
jiàn yì 建议 n. proposition
jiàn kāng 健康 n. health
jiàn kāng de 健康的 a.
  healthy
jiàn kāng de 健康的 a. robust
jiàn kāng de 健康的 a. well

jiàn tán de 健谈的 a. talkative
jiàn wàng de 健忘的 a forgetful
jiàn zhuàng de 健壮的 a. lusty
jiàn zhuàng de 健壮的 a.
  sturdy
jiàn jiǎn 渐减 n. decrement
jiàn xiǎo 渐小 v.i. taper
jiàn 溅 n splash
jiàn pō 溅泼 v.i. splash
jiàn 箭 n arrow
jiàn gǎn 箭杆 n. shaft
jiāng hú yī shù 江湖医术 n.
  quackery
jiāng bí tū rù 将鼻突入 v.
  nuzzle
jiāng jūn 将军 n checkmate
jiāng lái 将来 n future
jiāng bào píng 将刨平 v.t.
  plane
jiāng yìng 浆硬 v.t. starch
jiāng jú 僵局 n deadlock
jiāng jú 僵局 n. stalemate
jiāng shéng 缰绳 n. rein
jiāng 姜 n. ginger
jiǎng 讲 v.i. say
jiǎng 讲 v.i. speak
jiǎng 讲 v.t state
jiǎng 讲 v.i. talk
jiǎng 讲 v.t. tell
jiǎng dào 讲道 n. sermon
jiǎng dào tán 讲道坛 a. pulpit
jiǎng gù shi 讲故事 v.t. narrate
jiǎng huài huà 讲坏话 v.t.
  slander
jiǎng jià 讲价 v.t. bargain
jiǎng jiū lǐ yí 讲究礼仪 a.
  ceremonious
jiǎng shī 讲师 n. lecturer
jiǎng shù zhě 讲述者 n.
  narrator
jiǎng tán 讲坛 n. rostrum
jiǎng xiào hua 讲笑话 v.i. jest
jiǎng yǎn 讲演 v lecture
jiǎng 奖 n. award
jiǎng jīn 奖金 n bonus
jiǎng pǐn 奖品 n. prize
jiǎng shǎng 奖赏 v.t. reward
jiǎng xué jīn 奖学金 n.
  scholarship

jiǎng zhāng 奖章 n. badge
jiǎng zhāng 奖章 n. medal
jiǎng 桨 n. oar
jiǎng 桨 n paddle
jiàng jí 降级 v. t degrade
jiàng jià 降价 v. t. cheapen
jiàng dī 降低 v. t. debase
jiàng dī 降低 v.i. lower
jiàng lín dào 降临到 v. t befall
jiàng luò 降落 n. descent
jiàng luò 降落 n. landing
jiàng luò sǎn 降落伞 n.
  parachute
jiàng 酱 n. paste
jiàng yóu 酱油 n. sauce
jiāo chā diǎn 交叉点 n.
  intersection
jiāo chā diǎn 交叉点 n.
  junction
jiāo gěi 交给 v.t hand
jiāo huàn 交换 n. barter
jiāo huàn 交换 n exchange
jiāo huàn 交换 v. t exchange
jiāo huàn 交换 v. interchange
jiāo liú 交流 n. intercourse
jiāo pèi 交配 v.i. copulate
jiāo pèi 交配 v.t. mate
jiāo pèi fán zhí 交配繁殖 v.t
  breed
jiāo tán 交谈 v. t commune
jiāo tōng 交通 n. traffic
jiāo tōng chē liàng 交通车辆
  n. transportation
jiāo tōng gōng jù 交通工具 n.
  vehicle
jiāo wǎng 交往 v.t. associate
jiāo xiǎng qǔ 交响曲 n.
  symphony
jiāo yì 交易 n deal
jiāo yì 交易 n. transaction
jiāo zhàn 交战 n belligerency
jiāo zhàn guó 交战国 n
  belligerent
jiāo qū 郊区 n. suburb
jiāo qū de 郊区的 a.
  suburban
jiāo wài 郊外 n.pl. outskirts
jiāo yǎng 娇养 v. t cocker
jiāo ào 骄傲 n. pride

jiāo ào de 骄傲的 a. proud
jiāo shē yín yì de 骄奢淫逸的 a.
  voluptuous
jiāo náng zhuàng de 胶囊状的
  adj capsular
jiāo shuǐ 胶水 n. glue
jiāo shuǐ 胶水 n. mucilage
jiāo diǎn 焦点 n focus
jiāo diǎn de 焦点的 a focal
jiāo lù 焦虑 n agitation
jiāo lù 焦虑 v.i. worry
jiāo 教 v.t. teach
jiāo liáo 鹪鹩 n. wren
jiáo 嚼 v.t. masticate
jiǎo 角 n. horn
jiǎo dù 角度 n. angle
jiǎo luò 角落 n corner
jiǎo luò 角落 n. nook
jiǎo mó 角膜 n cornea
jiǎo chē 绞车 n. winch
jiǎo suì 绞碎 v.t. mince
jiǎo suǒ 绞索 n. noose
jiǎo xíng jià 绞刑架 n. gallows
jiǎo róu zào zuò 矫揉造作 n.
  mannerism
jiǎo zhèng 矫正 v.t. rectify
jiǎo huá 狡猾 n cunning
jiǎo huá 狡猾 n. guile
jiǎo huá de 狡猾的 a crafty
jiǎo huá de 狡猾的 a cunning
jiǎo huá de 狡猾的 a. sly
jiǎo huá de 狡猾的 a. tricky
jiǎo huá de 狡猾的 a. wily
jiǎo bàn 搅拌 v. t. & i. churn
jiǎo bàn qì 搅拌器 n whisk
jiǎo luàn 搅乱 v. t commove
jiǎo luàn 搅乱 v.t. unsettle
jiǎo rǔ jī 搅乳机 n. churn
jiǎo zhuó 搅浊 v.t. puddle
jiǎo 脚 n foot
jiǎo bù 脚步 n. step
jiǎo hòu gēn 脚后跟 n. heel
jiǎo huái 脚踝 n. ankle
jiǎo shǒu jià 脚手架 n. scaffold
jiǎo zhǐ 脚趾 n. toe
jiǎo zhuó 脚镯 n anklet
jiào 叫 v. t. call
jiào cuò 叫错 v.t. miscall
jiào hǎn 叫喊 v.i. shout

jiào hǎn 叫喊 v.i. yell

jiào mài xiǎo fàn 叫卖小贩 n. hawker

jiào rén zuò ǒu de 叫人作呕的 a. mawkish

jiào shēng 叫声 n. bellows

jiào shēng 叫声 n cry

jiào xiāo 叫嚣 n. hoot

jiào xǐng 叫醒 v.t. awake

jiào xǐng 叫醒 v.t. wake

jiào zuò 叫做 v.t. term

jiào dìng 校订 v. t edit

jiào dìng 校订 v.t. revise

jiào dìng 校订 n. revision

jiào chē 轿车 n. sedan

jiào chà de 较差的 a. inferior

jiào dàn de sè cǎi 较淡的色彩 v.t. tinge

jiào hǎo 较好 a better

jiào lǎo de 较老的 a elderly

jiào shǎo 较少 adv. less

jiào shǎo 较少 n less

jiào shǎo de 较少的 a. lesser

jiào xǐ huan 较喜欢 v.t. prefer

jiào xiǎo de 较小的 a. minor

jiào huáng zhì dù 教皇制度 n. papacy

jiào huì 教诲 n. tuition

jiào huì de 教诲的 a didactic

jiào pài 教派 n. sect

jiào qū 教区 n. parish

jiào qū mù shī 教区牧师 n. vicar

jiào shòu 教授 n. professor

jiào suō 教唆 v.t. abet

jiào suō 教唆 n. abetment

jiào suō 教唆 n. seduction

jiào suō fàn 教唆犯 n. barrator

jiào táng 教堂 n. church

jiào táng mù dì 教堂墓地 n. churchyard

jiào tiáo 教条 n doctrine

jiào tiáo 教条 n dogma

jiào tiáo de 教条的 a dogmatic

jiào yǎng yuàn 教养院 n. reformatory

jiào yù 教育 v. t educate

jiào yù 教育 n education

jiào yù xué 教育学 n. pedagogy

jiào yuán 教员 n. instructor

jiào xué dà gāng 教学大纲 n. syllabus

jiào 窖 n. vault

jiào cáng 窖藏 v.t. pit

jiào mǔ jūn 酵母菌 n. yeast

jiē duàn 阶段 n. gradation

jiē duàn 阶段 n. phase

jiē 接 n. catch

jiē chù 接触 n. contact

jiē chù 接触 v.t. touch

jiē dài 接待 n. reception

jiē féng chù 接缝处 n. commissure

jiē hé 接合 n. juncture

jiē jiàn 接见 v.t. interview

jiē jìn 接近 v.t. approach

jiē jìn 接近 prep. near

jiē jìn 接近 n. proximity

jiē jìn 接近 v.i. near

jiē lái 接来 v.t fetch

jiē lì bàng 接力棒 n baton

jiē shòu 接受 v accept

jiē shòu 接受 n acceptance

jiē shòu 接受 n embrace

jiē shòu zhě 接受者 n. receiver

jiē zhòng 接种 v.t. inoculate

jiē zhòng 接种 n. inoculation

jiē zhòng 接种 n. vaccination

jiē zhòng yuán 接种员 n. vaccinator

jiē 街 n. street

jiē dào 街道 n. avenue

jiē kāi 揭开 v.t. bare

jiē lù 揭露 n. revelation

jié 节 n. node

jié 节 n. stanza

jié mù 节目 n. programme

jié mù zhǔ chí rén 节目主持人 n. host

jié jiǎn de 节俭的 a. frugal

jié jiǔ 节酒 n. sobriety

jié rì 节日 n festival

jié rì 节日 n festivity

jié shěng 节省 n. retrenchment

jié shěng 节省 n. spare

jié yuē de 节约的 n. thrift

jié yuē de 节约的 a. thrifty

jié zhàng　节杖　*n.*　sceptre

jié zòu　节奏　*n*　rhythm

jié chū　杰出　*n.*　pre-eminence

jié chū de　杰出的　*a*　eminent

jié chū de　杰出的　*a.*
　outstanding

jié chū de　杰出的　*a.*
　pre-eminent

jié zuò　杰作　*n.*　masterpiece

jié　结　*n.*　knot

jié dài zi　结带子　*v.t.*　lace

jié gòu　结构　*n*　construction

jié gòu　结构　*n.*　structure

jié gòu shàng de　结构上的　*a.*
　structural

jié guǒ　结果　*n.*　outcome

jié guǒ　结果　*n.*　result

jié guǒ　结果　*n.*　upshot

jié guǒ shí de　结果实的　*a.*
　fruitful

jié hé　结合　*v. t*　combine

jié hé　结合　*v.t.*　fuse

jié hé　结合　*n.*　fusion

jié hé bìng　结核病　*n.*
　tuberculosis

jié hé de　结合的　*adj.*　conjunct

jié hūn　结婚　*v.t.*　wed

jié hūn qián de　结婚前的　*adj.*
　antenuptial

jié jú　结局　*n*　finish

jié lùn　结论　*n.*　conclusion

jié lùn xìng de　结论性的　*a*
　conclusive

jié méng　结盟　*v.t.*　ally

jié mó　结膜　*n.*　conjunctiva

jié shi de　结实的　*a*　firm

jié shi de　结实的　*a.*　stout

jié shù　结束　*v. t*　conclude

jié zā　结扎　*n*　tie

jié máo　睫毛　*n*　eyelash

jié qǔ　截取　*v.t.*　intercept

jiě chú　解除　*v.t*　absolve

jiě chú　解除　*n.*　relief

jiě chú guǎn lǐ　解除管理　*v.t.*
　decontrol

jiě chú wǔ zhuāng　解除武装
　v. t　disarm

jiě dòng　解冻　*v.i*　thaw

jiě fàng　解放　*n.*　emancipation

jiě fàng　解放　*v.t.*　liberate

jiě fàng　解放　*n.*　liberation

jiě fàng　解放　*n.*　manumission

jiě fàng nú lì　解放奴隶　*v.t.*
　manumit

jiě fàng zhě　解放者　*n.*　liberator

jiě gù　解雇　*n*　dismissal

jiě jiù　解救　*v.t.*　save

jiě jué　解决　*v.t.*　resolve

jiě jué　解决　*v.i.*　settle

jiě jué　解决　*n.*　solution

jiě kāi　解开　*v.t.*　undo

jiě kě　解渴　*v.t.*　slake

jiě pōu　解剖　*v. t*　dissect

jiě pōu　解剖　*n*　dissection

jiě pōu xué　解剖学　*n.*　anatomy

jiě sàn　解散　*v. t.*　dismiss

jiě shì　解释　*v. t*　elucidate

jiě shì　解释　*v. t.*　explain

jiě shì　解释　*n*　explanation

jiě shì　解释　*v.t.*　solve

jiě shì zhě　解释者　*n.*
　interpreter

jiě xī　解析　*n.*　resolution

jiě yào　解药　*n.*　antidote

jiè cí　介词　*n.*　preposition

jiè rù　介入　*n.*　intervention

jiè shào　介绍　*v.t.*　introduce

jiè shào　介绍　*n.*　introduction

jiè shào　介绍　*v.t.*　present

jiè shào de　介绍的　*a.*
　introductory

jiè　戒　*v.i.*　abstain

jiè jiǔ　戒酒　*n.*　temperance

jiè nǎi　戒奶　*v. t*　ablactate

jiè nǎi　戒奶　*n*　ablactation

jiè zhi　戒指　*n.*　ring

jiè mo　芥末　*n.*　mustard

jiè xiàn　界限　*n.*　bound

jiè xiàn　界限　*n.*　limit

jiè　借　*v. t*　borrow

jiè　借　*v.t.*　lend

jiè　借　*v.t.*　loan

jiè fāng　借方　*n*　debit

jiè kǒu　借口　*n*　excuse

jiè kǒu　借口　*n*　pretext

jiè chuāng　疥疮　*n.*　scabies

jīn tiān　今天　*adv.*　today

jīn tiān　今天　*n.*　today

jīn wǎn　今晚　*n.*　tonight
jīn wǎn　今晚　*adv.*　tonight
jīn de　金的　*a.*　golden
jīn jiàng　金匠　*n.*　goldsmith
jīn qián de　金钱的　*a.*
　monetary
jīn qián de　金钱的　*a.*
　pecuniary
jīn róng jiā　金融家　*n*　financier
jīn shǔ　金属　*n.*　metal
jīn shǔ de　金属的　*a.*　metallic
jīn shǔ sī　金属丝　*n.*　tinsel
jīn shǔ xiǎo hé　金属小盒　*n.*
　locket
jīn zì tǎ　金字塔　*n.*　pyramid
jīn tiē　津贴　*n.*　allowance
jīn tiē　津贴　*n*　benefit
jīn tiē　津贴　*n.*　subsidy
jīn dòu　筋斗　*n.*　somersault
jín guǎn　尽管　*conj.*
　notwithstanding
jín guǎn rú cǐ　尽管如此　*adv.*
　nonetheless
jín jín　仅仅　*adv.*　barely
jín jín　仅仅　*adv.*　only
jǐn āi　紧挨　*v.t.*　adjoin
jǐn de　紧　*a.*　tight
jǐn jí　紧急　*n.*　stringency
jǐn jí　紧急　*n.*　urgency
jǐn jí de　紧急的　*a.*　urgent
jǐn jí qíng kuàng　紧急情况　*n*
　emergency
jǐn kào　紧靠　*v*　abutted
jǐn shēn xiōng yī　紧身胸衣　*n*
　bodice
jǐn suō　紧缩　*v.t.*　retrench
jǐn wò　紧握　*n*　grip
jǐn yào guān tóu　紧要关头　*n.*
　conjuncture
jǐn zhāng bù ān de　紧张不安的
　a.　nervous
jǐn zhāng de　紧张的　*a.*　in-
　tense
jǐn biāo sài　锦标赛　*n.*
　tournament
jǐn duàn　锦缎　*n*　brocade
jǐn shèn de　谨慎的　*a.*　cautious
jǐn shèn de　谨慎的　*a.*　wary
jìn lì　尽力　*v.i*　endeavour

jìn bù　进步　*n.*　improvement
jìn bù　进步　*n.*　progress
jìn bù　进步　*v.i.*　progress
jìn bù de　进步的　*a.*　progressive
jìn de　近的　*a.*　close
jìn　近　*adv.*　anigh
jìn　近　*a.*　near
jìn　近　*prep.*　nigh
jìn de　近的　*adv.*　near
jìn shì　近视　*n.*　myopia
jìn shì de　近视的　*a.*　myopic
jìn shì de　近似的　*a.*　similar
jìn gōng　进攻　*n*　offensive
jìn huà　进化　*n*　evolution
jìn huò　进货　*v.t.*　stock
jìn jūn　进军　*v.i*　march
jìn kǒu huò　进口货　*n.*　import
jìn rén kǒng　进人孔　*n.*
　manhole
jìn rù　进入　*n*　entry
jìn rù　进入　*v.t.*　penetrate
jìn rù quán　进入权　*n.*
　admittance
jìn rù... zhī nèi　进入...之内　*prep.*
　into
jìn wǔ cān　进午餐　*v.i.*　lunch
jìn xíng fǎn xǐng　进行反省　*v.i.*
　introspect
jìn xíng jiāo yì　进行交易　*v.i*
　trade
jìn xíng mín yì cè yàn　进行民意
　测验　*v.t.*　poll
jìn xíng zhōng　进行中　*adv.*
　afoot
jìn zhǎn　进展　*n.*　advance
jìn jí　晋级　*n.*　promotion
jìn shēng　晋升　*n.*　advancement
jìn shēng　晋升　*v.t.*　promote
jìn jì　禁忌　*n.*　taboo
jìn jì de　禁忌的　*a*　taboo
jìn lìng　禁令　*n*　ban
jìn lìng　禁令　*n.*　injunction
jìn lìng　禁令　*n.*　prohibition
jìn　浸　*v.t*　dip
jìn　浸　*v.t.*　immerse
jìn　浸　*n.*　immersion
jìn　浸　*v.t.*　soak
jìn　浸　*n.*　soak
jìn tòu　浸透　*n.*　penetration

jìn tòu 浸透 *v.t.* steep

jìn yù 禁欲 *n.* ascetic

jìn yù de 禁欲的 *a.* ascetic

jìn yù zhǔ yì zhě 禁欲主义者 *n.* stoic

jìn zhǐ 禁止 *v.* ban

jìn zhǐ 禁止 *v.t* bar

jìn zhǐ 禁止 *v. t.* debar

jìn zhǐ 禁止 *v.t* forbid

jìn zhǐ 禁止 *v.t.* inhibit

jìn zhǐ 禁止 *n.* inhibition

jìn zhǐ 禁止 *v.t.* prohibit

jìn zhǐ 禁止 *v.t.* taboo

jìn zhǐ de 禁止的 *a.* prohibitive

jīng cháng 经常 *adv.* oft

jīng diǎn 经典 *n* canon

jīng dù 经度 *n.* longitude

jīng guò 经过 *adv* by

jīng guò 经过 *prep.* via

jīng jì 经济 *n* economy

jīng jì de 经济的 *a* economic

jīng jì rén 经纪人 *n* agent

jīng jì rén 经纪人 *n* broker

jīng jì shuāi tuì 经济衰退 *n.* recession

jīng jì xué 经济学 *n.* economics

jīng jì xué shàng de 经济学上的 *a* economical

jīng lì 经历 *v. t.* experience

jīng lì 经历 *v.t.* undergo

jīng lǐ 经理 *n.* manager

jīng lǐ de 经理的 *a.* managerial

jīng xiāo shāng 经销商 *n* dealer

jīng yàn 经验 *n* experience

jīng yàn fēng fù de 经验丰富的 *a.* veteran

jīng yíng xíng wéi 经营行为 *n.* dealing

jīng 惊 *a.* afraid

jīng dòng 惊动 *v.t* alarm

jīng pǎo 惊跑 *n.* stampede

jīng qí 惊奇 *v.t.* amaze

jīng qí 惊奇 *n.* amazement

jīng qí 惊奇 *n.* surprise

jīng qí 惊奇 *n* wonder

jīng tàn cí 惊叹词 *n* exclamation

jīng tuì 惊退 *n.* shy

jīng tuì 惊退 *v.i.* shy

jīng xià 惊吓 *n.* fright

jīng xià 惊吓 *n.* scare

jīng xià 惊吓 *v.t.* scare

jīng xiǎn de 惊险的 *a* breakneck

jīng yà 惊讶 *v.t.* astonish

jīng yà 惊讶 *n.* astonishment

jīng yà 惊讶 *v.i.* wonder

jīng yì 惊异 *v.i* marvel

jīng 茎 *n.* stem

jīng cǎi de 精彩的 *a* brilliant

jīng fǎng róng 精纺绒 *n.* worsted

jīng lì chōng pèi de 精力充沛的 *a.* vigorous

jīng liàn 精炼 *v.t.* refine

jīng liàn chǎng 精炼厂 *n.* refinery

jīng míng de 精明的 *a.* shrewd

jīng què dù 精确度 *n.* precision

jīng shen 精神 *n.* spirit

jīng shen báo mǎn de 精神饱满的 *a.* spirited

jīng shen bìng 精神病 *n.* insanity

jīng shen bìng 精神病 *n.* psychosis

jīng shen bìng huàn zhě 精神病患者 *n.* psychopath

jīng shen bìng xué 精神病学 *n.* psychiatry

jīng shen cuò luàn 精神错乱 *n.* lunacy

jīng shen jiàn quán de 精神健全的 *a.* sane

jīng shen kē yī sheng 精神科医生 *n.* psychiatrist

jīng shen xìng 精神性 *n.* spirituality

jīng tōng 精通 *n.* mastery

jīng tōng 精通 *n.* proficiency

jīng xì de 精细的 *a.* subtle

jīng yè 精液 *n.* semen

jīng yè de 精液的 *a.* seminal

jìng zhì 精致 *n.* refinement

jīng zǐ 精子 *n.* sperm

jīng 鲸 *n.* whale

jīng xū 鲸须 *n.* baleen

jǐng 井 *n.* well

jǐng 颈 *n.* nape

jǐng 颈 *n.* neck

jǐng sè 景色 *n.* outlook

jǐng bào 警报 *n* alarm

jǐng bào qì 警报器 *n.* siren

jǐng chá 警察 *n* constable

jǐng chá 警察 *n.* police

jǐng chá 警察 *n.* policeman

jǐng chá xiǎo duì zhǎng 警察小
队长 *n.* sergeant

jǐng gào 警告 *n.* admonition

jǐng gào 警告 *n.* caution

jǐng gào 警告 *v.t.* warn

jǐng gào 警告 *n.* warning

jǐng gào de 警告的 *a.*
monitory

jǐng jiè 警戒 *n.* vigilance

jǐng jué de 警觉的 *a.* alert

jǐng jué de 警觉的 *a.* vigilant

jǐng jué xìng 警觉性 *n.*
alertness

jìng de 净的 *v.t.* net

jìng huà 净化 *n.* purgation

jìng huà 净化 *n.* purification

jìng huà 净化 *v.t.* purify

jìng huà de 净化的 *a* purgative

jìng jì chǎng 竞技场 *n* arena

jìng jì chǎng 竞技场 *n.* lists

jìng sài 竞赛 *v. t* emulate

jìng sài zhě 竞赛者 *n.* player

jìng zhēng 竞争 *v. i* compete

jìng zhēng 竞争 *v. i* contend

jìng zhēng 竞争 *n.* rivalry

jìng zhēng 竞争 *n.* strife

jìng zhēng de 竞争的 *a*
competitive

jìng zhēng de 竞争的 *a.* rival

jìng zhēng zhě 竞争者 *n.* rival

jìng 胫 *n.* shin

jìng lǐ 敬礼 *n.* obeisance

jìng lǐ 敬礼 *n* salute

jìng wèi 敬畏 *n.* awe

jìng luán de 痉挛的 *a.*
spasmodic

jìng diàn fù yìn 静电复印 *v.t.*
xerox

jìng diàn gān rǎo 静电干扰 *n.*
static

jìng lì xué 静力学 *n.* statics

jìng mài 静脉 *n.* vein

jìng zhǐ 静止 *v.t.* still

jìng zhǐ 静止 *n.* stillness

jìng zhǐ de 静止的 *a.* quiet

jìng zhǐ de 静止的 *a.* still

jìng 镜 *n* mirror

jìng piàn 镜片 *n.* lens

jìng tóu 镜头 *n.* scene

jiū chá duì 纠察队 *n.* picket

jiū jié 纠结 *n.* tangle

jiū zhèng 纠正 *v.* aright

jiū zhèng 纠正 *v.t.* redress

jiū zhèng 纠正 *v.t.* right

jiǔ 九 *n.* nine

jiǔ shí 九十 *n.* ninety

jiǔ yuè 九月 *n.* September

jiǔ zuò de 久坐的 *a.* sedentary

jiǔ 酒 *n.* liquor

jiǔ 酒 *n.* wine

jiǔ bā 酒吧 *n.* bar

jiǔ bā 酒吧 *n.* saloon

jiǔ bēi 酒杯 *n.* goblet

jiǔ guǎn 酒馆 *n.* tavern

jiú guǐ 酒鬼 *n* bibber

jiú guǐ 酒鬼 *n* drunkard

jiǔ jīng 酒精 *n* alcohol

jiǔ lèi yǐn liào 酒类饮料 *n.*
intoxicant

jiù de 旧的 *a.* old

jiù chǐ 白齿 *n.* molar

jiù chǐ de 白齿的 *a* molar

jiù rèn 就任 *n* accession

jiù rèn de 就任的 *a.* inaugural

jiù shì 就是 *adv.* namely

jiù wèi 就位 *v.i.* perch

jiù zhí 就职 *n.* inauguration

jiù zhí 就职 *n.* induction

jiù hù chē 救护车 *n.* ambulance

jiù jì pǐn 救济品 *n.* alms

jiù shì zhǔ 救世主 *n.* messiah

jiù xīng 救星 *n.* saviour

jū liú 拘留 *n.* arrest

jū jìn 拘禁 *v.t.* imprison

jū liú de 居留的 *a.* resident

jū mín　居民　*n.*　inhabitant

jū mín　居民　*n*　resident

jū zhù　居住　*n*　dwelling

jū zhù　居住　*n.*　habitation

jū zhù　居住　*v.i.*　live

jū zhù yú　居住于　*v.t.*　inhabit

jū gōng　鞠躬　*v. t*　bow

jū gōng　鞠躬　*n*　bow

jú　局　*n.*　bureau

jú　局　*n.*　innings

jú　局　*n.*　round

jú bù huà　局部化　*v.t.*　localize

jú zi guǒ jiàng　橘子果酱　*n.*　marmalade

jǔ jué　咀嚼　*v. t*　chew

jǔ sàng　沮丧　*n*　dejection

jǔ lì　举例　*v.t.*　adduce

jǔ lì shuō míng　举例说明　*v.t.*　illustrate

jǔ qǐ　举起　*n*　uplift

jǔ xíng diǎn lǐ　举行典礼　*v.t.*　solemnize

jù dà　巨大　*n.*　magnitude

jù dà de　巨大的　*a*　enormous

jù dà de　巨大的　*a.*　gigantic

jù dà de　巨大的　*a.*　huge

jù dà de　巨大的　*a.*　tremendous

jù dà de　巨大的　*a.*　vast

jù làng　巨浪　*n*　billow

jù rén　巨人　*n.*　giant

jù shí　巨石　*n.*　megalith

jù shí de　巨石的　*a.*　megalithic

jù wù　巨物　*n.*　immensity

jù xiǎng　巨响　*n.*　bang

jù fǎ　句法　*n.*　syntax

jù zi　句子　*n.*　sentence

jù tǐ huà　具体化　*n*　embodiment

jù jué　拒绝　*v.t.*　negative

jù jué　拒绝　*n.*　refusal

jù jué　拒绝　*v.t.*　refuse

jù jué　拒绝　*v.t.*　reject

jù jué　拒绝　*n.*　rejection

jù jué　拒绝　*v.t.*　renounce

jù jué　拒绝　*v.t.*　repudiate

jù jué　拒绝　*n.*　repulse

jǔ xíng de　矩形的　*a.*　rectangular

jù lí　距离　*n*　distance

jù lè bù　俱乐部　*n*　club

jù biàn　剧变　*n.*　upheaval

jù dú de　剧毒的　*a.*　virulent

jù tòng　剧痛　*n.*　throe

jù yuàn　剧院　*n.*　theatre

jù zuò jiā　剧作家　*n*　dramatist

jù chǐ xíng de　锯齿形的　*a.*　zigzag

jù kāi　锯开　*v.t.*　saw

jù zǐ　锯子　*n.*　saw

jù fēng　飓风　*n.*　hurricane

jù huì　聚会　*n.*　party

jù jí　聚集　*n.*　clot

jù jí　聚集　*v. i.*　cluster

jù jí　聚集　*v. t*　convene

jù jí　聚集　*v.i*　mass

jù xiān àn xiān wéi　聚酰胺纤维　*n.*　nefalon

juān kuǎn　捐款　*n.*　donation

juān shuì　捐税　*n.*　tithe

juān zèng　捐赠　*v. t*　contribute

juān zèng　捐赠　*v. t*　donate

juān zèng jī jīn　捐赠基金　*v. t*　endow

juān zhù　捐助　*v.t.*　subscribe

juǎn　卷　*n.*　roll

juǎn qǔ　卷曲　*v*　curl

juǎn shōu　卷收　*v.t.*　furl

juǎn shù duō de　卷数多的　*a.*　voluminous

juàn zhóu　卷轴　*n.*　reel

jué dìng　决定　*v. t*　decide

jué dìng　决定　*n*　decision

jué dìng　决定　*v. t*　determine

jué dìng xìng de　决定性的　*adj.*　crucial

jué dìng xìng de　决定性的　*a*　decisive

jué dòu　决斗　*n*　duel

jué dòu　决斗　*v. i*　duel

jué xīn　决心　*n.*　determination

jué sè　角色　*n.*　character

jué sè　角色　*n.*　role

jué sè fēn pèi　角色分配　*n*　casting

jué xià miàn　掘下面　*v.t.*　undermine

jué chū　掘出　*v.t.*　unearth

jué duì　绝对　*a*　absolute

jué duì　绝对　*adv*　absolutely

jué duì de　绝对的　*a.*
　categorical

jué duì jiè jiǔ zhǔ yì　绝对戒酒
　主义　*n.*　teetotaller

jué duì zhōng shí de　绝对忠实
　的　*a.*　stalwart

jué jīng qī　绝经期　*n.*
　menopause

jué shí　绝食　*n*　fast

jué wàng　绝望　*n*　despair

jué wàng　绝望　*v. i*　despair

jué wú cuò wù de　绝无错误的
　a.　infallible

jué yuán tǐ　绝缘体　*n.*
　insulator

jué qǔ　攫取　*v.t.*　grab

jué jiàng　倔强　*n.*　perversity

jūn fēn　均分　*v.t.*　share

jūn bèi　军备　*n.*　armament

jūn dāo　军刀　*n.*　sabre

jūn duì　军队　*n.*　army

jūn duì　军队　*n*　battalion

jūn duì　军队　*n*　military

jūn huǒ　军火　*n.*　munitions

jūn shì de　军事的　*a.*　military

jūn shì jiā　军事家　*n.*　strategist

jūn tuán　军团　*n.*　legion

jūn tuán shì bīng　军团士兵　*n.*
　legionary

jūn xiào shēng　军校生　*n.*
　cadet

jūn xiè kù　军械库　*n.*　armoury

jūn yòng pǐn　军用品　*n.*
　ordnance

jūn zhǔ　君主　*n.*　sovereign

jūn zhǔ zhèng zhì　君主政治　*n.*
　monarchy

jùn　郡　*n.*　shire

jùn mǎ　骏马　*n.*　steed

K

kā fēi　咖啡　*n*　coffee

kā fēi diàn　咖啡店　*n.*　cafe

kǎ　卡　*n.*　card

kǎ chē　卡车　*n.*　truck

kāi cáo yú　开槽于　*v.t*　groove

kāi chǔ fāng　开处方　*v.t.*
　prescribe

kāi fā tiáo de yào shi　开发条的
　钥匙　*n.*　winder

kāi gōu　开沟　*v.t.*　trench

kāi huà　开化　*v. t*　civilize

kāi huā　开花　*v.i.*　bloom

kāi huā　开花　*v.i*　blossom

kāi kěn　开垦　*n*　reclamation

kāi qì chē de rén　开汽车的人　*n.*
　motorist

kāi shǐ　开始　*n*　begin

kāi shǐ　开始　*n.*　beginning

kāi shǐ　开始　*v. t*　commence

kāi shǐ　开始　*n*　commencement

kāi shǐ　开始　*v.t.*　initiate

kāi shǐ　开始　*n.*　onset

kāi shǐ　开始　*v.t.*　start

kāi shǐ　开始　*n*　start

kāi tóu　开头　*n.*　opening

kāi tóu　开头　*n.*　outset

kāi wán xiào　开玩笑　*v.t.*　banter

kāi wán xiào　开玩笑　*v.i.*　joke

kāi wán xiào　开玩笑　*v.i*　trifle

kāi wèi de　开胃的　*a.*　piquant

kāi zhǎn　开展　*v.t.*　wage

kāi zhāng　开张　*v.t.*　auspicate

kāi zhe de　开着的　*a.*　open

kāi zhī　开支　*n.*　expense

kāi zú mǎ lì　开足马力　*n.*　throttle

kǎi xuán de　凯旋的　*a.*
　triumphal

kǎi xuán shì　凯旋式　*n.*　triumph

kān tàn　勘探　*n*　exploration

kǎn　砍　*v.t.*　hew

kǎn fá　砍伐　*n.*　lop

kǎn tóu　砍头　*v. t.*　behead

kàn　看　*v.i*　look

kàn　看　*v.t.*　view

kàn bú jiàn de　看不见的　*a.*
　invisible

kàn dé jiàn de　看得见的　*a.*
　visible

kàn jiàn　看见　*v.t.*　see

kàn jiàn　看见　*v.t.*　sight

kān shǒu　看守　*v.i.*　guard

kān shǒu　看守　*n.*　warder

kān shǒu zhě 看守者 *n.* guardian

kàn zuò rén 看做人 *v.t.* personify

kāng kǎi 慷慨 *n* bounty

kāng kǎi 慷慨 *n.* generosity

kāng kǎi 慷慨 *n.* liberality

kāng kǎi de 慷慨的 *a.* generous

kāng kǎi de 慷慨的 *a.* liberal

kāng kǎi dì shǎng cì 慷慨地赏赐 *n.* largesse

kāng kǎi jí yǔ 慷慨给予 *v.t.* lavish

kāng kǎi jí yǔ de 慷慨给予的 *a.* munificent

kàng yì 抗议 *n.* protest

kǎo chá 考查 *v.t.* quiz

kǎo lǜ 考虑 *v. t* consider

kǎo lǜ 考虑 *n* consideration

kǎo lǜ 考虑 *v.t.* meditate

kǎo lǜ dào 考虑到 *prep.* considering

kǎo shì 考试 *n.* examination

kǎo wèn 拷问 *v.t.* torture

kǎo 烤 *v.t.* bake

kǎo 烤 *v.t.* roast

kǎo miàn bāo piàn 烤面包片 *n.* toast

kǎo ròu 烤肉 *n* roast

kào jìn 靠近 *prep* by

kē lín sī 科林斯 *n.* Corinth

kē xué 科学 *n.* science

kē xué de 科学的 *a.* scientific

kē xué jiā 科学家 *n.* scientist

kē shuì 瞌睡 *n.* doze

kē shuì de 瞌睡的 *a.* somnolent

ké 壳 *n.* shell

ké sou 咳嗽 *n.* cough

ké sou 咳嗽 *v. i.* cough

kě ài de 可爱的 *a.* adorable

kě ài de 可爱的 *a* darling

kě ài de 可爱的 *a.* lovely

kě bǎo shì de 可保释的 *a.* bailable

kě bēi de 可悲的 *a.* lamentable

ké bǐ de 可鄙的 *a* despicable

kě biàn de 可变的 *a.* variable

kě cè liáng de 可测量的 *a.* measurable

kě chá jué de 可察觉的 *adj* perceptible

ké chǐ de 可耻的 *a.* shameful

kě dòng de 可动的 *a.* movable

kě dòng xìng 可动性 *n.* mobility

kě fán zhí de 可繁殖的 *a* fertile

kě fèi zhǐ de 可废止的 *a.* revocable

kě fēn lí de 可分离的 *a.* separable

kě fù de 可付的 *a.* payable

kě jīng yíng de 可经营的 *a.* workable

kě jū zhù de 可居住的 *a.* inhabitable

kě jué chá de 可觉察的 *a.* appreciable

kě kǎ yīn 可卡因 *n* cocaine

kě kào de 可靠的 *a* credible

kě kào de 可靠的 *a.* reliable

kě kào de 可靠的 *a.* trustworthy

kě kuān shù de 可宽恕的 *a.* venial

kě lián 可怜 *v.t.* pity

kě lián de 可怜的 *a.* miserable

kě lián de 可怜的 *a.* pathetic

kě lián de 可怜的 *a.* piteous

kě lián de 可怜的 *a.* pitiful

kě mǎn zú de 可满足的 *a.* satiable

kě néng de 可能的 *a.* possible

kě néng xìng 可能性 *n.* likelihood

kě néng xìng 可能性 *n.* possibility

kě néng xìng 可能性 *n.* probability

kě nì de 可逆的 *a.* reversible

kě pà 可怕 *a.* terrible

kě pà de 可怕的 *a.* awful

kě pà de 可怕的 *a* dire

kě pà de 可怕的 *a.* fearful

kě pà de 可怕的 *a* formidable

kě pà de 可怕的 *a.* ghastly

kě pà de 可怕的 *a.* horrible
kě pà de 可怕的 *a.* monstrous
kě pà de 可怕的 *a.* uncanny
kě péi cháng de 可赔偿的 *a.* raparable
kě qīn pèi de 可钦佩的 *a.* admirable
kě qīn pèi de 可钦佩的 *a* creditable
kě rěn shòu de 可忍受的 *a* endurable
kě rěn shòu de 可忍受的 *a.* tolerable
kě róng de 可溶的 *a.* soluble
kě shí xíng de 可实行的 *a.* practicable
kě shí yòng de 可食用的 *a* eatable
kě shōu mǎi de 可收买的 *a.* venal
kě sù de 可塑的 *a.* malleable
kě tàn de 可叹的 *a* deplorable
kě tōng chuán de 可通船的 *a.* navigable
kě xǐ de 可洗的 *a.* washable
kě xié dài de 可携带的 *a.* portable
kě xié shāng de 可协商的 *a.* negotiable
kě xìn rèn de rén 可信任的人 *n.* trusty
kě xíng de 可行的 *a* feasible
ké yǐ 可以 *a* able
ké yǐ 可以 *v. t.* can
ké yǐ chī de 可以吃的 *a* edible
ké yǐ chú lǐ de 可以处理的 *a.* manageable
ké yí chuán de 可遗传的 *a.* heritable
kě yí de 可疑的 *a.* questionable
kě yí de 可疑的 *a.* suspect
kě yí de 可疑的 *a.* suspicious
ké yǐ jié hūn de 可以结婚的 *a.* marriageable
ké yǐ jiē shòu de 可以接受的 *a* acceptable

ké yǐ jiē shòu de 可以接受的 *a.* admissible
ké yǐ jiē shòu de 可以接受的 *a.* agreeable
ké yí qù de 可移去的 *a.* removable
ké yǐ yuán liàng de 可以原谅的 *a.* pardonable
kě yī zhì de 可医治的 *a* curable
kě yòng de 可用的 *a* available
kě yún xǔ de 可允许的 *a.* permissible
kě zēng de 可憎的 *a.* heinous
kě zēng de 可憎的 *a.* obnoxious
kē zhèng 苛政 *n.* tyranny
kè zhì 克制 *v.i.* refrain
kě zhōng zhǐ de 可终止的 *a.* terminable
kě zhuǎn yí de 可转移的 *a.* transferable
kě zhuī sù de 可追溯的 *a.* traceable
kě zì yóu xuǎn zé de 可自由选择的 *a.* optional
kě 渴 *n.* thirst
kě wàng 渴望 *adj.* agog
kě wàng 渴望 *a* eager
kě wàng 渴望 *v.i.* hanker
kě wàng 渴望 *n* hunger
kě wàng 渴望 *v.i* long
kě wàng 渴望 *n.* longing
kě wàng 渴望 *v.i.* thirst
kě wàng 渴望 *a.* wishful
kě wàng 渴望 *v.i.* yearn
kě wàng 渴望 *n.* yearning
kě wàng de 渴望的 *adj.* appetent
kě wàng de 渴望的 *adj.* athirst
kě wàng de 渴望的 *adv* avidly
kě wàng de 渴望的 *v.t.* crave
kě wàng de 渴望的 *a* desirous
kě wàng de 渴望的 *a.* wistful
kè 克 *n.* gramme
kè fú 克服 *v.t.* overcome
kè fú 克服 *v.t.* surmount
kè guān de 客观的 *a.* impersonal
kè guān de 客观的 *a.* objective

kè hù　客户　n customer
kè lā　克拉　n. carat
kè qi de　客气的　a. mannerly
kè rén　客人　n. guest
kè tīng　客厅　n drawing-room
kè tīng　客厅　n. parlour
kè　刻　v. t. carve
kè dù pán　刻度盘　n. dial
kè hén　刻痕　n. nick
kè shàng　刻上　v. t engrave
kè　课　n. lesson
kè chéng　课程　n. course
kè chéng　课程　n curriculum
kěn dìng　肯定　v.t. affirm
kěn dìng　肯定　v.t. assert
kěn dìng　肯定　a. sure
kěn dìng de　肯定的　a
　affirmative
kén qǐng　恳请　n. solicitation
kěn qiú　恳求　n adjuration
kěn qiú　恳求　n. entreaty
kěn qiú　恳求　v.t. implore
kěn qiú　恳求　n. plea
kěn qiú　恳求　v.i. plead
kěn qiú　恳求　v.t. solicit
kòng bái　空白　n. lacuna
kòng bái de　空白的　a blank
kōng de　空的　a. bare
kōng de　空的　a empty
kōng de　空的　a. hollow
kōng de　空的　a. vacant
kōng de　空的　a. void
kōng gé　空格　n blank
kōng jiān　空间　n. space
kōng jiān　空间　n. void
kōng jiān de　空间的　a. spatial
kōng qì　空气　n air
kōng qì de　空气的　a. airy
kòng quē　空缺　n. vacancy
kōng tán de　空谈的　a.
　platonic
kòng xián　空闲　n. leisure
kòng xián de　空闲的　a leisure
kōng zhōng dì　空中的　a. aerial
kǒng　孔　n. aperture
kǒng　孔　n. socket
kǒng què　孔雀　n. peacock
kǒng yǎn　孔眼　n eyelet
kǒng bù　恐怖　n dread

kǒng bù　恐怖　n fear
kǒng bù　恐怖　n. horror
kǒng bù　恐怖　n. terror
kǒng bù　恐怖　v.t. terrorize
kǒng bù fèn zǐ　恐怖分子　n.
　terrorist
kǒng bù zhǔ yì　恐怖主义　n.
　terrorism
kǒng hè　恐吓　v. t. cow
kǒng hè　恐吓　n. intimidation
kǒng hè　恐吓　v.t. threaten
kǒng huāng　恐慌　n. panic
kòng gào　控告　n accusation
kòng gào　控告　v.t. accuse
kòng gào　控告　v.t. impeach
kòng gào　控告　n.
　impeachment
kòng gào　控告　n. indictment
kòng gào　控告　v.t. sue
kòng zhì　控制　v. t control
kòng zhì　控制　n domination
kòng zhì　控制　n. hold
kòng zhì　控制　v.t. regulate
kòng zhì quán　控制权　n control
kǒu bí　口鼻　n. muzzle
kǒu cái　口才　n eloquence
kǒu chī　口吃　v.i. stammer
kǒu chī　口吃　n stammer
kóu chǐ bù qīng　口齿不清　n lisp
kǒu dai　口袋　n. pocket
kǒu hào　口号　n. slogan
kǒu hào　口号　n. watchword
kǒu kě de　口渴的　a. thirsty
kǒu shào　口哨　n whistle
kǒu shì　口试　n viva-voce
kǒu shì xīn fēi　口是心非　n
　duplicity
kǒu shù　口述　v. t dictate
kǒu shù　口述　n dictation
kǒu shù　口述　adv. orally
kǒu tóu de　口头的　a. oral
kǒu tóu de　口头的　a. verbal
kǒu tóu de　口头的　a viva-voce
kǒu tóu dì　口头地　adv.
　verbally
kǒu tóu shàng de　口头上的　adv.
　viva-voce
kǒu yīn　口音　n accent
kòu chú　扣除　v.t. deduct

kòu jǐn　扣紧　v. t.　button
kòu jǐn　扣紧　n　clasp
kòu liú　扣留　v. t　detain
kòu liú　扣留　v.t.　intern
kòu yā quán　扣押权　n.　lien
kòu zhù　扣住　n　buckle
kū sù　哭诉　v.i.　whine
kǔ　苦　a　bitter
kǔ ài　苦艾　n.　wormwood
kǔ gōng　苦工　n.　toil
kǔ lì　苦力　n　coolie
kǔ mèn　苦闷　v.t.　agonize
kǔ mèn　苦闷　n.　torture
kǔ nàn　苦难　n.　misery
kǔ nàn　苦难　n.　tribulation
kǔ nàn gēn yuán　苦难根源　n.
　　scourge
kú nǎo　苦恼　n.　anguish
kú nǎo　苦恼　n　distress
kú nǎo　苦恼　n.　trouble
kú nǎo　苦恼　n.　woe
kù cún　库存　n.　stock
kù zi　裤子　n. pl　trousers
kuā dà　夸大　v. t.　exaggerate
kuā zhāng　夸张　n. exaggeration
kuā zhāng biáo yǎn　夸张表演
　　v.t.　overact
kuā zhāng fǎ　夸张法　n.
　　hyperbole
kuài jì　会计　n.　accountant
kuài jì xué　会计学　n.
　　accountancy
kuài　块　n　block
kuài　块　n.　mass
kuài　块　n.　piece
kuài　快　adv.　speedily
kuài jīn　块金　n.　nugget
kuài cān　快餐　n.　snack
kuài chē　快车　n　express
kuài de　快的　a　express
kuài de　快的　a.　quick
kuài de　快的　a.　speedy
kuài ér hán hu dì shuō　快而含
　　糊地说　v.t.　jabber
kuài huo　快活　n　ease
kuài huo de　快活的　a.　jovial
kuài lè　快乐　n.　happiness
kuài lè　快乐　n.　joviality
kuài lè de　快乐的　a.　happy

kuài sù chuán　快速船　n.
　　greyhound
kuài sù de　快速的　a　fast
kuān chǎng　宽敞　a.　capacious
kuān chǎng de　宽敞的　a.
　　roomy
kuān chǎng de　宽敞的　a.
　　spacious
kuān dà　宽大　n.　lenience,
　　leniency
kuān dà cháng páo　宽大长袍
　　n.　toga
kuān dà de　宽大的　a.　lenient
kuān dà de　宽大的　a.　merciful
kuān de　宽的　a.　wide
kuān dù　宽度　n　breadth
kuān hóng dà liàng　宽宏大量　n.
　　magnanimity
kuān hóng dà liàng de　宽宏大量
　　的　a.　magnanimous
kuān kuò de　宽阔的　a　broad
kuān róng　宽容　n.　toleration
kuān róng de　宽容的　a.
　　tolerant
kuān shù　宽恕　n.　condonation
kuān shù　宽恕　n.　mercy
kuān shù　宽恕　n.　remission
kuān sōng cháng páo　宽松长袍
　　n.　robe
kuān sōng de　宽松的　a.　slack
kuān sōng de kù zi　宽松的裤子
　　n.　slacks
kuǎn dài　款待　n.　hospitality
kuǎn dài　款待　n　treat
kuáng bào　狂暴　v.i.　rampage
kuáng fèi　狂吠　n　yap
kuáng fēng　狂风　n.　gale
kuáng huān　狂欢　n.　revel
kuáng huān　狂欢　n.　revelry
kuáng huān zuò lè　狂欢作乐　v.i.
　　revel
kuáng nù　狂怒　adv.　amuck
kuáng nù de　狂怒的　a.　furious
kuáng quǎn bìng　狂犬病　n.
　　rabies
kuáng rè de　狂热的　a　fanatic
kuáng rè zhě　狂热者　n　fanatic
kuáng rén　狂人　n　mania
kuáng xiǎng　狂想　n.　vagary

kuàng qiě 况且 *adv.* moreover
kuàng 矿 *n* mine
kuàng gōng 矿工 *n.* miner
kuàng gōng 矿工 *n.* pitman
kuàng shí 矿石 *n.* ore
kuàng wù 矿物 *n.* mineral
kuàng wù de 矿物的 *a* mineral
kuàng wù xué 矿物学 *n.* mineralogy
kuàng wù xué jiā 矿物学家 *n.* mineralogist
kuàng yě kǒng bù zhèng 旷野恐怖症 *n.* agoraphobia
kuàng 框 *n* frame
kuī 盔 *n.* helmet
kuī jiǎ 盔甲 *n.* armour
kuī shì 窥视 *v.i.* peep
kuí níng 奎宁 *n.* quinine
kuí wú yǒu lì de 魁梧有力的 *a.* herculean
kuì yáng 溃疡 *n.* ulcer
kuì yáng de 溃疡的 *a.* ulcerous
kūn chóng 昆虫 *n.* bug
kūn chóng 昆虫 *n.* insect
kūn chóng xué 昆虫学 *n.* entomology
kǔn 捆 *n* bundle
kún bǎng 捆绑 *v.t.* lash
kùn fá de 困乏的 *a.* weary
kùn huò 困惑 *n.* perplexity
kùn huò 困惑 *n.* quandary
kùn jìng 困境 *n.* adversity
kùn jìng 困境 *n* dilemma
kùn jìng 困境 *n* fix
kùn jìng 困境 *n.* plight
kùn nan 困难 *n* rub
kùn nan de 困难的 *a* difficult
kùn rǎo 困扰 *v.t.* ail
kùn rǎo 困扰 *v.t.* baffle
kùn rǎo 困扰 *v.t.* perplex
kuò chōng 扩充 *n.* expansion
kuò dà 扩大 *n* amplification
kuò yīn qì 扩音器 *n* amplifier

L

lā 拉 *v.t* draw
lā 拉 *v.t.* pull

lā 拉 *n.* pull
lā 拉 *v.t.* trail
lā 拉 *v.t.* tug
lā 拉 *v.t.* zip
lā cháng 拉长 *v.t.* stretch
lā jǐn 拉紧 *n* strain
lā jǐn 拉紧 *n.* tension
lā liàn 拉链 *n.* zip
lā lǒng 拉拢 *v.t.* pack
lā mǐ zhǐ pái xì 拉米纸牌戏 *n.* rummy
lā piào 拉票 *v.t.* canvass
lā jī 垃圾 *n.* garbage
lā jī 垃圾 *n.* junk
lā jī 垃圾 *n.* litter
lā jī 垃圾 *n.* rubbish
lā jī 垃圾 *n.* trash
lā jī qì zhì chǎng 垃圾弃置场 *n.* tip
lā tā 邋遢 *n.* squalor
lā tā de 邋遢的 *a.* slovenly
lā tā de 邋遢的 *a.* squalid
lā tā nǚ rén 邋遢女人 *n.* slattern
lǎ ba 喇叭 *n.* speaker
lǎ ba 喇叭 *n.* trumpet
lǎ ba tǒng 喇叭筒 *n.* megaphone
lǎ ma 喇嘛 *n.* lama
là 蜡 *n.* wax
là zhú 蜡烛 *n.* candle
là jiāo 辣椒 *n* capsicum
là jiāo 辣椒 *n.* chilli
lái 来 *v.i.* come
lái fù qiāng 来复枪 *n* rifle
lái háng jī 来航鸡 *n.* leghorn
lái yuán 来源 *n.* source
lài zhàng 赖账 *v.t.* bilk
lán jié 拦截 *n.* interception
lán 栏 *n* column
lán gān 栏杆 *n.* rail
lán wěi 阑尾 *n.* appendix
lán wěi yán 阑尾炎 *n.* appendicitis
lán bǎo shí 蓝宝石 *n.* sapphire
lán sè 蓝色 *n* blue
lán 篮 *n.* basket
lǎn duò 懒惰 *n.* sloth
lǎn duò de 懒惰的 *a.* idle

lǎn duò de 懒惰的 *a.* indolent
lǎn duò de 懒惰的 *a.* lazy
lǎn duò de 懒惰的 *n.* slothful
lǎn hàn xié 懒汉鞋 *n.* loafer
lǎn rén 懒人 *n.* sluggard
lán sǎn dì xián dàng 懒散地闲
荡 *v.i.* loll
làn yòng 滥用 *n* abuse
làn yòng 滥用 *n.*
  misapplication
làn yòng 滥用 *n.* misuse
làn yòng 滥用 *v.t.* misuse
láng 狼 *n.* wolf
láng tūn hǔ yàn 狼吞虎咽 *n.*
  gobble
láng tūn hǔ yān dì chī 狼吞虎
咽地吃 *v.i.* scoff
lǎng dú 朗读 *v.t.* recite
lǎng mǔ jiǔ 朗姆酒 *n.* rum
làng dàng zǐ 浪荡子 *n*
  debauchee
làng fèi 浪费 *n.* prodigality
làng fèi 浪费 *n.* profligacy
làng fèi 浪费 *v.t.* riot
làng fèi 浪费 *v.t.* waste
làng fèi de 浪费的 *a.* prodigal
làng fèi de 浪费的 *a.* wasteful
làng màn de 浪漫的 *a.*
  romantic
làng màn shǐ 浪漫史 *n.*
  romance
láo dāo 唠叨 *n. & v. i* clack
láo dāo 唠叨 *n.* verbosity
láo dòng 劳动 *v.t.* modify
láo dòng 劳动 *v.i.* moil
láo gōng 劳工 *n.* labour
láo gōng 劳工 *n.* labourer
láo gōng 劳工 *n.* peon
láo kǔ de 劳苦的 *a.* painstaking
láo bǎn 老板 *n* boss
lǎo chǒu jué 老丑角 *n.*
  pantaloon
lǎo chú nǚ 老处女 *n.* spinster
lǎo hǔ 老虎 *n.* tiger
lǎo nián de 老年的 *a.* aged
lǎo shī 老师 *n.* teacher
lǎo xiōng 老兄 *n* mate
lè guān 乐观 *n.* optimism

lè guān de 乐观的 *a.* optimistic
lè guān de 乐观的 *a.* sanguine
lè guān zhě 乐观者 *n.* optimist
lè qù 乐趣 *n.* fun
lè yì 乐意 *n.* alacrity
lè yì 乐意 *n.* willingness
lè yì de 乐意的 *a.* willing
lè yì dì 乐意地 *adv.* readily
lè suǒ 勒索 *v.t* blackmail
lè suǒ shú jīn 勒索赎金 *v.t.*
  ransom
lēi mǎ shéng 勒马绳 *n* curb
lēi sǐ 勒死 *v.t.* strangle
léi 雷 *n.* thunder
léi míng shì de 雷鸣似的 *a.*
  thunderous
léi 镭 *n.* radium
lěi jī 累积 *v.t.* amass
lèi 泪 *n.* tear
lèi gǔ 肋骨 *n.* rib
lèi gǔ de 肋骨的 *adj.* costal
lèi bǐ 类比 *n.* analogy
lèi rén yuán 类人猿 *adj.*
  anthropoid
lèi shì de 类似的 *a.* akin
lèi sì 类似 *n.* parallelism
lèi xíng 类型 *n.* type
lěng dàn de 冷淡的 *a.* frigid
lěng dàn de 冷淡的 *a.*
  nonchalant
lěng de 冷的 *a* cold
lěng dòng 冷冻 *n.* refrigeration
lěng jìng 冷静 *n.* calm
lěng kù wú qíng de 冷酷无情的
  a. callous
lěng kù wú qíng de 冷酷无情的
  adj. merciless
lěng mò 冷漠 *n.* apathy
lěng què qì 冷却器 *n* cooler
lí 犁 *n.* plough
lí tóu 犁头 *n* colter
lí zǐ 梨子 *n.* pear
lí hūn 离婚 *n* divorce
lí kāi 离开 *adv.* away
lí kāi 离开 *v. i.* depart
lí kāi 离开 *n* departure
lí kāi 离开 *v.t.* leave
lí kāi 离开 *v.t.* quit
lí xīn de 离心的 *adj.* centrifugal

lí míng 黎明 *n* dawn
lǐ bài 礼拜 *n.* worship
lǐ bài yí shì de 礼拜仪式的 *a.* liturgical
lǐ jié 礼节 *n* etiquette
lǐ mào 礼貌 *n.* courtesy
lǐ mào 礼貌 *n.* manner
lǐ mào 礼貌 *n.* propriety
lí pǐn 礼品 *n.* present
lǐ wù 礼物 *n.* gift
lǐ yí de 礼仪的 *a.* ceremonial
lǐ zi 李子 *n.* plum
lǐ chéng bēi 里程碑 *n.* milestone
lǐ yǔ 俚语 *n.* slang
lǐ fà shī 理发师 *n.* barber
lǐ gōng zhuān kē xué xiào 理工专科学校 *n.* polytechnic
lí jiě 理解 *v.t.* apprehend
lí jiě 理解 *n.* apprehension
lí jiě 理解 *v. t* comprehend
lí jiě lì 理解力 *n* comprehension
lǐ lùn 理论 *n.* theory
lǐ lùn huà 理论化 *v.i.* theorize
lǐ lùn jiā 理论家 *n.* theorist
lǐ lùn shàng 理论上 *a.* theoretical
lǐ shì huì 理事会 *n.* council
lí xiǎng 理想 *n* ideal
lí xiǎng de 理想的 *a.* ideal
lí xiǎng ér bù shí jì de 理想而不实际的 *a.* quixotic
lí xiǎng guó 理想国 *n.* utopia
lí xiǎng zhǔ yì 理想主义 *n.* idealism
lí xiǎng zhǔ yì de 理想主义的 *a.* idealistic
lí xiǎng zhǔ yì zhě 理想主义者 *n.* idealist
lǐ xìng de 理性的 *a.* rational
lì liàng 力量 *n* force
lì liàng 力量 *n.* potency
lì liàng 力量 *n.* strength
lì qi 力气 *n.* might
lì chǎng 立场 *n.* standpoint
lì fǎ 立法 *n.* legislation
lì fǎ de 立法的 *a.* legislative

lì fǎ jī guān 立法机关 *n.* legislature
lì fǎ wěi yuán 立法委员 *n.* legislator
lì fāng tǐ de 立方体的 *a* cubical
lì fāng xíng 立方形 *n* cube
lì fāng xíng de 立方形的 *adj.* cubiform
lì jí 立即 *adv.* anon
lì jí 立即 *n.* instant
lì jí de 立即的 *a* immediate
lì kè 立刻 *adv.* forthwith
lì kè 立刻 *adv.* now
lì kè 立刻 *adv.* soon
lì kè 立刻 *adv.* straightway
lì kè de 立刻的 *a.* prompt
lì zhì zuò 立志做 *v.t.* aspire
lì shǐ 历史 *n.* history
lì shǐ de 历史的 *a.* historical
lì shǐ xìng de 历史性的 *a.* historic
lì shǐ xué jiā 历史学家 *n.* historian
lì qīng 沥青 *n.* tar
lì rùn 利润 *n.* profit
lì yòng 利用 *v. t* exploit
lì yòng 利用 *n.* utilization
lì yòng 利用 *v.t.* utilize
lì wài 例外 *n* exception
lì zi 栗子 *n.* chestnut
lì zi 例子 *n* example
lì zi 例子 *n.* instance
lì jí 痢疾 *n* dysentery
lián gēn bá qǐ 连根拔起 *v.t.* uproot
lián guàn xìng 连贯性 *n.* consistence,-cy
lián jié 连结 *v.t* link
lián jiē 连接 *v. t.* connect
lián jiē 连接 *v. t* couple
lián jiē zhe 连接着 *adj.* annectant
lián jié 连结 *v.t.* interlock
lián lěi 连累 *v.t.* incriminate
lián xù de 连续的 *adj.* consecutive
lián xù de 连续的 *adj.* continual
lián xù de 连续的 *a.* serial
lián xù de 连续的 *a.* successive

lián xù dì 连续地 adv
consecutively

lián xù pào hōng 连续炮轰
n. &v. t cannonade

lián xù tóu qiú bǐ sài 连续投球
比赛 n over

lián xù xìng 连续性 n
continuity

lián yī qún 连衣裙 n. frock

lián zǎi xiǎo shuō 连载小说 n.
serial

lián bāng 联邦 n.
commonwealth

lián bāng 联邦 n federation

lián bāng de 联邦的 a federal

lián hé qǐ yè 联合企业 n
complex

lián hé zhǔ yì zhě 联合主义者
n. unionist

lián jié 联结 n bond

lián luò 联络 n. liaison

lián méng 联盟 n. alliance

lián méng 联盟 n coalition

lián méng 联盟 n. league

lián xì 联系 v. t contact

lián bō 涟波 n. ripple

lián jià chū shòu 廉价出售 n.
sale

lián huā 莲花 n. lotus

lián dāo 镰刀 n. sickle

liǎn 脸 n face

liǎn de 脸的 a facial

liǎn hóng 脸红 adv ablush

liǎn hóng 脸红 n blush

liǎn hóng 脸红 v.i blush

liàn ài de 恋爱的 adj amatory

liàn xí 练习 v.t. practise

liàn jiāo 炼焦 v. t coke

liàn jīn shù 炼金术 n. alchemy

liàn jiē 链接 n. link

liàn tiáo 链条 n chain

liáng xīn 良心 n conscience

liáng 凉 a cool

liáng tíng 凉亭 n bower

liáng xié 凉鞋 n. sandal

liáng dù 量度 n. measurement

liǎng 两 a. two

liǎng bèi de 两倍的 a double

liǎng cì 两次 adv. twice

liǎng gè 两个 pron both

liǎng gè bù fen de 两个部分的
a. twofold

liǎng gè zì mǔ de 两个字母的
adj biliteral

liǎng nián yí cì de 两年一次的
adj biennial

liǎng xīng qī 两星期 n.
fortnight

liǎng xīng qī yí cì 两星期一次
adj bi-weekly

liǎng zhě zhī yī de 两者之一的
a. either

liǎng zhǐ shǒu tào 两指手套 n.
mitten

liǎng zú dòng wù 两足动物 n
biped

liàng de 亮的 a bright

liàng zǐ 量子 n. quantum

liáo fǎ 疗法 n. therapy

liáo cǎo de bǐ jì 潦草的笔迹 n
scrawl

liáo cǎo de zì 潦草的字 n.
scribble

liáo máo 燎毛 v.t. singe

liáo shǔ 僚属 n. minion

liáo tiān 聊天 n. chat

liáo tiān 聊天 v. i. chat

liào wàng tǎ 瞭望塔 n
belvedere

liǎo bù qǐ de 了不起的 a.
stupendous

liáo jiě 了解 v.t. realize

liáo yǎng yuàn 疗养院 n.
sanatorium

liè chū 列出 v.t. list

liè duì 列队 n. alignment

liè duì xíng jìn 列队行进 v.i. file

liè jǔ 列举 v. t. enumerate

liè quǎn 猎犬 n. hound

liè rén 猎人 n. hunter

liè rén 猎人 n. huntsman

liè yīng 猎鹰 n falcon

liè fèng 裂缝 n fissure

liè fèng 裂缝 n. slit

liè fèng 裂缝 n. tear

liè hén 裂痕 n crack

liè kāi 裂开 v. i crack

liè kāi 裂开 v.i. gape

liè kāi de 裂开的 *a* cleft
liè kǒu 裂口 *n*. rift
liè gǒu 鬣狗 *n*. hyaena, hyena
lín jìn de 邻近的 *a*. adjacent
lín jū 邻居 *n*. neighbour
lín rén shì de 邻人似的 *a*. neighbourly
lín qū 林区 *n*. woodland
lín wù guān 林务官 *n* forester
lín yè 林业 *n* forestry
lín shī 淋湿 *v.t.* shower
lín yù 淋浴 *n*. shower
lín 磷 *n*. phosphorus
lín suān yán 磷酸盐 *n*. phosphate
lìn sè de 吝啬的 *a*. mean
lìn sè de 吝啬的 *a*. miserly
lìn sè de rén 吝啬的人 *n*. miser
líng gǎn 灵感 *n*. inspiration
líng hún de 灵魂的 *a*. psychic
líng mǐn de 灵敏的 *a*. smart
líng mǐn de xiǎo liè gǒu 灵敏的小猎狗 *n*. terrier
líng qiǎo de 灵巧的 *adj*. deft
líng qiǎo de 灵巧的 *a*. skilful
líng 铃 *n* bell
líng mù 陵墓 *n*. mausoleum
líng 零 *n*. nil
líng 零 *n*. nought
líng 零 *n*. zero
líng shòu 零售 *v.t.* retail
líng shòu 零售 *n*. retail
líng shòu de 零售的 *a* retail
líng shòu shāng 零售商 *n*. retailer
líng dǎo néng lì 领导能力 *n*. leadership
líng dǎo zhě 领导者 *n*. leader
líng dǎo zhě 领导者 *n*. protagonist
líng háng 领航 *v.t.* pilot
líng qǔ fǔ xù jīn zhě 领取抚恤金者 *n*. pensioner
líng shòu zhě 领受者 *n*. recipient
líng tǔ 领土 *n*. territory
líng wù 领悟 *n*. realization
líng xiān 领先 *n*. lead

líng yáng 羚羊 *n*. antelope
lǐng yǎng 领养 *v.t.* adopt
lǐng yǎng 领养 *n* adoption
lǐng yáng lǎo jīn rén 领养老金人 *n* annuitant
lǐng yù 领域 *n* domain
lǐng yù 领域 *a*. realm
lìng 令 *n*. ream
lìng rén bú kuài de 令人不快的 *a*. disagreeable
lìng rén kǒng jù de 令人恐惧的 *a* dread
lìng rén nán wàng de 令人难忘的 *a*. imposing
lìng rén rù shén 令人入神 *v.t* fascinate
lìng rén tǎo yàn de 令人讨厌的 *a*. objectionable
lìng rén tǎo yàn de 令人讨厌的 *a*. repellent
lìng rén xiàn mù 令人羡慕 *a* enviable
lìng rén xiǎng wàng de 令人想望的 *a* desirable
lìng rén yàn fán de 令人厌烦的 *a*. irksome
lìng rén yàn juàn de 令人厌倦的 *a*. tiresome
lìng rén zēng wù de 令人憎恶的 *a*. loathsome
lìng rén zháo mí de shì wù 令人着迷的事物 *n*. fascination
lìng wài 另外 *a* another
liū bīng 溜冰 *v.i.* skate
liú chǎn 流产 *n*. miscarriage
liú de 硫的 *a*. sulphuric
liú dòng 流动 *n* flow
liú dòng 流动 *v.i* flow
liú dòng de 流动的 *a* fluid
liú fàng 流放 *n*. exile
liú làng 流浪 *v.i.* rove
liú làng de 流浪的 *a* vagabond
liú làng zhě 流浪者 *n*. rover
liú làng zhě 流浪者 *n*. vagabond
liú lèi 流泪 *v.i.* weep
liú lèi de 流泪的 *a*. tearful
liú lì de 流利的 *a* fluent
liú máng 流氓 *n*. gangster

liú máng de 流氓的 a. roguish

liú rù 流入 n. influx

liú shā 流沙 n. quicksand

liú xíng 流行 n fashion

liú xíng 流行 n. vogue

liú xīng 流星 n. meteor

liú xíng bìng 流行病 n epidemic

liú xíng de 流行的 a current

liú xíng de 流行的 a fashionable

liú xīng de 流星的 a. meteoric

liú xíng xìng gǎn mào 流行性感冒 n. influenza

liú xíng xìng sāi xiàn yán 流行性腮腺炎 n. mumps

liú xíng yīn yuè 流行音乐 n pop

liú xuè 流血 v. i bleed

liú huáng 硫磺 n. sulphur

liú lǎn 浏览 n browse

liú jiàn gé 留间隔 v.t. space

liú shēng jī 留声机 n. gramophone

liú xīn 留心 a. attentive

liú xīn 留心 n heed

liù 六 n., a six

liù shí 六十 n., a. sixty

liǔ 柳 n. willow

liǔ tiáo 柳条 n. wicker

liǔ yè dāo 柳叶刀 n. lancet

lóng lóng shēng 隆隆声 n. rumble

lóng 龙 n dragon

lóng juǎn fēng 龙卷风 n. tornado

lóng xiā 龙虾 n. lobster

lóng tou 笼头 n bridle

lóng zi 笼子 n. cage

lóng de 聋的 a deaf

lóu tī 楼梯 n. stair

lòu 漏 v.i. leak

lòu 漏 n. leakage

lòu dòng 漏洞 n. leak

lòu dòng 漏洞 n. loop-hole

lóu gé 楼阁 n. pavilion

lòu guǎn 瘘管 n fistula

lòu chū xiàn féng de 露出线缝的 a. seamy

lú bǐ 卢比 n. rupee

lú bù 卢布 n. rouble

lú 炉 n cooker

lú 炉 n. oven

lú chuáng 炉床 n. hearth

lú cí 鸬鹚 n. cormorant

lǔ tè shī qín 鲁特诗琴 n. lute

lù jūn 陆军 n. brigade

lù jūn zhǔn jiāng 陆军准将 n brigadier

lù qǔ 录取 v.t. matriculate

lù qǔ rù xué 录取入学 n. matriculation

lù yīn 录音 v.t tape

lù yīn dài 录音带 n. cassette

lù yīn dài 录音带 n. tape

lù yīn jī 录音机 n. recorder

lù 路 n. road

lù 路 n. way

lù xiàn 路线 n. route

lù zhàng 路障 n. barricade

lù 鹿 n deer

lù jiǎo 鹿角 n. antler

lù shuǐ 露水 n. dew

lǘ 驴 n. ass

lǘ jiào shēng 驴叫声 n bray

lǘ zǐ 驴子 n donkey

lǚ chéng 旅程 n drive

lǚ chéng 旅程 n. journey

lǚ guǎn 旅馆 n. hotel

lǚ guǎn 旅馆 n. inn

lǚ guǎn 旅馆 n. motel

lǚ kè 旅客 n. wayfarer

lǚ xíng 旅行 v.i. journey

lǚ xíng 旅行 n. tour

lǚ xíng 旅行 v.i. tour

lǚ xíng 旅行 v.i. travel

lǚ xíng 旅行 n travel

lǚ xíng 旅行 n. trip

lǚ xíng zhě 旅行者 n. tourist

lǚ xíng zhě 旅行者 n. traveller

lǚ yóu yè 旅游业 n. tourism

lǚ 铝 n. aluminium

lǚ suān yán 铝酸盐 n. aluminate

lǚ xíng 履行 n. fulfilment

lǜ shī 律师 n. lawyer

lǜ 率 n. rate

lǜ bǎo shí　绿宝石　n　emerald

lǜ huà　绿化　v.t.　afforest

lǜ sè　绿色　n　green

lǜ sè de　绿色的　a.　green

lǜ yè　绿叶　n.　greenery

lǜ qì　氯气　n　chlorine

lǜ fǎng　氯仿　n　chloroform

luǎn　卵　n.　spawn

luǎn cháo　卵巢　n.　ovary

luǎn xíng　卵形　n　oval

luǎn xíng de　卵形的　a.　oval

luàn diū　乱丢　v.t.　litter

luàn huā qián de rén　乱花钱的
　人　n.　spendthrift

luàn jiǎng　乱讲　v. t. & i　blab

luàn liú　乱流　n.　turbulence

luàn mō　乱摸　v.i.　fumble

luàn nào　乱闹　n.　rampage

luàn qī bā zāo de　乱七八糟的
　a.　topsy turvy

luàn qī bā zāo dì　乱七八糟地
　adv.　pell-mell

luán shēng de　孪生的　a　twin

luàn xiě　乱写　v.t.　scrawl

luàn xiě　乱写　v.t.　scribble

luàn yòng　乱用　v.t.
　misappropriate

lüè duó　掠夺　v.t.　depredate

lüè dài táo sè de　略带桃色的
　a.　pinkish

lüè jì　略记　v.t.　jot

lún　轮　n.　wheel

lún chàng　轮唱　n.　antiphony

lún jìn　轮尽　a.　maladroit

lún kuò　轮廓　n　contour

lún liú　轮流　v.t.　alternate

lún liú de　轮流的　a.　alternate

lún tāi　轮胎　n.　tyre

lùn tán　论坛　n.　forum

lùn tí de　论题的　a.　topical

lùn wén　论文　n.　thesis

lùn wén　论文　n.　treatise

luo suo　啰唆　v. i　blether

luó lè　罗勒　n.　basil

luó mǎ jiào huáng　罗马教皇
　n.　pope

luó wàng zǐ shù　罗望子树　n.
　tamarind

luó jí　逻辑　n.　logic

luó jí xué jiā　逻辑学家　n.
　logician

M

ma fēi　吗啡　n.　morphia

ma nǎ tiān cì shí wù　吗哪天赐食
　物　n.　manna

mā　妈　n　mum

mā ma　妈妈　n.　mamma

mā mī　妈咪　n.　mummy

má bì　麻痹　n.　palsy

má bì　麻痹　n.　paralysis

má bì de　麻痹的　a.　paralytic

má bù dài　麻布袋　n.　sack

má fan　麻烦　n.　ado

má fan　麻烦　v. t　bother

má fan shì qíng　麻烦事情　n.
　nuisance

má fēng bìng　麻疯病　n.
　leprosy

má fēng bìng de　麻疯病的　a.
　leprous

má mù de　麻木的　a.　numb

má què　麻雀　n.　sparrow

má zhěn　麻疹　n　measles

má zuì　麻醉　n　anaesthesia

má zuì　麻醉　n.　narcosis

má zuì jì　麻醉剂　n.　narcotic

má zuì yào　麻醉药　n.
　anaesthetic

má fēng bìng huàn zhě　癫疯病
　患者　n.　leper

mǎ　马　n.　horse

mǎ　马　n.　nag

mǎ ān　马鞍　n.　saddle

mǎ cáo　马槽　n.　manger

mǎ chē　马车　n.　barouche

mǎ chē　马车　n.　cart

mǎ chē　马车　n　chaise

mǎ chē　马车　n.　wagon

mǎ chē fū　马车夫　n　coachman

mǎ dá　马达　n.　motor

mǎ dèng　马镫　n.　stirrup

mǎ fàn zi　马贩子　n.　coper

mǎ jiù　马厩　n　stable

mǎ jù　马具　n.　harness

mǎ kù　马裤　n.　breeches

mǎ lā sōng cháng pǎo 马拉松长跑 n. marathon

mǎ líng shǔ 马铃薯 n. potato

mǎ mǔ qí tián jiǔ 马姆齐甜酒 n. malmsey

mǎ qiú 马球 n. polo

mǎ sài kè 马赛克 n. mosaic

mǎ xì tuán 马戏团 n. circus

mǎ xì tuán 马戏团 n. troupe

mǎ tou 码头 n. dock

mǎ tou fèi 码头费 n. wharfage

má yǐ 蚂蚁 n ant

mái 埋 v. t. bury

mái fú 埋伏 n. ambush

mái fú 埋伏 v.i. lurk

mái fú děng hòu 埋伏等候 v.t. waylay

mǎi 买 v. t. buy

mǎi 买 v.t. purchase

mǎi dōng xi 买东西 v.i. shop

mǎi fāng 买方 n. buyer

mài lì zhǒng 麦粒肿 n. stye

mài piàn 麦片 n. cereal

mài yá 麦芽 n. malt

mài bó 脉搏 n. pulse

mài luò mó 脉络膜 n choroid

mài nòng fēng sāo de rén 卖弄风骚的人 n flirt

mài 卖 v.t. sell

mài yín 卖淫 v.t. prostitute

mài yín 卖淫 n. prostitution

mǎn kǒu 满口 n. mouthful

mǎn kǒu kōng huà de rén 满口空话的人 n. windbag

mǎn yì 满意 n contentment

mǎn yì 满意 n. satisfaction

mǎn yì de 满意的 a. satisfactory

màn yóu 漫游 v.i. roam

mǎn zú 满足 n. gratification

mǎn zú 满足 n. satiety

mǎn zú 满足 v.t. satisfy

mǎn zú de 满足的 a. content

mǎn lèi 螨类 n. mite

màn 慢 a slow

màn dù 慢度 n. slowness

màn màn 慢慢 adv. slowly

màn màn de zǒu 慢慢地走 v.i. pace

màn pǎo 慢跑 v.t. jog

màn rán 慢燃 v.i. smoulder

màn sù 慢速 n crawl

màn xìng de 慢性的 a. chronic

màn bù 漫步 v.i. meander

màn bù 漫步 n ramble

màn bù 漫步 v.i. saunter

màn huà 漫画 n. caricature

màn huà 漫画 n comic

máng guǒ 芒果 n mango

máng 忙 a busy

máng lù de 忙碌的 a. pragmatic

máng 盲 a blind

máng cóng de 盲从的 a. slavish

máng wén 盲文 n braille

māo 猫 n. cat

māo tóu yīng 猫头鹰 n. owl

máo chóng 毛虫 n caterpillar

máo gě 毛葛 n. poplin

máo jīn 毛巾 n. towel

máo kǒng 毛孔 n. pore

máo lā 毛拉 n. mullah

máo pí 毛皮 n. fur

máo tǎn 毛毯 n blanket

máo xiàng 毛象 n. mammoth

máo yī 毛衣 n. sweater

máo zhī pǐn 毛织品 n woollen

máo 矛 n. spear

máo dùn 矛盾 n. antinomy

máo dùn 矛盾 n contradiction

máo shè 茅舍 n. hut

máo 锚 n. anchor

máo niú 氂牛 n. yak

mǎo dīng 铆钉 n. rivet

mào chōng 冒充 v.i. sham

mào dú de 冒渎的 a. sacrilegious

mào hào 冒号 n colon

mào pái 冒牌 n. imposture

mào pái shī rén 冒牌诗人 n. poetaster

mào pào 冒泡 v.i. seethe

mào wēi xiǎn 冒危险 v.t hazard

mào xiǎn 冒险 n adventure

mào xiǎn 冒险 n. risk

mào xiǎn 冒险 n. venture

mào xiǎn de 冒险的 a. venturesome

mào yān de 冒烟的 *a.* smoky
mào zi 帽子 *n.* cap
mào zi 帽子 *n.* hat
mào yì 贸易 *n* commerce
mào yì 贸易 *n.* trade
méi guī 玫瑰 *n.* rose
méi guī sè de 玫瑰色的 *a.*
　roseate
méi guī yuán 玫瑰园 *n.* rosary
méi lǐ mào de 没礼貌的 *a*
　unmannerly
méi xiǎng dào 没想到 *adv.*
　unawares
méi yǒu 没有 *n.* nothing
méi yǒu 没有 *prep.* without
méi yǒu jià zhí de 没有价值的
　a. worthless
méi yǒu tóu de 没有头的 *adj.*
　acephalous
méi yǒu yì yìde 没有意义的 *a.*
nonsensical
méi 眉 *n* brow
méi jiè wù 媒介物 *n* medium
méi 煤 *n* coal
méi yān nòng zāng 煤烟弄脏
　n. soot
méi yān nòng zāng 煤烟弄脏
　v.t. soot
méi yóu 煤油 *n.* kerosene
méi 霉 *n.* mildew
méi jūn 霉菌 *n.* mould
měi 每 *a* each
měi 每 *prep.* per
měi fēn zhōng de 每分钟的
　adv. minutely
měi liǎng gè yuè 每两个月 *adj*
bimensal
měi nián de 每年的 *a.* yearly
měi rì de 每日的 *a* daily
měi rì dì 每日地 *adv.* daily
měi yè de 每夜的 *adv.* nightly
měi yǐ 每一 *a* every
měi yuè 每月 *adv* monthly
měi yuè de 每月的 *a.* monthly
měi zhōu 每周 *adv.* weekly
měi dé 美德 *n.* virtue
méi gǎn 美感 *n.pl.* aesthetics
méi hǎo 美好 *n.* nicety

méi hǎo de shì wù 美好的事物
　n. fair
měi huà 美化 *v.t* beautify
měi huà le de dōng xi 美化了的
　东西 *n.* glorification
měi lì 美丽 *n* beauty
měi nǚ 美女 *n* belle
měi rén yú 美人鱼 *n.* mermaid
měi shǎo nǚ 美少女 *n.* nymph
měi wèi 美味 *n.* dainty
měi wèi de 美味的 *a.*
　toothsome
měi wèi de 美味的 *a* delicious
měi xué de 美学的 *a.* aesthetic
měi yuán 美元 *n* dollar
mèi lì 魅力 *n.* charm1
mèi lì 魅力 *n.* glamour
mèi lì 魅力 *n* spell
mén 门 *n* door
mén fáng 门房 *n.* usher
mén kǒu 门口 *n.* threshold
mén láng 门廊 *n.* porch
mén láng 门廊 *n.* portico
mén shuān 门闩 *n* bolt
mén shuān 门闩 *n.* latch
mén tú 门徒 *n* disciple
mén zhěn bìng rén 门诊病人 *n.*
　outpatient
mèn rè de 闷热的 *a.* muggy
mèn rè de 闷热的 *a.* stuffy
mèn rè de 闷热的 *a.* sultry
mèn 焖 *v.t.* stew
méng guó 盟国 *n.* ally
méng zhù yǎn 蒙住眼 *v.t*
　blindfold
méng lóng de 朦胧的 *a.* hazy
méng lóng dì chū xiàn 朦胧地出
　现 *v.i.* loom
měng chōng 猛冲 *v.i.* dash
měng dǎ 猛打 *v* crump
měng de yǎo zhù 猛地咬住 *v.t.*
　snap
měng gōng 猛攻 *n.* onslaught
měng jī 猛击 *v.t.* wallop
měng jī 猛击 *v.t.* whack
měng lā 猛拉 *v.t.* pluck
měng pū 猛扑 *n* pounce
měng tuī 猛推 *v.t.* thrust
měng yǎo 猛咬 *n* snap

měng zēng　猛增　*v.i.*　zoom

měng　锰　*n.*　manganese

mèng　梦　*n*　dream

mèng xiǎng de　梦想的　*a.*
visionary

mèng yóu zhě　梦游者　*n.*
somnambulist

mèng yóu zhèng　梦游症　*n.*
somnambulism

mī mī　咪咪　*n.*　mew

mī mī dì jiào　咪咪地叫　*v.i.*
mew

mí gōng　迷宫　*n.*　labyrinth

mí gōng　迷宫　*n.*　maze

mí huò　迷惑　*v.t*　bewitch

mí huò　迷惑　*n*　dazzle

mí huò　迷惑　*v.t.*　delude

mí huò　迷惑　*v.t.*　mesmerize

mí huò　迷惑　*n.*　puzzle

mí liàn　迷恋　*n.*　infatuation

mí lù　迷路　"*adv.,*"　astray

mí lù　迷路　*v.i.*　stray

mí lù zhě　迷路者　*n.*　straggler

mí lù zhě　迷路者　*n*　stray

mí luàn　迷乱　*n*　daze

mí xìn　迷信　*n.*　superstition

mí xìn shàng de　迷信上的　*a.*
superstitious

mí xìn zhāo hún zhě　迷信招魂
者　*n.*　spiritualist

mí zhù　迷住　*v. t.*　captivate

mí zhù　迷住　*v.t.*　obsess

mí　谜　*n*　enigma

mí yǔ　谜语　*n.*　conundrum

mí yǔ　谜语　*n.*　riddle

mí　醚　*n*　ether

mǐ　米　*n.*　metre

mǐ　米　*n.*　rice

mì fāng　秘方　*n.*　nostrum

mì mì　秘密　*n.*　secret

mì mì de　秘密的　*adj.*
clandestine

mì mì de　秘密的　*a.*
confidential

mì mì de　秘密的　*a.*　secretive

mì mì de　秘密的　*a.*
underhand

mì mì de　秘密的　*a.*　secret

mì shū　秘书　*n.*　secretary

mì shū chù　秘书处　*n.*
secretariat (e)

mì dù　密度　*n*　density

mì gào zhě　密告者　*n.*　informer

mì jí de　密集的　*a.*　intensive

mì mǎ　密码　*n*　code

mì mǎ xué　密码学　*n.*
cryptography

mì móu　密谋　*v. i.*　conspire

mì móu　密谋　*v.t.*　plot

mì qiè　密切　*a.*　intimate

mì qiè de guān xì　密切的关系　*n*
affinity

mì shǐ　密使　*n*　emissary

mì yǒu　密友　*n*　chum

mì fēng　蜜蜂　*n.*　bee

mì jiàn　蜜饯　*n.*　comfit

mì yuè　蜜月　*n.*　honeymoon

mián　棉　*n.*　cotton

mián bèi　棉被　*n.*　quilt

miǎn chú　免除　*v.t.*　rid

miǎn chú de　免除的　*a.*　exempt

miǎn fèi dì　免费地　*adv.*　gratis

miǎn yì　免疫　*n.*　immunity

miǎn yì de　免疫的　*a.*　immune

miǎn zhí　免职　*v. t*　depose

miǎn zuì　免罪　*n.*　impunity

mián qiǎng　勉强　*n.*　reluctance

mián qiǎng de　勉强的　*a.*
reluctant

miàn bāo　面包　*n*　bread

miàn bāo diàn　面包店　*n*　bakery

miàn bāo pí　面包皮　*n.*　crust

miàn bāo shī　面包师　*n.*　baker

miàn bāo zuò de　面包做的
v. t. & i　breaden

miàn duì　面对　*v.t*　face

miàn duì　面对　*v.t*　front

miàn duì miàn　面对面　*n.*
tete-a-tete

miàn fěn　面粉　*n*　flour

miàn fěn chǎng　面粉厂　*n.*　mill

miàn hóng　面红　*n*　flush

miàn jiá　面颊　*n*　cheek

miàn mào　面貌　*n.*　visage

miàn shā　面纱　*n.*　veil

miàn shì　面试　*n.*　interview

miáo　苗　*n*　shoot

miáo tiao　苗条　*a.*　trim

miáo tiao de 苗条的 *a.* slender

miáo tiao de 苗条的 *a.* slim

miáo huì 描绘 n. portrayal

miáo huì xiāo xiàng 描绘肖像 *v.t.* portray

miáo shù 描述 *v. t.* depict

miáo shù 描述 *v. t* describe

miáo shù 描述 *n* description

miáo shù 描述 *n.* presentation

miáo shù de 描述的 *a* descriptive

miáo zhǔn 瞄准 *v.i.* aim

miǎo 秒 *n* second

miǎo shì 藐视 *n.* scorn

miào fǎ 妙法 *n.* tip

miào yǔ 妙语 *n.* witticism

miào 庙 *n* temple

miē miē jiào 咩咩叫 *v. i* bleat

miè jué de 灭绝的 *a* extinct

miè shì 蔑视 *n* disdain

miè shì 蔑视 *v. t.* disdain

mín bīng 民兵 *n.* militia

mín gē 民歌 *n.* ballad

mín zhǔ de 民主的 *a* democratic

mín zhǔ zhèng zhì 民主政治 *n* democracy

mín zú zhǔ yì zhě 民族主义者 *n.* nationalist

mín gǎn de 敏感的 *a.* sensitive

mín gǎn xìng 敏感性 *n.* sensibility

mǐn jié 敏捷 *a.* agile

mǐn jié de 敏捷的 *a.* nimble

mǐn ruì 敏锐 *n.* acumen

míng cí 名词 *n.* noun

míng fù qí shí de 名副其实的 *a.* veritable

míng qì 名气 *n.* repute

míng rén 名人 *n* celebrity

míng shēng 名声 *n.* renown

míng shì 名士 *n.* personage

míng wàng 名望 *n* fame

míng yì shàng de 名义上的 *a.* nominal

míng yù 名誉 *n.* reputation

míng zi 名字 *n.* name

míng bai 明白 *v.t.* understand

míng bai de 明白的 *a* downright

míng lǎng 明朗 *n.* lucidity

míng liǎo de 明了的 *a.* articulate

míng tiān 明天 *n.* tomorrow

míng tiān 明天 *adv.* tomorrow

míng xī de 明晰的 *a.* lucid

míng xiǎn 明显 *a.* apparent

míng xiǎn de 明显的 *a.* manifest

míng xiǎn de 明显的 *a.* obvious

míng xiǎn de 明显的 *a.* palpable

míng xiǎn dì 明显地 *adv* clearly

míng yù 明喻 *n.* simile

míng zhì de 明智的 *a.* politic

míng zhì de 明智的 *a.* sensible

míng zhì de 明智的 *a.* wise

míng xiǎng 鸣响 *v.i* hoot

míng xiǎng 冥想 *v.i.* muse

míng xiǎng lù 冥想录 *n.* meditation

mìng lìng 命令 *n* command

mìng lìng 命令 *v. t* command

mìng lìng 命令 *n.* mandate

mìng lìng 命令 *v.t* order

mìng lìng 命令 *n.* writ

mìng míng 命名 *v.t.* name

mìng míng fǎ 命名法 *n.* nomenclature

mìng yùn 命运 *n* destiny

mìng yùn 命运 *n* doom

mìng yùn 命运 *n* fate

miù lùn 谬论 *n* fallacy

mō suǒ 摸索 *v.t.* grope

mó 膜 *n.* membrane

mó fàn 模范 *n.* paragon

mó fàn 模范 *n.* pattern

mó fǎng 模仿 *n.* imitation

mó fǎng 模仿 *v.t.* impersonate

mó fǎng 模仿 *n.* impersonation

mó fǎng zhě 模仿者 *n.* imitator

mó hú 模糊 *n.* ambiguity

mó hú 模糊 *n* blur

mó hú bù qīng 模糊不清 *n.* illegibility

mó hú de 模糊的 a. ambiguous

mó páng 模彷 v.t. ape

mó páng 模彷 v.t. imitate

mó páng 模彷 n. mimesis

mó páng 模彷 n mimicry

mó páng de 模彷的 a. mimic

mò fáng zhǔ 磨坊主 n. miller

mó cèng 磨蹭 n. shilly-shally

mó de rén 磨的人 n. sharpener

mó jiān 磨尖 v.t. sharpen

mó suì 磨碎 v.t grate

mó suì 磨碎 v.i. grind

mó suì 磨碎 v.t. mill

mó sǔn 磨损 n fray

mó cā 摩擦 v. t brustle

mó cā 摩擦 n. friction

mó gu 蘑菇 n. mushroom

mó guǐ 魔鬼 n. demon

mó guǐ 魔鬼 n devil

mó guǐ 魔鬼 n fiend

mó guǐ 魔鬼 n. satan

mó shù de 魔术的 a. magical

mó shù jiā 魔术家 n. magician

mò qī de 末期的 a. terminal

mò shēng rén 陌生人 n. stranger

mò lì 茉莉 n. jasmine

mò shōu 没收 v. t confiscate

mò shōu 没收 n confiscation

mò shōu 没收 v.t forfeit

mò sī kē rén 莫斯科人 n. muscovite

mò bù guān xīn 漠不关心 n. indifference

mò bù guān xīn de 漠不关心的 a. indifferent

mò rèn 默认 v.i. acquiesce

mò rèn 默认 n. acquiescence

mò shuǐ 墨水 n. ink

mò xiǎng de 默想的 a. meditative

mò yào 没药 n. myrrh

mó zhì pǐn 模制品 n mould

mōu 哞 v.i moo

mǒu chù 某处 adv. somewhere

mǒu wù 某物 pron. something

móu fǎn 谋反 n. rebellion

móu pàn de 谋叛的 a. insurgent

móu shì 谋士 n. tactician

mú bǎn 模板 n. stencil

mǔ ài de 母爱的 a. motherly

mǔ jī 母鸡 n. hen

mǔ láo hǔ 母老虎 n. tigress

mǔ lù 母鹿 n doe

mǔ mǎ 母马 n. mare

mǔ qīn 母亲 n mother

mǔ qīn de 母亲的 a. maternal

mǔ qīn shì de 母亲似的 a. motherlike

mǔ tǐ 母体 n matrix

mǔ xìng 母性 n. motherhood

mǔ yáng 母羊 n ewe

mǔ zhū 母猪 n. sow

mǔ lù 牡鹿 n. stag

mú zhǐ 拇指 n. thumb

mù 木 n. timber

mù cái 木材 n. wood

mù gōng 木工 n. carpentry

mù jiang 木匠 n. carpenter

mù nǎi yī 木乃伊 n mummy

mù ǒu 木偶 n. puppet

mù qín 木琴 n. xylophone

mù tǒng 木桶 n cask

mù xīng 木星 n. jupiter

mù zhì de 木制的 a. wooden

mù biāo 目标 n. aim

mù biāo 目标 n. goal

mù biāo 目标 n. target

mù bù shí dīng de 目不识丁的 a. illiterate

mù dèng kǒu dāi 目瞪口呆 adv. agape

mù dì 目的 n. intent

mù dì 目的 n. intention

mù dì 目的 n. objective

mù dì 目的 n. purpose

mù dì 目的 n. sake

mù dì dì 目的地 n destination

mù jī 目击 v.i. witness

mù jī zhě 目击者 n. witness

mù lù 目录 n. catalogue

mù lù 目录 n. content

mù qián 目前 adv. presently

mù chǎng 牧场 *n.* pasture

mù rén 牧人 *n.* herdsman

mù rén de 牧人的 *a.* pastoral

mù shī 牧师 *n* clergy

mù shī 牧师 *n.* parson

mù shī 牧师 *n.* preacher

mù yáng rén 牧羊人 *n.* shepherd

mù xu 苜蓿 *n.* lucerne

mù sī lín 穆斯林 *n.* nabob

mù dì 墓地 *n.* cemetery

mù zhì míng 墓志铭 *n* epitaph

mù jiān 幕间 *n.* interlude

N

ná chǎn zi chǎn 拿铲子铲 *v.t.* spade

ná dūn bù tuō 拿墩布拖 *v.t.* mop

ná xūn má dǎ 拿荨麻打 *v.t.* nettle

nǎ lǐ 哪里 *pron.* where

nǎ yí gè 哪一个 *a* which

nà bian de 那边的 *a.* yonder

nà gè 那个 *a.* that

nà gè 那个 *dem. pron.* that

nà gè 那个 *rel. pron.* that

nà yàng 那样 *adv.* that

nà yí gè 那一个 *pron.* which

nǎi 奶 *n.* milk

nǎi lào 奶酪 *n.* cheese

nǎi tóu 奶头 *n.* nipple

nǎi yóu 奶油 *n* cream

nǎi 氖 *n.* neon

nài jiǔ 耐久 *n.* endurance

nài lì 耐力 *n.* tolerance

nài xìng 耐性 *n.* patience

nài yòng de 耐用的 *a* durable

nán 南 *n.* south

nán 南 *a.* southerly

nán fāng de 南方的 *a.* south

nán fāng de 南方的 *a.* southern

nán fēi líng yáng 南非羚羊 *n* bontebok

nán guā 南瓜 *n.* pumpkin

nán jí 南极 *a.* antarctic

nán àn mó shī 男按摩师 *n.* masseur

nán dī yīn 男低音 *n.* bass

nán hái 男孩 *n* boy

nán nǚ tóng xiào 男女同校 *n.* co-education

nán rén 男人 *n.* man

nán xìng 男性 *n* male

nán xìng de 男性的 *a.* male

nán xìng de 男性的 *a.* virile

nán wū 男巫 *n.* wizard

nán zǐ 男子 *n.* manhood

nán zǐ qì 男子气 *n* manliness

nán nán zì yǔ 喃喃自语 *v.i.* mutter

nán biàn rèn de 难辨认的 *a.* illegible

nán de 难的 *adj.* hardy

nán diǎn 难点 *n* difficulty

nàn mín 难民 *n.* refugee

nán nài 难耐 *n.* impatience

nán shòu de 难受的 *a.* trying

nán wàng de 难忘的 *a.* memorable

nán xiāo huà de 难消化的 *a.* indigestible

nán yǐ kè fú de 难以克服的 *a.* insurmountable

nán yǐ míng liǎo de 难以明了的 *a.* intangible

nán yǐ zhì xìn de 难以置信的 *a.* incredible

nǎo 脑 *n* brain

nǎo mó yán 脑膜炎 *n.* meningitis

nào jù 闹剧 *n* farce

nào shì 闹事 *n* affray

nèi bù 内部 *n.* inside

nèi bù 内部 *n.* interior

nèi bù 内部 *n.* within

nèi bù de 内部的 *a.* inner

nèi bù de 内部的 *a* inside

nèi bù de 内部的 *a.* interior

nèi bù de 内部的 *a.* internal

nèi dì 内地 *n.* inland

nèi háng de 内行的 *a.* adept

nèi jiù 内疚 *n.* guilt

nèi lù de 内陆的 *a.* inland

nèi róng 内容 *n* content

nèi róng jiǎn jiè 内容简介 n. prospectus

nèi xīn de 内心的 a. innermost

nèi xīn shēn chù de 内心深处的 a. inmost

nèi yī 内衣 n. underwear

nèi zài de 内在的 a. intrinsic

nèi zàng 内脏 n. entrails

nèi zhèng de 内政的 a. municipal

néng dé dào de 能得到的 a. obtainable

néng jiàn dù 能见度 n. visibility

néng jiē nà de 能接纳的 a. receptive

néng lì 能力 n ability

néng lì 能力 n. capability

néng lì 能力 n competence

néng liàng 能量 n. energy

néng shēng chǎn de 能生产的 a. productive

néng yǎng huó de 能养活的 a. viable

ní gū ān 尼姑庵 n. nunnery

ní gǔ dīng 尼古丁 n. nicotine

ní lóng 尼龙 n. nylon

ní 泥 n. mud

ní chǎn 泥铲 n. trowel

ní huī zhuān 泥灰砖 n. marl

ní kuài 泥块 n. clod

ní nìng de 泥泞的 a. slushy

ní shā 泥沙 n. silt

ní tǔ 泥土 n clay

ní tǔ 泥土 n dirt

ní tǔ 泥土 n. soil

ní zhǎo 泥沼 n. mire

ní zhǎo 泥沼 n. slough

nǐ jì huà 拟计划 v.t. programme

nì míng 匿名 n. anonymity

nì míng de 匿名的 a. anonymous

nián 年 n. year

nián biǎo 年表 n. chronology

nián jiàn 年鉴 n. almanac

nián líng 年龄 n. age

nián qīng de 年轻的 a. young

nián qīng rén 年轻人 n. youngster

nián shào de 年少的 a. junior

nián shào zhě 年少者 n. junior

nián zhǎng de 年长的 a elder

nián zhǎng de 年长的 a. senior

nián zhǎng zhě 年长者 n elder

nián zhǎng zhě 年长者 n. senior

nián tǔ 粘土 n. adobe

nián de 粘的 a. sticky

nián hu hú de 粘糊糊的 a. slimy

nián tǔ 粘土 n. slime

nián yè 粘液 n. mucus

niàng jiǔ chǎng 酿酒厂 n distillery

niǎo 鸟 n bird

niǎo 鸟 n. jay

niǎo há 鸟蛤 v.i cockle

niǎo jiào 鸟叫 v.i. chirp

niǎo jiāo 鸟胶 n birdlime

niǎo jiào shēng 鸟叫声 n chirp

niǎo míng 鸟鸣 v.i. warble

niǎo shě 鸟舍 n. aviary

niǎo zhuàn 鸟啭 n warble

niǎo zuǐ 鸟嘴 n beak

niào 尿 n. urine

niào de 尿的 a. urinary

niào hú 尿壶 n. urinal

niē 捏 v.t. pinch

niē 捏 n. pinch

niè chǐ dòng wù 啮齿动物 n. rodent

niè 镍 n. nickel

níng jìng 宁静 n. serenity

níng jìng 宁静 n. tranquility

níng jìng de 宁静的 a. serene

nìng kě 宁可 adv. rather

níng méng 柠檬 n. lemon

níng méng de 柠檬的 adj. citric

níng méng shuǐ 柠檬水 n. lemonade

níng jié 凝结 v.t clot

níng rǔ 凝乳 n curd

níng shì 凝视 v.t daze

níng shì 凝视 n gaze

níng shì 凝视 n. stare

nǐng 拧 v.t wring

niú 牛 *n.* cattle
niú 牛 *n.* cow
niú 牛 *n.* ox
niú jiào 牛叫 *v.i.* low
niú mǎ fèn 牛马粪 *n.* muck
niú péng 牛棚 *n* byre
niú ròu 牛肉 *n* beef
niú tóu quǎn 牛头犬 *n* bulldog
niú zǎi kù 牛仔裤 *n.* jean
niǔ 扭 *v.t.* sprain
niǔ 扭 *v.t.* twist
niǔ dǎ 扭打 *n.* scuffle
niǔ dǎ 扭打 *v.i.* scuffle
niǔ dòng 扭动 *n* wriggle
niǔ jīn 扭筋 *n* wrick
niǔ qǔ 扭曲 *v.t* distort
niǔ qǔ de 扭曲的 *a.* tortuous
niǔ shāng 扭伤 *n.* sprain
niǔ shāng 扭伤 *v.t.* wrench
niú zhuǎn 扭转 *n.* twist
niú zhuǎn 扭转 *n.* wrench
niǔ kòu 纽扣 *n* button
nóng chǎng 农场 *n.* barton
nóng chǎng 农场 *n* farm
nóng fū 农夫 *n* farmer
nóng fū 农夫 *n.* peasant
nóng mín 农民 *n.* peasantry
nóng nú 农奴 *n.* serf
nóng shì 农事 *n.* husbandry
nóng xué 农学 *n.* agronomy
nóng yè 农业 *n* agriculture
nóng yè de 农业的 *a.* agrarian
nóng yè de 农业的 *a* agricultural
nóng yè jiā 农业家 *n.* agriculturist
nóng zuò wù 农作物 *n* crop
nóng pí jiǔ 浓啤酒 *n* ale
nóng hòu de 浓厚的 *a* dense
nóng 脓 *n.* pus
nóng dú bìng 脓毒病 *n.* sepsis
nóng dú xìng de 脓毒性的 *a.* septic
nóng zhǒng 脓肿 *n* abscess
nóng zhǒng 脓肿 *n* boil
nòng cuò 弄错 *v.t.* mistake

nòng duǎn 弄短 *v.t.* shorten
nòng gān 弄干 *v.i.* dry
nòng kōng 弄空 *v* empty
nòng kuān 弄宽 *v.t.* widen
nòng píng 弄平 *v.t.* level
nòng shàng bān diǎn 弄上斑点 *v.t.* spot
nòng shī 弄湿 *v.t.* moisten
nòng suān 弄酸 *v.t.* sour
nòng suì 弄碎 *v.t* crumble
nòng tián 弄甜 *v.t.* sweeten
nòng wān 弄弯 *v.t* curve
nòng zāng 弄脏 *v.t.* soil
nòng zāng 弄脏 *v.t.* stain
nòng zhǎi 弄窄 *v.t.* straiten
nòng zhòu 弄皱 *v.t.* ruffle
nú lì 奴隶 *n.* slave
nú lì 奴隶 *n.* thrall
nú lì de 奴隶的 *a.* servile
nú lì shēn fèn 奴隶身分 *n.* slavery
nú pú 奴仆 *n* menial
nú yì 奴役 *n.* thralldom
nǔ lì 努力 *n* effort
nǔ lì 努力 *v.i.* labour
nù huǒ 怒火 *n.* anger
nù shì 怒视 *v.i.* scowl
nǚ dī yīn 女低音 *n* alto
nǚ ér 女儿 *n* daughter
nǚ hái 女孩 *n.* girl
nǚ hēi rén 女黑人 *n.* negress
nǚ jì sī 女祭司 *n.* priestess
nǚ jiā tíng jiào shī 女家庭教师 *n.* governess
nǚ mào lèi 女帽类 *n.* millinery
nǚ mào tóu shì shāng 女帽头饰商 *n.* milliner
nǚ pú 女仆 *n.* maid
nǚ qún 女裙 *n.* skirt
nǚ rén 女人 *n.* woman
nǚ rén shì de 女人似的 *a* effeminate
nǚ shén 女神 *n.* goddess
nǚ shì 女士 *n.* lady
nǚ shī rén 女诗人 *n.* poetess
nǚ shì zhě 女侍者 *n.* waitress
nǚ wáng 女王 *n.* queen
nǚ wū 女巫 *n.* witch
nǚ xiào yǒu 女校友 *n* alumna

nǚ xìng 女性 *n* female
nǚ xìng 女性 *n.* womanhood
nǚ xìng de 女性的 *a* female
nǚ xìng de 女性的 *a* feminine
nǚ xiū dào yuàn 女修道院 *n* convent
nǚ xiū dào yuàn yuàn zhǎng 女修道院院长 *n.* prioress
nǚ yǎn yuán 女演员 *n.* actress
nǚ zhǔ jué 女主角 *n.* heroine
nǚ zhǔ rén 女主人 *n.* mistress
nǚ zǐ qì de 女子气的 *n.* womanish
nǚ zú zhǎng 女族长 *n.* matriarch
nuǎn huo de 暖和的 *a.* warm
nuè ji 疟疾 *n* ague
nuè ji 疟疾 *n.* malaria
nuè dài 虐待 *v.t.* abuse
nuè dài 虐待 *n.* mal-treatment
nuè dài 虐待 *v.t.* mistreat
nuè dài kuáng 虐待狂 *n.* sadism
nuè dài kuáng zhě 虐待狂者 *n.* sadist
nuó yòng 挪用 *n.* appropriation
nuò yán 诺言 *n* promise
nuò ruò 懦弱 *n.* cowardice

O

ǒu tù 呕吐 *v.t.* vomit
ǒu tù 呕吐 *n* vomit
ōu dǎ 殴打 *v.t.* assault
ōu dǎ 殴打 *n.* welt
ōu 鸥 *n.* gull
ǒu xiàng 偶像 *n.* idol

P

pá 爬 *v.i* climb
pá 爬 *v.t* crawl
pá 爬 *v.i* creep
pá xíng 爬行 *n* scramble
pá xíng dòng wù 爬行动物 *n.* reptile

pà lǎo po de 怕老婆的 *a.* henpecked
pà yǎng de 怕痒的 *a.* ticklish
pāi 拍 *v.i* bat
pāi 拍 *n* pat
pāi chì 拍翅 *v.t* flutter
pāi diàn bào 拍电报 *v.t.* wire
pāi mài 拍卖 *n* auction
pāi mài 拍卖 *v.t.* auction
pāi shè 拍摄 *v.t* film
pāi shǒu 拍手 *v. i.* clap
pāi zi 拍子 *n* beat
pāi zi 拍子 *n* pulse
pái huái 徘徊 *v.i.* linger
pái huái 徘徊 *v.i.* loiter
pái huái 徘徊 *n.* lurch
pái huái 徘徊 *v.t.* maunder
pái 排 *n.* platoon
pái 排 *n.* row
pái chì 排斥 *v.t.* ostracize
pái chì de 排斥的 *a.* repulsive
pái chú 排除 *v. t* exclude
pái chū 排出 *v. t* drain
pái duì 排队 *v.i.* line
pái liè 排列 *n.* array
pái liè 排列 *n.* permutation
pái liè 排列 *v.t.* range
pái qì kǒu 排气口 *n.* vent
pái shuǐ 排水 *n* drainage
pái shuǐ gōu 排水沟 *n* drain
pái shuǐ gōu 排水沟 *n.* gutter
pái shuǐ xì tǒng 排水系统 *n.* sewerage
pái wū 排屋 *n.* terrace
pái yǎn 排演 *v.t.* rehearse
pái zhe duì qián jìn 排着队前进 *v.i* troop
pái zì gōng rén 排字工人 *n.* compositor
pái zi 牌子 *n* brand
pài gěi gōng zuò 派给工作 *v.t.* task
pān dēng 攀登 *v. i* clamber
pān dēng 攀登 *n.* climb
pān dēng 攀登 *v.i.* scale
pān yuán 攀缘 *v.i.* scramble
pān yuán zhí wù 攀缘植物 *n* creeper
pán 盘 *n.* tray

pán rào 盘绕 v.t. wreathe

pán shān dì zǒu 蹒跚地走 v.i. reel

pán shí 磐石 n. monolith

pàn duàn 判断 n estimation

pàn duàn 判断 n. judgement

pàn duàn cuò 判断错 v.t. misjudge

pàn jué 判决 v.t. adjudge

pàn jué 判决 v.t. sentence

pàn jué bù dāng de 判决不当 的 a. injudicious

pàn biàn de 叛变的 a. mutinous

pàn guó zuì 叛国罪 n. treason

pàn luàn 叛乱 n. insurrection

pàn nì zhě 叛逆者 n. traitor

pàn nì zuì 叛逆罪 n. parricide

pàn tú 叛徒 n. rebel

páng dà de 庞大的 a bulky

páng dà de 庞大的 a mammoth

páng biān 旁边 n. aside

páng guān zhě 旁观者 n. on-looker

páng lù 旁路 n bypass

páng guāng 膀胱 n bladder

páng xiè 螃蟹 n crab

pāo chū 抛出 v.i. heave

pāo máo 抛锚 n anchorage

pāo qì 抛弃 n. repudiation

pāo shè wù 抛射物 n. projectile

páo xiāo 咆哮 v. i bellow

páo xiāo 咆哮 v.i. growl

páo xiāo shēng 咆哮声 n growl

pǎo 跑 v.i. run

pǎo bù 跑步 n. run

pǎo bù zhě 跑步者 n. runner

pào cài 泡菜 n. pickle

pào mò 泡沫 n foam

pào pào 泡泡 n bubble

pēi tāi 胚胎 n embryo

péi bàn 陪伴 v.t. accompany

péi shěn tuán 陪审团 n. jury

péi shěn yuán 陪审员 n. juror

péi shěn yuán 陪审员 n. juryman

péi cháng 赔偿 v.t compensate

péi cháng 赔偿 n compensation

péi cháng 赔偿 v.t. recompense

péi cháng 赔偿 n. recompense

péi cháng 赔偿 n redress

pèi é 配额 n. quota

pèi hé de 配合的 a co-operative

pèi jǐ 配给 n. allocation

pèi jǐ 配给 n. ration

pèi ǒu 配偶 n. consort

pèi ǒu 配偶 n. spouse

pēn 喷 v.t. spray

pēn 喷 v.t. spray

pēn chū 喷出 v. t. eject

pēn chū 喷出 v.i. puff

pēn chū 喷出 v.i. spout

pēn chū 喷出 v.i. spurt

pēn guǎn 喷管 n. spout

pēn shè liú 喷射流 n. jet

pēn shuǐ chí 喷水池 n. fountain

pēn xiǎng bí zi 喷响鼻子 v.i. snort

pén 盆 n. basin

pēng de shēng yīn 砰的声音 n slam

pēng de yì shēng 砰的一声 n. thud

pēng de yì shēng zhòng jī 砰的 一声重击 v.i. thud

pēng dì guān shàng 砰地关上 v.t. slam

pēng 嘭 n. bam

pēng tiáo 烹调 v. t cook

péng you 朋友 n. friend

péng you 朋友 n. kith

péng you 朋友 n. mate

péng wū 棚屋 a. shanty

pèng zhuàng 碰撞 v. i. collide

pèng zhuàng 碰撞 n collision

pèng zhuàng 碰撞 n crash

pèng zhuàng 碰撞 v. t. clash

pī 批 n batch

pī fā 批发 n. wholesale

pī fā de 批发的 a wholesale

pī fā shāng 批发商 n. wholesaler

pī píng 批评 n. censure

pī píng 批评 n criticism

pī píng　批评　v. t criticize
pī píng jiā　批评家　n critic
pī zhǔn　批准　v.t approbate
pī zhǔn　批准　n. approval
pī zhǔn　批准　v.t. approve
pī zhǔn　批准　v.t. authorize
pī zhǔn　批准　v.t. ratify
pī zhǔn jí yǔ zhuān lì　批准给予
　专利　v.t. patent
pī shuāng　砒霜　n arsenic
pī jiān　披肩　n. cape
pī jiān　披肩　n. shawl
pī　劈　v.t. hack
pī chéng suì piàn　劈成碎片　v.t.
　splinter
pī kāi　劈开　n split
pī lǐ pā lā　噼里啪啦　v.t. crackle
pí　皮　n. peel
pí dài　皮带　n belt
pí fū　皮肤　n. skin
pí gé　皮革　n. leather
pí jiā　皮夹　n. wallet
pí zhěn　皮疹　a. rash
pí jiǔ　啤酒　n beer
pí jiǔ chǎng　啤酒厂　n brewery
pí jiǔ cù　啤酒醋　n alegar
pí　脾　n. spleen
pí qi　脾气　n. temper
pí pá lèi yuè qì　琵琶类乐器
　n. lyre
pí juàn　疲倦　v.t. tire
pí juàn　疲倦　v.t. & i weary
pí juàn de　疲倦的　a. weary
pí láo　疲劳　n fatigue
pì gu　屁股　n buttock
pǐ xìng　癖性　n. proclivity
piān ài　偏爱　n. preference
piān jī de　偏激的　a extreme
piān jī fèn zi　偏激份子　n
　extremist
piān jiàn　偏见　n. prejudice
piān lí　偏离　v. i deviate
piān pì de　偏僻的　a. remote
piān xīn　偏心　n bias
piān xīn　偏心　n. partiality
pián yi　便宜　a cheap
pián yi huò　便宜货　n. bargain
piàn kè　片刻　adv. awhile
piàn kè　片刻　n. moment

piàn　骗　v. t beguile
piàn　骗　v.t gull
piàn　骗　v.t. rook
piàn qǔ　骗取　n. swindler
piàn rén de　骗人的　a crook
piàn zi　骗子　n. cheat
piàn zi　骗子　n. fraud
piàn zi　骗子　n. impostor
piàn zi　骗子　n. rook
piàn zi　骗子　n. sharper
piàn zi　骗子　n. trickster
piāo fú　漂浮　adv. afloat
piāo dàng　飘荡　v.t. waft
piǎo bái　漂白　v. t. & i blanch
piǎo bái　漂白　v. t bleach
piào　票　n. ticket
piào liang　漂亮　a beautiful
piào liang　漂亮　n. prettiness
piào liang de　漂亮的　a pretty
piě hào　撇号　n. apostrophe
pīn mìng gōng zuò　拼命工作
　v.i. slave
pīn xiě　拼写　v.t. spell
pín jí de　贫瘠的　adj. arid
pín mín kū　贫民窟　n. slum
pín qióng　贫穷　n. poverty
pín qióng de　贫穷的　a. needy
pín xuè　贫血　n anaemia
pín dào　频道　n channel
pín lǜ　频率　n. frequency
pǐn dé gāo shàng de　品德高尚
　的　a. virtuous
pǐn wèi　品味　v.t. savour
pǐn xíng bù liáng　品行不良　n.
　misbehaviour
pǐn zhì zhèng míng　品质证明　n.
　hallmark
pín zhǒng　品种　n breed
píng cháng de　平常的　a. casual
píng dàn wú wèi de　平淡无味的
　adj. bland
píng de　平的　a. plane
píng děng　平等　n equality
píng děng　平等　n. parity
píng dì　平地　n flat
píng fán　平凡　adv. ordinarily
píng fán de　平凡的　a. banal
píng fán de　平凡的　a.
　commonplace

píng fáng　平房　n　bungalow
píng fēn　平分　v. t　bisect
píng héng　平衡　n. balance
píng héng　平衡　v.t. balance
píng héng　平衡　n poise
píng huá de　平滑的　a. glossy
píng jìng　平静　v.t. tranquillize
píng jìng　平静　n. calm
píng jìng　平静　v.t. quiet
píng jìng de　平静的　a.
　peaceful
píng jūn de　平均的　a. average
píng jūn shù　平均数　n.
　average
píng jūn shù　平均数　n. mean
píng jūn wéi　平均为　v.t.
　average
píng miàn　平面　n plane
píng mín　平民　n civilian
píng mín　平民　n. commoner
píng mín　平民　n. populace
píng mín de　平民的　a civil
píng shí de　平时的　a. usual
píng tǎn de　平坦的　a even
píng tǎn de　平坦的　a flat
píng tǎn de　平坦的　a level
píng wén xì bù　平纹细布　n.
　muslin
píng xī　平息　v.t. pacify
píng xíng de　平行的　a. parallel
píng xíng sì biān xíng　平行四
　边形　n. parallelogram
píng yuán　平原　n. plain
píng gū　评估　v.t. assess
píng gū　评估　v. t evaluate
píng jià　评价　v.t. appraise
píng jià　评价　n. assessment
píng lùn　评论　v. i comment
píng lùn　评论　n comment
píng lùn　评论　n commentary
píng lùn　评论　n. remark
píng lùn　评论　v.t. remark
píng lùn　评论　n review
píng lùn yuán　评论员　n
　commentator
píng guǒ　苹果　n. apple
píng dān　凭单　n. voucher
píng　瓶　n bottle
pō fù　泼妇　n. shrew

pò hài　迫害　v.t. persecute
pò hài　迫害　n. persecution
pò shǐ　迫使　v.t. oblige
pò shǐ　迫使　v.t. pressurize
pò chǎn　破产　n. bankrupt
pò chǎn　破产　n. bankruptcy
pò chǎn　破产　n. insolvency
pò huài　破坏　v. t. corrupt
pò huài　破坏　v. t destroy
pò huài　破坏　n. ravage
pò huài　破坏　n. wrack
pò huài　破坏　v.t. wreck
pò huài de　破坏的　a. subversive
pò huài huó dòng　破坏活动　n.
　sabotage
pò jiù de　破旧的　a. shabby
pò jiù de　破旧的　a. threadbare
pò liè　破裂　n. rupture
pò liè　破裂　v.t. rupture
pò suì　破碎　v.t fracture
pò suì　破碎　n smash
pò sǔn　破损　n breakage
pò xiǎo　破晓　v. i. dawn
pū bǎn　铺板　v.t. plank
pū dì bǎn　铺地板　v.t floor
pū shè　铺设　v.t. pave
pú rén　仆人　n. lackey
pú rén　仆人　n. servant
pú tao　葡萄　n. grape
pú tao gān　葡萄干　n. raisin
pú tao shōu huò　葡萄收获　n.
　vintage
pú tao táng　葡萄糖　n. glucose
pú gōng yīng　蒲公英　n.
　dandelion
pǔ sù　朴素　n. rusticity
pǔ biàn　普遍　n. prevalence
pǔ biàn de　普遍的　a. general
pǔ biàn de　普遍的　a. prevalent
pǔ biàn xìng　普遍性　n.
　universality
pǔ jí de　普及的　a. widespread
pǔ pǔ tōng tōng de　普普通通的
　a. mediocre
pǔ tōng　普通　n. mediocrity
pǔ tōng de　普通的　a. ordinary
pǔ tōng de　普通的　a standard
pǔ tōng de　普通的　a.
　workaday

pǔ tōng zhào piàn 普通照片 *n.* still

pù bù 瀑布 *n.* waterfall

Q

qī 七 *n.* seven

qī 七 *a* seven

qī zuǐ bā zuǐ dì shuō 七嘴八嘴 地说 *v.i.* gabble

qī shí 七十 *n., a* seventy

qī mù 栖木 *n.* perch

qī xī 栖息 *v.i.* roost

qī xī dì 栖息地 *n.* habitat

qī 妻 *n.* wife

qī fu 欺负 *v. t.* bully

qī piàn 欺骗 *n* deceit

qī piàn 欺骗 *v. t* deceive

qī piàn 欺骗 *n* deception

qī piàn 欺骗 *v.t* hoax

qī piàn 欺骗 *n.* swindle

qī piàn 欺骗 *n.* trickery

qī piàn 欺骗 *v.t.* impose

qī zhà de 欺诈的 *a.* fraudulent

qī dài 期待 *n.* expectation

qī jiān 期间 *n* duration

qī jiān 期间 *n.* session

qī kān 期刊 *n.* periodical

qī qī chā chā dì jiào 喊喊喳喳 地叫 *v.i.* twitter

qí cì de 其次的 *a.* next

qí cì de 其次的 *a.* other

qí hòu de 其后的 *a.* subsequent

qí jiān 其间 *adv.* meanwhile

qí tā 其他 *adv* else

qí dǎo 祈祷 *n.* invocation

qí dǎo 祈祷 *v.i.* pray

qí dǎo 祈祷 *n.* prayer

qí qiú 祈求 *v.t.* conjure

qí qiú 祈求 *v.t.* invoke

qí guài de 奇怪的 *adj* bizarre

qí guài de 奇怪的 *a.* grotesque

qí guài de 奇怪的 *a.* queer

qí jì 奇迹 *n.* miracle

qí jì bān de 奇迹般的 *a.* miraculous

qí miào de 奇妙的 *a* fantastic

qí tè 奇特 *n.* singularity

qí tè de 奇特的 *a.* peculiar

qí yì de 奇异的 *a.* marvellous

qí yì de 奇异的 *a.* wondrous

qí yì shì wù 奇异事物 *n.* marvel

qí shì 歧视 *n* discrimination

qí 骑 *v.t.* ride

qí bīng 骑兵 *n.* cavalry

qí bīng 骑兵 *n.* trooper

qí bīng lián 骑兵连 *n.* troop

qí bīng zhōng duì 骑兵中队 *n.* squadron

qí mǎ 骑马 *n* ride

qí mǎ màn pǎo 骑马慢跑 *n* canter

qí shì 骑士 *n.* bayard

qí shì 骑士 *n* chevalier

qí shì 骑士 *n* knight

qí shì de 骑士的 *a.* chivalrous

qí shì qì gài 骑士气概 *n.* chivalry

qí shǒu 骑手 *n.* rider

qí zì xíng chē de rén 骑自行车 的人 *n* cyclist

qí qū bù píng de 崎岖不平的 *adj* bumpy

qí qū de 崎岖的 *a.* rugged

qí 旗 *n.* banner

qí zi 旗子 *n* flag

qí 鳍 *n* fin

qǐ gài 乞丐 *n* beggar

qǐ tǎo 乞讨 *v.i* cadge

qǐ yè 企业 *n* enterprise

qǐ qiú 企求 *n.* conation

qǐ tú 企图 *v.t.* essay

qǐ fā 启发 *v.t.* enlighten

qǐ cǎo 起草 *v.t* draft

qǐ cǎo rén 起草人 *n* draftsman

qǐ chū 起初 *n.* inception

qǐ chuò hào 起绰号 *v.t.* nickname

qǐ dà làng 起大浪 *v.i.* surge

qǐ fǎn yìng 起反应 *v.i.* react

qǐ fú 起伏 *v.i.* undulate

qǐ sù 起诉 *v.t.* indict

qǐ sù 起诉 *v.t.* prosecute

qǐ yì 起义 *n.* uprising

qǐ yì zhě　起义者　*n.*　insurgent
qǐ zhòu　起皱　*v.*　crimp
qǐ yīn　起因　*n.*　cause
qì fēn　气氛　*n.*　atmosphere
qì hòu　气候　*n.*　climate
qì qiú　气球　*n.*　balloon
qì sè　气色　*n*　complexion
qì tǐ　气体　*n.*　gas
qì tǐ de　气体的　*a.*　gassy
qì tǐ huà　气体化　*v.t.*　aerify
qì wèi　气味　*n.*　scent
qì wèi　气味　*n.*　smell
qì xī　气息　*n*　breath
qì xiàng xué　气象学　*n.*
　meteorology
qì xiàng xué jiā　气象学家　*n.*
　meteorologist
qì yā jì　气压计　*n*　barometer
qì zhì　气质　*n.*　temperament
qì chē　汽车　*n.*　automobile
qì yóu　汽油　*n.*　petrol
qì jù　契据　*n.*　muniment
qì yuē　契约　*n.*　compact
qì yuē　契约　*n.*　testament
qì cí zhuān　砌瓷砖　*v.t.*　tile
qì guān　器官　*n.*　organ
qì jù　器具　*n.*　appliance
qià dàng　恰当　*n.*　adequacy
qià dàng de　恰当的　*a.*　apposite
qiān　千　*a*　thousand
qiān fēn chǐ　千分尺　*n.*
　micrometer
qiān jīn dǐng　千斤顶　*n.*　jack
qiān zhōu nián jì niàn　千周年
　纪念　*n.*　millennium
qiān zú chóng　千足虫　*n.*
　millipede
qiān yí　迁移　*n.*　transfer
qiān　铅　*n.*　lead
qiān bǐ　铅笔　*n.*　pencil
qiān míng　签名　*n.*　autograph
qiān míng　签名　*n.*　signature
qiān míng yú　签名于　*v.t.*　sign
qiān zì rén　签字人　*n.*　signatory
qiān xū　谦虚　*n.*　humility
qiān xū　谦虚　*n*　modesty
qiān xū de　谦虚的　*a.*　modest
qiān xùn de　谦逊的　*a.*　humble
qiān lián　牵连　*v.t.*　implicate

qiān lián　牵连　*n.*　implication
qiān xiàn mù ǒu　牵线木偶　*n.*
　marionette
qiān yǐn　牵引　*n*　draw
qiān yǐn　牵引　*n.*　traction
qián bì　前臂　*n*　forearm
qián jiǎo　前脚　*n*　foreleg
qián mian　前面　*adv.*　ahead
qián mian　前面　*n.*　front
qián rèn　前任　*n.*　predecessor
qián shào　前哨　*n.*　outpost
qián zhě　前者　*pron*　former
qián zhuì　前缀　*n.*　prefix
qián zòu　前奏　*n.*　prelude
qián zòu qǔ　前奏曲　*n.*　overture
qiǎn de　浅的　*a.*　shallow
qián　钱　*n.*　money
qián bāo　钱包　*n.*　purse
qián zi　钳　*n. pl.*　tongs
qián zi　钳子　*n*　clamp
qián chéng　虔诚　*n.*　piety
qián chéng de　虔诚的　*a.*　godly
qián chéng de　虔诚的　*a.*　pious
qián chéng de　虔诚的　*a.*
　religious
qiǎn kǒu wù　箝口物　*n.*　gag
qiǎn tān　浅滩　*n*　shoal
qián fú xìng de　潜伏性的　*a.*
　latent
qián néng　潜能　*n.*　potential
qián shuǐ　潜水　*n*　dive
qián shuǐ　潜水　*v.i.*　submerge
qián tǐng　潜艇　*n.*　submarine
qián zài xìng　潜在性　*n.*
　potentiality
qián fǎn　遣返　*v.t.*　repatriate
qiǎn sòng huí guó　遣送回国　*n.*
　repatriation
qiǎn zé　谴责　*v. t.*　censure
qiǎn zé　谴责　*n*　condemnation
qiǎn zé　谴责　*n.*　denunciation
qiǎn zé　谴责　*n.*　reprimand
qiǎn zé　谴责　*v.t.*　reprimand
qiàn shèn zhòng de　欠慎重的　*a.*
　indiscreet
qiāng　枪　*n.*　gun
qiáng dà de　强大的　*a.*　mighty
qiáng dào　强盗　*n.*　bandit
qiáng dào　强盗　*n.*　dacoit

qiáng dào 强盗 *n.* robber
qiáng diào 强调 *v.t* accent
qiáng diào 强调 *n* emphasis
qiáng diào 强调 *v. t* emphasize
qiáng diào 强调 *v.t* stress
qiáng diào de 强调的 *a*
  emphatic
qiáng dù 强度 *n.* intensity
qiáng huà 强化 *n* consolidation
qiáng jiān 强奸 *n.* rape
qiáng jiān 强奸 *v.t.* rape
qiáng liè dǎ jī 强烈打击 *v.t.*
  pound
qiáng liè kàng yì 强烈抗议 *a.*
  outcry
qiǎng pò 强迫 *v. t* compel
qiǎng pò 强迫 *n* compulsion
qiǎng pò 强迫 *v.t* force
qiáng qiǎng 强抢 *n* abaction
qiáng qiǎng zhě 强抢者 *n*
  abactor
qiǎng zhì de 强制的 *a* com
  pulsory
qiǎng zhì de 强制的 *a* forcible
qiáng zhuàng de 强壮的 *a.*
  hale
qiáng zhuàng de 强壮的 *a.*
  manly
qiáng zhuàng de 强壮的 *a.*
  muscular
qiáng 墙 *n.* wall
qiáng wēi sè de 蔷薇色的 *a.*
  rosy
qiǎng 抢 *v.t.* snatch
qiǎng duó 抢夺 *n* plunder
qiǎng duó 抢夺 *v.t.* rob
qiǎng duó 抢夺 *v.t.* snatch
qiǎng jié 抢劫 *n.* dacoity
qiǎng jié 抢劫 *v.i.* maraud
qiǎng jié 抢劫 *v.t.* plunder
qiǎng jié 抢劫 *n.* robbery
qiǎng jié 抢劫 *n* spoil
qiǎng jié zhě 抢劫者 *n.*
  marauder
qiǎng jiù 抢救 *n.* salvage
qiǎng jiù 抢救 *v.t.* salvage
qiǎng qù 抢去 *v.t.* wrest
qiǎng xiān zhàn jù 抢先占据 *n.*
preoccupation

qiáo 桥 *n* bridge
qiāo 敲 *v.t.* knock
qiāo gǔ 敲鼓 *v.i.* drum
qiāo zhà 敲诈 *n* blackmail
qiáo cuì 憔悴 *v.i.* languish
qiáo cuì de 憔悴的 *a.* haggard
qiǎo hé 巧合 *v. i* coincide
qiǎo kè lì 巧克力 *n* chocolate
qiǎo miào 巧妙 *n.* subtlety
qiǎo miào de 巧妙的 *a.* artful
qiǎo miào de 巧妙的 *a.*
  masterly
qiǎo yú mó fǎng de rén 巧于模
  仿的人 *n* mimic
qiào bì 峭壁 *n* bluff
qiào 鞘 *n.* scabbard
qiào kāi 撬开 *v.t.* lever
qiē 切 *v. t* chop
qiē 切 *v. t* cut
qiē chú 切除 *n.* removal
qiē duàn 切断 *v.t.* sever
qiē duàn zhě 切断者 *n.*
  mutilation
qiē kāi 切开 *v.t.* slit
qiē xià 切下 *v.t.* slice
qiē xiàn 切线 *n.* tangent
qié zi 茄子 *n* brinjal
qiè 妾 *n* concubine
qīn ài 亲爱 *n.* endearment
qīn ài de 亲爱的 *n* darling
qīn ài de 亲爱的 *a* dear
qīn ài de 亲爱的 *a.* loving
qīn jìn de 亲近的 *a* conversant
qīn mì 亲密 *n.* intimacy
qīn qi 亲戚 *n.* kin
qīn qi 亲戚 *n.* relative
qīn qiè 亲切 *n.* amiability
qīn qiè de 亲切的 *a.* amiable
qīn qiè de 亲切的 *a* cordial
qīn qiè de 亲切的 *a* kind
qīn shǔ guān xi 亲属关系 *n.*
  kinship
qīn xìn 亲信 *n.* henchman
qīn fàn 侵犯 *v.t.* infringe
qīn lüè 侵略 *v.t.* invade
qīn lüè zhě 侵略者 *n.* aggressor
qīn rù 侵入 *n.* invasion
qīn rù 侵入 *n.* irruption
qīn rù 侵入 *v.i.* trespass

qīn shí 侵蚀 *v. t* erode

qīn shí 侵蚀 *n* erosion

qīn tūn 侵吞 *n.*
misappropriation

qīn zhàn 侵佔 *v. i* encroach

qīn zhàn 侵占 *v.t.* usurp

qín fèn 勤奋 *n* diligence

qín fèn de 勤奋的 *a.* strenuous

qín miǎn de 勤勉的 *a* diligent

qín miǎn de 勤勉的 *a.*
industrious

qín shòu 禽兽 *n* brute

qīng chūn qī 青春期 *n.*
adolescence

qīng chūn qī 青春期 *n.*
puberty

qīng guāng yǎn 青光眼 *n*
amaurosis

qīng guāng yǎn 青光眼 *n.*
glaucoma

qīng nián 青年 *n.* lad

qīng nián de 青年的 *a.*
youthful

qīng nián men 青年们 *n*
young

qīng shào nián 青少年 *n.*
teenager

qīng shào nián de 青少年的 *a.*
adolescent

qīng tóng 青铜 *n. & adj*
bronze

qīng wā 青蛙 *n.* frog

qīng wā shēng 青蛙声 *n.*
croak

qīng kè de 顷刻的 *a.*
momentary

qīng dǎ 轻打 *v.t.* tap

qīng de 轻的 *a* light

qīng diǎn shuǐ miàn 轻点水面
v.i. dap

qīng jī 轻击 *v.t.* tip

qīng kuài 轻快 *n.* agility

qīng kuài de 轻快的 *adj* brisk

qīng miè 轻蔑 *n* contempt

qīng miè 轻蔑 *n.* slight

qīng miè de 轻蔑的 *a*
contemptuous

qīng pāi 轻拍 *v.t.* pat

qīng qīng dì 轻轻地 *adv.* lightly

qīng shì 轻视 *v. t* despise

qīng shì 轻视 *v.t.* slight

qīng shuài 轻率 *n* flippancy

qīng shuài 轻率 *n.* imprudence

qīng shuài 轻率 *n.* levity

qīng shuài de 轻率的 *a.* hasty

qīng shuài de 轻率的 *a.*
impetuous

qīng shuài de 轻率的 *a.*
imprudent

qīng sōng de 轻松的 *a.*
mercurial

qīng tiào 轻跳 *n* skip

qīng tiāo de 轻佻的 *a.* frivolous

qīng tuī 轻推 *v.t.* nudge

qīng wēi de 轻微的 *a.* slight

qīng xìn 轻信 *n* credulity

qīng 氢 *n.* hydrogen

qīng chú 清除 *n* clearance

qīng chú 清除 *v.t.* purge

qīng chu de 清楚的 *a* clear

qīng chu de 清楚的 *a* distinct

qīng chu de 清楚的 *a.* explicit

qīng dān 清单 *n.* list

qīng jiào tú 清教徒 *n.* puritan

qīng jiào tú de 清教徒的 *a.*
puritanical

qīng jié 清洁 *v. t* clean

qīng lián de 清廉的 *a.*
incorruptible

qīng sǎo gōng rén 清扫工人 *n.*
sweeper

qīng suàn 清算 *v.t.* liquidate

qīng qī 清漆 *n.* varnish

qīng xǐ 清洗 *v. t* cleanse

qīng xī 清晰 *n* clarity

qīng xī de 清晰的 *a.* legible

qīng xī de 清晰的 *a.* vivid

qīng xǐng de 清醒的 *a*
conscious

qīng xǐng de 清醒的 *a.* sober

qīng zhēn sì 清真寺 *n.* mosque

qīng fù 倾覆 *n* overthrow

qīng pén dà yǔ 倾盆大雨 *n*
downpour

qīng xiàng 倾向 *n.* inclination

qīng xiàng 倾向 *v.i.* incline

qīng xiàng 倾向 *n.* tendency

qīng xié 倾斜 *v.i.* slope

qīng xié 倾斜 *v.i.* tilt

qīng xié 倾斜 *n.* tilt

qīng xié de 倾斜的 *adj.* declivous

qīng xié de 倾斜的 *a.* oblique

qǐng qiú 请求 *v.t.* entreat

qǐng qiú 请求 *n* request

qíng fù 情妇 *n.* courtesan

qíng jié 情节 *n.* plot

qíng jié jù 情节剧 *n.* melodrama

qíng kuàng 情况 *n* circumstance

qíng kuàng 情况 *n.* situation

qíng rén 情人 *n.* paramour

qíng xù 情绪 *n.* sentiment

qǐng yuàn 请愿 *n.* petition

qǐng yuàn 请愿 *v.t.* petition

qǐng yuàn rén 请愿人 *n.* petitioner

qǐng yuàn zhě 请愿者 *n.* suitor

qìng hè 庆贺 *v.t* felicitate

qìng zhù 庆祝 *v.t. & i.* celebrate

qìng zhù huó dòng 庆祝活动 *n.* celebration

qióng 穷 *a.* poor

qióng jìng 穷境 *n.* predicament

qióng kùn 穷困 *n.* privation

qióng rén 穷人 *n.* pauper

qiū zhěn 丘疹 *n.* pimple

qiū bǐ tè 邱比特 *n* Cupid

qiū bō 秋波 *n* ogle

qiū qiān 秋千 *n* swing

qiū tiān 秋天 *n.* autumn

qiú 求 *v.t.* beg

qiú ài 求爱 *v.t.* court

qiú ài qī 求爱期 *n.* courtship

qiú hūn 求婚 *v.t.* propose

qiú yuán 求援 *n.* recourse

qiú fàn 囚犯 *n.* prisoner

qiú 球 *n.* ball

qiú 球 *n.* globe

qiú 球 *n.* orb

qiú 球 *n.* sphere

qiú de 球的 *a.* spherical

qiú pāi 球拍 *n* bat

qū bié 区别 *v.t.* discriminate

qū bié 区别 *n* distinction

qū bié 区别 *v.i* distinguish

qū fēn 区分 *n.* partition

qū yù 区域 *n* district

qū yù xìng de 区域性的 *a.* zonal

qǔ diào 曲调 *n.* tune

qū gùn qiú 曲棍球 *n.* hockey

qū jiě 曲解 *v.t.* misrepresent

qū xiàn 曲线 *n* curve

qū zhé xiàn tiáo 曲折线条 *n.* zigzag

qū cóng 屈从 *v.t.* abase

qū cóng 屈从 *n* abasement

qū cóng 屈从 *n.* subjection

qū fú 屈服 *n.* submission

qū fú 屈服 *v.i.* succumb

qū fú 屈服 *v.i.* yield

qū shì 趋势 *n.* trend

qú 渠 *n.* trench

qǔ dé 取得 *n* acquest

qǔ huí 取回 *v.t.* retrieve

qǔ xiāo 取消 *v.t.* cancel

qǔ xiāo 取消 *n* cancellation

qǔ xiāo zī gé 取消资格 *n* disqualification

qǔ xiāo zī gé 取消资格 *v.t.* disqualify

qū bì jì 驱避剂 *n* repellent

qū zhú chū jìng 驱逐出境 *v.t.* deport

qù 去 *v.i.* go

qù ké 去壳 *v.t.* shell

qù sǐ 去死 *adj.* alamort

qù yě cān 去野餐 *v.i.* picnic

quān 圈 *n.* loop

quān tào 圈套 *n. pl.* toils

quán guì 权贵 *n.* magnate

quán lì 权力 *n.* authority

quán lì 权力 *n.* power

quán lì 权利 *n* right

quán yí zhī jì 权宜之计 *a* expedient

quán zhòng 权重 *n.* weightage

quán bù 全部 *a.* all

quán bù 全部 *n.* lot

quán bù 全部 *adv.* throughout

quán bù 全部 *a.* whole
quán bù de 全部的 *a* entire
quán bù de 全部的 *a* overall
quán chéng de 全程的 *a* through
quán guó xìng de 全国性的 *a.* national
quán jǐng 全景 *n.* panorama
quán miàn de 全面的 *a* comprehensive
quán néng 全能 *n.* omnipotence
quán néng de 全能的 *a.* almighty
quán néng de 全能的 *a.* omnipotent
quán qiú de 全球的 *a.* global
quán rán de 全然的 *a* utter
quǎn rú xué zhě 犬儒学者 *n* cynic
quán shēn de 全身的 *adv.* bodily
quán shén guàn zhù de 全神贯注的 *a.* rapt
quán shèng qī 全盛期 *n.* heyday
quán shèng qī 全盛期 *n.* prime
quán shì jiè de 全世界的 *a.* universal
quán sù bēn pǎo 全速奔跑 *v.i.* sprint
quán tǐ 全体 *n.* totality
quán tǐ yǎn yuán 全体演员 *n.* cast
quán wú de 全无的 *a* devoid
quán xīn quán yì de 全心全意的 *a.* whole-hearted
quán zhī 全知 *n.* omniscience
quán yù 痊愈 *v.i.* heal
quán jī 拳击 *n* boxing
quán tou 拳头 *n* fist
quàn dǎo 劝导 *v. t.* counsel
quàn gào 劝告 *v.t.* advise
quàn zǔ 劝阻 *v. t* dissuade
quē diǎn 缺点 *n* defect
quē diǎn 缺点 *n* drawback
quē fá 缺乏 *n* dearth
quē fá 缺乏 *v.t.* lack

quē fá 缺乏 *n.* scarcity
quē fá de 缺乏的 *a.* scanty
quē kǒu 缺口 *n.* notch
quē xí 缺席 *n* absence
quē xí 缺席 *a* absent
quē xí 缺席 *v.t* absent
quē xí 缺席 *v.t.* miss
qué zi 瘸子 *n* cripple
què dìng 确定 *n* confirmation
què dìng de 确定的 *a* certain
què dìng xìng 确定性 *n.* certainty
què lì 确立 *n* establishment
què rèn 确认 *v. t* confirm
què shí de 确实的 *a* concrete
què 鹊 *n.* magpie
qún dài guān xi 裙带关系 *n.* nepotism
qún 群 *n* cluster
qún 群 *n.* horde
qún jí 群集 *n* muster
qún jí 群集 *v.t.* throng
qún mó diàn 群魔殿 *n.* pandemonium
qún shè 群射 *n.* volley
qún shè 群射 *v.t* volley
qún zhòng xí jī 群众袭击 *v.t.* mob

R

rán ér 然而 *conj* however
rán ér 然而 *conj.* nevertheless
rán hòu 然后 *adv.* then
rán liào 燃料 *n.* fuel
rán shāo 燃烧 *v.i* blaze
rán shāo 燃烧 *v. t* burn
rán shāo 燃烧 *v.i* flame
rǎn 染 *v. t* dye
rǎn 染 *v.t.* tincture
rǎn liào 染料 *n* dye
ràng 让 *v.t.* let
ràng bù 让步 *n* concession
ráo shé 饶舌 *v. t.* chatter
rǎo luàn 扰乱 *v. t* disturb
rào guò 绕过 *v.t.* round
rě qǐ 惹起 *v.t* occasion
rě qǐ 惹起 *v.t.* provoke

rě rén ài de　惹人爱的　*a.* lovable

rè　热　*n.* heat

rè　热　*a.* hot

rè ài　热爱　*adj.* avid

rè ài　热爱　*n* devotion

rè cháo　热潮　*n* craze

rè dài　热带　*n.* tropic

rè dài　热带　*a.* tropical

rè de　热的　*a* fervent

rè liàng　热量　*n.* calorie

rè liè　热烈　*n.* vehemence

rè liè de　热烈的　*a.* passionate

rè liè de　热烈的　*a.* vehement

rè liè huān yíng　热烈欢迎　*n.* ovation

rè qiè yāo qiú　热切要求　*a.* solicitous

rè qíng　热情　*n.* ardour

rè qíng　热情　*adv.* avidity

rè qíng　热情　*n* fervour

rè qíng　热情　*n.* passion

rè qíng　热情　*n.* verve

rè qíng　热情　*n.* zeal

rè qíng　热情　*n.* zest

rè qíng de　热情的　*a* enthusiastic

rè shuǐ píng　热水瓶　*n.* thermos (flask)

rè xīn　热心　*n* enthusiasm

rè xīn de　热心的　*a.* ardent

rè xīn de　热心的　*a.* keen

rè xīn de　热心的　*a.* zealous

rè xīn zhě　热心者　*n.* zealot

rén　人　*n.* people

rén　人　*n.* person

rén dào zhǔ yì de　人道主义的　*a* humanitarian

rén gé huà　人格化　*n.* personification

rén kǒu　人口　*n.* population

rén kǒu diào chá　人口调查　*n.* census

rén kǒu duō de　人口多的　*a.* populous

rén lèi　人类　*a.* human

rén lèi　人类　*n.* humanity

rén lèi　人类　*n.* mankind

rén lì chē　人力车　*n.* rickshaw

rén qún　人群　*n* crowd

rén shēn bǎo hù quán　人身保护权　*n.* habeas corpus

rén shì bù mén　人事部门　*n.* personnel

rén shì bù xǐng　人事不省　*n.* insensibility

rén tǐ mó xíng　人体模型　*n.* mannequin

rén xíng dào　人行道　*n.* pavement

rén zào de　人造的　*a.* artificial

rén zào de　人造的　*a.* synthetic

rén zào nǎi yóu　人造奶油　*n.* margarine

rén zào wèi xīng　人造卫星　*n.* satellite

rén zào wèi xīng　人造卫星　*n.* sputnik

rén zhì　人质　*n.* hostage

rén cí　仁慈　*n.* goodness

rén cí de　仁慈的　*adj* benign

rén cí dì　仁慈地　*adv* benignly

rěn nài　忍耐　*v.t.* endure

rěn nài bú zhù de　忍耐不住的　*a.* insupportable

rèn chū　认出　*v.t.* recognize

rèn kě　认可　*n.* recognition

rèn wéi　认为　*v.i.* deem

rèn wéi　认为　*v.t* figure

rèn wéi　认为　*v.t.* opine

rèn wéi　认为　*v.t.* reckon

rèn wéi　认为　*v.t.* repute

rèn zhēn　认真　*a* earnest

rèn zhēn de　认真的　*a* elaborate

rèn zhēn zuò　认真做　*v.t* elaborate

rèn hé　任何　*a.* any

rèn hé　任何　*adv.* any

rèn hé shì wù　任何事物　*n.* aught

rèn wù　任务　*n.* task

rén xìng　任性　*n.* caprice

rén xìng de　任性的　*a.* petulant

rén xìng de　任性的　*a.* wayward

rèn yì de　任意的　*a.* arbitrary

rèn yì de　任意的　*a.* random

rēng　扔　*v.t.* throw

rēng　扔　*n.* throw

rì bào 日报 n. daily
rì cháng de 日常的 a routine
rì cháng gōng zuò 日常工作 n. routine
rì cháng shǐ yòng de 日常使用的 a. informal
rì cháng yǐn shí 日常饮食 n diet
rì jì 日记 n diary
rì jì 日记 n. journal
rì lì 日历 n. calendar
rì luò 日落 n set
rì qī 日期 n date
rì yuán 日元 n. Yen
róng yù 荣誉 n. glory
róng yù 荣誉 n. honour
róng guāng huàn fā 容光焕发 v. i beam
róng guāng huàn fā de 容光焕发的 n. radiance
róng liàng 容量 n. capacity
róng mào 容貌 n. countenance
róng nà 容纳 v.t accommodate
róng rěn 容忍 v.i abide
róng xǔ 容许 v.t. tolerate
róng yì de 容易的 a easy
róng yì de 容易的 a facile
róng jì 溶剂 n solvent
róng jiě 溶解 v.t dissolve
róng jiě dù 溶解度 n. solubility
róng huà 熔化 v.i. melt
róng huà le de 熔化了的 a. molten
róng liàn 熔炼 v.t. smelt
róng lú 熔炉 n. crevet
róng lú 熔炉 n forge
róng yán 熔岩 n. lava
róng shù 榕树 n. banyan
róng xuě 融雪 n thaw
róng 绒 n. nap
rǒng cháng de 冗长的 a. interminable
rǒng cháng de 冗长的 a. lengthy
rǒng cháng de 冗长的 a. verbose
rǒng cháng fá wèi 冗长乏味 n. tedium

rǒng cháng fá wèi de 冗长乏味的 a. tedious
ròu 肉 n flesh
ròu 肉 n. meat
ròu guì fěn 肉桂粉 n cinnamon
ròu tāng 肉汤 n broth
ròu tǐ de 肉体的 a corporal
róu ruǎn 柔软 n. soft
róu ruǎn de 柔软的 a. supple
róu ruò de 柔弱的 a delicate
róu ruò de 柔弱的 a. weak
róu shùn de 柔顺的 a flexible
rú cǐ 如此 adv. so
rú guǒ 如果 conj. if
rú chóng 蠕虫 n. worm
rú dòng 蠕动 v.i. writhe
rú dòng zhe qián jìn 蠕动着前进 v.i. wriggle
rǔ dàn gāo 乳蛋糕 n custard
rǔ fáng 乳房 n. udder
rǔ fáng de 乳房的 a. mammary
rǔ pǐn diàn 乳品店 n dairy
rǔ táng 乳糖 n. lactose
rǔ tóu 乳头 n. teat
rǔ mà 辱骂 v.t. taunt
rù 入 v. t enter
rù chǎng 入场 n entrance
rù chǎng fèi 入场费 n. admission
rù kǒu 入口 n. portal
rù shì shuì 入市税 n. octroi
ruǎn báo bù 软薄布 n. mull
ruǎn kuài 软块 n. mush
ruǎn mù sāi 软木塞 n. cork
ruì shì de 瑞士的 a Swiss
ruì shì rén 瑞士人 n. Swiss
ruì lì 锐利 n. keenness
ruì lì de 锐利的 adj. cultrate
ruì lì de 锐利的 a. sharp
ruì zhì 睿智 n. sagacity
rùn huá 润滑 n. lubrication
rùn huá yóu 润滑油 n. lubricant
rùn shì 润饰 v.t. retouch
ruò 弱 n. weakness
ruò de 弱的 a. infirm

S

să 洒 v. t. sprinkle
să xiāng shuǐ yú 洒香水于 v.t. perfume
sā shí huī 撒石灰 v.t lime
sā wǎng 撒网 v.t. net
sāi mǎn 塞满 v. t cram
sāi mǎn 塞满 v.t. stuff
sāi zi 塞子 n. plug
sài huì 赛会 n. pageant
sài pǎo 赛跑 v.i race
sān 三 a three
sān bèi de 三倍的 a. triplicate
sān bù fen de 三部分的 a. triple
sān chóng chàng 三重唱 n. trio
sān cì 三次 adv. thrice
sān fèn zhōng zhī yī 三份中之一 n triplicate
sān gè rén 三个人 n. three
sān jiǎo jià 三脚架 n. tripod
sān jiǎo xíng 三角形 n. triangle
sān jiǎo xíng de 三角形的 a. triangular
sān jiǎo zhōu 三角洲 n delta
sān lún chē 三轮车 n. tricycle
sān míng zhì 三明治 n. sandwich
sān sè de 三色的 a. tricolour
sān sè qí 三色旗 n tricolour
sān shí 三十 a thirty
sān shí de jì hao 三十的记号 n. thirty
sān wèi yì tǐ 三位一体 n. trinity
sān yuè 三月 n. March
sǎn 伞 n. umbrella
sàn bō 散播 v.t. strew
sàn bù 散布 v. t bestrew
sàn bù 散步 v.i. stroll
sàn bù 散步 n stroll
sàn bù 散步 n walk
sàn fā 散发 v.t. radiate
sàn kāi 散开 v.i. straggle
sǎn wén 散文 n. prose

sǎn wén de 散文的 a. prosaic
sāng 桑 n. mulberry
sàng shī 丧失 v. t. bereave
sàng shī 丧失 n forfeiture
sàng shī míng yù 丧失名誉 n disrepute
sàng shī qīn yǒu 丧失亲友 n bereavement
sāo chù 搔触 v.t. tickle
sāo dòng 骚动 n. tumult
sāo dòng 骚动 n. turmoil
sāo dòng de 骚动的 a. tempestuous
sāo luàn 骚乱 n commotion
sāo luàn 骚乱 n unrest
sāo luàn de 骚乱的 a. turbulent
sāo rǎng 骚嚷 n. uproar
sāo rǎo 骚扰 v.t. harass
sāo rǎo 骚扰 n. harassment
sǎo 扫 v.i. sweep
sǎo miáo 扫描 v.t. scan
sào zhou 扫帚 n broom
sè cǎi 色彩 n. tint
sè lā 色拉 n. salad
sēn lín 森林 n forest
sēn lín 森林 n. woods
sēn lín de 森林的 a. sylvan
sēng lǚ 僧侣 n. monk
shā 杀 v.t. kill
shā 杀 n. kill
shā chóng jì 杀虫剂 n. insecticide
shā chóng jì 杀虫剂 n. pesticide
shā fù zhě 杀父者 n. patricide
shā jià 杀价 v.i. haggle
shā jūn jì 杀菌剂 n. germicide
shā mǔ de 杀母的 a. matricidal
shā mǔ zuì 杀母罪 n. matricide
shā rén fàn xiōng shǒu 杀人犯凶手 n. murderer
shā rén zhě 杀人者 n. homicide
shā sǐ 杀死 v.t. slay
shā yīng 杀婴 n. infanticide
shā 沙 n. sand
shā de 沙的 a. sandy
shā fā 沙发 n. sofa

shā mò　沙漠　*n* desert
shā mò de lǜ zhōu　沙漠的绿洲
　n. oasis
shā tān　沙滩　*n.* beach
shā yǎ de　沙哑的　*a.* hoarse
shā yǎ de　沙哑的　*a.* throaty
shā xiàn　纱线　*n.* yarn
shā mù　杉木　*n* fir
shā chē　刹车　*n* brake
shā chē　刹车　*v. t* brake
shā chē huá xíng　刹车滑行　*v.i.*
　skid
shǎ de　傻的　*a.* silly
shǎ guā　傻瓜　*n* blockhead
shǎ guā　傻瓜　*n* burk
shǎ guā　傻瓜　*n.* coot
shǎ guā　傻瓜　*n.* loggerhead
shǎ qì de　傻气的　*a.* apish
shǎ zi　傻子　*n.* simpleton
shā yú　鲨鱼　*n.* shark
shāi　筛　*n.* sieve
shāi　筛　*v.t.* sieve
shāi　筛　*v.t.* sift
shāi diào　筛掉　*v.t.* winnow
shài　晒　*v.t.* sun
shài hēi　晒黑　*v.i.* tan
shài tài yáng　晒太阳　*v.i.* bask
shān　山　*n.* mount
shān　山　*n.* mountain
shān dòng　山洞　*n.* cave
shān duō de　山多的　*a.*
　mountainous
shān fēng　山峰　*n.* peak
shān gǔ　山谷　*n.* valley
shān máo jǔ　山毛榉　*n.* beech
shān yáng　山羊　*n.* goat
shān yáng zuò　山羊座　*n*
　Capricorn
shān zhā　山楂　*n.* hawthorn
shān chú　删除　*v. t* delete
shān chú　删除　*v. t* erase
shān jié　删节　*v.t* abridge
shān hú　珊瑚　*n* coral
shān dòng　煽动　*v.t.* instigate
shān dòng　煽动　*n.* instigation
shān dòng sāo luàn　煽动骚乱
　n. sedition
shān dòng xìng de　煽动性的
　a. seditious

shǎn bì　闪避　*v. t* elude
shǎn guāng　闪光　*v.i* flare
shǎn guāng　闪光　*n* flash
shǎn guāng　闪光　*v.i.* glance
shǎn guāng　闪光　*n.* sparkle
shǎn guāng　闪光　*n.* twinkle
shǎn liàng　闪亮　*v.i.* sparkle
shǎn shuò　闪烁　*n* flicker
shǎn shuò　闪烁　*v.i.* glitter
shǎn shuò　闪烁　*n* glitter
shǎn shuò　闪烁　*n.* scintillation
shǎn shuò　闪烁　*v.i.* twinkle
shǎn yào　闪耀　*n* flare
shǎn yào guāng　闪耀光　*n.* glare
shàn xīn　善心　*n* benevolence
shàn biàn de　善变的　*a.*
　capricious
shàn yì　善意　*n.* goodwill
shàn yú chuàng zào de　善于创
　造的　*a.* inventive
shàn cháng　擅长　*n.* adept
shàn yǎng fèi　赡养费　*n.* alimony
shāng　伤　*n.* wound
shāng hài　伤害　*n.* harm
shāng hài　伤害　*v.t* harm
shāng hài　伤害　*n* hurt
shāng hài　伤害　*v.t.* injure
shāng hài　伤害　*n.* injury
shāng hài　伤害　*v.t.* outrage
shāng hài　伤害　*v.t.* wound
shāng hán　伤寒　*n.* typhoid
shāng hén　伤痕　*n* bruise
shāng kǒu　伤口　*n* cut
shāng wáng　伤亡　*n* bloodshed
shāng xīn　伤心　*v.t.* hurt
shāng xīn　伤心　*v.i.* grieve
shāng　商　*n.* monger
shāng　商　*n.* quotient
shāng pǐn　商品　*n.* commodity
shāng pǐn　商品　*n.* merchandise
shāng rén　商人　*n.* merchant
shāng rén　商人　*n.* trader
shāng rén　商人　*n.* tradesman
shāng tǎo huì　商讨会　*n*
　consultation
shāng yè de　商业的　*a*
　commercial
shāng yè de　商业的　*a.*
　mercantile

shāng yè zhōng xīn 商业中心 n. mart

shàng 上 prep upon

shàng àn 上岸 adv. ashore

shàng chē 上车 adv aboard

shàng chuán 上船 v. t. board

shàng děng rén 上等人 n. gentry

shàng dì 上帝 n. god

shàng è 上轭 v.t. yoke

shàng guāng jì 上光剂 n. polish

shàng mian 上面 prep. above

shàng mian 上面 n. top

shàng mian de 上面的 a. upper

shàng qù 上去 adv. on

shàng sè 上色 v. t colour

shàng shēng 上升 v.t. ascend

shàng shēng 上升 n. ascent

shàng sù 上诉 n. appeal

shàng sù rén 上诉人 n. appellant

shàng wǎn jù 上挽具 v.t harness

shàng wǔ 上午 n forenoon

shàng xià wén 上下文 n context

shàng xiào 上校 n. colonel

shàng yǎn 上演 v.t. stage

shàng yǐn 上瘾 v.t. addict

shàng yǐn zhě 上瘾者 n. addict

shàng yóu 上油 v.t oil

shàng yóu qī 上油漆 v.t. paint

shàng wèi jué dìng 尚未决定 n. subjudice

shāo bēi 烧杯 n beaker

shāo huǒ 烧火 v.t. stoke

shāo jiāo 烧焦 v.t. scorch

shāo jiāo 烧焦 n singe

shāo píng 烧瓶 n flask

shāo shāng 烧伤 n burn

shāo zháo 烧着 adv. aflame

shǎo de 少的 a. less

shǎo liàng 少量 n. jot

shǎo liàng 少量 n. modicum

shǎo liàng 少量 n. morsel

shǎo liàng 少量 n. paucity

shǎo liàng de jiǔ 少量的酒 n dram

shǎo liàng jīn tiē 少量津贴 n. pittance

shǎo shù 少数 n. handful

shǎo shù 少数 n. minority

sháo xǔ 少许 n lick

sháo xǔ 少许 n. little

sháo xǔ 少许 n. tinge

shǎo yú 少于 prep below

sháo zi 勺子 n. ladle

shào fù 少妇 n. wench

shào nián 少年 n. youth

shào nǚ 少女 n. damsel

shào nǚ 少女 n. lass

shào nǚ de 少女的 a. girlish

shào bīng 哨兵 n. sentinel

shào bīng 哨兵 n. sentry

shē chǐ 奢侈 n extravagance

shē chǐ 奢侈 n. luxury

shē chǐ de 奢侈的 a extravagant

shē chǐ de 奢侈的 a. sumptuous

shē chǐ pǐn 奢侈品 n. superfluity

shé 舌 n. tongue

shé 蛇 n. serpent

shé 蛇 n. snake

shè huì 社会 n. society

shè huì de 社会的 n. social

shè huì dì wèi 社会地位 n caste

shè huì xué 社会学 n. sociology

shè huì zhǔ yì 社会主义 n socialism

shè huì zhǔ yì zhě 社会主义者 n,a socialist

shè lùn 社论 n editorial

shè qū 社区 n. community

shè bèi 设备 n equipment

shè fǎ 设法 adv. somehow

shè jì 设计 v. t. design

shè jì 设计 n. design

shè shī 设施 n facility

shè zài 设在 v.t. base

shè liè 涉猎 n. dip

shè jí 射击 n. shot

shè miǎn 赦免 v.t. assoil

shè miǎn 赦免 v.t. pardon

shè shì de 摄氏的 a. centigrade

shè yǐng 摄影 n. photography

shè yǐng shī 摄影师 n. photographer

shè yǐng yòng de 摄影用的 a. photographic

shè xiāng 麝香 n. musk

shè xiāng māo 麝香猫 n. mongoose

shēn qǐng 申请 n. application

shēn qǐng 申请 v.t. apply

shēn qǐng rén 申请人 n. applicant

shēn qǐng zhě 申请者 n. claimant

shēn 伸 n stretch

shēn yín 呻吟 v.i. groan

shēn yín 呻吟 n groan

shēn yín 呻吟 v.i. moan

shēn yín shēng 呻吟声 n. moan

shēn 身 n body

shēn cháng 身长 n. stature

shēn fèn 身份 n. identity

shēn fèn gāo de nán zǐ hé shēn fèn dī de nǚ zǐ jié hūn de 身份高男子和身份低女子结婚 a. morganatic

shēn fèn zhèng míng 身分证明 n. indentification

shēn tǐ de 身体的 a bodily

shēn tǐ de 身体的 a. physical

shēn shì 绅士 n. gentleman

shēn ài de 深爱的 a beloved

shēn chù 深处 n abyss

shēn de 深的 a. deep

shēn dù 深度 n depth

shēn dù 深度 n. profundity

shēn hóng sè 深红色 n crimson

shēn kǎn 深砍 n slash

shēn kēng 深坑 n. pit

shēn qíng de 深情的 a. affectionate

shēn shēn kǎn rù 深深砍入 v.t. slash

shēn sī shú lǜ de 深思熟虑的 a deliberate

shén me 什么 pron. what

shén me de 什么的 a. what

shén me dì fang dōu bú dào 什么地方都不到 adv. nowhere

shén 神 n. deity

shén 神 n divinity

shén fù 神父 n. priest

shén huà 神话 n. myth

shén huà de 神话的 a. mythical

shén huà de 神话的 a. mythological

shén huà xué 神话学 n. mythology

shén jīng 神经 n. nerve

shén jīng bìng xué 神经病学 n. neurology

shén jīng bìng zhuān kē yī sheng 神经病专科医生 n. neurologist

shén jīng jī néng bìng 神经机能病 n. neurosis

shén mì 神秘 n. mystery

shén mì 神秘 n. mysticism

shén mì de 神秘的 a. mysterious

shén mì de 神祕的 a. mystic

shén mì de 神秘的 a. occult

shén mì zhǔ yì zhě 神祕主义者 n mystic

shén qiāng shǒu 神枪手 n. marksman

shén quán zhèng zhì 神权政治 n. theocracy

shén sè 神色 n. look

shén shèng 神圣 n. sanctity

shén shèng de 神圣的 a divine

shén shèng de 神圣的 a. holy

shén shèng de 神圣的 a. sacred

shén shèng huà 神圣化 n. sanctification

shén xìng 神性 n. godhead

shén xué 神学 n. theology

shén xué jiā 神学家 n. theologian

shén xué shàng de 神学上的 a. theological

shén zhì jiàn quán 神智健全 n. sanity

shén zhí rén yuán 神职人员 n. priesthood

shěn chá 审查 n. audit

shěn chá 审查 v.t. censor

shěn chá 审查 n. censorship

shěn chá guān 审查官 n. censor

shěn jì 审计 v.t. audit

shěn jì yuán 审计员 n. auditor

shěn pàn 审判 n. trial

shěn shèn 审慎 n. prudence

shěn shèn de 审慎的 a. prudent

shěn shèn de 审慎的 a. prudential

shěn wèn 审问 v.t. interrogate

shěn wèn 审问 n. interrogation

shěn xùn 审讯 n. inquest

shèn chū 渗出 v.i. ooze

shèn chū 渗出 v.i. seep

shèn lòu 渗漏 n. ooze

shèn yuǎn dì 甚远地 adv. far

shèn zhì 甚至 adv even

shèn zhòng 慎重 n discretion

shèn zhòng de 慎重的 adj. circumspect

shèn 肾 n. kidney

shēng gāo 升高 v.t. lift

shēng qǐ 升起 v.t. hoist

shēng qǐ 升起 v. rise

shēng bìng de 生病的 a. ill

shēng cài 生菜 n. cabbage

shēng chǎn 生产 v.t. manufacture

shēng chǎn 生产 v.t. produce

shēng chǎn liàng 生产量 n yield

shēng chán pǐn 生产品 n. produce

shēng cún 生存 n. subsistence

shēng cún 生存 n. survival

shēng de 生的 a. raw

shēng dòng de 生动的 a. picturesque

shēng gēn 生根 v.i. root

shēng jì 生计 n. livelihood

shēng jì 生计 n living

shēng miàn tuán 生面团 n dough

shēng mìng 生命 n being

shēng mìng 生命 n life

shēng qián de 生前的 a. previous

shēng wù 生物 n creature

shēng wù 生物 n. organism

shēng wù xué 生物学 n biology

shēng wù xué jiā 生物学家 n biologist

shēng xiù 生锈 v.i rust

shēng xiù de 生锈的 a. rusty

shēng yá 生牙 v.i. teethe

shēng yi 生意 n business

shēng yi rén 生意人 n businessman

shēng zhǎng 生长 n. growth

shēng zhí de 生殖的 a. reproductive

shēng yù lì 生育力 n fertility

shēng chēng 声称 v.t. allege

shēng chēng 声称 v. t claim

shēng chēng 声称 v.t. profess

shēng chēng 声称 v.t. purport

shēng míng 声明 v.t. avow

shēng míng 声明 n. protestation

shēng míng láng jí 声名狼藉 a. infamous

shēng míng láng jiè de 声名狼藉的 a. notorious

shēng yīn 声音 n. noise

shēng yīn 声音 n. voice

shēng yīn de 声音的 a acoustic

shēng yīn de 声音的 a. sonic

shēng yīn de 声音的 n sound

shēng yīn de 声音的 a. vocal

shēng yīn shā yǎ de 声音沙哑的 a. husky

shēng yuán 声援 v. t. champion

shéng 绳 n. rope

shéng zi 绳子 n cord

shéng zi 绳子 n. string

shěng 省 n. province

shěng de 省的 a. provincial

shěng qù 省去 v.t. omit

shèng dàn jié 圣诞节 n Christmas

shèng dàn jié 圣诞节 n. Xmas

shèng dì 圣地 n. shrine

shèng fèng 圣俸 n benefice

shèng gē 圣歌 n chant

shèng gē 圣歌 n. hymn

shèng jié de 圣洁的 a. saintly

shèng jīng　圣经　*n*　bible
shèng jīng　圣经　*n.*　scripture
shèng lǐ　圣礼　*n.*　sacrament
shèng rén　圣人　*n.*　sage
shèng rén　圣人　*n.*　saint
shèng shī　圣诗　*n.*　psalm
shèng guò　胜过　*v.t.*　outdo
shèng guò　胜过　*v.t.*　outshine
shèng guò qí tā　胜过其他　*v.i*
　excel
shèng lì　胜利　*n.*　victory
shèng lì de　胜利的　*a.*
　victorious
shèng lì zhě　胜利者　*n.*　victor
shèng lì zhě　胜利者　*n.*　winner
shèng guān　盛观　*n.*　pageantry
shèng xíng　盛行　*v.i.*　prevail
shèng yú　剩余　*n.*　surplus
shèng yú bù fen　剩余部分　*n*
　rest
shèng yú wù　剩余物　*n.*
　remainder
shèng yú wù　剩余物　*n.*
　remains
shī tǐ　尸体　*n*　corpse
shī bài　失败　*n*　defeat
shī bài　失败　*v.i*　fail
shī bài　失败　*n*　failure
shī bài de　失败的　*adj*　abortive
shī bài zhě　失败者　*n*　underdog
shī cè　失策　*n*　blunder
shī míng　失明　*n*　ablepsy
shī míng　失明　*n*　blindness
shī mián de　失眠的　*a.*　wakeful
shī lǐ de　失礼的　*a*　discourteous
shī shì　失事　*n.*　wreck
shī tiáo　失调　*n.*　mal adjustment
shī shì　失事　*n.*　wreckage
shī wù　失误　*n*　bungle
shī yì　失忆　*n*　amnesia
shī zōng　失踪　*n*　disappearance
shī　诗　*n.*　poem
shī　诗　*n.*　poesy
shī　诗　*n.*　poetry
shī　诗　*n.*　verse
shī de　诗的　*a.*　poetic
shī lǜ　诗律　*n.*　versification
shī rén　诗人　*n.*　bard
shī rén　诗人　*n.*　poet

shī xué　诗学　*n.*　poetics
shī dì　湿地　*n.*　marsh
shī de　湿的　*a.*　wet
shī dù　湿度　*n.*　humidity
shī rùn　湿润　*n.*　wetness
shī rùn de　湿润的　*a.*　moist
shī zi　虱子　*n.*　louse
shī féi yú　施肥于　*v.t.*　manure
shī liè　狮鬣　*n.*　mane
shī zi　狮子　*n*　lion
shī zi de　狮子的　*a*　leonine
shī zi zuò　狮子座　*n.*　Leo
shí　十　*n., a*　ten
shí bā　十八　*a*　eighteen
shí duō suì　十多岁　*n. pl.*　teens
shí èr　十二　*n.*　twelve
shí èr　十二　*num.*　twelve
shí èr rì　十二日　*n.*　twelfth
shí èr yuè　十二月　*n*　december
shí fēn zhī yì shēng　十分之一升
　n.　decillion
shí jìn wèi de　十进位的　*a*
　decimal
shí jiǔ　十九　*n.*　nineteen
shí liù　十六　*n., a.*　sixteen
shí nián　十年　*n*　decade
shí qī　十七　*n., a*　seventeen
shí sān　十三　*n.*　thirteen
shí sān　十三　*a*　thirteen
shí sì　十四　*n.*　fourteen
shí sì háng shī　十四行诗　*n.*
　sonnet
shí wǔ　十五　*n*　fifteen
shí yì　十亿　*n*　billion
shí yī　十一　*n*　eleven
shí yí yuè　十一月　*n.*　November
shí yuè　十月　*n.*　October
shí zhōu nián　十周年　*n.*
　decennary
shí zì jià　十字架　*n*　cross
shí zì jià　十字架　*n.*　rood
shí zì jūn　十字军　*n*　crusade
shí zì lù kǒu　十字路口　*n.*
　crossing
shí zú de　十足的　*n.*　arrant
shí jǐn nóng tāng　什锦浓汤　*n.*
　hotchpotch
shí guān　石棺　*n*　cist
shí huī　石灰　*n.*　lime

shí huī guāng　石灰光　*n.*
　limelight
shí jiang　石匠　*n.* mason
shí là　石蜡　*n.* paraffin
shí mián　石棉　*n.* asbestos
shí tou　石头　*n.* rock
shí tou　石头　*n.* stone
shí tou de　石头的　*a.* stony
shí yóu　石油　*n.* petroleum
shí zào jiàn zhù　石造建筑　*n.*
　masonry
shí jì shàng　实际上　*adv.*
　actually
shí jì de　实际的　*a.* practical
shí jiàn　实践　*v.t.* fulfil
shí jiàn　实践　*n.* practice
shí tǐ　实体　*n* entity
shí xíng　实行　*n* execution
shí tǐ huà de　实体化的　*a.*
　incarnate
shí tǐ shàng　实体上　*adv.*
　substantially
shí yàn shì　实验室　*n.*
　laboratory
shí xí shēng　实习生　*n.* trainee
shí xiàn　实现　*v.t.* achieve
shí xiàn　实现　*v.t.* materialize
shí xíng zhě　实行者　*n.*
　prosecutor
shí yàn　实验　*n* experiment
shí yòng xìng　实用性　*n.*
　practicability
shí yòng zhǔ yì　实用主义　*n.*
　pragmatism
shí zai　实在　*n.* reality
shí zai de　实在的　*a.* tangible
shí zhì　实质　*n* essence
shí cháng fā shēng de　时常发
　生的　*a.* frequent
shí dài　时代　*n* epoch
shí dài　时代　*n* era
shí dài cuò wù　时代错误　*n*
　anachronism
shí jī zhèng hǎo de　时机正好
　的　*a.* well-timed
shí jiān　时间　*n.* time
shí jiān biǎo　时间表　*n.*
　schedule

shí jiān de xiāo shì　时间的消逝
　n lapse
shí qī　时期　*n.* period
shí shàng　时尚　*n* fad
shí tài　时态　*n.* tense
shí zhuāng mó tè ér　时装模特儿
　n. model
shí bié　识别　*v.t.* identify
shí　蚀　*n* eclipse
shí mù de　蚀木的　*a.*
　xylophagous
shí fǔ dòng wù　食腐动物　*n.*
　scavenger
shí pǔ　食谱　*n.* recipe
shí rén zú　食人族　*n.*
　androphagi
shí pǐn chǔ cún shì　食品储存室
　n. pantry
shí pǐn shāng　食品商　*n.* grocer
shí pǐn zá huò diàn　食品杂货店
　n. grocery
shí táng　食堂　*n.* canteen
shí wù　食物　*n.* eatable
shí wù　食物　*n* food
shí,wù　食物　*n.* sustenance
shí zhǐ　食指　*n* forefinger
shǐ guān　史官　*n.* annalist
shǐ qián de　史前的　*a.*
　prehistoric
shǐ shī　史诗　*n* epic
shǐ àn dàn　使暗淡　*v. t* dim
shǐ ān jìng　使安静　*v.t.* silence
shǐ ān jìng de　使安静的　*a.*
　sedative
shǐ ān yì　使安逸　*v. t* ease
shǐ bái　使白　*v.t.* whiten
shǐ bēi shāng　使悲伤　*v.t.*
　aggrieve
shǐ biàn cāng bái　使变苍白　*v.i.*
　pale
shǐ biàn kǔ　使变苦　*v. t* embitter
shǐ biàn xíng　使变形　*v.t.*
　transfigure
shǐ biàn yìng　使变硬　*v.t.* harden
shǐ biàn zhì　使变质　*v.t.* vitiate
shǐ bú miè　使不灭　*v.t.*
　immortalize
shǐ bù yú kuài　使不愉快　*v. t*
　displease

shǐ chán jié 使缠结 *v.t.* tangle
shǐ cháo shī 使潮湿 *v. t.* damp
shǐ chén jiù 使陈旧 *v.t.* stale
shǐ chéng bǐ lì 使成比例 *v.t.* proportion
shǐ chéng cán fèi 使成残废 *v.t.* lame
shǐ chéng duì 使成对 *v.t.* pair
shǐ chéng gū ér 使成孤儿 *v.t* orphan
shǐ chéng guǎ fu 使成寡妇 *v.t.* widow
shǐ chéng kuài zhuàng 使成块状 *v.t.* lump
shǐ chéng píng xíng 使成平行 *v.t.* parallel
shǐ chéng sān bèi 使成三倍 *v.t.* triplicate
shǐ chéng sì bèi 使成四倍 *v.t.* quadruple
shǐ chéng tōng sú xìng 使成通俗性 *v.t.* popularize
shǐ chéng wéi bì xū 使成为必需 *v.t.* necessitate
shǐ chū guǐ 使出轨 *v. t.* derail
shǐ chǔ yú wēi xiǎn 使处于危险 *v.t.* imperil
shǐ chuān yī 使穿衣 *v.t* dress
shǐ chuān yī fu 使穿衣服 *v.t.* vest
shǐ cóng shǔ 使从属 *v.t.* subordinate
shǐ dài nú zǐ qì 使带女子气 *v.t.* womanise
shǐ dào dé bài huài 使道德败坏 *v.t.* demoralize
shǐ dēng jī 使登基 *v.t* enthrone
shǐ diān bǒ 使颠簸 *v.t.* jolt
shǐ diū liǎn 使丢脸 *v.t.* humiliate
shǐ duàn nǎi 使断奶 *v.t.* wean
shǐ duàn zhī 使断肢 *v.t.* mutilate
shǐ duò luò 使堕落 *v. t.* debauch
shǐ duò luò 使堕落 *v.t.* pervert
shǐ fā dāi 使发呆 *v.t.* stupefy
shǐ fā dǒu 使发抖 *v.i.* shiver

shǐ fā kuáng 使发狂 *v.t* dement
shǐ fā liàng 使发亮 *v. t* brighten
shǐ fā wěi shì 使发伪誓 *v.t.* perjure
shǐ fán nǎo 使烦恼 *v.t.* annoy
shǐ fán nǎo 使烦恼 *v.t.* fret
shǐ fán nǎo 使烦恼 *v.t.* trouble
shǐ fán nǎo 使烦恼 *v.t.* vex
shǐ fán xiǎng 使反响 *v. t* echo
shǐ fáng shuǐ 使防水 *v.t.* waterproof
shǐ fāng zhèng 使方正 *v.t.* square
shǐ fēi pǎo 使飞跑 *v.t.* gallop
shǐ fēn kāi 使分开 *v.t.* part
shǐ fēn kāi 使分开 *v.t.* separate
shǐ fēn lí 使分离 *v. t* detach
shǐ fēn lí 使分离 *v. t* disconnect
shǐ fēn lí 使分离 *v.t.* segregate
shǐ fēn liè 使分裂 *v. t* disrupt
shǐ fěn suì 使粉碎 *v.t.* shatter
shǐ fēng fù 使丰富 *v. t* enrich
shǐ fú cóng 使服从 *v.t.* subject
shǐ fú cóng 使服从 *v.t.* submit
shǐ fǔ fú 使俯伏 *v.t.* prostrate
shǐ fù yuán 使复原 *v.t.* reinstate
shǐ gǎn dòng 使感动 *v.t.* inspire
shǐ gāo guì 使高贵 *v. t.* ennoble
shǐ gāo xìng 使高兴 *v. t.* delight
shǐ gāo xìng 使高兴 *v.t.* please
shǐ gé lí 使隔离 *v.t.* isolate
shǐ gé lí 使隔离 *v.t.* seclude
shǐ gèng huài 使更坏 *v.t.* worsen
shǐ gēng xīn 使更新 *v.t.* renew
shǐ gōng zuò 使工作 *v.t.* work
shǐ gù dìng 使固定 *v.t* fix
shǐ gū lì 使孤立 *v.t* maroon
shí guǎn guǎn yuán 使馆馆员 *n.* attache
shǐ guó jiā huà 使国家化 *v.t.* nationalize
shǐ hé fǎ huà 使合法化 *v.t.* legalize
shǐ hé huǎn 使和缓 *v.t.* moderate
shǐ hé jiě 使和解 *v.t.* reconcile
shǐ hé lǐ 使合理 *v.t.* rationalize
shǐ hēi 使黑 *v. t.* blacken

shǐ hòu 使厚 *v.i.* thicken

shǐ huà chéng zhǐ jiāng 使化成纸浆 *v.t.* pulp

shǐ huái yí 使怀疑 *v.t.* misgive

shǐ huǎn hé 使缓和 *v.t.* temper

shǐ huàn huáng da 使患黄疸 *v.t.* jaundice

shǐ huī xīn 使灰心 *v.t* deject

shǐ hùn hé 使混合 *v.t.* intermingle

shǐ hùn hé 使混合 *v.t.* mingle

shǐ hùn luàn 使混乱 *v.t.* muddle

shǐ huó huà 使活化 *v.t.* activate

shǐ jī dòng 使激动 *v.t.* thrill

shǐ jiā bèi 使加倍 *v.t* double

shǐ jiā bèi 使加倍 *v.t* duplicate

shǐ jiǎn dào zuì shǎo 使减到最少 *v.t.* minimize

shǐ jiàn mǎn ní nìng 使溅满泥泞 *v.t.* mire

shǐ jiān mò 使缄默 *v.t* muzzle

shǐ jiān qiáng 使坚强 *v.t.* fortify

shǐ jián shǎo 使减少 *v.t* dwindle

shǐ jiāng huà 使僵化 *v.t.* ossify

shǐ jiāng yìng 使僵硬 *v.t.* stiffen

shǐ jìn huà 使进化 *v.t* evolve

shǐ jìn zài shuǐ zhōng 使浸在水中 *v.t.* swamp

shǐ jǐn zhāng 使紧张 *v.t.* strain

shǐ jǐn zhāng 使紧张 *a.* tense

shǐ jīng pí lì jìn 使精疲力尽 *v.t.* exhaust

shǐ jīng qí 使惊奇 *v.t.* surprise

shǐ jīng táo 使惊逃 *v.i* stampede

shǐ jīng xià 使惊吓 *v.t.* frighten

shǐ jiǒng pò 使窘迫 *v.t* embarrass

shǐ jiù zhí 使就职 *v.t.* induct

shǐ jù jí 使聚集 *v.t.* gather

shǐ jù jiāo 使聚焦 *v.t* focus

shǐ jǔ sàng 使沮丧 *v.t* depress

shǐ jù tǐ huà 使具体化 *v.t.* embody

shǐ jù tǐ huà 使具体化 *v.t.* incarnate

shǐ juǎn rù 使卷入 *v.t* entangle

shǐ jué yuán 使绝缘 *v.t.* insulate

shǐ kǒng jù 使恐惧 *v.t.* horrify

shǐ kōng qì liú tōng 使空气流通 *v.t.* ventilate

shǐ kú nǎo 使苦恼 *v.t* distress

shǐ kuài huo 使快活 *v.t* enliven

shǐ kuài lè 使快乐 *v.t* entertain

shǐ kuáng xǐ 使狂喜 *v.t* enrapture

shǐ kuì bài 使溃败 *v.t.* rout

shǐ kùn huò 使困惑 *v.t.* perpetuate

shǐ kùn huò 使困惑 *v.t.* puzzle

shǐ lěng què 使冷却 *v.t.* refrigerate

shǐ lǐ xiǎng huà 使理想化 *v.t.* idealize

shǐ liú 使流 *v.i.* stream

shǐ luǒ lù 使裸露 *v.t.* denude

shǐ má bì 使麻痹 *v.t.* paralyse

shǐ máng rán 使茫然 *v.t* dazzle

shǐ máng yú 使忙于 *v.t* engage

shǐ mí liàn 使迷恋 *v.t.* infatuate

shǐ mí zhù 使迷住 *v.t* enchant

shǐ miǎn chú 使免除 *v.t.* exempt

shǐ miǎn yì 使免疫 *v.t.* immunize

shǐ mìng 使命 *n.* commission

shǐ mó hu 使模糊 *v.t* blear

shǐ néng gòu 使能够 *v.t* enable

shǐ nián qīng 使年轻 *v.t.* rejuvenate

shǐ níng gù 使凝固 *v.t* concrete

shǐ nuǎn 使暖 *v.t.* warm

shǐ ǒu tù 使呕吐 *v.t.* gag

shǐ pái chū tǐ yè 使排出体液 *v.t.* sap

shǐ péng zhàng 使膨胀 *v.t.* expand

shǐ pí juàn 使疲倦 *v.t.* weary

shǐ pín qióng 使贫穷 *v.t.* depauperate

shǐ pín qióng 使贫穷 *v.t.* impoverish

shǐ píng héng 使平衡 *v.t.* poise

shǐ píng jìng 使平静 v.t. lull

shǐ píng tǎn 使平坦 v. t even

shǐ qǐ lián yī 使起涟漪 v.t. ripple

shǐ qǐ pào mò 使起泡沫 v.t foam

shǐ qīng xié 使倾斜 v.t. slant

shǐ qīng xīn 使倾心 v. t enamour

shǐ qīng xīn 使清新 v.t. refresh

shǐ quán shén guàn zhù 使全神贯注 v.t engross

shǐ quán shén guàn zhù 使全神贯注 v.t. preoccupy

shǐ rén gǎn dòng de 使人感动的 a. sensational

shǐ rén kǒu jù jū zài 使人口聚居在 v.t. populate

shǐ róu ruǎn 使柔软 v.t. limber

shǐ rù guó jí 使入国籍 v.t. naturalize

shǐ rù wǔ 使入伍 v. t enlist

shǐ rù xué 使入学 v. t enrol

shǐ ruǎn huà 使软化 v.t. soften

shǐ rùn huá 使润滑 v.t. lubricate

shǐ sāi mǎn 使塞满 v.t. jam

shǐ sàng shī guāng zé 使丧失光泽 v.t. tarnish

shǐ sàng shī míng yù 使丧失名誉 v. t dishonour

shǐ shǎn guāng 使闪光 v.t flash

shǐ shǎn shuò 使闪烁 v.t flicker

shǐ shàng àn 使上岸 v.i. land

shǐ shàng fēi jī 使上飞机 v. t embark

shǐ shén mì huà 使神秘化 v.t. mystify

shǐ shén shèng 使神圣 v.t. sanctify

shǐ shèn tòu 使渗透 v.t. saturate

shǐ shēng fǎn gǎn 使生反感 v.t. scandalize

shǐ shēng huá 使升华 v.t. sublimate

shǐ shī qù néng lì 使失去能力 v. t disable

shǐ shī tòu 使湿透 v. t drench

shǐ shī wàng 使失望 v. t. disappoint

shǐ shì yìng 使适应 v.t. orient

shǐ shòu hài 使受害 v.t. victimize

shǐ shòu jīng 使受精 v.t fertilize

shǐ shòu xǐ ài 使受喜爱 v.t endear

shǐ shuāi ruò 使衰弱 v. t. enfeeble

shǐ sōng chí 使松弛 v.t. relax

shǐ táo zuì 使陶醉 v.t. intoxicate

shǐ téng tòng 使疼痛 v.t. pain

shǐ tǐ tǒng huà 使体统化 v.t. systematize

shǐ tíng bó 使停泊 v.t moor

shǐ tíng zhǐ 使停止 v. t. halt

shǐ tōng fēng 使通风 v.t. wind

shǐ tòng kǔ 使痛苦 v.t. rack

shǐ tǒng yī 使统一 v.t. standardize

shǐ tòu bú guò qì lái 使透不过气来 v.t. smother

shǐ tóu rù 使投入 v.t. plunge

shǐ wán jié 使完结 v.t end

shǐ wán měi 使完美 v.t. perfect

shǐ wéi nán 使为难 v.t. nonplus

shǐ wěn dìng 使稳定 v.t. stabilize

shǐ wěn gù 使稳固 v.t. steady

shǐ wù rù qí tú 使误入歧途 v.t. misguide

shǐ wú xiào 使无效 v.t. nullify

shǐ xí guàn 使习惯 v.t. accustom

shǐ xí guàn yú 使习惯于 v. t. habituate

shǐ xǐ yuè 使喜悦 v.t. gladden

shǐ xiàn dài huà 使现代化 v.t. modernize

shǐ xiàn luó wǎng 使陷罗网 v. t. entrap

shǐ xiāng děng 使相等 v. t. equalize

shǐ xiāng děng 使相等 v. t equate

shǐ xiāo sàn 使消散 v.t. scatter

shǐ xīng fèn 使兴奋 v. t electrify

shǐ xīng fèn 使兴奋 *v. t* excite

shǐ xiū kuì 使羞愧 *v.t.* abash

shǐ xiū kuì 使羞愧 *v.t.* shame

shǐ xuán zhuǎn 使旋转 *v.t.* wheel

shǐ yàn nì 使厌腻 *v.t.* satiate

shǐ yǎn sè 使眼色 *n* wink

shǐ yòng 使用 *v.t.* ply

shǐ yòng 使用 *n.* use

shǐ yòng duō zhǒng yǔ yán de rén 使用多种语言的人 *n.* polyglot

shǐ yōu chóu 使忧愁 *v.t.* sadden

shǐ yōu měi 使优美 *v.t.* grace

shǐ yǒu shāng hén 使有伤痕 *v.t.* scar

shǐ yǒu yìn xiàng 使有印象 *v.t.* impress

shì yú jū zhù de 适于居住的 *a.* habitable

shǐ zài jié hé 使再结合 *v.t.* rejoin

shǐ zài shēng 使再生 *v.t.* regenerate

shǐ zháo mí 使着迷 *v. t* bemuse

shí zhě 使者 *n.* herald

shǐ zhèn dòng 使震动 *v.t.* shock

shǐ zhèn jīng 使震惊 *v.t* astound

shǐ zhèng cháng huà 使正常化 *v.t.* normalize

shí zhì de 实质的 *a.* substantial

shǐ zhì xī 使窒息 *v.t* suffocate

shǐ zhōng lì huà 使中立化 *v.t.* neutralize

shǐ zhōng zhǐ 使终止 *v.t.* terminate

shǐ zhuǎn huà 使转化 *v.t.* invert

shǐ zuì 使醉 *n.* intoxication

shǐ zuò nú lì 使做奴隶 *v.t.* enslave

shǐ zuò xià 使坐下 *v.t.* seat

shǐ... jǔ sàng 使...沮丧 *v. t* dishearten

shǐ shén shèng 使神圣 *v.t.* hallow

shǐ shī 使湿 *v.t.* wet

shì bīng 士兵 *n.* soldier

shì qì 士气 *n.* morale

shì jì 世纪 *n.* century

shì jiān de 世间的 *a.* worldly

shì jiè 世界 *n.* world

shì sú de 世俗的 *a.* temporal

shì fàn 示范 *v. t* demonstrate

shì fàn 示范 *n.* demonstration

shì 市 *n.* town

shì chǎng 市场 *n* market

shì zhǎng 市长 *n.* mayor

shì zì zhì zhǔ yì 市自治主义 *n.* municipality

shì zhě 侍者 *n.* waiter

shì dàng 适当 *adv* pat

shì dàng de 适当的 *a.* adequate

shì dàng de 适当的 *a.* advisable

shì dàng de 适当的 *a.* appropriate

shì dàng de 适当的 *a.* proper

shì dàng de 适当的 *a.* seemly

shì dàng dì 适当地 *adv* duly

shì dàng dì wèi 适当地位 *n.* niche

shì dàng xìng 适当性 *n* advisability

shì dù de 适度的 *a.* moderate

shì hé 适合 *a.* applicable

shì hé 适合 *v.t* fit

shì hé 适合 *n.* suitability

shì hé de 适合的 *adj* apposite

shì hé de 适合的 *a.* suitable

shì hé yú jì jié de 适合于季节的 *a.* seasonable

shì hé gēng zhòng de 适合耕种的 *adj* arable

shì liàng yòng yào 适量用药 *n.* overdose

shì xiāo de 适销的 *a.* salable

shì yí de 适宜的 *a* fit

shì yìng 适应 *v.t* acclimatise

shì yìng 适应 *v.t.* adapt

shì wù 饰物 *n* accessory

shì 是 *v.* be

shì 是 *adv.* yes

shì nèi de 室内的 *a.* indoor

shì jué de　视觉的　*a.*　visual
shì lì　视力　*n.*　sight
shì lì　视力　*n.*　vision
shì wǎng mó　视网膜　*n.*　retina
shì　试　*v.i.*　try
shì xià　试下　*v.t.*　sample
shì yàn　试验　*v.t.*　test
shì yòng　试用　*n.*　probation
shì　事　*n.*　matter
shì gù　事故　*n.*　contingency
shì jiàn　事件　*n*　event
shì jiàn　事件　*n.*　happening
shì jiàn　事件　*n.*　incident
shì shí　事实　*n*　fact
shì xiān　事先　*adv.*　beforehand
shì jūn　弑君　*n.*　regicide
shì lì　势利　*n.*　snobbery
shì lì de　势利的　*v*　snobbish
shì fàng　释放　*v.t.*　enfranchise
shì fàng　释放　*v.t*　free
shì fàng　释放　*v.t.*　loose
shì fàng　释放　*v.t.*　release
shì fàng xuān shì　释放宣誓　*n.*　parole
shì yì　释义　*v.t.*　paraphrase
shì hào　嗜好　*n.*　hobby
shì yán　誓言　*n.*　oath
shì yuē　誓约　*n.*　covenant
shì yuē　誓约　*n.*　vow
shōu dào　收到　*v.t.*　receive
shōu fèi　收费　*v. t.*　charge
shōu fèi biǎo　收费表　*n.*　tariff
shōu gē　收割　*v.t.*　mow
shōu gē　收割　*v.t.*　reap
shōu gē jī　收割机　*n.*　harvester
shōu gē jī　收割机　*n.*　reaper
shōu huò　收获　*n.*　harvest
shōu jí　收集　*v. t*　collect
shōu jí jiā　收集家　*n*　collector
shōu jiàn rén　收件人　*n.*　addressee
shōu jǐn　收紧　*v.t.*　tighten
shōu jù　收据　*n.*　receipt
shōu kuǎn rén　收款人　*n.*　payee
shōu rù　收入　*n.*　income
shōu rù　收入　*n.*　proceeds
shōu shi　收拾　*v.t.*　tidy
shōu suō　收缩　*v. t*　contract

shōu tīng zhě　收听者　*n.*　listener
shōu qǔ fù jiā fèi　收取附加费　*v.t.*　surcharge
shōu yì　收益　*n.*　lucre
shōu yīn jī　收音机　*n.*　radio
shōu yín yuán　收银员　*n.*　cashier
shǒu　手　*n*　hand
shǒu bì　手臂　*n.*　arm
shǒu cè　手册　*n*　brochure
shǒu cè　手册　*n.*　handbook
shǒu cè　手册　*n*　manual
shǒu de　手的　*a.*　manual
shóu gǎo　手稿　*n.*　manuscript
shóu gǎo　手稿　*n.*　script
shǒu gōng　手工　*n.*　handiwork
shǒu gōng de　手工的　*a*　mechanic
shǒu gōng yì　手工艺　*n.*　handicraft
shǒu kào　手铐　*n*　cuff
shǒu kào　手铐　*n.*　handcuff
shǒu liàn　手链　*n*　bracelet
shǒu liú dàn　手榴弹　*n.*　grenade
shǒu pà　手帕　*n.*　handkerchief
shǒu qiāng　手枪　*n.*　pistol
shǒu shì　手势　*n.*　gesture
shǒu tào　手套　*n.*　glove
shǒu xiàng shù　手相术　*n.*　palmist
shǒu xiàng shù　手相术　*n.*　palmistry
shǒu yì　手艺　*n*　craft
shǒu yì　手艺　*n.*　workmanship
shóu zhǎng　手掌　*n.*　palm
shóu zhǐ　手指　*n*　finger
shǒu zhuó　手镯　*n.*　bangle
shǒu zú zhī qíng　手足之情　*n*　brotherhood
shǒu hòu　守候　*v.i*　scout
shǒu líng　守灵　*n*　wake
shǒu yè　守夜　*n.*　vigil
shǒu dū　首都　*n.*　capital
shǒu dū　首都　*n.*　metropolis
shóu líng　首领　*n.*　chieftain
shǒu wèi de　首位的　*a.*　premier
shǒu xiān　首先　*adv*　first
shǒu xiàng　首相　*n*　premier
shǒu yào de　首要的　*a.*　chief

shǒu zì mǔ 首字母 *n.* initial
shòu liè 狩猎 *n* hunt
shòu dà zhòng huān yíng 受大众欢迎 *n.* popularity
shòu hài rén 受害人 *n.* victim
shòu huān yíng de 受欢迎的 *a.* popular
shòu huān yíng de 受欢迎的 *a.* welcome
shòu kǔ 受苦 *v.t.* suffer
shòu shàn yǎng rén 受赡养人 *n* dependant
shòu xǐ 受洗 *v.t.* baptize
shòu tuō rén 受托人 *n.* trustee
shòu zhī pèi de 受支配的 *a* subject
shòu quán 授权 *v. t* empower
shòu yǔ 授予 *n* grant
shòu huò tān 售货摊 *n.* stall
shòu huò yuán 售货员 *n.* salesman
shòu qún 兽群 *n* flock
shòu qún 兽群 *n.* herd
shòu xìng 兽性 *n.* savagery
shòu xué 兽穴 *n* den
shòu xué 兽穴 *n.* lair
shòu yī de 兽医的 *a.* veterinary
shòu de 瘦的 *a.* lank
shòu de 瘦的 *a.* thin
shòu ròu 瘦肉 *n.* lean
shū 书 *n* book
shū bāo 书包 *n.* satchel
shū chóng 书虫 *n* book-worm
shū dāi zi 书呆子 *n.* pedant
shū dāi zi de 书呆子的 *a* bookish
shū fǎ 书法 *n* calligraphy
shū fáng 书房 *n.* study
shū mù 书目 *n* bibliography
shū mù biān zhě 书目编者 *n* bibliographer
shū qiān 书签 *n.* book-mark
shū shāng 书商 *n* book-seller
shū xìn 书信 *n.* missive
shū zhuō 书桌 *n* desk
shū qíng de 抒情的 *a.* lyric
shū qíng shī diào de 抒情诗调的 *a.* lyrical

shū qíng shī rén 抒情诗人 *n.* lyricist
shū jī zhǔ jiāo 枢机主教 *n.* cardinal
shū bai 叔伯 *n.* uncle
shū fu 舒服 *n.* comfort
shū fu de 舒服的 *a* comfortable
shū shì de 舒适的 *a.* cosy
shū shì de 舒适的 *a.* cozy
shū shì de 舒适的 *a.* snug
shū sàn 疏散 *n* evacuation
shū 梳 *n* comb
shū hu 疏忽 *n.* negligence
shū hu 疏忽 *n.* oversight
shū sàn 疏散 *v. t* evacuate
shū yuǎn 疏远 *v.t.* alienate
shū chū pǐn 输出品 *n* export
shū jīng guǎn qiē chú shǒu shù 输精管切除手术 *n.* vasectomy
shū qù 输去 *v.t.* lose
shú rén 熟人 *n.* acquaintance
shū rù 输入 *v.t.* import
shū rù 输入 *n.* infusion
shū rù 输入 *n.* input
shū shuǐ guǎn 输水管 *n* aqueduct
shū sòng 输送 *v. t.* convey
shū cài 蔬菜 *n.* vegetable
shū cài de 蔬菜的 *a.* vegetable
shú huí 赎回 *n.* redemption
shú jīn 赎金 *n.* ransom
shú zuì 赎罪 *v.i.* atone
shú zuì 赎罪 *n.* atonement
shú dú 熟读 *n.* perusal
shú dú 熟读 *v.t.* peruse
shú liàn de 熟练的 *a.* proficient
shú liàn de 熟练的 *a.* versed
shú lǜ 熟虑 *n* deliberation
shú shí diàn 熟食店 *n* deli
shú xī 熟悉 *v.t.* acquaint
shú xī de 熟悉的 *adj.* conversant
shú xī de 熟悉的 *a* familiar
shǔ xìng 属性 *n.* attribute
shǔ yú 属于 *v. i* belong
shǔ guāng 曙光 *n* aurora
shǔ 鼠 *n.* rat
shù shì 术士 *n.* sorcerer

shù yǔ 术语 n. terminology
shù yǔ de 术语的 a. terminological
shù 束 n bunch
shù 束 n. sheaf
shù fù 束缚 n bondage
shù fù 束缚 v. t curb
shù fù 束缚 n fetter
shù fù 束缚 v.t. shackle
shù kuàng 竖框 n. mullion
shù qín 竖琴 n. harp
shù 树 n. tree
shù lí 树篱 n. hedge
shù gàn 树干 n. trunk
shù pí 树皮 n. bark
shù yè 树叶 n foliage
shù yè 树液 n. sap
shù zhī 树枝 n branch
shù zhuāng 树桩 n. stump
shù kǒu 漱口 v.i. gargle
shù 数 v. t. count
shù de 数的 a. numeral
shù liàng 数量 n amount
shù liàng 数量 n. quantity
shù liàng de 数量的 a. quantitative
shù liàng shàng shèng guò 数量上胜过 v.t. outnumber
shù xué 数学 n mathematics
shù xué de 数学的 a. mathematical
shù xué jiā 数学家 n. mathematician
shù zì 数字 n digit
shù zì 数字 n figure
shù zì de 数字的 a. numerical
shuā zi 刷子 n brush
shuǎ nòng 耍弄 v.t. juggle
shuāi bài 衰败 n downfall
shuāi jié 衰竭 n. prostration
shuāi tuì 衰退 v. i ebb
shuāi wēi de 衰微的 a decadent
shuāi dǎo 摔倒 v.i. stumble
shuāi jiāo 摔跤 v.i. wrestle
shuāi jiāo yùn dòng yuán 摔跤运动员 n. wrestler
shuān jǐn 拴紧 v.t fasten
shuān xì 拴系 v.t. tether

shuāng 双 pref bi
shuāng bāo tāi 双胞胎 n. twin
shuāng bèi 双倍 n double
shuāng fāng de 双方的 a both
shuāng fèn de 双份的 a duplicate
shuāng guān yǔ 双关语 n. pun
shuāng jiǎo de 双角的 adj. biangular
shuāng rèn cháng jiàn 双刃长剑 n. rapier
shuāng xìng liàn de 双性恋的 adj. bisexual
shuāng yǔ de 双语的 a bilingual
shuāng zhóu de 双轴的 adj biaxial
shuāng 霜 n. frost
shuí 谁 pron. who
shuí 谁 pron. whom
shuí guǒ 水果 n. fruit
shuí tǒng 水桶 n bucket
shuí shǒu 水手 n. mariner
shuǐ 水 n. water
shuǐ bà 水坝 n dam
shuǐ dào tián 水稻田 n. paddy
shuí de 谁的 pron. whose
shuǐ de 水的 a. watery
shuǐ diāo 水貂 n. mink
shuǐ fèn 水分 n. moisture
shuǐ guǎn 水管 n. hose
shuǐ guǎn gōng rén 水管工人 n. plumber
shuǐ hú 水壶 n. jug
shuǐ huā 水花 n spray
shuǐ ní 水泥 n. cement
shuǐ niú 水牛 n. buffalo
shuǐ pào 水泡 n blain
shuǐ pào 水泡 n bleb
shuǐ pào 水泡 n blister
shuǐ jīng 水晶 n crystal
shuǐ kēng 水坑 n. puddle
shuǐ kù 水库 n. reservoir
shuì kuǎn 税款 n. levy
shuǐ liú 水流 n current
shuǐ lóng tou 水龙头 n. tap
shuǐ lù liǎng qī de 水陆两栖的 adj amphibious
shuǐ tǎ 水獭 n. otter
shuǐ xiān 水仙 n narcissus

shuǐ xiān huā 水仙花 *n.* daffodil

shuǐ yín 水银 *n.* mercury

shuǐ yín 水银 *n.* quicksilver

shuǐ zhá 水闸 *n.* sluice

shuǐ zhì 水蛭 *n.* leech

shuǐ zú guǎn 水族馆 *n.* aquarium

shuì 睡 *v.i.* sleep

shuì 税 *n.* tax

shuì jiào shí jiān 睡觉时间 *n.* bed-time

shuì mián zhě 睡眠者 *n.* sleeper

shuì mián 睡眠 *n.* sleep

shuì mián 睡眠 *v.i.* slumber

shuì shōu 税收 *n.* revenue

shuì yī 睡衣 *n.* gown

shuì zháo 睡着 *adv.* asleep

shǔn xī 吮吸 *v.t.* suckle

shùn cóng 顺从 *n.* compliance

shùn cóng de 顺从的 *a* amenable

shùn cóng de 顺从的 *adj.* compliant

shùn cóng de 顺从的 *a.* submissive

shùn shì liáo fǎ 顺势疗法 *n.* homeopathy

shùn shì liáo fǎ de yī sheng 顺势疗法的医生 *n.* homoeopath

shùn zhe 顺着 *prep.* up

shuō chū 说出 *v.t.* mouth

shuō fǎ 说法 *n.* parlance

shuō fú 说服 *v. t* convince

shuō fú 说服 *v.t.* persuade

shuō fú lì 说服力 *n.* persuasion

shuō huǎng 说谎 *v.i* lie

shuō huǎng zhě 说谎者 *n.* liar

shuō jiào 说教 *v.i.* sermonize

shuō míng 说明 *v.t.* account

shuō shuāng guān yǔ 说双关语 *v.i.* pun

sī fǎ 司法 *n.* judicature

sī fǎ de 司法的 *a.* judicial

sī fǎ quán 司法权 *n.* jurisdiction

sī jī 司机 *n.* chauffeur

sī jī 司机 *n* driver

sī lìng 司令 *n* commandant

sī lú 司炉 *n.* stoker

sī bēn 私奔 *v.i* elope

sī rén de 私人的 *a.* personal

sī rén de 私人的 *a.* private

sī rén jiào shī 私人教师 *n.* tutor

sī shēng de 私生的 *a.* illegitimate

sī shēng zǐ 私生子 *n.* bastard

sī tōng 私通 *n* amour

sī xíng 私刑 *v.t.* lynch

sī shuì 思睡 *n.* somnolence

sī xiǎng 思想 *n* thought

sī xiǎng jiā 思想家 *n.* thinker

sī 丝 *n.* silk

sī dài de 丝带的 *a.* lacy

sī de 丝的 *a.* silken

sī yí yàng de 丝一样的 *a.* silky

sī wǎng de 丝网的 *a.* webby

sī 嘶 *v.i.* neigh

sī sī shēng 嘶嘶声 *n* hiss

sī míng shēng 嘶鸣声 *n.* neigh

sī 撕 *v.t.* rip

sī kāi 撕开 *n.* avulsion

sī kāi 撕开 *v.t.* tear

sī suì 撕碎 *v.t* tatter

sǐ 死 *v.i* decease

sǐ de 死的 *a* dead

sǐ de 死的 *a.* mortal

sǐ hòu 死后 *a.* post-mortem

sǐ hòu de 死后的 *a.* posthumous

sǐ jì yìng bèi 死记硬背 *n.* rote

sǐ lù 死路 *n.* impasse

sǐ shī 死尸 *n.* stiff

sǐ xíng de 死刑的 *a.* capital

sǐ wáng lù 死亡率 *n.* mortality

sǐ wáng 死亡 *n* death

sǐ wáng 死亡 *n* decease

sǐ wáng 死亡 *v.i* die

sǐ wáng 死亡 *v.i.* perish

sì 四 *n.* four

sì biān xíng de 四边形的 *a.&n.* quadrilateral

sì bèi de 四倍的 *a.* quadruple

sì [liù] rén dà jiào 四[六]人大轿 *n.* palanquin

sì děng fēn 四等分 *v.t.* quarter

sì fāng yuàn 四方院 *n.* quadrangle

sì fēn yīn fú 四分音符 *n.* crotchet

sì fēn zhī yī 四分之一 *n.* quarter

sì lún yùn huò mǎ chē 四轮运货马车 *n.* wain

sì shí 四十 *n.* forty

sì zú dòng wù 四足动物 *n.* quadruped

sì yuàn 寺院 *n.* monastery

sì liào 饲料 *n* fodder

sōng chí 松弛 *n.* laxity

sōng chí 松弛 *n.* relaxation

sōng chí de 松弛的 *a* flabby

sōng de 松的 *a.* lax

sōng de 松的 *a.* loose

sōng jié yóu 松节油 *n.* turpentine

sōng kāi 松开 *v.t.* loosen

sōng shù 松树 *n.* pine

sōng shǔ 松鼠 *n.* squirrel

sǒng 耸 *v.t.* shrug

sǒng jiān 耸肩 *n* shrug

sòng cí 颂词 *n.* panegyric

sòng gē 颂歌 *n* carol

sòng gē 颂歌 *n.* ode

sòng qiū bō 送秋波 *v.t.* ogle

sòng xìn rén 送信人 *n.* messenger

sòng yáng 颂扬 *v.t.* extol

sōu chá 搜查 *v.t.* raid

sōu xún 搜寻 *n.* search

sōu xún 搜寻 *v.t.* search

sōu sōu zuò shēng 飕飕作声 *v.i.* whiz

sū gé lán de 苏格兰的 *a.* scotch

sū gé lán rén 苏格兰人 *n.* Scot

sū gé lán wēi shì jì 苏格兰威士忌 *n.* scotch

sū xǐng 苏醒 *v.i.* revive

sú huà 俗话 *n* byword

sú lì de 俗丽的 *a.* gaudy

sú rén 俗人 *n.* worldling

sù sòng 诉讼 *n.* litigation

sù sòng dāng shì rén 诉讼当事人 *n.* litigant

sù zhū 诉诸 *v.i.* resort

sù dù 速度 *n* pace

sù dù 速度 *n.* speed

sù dù 速度 *n.* velocity

sù jì 速记 *n.* stenography

sù jì yuán 速记员 *n.* stenographer

sù mìng lùn 宿命论 *n.* predestination

sù shè 宿舍 *n.* hostel

sù shí de 素食的 *a* vegetarian

sù shí zhě 素食者 *n.* vegetarian

sù jìng 肃静 *v.t.* hush

sù náng 嗉囊 *n.* craw

sù 粟 *n.* millet

sù zào 塑造 *v.t* shape

suān 酸 *n* acid

suān chéng 酸橙 *n.* lime

suān de 酸的 *a* acid

suān de 酸的 *a.* sour

suān xìng 酸性 *n.* acidity

suàn cuò 算错 *v.t.* miscalculate

suàn cuò 算错 *n.* miscalculation

suàn shù 算术 *n.* arithmetic

suàn shù de 算术的 *a.* arithmetical

suī rán 虽然 *conj.* albeit

suī rán 虽然 *conj.* although

suī rán 虽然 *prep.* notwithstanding

suī rán 虽然 *adv.* notwithstanding

suī rán 虽然 *conj.* though

suī rán … dàn shì 虽然…但是 *conj.* yet

suí bǐ 随笔 *n.* essay

suí bǐ zuò jiā 随笔作家 *n* essayist

suí háng de 随行的 *a.* attendant

suí háng rén yuán 随行人员 *n.* retinue

suí shēn yòng jù 随身用具 *n.pl* paraphernalia

suì bō li 碎玻璃 *n.* cullet

suì bù 碎布 *n.* rag

suì bù 碎布 *n.* tatter

suì mài yá 碎麦芽 *n.* mash

suì piàn 碎片 *n.* fragment

suì piàn 碎片 *n.* scrap

suì piàn 碎片 *n.* splinter
suì xiè 碎屑 *n* crumb
suì zhuān 碎砖 *n.* rubble
suì dào 隧道 *n.* tunnel
sǔn hài 损害 *n* blight
sǔn hài 损害 *n.* damage
sǔn hài 损害 *v.t.* damage
sǔn hài 损害 *n* mischief
sǔn hài 损害 *v.i.* tamper
sǔn hào 损耗 *n.* wastage
sǔn huài 损坏 *v.t* break
sǔn huài 损坏 *v.t.* mangle
sǔn huài 损坏 *v.t.* spoil
sǔn shī 损失 *n.* loss
sǔn shī cǎn zhòng de 损失惨重
  的 *a* disastrous
suō 梭 *n.* shuttle
suō duǎn 缩短 *v.i* shrink
suō lǒng 缩拢 *v.t.* purse
suō shuǐ 缩水 *n.* shrinkage
suō tóng zhèng 缩瞳症 *n.*
  myosis
suō wēi jiāo juǎn 缩微胶卷 *n.*
  microfilm
suō xiǎo 缩小 *v.t.* narrow
suō xiě 缩写 *v.t.* abbreviate
suō xiě 缩写 *n* abbreviation
suǒ shì 琐事 *n.* trifle
suǒ zài dì 所在地 *n.* locus
suó yǐ 所以 *conj.* so
suó yǐ 所以 *adv.* therefore
suó yǐ 所以 *adv.* thus
suó yǒu 所有 *pron* all
suó yǒu quán 所有权 *n.*
  ownership
suó yǒu zhě 所有者 *n.*
  proprietor
suǒ suì de 琐碎的 *a.* petty
suǒ xì de 琐细的 *a.* trivial
suǒ 锁 *n.* lock
suǒ 锁 *v.t* lock
suǒ mén 锁门 *v.t* bolt
suó yǐn 索引 *n.* index

T

tā 它 *pron.* it
tā 她 *pron.* her

tā 她 *pron.* she
tā de 她的 *a* her
tā 他 *pron.* he
tā 他 *pron.* him
tā de 他的 *pron.* his
tā men 他们 *pron.* them
tā men de dōng xi 他们的东西
  a. their
tā men de dōng xi 他们的东西
  pron. theirs
tǎ 塔 *n.* pagoda
tǎ 塔 *n.* tower
tà bǎn 踏板 *n.* pedal
tà bù 踏步 *n.* rung
tái 台 *n.* dais
tái fēng 台风 *n.* typhoon
tái gāo 抬高 *v.t* elevate
tái qǐ 抬起 *v.t.* jack
tái xiǎn 苔藓 *n.* moss
tái yīng 苔莺 *n.* warbler
tài 太 *adv.* too
tài yuǎn 太远 *adv.* afield
tài fēi táng 太妃糖 *n.* toffee
tài gǔ de 太古的 *a.* immemorial
tài jiàn 太监 *n* eunuch
tài kōng rén 太空人 *n.* astronaut
tài píng jiān 太平间 *n.* mortuary
tài yáng 太阳 *n.* sun
tài yáng bān de 太阳般的 *a.*
  sunny
tài yáng de 太阳的 *a.* solar
tài yáng xué 太阳穴 *n.* temple
tài dù 态度 *n.* attitude
tān chán dì jǔ jué 贪馋地咀嚼
  v.t. munch
tān chī de 贪吃的 *a.* voracious
tān lán 贪婪 *n* cupidity
tān lán de 贪婪的 *a.* greedy
tān liàn jiǔ sè de 贪恋酒色的 *n.*
  voluptuary
tān qián 贪钱 *n.* avarice
tān qiú 贪求 *v.t.* covet
tān wū 贪污 *n.* corruption
tān yù 贪慾 *n.* greed
tān yù de 贪欲的 *a.* lustful
tān zi 摊子 *n* booth
tán huà 谈话 *v.t.* converse
tán huà 谈话 *n* discourse
tán pàn 谈判 *n.* nagotiation

tán pàn 谈判 v.i parley
tán pàn zhě 谈判者 n. negotiator
tán huí 弹回 v.i. rebound
tán huí 弹回 n. repercussion
tán xiāng mù 檀香木 n. sandalwood
tán 痰 n. sputum
tán yú 痰盂 n. spittoon
tǎn bái 坦白 n confession
tǎn bái de 坦白的 a. frank
tǎn shuài 坦率 n. candour
tàn 探 v.t. visit
tàn cè 探测 v.t detect
tàn qì 叹气 n. sigh
tàn qì 叹气 v.i. sigh
tàn suǒ 探索 n probe
tàn suǒ 探索 n. quest
tàn xiǎn 探险 v.t explore
tàn 碳 n. carbon
tàn huà wù 碳化物 n. carbide
tàn suān jiǎ 碳酸钾 n. potash
tāng 汤 n. soup
táng 糖 n. candy
táng 糖 n. sugar
táng 糖 n sweet
táng 糖 n. sweetmeat
táng guǒ diǎn xin 糖果点心 n confectionery
táng guǒ diǎn xin diàn 糖果点心店 n confectioner
táng jiāng 糖浆 n molasses
táng jiāng 糖浆 n. syrup
táng jīng 糖精 n. saccharin
táng niào bìng 糖尿病 n diabetes
tàng píng 烫平 v.t. iron
tàng píng 烫平 v.t. smooth
táng yǐ 躺椅 n chaise
táo 逃 v.i flee
táo bì 逃避 n elusion
táo bì 逃避 n escape
táo bì 逃避 v.t evade
táo bì 逃避 n evasion
táo bì 逃避 v.i. shirk
táo bì 逃避 v.t. shunt
táo bì zhě 逃避者 n. shirker
táo fàn 逃犯 n. outlaw
táo wáng de 逃亡的 a. fugitive

táo wáng zhě 逃亡者 n. fugitive
táo zi 桃子 n. peach
táo zǒu 逃走 v.i abscond
táo zǒu 逃走 v.i decamp
táo zǒu 逃走 v.i escape
táo huā xīn mù 桃花心木 n. mahogany
táo cí 陶瓷 n ceramics
táo qì 陶器 n. crockery
táo qì 陶器 n. pottery
táo tǔ 陶土 n argil
tǎo hǎo nǚ rén 讨好女人 v.i. spark
tǎo jià guò gāo 讨价过高 v.t. overcharge
tǎo lùn 讨论 v.t. discuss
tǎo lùn 讨论 n. moot
tǎo yàn 讨厌 a abominable
tǎo yàn 讨厌 v.t dislike
tǎo yàn de 讨厌的 a. odious
tǎo yàn de 讨厌的 a. offensive
tǎo yàn de 讨厌的 a. repugnant
tǎo yàn de 讨厌的 a. troublesome
tǎo yàn de rén 讨厌的人 n. gadfly
tào shān 套衫 n. pullover
tè bié dà de 特别大的 a. outsize
tè bié de 特别的 a especial
tè bié de 特别的 a. particular
tè bié de 特别的 a. special
tè dìng de 特定的 a. specific
tè jì 特技 n stunt
tè jí de 特级的 a. superfine
tè pài yuán 特派员 n. commissioner
tè quán 特权 n. prerogative
tè quán 特权 n. privilege
tè sè 特色 n feature
tè shè 特赦 n. pardon
tè xǔ jīng yíng quán 特许经营权 n. frachise
tè zhēng 特征 n. trait
téng běn zhí wù 藤本植物 n. vine
téng hú 藤壶 n barnacles
téng tòng 疼痛 n. ache
téng tòng 疼痛 v.i. ache
téng tòng de 疼痛的 a. painful

tī 梯 *n.* ladder

tī 踢 *n.* kick

tī 踢 *v.t.* kick

tī mǎ cì 踢马刺 *n.* spur

tí chū 提出 *v.t.* tender

tí chū gòng kǎo lǜ 提出供考虑 *v.t.* propound

tí cí yuán 提词员 *n.* prompter

tí dào 提到 *v.t.* mention

tí gāo 提高 *v.t.* raise

tí gōng 提供 *v.t.* offer

tí gōng 提供 *v.i.* provide

tí gōng xiāo xi de 提供消息的 *a.* informative

tí gōng yǐn shí 提供饮食 *v.i* cater

tí jí 提及 *n.* mention

tí jiāo 提交 *v.t.* refer

tí jiāo 提交 *v.t* file

tí kuǎn 提款 *n.* withdrawal

tí mù 题目 *n.* title

tí shěn 提审 *v.* arraign

tí shì 提示 *n* cue

tí shì 提示 *n.* hint

tí shì 提示 *v.t.* prompt

tí xǐng 提醒 *v.t.* caution

tí xǐng 提醒 *v.t.* remind

tí xǐng de rén 提醒的人 *n.* reminder

tí yì 提议 *n* offer

tí yì 提议 *v.t.* suggest

tí yì 提议 *n.* suggestion

tí zì 题字 *n.* inscription

tí zǐ gān 提子干 *n.* currant

tí 蹄 *n.* hoof

tǐ cāo 体操 *n.* gymnastics

tǐ cāo de 体操的 *a.* gymnastic

tǐ cāo yùn dòng yuán 体操运动员 *n.* gymnast

tǐ gé 体格 *n* build

tǐ gé 体格 *n.* physique

tǐ tiē de 体贴的 *a.* considerate

tǐ tiē rén de 体贴人的 *a.* thoughtful

tǐ wēn biǎo 体温表 *n.* thermometer

tǐ yù chǎng 体育场 *n.* stadium

tǐ yù guǎn 体育馆 *n.* gymnasium

tǐ zhòng 体重 *n.* weight

tì 剃 *v.t.* shave

tì dāo 剃刀 *n.* razor

tì dāo 剃刀 *n* shave

tì fā 剃发 *n.* tonsure

tì dài de 替代的 *a.* vicarious

tì zuì gāo yáng 替罪羔羊 *n.* scapegoat

tiān 天 *n* day

tiān 天 *n.* sky

tiān cái 天才 *n.* genius

tiān cì 天赐 *n.* godsend

tiān é 天鹅 *n.* swan

tiān é róng 天鹅绒 *n.* velvet

tiān fù 天赋 *n.* aptitude

tiān huā 天花 *n.* smallpox

tiān huā bǎn 天花板 *n.* ceiling

tiān mìng 天命 *n.* providence

tiān qì 天气 *n* weather

tiān qǐ de 天启的 *a.* oracular

tiān rán cí shí 天然磁石 *n.* loadstone

tiān rán de 天然的 *a.* natural

tiān shàng de 天上的 *adj* celestial

tiān shàng de 天上的 *a.* heavenly

tiān shēng de 天生的 *a.* inborn

tiān shēng de 天生的 *a.* innate

tiān shǐ 天使 *n* angel

tiān shǐ cháng 天使长 *n* archangel

tiān táng 天堂 *n.* heaven

tiān táng 天堂 *n.* paradise

tiān wén tái 天文台 *n.* observatory

tiān wén xué 天文学 *n.* astronomy

tiān wén xué jiā 天文学家 *n.* astronomer

tiān xiàn 天线 *n.* aerial

tiān yì de 天意的 *a.* providential

tiān zhēn 天真 *a.* artless

tiān zhēn 天真 *n.* naivety

tiān zhēn de 天真的 *a.* naive

tiān zhēn làn màn 天真烂漫 *n.* naivete

tiān zhēn wú xié 天真无邪 *n.* innocence

tiān zhǔ jiāo de 天主教的 *a.* catholic

tiān zhǔ jiāo de 天主教的 *a.* papal

tián dì 田地 *n* field

tián jìng yùn dòng 田径运动 *n.* athletics

tián yuán shēng huó 田园生活 *n.* rustication

tiān jiā 添加 *n.* addition

tián 甜 *a.* sweet

tián cài 甜菜 *n* beet

tián guā 甜瓜 *n.* melon

tián wèi 甜味 *n.* sweetness

tiǎn 舔 *v.t.* lick

tiáo dài 条带 *n.* strip

tiáo jiàn 条件 *n* condition

tiáo kuǎn 条款 *n* clause

tiáo wén 条纹 *n.* stripe

tiāo ti 挑剔 *v.t* cavil

tiāo xuǎn chū lái de 挑选出来的 *a* select

tiáo gēng 调羹 *n.* spoonful

tiáo hé de 调和的 *a.* consonant

tiáo hé pǐn 调和品 *n.* concoction

tiáo jié 调节 *v.t.* screw

tiáo jiě 调解 *n.* mediation

tiáo jié qì 调节器 *n.* regulator

tiáo jiě rén 调解人 *n.* mediator

tiáo pí de 调皮的 *a* arch

tiáo qíng 调情 *v.i* flirt

tiáo sè bǎn 调色板 *n.* palette

tiáo tíng 调停 *v.i.* mediate

tiáo wèi 调味 *v.t.* season

tiáo wèi 调味 *v.t.* relish

tiáo wèi pǐn 调味品 *n* dressing

tiáo xì 调戏 *v.t.* molest

tiáo xì 调戏 *n.* molestation

tiáo zhěng 调整 *v.t.* adjust

tiáo zhěng 调整 *n.* adjustment

tiáo zhěng 调整 *v.t.* modulate

tiáo zhì 调制 *v.t* concoct

tiáo yīn 调音 *v.t* key

tiǎo bō de 挑拨的 *a.* provocative

tiǎo suō zhě 挑唆者 *v.t* foment

tiǎo zhàn 挑战 *n.* challenge

tiǎo zhàn 挑战 *v.t.* challenge

tiào 跳 *v.i.* spring

tiào dòng 跳动 *n.* jump

tiào dòng 跳动 *v.i.* palpitate

tiào dòng 跳动 *v.i.* pulse

tiào dòng 跳动 *n.* throb

tiào sǎn zhě 跳伞者 *n.* parachutist

tiào shéng 跳绳 *v.i.* skip

tiào shuǐ 跳水 *v.i* dive

tiào lán 跳栏 *n.* hurdle

tiào wǔ 跳舞 *v.t.* dance

tiào yuè 跳跃 *v.i* jump

tiào yuè 跳跃 *n* leap

tiào yuè 跳跃 *v.i.* vault

tiē biāo qiān yú 贴标签于 *v.t.* label

tiē qiē 贴切 *adv* appositely

tiē shàng 贴上 *v.t.* affix

tiě chǎn 铁铲 *n.* shovel

tiě dá ní hào 铁达尼号 *a.* Titanic

tiě jiang 铁匠 *n* blacksmith

tiě jiang 铁匠 *n.* smith

tiě lù 铁路 *n.* railway

tiě shǒu tào 铁手套 *n.* gauntlet

tīng 听 *v.i.* listen

tīng bú jiàn de 听不见的 *a.* inaudible

tīng dào 听到 *v.t.* hear

tīng dào de 听到的 *a* audible

tīng jué de 听觉的 *adj.* auditive

tīng tǒng 听筒 *n.* stethoscope

tíng bó 停泊 *v.i.* moor

tíng chē 停车 *v.i.* park

tíng chē 停车 *n* stop

tíng liú 停留 *v.i.* stay

tíng shī shì 停尸室 *n.* morgue

tíng yè 停业 *n.* closure

tíng zhàn 停战 *n.* truce

tíng zhí 停职 *n.* suspension

tíng zhì 停滞 *n.* stagnation

tíng zhǐ 停止 *v.t* discontinue

tíng zhǐ 停止 *n* halt

tíng zhǐ 停止 *n.* standstill

tíng zhǐ 停止 *v.t.* stop

tíng zhì bù liú 停滞不流 *v.i.* stagnate

tíng zhì de 停滞的 *a.* stagnant

tíng yuàn 庭院 *n.* courtyard

tōng biàn de 通便的 a laxative
tōng cháng 通常 adv. generally
tōng cháng 通常 adv. usually
tōng diàn 通电 v.t. galvanize
tōng fēng 通风 n draught
tōng fēng 通风 n. ventilation
tōng fēng shè bèi 通风设备 n. ventilator
tōng guò 通过 v.i. pass
tōng guò 通过 adv. through
tōng huò jǐn suō 通货紧缩 n. deflation
tōng huò péng zhàng 通货膨胀 n. inflation
tōng xìn 通信 n. correspondence
tōng xìn 通信 n. message
tōng xíng 通行 n pass
tōng xíng 通行 n. passage
tōng xíng fèi 通行费 n. toll
tōng xùn 通讯 n. communication
tōng zhī 通知 v.t. inform
tōng zhī 通知 n. notice
tōng zhī 通知 n. notification
tōng zhī 通知 v.t. notify
tóng děng de 同等的 a. tantamount
tóng děng de rén 同等的人 n. peer
tóng jū 同居 v.t cohabit
tóng huà 同化 v. assimilate
tóng huà 同化 n assimilation
tóng qíng 同情 v.t commiserate
tóng qíng 同情 n compassion
tóng qíng 同情 n. pity
tóng qíng de 同情的 a. sympathetic
tóng qíng xīn 同情心 n. sympathy
tóng shàng 同上 n. ditto
tóng shì 同事 n. associate
tóng shì 同事 n colleague
tóng shì 同事 n fellow
tóng shí fā shēng de 同时发生的 a. simultaneous
tóng xìng liàn de 同性恋的 a. gay

tóng xìng míng de rén 同姓名的人 n. namesake
tóng yàng dì 同样地 adv. likewise
tóng yì 同意 v.t. accede
tóng yì 同意 v.i. agree
tóng yì 同意 n. assent
tóng yì 同意 v.i consent
tóng yì cí 同义词 n. synonym
tóng yì de 同义的 a. synonymous
tóng yī de 同一的 a. identical
tóng zhì 同志 n. comrade
tóng zhǒng de 同种的 a. homogeneous
tóng zhù zhě 同住者 n. inmate
tóng zú de 同族的 adj cognate
tóng... yí yàng 同...一样 adv. as
tóng huà jù 童话剧 n. pantomime
tóng nián 童年 n boyhood
tóng nián 童年 n. childhood
tóng 铜 n copper
tóng luó 铜锣 n. gong
tǒng 桶 n. barrel
tǒng 桶 n. pail
tǒng 桶 n. tub
tǒng jì de 统计的 a. statistical
tǒng jì xué jiā 统计学家 n. statistician
tǒng jì xué jiā 统计学家 n. statistics
tǒng yī 统一 n. unification
tǒng yī tǐ 统一体 n. unity
tǒng zhì 统治 v.t. govern
tǒng zhì 统治 n. governance
tǒng zhì 统治 v.t. master
tǒng zhì 统治 n reign
tǒng zhì 统治 v.t. rule
tǒng zhì quán 统治权 n dominion
tǒng zhì zhě 统治者 n. lord
tòng 痛 n. pain
tòng chù 痛处 n sore
tòng dǎ 痛打 v.t. lambaste
tòng de 痛的 a. sore
tòng fēng 痛风 n. gout
tòng mà 痛骂 v.t belabour
tòng kǔ 痛苦 n. affliction

tòng kǔ 痛苦 *n.* agony
tòng kǔ de 痛苦的 *a.* grievous
tòng kū 恸哭 *v.i.* wail
tòng kū 恸哭 *n* wail
tōu 偷 *v.i.* steal
tōu kàn 偷看 *n* peep
tōu lǎn 偷懒 *v.i.* laze
tōu lǎn de 偷懒的 *a.* sluggish
tōu qiè 偷窃 *n.* theft
tōu tōu táo zǒu 偷偷逃走 *v.i.* sneak
tóu 头 *n.* head
tóu nǎo jīng míng de 头脑精明的 *a.* judicious
tóu fa 头发 *n* hair
tóu gǔ 头骨 *n.* skull
tóu jīn 头巾 *n.* kerchief
tóu pán 头盘 *n* appetizer
tóu pí 头皮 *n* scalp
tóu pí xiè 头皮屑 *n* dandruff
tóu tòng 头痛 *n.* headache
tóu 投 *v.t* fling
tóu 投 *v.t.* pitch
tóu bǎo 投保 *v.i.* insure
tóu biāo 投标 *n* bid
tóu biāo 投标 *n* tender
tóu biāo rén 投标人 *n* bidder
tóu dàn shǒu 投弹手 *n* bomber
tóu piào 投票 *v.i.* ballot
tóu piào 投票 *n.* poll
tóu piào 投票 *v.i.* vote
tóu piào quán 投票权 *n.* suffrage
tóu piào rén 投票人 *n.* voter
tóu qiú 投球 *v.i* bowl
tóu qiú yuán zuǒ cè de wài cháng shǒu chǎng yuán 投球员左侧的外场守场员 *n.* mid-off
tóu shè 投射 *v.t.* cast
tóu shí qì 投石器 *n.* sling
tóu shǒu 投手 *n.* pitcher
tóu xiáng 投降 *v.t* capitulate
tóu xiáng 投降 *n* surrender
tóu yǐng 投影 *n.* projection
tóu zhì 投掷 *v.t.* toss
tóu zī 投资 *v.t.* invest
tóu zī 投资 *n.* investment
tóu zǐ 骰子 *n.* dice

tòu zhī 透支 *n.* overdraft
tòu lù 透露 *v.t* disclose
tòu míng de 透明的 *a.* transparent
tòu zhī 透支 *v.t.* overdraw
tū de 秃的 *a.* bare
tū jiù 秃鹫 *n.* vulture
tū biàn de 突变的 *a.* mutative
tū chū 突出 *n.* hernia
tū chū 突出 *n.* prominence
tū chū de 突出的 *a.* prominent
tū jī 突击 *n.* onrush
tū jī 突击 *n.* sally
tū jī 突击 *v.i.* sally
tū jìn 突进 *v.i* lunge
tū rán 突然 *n.* sudden
tū rán de 突然的 *a* abrupt
tū rán de 突然的 *a* snap
tū rán jiān 突然间 *adv.* suddenly
tū rán jīng guò 突然经过 *v.i.* leap
tū rán pēn chū 突然喷出 *n* spurt
tū rán yí zhèn 突然一阵 *n.* gust
tū xí 突袭 *v.i.* pounce
tū xí 突袭 *n.* raid
tū xí 突袭 *n* swoop
tú biǎo 图表 *n.* chart
tú biǎo 图表 *n* diagram
tú biǎo 图表 *n.* graph
tú huà 图画 *n* drawing
tú huà 图画 *n.* picture
tú shū guǎn 图书馆 *n.* library
tú shū guǎn yuán 图书馆员 *n.* librarian
tú xiàng 图像 *n.* image
tú céng 涂层 *n* coating
tú huáng yóu 涂黄油 *v.t* butter
tú là de 涂蜡的 *adj.* cerated
tú là yú 涂蜡于 *v.t.* wax
tú mǒ 涂抹 *v.t.* daub
tú qīng qī yú 涂清漆于 *v.t.* varnish
tú yǐ huī ní 涂以灰泥 *v.t.* plaster
tú yóu 涂油 *v.t.* anoint
tú zhī yú 涂脂于 *v.t* grease
tú dì 徒弟 *n.* apprentice
tú fū 屠夫 *n* butcher
tú shā 屠杀 *v.t* butcher

tú shā 屠杀 *v.t.* massacre
tú shā 屠杀 *n.* slaughter
tú zǎi 屠宰 *v.t.* slaughter
tǔ dì 土地 *n.* ground
tǔ dì 土地 *n* mould
tǔ dì de 土地的 *a.* territorial
tǔ dūn 土墩 *n.* mound
tǔ zhì de 土制的 *a* earthen
tǔ zhù 土著 *n* native
tǔ 吐 *v.i.* spit
tù zi 兔子 *n.* rabbit
tuán 团 *n.* regiment
tuán jié 团结 *v.i.* unite
tuán jié yí zhì 团结一致 *n.*
　solidarity
tuán tǐ 团体 *n.* confraternity
tuán tǐ 团体 *n.* guild
tuī 推 *v.t.* jostle
tuī 推 *v.t.* push
tuī 推 *n.* push
tuī 推 *v.t.* shove
tuī 推 *n.* shove
tuī cè 推测 *v.t* conjecture
tuī cè 推测 *v.t.* presume
tuī cè 推测 *v.i.* speculate
tuī cè 推测 *n.* speculation
tuī cè 推测 *v.t.* suppose
tuī cè 推测 *n.* supposition
tuī cè 推测 *n.* surmise
tuī cè 推测 *v.t.* surmise
tuī dòng 推动 *v.i.&n* budge
tuī duàn 推断 *v.t.* infer
tuī fān 推翻 *v.t.* overthrow
tuī fān 推翻 *v.t.* subvert
tuī jǐ 推挤 *n.* jostle
tuī jiàn 推荐 *v.t.* nominate
tuī jiàn 推荐 *n.* nomination
tuī jiàn 推荐 *v.t.* recommend
tuī jiàn 推荐 *n.*
　recommendation
tuī jiàn shū 推荐书 *n.*
　testimonial
tuī jiàn xìn 推荐信 *n* thrust
tuī jìn 推进 *v.t.* propel
tuī lùn 推论 *n.* inference
tuī lùn 推论 *v.i.* reason
tuī mó de rén 推磨的人 *n.*
　grinder
tuī xíng 推行 *v.t.* enforce

tuī xuǎn 推选 *v.t* elect
tuǐ 腿 *n.* leg
tuì bù 退步 *v.i.* backslide
tuì xiū 退休 *n.* retirement
tuì xiū jīn 退休金 *n.* pension
tuì què 退却 *v.i.* recoil
tuì suō 退缩 *v.i.* cower
tuì wǔ jūn rén 退伍军人 *n.*
　veteran
tuì xià de pí 蜕下的皮 *n.* slough
tuì sè 褪色 *v.i* fade
tūn 吞 *v.t.* swallow
tūn mò 吞没 *v.t* engulf
tūn mò 吞没 *v.t.* merge
tūn shí 吞食 *v.t* devour
tūn yàn 吞咽 *n.* gulp
tūn yàn 吞咽 *n.* swallow
tún bù 臀部 *n* hip
tuō ér suǒ 托儿所 *n.* nursery
tuō lí 脱离 *n.* secession
tuō lì 脱粒 *v.t.* thresh
tuō lí zhǔ yì zhě 脱离主义者 *n.*
　secessionist
tuō luò wù 脱落物 *n* shed
tuō huàn 脱换 *v.i.* moult
tuō zhī nǎi 脱脂奶 *n* buttermilk
tuō 拖 *v.t* drag
tuō bǎ 拖把 *n.* mop
tuō chē 拖车 *n* limber
tuō chē 拖车 *n.* trailer
tuō lā jī 拖拉机 *n.* tractor
tuō lěi 拖累 *n* drag
tuō xié 拖鞋 *n.* slipper
tuō yán 拖延 *n.* procrastination
tuō yè 拖曳 *v.i.* shuffle
tuó bèi 驼背 *n* stoop
tuó niǎo 鸵鸟 *n.* ostrich
tuǒ xié 妥协 *n* compromise
tuǒ xié 妥协 *v.t* compromise
tuò huāng zhě 拓荒者 *n.*
　pioneer
tuò mo 唾沫 *n* spittle
tuò yè 唾液 *n.* saliva
tuò yè 唾液 *n* spit

wā 挖 *v.t.* dig

wā dòng 挖洞 *v.t* hole

wā háo wéi rǎo 挖壕围绕 *v.t.* moat

wā jué 挖掘 *n* dig

wā jué 挖掘 *n.* excavation

wā kōng 挖空 *v.t.* excavate

wǎ tè 瓦特 *n.* watt

wà 袜 *n.* hosiery

wà dài 袜带 *n.* garter

wài biǎo 外表 *n* appearance

wài biǎo shàng 外表上 *adv.* outwardly

wài de 外的 *a.* outer

wài guān 外观 *n.* guise

wài guān 外观 *adv* outward

wài guó de 外国的 *a* foreign

wài guó huà 外国话 *n.* lingo

wài guó qì pài de 外国气派的 *a.* outlandish

wài guó rén 外国人 *a.* alien

wài guó rén 外国人 *n* foreigner

wài háng 外行 *n.* layman

wài háng de 外行的 *a.* lay

wài jiā de 外加的 *adj* adscititious

wài jiāo 外交 *n* diplomacy

wài jiāo de 外交的 *a* diplomatic

wài jiāo guān 外交官 *n* diplomat

wài ké 外壳 *n.* husk

wài kē shǒu shù 外科手术 *n.* surgery

wài kē yī sheng 外科医生 *n.* surgeon

wài lái zhě 外来者 *n.* outsider

wài mào 外貌 *n.* physiognomy

wài miàn 外面 *n* without

wài miàn de 外面的 *a* external

wài miàn de 外面的 *n* outside

wài tào 外套 *n.* jacket

wài xíng 外形 *n.* outline

wài yī 外衣 *n* coat

wān 弯 *n* bend

wān 弯 *v.t* bend

wān de 弯的 *n* bent

wān qū 弯曲 *v.t.* crankle

wān qū de 弯曲的 *a.* sinuous

wān qū de 弯曲的 *v.i.* snake

wān yāo 弯腰 *v.i.* stoop

wān dòu 豌豆 *n.* pea

wán chéng 完成 *v.t.* accomplish

wán chéng 完成 *v.t* complete

wán chéng 完成 *n* completion

wán chéng 完成 *v.t* finish

wán chéng le de 完成了的 *a* accomplished

wán jié 完结 *n.* close

wán měi 完美 *n.* perfection

wán měi de 完美的 *a.* perfect

wán quán 完全 *adv* all

wán quán dì 完全地 *adv* entirely

wán quán dì 完全地 *adv.* full

wán quán dì 完全地 *adv.* fully

wán quán dì 完全地 *adv.* stark

wán quán dì 完全地 *adv.* utterly

wán quán dì 完全地 *adv.* wholly

wán zhěng 完整 *n.* integrity

wán zhěng de 完整的 *a* complete

wán zhěng de 完整的 *a.* intact

wán 玩 *v.i.* play

wán hū 玩忽 *a.* negligent

wán jù 玩具 *n.* toy

wán nòng 玩弄 *v.i.* toy

wán nòng guǐ biàn 玩弄诡辩 *n.* sophistication

wán shuǐ 玩水 *v.i.* dabble

wán xiào 玩笑 *n.* banter

wán gù 顽固 *n* bigot

wán gù 顽固 *n* bigotry

wán gù 顽固 *n.* obduracy

wán gù de 顽固的 *a* bigot

wán gù de 顽固的 *a.* headstrong

wán gù de 顽固的 *a.* obdurate

wán gù de 顽固的 *a.* obstinate

wán gù de 顽固的 *a.* stubborn

wán pí de 顽皮的 *a.* naughty

wán pí gū niang 顽皮姑娘 *n.* minx

wán tóng 顽童 *n.* urchin

wǎn cān 晚餐 *n* dinner

wǎn de 晚的 *a.* late

wǎn gē 挽歌 *n* elegy

wǎn gē 挽歌 *n.* monody

wǎn huí 挽回 *v.t.* redeem

wǎn 碗 *n* bowl

wàn shòu jú 万寿菊 *n.* marigold

wàn suì 万岁 *interj.* hurrah

wàn yīng jiě dú yào 万应解毒药 *n.* mithridate

wàn yīng yào 万应药 *n.* panacea

wàn 腕 *n.* wrist

wàn gǔ 腕骨 *n.* carpal

wáng guó 王国 *n.* kingdom

wáng pái 王牌 *n.* trump

wáng shì chéng yuán 王室成员 *n.* royalty

wáng shì de 王室的 *a.* royal

wáng shì shǒu lín rén 王室守林人 *n.* ranger

wáng wèi 王位 *n.* throne

wáng zǐ 王子 *n.* prince

wáng zǐ de 王子的 *a.* princely

wǎng 网 *n.* net

wǎng qiú 网球 *n.* tennis

wǎng yǎn zhī wù 网眼织物 *n.* network

wǎng zhuàng wù 网状物 *n.* mesh

wǎng qián 往前 *adv.* forth

wǎng xià 往下 *prep* down

wǎng rán dì 枉然地 *adv.* vainly

wàng ēn fù yì 忘恩负义 *n.* ingratitude

wàng jì 忘记 *v.t* forget

wàng yuǎn jìng 望远镜 *n.* binocular

wàng yuǎn jìng 望远镜 *n.* telescope

wēi hài 危害 *v.t.* jeopardize

wēi jí 危及 *v.t.* endanger

wēi jī 危机 *n* crisis

wēi jī de 危机的 *a* critical

wēi xiǎn 危险 *n.* danger

wēi xiǎn 危险 *n.* hazard

wēi xiǎn 危险 *n.* jeopardy

wēi xiǎn 危险 *n.* peril

wēi xiǎn de 危险的 *a* dangerous

wēi xiǎn de 危险的 *a.* perilous

wēi xiǎn de 危险的 *a.* risky

wēi hè 威吓 *v.t* daunt

wēi shè 威慑 *v.t.* overawe

wēi shì jì jiǔ 威士忌酒 *n.* whisky

wēi xié 威胁 *v.t.* intimidate

wēi xié 威胁 *n* menace

wēi xié 威胁 *n.* threat

wēi xìn 威信 *n.* prestige

wēi yán de 威严的 *a.* august

wēi bō 微波 *n.* microwave

wēi bù zú dào de 微不足道的 *n.* pigmy

wēi bù zú dào de 微不足道的 *a.* negligible

wēi fēng 微风 *n* breeze

wēi fēng 微风 *n.* zephyr

wēi hóng de 微红的 *a.* reddish

wēi lì 微粒 *n.* particle

wēi ruò de 微弱的 *a* faint

wēi ruò de 微弱的 *a* feeble

wēi shuì 微睡 *n.* slumber

wēi wēn de 微温的 *a.* lukewarm

wēi xiào 微笑 *n.* smile

wēi xiào 微笑 *v.i.* smile

wēi xiǎo de 微小的 *a.* puny

wēi xiǎo huà xiàng 微小画像 *n.* miniature

wēi zuì de 微醉的 *a.* tipsy

wéi 为 *prep* for

wéi hài de 为害的 *a.* mischievous

wéi mǎ dìng tí tiě 为马钉蹄铁 *v.t.* shoe

wéi nán de 为难的 *a.* awkward

wéi shǒu 为首 *v.t* head

wéi chǎng 围场 *n.* yard

wéi gōng 围攻 *v.t* besiege

wéi jīn 围巾 *n.* muffler

wéi jīn 围巾 *n.* scarf

wéi qiáng 围墙 *n.* bawn

wéi qiáng 围墙 *n* fence

wéi qún 围裙 *n.* apron

wéi rào 围绕 *v.t.* begird

wéi rào 围绕 *v.t.* encircle

wéi rào 围绕 *v.t* girdle

wéi zhù 围住 *v.t.* picket

wéi zhù 围住 *v.t.* surround

wéi fǎ 违法 *n* breach

wéi fǎ de 违法的 *a.* illegal

wéi fàn 违犯 *n.* infringement

wéi fǎn 违反 *v.t* disobey

wéi fǎn 违反 *n.* transgression

wéi fǎn 违反 *v.t.* violate

wéi fǎn 违反 *n.* violation

wéi kàng 违抗 *n* defiance

wéi yuē 违约 *n.* default

wéi lì shì tú 唯利是图 *n.* venality

wéi wù zhǔ yì 唯物主义 *n.* materialism

wéi yī de 唯一的 *a.* only

wéi yī de 唯一的 *a* sole

wéi chí 维持 *v.t.* maintain

wéi chí shēng huó 维持生活 *v.i.* subsist

wéi shēng sù 维生素 *n.* vitamin

wéi xiū 维修 *n.* maintenance

wéi 桅 *n.* mast

wěi jūn zǐ 伪君子 *n.* hypocrite

wěi zào 伪造 *v.t* fabricate

wěi zào 伪造 *v.t* forge

wěi zào de 伪造的 *a.* spurious

wěi zào pǐn 伪造品 *n* forgery

wěi zào zhě 伪造者 *n.* counterfeiter

wěi shàn 伪善 *n.* hypocrisy

wěi shàn de 伪善的 *a.* hypocritical

wěi shì 伪誓 *n.* perjury

wěi ba 尾巴 *n.* tail

wěi bù 尾部 *n.* stern

wěi pài wéi dài biǎo 委派为代表 *v.t* delegate

wěi qu 委屈 *n.* grievance

wěi rèn 委任 *v.t.* accredit

wěi rèn 委任 *v.t.* appoint

wěi tuō 委托 *v.i* confide

wěi tuō 委托 *v.t.* consign

wěi tuō 委托 *n.* consignment

wěi tuō 委托 *v.t* entrust

wěi yuán 委员 *n.* councillor

wěi yuán huì 委员会 *n* committee

wěi dù 纬度 *n.* latitude

wěi xiè 猥亵 *n.* obscenity

wěi xiè de 猥亵的 *a.* obscene

wèi shēng 卫生 *n.* hygiene

wèi shēng de 卫生的 *a.* hygienic

wèi shēng de 卫生的 *a.* sanitary

wèi shén me 为什么 *adv.* why

wèi bì 未必 *adv.* surely

wèi bì yǒu de 未必有的 *a.* unlikely

wèi chéng nián 未成年 *n.* immaturity

wèi chéng nián zhě 未成年者 *n* minor

wèi jué dìng de 未决定的 *a* pending

wèi kāi huà de 未开化的 *a.* savage

wèi hūn rén shì 未婚人士 *n* agamist

wèi hūn de 未婚的 *a* maiden

wèi lái de 未来的 *a.* future

wèi lí cháo de chú 未离巢的雏 *n.* nestling

wèi wán chéng de 未完成的 *a.* incomplete

wèi yú 位于 *v.t.* locate

wèi zhi 位置 *n.* lay

wèi zhi 位置 *n.* location

wèi zhi 位置 *n.* position

wèi 味 *n* flavour

wèi 味 *n.* smack

wèi de 胃的 *a.* gastric

wèi kǒu 胃口 *n.* appetite

wèi suō 畏缩 *v.i.* cringe

wèi suō 畏缩 *n.* recoil

wèi suō 畏缩 *v.i.* wince

wèi 喂 *v.t* feed

wèi mǎ 喂马 *v.t* groom

wèi yǔ 谓语 *n.* predicate

wèi wèn 慰问 *n* condolence

wēn hé de 温和的 *a.* gentle

wēn hé de 温和的 *a.* mild

wēn hé de 温和的 *a.* placid

wēn hé de 温和的 *a.* temperate

wēn hé dì 温和地 *adv.* kindly

wēn nuǎn 温暖 *n.* warmth

wēn rè de 温热的 *a.* thermal

wēn róu de 温柔的 *a* tender

wēn shùn de 温顺的 *a* docile

wēn shùn de 温顺的 *a.* meek

wēn shùn de 温顺的 *a.* tame

wēn xí 温习 *v.t.* review

wēn yì 瘟疫 *n.* pestilence

wēn yì 瘟疫 *n.* plague

wén huà 文化 *n* culture

wén huà de 文化的 *a* cultural

wén jiàn 文件 *n* document
wén jiàn 文件 *n* file
wén jiàn jiá 文件夹 *n.* portfolio
wén jù 文具 *n.* stationery
wén jù shāng 文具商 *n.*
stationer
wén máng 文盲 *n.* illiteracy
wén míng shè huì 文明社会 *n.*
civilization
wén píng 文凭 *n* diploma
wén xué 文学 *n.* literature
wén xué de 文学的 *a.* literary
wén xué jiā 文学家 *n.*
litterateur
wén yǎ 文雅 *n.* urbanity
wén yuán 文员 *n* clerk
wén zhāng 文章 *n* article
wén shēn 纹身 *n.* tattoo
wén shēn 纹身 *v.i.* tattoo
wén 蚊 *n.* mosquito
wén 闻 *v.t* nose
wén 闻 *v.t.* smell
wén 闻 *n* sniff
wén chū 闻出 *v.t.* scent
wěn 吻 *n.* kiss
wěn 吻 *v.t.* kiss
wěn hé 吻合 *v.i.* tally
wěn dìng 稳定 *n.* stabilization
wěn dìng de 稳定的 *a.* stable
wěn dìng xìng 稳定性 *n.*
stability
wēn dù 温度 *n.* temperature
wěn gù de 稳固的 *n.* steadiness
wěn gù de 稳固的 *a.* steady
wèn 问 *v.t.* ask
wèn hòu 问候 *v.t.* greet
wèn hòu 问候 *n.* regard
wèn hòu 问候 *n.* salutation
wèn juǎn 问卷 *n.* questionnaire
wèn tí 问题 *n.* issue
wèn tí 问题 *n.* problem
wèn tí 问题 *n.* question
wēng wēng jiào 嗡嗡叫 *v.i*
buzz
wēng wēng shēng 嗡嗡声 *n*
hum
wēng wēng shēng 嗡嗡声 *n.*
buzz
wō 窝 *n.* cavity

wō lún jī 涡轮机 *n.* turbine
wō niú 蜗牛 *n.* snail
wò pū 卧铺 *n* berth
wò zhù 握住 *v.t* hold
wǒ 我 *pron.* I
wǒ 我 *pron.* me
wǒ de 我的 *pron.* mine
wǒ de 我的 *a.* my
wǒ men de 我们的 *pron.* our
wǒ zì jǐ 我自己 *pron.* myself
wū mù 乌木 *n* ebony
wū tuō bāng de 乌托邦的 *a.*
utopian
wū yā 乌鸦 *n* crow
wū diǎn 污点 *n.* blot
wū diǎn 污点 *n.* slur
wū diǎn 污点 *n.* stain
wū diǎn 污点 *n.* taint
wū huì 污秽 *n* filth
wū huì de 污秽的 *a* filthy
wū jī 污迹 *n.* daub
wū rǎn 污染 *v.t.* contaminate
wū rǎn 污染 *v.t.* pollute
wū rǎn 污染 *n.* pollution
wū rǎn 污染 *v.t.* taint
wū shuǐ 污水 *n.* sewage
wū shuǐ cáo 污水槽 *n* sink
wū shuǐ dào 污水道 *n* sewer
wū shuǐ kēng 污水坑 *n.*
cesspool
wū shī 巫师 *n.* necromancer
wū shù 巫术 *n.* sorcery
wū shù 巫术 *n.* witchery
wū yè 呜咽 *v.i.* whimper
wū dǐng 屋顶 *n.* roof
wū wài cè suǒ 屋外厕所 *n.*
outhouse
wú bǐ de 无比的 *a.*
incomparable
wú bǐ de 无比的 *a.* matchless
wú bǐ de 无比的 *a.* nonpareil
wú bǐ de 无比的 *a.* peerless
wú bǐ de rén [dōng xi] 无比的
人[东西] *n.* nonpareil
wú biān de 无边的 *a.* immense
wú cái zhì de 无才智的 *a.* witless
wú chā bié de 无差别的 *a.*
indiscriminate
wú chǐ de 无耻的 *a.* shameless

wú cóng zhuō mō de 无从捉摸的 *a* elusive

wú dí de 无敌的 *a.* invincible

wú dǐ de 无低的 *a.* baseless

wú fǎ jì shù de 无法计数的 *a.* incalculable

wú fǎ rěn shòu de 无法忍受的 *a.* intolerable

wú fǎ shí shī 无法实施 *n.* impracticability

wú guān de 无关的 *a.* irrelevant

wú guān de 无关的 *a.* irrespective

wú guān jǐn yào de 无关紧要的 *a.* insignificant

wú guāng zé de 无光泽的 *a.* lacklustre

wú guǒ de zhí wù 无果的植物 *adj.* acarpous

wú huā guǒ 无花果 *n* fig

wú jì huà de 无计划的 *a.* haphazard

wú jì lǜ 无纪律 *n.* indiscipline

wú jià de 无价的 *a.* invaluable

wú jīng dǎ cǎi de 无精打采的 *a.* listless

wú jīng yàn 无经验 *n.* inexperience

wú jūn de 无菌的 *a.* sterile

wú lài 无赖 *n* cad

wú lài 无赖 *n.* knave

wú lài 无赖 *n.* rascal

wú lì 无力 *n* disability

wú lǐ 无礼 *n.* impertinence

wú lǐ 无礼 *n.* indecency

wú lǐ 无礼 *n.* insolence

wú lì cháng huán de 无力偿还的 *a.* insolvent

wú lì de 无力的 *a.* impotent

wú lì de 无力的 *a.* nerveless

wú lǐ de 无礼的 *a.* impolite

wú lǐ de 无礼的 *a.* insolent

wú lì qi 无力气 *n.* lethargy

wú lùn nǎ lǐ 无论哪里 *adv.* wherever

wú lùn nà yí gè 无论那一个 *pron* whichever

wú lùn rú hé 无论如何 *adv.* anyhow

wú lùn rú hé 无论如何 *adv.* however

wú lùn shén me 无论什么 *pron.* whatever

wú lùn shuí 无论谁 *pron.* whoever

wú néng 无能 *n.* inability

wú néng lì 无能力 *n.* impotence

wú néng lì 无能力 *n.* incapacity

wú néng lì de 无能力的 *a.* incapable

wú néng lì de 无能力的 *a.* incompetent

wú qíng de 无情的 *a.* inexorable

wú qíng de 无情的 *a.* pitiless

wú qíng de 无情的 *a.* relentless

wú rén 无人 *pron.* nobody

wú rén cāo zuò de 无人操作的 *a.* unmanned

wú sè de 无色的 *adj* achromatic

wú shén lùn 无神论 *n* atheism

wú shén lùn zhě 无神论者 *n* antitheist

wú shén lùn zhě 无神论者 *n* atheist

wú shēng 无声 *n.* silence

wú shēng de 无声的 *a.* silent

wú shēng mìng de 无生命的 *a.* inanimate

wú shēng mìng de 无生命的 *a.* lifeless

wú shì zì rǎo 无事自扰 *v.i* fuss

wú shù 无数 *n.* million

wú shù 无数 *n.* myriad

wú shù de 无数的 *a.* countless

wú shù de 无数的 *a.* innumerable

wú shù de 无数的 *a* myriad

wú shù de 无数的 *a.* numberless

wú sī de 无私的 *a.* selfless

wú suǒ bú zài 无所不在 *n.* omnipresence

wú suǒ bú zài de 无所不在的 *a.* omnipresent

wú suǒ bù zhī de 无所不知的 *a.* omniscient

wú tóu guài tāi 无头怪胎 *n.*
acephalus

wú wèi 无味 *n.* insipidity

wú wèi de 无味的 *a.* insipid

wú xī wàng de 无希望的 *a.*
hopeless

wú xiá cī de 无瑕疵的 *a.*
stainless

wú xiàn 无限 *n.* infinity

wú xiàn de 无限的 *a.*
immeasurable

wú xiàn de 无限的 *a.* indefinite

wú xiàn de 无限的 *a.* infinite

wú xiàn de 无限的 *a.* limitless

wú xiàn de 无限的 *a.*
measureless

wú xiàn de 无线的 *a.* wireless

wú xiàn diàn 无线电 *n* wireless

wú xiào 无效 *n.* nullification

wú xiào de 无效的 *a.*
ineffective

wú xiào de 无效的 *a.* invalid

wú xiào de 无效的 *a.* null

wú xiào de 无效的 *v.* void

wú xiào lì de 无效力的 *a.*
inoperative

wú xíng de 无形的 *adj.*
aeriform

wú xíng de 无形的 *a.*
immaterial

wú xìng dòng wù 无性动物 *n*
neuter

wú xiù chèn shān 无袖衬衫 *n*
chemise

wú yào kě jiù de 无药可救的 *a.*
incorrigible

wú yì 无益 *n.* futility

wú yì de 无意的 *adv.*
unwittingly

wú yí gè 无一个 *pron.* none

wú yì shí de 无意识的 *a.*
senseless

wú yì yì 无意义 *n.*
insignificance

wú yì yì 无异议 *n.* unanimity

wú yì yì de 无意义的 *a.*
meaningless

wú yì zhōng tīng dào 无意中听
到 *v.t.* overhear

wú yòng de 无用的 *a.* futile

wú yòng de 无用的 *a.* waste

wú zhèng fǔ 无政府 *n* anarchy

wú zhèng fǔ zhǔ yì 无政府主义
n. anarchism

wú zhèng fǔ zhǔ yì zhě 无政府
主义者 *n* anarchist

wú zhēng lùn zhī yú dì de 无争论
之余地的 *a.* indisputable

wú zhī 无知 *n.* ignorance

wú zhī 无知 *n.* nescience

wú zhī de 无知的 *a.* ignorant

wú zhī jué de 无知觉的 *a.*
insensible

wú zhì xù 无秩序 *n.* misrule

wú zhù de 无助的 *a.* helpless

wú zuì de 无罪的 *a.* innocent

wú zuì de pàn jué 无罪的判决 *n.*
acquittal

wú rǔ 侮辱 *v.t.* affront

wú rǔ 侮辱 *n* affront

wú rǔ 侮辱 *n.* insult

wú rǔ 侮辱 *v.t.* insult

wū rǔ 污辱 *v.t.* attaint

wú rǔ de 侮辱的 *a.* abusive

wú gōng 蜈蚣 *n.* centipede

wǔ 五 *n* five

wǔ jiǎo xíng 五角形 *n.* pentagon

wǔ shí 五十 *n.* fifty

wǔ shí zhōu nián jì niàn 五十周
年纪念 *n.* jubilee

wǔ yuè 五月 *n.* May

wǔ cān 午餐 *n.* lunch

wǔ shuì 午睡 *n.* siesta

wǔ yè 午夜 *n.* midnight

wǔ qì 武器 *n.* arsenal

wǔ qì 武器 *n.* weapon

wǔ shì 武士 *n.* warrior

wǔ tái 舞台 *n.* stage

wǔ 舞 *n* dance

wù dǎo 误导 *v.t.* misdirect

wù huì 误会 *v.t.* misconstrue

wù huì 误会 *v.t.* misunderstand

wù huì 误会 *n.* misunderstanding

wù jiě 误解 *v.t.* misapprehend

wù jiě 误解 *n* misapprehension

wù jiě 误解 *v.t.* misconceive

wù jiě 误解 *n.* misconception

wù xìn 误信 *n.* misbelief

wù lǐ xué 物理学 *n.* physics

wù lǐ xué jiā 物理学家 *n.* physicist

wù pǐn 物品 *n.* ware

wù tǐ 物体 *n.* object

wù zhì 物质 *n.* substance

wù zhì de 物质的 *a.* material

wù zhǔ 物主 *n.* owner

wù 雾 *n.* mist

wù 雾 *n* fog

X

X guāng X光 *n.* x-ray

X shè xiàn de X射线的 *a.* x-ray

xī bān yá de 西班牙的 *a.* Spanish

xī bān yá rén 西班牙人 *n.* Spaniard

xī bān yá rén 西班牙人 *n.* Spanish

xī fāng 西方 *n.* occident

xī fāng 西方 *n.* west

xī fāng de 西方的 *a.* occidental

xī fāng de 西方的 *a.* west

xī fāng de 西方的 *a.* western

xī guā 西瓜 *n.* water-melon

xī lán huā 西兰花 *n.* broccoli

xī kè mò 西克莫 *n.* sycamore

xī zhuāng bèi xīn 西装背心 *n.* waistcoat

xī rù 吸入 *v.i.* inhale

xī rù 吸入 *n.* suck

xī shōu 吸收 *v.t* absorb

xī shōu 吸收 *v.t.* incorporate

xī yǐn 吸引 *v.t.* appeal

xī yǐn 吸引 *v.t.* attract

xī yǐn 吸引 *n.* attraction

xī yǐn 吸引 *v.t.* beckon

xī yǐn 吸引 *v.t.* charm

xī yǐn rén de 吸引人的 *a.* attractive

xī yǐn zhù 吸引住 *v.t.* rivet

xī là de 希腊的 *a* Greek

xī là rén 希腊人 *n.* Greek

xī wàng 希望 *v.t.* hope

xī wàng 希望 *n* hope

xī shēng 牺牲 *v.t.* sacrifice

xī shēng de 牺牲的 *a.* sacrificial

xī miè 熄灭 *v.t* extinguish

xī miè 熄灭 *v.t.* quench

xī niú 犀牛 *n.* rhinoceros

xī han de 稀罕的 *a.* scarce

xī shì 稀释 *v.t* dilute

xī shì de 稀释的 *a* dilute

xī shū 稀疏 *v.t.* thin

xī shū de 稀疏的 *a.* sparse

xī xì 嬉戏 *v.i.* frolic

xī yì 蜥蜴 *n.* lizard

xī 膝 *n.* knee

xí guàn 习惯 *n.* habit

xí guàn 习惯 *n* wont

xí guàn de 习惯的 *a.* wonted

xí guàn yú 习惯于 *a.* accustomed

xí sú 习俗 *n.* custom

xí jī 袭击 *n.* assault

xí jī 袭击 *n.* attack

xí jī 袭击 *v.t.* attack

xǐ 洗 *v.t.* wash

xǐ 洗 *n* wash

xí lǐ 洗礼 *n.* baptism

xí zǎo 洗澡 *n* ablution

xí zǎo 洗澡 *v.t* bathe

xǐ ěr qì 洗耳器 *n.* aurilave

xǐ jié 洗劫 *v.i.* loot

xǐ jié 洗劫 *v.t.* ransack

xǐ liǎn pén 洗脸盆 *n.* lavatory

xǐ tóu fa 洗头发 *v.t.* shampoo

xǐ tóu jì 洗头剂 *n.* shampoo

xǐ yǎn yào shuǐ 洗眼药水 *n* eyewash

xǐ yè 洗液 *n.* lotion

xǐ yī 洗衣 *v.t.* launder

xǐ yī diàn 洗衣店 *n.* laundry

xǐ yī jī 洗衣机 *n.* washer

xǐ yī nǚ gōng 洗衣女工 *n.* laundress

xǐ zhǐ pái 洗纸牌 *n.* shuffle

xǐ ài 喜爱 *n* favour

xǐ ài de 喜爱的 *a* favourite

xǐ bú zì jìn de 喜不自禁的 *a.* hilarious

xǐ huan 喜欢 *v.t.* like

xǐ huan chǎo jià de 喜欢吵架的 *a.* quarrelsome

xǐ huan de 喜欢的 *a* fond

xǐ huan chǎo jià de 喜欢吵架的 *a.* quarrelsome

xǐ huan de 喜欢的 *a* fond

xǐ huan de shì wù 喜欢的事物 *n* favourite

xǐ jù 喜剧 *n.* comedy

xǐ jù jiā 喜剧家 *n.* comedian

xǐ nù wú cháng de 喜怒无常的 *a.* moody

xǐ qìng de 喜庆的 *a* festive

xì jù 戏剧 *n* drama

xì jù de 戏剧的 *a* comic

xì jù de 戏剧的 *a* dramatic

xì jù de 戏剧的 *a.* theatrical

xì nòng 戏弄 *v.t.* rag

xì nòng 戏弄 *v.t.* tease

xì xuè 戏谑 *n.* raillery

xì gōng mù jiang 细工木匠 *n.* joiner

xì bāo 细胞 *n.* cell

xì bāo de 细胞的 *adj* cellular

xì jié 细节 *n* detail

xì jūn 细菌 *n.* bacteria

xì wēi chā bié 细微差别 *n.* nuance

xì xiǎng 细想 *v.t* contemplate

xì xiǎng 细想 *v.t.* mull

xì xiǎo de 细小的 *a.* minute

xì xiǎo de 细小的 *a.* small

xì yǔ 细雨 *n* drizzle

xì zhī 细枝 *n.* twig

xì bó 系泊 *n.* moorings

xì liè 系列 *n* collection

xì liè 系列 *n.* series

xì shéng 系绳 *n.* tether

xì shù 系数 *n.* coefficient

xì tǒng 系统 *n.* system

xiā gǎo 瞎搞 *v.i* fiddle

xiá cī 瑕疵 *n* blemish

xiá cī 瑕疵 *n* flaw

xiá dào 狭道 *n.* defile

xiá gǔ 峡谷 *n.* ravine

xià 下 *adv* down

xià bā 下巴 *n.* chin

xià báo 下雹 *v.i* hail

xià chén 下沉 *v.i.* sink

xià cì 下次 *adv.* next

xià diē 下跌 *v.i.* fall

xià è 下颚 *n.* maxilla

xià fù bù 下腹部 *n.* midriff

xià hu 吓唬 *v.t.* terrify

xià jiàn de rén 下贱的人 *n* churl

xià jiàng 下降 *v.t.* avale

xià jiàng 下降 *n* decline

xià jiàng 下降 *v.i.* descend

xià jiàng de 下降的 *a* downward

xià liú de 下流的 *a.* indecent

xià liú de 下流的 *a.* nasty

xià máo mao yǔ 下毛毛雨 *v.i* drizzle

xià mian 下面 *adv* below

xià mian 下面 *adv* beneath

xià mian 下面 *prep* beneath

xià mian de 下面的 *a.* nether

xià mian de 下面的 *a* under

xià pàn duàn 下判断 *v.i.* judge

xià xuě 下雪 *v.i.* snow

xià yǔ 下雨 *v.i.* rain

xià dāi de 吓呆的 *a.* aghast

xià yí tiào 吓一跳 *v.t.* startle

xià jì de 夏季的 *adj* aestival

xià tiān 夏天 *n.* summer

xiān nǚ 仙女 *n.* fairy

xiān rén zhǎng 仙人掌 *n.* cactus

xiān fēng 先锋 *n.* spearhead

xiān jiàn zhī míng 先见之明 *n* foresight

xiān jué tiáo jiàn 先决条件 *n* prerequisite

xiān lì 先例 *n.* antecedent

xiān lì 先例 *n.* precedent

xiān lìng 先令 *n.* shilling

xiān qián de 先前的 *a.* antecedent

xiān qū zhě 先驱者 *n.* precursor

xiān sheng 先生 *n.* Messrs

xiān sheng 先生 *n.* mister

xiān sheng 先生 *n.* sir

xiān yú 先于 *v.* precede

xiān zhī 先知 *n.* oracle

xiān wéi 纤维 *n* fibre

xián chě 闲扯 *n.* prattle

xián guàng yú 闲逛于 *v.t.* ramble

xián hún 闲混 *v.i.* lounge

xián liáo 闲聊 *n.* gossip

xián liáo 闲聊 *v.i.* prattle

xián sǎn 闲散 *n.* idleness

xián míng de 贤明的 *a.* sage

xián wèi nóng de 咸味浓的 a. salty

xián wù 嫌恶 n dislike

xián yí 嫌疑 n. suspicion

xián yí fàn 嫌疑犯 n suspect

xiǎn hè 显赫 n eminance

xiǎn rán de 显然的 a. evident

xiǎn shì 显示 n display

xiǎn wēi jìng 显微镜 n. microscope

xiǎn wēi jìng de 显微镜的 a. microscopic

xiǎn wēi xué 显微学 n. micrology

xiǎn xiàn 显现 n. manifestation

xiǎn yào rén wù 显要人物 n. notability

xiǎn zhù de 显著的 a. conspicuous

xiǎn zhù de 显著的 a. salient

xiǎn è de 险恶的 a. sinister

xiǎn jùn de 险峻的 a. steep

xiàn 县 n. county

xiàn chǎng 现场 n. locale

xiàn chǎng 现场 n. site

xiàn dài de 现代的 a contemporary

xiàn dài de 现代的 a. modern

xiàn dài xìng 现代性 n. modernity

xiàn jīn 现金 n. cash

xiàn shì de 现世的 a. mundane

xiàn shí zhǔ yì zhě 现实主义者 n. realist

xiàn xiàng 现象 n. phenomenon

xiàn xiàng de 现象的 a. phenomenal

xiàn zài de 现在的 a. present

xiàn zhì 限制 v bound

xiàn zhì 限制 v.t confine

xiàn zhì 限制 v.t. limit

xiàn zhì 限制 n. limitation

xiàn zhì 限制 v.t. restrict

xiàn zhì 限制 n. restriction

xiàn zhì 限制 n. stricture

xiàn 线 n. line

xiàn 线 n. thread

xiàn lù 线路 n. circuit

xiàn lù 线路 n. wiring

xiàn suǒ 线索 n clue

xiàn tuán 线团 n. clew

xiàn fǎ 宪法 n constitution

xiàn zhāng 宪章 n charter

xiàn jì 献祭 v.t. consecrate

xiàn mèi 献媚 v.t beslaver

xiàn shēn 献身 v.t devote

xiàn jǐng 陷阱 n. pitfall

xiàn jǐng 陷阱 n. snare

xiàn jǐng 陷阱 n. trap

xiàn rù 陷入 n. slump

xiàn rù ní zhǎo 陷入泥沼 v.t. slough

xiàn 腺 n. gland

xiàn mù 羡慕 v envy

xiāng chóu 乡愁 n. nostalgia

xiāng cūn de 乡村的 a. rustic

xiāng shēn 乡绅 n. squire

xiāng xia de 乡下的 a. rural

xiāng xia rén 乡下人 n boor

xiāng xia rén 乡下人 n rustic

xiāng xia xí qì 乡下习气 n. provincialism

xiāng 香 n. incense

xiāng cài 香菜 n. coriander

xiāng jiāo 香蕉 n. banana

xiāng liào 香料 n. spice

xiāng lú 香炉 n censer

xiāng shuǐ 香水 n. perfume

xiāng wèi 香味 n. fragrance

xiāng yān 香烟 n. cigarette

xiāng zhī shù 香脂树 n. balsam

xiāng zhī yóu 香脂油 n. balm

xiāng chèn de 相称的 a becoming

xiāng dāng 相当 adv. pretty

xiāng dāng 相当 adv. quite

xiāng dāng dà de 相当大的 a considerable

xiāng dāng dà de 相当大的 a. sizable

xiāng dāng de 相当的 a equivalent

xiāng děng de 相等的 a equal

xiāng duì de 相对的 a. opposite

xiāng duì wù 相对物 n. counterpart

xiāng fǎn 相反 n. antipodes

xiāng fǎn 相反 n reverse
xiāng fǎn de 相反的 a contrary
xiāng fǎn de 相反的 a. reverse
xiāng fǎn dì 相反地 adv.
  backward
xiāng guān 相关 n. correlation
xiāng hù guān lián 相互关联
  v.t. correlate
xiāng hù yī lài de 相互依赖的
  a. interdependent
xiāng hùn hé 相混合 v.i mix
xiāng pèi 相配 v.i. match
xiāng sì 相似 adv alike
xiāng sì 相似 v.t. resemble
xiāng sì 相似 n. similarity
xiāng sì 相似 n. similitude
xiāng sì chù 相似处 n.
  resemblance
xiāng sì de 相似的 a. analogous
xiāng sì de 相似的 a. like
xiāng sì wù 相似物 n. likeness
xiāng tóng 相同 a. alike
xiāng tóng de 相同的 a. same
xiāng xìn 相信 v.t believe
xiāng 箱 n box
xiāng 箱 n. case
xiāng 箱 n. casing
xiāng bǎn 镶板 n. panel
xiāng biān 镶边 v.t border
xiāng yǐ bǎo shí 镶以宝石 v.t.
  jewel
xiáng shù 详述 v.t detail
xiáng shù 详述 v.t. recount
xiáng xì qíng jié 详细情节 n.
  particular
xiáng xì shuō míng 详细说明
  v.t. specify
xiáng yǒu shēng wàng de 享有
  声望的 a. prestigious
xiǎng shòu 享受 v.t enjoy
xiǎng 响 v.i. sound
xiǎng 想 v.t. think
xiǎng shuì de 想睡的 a. sleepy
xiǎng xiàng 想像 v.t conceive
xiǎng xiàng 想象 v.t fancy
xiǎng xiàng 想像 v.t. imagine
xiǎng xiàng 想像 v.t. picture
xiǎng xiàng 想像 v.t. visualize

xiǎng xiàng de 想像的 a.
  imaginary
xiǎng xiàng de 想像的 a.
  imaginative
xiǎng xiàng lì 想像力 n.
  imagination
xiǎng yào 想要 v.t desire
xiǎng yào 想要 v.t. want
xiàng 向 prep. towards
xiàng … tóu rēng shí tou 向…投
  扔石头 v.t. stone
xiàng běi fāng 向北方 adv. north
xiàng dōng 向东 adv east
xiàng hòu 向后 adv. aback
xiàng hòu 向后 adv. back
xiàng nán fāng 向南方 adv
  south
xiàng nèi 向内 adv. inwards
xiàng nèi de 向内的 a. inward
xiàng qián 向前 adv. onwards
xiàng qián de 向前的 a. forward
xiàng qián de 向前的 a. onward
xiàng qián dì 向前地 adv
  forward
xiàng shàng 向上 adv. up
xiàng shàng de 向上的 a.
  upward
xiàng wài 向外 adv outwards
xiàng wài de 向外的 a. outward
xiàng xī 向西 adv. west
xiàng xī 向西 adv. westerly
xiàng xī de 向西的 a. westerly
xiàng xià 向下 adv downwards
xiàng xià dì 向下地 adv
  downward
xiàng xià měng chōng 向下猛冲
  v.i. swoop
xiàng yòu 向右 adv right
xiàng zhè biān 向这边 adv.
  hither
xiàng... zhì yì 向…致意 v.t. salute
xiàng jī 相机 n. camera
xiàng piàn 相片 n photo
xiàng piàn 相片 n photograph
xiàng mù 项目 n. item
xiàng quān 项圈 n. necklace
xiàng 象 n elephant
xiàng 象 prep like
xiàng bí chóng 象鼻虫 n. weevil

xiàng fū 象夫 *n.* mahout

xiàng shēng cí 象声词 *n.* onomatopoeia

xiàng shì 象是 *v.i.* seem

xiàng yá 象牙 *n.* ivory

xiàng zhēng 象征 *n* emblem

xiàng zhēng 象征 *v.t.* symbolize

xiàng zhēng de 象征的 *a.* symbolic

xiàng zhēng shóu fǎ 象征手法 *n.* symbolism

xiàng sì biān xíng de 像四边形的 *a.* quadrangular

xiàng niú nǎi de 像牛奶的 *a.* milky

xiàng tiān é róng de 像天鹅绒的 *a.* velvety

xiàng jiāo 橡胶 *n.* rubber

xiàng shù 橡树 *n.* oak

xiàng zǐ 橡子 *n.* acorn

xiāo xiàng 肖像 *n.* imagery

xiāo xiàng 肖像 *n.* portrait

xiāo xiàng huà 肖像画 *n.* portraiture

xiāo dú 消毒 *n.* sterilization

xiāo dú 消毒 *v.t.* sterilize

xiāo fèi 消费 *v.t* consume

xiāo fèi 消费 *n* consumption

xiāo fèi 消费 *n* expenditure

xiāo fèi liàng 消费量 *n* consumption

xiāo fèi shuì 消费税 *n* excise

xiāo guò dú de 消过毒的 *a.* antiseptic

xiāo huà 消化 *v.t.* digest

xiāo huà 消化 *v.t.* stomach

xiāo huà bù liáng 消化不良 *n.* indigestion

xiāo huà lì 消化力 *n* digestion

xiāo jí xìng 消极性 *n.* negative

xiāo jiǎn 消减 *v.t* curtail

xiāo miè 消灭 *n.* obliteration

xiāo miè hén jì 消灭痕迹 *v.t.* obliterate

xiāo mó 消磨 *v.t.* while

xiāo qiǎn 消遣 *n.* pastime

xiāo qiǎn 消遣 *n.* recreation

xiāo qù 消去 *v.t* efface

xiāo shì 消逝 *n* elapse

xiāo shī 消失 *v.i* disappear

xiāo shī 消失 *v.i.* vanish

xiāo shòu 消瘦 *v.i.* pine

xiāo xi 消息 *n.* information

xiāo xi 消息 *n.pl.* tidings

xiāo yīn qì 消音器 *n.* silencer

xiāo yè 宵夜 *n.* supper

xiāo jìn lìng 宵禁令 *n* curfew

xiāo shòu zhě 销售者 *n.* seller

xiāo zhāng de 嚣张的 *a.* arrogant

xiáo chǒu 小丑 *n* buffoon

xiáo chǒu 小丑 *n* clown

xiáo jiě 小姐 *n.* miss

xiáo pǎo 小跑 *n* trot

xiǎo qiǎo de 小巧的 *a.* dainty

xiǎo 小 *n.* smallness

xiǎo bǎ 小把 *n.* wisp

xiǎo biàn 小便 *v.i.* urinate

xiǎo biàn 小便 *n.* urination

xiǎo biǎn dòu 小扁豆 *n.* lentil

xiǎo bìng 小病 *n.* ailment

xiǎo bō li guǎn 小玻璃管 *n.* cuvette

xiǎo bù fèn 小部份 *n.* fraction

xiǎo cè zǐ 小册子 *n* booklet

xiǎo cè zǐ 小册子 *n* brochure

xiǎo cè zǐ 小册子 *n.* pamphlet

xiǎo cè zǐ 小册子 *n* tract

xiǎo cè zǐ zuò zhě 小册子作者 *n.* pamphleteer

xiǎo cháo 小潮 *a.* neap

xiǎo cūn 小村 *n.* hamlet

xiǎo dǎo 小岛 *n.* isle

xiǎo dāo 小刀 *n.* knife

xiǎo de 小的 *a.* little

xiǎo duì 小队 *n.* squad

xiǎo é luǎn shí 小鹅卵石 *n.* pebble

xiǎo fàn 小贩 *n.* vendor

xiǎo fèi 小费 *n* fee

xiǎo fèi 小费 *n.* gratuity

xiǎo fèi 小费 *v.t.* tip

xiǎo hé 小河 *n.* rivulet

xiǎo gǒu 小狗 *n.* puppy

xiǎo gǒu 小狗 *n.* whelp

xiǎo gǔ 小谷 *n* dale

xiǎo hú zǐ 小胡子 *n.* moustache

xiǎo huán 小环 *n* annulet

xiǎo jiān tǎ 小尖塔 *n.* pinnacle

xiǎo jiào táng 小教堂 *n.* chapel

xiǎo jīng líng 小精灵 *n* elf

xiǎo kuài dì tǎn 小块地毯 *n.* rug

xiǎo liú máng 小流氓 *n.* hooligan

xiǎo lù 小路 *n.* lane

xiǎo lù 小路 *n.* path

xiǎo luó bo 小萝卜 *n.* radish

xiǎo mài 小麦 *n* far

xiǎo mài 小麦 *n.* wheat

xiǎo māo 小猫 *n.* kitten

xiǎo mén 小门 *n.* wicket

xiǎo niú 小牛 *n.* calf

xiǎo pài xì 小派系 *n* faction

xiǎo píng 小瓶 *n.* vial

xiǎo pù bù 小瀑布 *n.* cascade

xiǎo qi de 小气的 *a.* niggardly

xiǎo qi de 小气的 *a.* stingy

xiǎo qi guǐ 小气鬼 *n.* niggard

xiǎo qiū 小丘 *n.* hillock

xiǎo shān 小山 *n.* hill

xiǎo shān yáng 小山羊 *n.* kid

xiǎo shù 小树 *n.* sapling

xiǎo shǔ 小鼠 *n.* mouse

xiǎo shù lín 小树林 *n.* coppice

xiǎo shuì 小睡 *n* nap

xiǎo shuì yī 小睡衣 *n.* nightie

xiǎo shuō 小说 *n* novel

xiǎo shuō 小说 *n* fiction

xiǎo shuō jiā 小说家 *n.* novelist

xiǎo tí qín 小提琴 *n* fiddle

xiǎo tí qín 小提琴 *n.* violin

xiǎo tí qín jiā 小提琴家 *n.* violinist

xiǎo wū 小屋 *n.* cote

xiǎo wū 小屋 *n* cottage

xiǎo wū 小屋 *n.* lodge

xiǎo xī 小溪 *n.* beck

xiǎo xī 小溪 *n.* brook

xiǎo xī 小溪 *n.* creek

xiǎo xī 小溪 *n.* stream

xiǎo xī 小溪 *n.* streamlet

xiǎo xiàng 小巷 *n.* alley

xiǎo xiàng quān 小项圈 *n.* necklet

xiǎo xīn 小心 *a* careful

xiǎo xíng mó tuō chē 小型摩托车 *n.* scooter

xiǎo xíng qì jiàn 小型器件 *a.* miniature

xiǎo xué jiào shī 小学教师 *n.* pedagogue

xiǎo yǐn xiū yuàn yuàn zhǎng 小隐修院院长 *n* prior

xiǎo zhēng lùn 小争论 *n.* skirmish

xiǎo zhī 小枝 *n.* sprig

xiào 笑 *v.i* chuckle

xiào 笑 *n.* laugh

xiào 笑 *v.i* laugh

xiào bǐng 笑柄 *n.* mockery

xiào hua 笑话 *n.* jest

xiào hua 笑话 *n.* joke

xiào shēng 笑声 *n.* laughter

xiào shùn de 孝顺的 *a* dutiful

xiào guǒ 效果 *n* effect

xiào lǜ 效率 *n* efficiency

xiào lǜ gāo de 效率高的 *a* efficient

xiào yòng 效用 *n.* utility

xiào zhǎng 校长 *n.* principal

xiào chuǎn 哮喘 *n.* asthma

xiē zhù 楔住 *v.t.* wedge

xiē zi 楔子 *n.* wedge

xiē sī dǐ lǐ de 歇斯底里的 *a.* hysterical

xiē sī dǐ lǐ zhèng 歇斯底里症 *n.* hysteria

xiē zi 蝎子 *n.* scorpion

xié dìng 协定 *n.* treaty

xié huì 协会 *n.* association

xié huì 协会 *n.* union

xié shāng 协商 *v.t* concert

xié shāng 协商 *v.i* confer

xié shāng 协商 *v.t* consult

xié tiáo 协调 *v.t* co-ordinate

xié tiáo 协调 *n* co-ordination

xié tiáo de 协调的 *a.* co-ordinate

xié yì shū 协议书 *n.* agreement

xié è 邪恶 *n* evil

xié è de 邪恶的 *a* evil

xié è de 邪恶的 *a.* sinful

xié è de 邪恶的 *a.* vicious

xié è de 邪恶的 *a.* wicked

xié jiào 邪教 *n* cult

xié pò 胁迫 *v.t* menace

xié pō 斜坡 *n* slant

xié pō 斜坡 *n.* slope

xié shì 斜视 *n* squint

xié tǐ de 斜体的 *a.* italic

xié tǐ zì 斜体字 *n.* italics

xié zhuó yǎn kàn 斜着眼看 *v.i.* squint

xié 鞋 *n.* shoe

xié dǐ 鞋底 *n.* sole

xié dài 携带 *adj.* borne

xié jiang 鞋匠 *n* cobbler

xiě 写 *v.t.* pen

xiě 写 *v.t.* write

xiě shí zhǔ yì 写实主义 *n.* realism

xiě zài hòu bian de 写在后边的 *adj.* adscript

xiě zhuàn lüè 写传略 *v.t.* profile

xiě lín lín de 血淋淋的 *a* bloody

xiè lòu 泄露 *v.t* divulge

xiè chū 泻出 *v.i.* spill

xiè jì 泻剂 *n.* purgative

xiè yào 泻药 *n.* laxative

xiè chú fù hè 卸除负荷 *v.t.* unburden

xiè huò 卸货 *n.* discharge

xiè xià 卸下 *v.t* discharge

xiè dú 亵渎 *v.t.* profane

xiè dú de 亵渎的 *a.* profane

xiè dú shèng wù 亵渎圣物 *n.* sacrilege

xīn 心 *n.* heart

xīn 心 *n.* mind

xīn ài de rén 心爱的人 *n* beloved

xīn jì 心悸 *n.* palpitation

xīn jiǎo tòng 心绞痛 *n* angina

xīn lǐ 心理 *n.* mentality

xīn lǐ liáo fǎ 心理疗法 *n.* psychotherapy

xīn lǐ xué 心理学 *n.* psychology

xīn lǐ xué jiā 心理学家 *n.* psychologist

xīn líng 心灵 *n.* psyche

xīn líng 心灵 *n.* soul

xīn líng de 心灵的 *a.* psychological

xīn líng de 心灵的 *a.* spiritual

xīn líng gǎn yìng 心灵感应 *n.* telepathy

xīn líng gǎn yìng de 心灵感应的 *a.* telepathic

xīn líng gǎn yìng zhě 心灵感应者 *n.* telepathist

xīn qíng 心情 *n.* mood

xīn xù bù níng 心绪不宁 *v.t.* perturb

xīn zàng de 心脏的 *adj* cardiacal

xīn zàng xíng de 心脏形的 *adj.* cordate

xīn zhì shuāi ruò 心智衰弱 *v.t* fatigue

xīn kǔ gōng zuò 辛苦工作 *v.i.* toil

xīn là 辛辣 *n.* pungency

xīn là de 辛辣的 *a.* spicy

xīn suān 辛酸 *n.* poignancy

xīn suān de 辛酸的 *a.* poignant

xīn shǎng 欣赏 *n.* admiration

xīn shǎng 欣赏 *v.t.* admire

xīn shǎng 欣赏 *v.t.* appreciate

xīn 锌 *n.* zinc

xīn bīng 新兵 *n.* recruit

xīn chén dài xiè 新陈代谢 *n.* metabolism

xīn de 新的 *a.* new

xīn láng 新郎 *n.* bridegroom

xīn láng 新郎 *n.* groom

xīn niáng 新娘 *n* bride

xīn qí 新奇 *n.* novelty

xīn shí qì shí dài de 新石器时代的 *a.* neolithic

xīn shǒu 新手 *n.* novice

xīn tāi miàn 新胎面 *n.* retread

xīn wén 新闻 *n.* news

xīn wén jì zhě 新闻记者 *n.* journalist

xīn wén yè 新闻业 *n.* journalism

xīn xiān de 新鲜的 *a.* fresh

xīn yǐng de 新颖的 *a.* novel

xīn zhǎng chū de ròu 新长出的肉 *n* quick

xīn shuǐ 薪水 *n* emolument

xīn shuǐ 薪水 *n.* salary

xīn zī 薪资 *n* pay

xìn 信 *n* letter

xìn hào 信号 n. signal

xìn fēng 信封 n envelope

xìn lài 信赖 v.i. depend

xìn niàn 信念 n creed

xìn rèn 信任 n. reliance

xìn rèn 信任 v.t trust

xìn rèn de 信任的 a. trustful

xìn tú 信徒 n. apostle

xìn tú 信徒 n. votary

xìn xīn 信心 n confidence

xìn xīn 信心 n faith

xìn yǎng 信仰 n belief

xìn yòng 信用 n credit

xīng fèn 兴奋 adv. aglow

xīng fèn de 兴奋的 adj alacrious

xīng fèn jì 兴奋剂 n agonist

xīng fèn jì 兴奋剂 n. stimulant

xīng lóng 兴隆 v.i. prosper

xīng wàng 兴旺 v.i. thrive

xīng hào 星号 n. asterisk

xīng qī 星期 n. week

xīng qī liù 星期六 n. Saturday

xīng qī rì 星期日 n. Sunday

xīng qī sān 星期三 n. Wednesday

xīng qī sì 星期四 n. Thursday

xīng qī wǔ 星期五 n. Friday

xīng qī yī 星期一 n. Monday

xīng qún 星群 n. asterism

xīng xì 星系 n. galaxy

xīng xing 星星 n. star

xīng zhuàng de 星状的 adj. asteroid

xīng zuò 星座 n. constellation

xīng yún 星云 n. nebula

xíng 行 v.i. step

xíng cì 行刺 v.t. assassinate

xíng li 行李 n. baggage

xíng li 行李 n. luggage

xíng rén 行人 n. pedestrian

xíng shǒu yín 行手淫 v.i. masturbate

xíng wéi 行为 n. act

xíng wéi 行为 n behaviour

xíng wéi 行为 n deed

xíng wéi bú zhèng 行为不正 n. misconduct

xíng wéi jú zhǐ 行为举止 n conduct

xíng xīng 行星 n. planet

xíng xīng de 行星的 a. planetary

xíng zhèng 行政 n. administration

xíng zhèng de 行政的 a. administrative

xíng zhèng qū 行政区 n canton

xíng zhèng rén yuán 行政人员 n. administrator

xíng fá de 刑罚的 a. penal

xíng chéng 形成 v.t. form

xíng róng cí 形容词 n. adjective

xíng tài 形态 n. modality

xíng xíng sè sè de 形形色色的 a. multifarious

xíng zhuàng 形状 n. shape

xǐng lái 醒来 v.i. rouse

xǐng 醒 a awake

xìng qù 兴趣 n. interest

xìng 杏 n. apricot

xìng rén 杏仁 n. almond

xìng 性 n. gender

xìng 性 n. sex

xìng ài de 性爱的 a erotic

xìng bié 性别 n. sexuality

xìng de 性的 a. sexual

xìng qíng bào zào 性情暴躁 a. temperamental

xìng qíng gǔ guài de rén 性情古怪的人 n. jerk

xìng zhì de 性质的 a. qualitative

xìng 姓 n. surname

xìng fú 幸福 n felicity

xìng yùn de 幸运的 a. fortunate

xìng yùn de 幸运的 a. lucky

xìng yùn dì 幸运地 adv. luckily

xiōng di 兄弟 n brother

xiōng di de 兄弟的 a. fraternal

xiōng di shā hài de xíng wéi 兄弟杀害的行为 n. fratricide

xiōng měng de 凶猛的 a fierce

xiōng shā 凶杀 n. murder

xiōng shā 凶杀 v.t. murder

xiōng shǒu 凶手 n cain

xiōng shǒu 凶手 n. thug

xiōng 胸 n breast

xiōng bù 胸部 n bosom

xiōng bù 胸部 *n* chest

xióng biàn de 雄辩的 *a* eloquent

xióng é 雄鹅 *n.* gander

xióng māo 雄猫 *n.* tomcat

xióng rén yú 雄人鱼 *n.* merman

xióng 熊 *n* bear

xiū gēng de 休耕的 *a* fallow

xiū huì 休会 *v.t.* prorogue

xiū huì 休会 *n.* recess

xiū xi 休息 *n* break

xiū xi 休息 *n.* repose

xiū xi 休息 *v.i.* repose

xiū xi 休息 *v.i.* rest

xiū xi suǒ 休息所 *n.* roost

xiū xián shì 休闲室 *n.* lounge

xiū zhàn 休战 *n.* armistice

xiū bǔ 修补 *v.t.* mend

xiū bǔ 修补 *v.t.* patch

xiū bǔ 修补 *v.t.* piece

xiū bǔ jiàng 修补匠 *n.* tinker

xiū cí 修辞 *n.* rhetoric

xiū cí xué de 修辞学的 *a.* rhetorical

xiū dào shēng huó 修道生活 *n* monasticism

xiū dào yuàn 修道院 *n.* abbey

xiū dào yuàn 修道院 *n.* cloister

xiū gǎi 修改 *n* alteration

xiū gǎi 修改 *v.t.* amend

xiū gǎi 修改 *n.* amendment

xiū gǎi 修改 *n.pl.* amends

xiū jiǎn 修剪 *v.t.* prune

xiū jiǎn 修剪 *n* trim

xiū jiǎn 修剪 *v.t.* trim

xiū lǐ 修理 *n.* repair

xiū nǔ 修女 *n.* nun

xiū nǔ tóu jin 修女头巾 *n.* wimple

xiū zhǐ jia 修指甲 *n.* manicure

xiū chǐ 羞耻 *n.* shame

xiū qiè 羞怯 *n.* timidity

xiū qiè de 羞怯的 *a.* sheepish

xiù zi 袖子 *n* sleeve

xiù 嗅 *v.i.* sniff

xiù chū liè wù 嗅出猎物 *v.i.* wind

xiù 锈 *n.* rust

xū gòu de 虚构的 *a* fictitious

xū gòu de shì 虚构的事 *n* figment

xū huàn de 虚幻的 *adj* mock

xū jiǎ de 虚假的 *a.* mendacious

xū kuā de 虚夸的 *a.* pompous

xū nǐ 虚拟 *a* virtual

xū ruò 虚弱 *n* debility

xū ruò 虚弱 *n.* infirmity

xū ruò de (rén) 虚弱的(人) *n.* weakling

xū wěi 虚伪 *n.* pretence

xū wú zhǔ yì 虚无主义 *n.* nihilism

xū zhāng shēng shì 虚张声势 *v.t* bluff

xū qiú 需求 *n* demand

xū qiú 需求 *n.* requirement

xū yào 需要 *n.* need

xū yào 需要 *v.t.* require

xū yào 需要 *n* want

xū yào de 需要的 *a.* needful

xú dé jìn de 徐得尽的 *n.* aliquot

xú fēi 徐非 *conj.* unless

xú kě 许可 *v.t.* license

xú kě 许可 *n.* permission

xú kě zhèng 许可证 *n.* permit

xǔ duō 许多 *n.* multitude

xǔ duō de 许多的 *a.* many

xǔ duō de 许多的 *a.* numerous

xǔ nuò 许诺 *v.t.* pledge

xǔ pèi 许配 *v.t* betroth

xù 序 *n* foreword

xù 序 *n.* preface

xù liè 序列 *n.* sequence

xù yán 序言 *n.* prologue

xù shù 叙述 *n.* narration

xù shù 叙述 *v.t.* relate

xù shù de 叙述的 *a.* narrative

xù jí 续集 *n.* sequel

xuān bù 宣布 *v.t.* announce

xuān bù 宣布 *n.* announcement

xuān bù 宣布 *v.t.* declare

xuān bù 宣布 *v.t.* proclaim

xuān chēng 宣称 *n* claim

xuān chuán 宣传 *v.t.* advertise

xuān chuán 宣传 *n.* propaganda

xuān chuán 宣传 *n.* propagation

xuān chuán 宣传 *n.* publicity

xuān chuán 宣传 *v.t.* publicize

xuān chuán zhě 宣传者 *n.* propagandist

xuān gào 宣告 *n* declaration

xuān pàn wú zuì 宣判无罪 *v.t.* acquit

xuān pàn yǒu zuì 宣判有罪 *v.t.* convict

xuān shì hòu shì fàng 宣誓后释放 *v.t.* parole

xuān shì shū 宣誓书 *n* affidavit

xuān yán 宣言 *n.* manifesto

xuān yán 宣言 *n.* proclamation

xuān huá 喧哗 *n* babel

xuān nào 喧闹 *n.* racket

xuān nào de 喧闹的 *a.* uproarious

xuān nào wán shuǎ 喧闹玩耍 *v.i.* romp

xuān nào yóu wán 喧闹游玩 *n.* romp

xuān rǎng 喧嚷 *v.i* bray

xuān xiāo 喧嚣 *n* din

xuán xué 玄学 *n.* metaphysics

xuán xué de 玄学的 *a.* metaphysical

xuán lǜ 旋律 *n.* melody

xuán lǜ de 旋律的 *a.* melodious

xuán wō 旋涡 *n.* whirlpool

xuán zhuǎn 旋转 *v.i.* revolve

xuán zhuǎn 旋转 *v.i.* rotate

xuán zhuǎn 旋转 *n.* rotation

xuán zhuǎn 旋转 *n* whirl

xuán zhuǎn 旋转 *v.t.* pivot

xuán zhuǎn de 旋转的 *a.* rotary

xuán zhuǎn mù mǎ 旋转木马 *n.* whirligig

xuán guà 悬挂 *v.t.* hang

xuán guà 悬挂 *n.* suspense

xuán yá 悬崖 *n.* cliff

xuǎn jǔ 选举 *n* election

xuǎn jǔ 选举 *n.* vote

xuǎn jǔ qū 选举区 *n* electorate

xuǎn chū 选出 *v.t.* single

xuǎn jí 选集 *n.* anthology

xuǎn mín 选民 *n.* constituent

xuǎn piào 选票 *n* ballot

xuǎn qū 选区 *n* constituency

xuǎn zé 选择 *n.* choice

xuǎn zé 选择 *v.t.* choose

xuǎn zé 选择 *v.i.* opt

xuǎn zé 选择 *n.* option

xuǎn zé 选择 *n.* pick

xuǎn zé 选择 *v.t.* select

xuǎn zé 选择 *n.* selection

xuǎn zé de 选择的 *a.* selective

xuǎn 癣 *n.* ringworm

xuàn fēng 旋风 *n.* cyclone

xuàn fēng 旋风 *n.* whirlwind

xuàn yào 炫耀 *n.* pomposity

xuē... pí xiāo...皮 *v.t.* peel

xuē ruò 削弱 *v.t.&i* weaken

xuē zi 靴子 *n* boot

xué 学 *v.i.* learn

xué huì 学会 *n.* institute

xué jiū shì de 学究式的 *a.* pedantic

xué qī 学期 *n.* semester

xué qī 学期 *n.* term

xué sheng 学生 *n.* pupil

xué sheng 学生 *n.* student

xué shì 学士 *n.* bachelor

xué shù de 学术的 *a* academic

xué wèi 学位 *n.* qualification

xué wèi 学位 *n* degree

xué xí 学习 *n.* learning

xué xí 学习 *v.i.* study

xué xí zhě 学习者 *n.* learner

xué xiào 学校 *n.* school

xué xiào de 学校的 *a.* scholastic

xué yàng 学样 *v.t* mimic

xué yuàn 学院 *n* academy

xué yuàn 学院 *n* college

xué zhě 学者 *n.* scholar

xuě 雪 *n.* snow

xuě jiā 雪茄 *n.* cigar

xuě jiā yān 雪茄烟 *n* cheroot

xuě shuǐ 雪水 *n.* slush

xuě sōng 雪松 *n.* cedar

xuè 血 *n* blood

xuè tǒng 血统 *n.* lineage

xūn má 荨麻 *n.* nettle

xūn yī cǎo 薰衣草 *n.* lavender

xūn ròu 熏肉 *n.* bacon

xún háng 巡航 *v.i.* cruise

xún luó 巡逻 *v.i.* patrol

xún luó 巡逻 *n* patrol

xún yáng jiàn 巡洋舰 *n* cruiser

xún mì shī shì chuán zhǐ zhě 寻
  觅失事船只者 *n.* wrecker
xún qiú 寻求 *v.t.* seek
xún zhǎo 寻找 *v.t.* quest
xún wèn 询问 *n.* inquiry
xún wèn 询问 *v.t* query
xún huán 循环 *n* circulation
xún huán 循环 *n* cycle
xún huán de 循环的 *a* cyclic
xún huán de 循环的 *a.*
  recurrent
xùn dǎo 训导 *v.t.* moralize
xùn liàn 训练 *v.t.* train
xùn liàn 训练 *n.* training
xùn sù 迅速 *n.* rapidity
xùn sù de 迅速的 *adv.* apace
xùn sù de 迅速的 *a.* swift
xùn sù qián jìn 迅速前进 *v.i.*
  speed
xùn fú 驯服 *v.t.* tame
xùn jiāo 殉教 *n.* martyrdom
xùn jiāo zhě 殉教者 *n.* martyr

Y

yā 压 *v.t.* press
yā biǎn 压扁 *v.t.* squash
yā zhì 压制 *v.t.* oppress
yā zhì 压制 *n.* oppression
yā zhì 压制 *v.t.* quell
yā zhì 压制 *n.* repression
yā zhì de 压制的 *a.* oppressive
yā dǎo 压倒 *v.t.* overwhelm
yā fú 压服 *v.t.* overpower
yā lì 压力 *n.* pressure
yā lì 压力 *n.* stress
yā pò 压迫 *v.t.* weigh
yā pò zhě 压迫者 *n.* oppressor
yā suō 压缩 *v.t.* compress
yā suō 压缩 *v.t* condense
yā suō 压缩 *v.t.* constrict
yā suō de 压缩的 *a.* compact
yā tóu yùn 押头韵 *v.* alliterate
yā tóu yùn 押头韵 *n.*
  alliteration
yā yùn 押韵 *n.* rhyme
yā yùn 押韵 *v.i.* rhyme
yā jiào 鸦叫 *v.i.* caw

yā jiào shēng 鸦叫声 *n.* caw
yā piàn 鸦片 *n.* opium
yā 鸭 *n.* duck
yā jiào shēng 鸭叫声 *n* quack
yá chǐ 牙齿 *n.* tooth
yá chuáng 牙床 *n.* gum
yá kē yī sheng 牙科医生 *n*
  dentist
yá tòng 牙痛 *n.* toothache
yǎ ba 哑巴 *n.* mute
yǎ de 哑的 *a* dumb
yǎ de 哑的 *a.* mute
yǎ jù yǎn yuán 哑剧演员 *n.*
  mime
yǎ jù yǎn yuán 哑剧演员 *n.*
  mummer
yǎ zhì dà fāng de 雅致大方的 *a.*
  tasteful
yà má bù 亚麻布 *n.* linen
yà má zi 亚麻子 *n.* linseed
yān 烟 *v.i.* smoke
yān cǎo 烟草 *n.* tobacco
yān chén 烟尘 *n.* smoke
yān cōng 烟囱 *n.* chimney
yān dì 烟蒂 *n.* stub
yān wù 烟雾 *n.* smog
yān mò 淹没 *v.t* flood
yān mò 淹没 *v.t.* whelm
yān niú 阉牛 *n* bullock
yān gē 阉割 *v.t.* geld
yān zhì 腌制 *v.t* pickle
yān 腌 *v.t.* condite
yán cháng 延长 *v.t.* prolong
yán cháng 延长 *n.* prolongation
yán chí 延迟 *v.t.&i.* delay
yán chí 延迟 *v.t.* postpone
yán chí 延迟 *v.i.* procrastinate
yán hòu 延后 *v.t.* adjourn
yán qī 延期 *n.* adjournment
yán qī 延期 *n.* postponement
yán shēn 延伸 *v.t* extend
yán cí 言辞 *n.* utterance
yán yǔ 言语 *n.* speech
yán gé 严格 *n.* severity
yán gé de 严格的 *a.* rigorous
yán gé de 严格的 *a.* stark
yán gé de 严格的 *a.* strict
yán gé zhí xíng jì lù de rén 严格
  执行纪律的人 *n.* martinet

yán lì 严厉 *n.* rigour
yán lì de 严厉的 *a.* stern
yán lì de 严厉的 *a.* stringent
yán lì jù jué 严厉拒绝 *v.t.*
   rebuff
yán lì pī píng 严厉批评 *v.t.*
   castigate
yán lìng 严令 *v.t.* adjure
yán mì de 严密的 *a* thorough
yán shǒu shí jiān 严守时间 *n.*
   punctuality
yán sù 严肃 *n.* solemnity
yán sù de 严肃的 *a.* austere
yán sù de 严肃的 *a.* grave
yán sù de 严肃的 *a.* solemn
yán zhòng de 严重的 *a* serious
yán zhòng de 严重的 *a.* severe
yán rè de 炎热的 *a.* torrid
yán zhèng xìng de 炎症性的 *a.*
   inflammatory
yán zhe 沿着 *prep.* along
yán jiū 研究 *v.i.* research
yán 盐 *n.* salt
yán de 盐的 *a.* saline
yán shuǐ 盐水 *n* brine
yán xìng 盐性 *n.* salinity
yán sè 颜色 *n* colour
yǎn de 眼的 *a.* optic
yǎn huā de 眼花的 *a.* giddy
yǎn jing 眼睛 *n* eye
yǎn jing de 眼睛的 *a.* ocular
yǎn jìng shāng 眼镜商 *n.*
   optician
yǎn jing shé 眼睛蛇 *n* cobra
yǎn kē yī sheng 眼科医生 *n.*
   oculist
yǎn qiú 眼球 *n* eyeball
yǎn 演 *v.i.* act
yǎn jiǎng 演讲 *n.* lecture
yǎn jiǎng 演讲 *n.* oration
yǎn jiǎng 演讲 *n* talk
yǎn jiǎng shù 演讲术 *n.*
   oratory
yǎn jiǎng zhě 演讲者 *n.* orator
yǎn chàng huì 演唱会 *n.*
   concert
yǎn chū 演出 *n.* acting
yǎn chū 演出 *n.* performance
yǎn chū 演出 *n.* show

yǎn shuō de 演说的 *a.* oratorical
yǎn xí 演习 *n* drill
yǎn yuán 演员 *n.* actor
yǎn zhǔ jué 演主角 *v.t.* star
yǎn tǐ 掩体 *n* blindage
yǎn bì 掩蔽 *v.t.* screen
yǎn shì 掩饰 *v.t.* mask
yǎn shì 掩饰 *n.* masquerade
yǎn shì 掩饰 *v.t.* whitewash
yǎn shǔ 鼹鼠 *n.* mole
yàn shì zhě 厌世者 *n.*
   misanthrope
yàn xià 咽下 *v.t* down
yàn shī 验尸 *n.* post-mortem
yàn huì 宴会 *n.* banquet
yàn huì 宴会 *n* feast
yàn huì 宴会 *n.* wassail
yàn huì de 宴会的 *adj.* convivial
yàn qǐng 宴请 *v.t.* banquet
yàn qǐng 宴请 *v.t.* dine
yàn yǔ 谚语 *n.* adage
yàn yǔ de 谚语的 *a.* proverbial
yàn mài 燕麦 *n.* oat
yàn zi 燕子 *n.* swallow
yáng 羊 *n.* sheep
yáng jiào shēng 羊叫声 *n* bleat
yáng máo 羊毛 *n* fleece
yáng máo 羊毛 *n.* wool
yáng máo de 羊毛的 *a.* woollen
yáng ròu 羊肉 *n.* mutton
yáng xián fēng 羊癫疯 *n*
   epilepsy
yáng tái 阳台 *n.* balcony
yáng tái 阳台 *n.* veranda
yáng cōng 洋葱 *n.* onion
yáng 洋 *n.* ocean
yáng wá wa 洋娃娃 *n* doll
yáng shù 杨树 *n.* poplar
yǎng lǎo jīn 养老金 *n.* annuity
yǎng fēng chǎng 养蜂场 *n.*
   apiary
yǎng fēng yè 养蜂业 *n.*
   apiculture
yǎng tù chǎng 养兔场 *n.* warren
yǎng yù 养育 *v.t.* foster
yǎng yù 养育 *v.t.* nurture
yǎng yù 养育 *v.t.* rear
yǎng 痒 *n.* itch
yǎng qì 氧气 *n.* oxygen

yàng běn 样本 *n.* sample
yàng běn 样本 *n.* specimen
yāo guài 妖怪 *n* bogle
yāo shù 妖术 *n.* witchcraft
yāo qiú 要求 *v.t* demand
yāo qiú 要求 *v.t.* request
yāo 腰 *n.* waist
yāo bù 腰部 *n* small
yāo dài 腰带 *n.* girdle
yāo dài 腰带 *n.* waistband
yāo ròu 腰肉 *n.* loin
yāo qǐng 邀请 *v.* invitation
yāo qǐng 邀请 *v.t.* invite
yáo yán 谣言 *n* canard
yáo yán 谣言 *n.* hearsay
yáo yán 谣言 *n.* rumour
yáo kòng qì 遥控器 *n.* controller
yáo bǎi 摇摆 *v.i.* sway
yáo bǎi 摇摆 *v.i.* swing
yáo bǎi 摇摆 *n* wag
yáo chuán 谣传 *v.t.* rumour
yáo dòng 摇动 *v.t.* rock
yáo dòng 摇动 *n* shake
yáo dòng 摇动 *n* sway
yáo huàng 摇晃 *n.* stagger
yáo huàng 摇晃 *v.i* wobble
yáo huàng dì xuán guà 摇晃地悬挂 *v.t* dangle
yáo lán 摇篮 *n* cradle
yáo lán chē 摇篮车 *n.* perambulator
yáo lán qǔ 摇篮曲 *n.* lullaby
yáo yáo bǎi bǎi 摇摇摆摆 *v.i.* stagger
yáo yáo bǎi bǎi dì zǒu 摇摇摆摆地走 *v.i.* waddle
yáo tiǎo de shū nǔ 窈窕的淑女 *n.* sylph
yáo 窑 *n.* kiln
yǎo 咬 *v.t.* bite
yǎo zhe shé shuō 咬着舌说 *v.t.* lisp
yào 要 *v.t.* need
yào diǎn 要点 *n.* gist
yào jǐn 要紧 *v.i.* matter
yào sài 要塞 *n.* stronghold
yào sù 要素 *n* element
yào shi 钥匙 *n.* key

yào 药 *n* cure
yào cǎo 药草 *n.* herb
yào fáng 药房 *n* dispensary
yào fáng 药房 *n.* pharmacy
yào fāng 药方 *n.* prescription
yào gāo 药膏 *n.* ointment
yào jì shī 药剂师 *n* druggist
yào jiǔ 药酒 *n.* tincture
yào piàn 药片 *n.* tablet
yào pǐn 药品 *n.* physic
yào wán 药丸 *n.* pill
yào wù 药物 *n.* remedy
yào wù 药物 *n.* medicament
yē ké xiān wéi 椰壳纤维 *n* coir
yē zi 椰子 *n* coconut
yě xǔ 也许 *adv.* perhaps
yě bú 也不 *conj* nor
yě bú 也不 *conj.* neither
yě cān 野餐 *n.* picnic
yě mán 野蛮 *a.* barbarism
yě mán 野蛮 *a.* barbarism
yě mán rén 野蛮人 *n.* barbarian
yě niú 野牛 *n* bison
yě shēng de 野生的 *a.* wild
yě shòu 野兽 *n* beast
yě shòu yí yàng de 野兽一样的 *a* beastly
yě tù 野兔 *n.* hare
yě xīn bó bó de 野心勃勃的 *a.* ambitious
yě yíng 野营 *v.i.* camp
yè 叶 *n.* leaf
yè 页 *n.* page
yè yú ài hào zhě 业余爱好者 *n.* amateur
yè jiān de 夜间的 *a.* nocturnal
yè yīng 夜莺 *n.* nightingale
yè wǎn 夜晚 *n.* night
yè huà 液化 *v.t.* liquefy
yè tǐ 液体 *n* fluid
yè tǐ 液体 *n* liquid
yè tǐ de 液体的 *a.* liquid
yī 一 *art* an
yī 一 *a.* a
yī 一 *a.* one
yī 一 *pron.* one
yī bàn 一半 *n.* half
yī bàn de 一半的 *a* half
yī bā zhang 一巴掌 *n.* slap

yī bǎi zhōu nián 一百週年 *n.* centenary

yī bǎi zhōu nián de 一百週年的 *adj.* centennial

yī bù fen de 一部分的 *a.* partial

yī bùyī bù tuī yí 一步一步推移 *v.i.* tick

yī biān 一边 *adv.* aside

yī cān 一餐 *n* feed

yī cān 一餐 *n.* meal

yī chuàn 一串 *v.t.* string

yī chuī 一吹 *n.* whiff

yī cì 一次 *adv.* once

yī cì 一刺 *n.* prick

yī dà qún rén 一大群人 *n.* throng

yī dài 一代 *n.* generation

yī dìng 一定 *v.* must

yī dìng de 一定的 *a* definite

yī dá 一打 *n.* dozen

yī diǎn diǎn dì yǎo xià 一点点地咬下 *v.t.* nibble

yī diánr 一点儿 *n* bit

yī diánr 一点儿 *adv.* somewhat

yī diǎn yě bú 一点也不 *adv.* none

yī diǎn yī diǎn de yǎo 一点一点的咬 *n* nibble

yī duī 一堆 *n* lot

yī duàn qíng jié 一段情节 *n* episode

yī duì 一队 *n.* queue

yī duì 一对 *n* couple

yī duì 一对 *n.* pair

yī duì gòng è niú 一对共轭牛 *n.* span

yī fèn 一份 *n* share

yī fèn 一份 *n* portion

yī fū yī qī de 一夫一妻的 *a.* monogynous

yī fū yī qī zhì 一夫一妻制 *n.* monogamy

yī gè guì zú 一个贵族 *n.* aristocrat

yī huìr 一会儿 *n.* while

yī jī 一击 *n* stroke

yī jì 一剂 *n* dose

yī kǒu 一口 *n* bite

yī lǚ tóu fa 一缕头发 *n* lock

yī mǒ 一抹 *n.* stroke

yī nián yī cì 一年一次 *adv.* yearly

yī nián yī cì de 一年一次的 *a.* annual

yī piàn 一片 *n.* slice

yī piē 一瞥 *n.* glance

yī piē 一瞥 *n.* glimpse

yī qí 一齐 *adv.* along

yī qí 一齐 *adv.* altogether

yī qí 一齐 *adv.* together

yī qí 一齐 *n.* unison

yī qiān 一千 *n.* chiliad

yī qiān gè 一千个 *n.* thousand

yī qiè 一切 *n* all

yī quān 一圈 *n.* lap

yì shén chóng bài 一神崇拜 *n.* monolatry

yì shén jiāo 一神教 *n.* monotheism

yì shén lùn zhě 一神论者 *n.* monotheist

yī shí de xìng zhì 一时的兴致 *n.* whim

yī shù 一束 *n.* skein

yī tào 一套 *n.* suite

yī tào yī fu 一套衣服 *n.* suit

yī tiáo miàn bāo 一条面包 *n.* loaf

yī wō 一窝 *n* brood

yī xíng 一行 *n.* row

yī yè gōng fu 一夜工夫 *adv.* overnight

yī zhōu yī cì de 一周一次的 *a.* weekly

yī zhèn 一阵 *n* bout

yī zhèn jù tòng 一阵剧痛 *n.* pang

ī zhèn pēn yān 一阵喷烟 *n.* puff

yī zhì 一致 *n.* accord

yī zhì 一致 *n.* conformity

yī zhì 一致 *n.* oneness

yī zhì de 一致的 *a* congenial

yī zhì de 一致的 *a* consistent

yī zhì tóng yì de 一致同意的 *a.* unanimous

yī chú 衣橱 *n.* wardrobe

yī dà xiǎo pái liè 依大小排列 v.t. size

yī fu 衣服 n. clothes

yī fu 衣服 n dress

yī fu 衣服 n. garment

yī fu lèi 衣服类 n clothing

yī lǐng 衣领 n collar

yī hǎo 医好 v.t. cure

yī liáo de 医疗的 a. medical

yī sheng 医生 n doctor

yī sheng 医生 n. medico

yī shī 医师 n. physician

yī yào 医药 n. medicine

yī yào de 医药的 a. medicinal

yī yuàn 医院 n. hospital

yī lài 依赖 n anaclisis

yī lài 依赖 n dependence

yī lài 依赖 v.i. rely

yī lài de 依赖的 a dependent

yí qì 仪器 n. apparatus

yí qì de 仪器的 a. instrumental

yí shì 仪式 n. ceremony

yí shì 仪式 n. rite

yí shì 仪式 n. ritual

yí shì de 仪式的 a. ritual

yí zhàng guān 仪仗官 n. beadle

yí wéi píng dì 夷为平地 v.t. raze

yí dòng 移动 v.t. remove

yí dòng de 移动的 adj ambulant

yí jū 移居 v.i. migrate

yí jū 移居 n. transmigration

yí mín 移民 n. immigrant

yí mín 移民 n. immigration

yí mín zhě 移民者 n. migrant

yí mín zhě 移民者 n. settler

yí rù 移入 v.i. immigrate

yí zhí 移植 v.t. transplant

yí zhì 移置 v.t displace

yí zhù 移住 n. migration

yí zhǔ 遗嘱 n. will

yí 姨 n. aunt

yí chǎn 遗产 n. heritage

yí chǎn 遗产 n. inheritance

yí chǎn 遗产 n. legacy

yí chǎn 遗产 n. patrimony

yí chuán 遗传 n. heredity

yí chuán de 遗传的 n. hereditary

yí hàn 遗憾 n regret

yí jì 遗迹 n. relic

yí jì 遗迹 n. vestige

yí liú 遗留 v.t. bequeath

yí lòu 遗漏 n. omission

yí qì 遗弃 v.t. abandon

yí huò 疑惑 n. misgiving

yí huò 疑惑 n. mistrust

yí wèn 疑问 n doubt

yí wèn 疑问 n. query

yí wèn cí 疑问词 n interrogative

yí wèn de 疑问的 a. interrogative

yǐ dào jié hūn nián líng de 已到结婚年龄的 a. nubile

yǐ fèi qì de 已废弃的 a. obsolete

yǐ jing 已经 adv. already

yǐ cháng máo gōng jī 以长矛攻击 v.t. lance

yǐ chí yǎo qǐ 以匙舀起 v.t. spoon

yǐ féi zào xǐ 以肥皂洗 v.t. soap

yǐ héng mù wéi lán 以横木围栏 v.t. rail

yǐ hòu 以后 conj. after

yǐ hòu 以后 adv. since

yǐ lái …以来 conj. since

yǐ líng shòu fāng shì 以零售方式 adv. retail

yǐ miǎn 以免 conj. lest

yǐ qián 以前 adv. before

yǐ qián 以前 adv formerly

yǐ qīng shuǐ chōng xǐ 以清水冲洗 v.t. rinse

yǐ quán zhòng jī 以拳重击 v.t. punch

yǐ shàng 以上 adv above

yǐ sháo yǎo qǔ 以勺舀取 v.t. ladle

yǐ tí bā dì 以蹄扒地 v.t. paw

yǐ tián yán mì yǔ yòu huò 以甜言蜜语诱惑 v.t. wheedle

yǐ wù huàn wù 以物换物 v.t. barter

yǐ zhì 以致 conj. that

yǐ zhí yuán shēn fēn 以职员身分 adv. officially

yǐ kào 倚靠 v.i. lean

yǐ zi 椅子 n. chair

yǐ zi 椅子 n. ottoman

yì wù de 义务的 *a.* obligatory

yì fèn 义愤 *n.* outrage

yì chéng biǎo 议程表 *n.* agenda

yì dìng 议定 *v.t.* negotiate

yì shù 艺术 *n.* art

yì shù de 艺术的 *a.* artistic

yì shù jiā 艺术家 *n.* artist

yì cháng 异常 *n* anomaly

yì cháng 异常 *adv.* singularly

yì cháng de 异常的 *a* anomalous

yì xiǎng tiān kāi de 异想天开的 *a.* whimsical

yì yì 异议 *n* demur

yì shì 轶事 *n.* anecdote

yì zhì 抑制 *v.t.* mortify

yì zhì 抑制 *v.t.* restrain

yì yù [zhèng] 抑郁[症] *n* depression

yì dú dì 易读地 *adv.* legibly

yì fǔ huài de 易腐坏的 *a.* perishable

yì huài de 易坏的 *a* flimsy

yì kū de 易哭的 *a* maudlin

yì lǐ jiě de 易理解的 *a.* intelligible

yì nù de 易怒的 *a* cross

yì nù de 易怒的 *a.* irritable

yì nù de 易怒的 *a.* touchy

yì nù de 易怒的 *a.* waspish

yì rán de 易燃的 *a.* inflammable

yì shòu piàn zhī rén 易受骗之人 *n* gull

yì wàng 易忘 *n.* oblivion

yì wàng de 易忘的 *a.* oblivious

yì mǎ 驿马 *n.* relay

yì miáo 疫苗 *n.* vaccine

yì lì 毅力 *n.* perseverance

yì lì 毅力 *n.* stamina

yì dà lì de 意大利的 *a.* Italian

yì dà lì rén 意大利人 *n.* Italian

yì jiàn 意见 *n.* notion

yì jiàn 意见 *n.* opinion

yì si 意思 *n.* meaning

yì si 意思 *a.* meaningful

yì wài 意外 *n* accident

yì wài shì gù 意外事故 *n.* misadventure

yì yì 意译 *n.* paraphrase

yì yì 意义 *n.* purport

yì yì 意义 *n.* signification

yì yù 意欲 *v.t.* purpose

yì zài jìn zhǐ de 意在禁止的 *a.* prohibitory

yì zhì lì 意志力 *n.* volition

yì chū 溢出 *n* spill

yì sǐ 缢死 *v.t.* throttle

yì 翼 *n.* wing

yīn cǐ 因此 *adv.* hence

yīn cǐ 因此 *adv.* thence

yīn cǐ 因此 *adv.* thereby

yīn guǒ guān xi 因果关系 *n* causality

yīn guǒ guān xi de 因果关系的 *adj.* causal

yīn sù 因素 *n* factor

yīn wèi 因为 *conj.* as

yīn wèi 因为 *conj.* because

yīn wèi 因为 *conj.* for

yīn àn de 阴暗的 *a* cheerless

yīn àn de 阴暗的 *a.* shadowy

yīn chù 阴处 *n.* shade

yīn dào 阴道 *n.* vagina

yīn gōu 阴沟 *n.* culvert

yīn jiān de zhū shén 阴间的诸神 *a.* manful

yīn jīng 阴茎 *n.* penis

yīn lì de 阴历的 *a.* lunar

yīn móu 阴谋 *n.* conspiracy

yīn móu 阴谋 *n* intrigue

yīn shī de 阴湿的 *adj.* dank

yīn diào 音调 *v.t.* tune

yīn jié 音节 *n.* syllable

yīn jié de 音节的 *a.* syllabic

yīn liàng 音量 *n.* volume

yīn xiǎng xiào guǒ 音响效果 *n.* acoustics

yīn yuè 音乐 *n.* music

yīn yuè de 音乐的 *a.* musical

yīn yuè jiā 音乐家 *n.* musician

yīn qīn 姻亲 *n.* in-laws

yīn qín 殷勤 *n.* complaisance

yīn qín de 殷勤的 *adj.* complaisant

yín sòng 吟诵 *n.* recitation

yín dàng de 淫荡的 *a.* lascivious

yín dàng de 淫荡的 *a.* lewd

yín 银 *n.* silver
yín de 银的 *a* silver
yín háng 银行 *n.* bank
yín háng bào gào dān 银行报告
单 *n.* statement
yín háng jia 银行家 *n.* banker
yín mù 银幕 *n.* screen
yǐn dǎo 引导 *v.t.* usher
yǐn qǐ 引起 *v.t* beget
yǐn qǐ 引起 *v.t* cause
yǐn qǐ 引起 *v.t* effect
yǐn qǐ 引起 *v.t* evoke
yǐn lì 引力 *n.* gravitation
yǐn qíng 引擎 *n* engine
yǐn rén lián mǐn de 引人怜悯的
a. pitiable
yǐn rù 引入 *v.t.* adhibit
yǐn rù qí tú 引入歧途 *v.t.*
mislead
yǐn yán 引言 *n.* preamble
yǐn yòng 引用 *v.t* cite
yǐn yòng 引用 *v.t* quote
yǐn yòu 引诱 *v.t.* entice
yǐn yòu 引诱 *v.t.* induce
yǐn yòu 引诱 *n.* inducement
yǐn yòu jì 引诱剂 *n.* lure
yǐn 饮 *v.t* drink
yǐn liào 饮料 *n* drink
yǐn liào 饮料 *n.pl* victuals
yǐn pǐn 饮品 *n* beverage
yǐn cáng 隐藏 *v.t* bemask
yǐn dùn zhě 隐遁者 *n.* recluse
yǐn jū 隐居 *v.i.* retire
yǐn jū chù 隐居处 *n.* hermitage
yǐn mán 隐瞒 *v.t.* conceal
yǐn shì 隐士 *n.* hermit
yǐn sī 隐私 *n.* privacy
yǐn tuì 隐退 *n.* seclusion
yǐn tuì de 隐退的 *a.* secluded
yǐn 瘾 *n.* addiction
yìn 印 *v.t.* imprint
yìn 印 *n.* imprint
yìn cuò 印错 *n.* misprint
yìn cuò 印错 *v.t.* misprint
yìn dù de 印度的 *a.* Indian
yìn xiàng 印象 *n.* impression
yìn zhāng 印章 *n.* seal
yīng dé wù 应得物 *n* due

yīng fù zé de 应负责的 *a.*
answerable
yīng nà shuì de 应纳税的 *a.*
taxable
yīng shòu zūn jìng de 应受尊敬
的 *a.* reverend
yīng yǔn 应允 *v.i* comply
yīng bàng 英镑 *n.* pound
yīng cùn 英寸 *n.* inch
yīng gé lán 英格兰 *n* albion
yīng guó de 英国的 *adj* british
yīng guó huò bì 英国货币 *n.*
sterling
yīng guó huò bì de 英国货币的
a. sterling
yīng jùn de 英俊的 *a.* handsome
yīng lǐ 英里 *n.* mile
yīng lǐ shù 英里数 *n.* mileage
yīng mǔ 英亩 *n.* acre
yīng mǔ shù 英亩数 *n.* acreage
yīng xióng 英雄 *n.* hero
yīng xún 英寻 *n* fathom
yīng yǒng 英勇 *n.* heroism
yīng yǒng 英勇 *n.* prowess
yīng yǒng 英勇 *n.* valour
yīng yǒng de 英勇的 *a.* gallant
yīng yǒng de 英勇的 *a.* heroic
yīng yǒng de 英勇的 *a.* valiant
yīng yǔ 英语 *n* English
yīng hái 婴孩 *n.* bantling
yīng wǔ 鹦鹉 *n.* parrot
yīng 鹰 *n* eagle
yīng 鹰 *n* hawk
yíng 赢 *n* win
yíng tóu suì làng 迎头碎浪 *n.*
surf
yǐng 影 *n.* shadow
yíng xiǎng 影响 *v.t.* affect
yíng xiǎng 影响 *n.* impact
yíng xiǎng 影响 *v.t.* influence
yíng xiǎng lì 影响力 *n.* influence
yíng de 营的 *adj* castral
yíng yǎng 营养 *n.* nurture
yíng yǎng 营养 *n.* aliment
yíng yǎng 营养 *n.* nourishment
yíng yǎng 营养 *n.* nutrition
yíng yǎng bù liáng 营养不良 *n.*
malnutrition

yíng yǎng de 营养的 a. nutritive

yíng dé 赢得 v.t. win

yíng dé rén zhù yì de 赢得人注意的 a. winsome

yìng dá zhě 应答者 n. respondent

yìng shì zhě 应试者 n examinee

yìng fù 应付 v.i cope

yìng fù 应付 v.t. tackle

yìng bǎ zì jǐ jǐ jìn 硬把自己挤进 v.t. intrude

yìng bì 硬币 n coin

yìng de 硬的 a. hard

yìng zhí bǎn 硬纸板 n. cardboard

yōng hù 拥护 v.t. advocate

yōng rén 佣人 n domestic

yōng yǒu 拥有 v.t. own

yōng yǒu 拥有 v.t. possess

yóng jiǔ 永久 n. permanence

yóng jiǔ de 永久的 a. lasting

yóng jiǔ de 永久的 a. permanent

yóng yuǎn 永远 n eternity

yóng yuǎn 永远 adv forever

yóng yuǎn de 永远的 a. eternal

yǒng bú 永不 adv. never

yǒng héng de 永恒的 a abiding

yǒng héng de 永恆的 a. everlasting

yǒng chū 涌出 v.i. well

yóng gǎn 勇敢 n bravery

yóng gǎn de 勇敢的 a brave

yóng gǎn de 勇敢的 a. courageous

yóng gǎn de 勇敢的 a. mettlesome

yóng gǎn xíng wéi 勇敢行为 n. gallantry

yóng měng de 勇猛的 a. interpid

yǒng qì 勇气 n. courage

yǒng qì 勇气 n. mettle

yǒng qì 勇气 n pluck

yòng 用 n access

yòng 用 v.t. use

yòng biāo qiāng chuō 用标枪戳 v.t. spear

yòng bù qiāng shè jī 用步枪射击 v.t. rifle

yòng cí bù dāng 用词不当 n. misnomer

yòng dà lián dāo gē 用大镰刀割 v.t. scythe

yòng dài zi kǔn zā 用带子捆扎 v.t. strap

yòng dào cǎo děng gài wū dǐng 用稻草等盖屋顶 v.t. thatch

yòng diàn shì guǎng bō 用电视广播 v.t. telecast

yòng dìng dīng láo 用钉钉牢 v.t. nail

yòng fǎ 用法 n. usage

yòng fáng fǔ yào wù 用防腐药物 v.t embalm

yòng gōng shì biǎo shì 用公式表示 v.t formulate

yòng guǐ biàn qī piàn 用诡辩欺骗 v.t. sophisticate

yòng hǎi mián cā 用海绵擦 v.t. sponge

yòng jiǎo chē diào qǐ 用绞车吊起 v.t. windlass

yòng jiǎo tà dòng 用脚踏动 v.t. pedal

yòng jiǎo zhǐ cǎi 用脚趾踩 v.t. toe

yòng jù 用具 n. utensil

yòng lí ba wéi zhù 用篱笆围住 v.t fence

yòng lì dì 用力地 adv. headlong

yòng lì qīng pū 用沥青铺 v.t. tar

yòng lì tóu zhì 用力投掷 v.t. hurl

yòng mǎ dāo kǎn 用马刀砍 v.t. sabre

yòng mú bǎn shuā yìn 用模板刷印 v.i. stencil

yòng qiān bǎn yìn shuā 用铅版印刷 v.t. stereotype

yòng qiān bǐ xiě huò tú 用铅笔写或涂 v.t. pencil

yòng qiáng wéi zhù 用墙围住 v.t. wall

yòng qún zi fù gài 用裙子覆盖 v.t. skirt

yòng rén lì tuī dòng 用人力推动 v.t. manhandle

yòng shóu zhǎng fǔ mó 用手掌抚摩 v.t. palm

yòng shóu zhǐ bō nòng 用手指拨弄 v.t finger

yòng shù lí wéi 用树篱围 v.t hedge

yòng táng zhǔ 用糖煮 v.t. candy

yòng tào suǒ bǔ zhuō 用套索捕捉 v.t. noose

yòng téng tiáo dǎ 用藤条打 v.t. cane

yòng wú xiàn diàn fā sòng 用无线电发送 v.t. radio

yòng X guāng jiǎn chá 用X光检查 v.t. x-ray

yòng xiāng fén 用香焚 v.t. incense

yòng xiǎo shū xiě tǐ de 用小书写体的 a. minuscule

yòng xìng míng de shǒu zì mǔ qiān míng 用姓名的首字母签名 v.t initial

yòng yán cí biǎo dá 用言辞表达 v.t word

yòng yǔ 用语 n diction

yòng yú léi xí jī 用鱼雷袭击 v.t. torpedo

yòng zhǐ jù cè liáng de rén 用指距测量的人 n. spanner

yòng zhù shè qì guàn gài 用注射器灌溉 v.t. syringe

yòng zhuāng chēng chí 用桩撑持 v.t. stake

yōu diǎn 优点 n excellency

yōu diǎn 优点 n. merit

yōu huì quàn 优惠券 n. coupon

yōu liáng de 优良的 a. excellent

yōu róu guǎ duàn 优柔寡断 n. indecision

yōu róu guǎ duàn 优柔寡断 v.i. shilly-shally

yōu shì 优势 n. predominance

yōu shì 优势 n. preponderance

yōu xiān quán 优先权 n. priority

yōu xiān 优先 n. precedence

yōu xiān de 优先的 a. preferential

yōu xiù 优秀 n. excellence

yōu xiù de 优秀的 a. superior

yōu yǎ 优雅 n. grace

yōu yǎ de 优雅的 adj elegant

yōu chóu de 忧愁的 a. sad

yōu lù 忧虑 a anxiety

yōu lù de 忧虑的 a. anxious

yōu yù 忧郁 a blue

yōu yù 忧郁 n. melancholy

yōu yù (zhèng) de 忧郁(症)的 a. melancholic

yōu yù bìng 忧郁病 n. melancholia

yōu yù de 忧郁的 adj melancholy

yōu yuè 优越 n. superiority

yōu àn 幽暗 n. gloom

yōu huì 幽会 n. tryst

yōu líng 幽灵 n. spectre

yōu mò 幽默 n. humour

yōu mò de huà 幽默的话 n. pleasantry

yōu mò zuò jiā 幽默作家 n. humorist

yōu xián de 悠闲的 a. leisurely

yóu shǐ zhì zhōng 由始至终 prep. throughout

yóu yú 由于 prep. with

yóu 油 n. oil

yóu cáo chē 油槽车 n. tanker

yóu de 油的 a. oily

yóu jī 油迹 n. smear

yóu nì de 油腻的 a. greasy

yóu qī 油漆 n. paint

yóu zhà 油炸 v.t. fry

yóu dài 邮袋 n. pouch

yóu dì 邮递 n mail

yóu dì 邮递 v.t. post

yóu dì yuán 邮递员 n. postman

yóu fèi 邮费 n. postage

yóu jì 邮寄 v.t. mail

yóu jiàn 邮件 n. mail

yóu jú 邮局 n. post-office

yóu piào 邮票 n. stamp

yóu zhèng 邮政 n. post

yóu zhèng de 邮政的 *a.* postal

yóu zhèng jú zhǎng 邮政局长 *n.* postmaster

yóu mù 柚木 *n.* teak

yóu tài rén 犹太人 *n.* Jew

yóu yù 犹豫 *v.i.* hesitate

yóu yù 犹豫 *n.* hesitation

yóu yù bú dìng de 犹豫不定的 *a.* hesitant

yóu 疣 *n.* wart

yóu dàng 游荡 *v.i.* wander

yóu jī duì 游击队 *n.* guerilla

yóu jī duì yuán 游击队员 *n.* partisan

yóu mù de 游牧的 *a.* nomadic

yóu mù mín de yì yuán 游牧民的一员 *n.* nomad

yóu shǒu hǎo xián 游手好闲 *v.i.* dawdle

yóu shǒu hǎo xián 游手好闲 *v.i.* loaf

yóu shǒu hǎo xián de rén 游手好闲的人 *n.* idler

yóu shuǐ 游水 *v.i.* swim

yóu tǐng 游艇 *n.* yacht

yóu xì 游戏 *n.* game

yóu xì 游戏 *n.* play

yóu xíng 游行 *n.* parade

yóu xíng 游行 *v.t.* parade

yóu yí bú dìng 游移不定 *v.i.* vacillate

yóu yǒng 游泳 *n* swim

yóu yǒng zhě 游泳者 *n.* swimmer

yǒu hǎo 友好 *n.* amity

yǒu ài 友爱 *n.* fraternity

yóu diǎn 有点 *adv.* something

yóu lǐ de 有理的 *a.* justifiable

yǒu 有 *v.t.* have

yǒu jià zhí 有价值 *v.t* merit

yǒu ài xīn de 有爱心的 *a* be nevolent

yǒu bāng zhù de 有帮助的 *a.* helpful

yǒu bào chóu de 有报酬的 *a.* remunerative

yǒu báo wù de 有薄雾的 *a.* misty

yǒu bèi xuán jǔ zī gé de 有被选举资格的 *a* eligible

yǒu bìng de 有病的 *a.* invalid

yǒu bìng de 有病的 *a.* sickly

yǒu bù tóng 有不同 *v.i.* vary

yǒu cì de 有刺的 *a.* barbed

yǒu cí xìng de 有磁性的 *a.* magnetic

yǒu cì xù de 有次序的 *a.* methodical

yǒu dài dòng wù 有袋动物 *n.* marsupial

yǒu dí yì de 有敌意的 *a.* inimical

yǒu dú de 有毒的 *a.* poisonous

yǒu dú de 有毒的 *a.* venomous

yǒu dú xiě néng lì de 有读写能力的 *a.* literate

yǒu fēn cùn de 有分寸的 *a* decent

yǒu fēng de 有风的 *a.* windy

yǒu gǎn jué lì de 有感觉力的 *a.* sentient

yǒu gǎn jué xìng 有感觉性 *n.* sentience

yǒu guān 有关 *n.* relevance

yǒu guān de 有关的 *a.* pertinent

yǒu guān lián de 有关联的 *a.* relevant

yǒu guān xi de 有关系的 *a.* associate

yǒu guān xi de 有关系的 *a.* relative

yǒu guāng zé de 有光泽的 *a.* lustrous

yǒu guò shī de 有过失的 *a* faulty

yǒu hài de 有害的 *a.* injurious

yǒu hài de 有害的 *a* malign

yǒu hài de 有害的 *a.* noxious

yǒu hài de 有害的 *a.* pernicious

yǒu hài dì 有害地 *adv.* ill

yǒu jī de 有机的 *a.* organic

yǒu jià zhí de 有价值的 *a.* valuable

yǒu jiǎo de 有角的 *a.* angular

yǒu jié zòu de 有节奏的 *a.* rhythmic

yǒu kě néng de 有可能的 *a.* apt

yǒu lǐ 有礼 *n.* politeness

yǒu míng de 有名的 *a.* renowned

yǒu lì de 有利的 *a.* advantageous

yǒu lì de 有利的 *a* beneficial

yǒu lì de 有力的 *a* forceful

yǒu lì de 有力的 *a.* strong

yǒu lǐ mào de 有礼貌的 *a.* courteous

yǒu lǐ mào de 有礼貌的 *a.* polite

yǒu lǐ mào de 有礼貌的 *a.* urbane

yǒu lì rùn de 有利润的 *a.* profitable

yǒu lì yì de 有利益的 *a.* lucrative

yǒu lì yú 有利于 *v.t.* benefit

yǒu liáo xiào de 有疗效的 *a* curative

yǒu nǎi de 有奶的 *a.* milch

yǒu nài xìng de 有耐性的 *a.* patient

yǒu nán zǐ qì de 有男子气的 *a.* masculine

yǒu nán zǐ qì gài de 有男子气概的 *a.* manlike

yǒu néng lì de 有能力的 *a.* capable

yǒu néng lì de 有能力的 *a.* competent

yǒu níng jù lì de 有凝聚力的 *adj* cohesive

yǒu piān jiàn 有偏见 *v.t* bias

yǒu piān tǎn de 有偏袒的 *a.* partisan

yǒu qián lì de 有潜力的 *a.* potential

yǒu qù de 有趣的 *a.* interesting

yǒu qù de 有趣的 *a.* laughable

yǒu quán lì de 有权力的 *a.* powerful

yǒu quán wēi de 有权威的 *a.* authoritative

yǒu quán wēi de 有权威的 *a.* magisterial

yǒu quē xiàn de 有缺陷的 *adj.* deficient

yǒu rén 有人 *pron.* somebody

yǒu rén 有人 *pron.* someone

yǒu rén qíng de 有人情的 *a.* humane

yǒu róng jiě lì de 有溶解力的 *a.* solvent

yǒu shén lùn 有神论 *n.* theism

yǒu shén lùn zhě 有神论者 *n.* theist

yǒu shēng qì de 有生气的 *a.* animate

yǒu shí 有时 *adv.* sometimes

yǒu shuō fú lì de 有说服力的 *adj.* cogent

yǒu tán xìng 有弹性 *a* elastic

yǒu tiān cái de 有天才的 *a.* gifted

yǒu tiáo jiàn de 有条件的 *a* conditional

yǒu tiáo lǐ de 有条理的 *a* coherent

yǒu wèi 有味 *v.i.* smack

yǒu wèi de 有味的 *a.* odorous

yǒu wēi yán de 有威严的 *a.* lordly

yǒu xì tǒng de 有系统的 *a.* systematic

yǒu xī wàng de 有希望的 *a.* hopeful

yǒu xī wàng de 有希望的 *a.* promising

yǒu xiàn de 有限的 *a* finite

yǒu xiàn de 有限的 *a.* limited

yǒu xiān jiàn zhī míng de 有先见之明的 *a.* provident

yǒu xiāng dāng shēn fèn de rén 有相当身分的人 *n.* somebody

yǒu xiào 有效 *a* effective

yǒu xiào de 有效的 *a.* potent

yǒu xiào de 有效的 *a.* valid

yǒu xiāo lù de 有销路的 *a.* marketable

yǒu xiào xìng 有效性 *n.* validity

yǒu xiào yòng de 有效用的 *a.* utilitarian

yǒu xiē rén 有些人 *pron.* some

yǒu xìn xīn 有信心 *a.* confident

yǒu xìng gǎn de 有性感的 *n.* sexy

yǒu xué wen de 有学问的 *a.* learned

yǒu xué wen de 有学问的 *a.* scholarly

yǒu yǎn lì de rén 有眼力的人 *n.* visionary

yǒu yàng zi de 有样子的 *a.* shapely

yǒu yì de 有翼的 *adj.* aliferous

yǒu yì de 有益的 *a.* salutary

yǒu yì de 有益的 *a.* wholesome

yǒu yì si 有意思 *v.t* mean

yǒu yì wù de 有义务的 *a.* liable

yǒu yì yì 有意义 *n.* significance

yǒu yì yú 有益于 *v.t.* avail

yǒu yì yú 有益于 *v.t.* profit

yǒu yíng xiǎng de 有影响的 *a.* influential

yǒu yíng yǎng de 有营养的 *a.* nutritious

yǒu yòng de 有用的 *a* favourable

yǒu yòng de 有用的 *a.* serviceable

yǒu yòng de 有用的 *a.* useful

yǒu yuē shù lì de 有约束力的 *a* binding

yǒu zé rèn 有责任 *a* accountable

yǒu zé rèn de 有责任的 *a.* responsible

yǒu zhàn dòu jing shen de rén 有战斗精神的人 *n* militant

yǒu zhèng zhuàng de 有症状的 *a.* symptomatic

yǒu zhì xù de 有秩序的 *a.* orderly

yǒu zhì zhě 有志者 *n.* aspirant

yǒu zhù yú 有助于 *v.t.* advantage

yǒu zhù yú bǎo cún de 有助于保存的 *a.* preservative

yǒu zī gé 有资格 *v.t.* entitle

yǒu zī gé 有资格 *v.i.* qualify

yǒu zuì de 有罪的 *a* culpable

yǒu zuì pàn jué 有罪判决 *n* conviction

yòu ér chuáng 幼儿床 *n.* cot

yòu ér chuáng 幼儿床 *n.* crib

yòu shòu 幼兽 *n* cub

yòu yá 幼芽 *n.* chit

yòu yá 幼芽 *n* sprout

yòu zhì 幼稚 *a.* childish

yòu zhì de 幼稚的 *adj* callow

yòu zhì de 幼稚的 *a.* infantile

yòu zhì de 幼稚的 *a.* juvenile

yòu zhì de 幼稚的 *a.* puerile

yòu zhì yuán 幼稚园 *n.* kindergarten ;

yòu 釉 *n* glaze

yòu bǔ 诱捕 *v.t.* trap

yòu ěr 诱饵 *n* bait

yòu guǎi 诱拐 *v.t.* abduct

yòu guǎi 诱拐 *n* abduction

yòu huò 诱惑 *v.t.* allure

yòu huò 诱惑 *n* allurement

yòu huò 诱惑 *v.t.* lure

yòu huò 诱惑 *v* seduce

yòu huò 诱惑 *v.t.* tempt

yòu huò 诱惑 *n.* temptation

yòu huò de 诱惑的 *a* seductive

yòu huò zhě 诱惑者 *n.* tempter

yū fǔ 迂腐 *n.* pedantry

yū huí de 迂回的 *adj* anfractuous

yū jī 淤积 *v.t.* silt

yú shì 于是 *conj.* whereupon

yú é 余额 *n.* balance

yú 鱼 *n* fish

yú léi 鱼雷 *n.* torpedo

yú miáo 鱼苗 *n* fry

yú qún 鱼群 *n.* shoal

yú zǐ 鱼子 *n.* roe

yú lè 娱乐 *v.t.* amuse

yú lè 娱乐 *n* amusement

yú lè 娱乐 *n.* entertainment

yú chuán 渔船 *n* smack

yú fū 渔夫 *n* fisherman

yú kuài 愉快 *n* enjoyment

yú kuài 愉快 *n.* pleasure

yú kuài de 愉快的 *a.* jolly

yú kuài de 愉快的 *a* merry

yú kuài de 愉快的 *a.* pleasant

yú kuài de nián qīng rén 愉快的年轻人 *n.* spark

yú bèn 愚笨 *n.* stupidity

yú bèn de 愚笨的 *adj.* daft

yú chǔn 愚蠢 *n* folly

yú chǔn de 愚蠢的 *a* foolish

yú chǔn de 愚蠢的 *a.* idiotic

yú chǔn de 愚蠢的 *a* stupid

yú dùn de 愚钝的 *a* dull

yú nòng 愚弄 *v.t.* trick

yú rén 愚人 *n* fool

yǔ... lí hūn 与...离婚 *v.t* divorce

yǔ... niǔ dǎ 与...扭打 *n.* grapple

yǔ zhòu 宇宙 *n.* universe

yǔ zhòu de 宇宙的 *adj.* cosmic

yǔ máo 羽毛 *n* feather

yǔ máo qiú 羽毛球 *n.* badminton

yǔ máo qiú 羽毛球 *n.* shuttlecock

yǔ shā 羽纱 *n* camlet

yǔ 雨 *n* rain

yǔ jì 雨季 *n.* monsoon

yǔ yún 雨云 *n.* nimbus

yǔ fǎ jiā 语法家 *n.* grammarian

yǔ fǎ xué 语法学 *n.* grammar

yǔ qì 语气 *n.* tone

yǔ wén xué 语文学 *n.* philology

yǔ wén xué de 语文学的 *a.* philological

yǔ wén xué zhě 语文学者 *n.* philologist

yǔ yán 语言 *n.* language

yǔ yán de 语言的 *a.* lingual

yǔ yán de 语言的 *a.* linguistic

yǔ yán fēng gé 语言风格 *n.* locution

yǔ yán xué 语言学 *n.* linguistics

yǔ yán xué jiā 语言学家 *n.* linguist

yǔ yīn de 语音的 *a.* phonetic

yǔ yīn xué 语音学 *n.* phonetics

yù 玉 *n.* jade

yù mǐ 玉米 *n* corn

yù shǔ shǔ 玉蜀黍 *n.* maize

yù jīn gēn fěn 郁金根粉 *n.* turmeric

yù jīn xiāng 郁金香 *n.* curcuma

yù mèn de 郁闷的 *a.* morose

yù yù bú lè 郁郁不乐 *v.i.* mope

yù bào 预报 *v.t* herald

yù cè 预测 *v.t* forecast

yù dìng 预定 *n.* reservation

yù dìng 预订 *v.t.* reserve

yù fáng 预防 *n.* precaution

yù fáng 预防 *n.* prevention

yù fáng de 预防的 *a.* precautionary

yù fáng de 预防的 *a.* preventive

yù fáng jiē zhòng 预防接种 *v.t.* vaccinate

yù gǎn 预感 *n.* hunch

yù gǎn 预感 *n.* premonition

yù jì 预计 *n.* anticipation

yù jì 预计 *n* bet

yù jiàn 预见 *v.t* foresee

yù liào 预料 *v.t.* anticipate

yù liào 预料 *v.t.* presuppose

yù móu 预谋 *n* forethought

yù móu 预谋 *n.* premeditation

yù qī 预期 *n* antedate

yù qī 预期 *v.t* expect

yù qī de 预期的 *a.* prospective

yù suàn 预算 *n* budget

yù xiān jǐng gào 预先警告 *v.t* forewarn

yù xiān jué dìng 预先决定 *v.t.* predetermine

yù xiān kǎo lǜ 预先考虑 *v.t.* premeditate

yù xiān wǔ zhuāng 预先武装 *v.t* forearm

yù xiān zǔ zhǐ 预先阻止 *v.t* forestall

yù xiǎng 预想 *n* forecast

yù yán 预言 *v.t* foretell

yù yán 预言 *n.* prediction

yù yán 预言 *n.* prophecy

yù yán 预言 *v.t.* prophesy

yù yǎn 预演 *n.* rehearsal

yù yán de 预言的 *a.* prophetic

yù yán zhě 预言者 *n.* prophet

yù yán zhě 预言者 *n.* seer

yù yuē 预约 *n.* appointment

yù zhào 预兆 *n.* auspice

yù zhào 预兆 *n* forerunner

yù zhào 预兆 *n.* omen

yù zhī 预知 *n.* foreknowledge

yù zhī 预知 *v.t.* predict

yù zhī 预知 *n.* prescience

yù gāng 浴缸 *n* bath

yù wàng 欲望 *n.* appetence

yù wàng 欲望 *n.* appetite

yù wàng 欲望 n desire
yù wàng 欲望 n. lust
yù jiàn 遇见 v.t encounter
yù jiàn 遇见 v.t. meet
yù nàn zhě 遇难者 n. casualty
yù yán 寓言 n apologue
yù yán 寓言 n. fable
yù yán 寓言 n. parable
yù yì 寓意 n. allegory
yù yì 寓意 n. moral
yù zú 狱卒 n. jailer
yù hé 愈合 v.t. conglutinate
yuán shuài 元帅 n marshal
yuán yīn 元音 n. vowel
yuán yì 园艺 n. horticulture
yuán yì jiā 园艺家 n. gardener
yuán gào 原告 n. plaintiff
yuán lǐ 原理 n. rationale
yuán liàng 原谅 v.t excuse
yuán liàng 原谅 v.t forgive
yuán shǐ de 原始的 a. original
yuán shǐ de 原始的 a. primeval
yuán shǐ rén 原始人 n savage
yuán wén de 原文的 n. textual
yuán wù 原物 n original
yuán xíng 原型 n. prototype
yuán yīn 原因 n. reason
yuán zé 原则 n. creed
yuán zé 原则 n. principle
yuán zé 原则 n. tenet
yuán zǐ 原子 n. atom
yuán zǐ de 原子的 a. atomic
yuán zǐ hé 原子核 n. nucleus
yuán zǐ hé de 原子核的 a. nuclear
yuán zhù mín 原住民 n.pl aborigines
yuán dǐng 圆顶 n dome
yuán mù 圆木 n. log
yuán pán 圆盘 n. disc
yuán quān 圆圈 n. circle
yuán xíng 圆形 a circular
yuán xíng de 圆形的 a. round
yuán zhōu 圆周 n. circumference
yuán zhù xíng 圆柱型 n cylinder
yuán zhuī xíng 圆锥形 n. cone
yuán zhù 援助 n aid

yuán zhù 援助 n. succour
yuán jiù 援救 v.t. rescue
yuán jiù 援救 n rescue
yuán 猿 n ape
yuǎn 远 adv. afar
yuǎn de 远的 a distant
yuǎn de 远的 a far
yuǎn jǐng 远景 n. perspective
yuǎn jǐng 远景 n. vista
yuǎn shì de 远视的 a. telescopic
yuǎn zhēng 远征 n expedition
yuǎn zú 远足 n. excursion
yuàn xì 院系 n faculty
yuàn zhǎng 院长 n. dean
yuàn hèn 怨恨 n grudge
yuàn hèn 怨恨 n. resentment
yuàn hèn 怨恨 n. spite
yuàn yán 怨言 n complaint
yuàn yán 怨言 n. quarrel
yuàn 愿 v.t. wish
yuàn néng 愿能 v may
yuàn wàng 愿望 n. wish
yuàn yì 愿意 v.t. will
yuē hǎo de 约好的 a. promissory
yuē huì 约会 v.t date
yuē huì 约会 n. engagement
yuē huì 约会 n. rendezvous
yuē shù de 约束的 a. restrictive
yuè 月 n. month
yuè guì shù 月桂树 n laurel
yuè jīng 月经 n. menses
yuè jīng bú diào 月经不调 n amenorrhoea
yuè jīng de 月经的 a. menstrual
yuè jīng qī jiān 月经期间 n. menstruation
yuè kān 月刊 n monthly
yuè liang 月亮 n. moon
yuè qì yǎn zòu zhě 乐器演奏者 n. instrumentalist
yuè tuán 乐团 n. band
yuè guò 越过 v.t hurdle
yuè guò 越过 adv over
yuè guò… 越过… prep. over
yuè jiè 越界 v.t. transgress
yūn jué 晕厥 n. swoon
yún 云 n. cloud
yún mǔ 云母 n. mica

yún què 云雀 *n.* lark
yún xǔ 允许 *v.t.* allow
yún xǔ 允许 *n.* consent
yún xǔ 允许 *v.t.* consent
yún xǔ 允许 *v.t.* grant
yún xǔ 允许 *v.t.* permit
yún xǔ 允许 *v.t.* vouchsafe
yǔn nuò 允诺 *v.t* promise
yùn fù qīng sōng 孕腹轻松 *n.*
  lightening
yùn dòng 运动 *n.* campaign
yùn dòng 运动 *n.* exercise
yùn dòng 运动 *n.* motion
yùn dòng 运动 *n.* sport
yùn dòng 运动 *v.i.* sport
yùn dòng de 运动的 *a.* athletic
yùn dòng de 运动的 *a.* sportive
yùn dòng huì 运动会 *n.* meet
yùn dòng shān 运动衫 *n.* jersey
yùn dòng yuán 运动员 *n.*
  athlete
yùn dòng yuán 运动员 *n.*
  sportsman
yùn hé 运河 *n.* canal
yùn qi 运气 *n.* luck
yùn shū 运输 *n* conveyance
yùn shū 运输 *v.t.* transport
yùn shū 运输 *n.* transit
yùn shū fèi 运输费 *n.* cartage
yùn shū gōng jù 运输工具 *n.*
  transport
yùn shū xíng 运输行 *n.* carrier
yùn sòng 运送 *v.t* ferry
yùn xíng 运行 *v.i* function
yùn yòng 运用 *v.t.* wield
yùn lǜ xué 韵律学 *n.* prosody
yùn chuán 晕船 *n.* nausea
yùn dǒu 熨斗 *n.* iron

Z

zā 咂 *v.t.* suck
zā zuǐ 咂嘴 *v.t.* smack
zá cǎo 杂草 *n.* weed
zá duō de 杂多的 *a.* sundry
zá huò shāng 杂货商 *n.*
  milliner
zá jì 杂记 *n.* miscellany

zá jì yǎn yuán 杂技演员 *n.*
  acrobat
zá luàn 杂乱 *n* disorder
zá sè de 杂色的 *a.* motley
zá zhì 杂质 *n.* impurity
zá zhǒng 杂种 *n* hybrid
zá zhǒng de 杂种的 *a.* hybrid
zá zhǒng gǒu 杂种狗 *a* mongrel
zāi huò 灾祸 *n* disaster
zāi nàn 灾难 *n.* calamity
zāi péi zhě 栽培者 *n.* grower
zài 在 *prep.* at
zài … de qī jiān 在…的期间
  prep during
zài … de xià mian 在…的下面
  prep. underneath
zài … nèi 在…内 *v.t.* withhold
zài … nèi 在…内 *prep.* within
zài … shàng 在…上 *prep.* on
zài … shàng 在…上 *v.i.* stamp
zài … shàng qiàn bǎn zi 在…上
  嵌板子 *v.t.* panel
zài … xià 在…下 *prep.* under
zài … zhī shàng 在…之上 *prep*
  outside
zài chuán wài 在船外 *adv.*
  overboard
zài chuáng shàng 在床上 *adv.*
  abed
zài fǎ tíng xiāng zhēng 在法庭相
  争 *v.t.* litigate
zài hé chù 在何处 *adv.*
  whereabouts
zài hù nèi 在户内 *adv.* indoors
zài lǐ miàn 在里面 *adv.* inside
zài nà bian 在那边 *adv.* yonder
zài nǎ fāng miàn 在哪方面 *adv.*
  wherein
zài nà lǐ 在那里 *adv.* there
zài nà lǐ 在那里 *ad.* whereat
zài nǎ lǐ 在哪里 *adv.* where
zài nèi 在内 *adv.* within
zài shàng mian 在上面 *adv.* aloft
zài shàng mian 在上面 *adv.*
  upwards
zài shì chǎng shàng chū shòu 在
  市场上出售 *v.t* market

zài tóu qiú yuán yòu cè de wài cháng shǒu chǎng yuán 在投球员右侧的外场守场员 *n.* mid-on

zài wài bù 在外部 *adv.* without

zài wài miàn 在外面 *adv* outside

zài xià 在下 *adv* under

zài xià mian 在下面 *adv.* underneath

zài xiān de 在先的 *a.* prior

zài zhè lǐ 在这里 *adv.* here

zài zhè lǐ fù jìn 在这里附近 *adv.* hereabouts

zài zhī qián 在之前 *v.t.* antecede

zài zhí zhě 在职者 *n.* incumbent

zài zhōng jiān 在中间 *prep.* amid

zài... qī jiān 在...期间 *prep.* in

zài... zhī nèi 在...之内 *prep.* inside

zài 再 *adv.* again

zài bǎn 再版 *v.t.* reprint

zài cì xíng chéng 再次形成 *adj* anamorphous

zài huì 再会 *interj.* farewell

zài jiàn 再见 *interj.* bye-bye

zài jiàn 再见 *interj.* good-bye

zài shēng 再生 *n.* rebirth

zài shēng 再生 *v.t.* reproduce

zài xiàn 再现 *n.* recurrence

zài xí lǐ 再洗礼 *n* anabaptism

zàn chéng 赞成 *v.i.* assent

zàn chéng 赞成 *v.t* favour

zàn chéng rén 赞成人 *n.* seconder

zàn měi 赞美 *v.t.* glorify

zàn měi 赞美 *n* laud

zàn shí de 暂时的 *a.* provisional

zàn shí de 暂时的 *a.* temporary

zàn shí de 暂时的 *a.* transitory

zàn shí tíng zhǐ 暂时停止 *v.t.* suspend

zàn shí xìng 暂时性 *n.* provisonality

zàn tíng 暂停 *n.* pause

zàn tíng 暂停 *v.i.* pause

zàn yáng 赞扬 *n.* compliment

zàn yáng 赞扬 *v.t* compliment

zàn yáng 赞扬 *v.t* exalt

zàn zhù 赞助 *n.* patronage

zàn zhù 赞助 *v.t.* sponsor

zàn zhù rén 赞助人 *n.* patron

zàn zhù zhě 赞助者 *n.* sponsor

zāng wù 赃物 *n* booty

zāng wù 赃物 *n.* loot

zàng hóng huā 藏红花 *n.* saffron

zàng lǐ 葬礼 *n* burial

zàng lǐ 葬礼 *n.* funeral

zāo yù 遭遇 *n.* encounter

záo suì dào 凿隧道 *v.i.* tunnel

záo zi 凿子 *n* chisel

zǎo 早 *adv* early

zǎo cān 早餐 *n* breakfast

záo chǎn 早产 *v.i.* miscarry

záo chǎn de 早产的 *a.* premature

zǎo chén 早晨 *n.* morning

zǎo rì de 早日的 *a* early

zǎo 蚤 *n.* flea

zào bì chǎng 造币厂 *n* mint

zào fǎn 造反 *v.i.* rebel

zào wō 造窝 *v.i.* nestle

zé bèi 责备 *v.t.* chide

zé bèi 责备 *v.t.* reproach

zé bèi 责备 *n.* reproach

zé bèi 责备 *n.* reproof

zé bèi 责备 *v.t* upbraid

zé guài 责怪 *v.t* blame

zé mà 责骂 *v.t.* scold

zé rèn 责任 *n* blame

zé rèn 责任 *n* charge

zé rèn 责任 *n* duty

zé rèn 责任 *n.* liability

zé rèn 责任 *n.* obligation

zé rèn 责任 *n.* onus

zé rèn 责任 *n.* responsibility

zé rèn 责任 *n.* trust

zéi 贼 *n* burglar

zéi 贼 *n.* thief

zěn me 怎么 *interj.* what

zěn yàng 怎样 *adv.* how

zēng bǔ 增补 *n.* supplement

zēng bǔ de 增补的 *a.* supplementary

zēng gāo 增高 *v.t.* heighten

zēng jiā 增加 *v.t.* maximize

zēng jiā 增加 *v.t.* accrete

zēng jiā 增加 *v.t.* augment

zēng jiā 增加 *n.* augmentation

zēng jiā 增加 *v.t.* increase

zēng jiā 增加 *n* increase

zēng jiā 增加 *n.* rise

zēng jìn 增进 *v.t* further

zēng jìn 增进 *v.t.* gain

zēng shēng 增生 *n.* concrescence

zēng wēi yán 增威严 *v.t* dignify

zēng wù 憎恶 *v.t.* loathe

zēng yì 增益 *n* gain

zēng zhǎng 增长 *n* accrementition

zēng zhí 增值 *v.i.* accrue

zēng zhí 增值 *n.* increment

zēng zhì sān bèi 增至三倍 *v.i.* triple

zēng hèn 憎恨 *v.t.* hate

zèng 赠 *v.t* bestow

zèng sòng rén 赠送人 *n* donor

zhá 闸 *n.* gate

zhá yǎn 眨眼 *v.t.&i* blink

zhá yǎn 眨眼 *v.i.* wink

zhà qǔ 诈取 *v.t* fleece

zhà qǔ 诈取 *v.t.* swindle

zhà 炸 *v.t* bomb

zhà dàn 炸弹 *n* bomb

zhà làn 炸烂 *v.i* blast

zhà yào 炸药 *n.* explosive

zhà chū wù 榨出物 *n* extract

zhà qǔ 榨取 *v.t* extract

zhāi jiè 斋戒 *v.i* fast

zhāi 摘 *v.t.* pick

zhāi yào 摘要 *n* abridgement

zhāi yào 摘要 *n* abstract

zhāi yào 摘要 *n.* breviary

zhāi yào 摘要 *n.* digest

zhāi yào 摘要 *n.* precis

zhǎi 窄 *a.* narrow

zhài 债 *n.pl.* arrears

zhài wù 债务 *n* debt

zhài wù rén 债务人 *n* debtor

zhài zhǔ 债主 *n* creditor

zhān hé de 粘合的 *a.* adhesive

zhān hé jì 粘合剂 *n.* adhesive

zhān xiàn 粘线 *a* crazy

zhān zhù 粘住 *n.* adhesion

zhǎn 斩 *v.t.* lop

zhǎn lǎn 展览 *n.* exhibition

zhǎn lǎn pǐn 展览品 *n.* exhibit

zhǎn chū 展出 *v.t* exhibit

zhǎn kāi 展开 *v.t.* deploy

zhǎn wàng 展望 *n.* prospect

zhàn xīng xué 占星学 *n.* astrology

zhàn xīng xué jiā 占星学家 *n.* astrologer

zhàn yòng 占用 *v.t.* occupy

zhàn yòng zhě 占用者 *n.* occupier

zhàn yǒu 占有 *n.* occupancy

zhàn yǒu 占有 *n.* tenure

zhàn yǒu rén 占有人 *n.* occupant

zhàn yōu shì 占优势 *v.i.* predominate

zhàn yōu shì 占优势 *v.i.* preponderate

zhàn yōu shì de 占优势的 *a* dominant

zhàn zhú dǎo dì wèi de 占主导地位的 *a.* predominant

zhàn chē 战车 *n* chariot

zhàn dòu 战斗 *n* battle

zhàn dòu 战斗 *a.* combatant

zhàn dòu zhōng dì 战斗中的 *a.* militant

zhàn lì 战栗 *n* shudder

zhàn lì 战栗 *v.i.* tremble

zhàn lì pǐn 战利品 *n.* trophy

zhàn lüè de 战略的 *a.* strategic

zhàn shèng 战胜 *v.t.* worst

zhàn shì 战士 *n* combatant

zhàn zhēng 战争 *n.* war

zhàn zhēng 战争 *n.* warfare

zhàn zhēng de 战争的 *a.* martial

zhàn dé zhù de 站得住的 *a.* tenable

zhàn lì 站立 *v.i.* stand

zhàn lì 站立 *n.* standing

zhàn tái 站台 *n.* platform

zhāng 章 *n.* chapter

zhāng láng 蟑螂 *n* cockroach

zhāng nǎo 樟脑 *n.* camphor

zhāng tiē 张帖 *v.t.* post

zhāng zhān wù 张粘物 *n.* sticker

zhǎng bèi 长辈 *n.* seniority

zhǎng dé kuài 长得快 *v.t.* outgrow

zhǎng guān 长官 *n.* prefect

zhǎng máo chuí ěr gǒu 长毛垂耳狗 *n.* spaniel

zhǎng yá 长牙 *n.* tusk

zhǎng wò 掌握 *n* clutch

zhǎng shēng 掌声 *n.* applause

zhàng fu 丈夫 *n* husband

zhàng peng 帐篷 *n.* tent

zhàng dān 账单 *n* bill

zhàng hào 账号 *n.* account

zhàng ài 障碍 *n.* barrier

zhàng ài 障碍 *n* handicap

zhàng ài 障碍 *n.* impediment

zhàng ài wù 障碍物 *n.* obstacle

zhāo dài 招待 *v.t.* serve

zhāo dài 招待 *v.i.* tend

zhāo hu 招呼 *v.t* hail

zhāo hún shù 招魂术 *n.* spiritualism

zhāo jí 招集 *v.t.* assemble

zhāo shǒu 招手 *v.t* beckon

zhāo zhì 招致 *v.t.* incur

zháo huǒ 着火 *adv.* ablaze

zháo mí 着迷 *v.i* swoon

zháo mó 着魔 *n.* obsession

zhǎo 爪 *n* claw

zhǎo 爪 *n.* paw

zhǎo dì 沼地 *n.* swamp

zhǎo dì de 沼地的 *a.* marshy

zhǎo zé 沼泽 *n* bog

zhào jí 召集 *v.t.* array

zhào jí 召集 *v.t.* convoke

zhào jí rén 召集人 *n* convener

zhào gù 照顾 *n.* care

zhào liàng de 照亮的 *v.i.* alight

zhào liào 照料 *v.t* nurse

zhào míng 照明 *v.t.* illuminate

zhào míng 照明 *n.* illumination

zhào pī fā 照批发 *adv.* wholesale

zhào xiàng 照相 *v.t.* photograph

zhào shān 罩衫 *n.* overall

zhào shān 罩衫 *n.* smock

zhào zi 罩子 *n* bonnet

zhē 遮 *v.t.* shade

zhē bì 遮蔽 *v.t.* cover

zhē bì 遮蔽 *v.t.* obscure

zhē bì 遮蔽 *v.t.* veil

zhē yǎn 遮眼 *v.t.* hoodwink

zhē yīn 遮阴 *v.t.* overshadow

zhē zhù 遮住 *v.t* shadow

zhé céng 折层 *n* fold

zhé dié 折叠 *v.t* fold

zhé duàn 折断 *adv.* asunder

zhé kòu 折扣 *n* discount

zhé mó 折磨 *v.t.* afflict

zhé mó 折磨 *v.t* bedevil

zhé mó 折磨 *n.* ordeal

zhé mó 折磨 *v.t.* plague

zhé mó 折磨 *v.t.* torment

zhé mó zhě 折磨者 *n.* torment

zhé xué 哲学 *n.* philosophy

zhé xué de 哲学的 *a.* philosophical

zhé xué jiā 哲学家 *n.* philosopher

zhé hén 摺痕 *n* crease

zhé jì 辙迹 *n.* rut

zhè yàng de 这样的 *a.* such

zhè yàng de rén 这样的人 *pron.* such

zhēn jié 贞节 *n.* chastity

zhēn jié de 贞节的 *a.* chaste

zhēn 针 *n.* needle

zhēn 针 *n.* pin

zhēn de 针的 *a.* spinal

zhēn jiǎo 针脚 *n.* stitch

zhēn chá 侦察 *v.i.* spy

zhēn chá yuán 侦察员 *n* scout

zhēn tàn 侦探 *n.* detective

zhēn tàn de 侦探的 *a* detective

zhēn ài 珍爱 *v.t.* treasure

zhēn guì de 珍贵的 *a.* precious

zhēn shì 珍视 *v.t.* prize

zhēn xī 珍惜 *v.t.* cherish

zhēn de 真的 *a.* real

zhēn jūn 真菌 *n.* fungus

zhēn kōng 真空 *n.* vacuum

zhēn shí 真实 *n.* sincerity

zhēn shí de 真实的 *a.* actual

zhēn shí de 真实的 *a.* true
zhēn shí dì 真实地 *adv.* really
zhēn xiàng 真相 *n.* truth
zhēn zhèng de 真正的 *a.* authentic
zhēn zhèng de 真正的 *a* bonafide
zhēn zhèng de 真正的 *a.* genuine
zhēn zhèng de 真正的 *a.* straightforward
zhēn zhì de 真挚的 *a.* sincere
zhēn 砧 *n.* anvil
zhēn zhū 珍珠 *n.* pearl
zhěn suǒ 诊所 *n.* clinic
zhěn duàn 诊断 *v.t* diagnose
zhěn duàn 诊断 *n* diagnosis
zhěn tou 枕头 *n* pillow
zhèn dòng 振动 *v.i.* vibrate
zhèn dòng 震动 *n.* pulsation
zhèn dòng 震动 *n.* quiver
zhèn dòng 震动 *n.* shock
zhèn dòng 震动 *n.* tremor
zhèn dòng 震动 *n.* vibration
zhèn dòng de 震动的 *a.* shaky
zhèn yáo 震摇 *n.* jolt
zhèn jìng 镇静 *v.t.* calm
zhèn jìng 镇静 *n.* composure
zhèn jìng de 镇静的 *adj* calmative
zhèn jìng jì 镇静剂 *n* sedative
zhèn qū 镇区 *a.* township
zhèn yā 镇压 *v.t.* repress
zhèn yā 镇压 *v.t.* stifle
zhèn yā 镇压 *v.t.* suppress
zhèn yā 镇压 *n.* suppression
zhēng 争 *v.i.* vie
zhēng biàn 争辩 *v.t.* argue
zhēng biàn 争辩 *v.t* contest
zhēng chǎo 争吵 *v.t* bicker
zhēng chǎo 争吵 *v.i.* row
zhēng chǎo 争吵 *v.i.* wrangle
zhēng dòu 争斗 *n.* tussle
zhēng lùn 争论 *n.* altercation
zhēng lùn 争论 *n.* conflict
zhēng lùn 争论 *n* contention
zhēng lùn 争论 *n* controversy
zhēng lùn 争论 *v.t.* debate
zhēng lùn 争论 *n* dispute

zhēng lùn 争论 *v.i* dispute
zhēng lùn 争论 *n.* wrangle
zhēng fú 征服 *v.t* conquer
zhēng fú 征服 *n* conquest
zhēng fú 征服 *v.t.* subdue
zhēng fú 征服 *v.t.* subjugate
zhēng fú 征服 *n.* subjugation
zhēng mù 征募 *v.t.* recruit
zhēng shōu 征收 *n.* imposition
zhēng shōu 征收 *v.t.* levy
zhēng shōu 征收 *v.t.* toll
zhēng shuì 征税 *v.t.* tax
zhēng shuì 征税 *n.* taxation
zhēng yòng 征用 *v.t.* requisition
zhēng zhá 挣扎 *v.i.* struggle
zhēng fā 蒸发 *v.i* evaporate
zhēng fā 蒸发 *v.i.* steam
zhēng fā 蒸发 *v.t.* vaporize
zhēng liú 蒸馏 *v.t* distil
zhēng lóng 蒸笼 *n.* steamer
zhēng qì 蒸汽 *n* steam
zhēng qì 蒸气 *n.* vapour
zhēng qì de 蒸气的 *a.* vaporous
zhēng jiù 拯救 *n.* salvation
zhěng 整 *v.t* create
zhěng dùn 整顿 *v.t.* straighten
zhěng jié de 整洁的 *a.* neat
zhěng jié de 整洁的 *a.* smug
zhěng lǐ 整理 *v.t.* make
zhěng lǐ 整理 *v.t* marshal
zhěng lǐ 整理 *v.t* sort
zhěng qí 整齐 *n.* tidiness
zhěng qí de 整齐的 *a.* tidy
zhěng tǐ 整体 *n* whole
zhèng 正 *adv* due
zhèng cháng de 正常的 *a.* normal
zhèng cháng zhuàng tài 正常状态 *n.* normalcy
zhèng dāng de 正当的 *a.* righteous
zhèng de 正的 *a.* plus
zhèng de 正的 *a.* positive
zhèng fāng xíng 正方形 *n.* square
zhèng fāng xíng de 正方形的 *a* square
zhèng hào 正号 *n* plus
zhèng hǎo 正好 *adv.* just

zhèng què 正确 *adv* aright
zhèng què de 正确的 *a* correct
zhèng què de 正确的 *a*. right
zhèng shì de 正式的 *a* formal
zhèng shì de 正式的 *a*. official
zhèng shì qǐng qiú 正式请求 *n*. requisition
zhèng shì tuō lí 正式脱离 *v.i.* secede
zhèng tǒng pài de 正统派的 *a*. orthodox
zhèng tǒng pài de guān niàn 正统派的观念 *n*. orthodoxy
zhèng wén 正文 *n*. text
zhèng wǔ 正午 *n*. midday
zhèng wǔ 正午 *n*. noon
zhèng yì 正义 *n*. justice
zhèng zhí de 正直的 *a*. just
zhèng jù 证据 *n* evidence
zhèng jù 证据 *n*. proof
zhèng jù 证据 *n*. testimony
zhèng míng 证明 *v.t.* justify
zhèng míng 证明 *v.t.* prove
zhèng míng rén 证明人 *n*. deponent
zhèng míng wú gū 证明无辜 *n*. vindication
zhèng míng zhèng dāng 证明正当 *n*. justification
zhèng shí 证实 *n* affirmation
zhèng shí 证实 *v.t.* attest
zhèng shí 证实 *v.t.* certify
zhèng shí 证实 *v.t.* corroborate
zhèng shí 证实 *v.t.* substantiate
zhèng shí 证实 *n*. substantiation
zhèng shí 证实 *v.i.* testify
zhèng shí 证实 *v.t.* validate
zhèng shí 证实 *n*. verification
zhèng shí 证实 *v.t.* verify
zhèng shū 证书 *n*. certificate
zhèng zhòng dì xuān bù 郑重地宣布 *v.t.* vow
zhèng biàn 政变 *n*. coup
zhèng fǔ 政府 *n*. government
zhèng zhì 政治 *n*. politics
zhèng zhì de 政治的 *a*. political
zhèng zhì jiā 政治家 *n*. politician

zhèng zhì jiā 政治家 *n*. statesman
zhèng zhì zǔ zhī 政治组织 *n*. polity
zhèng zhuàng 症状 *n*. symptom
zhī hòu 之后 *prep*. after
zhī hòu 之后 *adv*. afterwards
zhī jiān 之间 *prep* between
zhī qián 之前 *adv*. ago
zhī qián 之前 *prep* before
zhī qián 之前 *conj* before
zhī qián 之前 *prep*. afore
zhī zhōng 之中 *prep*. among
zhī zhōng 之中 *prep*. amongst
zhī chēng 支撑 *v.t.* prop
zhī chēng 支撑 *v.t.* sustain
zhī chí 支持 *v.t.* second
zhī chí 支持 *v.i.* side
zhī chí 支持 *v.t.* support
zhī chí 支持 *n*. support
zhī chí 支持 *v.t* uphold
zhī chí wù 支持物 *n* brace
zhī fù 支付 *v.t.* pay
zhī liú 支流 *n*. tributary
zhī liú de 支流的 *a*. tributary
zhī pèi 支配 *v.t* dominate
zhī piào 支票 *n*. cheque
zhī wàn zhàng 支腕杖 *n*. maulstick
zhī wú 支吾 *v.i* falter
zhī zhù 支柱 *n*. mainstay
zhī zhù 支柱 *n* stake
zhī 汁 *n* juice
zhī zhī jiào 吱吱叫 *v.i* cheep
zhī 肢 *n*. limb
zhī 织 *v.t.* weave
zhī bù jī 织布机 *n* loom
zhī gōng 织工 *n*. weaver
zhī huā zhào tǎn 织花罩毯 *n*. tapestry
zhī dào 知道 *a*. aware
zhī dào 知道 *v.t.* know
zhī jǐ 知己 *n* confidant
zhī jué 知觉 *n*. perception
zhī jué de 知觉的 *a*. perceptive
zhī shí 知识 *n*. knowledge
zhī shí 知识 *n*. lore
zhī shí fèn zǐ 知识分子 *n*. intellectual

zhī shí jiè 知识界 n. intelligentsia

zhī zú 知足 v.t content

zhī tiáo 枝条 n. withe

zhī jia cuò 指甲锉 n file

zhī fáng 脂肪 n fat

zhī fáng 脂肪 n grease

zhī zhū 蜘蛛 n. spider

zhī zhū wǎng 蜘蛛网 n cobweb

zhī zhū wǎng 蜘蛛网 n. web

zhí dá yuán 执达员 n. bailiff

zhí shì 执事 n. deacon

zhí xíng 执行 v.t execute

zhí xíng 执行 v.t. implement

zhí xíng 执行 n. prosecution

zhí zhào 执照 n. licence

zhí zhào 执照 n. warrant

zhí 直 adv. straight

zhí cháng 直肠 n. rectum

zhí chǐ 直尺 n. ruler

zhí dào ⋯ wéi zhǐ 直到⋯为止 prep. till

zhí dào ⋯ wéi zhǐ 直到⋯为止 n.conj. till

zhí dào ⋯ wéi zhǐ 直到⋯为止 conj until

zhí jiē de 直接的 a direct

zhí jìng 直径 n diameter

zhí jué 直觉 n. instinct

zhí jué 直觉 n. intuition

zhí jué de 直觉的 a. instinctive

zhí jué de 直觉的 a. intuitive

zhí lì 直立 n erection

zhí lì de 直立的 a erect

zhí shuài de rén 直率的人 a. outspoken

zhí tǐng de 直挺的 a. straight

zhí nǚ 侄女 n. niece

zhí zi 侄子 n. nephew

zhí dé ⋯ 值得⋯ a worth

zhí dé chēng zàn de 值得称赞的 a. praiseworthy

zhí dé de 值得⋯的 a. worthy

zhí dé jiǎng lì de 值得奖励的 a. meritorious

zhí dé zàn měi de 值得赞美的 a. commendable

zhí dé zàn shǎng de 值得赞赏的 a. laudable

zhí dé zūn jìng de 值得尊敬的 a. venerable

zhí děi zhù yì de 值得注意的 a. notable

zhí děi zhù yì de 值得注意的 a. noteworthy

zhí děi zhù yì de 值得注意的 a. remarkable

zhí wèi 职位 n post

zhí yè 职业 n. occupation

zhí yè 职业 n. profession

zhí yè 职业 n. vocation

zhí yè shēng yá 职业生涯 n. career

zhí yuán 职员 n. staff

zhí yuán de 职员的 a clerical

zhí mín de 殖民的 a colonial

zhí mín dì 殖民地 n colony

zhí wù 植物 n. plant

zhí wù 植物 n. vegetation

zhí wù qún 植物群 n flora

zhí wù xué 植物学 n botany

zhǐ 纸 n. paper

zhǐ chū 指出 v.t. indicate

zhǐ chū 指出 v.t. point

zhǐ dǎo 指导 v.t direct

zhǐ dǎo 指导 n. guidance

zhǐ dǎo 指导 v.t. guide

zhǐ dìng dài lǐ rén 指定代理人 v.t depute

zhǐ huī guān 指挥官 n commander

zhǐ huī jiā 指挥家 n conductor

zhǐ lìng 指令 n. instruction

zhǐ nán 指南 n. guide

zhǐ nán zhēn 指南针 n compass

zhǐ pài 指派 v.t. assign

zhǐ shì 指示 v.t denote

zhǐ shì 指示 n. indication

zhǐ shì 指示 v.t. instruct

zhǐ shì qì 指示器 n. indicator

zhǐ zé 指责 v.t. condemn

zhǐ zé 指责 n. rebuke

zhǐ jiāng 纸浆 n. pulp

zhǐ jiāng zhuàng de 纸浆状的 a. pulpy

zhǐ jīn 纸巾 n. tissue

zhì jīn 至今 *adv.* hitherto

zhì xiàng 志向 *n.* aspiration

zhì yuàn zhě 志愿者 *n.* volunteer

zhì dì 质地 *n.* texture

zhì liàng 质量 *n.* quality

zhì jīn xué 冶金学 *n.* metallurgy

zhì liáo 治疗 *v.t* remedy

zhì liáo 治疗 *n.* treatment

zhì biǎo rén 制表人 *n.* tabulation

zhì biǎo rén 制表人 *n.* tabulator

zhì cái 制裁 *n.* sanction

zhì chéng báo bǎn 制成薄板 *v.t.* laminate

zhì chéng biǎo gé 制成表格 *v.t.* tabulate

zhì chéng dòng huà 制成动画 *v.t.* animate

zhì chéng sān míng zhì 制成三明治 *v.t.* sandwich

zhì dìng fǎ lǜ 制定法律 *v.t* enact

zhì dìng fǎ lǜ 制定法律 *v.i.* legislate

zhì dìng zhì cái guī zé 制定制裁规则 *v.t.* sanction

zhì dòng qì 制动器 *n* skid

zhì fú 制服 *n.* livery

zhì gé chǎng 制革厂 *n.* tannery

zhì gé gōng rén 制革工人 *n.* tanner

zhì yào gōng sī 制药公司 *n.* compounder

zhì zào 制造 *n* fabrication

zhì zào 制造 *n* make

zhì zào 制造 *n.* production

zhì zào shāng 制造商 *n* manufacturer

zhì zào yè zhě 制造业者 *n* manufacture

zhì zào zhě 制造者 *n.* maker

zhì mìng de 致命的 *a* deadly

zhì mìng de 致命的 *a* fatal

zhì mìng de 致命的 *a.* lethal

zhì gù 桎梏 *n.* shackle

zhì liú fèi 滞留费 *n.* demurrage

zhì chǐ 智齿 *n.* wisdom-tooth

zhì huì 智慧 *n.* wisdom

zhì huì de 智慧的 *a.* mental

zhì lì 智力 *n.* intellect

zhì lì 智力 *n.* intelligence

zhì lì 智力 *n.* wit

zhì lì cè yàn 智力测验 *n.* quiz

zhì lì de 智力的 *a.* intellectual

zhì zhě 智者 *n.* sophist

zhì 痔 *n.* piles

zhì qián bì jué dìng 掷钱币决定 *n* toss

zhì tóu zǐ 掷骰子 *v.i.* dice

zhì xī 窒息 *n* apnoea

zhì xī 窒息 *n.* strangulation

zhì xī 窒息 *n.* suffocation

zhì yú diàn nèi sì fèng 置于殿内祀奉 *v.t* enshrine

zhì yú xiǎn jìng 置于险境 *v.t.* peril

zhōng bù dì qū 中部地区 *n.* midland

zhōng děng de 中等的 *a.* middling

zhōng diàn 中殿 *n.* nave

zhōng duàn 中断 *n* abruption

zhōng duàn 中断 *v.t.* interrupt

zhōng gǔ de 中古的 *a.* medieval

zhōng hào chǐ cùn 中号尺寸 *a* medium

zhōng hé suān de 中和酸的 *adj.* antacid

zhōng jiān 中间 *n.* midst

zhōng jiān 中间 *n* middle

zhōng jiān de 中间的 *a.* intermediate

zhōng jiān de 中间的 *a.* median

zhōng jiān de 中间的 *a.* mid

zhōng jiān de 中间的 *a.* middle

zhōng jiān rén 中间人 *n.* intermediary

zhōng jiān rén 中间人 *n.* middleman

zhōng lì de 中立的 *a.* neutral

zhōng piān xiǎo shuō 中篇小说 *n.* novelette

zhōng shì jì de 中世纪的 *a.* medieval

zhōng shū 中枢 *n.* pivot

zhōng wèi 中尉 *n.* lieutenant

zhōng xīn 中心 *n* center
zhōng xīn 中心 *n* centre
zhōng xīn de 中心的 *a.* central
zhōng xìng de 中性的 *a.* neuter
zhōng zǐ 中子 *n.* neutron
zhōng diǎn zhàn 终点站 *n.* terminus
zhōng jí 终极 *a.* ultimate
zhōng shēn de 终身的 *a.* lifelong
zhōng zhǐ 终止 *v.i* abort
zhōng zhǐ 终止 *v.i.* cease
zhōng zhǐ 终止 *n.* termination
zhōng chéng 忠诚 *n.* allegiance
zhōng chéng de 忠诚的 *a.* loyal
zhōng chéng de rén 忠诚的人 *n.* loyalist
zhōng gào 忠告 *n.* counsel
zhōng shí 忠实 *n* fidelity
zhōng shí de 忠实的 *a* faithful
zhōng shí de chéng yuán 忠实的成员 *n* stalwart
zhōng xīn 忠心 *n.* loyalty
zhōng bǎi 钟摆 *n.* pendulum
zhōng biǎo 钟表 *n.* clock
zhōng shēng 钟声 *n* toll
zhōng tóu 钟头 *n.* hour
zhōng xīn dì 衷心地 *adv.* heartily
zhǒng dà 肿大 *v.i.* swell
zhǒng kuài 肿块 *n.* lump
zhǒng liú 肿瘤 *n.* tumour
zhǒng zhàng 肿胀 *v.i.* strut
zhǒng zhàng 肿胀 *n* swell
zhǒng 种 *v.t.* sow
zhǒng lèi 种类 *n.* category
zhǒng lèi 种类 *n* classification
zhǒng lèi 种类 *n.* kind
zhǒng lèi 种类 *n.* sort
zhǒng lèi 种类 *n.* species
zhǒng lèi 种类 *n.* variety
zhǒng mǎ 种马 *n.* stallion
zhǒng zi 种子 *n.* seed
zhǒng zú de 种族的 *a.* racial
zhǒng zú zhǔ yì 种族主义 *n.* racialism
zhòng shāng 中伤 *v.t.* backbite

zhòng shāng 中伤 *v.t.* defame
zhòng shāng 中伤 *v.t.* libel
zhòng shāng 中伤 *v.t.* vilify
zhòng cái 仲裁 *v.t.* arbitrate
zhòng cái 仲裁 *n.* arbitration
zhòng cái rén 仲裁人 *n.* arbitrator
zhòng xià 仲夏 *n.* midsummer
zhòng zhí 种植 *v.t.* grow
zhòng zhí 种植 *v.t.* plant
zhòng zhí yuán 种植园 *n.* plantation
zhòng dà de 重大的 *a.* momentous
zhòng de 重的 *a.* hefty
zhòng de 重的 *a.* massive
zhòng de 重的 *a.* weighty
zhòng jī 重击 *n.&v.t.* thump
zhòng shì 重视 *v.t.* value
zhòng yào de 重要的 *a.* important
zhòng yào de 重要的 *a.* significant
zhòng yào de 重要的 *a.* vital
zhòng yào xìng 重要性 *n.* importance
zhōu zhǎng 州长 *n.* governor
zhōu qī xìng piān tóu tòng 周期性偏头痛 *n.* migraine
zhōu wéi 周围 *prep.* around
zhōu wéi 周围 *n.* periphery
zhōu wéi de 周围的 *adj.* ambient
zhōu wéi de shì wù 周围的事物 *n.* surroundings
zhōu kān 周刊 *n.* weekly
zhōu 洲 *n* continent
zhōu 粥 *n.* porridge
zhóu 轴 *n.* axis
zhǒu 肘 *n* ancon
zhǒu 肘 *n* elbow
zhòu 咒 *n* curse
zhòu biān 皱边 *n.* frill
zhòu méi 皱眉 *n.* frown
zhòu méi tóu 皱眉头 *v.i* frown
zhòu qǐ 皱起 *v.t.* wrinkle
zhòu wén 皱纹 *n.* furrow
zhòu wén 皱纹 *n.* wrinkle
zhòu zhě 皱褶 *n* crimple

zhū hóng sè 朱红色 *n.* vermillion

zhū hóng sè de 朱红色的 *a.* vermillion

zhū shā 朱砂 *n* cinnabar

zhū rú 侏儒 *n.* pygmy

zhū bǎo 珠宝 *n.* jewel

zhū bǎo hé 珠宝盒 *n* casket

zhū bǎo shāng 珠宝商 *n.* jeweller

zhū zi 珠子 *n* bead

zhū 猪 *n.* pig

zhū 猪 *n.* swine

zhū bí zi 猪鼻子 *n.* snout

zhū juàn 猪圈 *n.* sty

zhū ròu 猪肉 *n.* pork

zhū yóu 猪油 *n.* lard

zhú mǎ 竹马 *n.* hobby-horse

zhú yù 竹芋 *n.* arrowroot

zhú zi 竹子 *n.* bamboo

zhú chū 逐出 *v.t* evict

zhú chū 逐出 *n* eviction

zhú chū 逐出 *n.* expulsion

zhú chū 逐出 *v.t.* oust

zhú chū 逐出 *v.t.* out-balance

zhú chū jiào huì 逐出教会 *v.t.* excommunicate

zhú jiàn de 逐渐的 *a.* gradual

zhú jiàn xuē báo 逐渐削薄 *v.t.* whittle

zhú zì de 逐字的 *a.* verbatim

zhú zì dì 逐字地 *adv.* verbatim

zhú tuì 逐退 *v.t.* repel

zhú huā 烛花 *n.* snuff

zhǔ kǎo zhě 主考者 *n* examiner

zhǔ chí 主持 *v.i.* officiate

zhǔ chí 主持 *v.i.* preside

zhǔ dòng xíng dòng 主动行动 *n.* initiative

zhǔ guān de 主观的 *a.* subjective

zhǔ jiāo 主教 *n* bishop

zhǔ jiāo guàn 主教冠 *n.* mitre

zhǔ quán 主权 *n.* sovereignty

zhǔ rén 主人 *n.* master

zhǔ tí 主题 *n.* motif

zhǔ tí 主题 *n.* subject

zhǔ tí 主题 *n.* theme

zhǔ tí 主题 *n.* topic

zhǔ tí de 主题的 *a.* thematic

zhǔ xí 主席 *n* chairman

zhǔ xiū kè 主修课 *n* major

zhǔ yào chéng shì de 主要城市的 *a.* metropolitan

zhǔ yào de 主要的 *a.* cardinal

zhǔ yào de 主要的 *a* main

zhǔ yào de 主要的 *a.* major

zhǔ yào de 主要的 *a.* prime

zhǔ yào de 主要的 *a* staple

zhǔ yào dì 主要地 *adv.* mainly

zhǔ yào dì 主要地 *adv.* primarily

zhǔ yi 主意 *n.* idea

zhù 住 *v.i* dwell

zhù 住 *v.i.* reside

zhù mǎn rén 住满人 *v.t.* people

zhù sù 住宿 *n.* accommodation

zhù suǒ 住所 *n* abode

zhù suǒ 住所 *n* domicile

zhù zhái 住宅 *n.* residence

zhù chǎn shì 助产士 *n.* midwife

zhù shǒu 助手 *n.* assistant

zhù dìng 注定 *v.t.* doom

zhù rù 注入 *v.t.* infuse

zhù shè 注射 *v.t.* inject

zhù shè 注射 *n.* injection

zhù shè qì 注射器 *n.* syringe

zhù shì 注视 *adv* agaze

zhù shì 注视 *v.t* behold

zhù shì 注视 *v.i.* gaze

zhù shì 注视 *v.t.* watch

zhù shuǐ yú 注水于 *v.t.* water

zhù yì 注意 *n.* attention

zhù yì 注意 *v.t.* heed

zhù yì 注意 *v.t.* mind

zhù yì 注意 *v.t.* notice

zhù yì de 注意的 *a.* mindful

zhù yì de 注意的 *a.* watchful

zhù zi 柱子 *n.* pillar

zhù zhā 驻扎 *v.t.* station

zhù mù de 蛀木的 *a.* xylophilous

zhù hè 祝贺 *n* congratulation

zhù fú 祝福 *n* benison

zhù fú 祝福 *v.t* bless

zhù tiě 铸铁 *n* cast-iron

zhù cháo 筑巢 *v.t.* nest

zhù dī 筑堤 *n* embankment

zhù míng de 著名的 *a.* well-known

zhù zào 铸造 *v.t.* mint

zhù zào chǎng 铸造厂 *n.* foundry

zhuā 抓 *n.* scratch

zhuā 抓 *v.t.* scratch

zhuā jǐn 抓紧 *v.t.* grip

zhuā zhù 抓住 *v.t.* catch

zhuā zhù 抓住 *v.i.* grapple

zhuā zhù 抓住 *v.t.* grasp

zhuā zhù 抓住 *v.t.* seize

zhuān cháng 专长 *n.* speciality

zhuān dì gōng sī 专递公司 *n.* courier

zhuān gōng 专攻 *v.i.* specialize

zhuān hèng de 专横的 *a* autocratic

zhuān jí 专辑 *n.* album

zhuān jiā 专家 *n* expert

zhuān jiā 专家 *n.* specialist

zhuān lì de 专利的 *a.* patent

zhuān lì pǐn 专利品 *n.* monopoly

zhuān lì quán 专利权 *n* patent

zhuān lì zhě 专利者 *n.* monopolist

zhuān lùn 专论 *n.* monograph

zhuān mén de 专门的 *a* expert

zhuān mén huà 专门化 *n.* specialization

zhuān mén shù yǔ 专门术语 *n.* jargon

zhuān tí tǎo lùn huì 专题讨论会 *n.* seminar

zhuān tí tǎo lùn huì 专题讨论会 *n.* symposium

zhuān xīn 专心 *n.* concentration

zhuān xīn de 专心的 *a.* intent

zhuān yè cí diǎn 专业词典 *n.* glossary

zhuān yè de 专业的 *a.* professional

zhuān yǒu de 专有的 *a.* proprietary

zhuān 砖 *n* brick

zhuǎn biàn 转变 *v.t.* switch

zhuǎn biàn 转变 *n.* transition

zhuǎn dòng 转动 *v.i.* turn

zhuǎn huà 转化 *v.t* convert

zhuǎn huàn 转换 *n* conversion

zhuǎn jì 转寄 *v.t* forward

zhuǎn ràng 转让 *v.t.* transfer

zhuǎn wān 转弯 *n* turn

zhuǎn yí 转移 *v.t.* deflect

zhuǎn yí 转移 *v.t* divert

zhuǎn yí 转移 *v.t.* shift

zhuǎn zǐ 转子 *n.* armature

zhuǎn zū 转租 *v.t.* sublet

zhuàn jì 传记 *n* biography

zhuàn jì zuò jiā 传记作家 *n* biographer

zhuàn lüè 传略 *n.* profile

zhuàn dé 赚得 *v.t* earn

zhuāng jia hàn 庄稼汉 *n.* ploughman

zhuāng yán 庄严 *n.* grandeur

zhuāng yán 庄严 *n.* stateliness

zhuāng yán de 庄严的 *a.* majestic

zhuāng yán de 庄严的 *a.* stately

zhuāng yuán 庄园 *n.* manor

zhuāng yuán de 庄园的 *a.* manorial

zhuāng zhòng de 庄重的 *a.* grand

zhuāng 桩 *n.* pale

zhuāng bàn 装扮 *v.t.* adorn

zhuāng bèi 装备 *v.t.* arm

zhuāng bèi 装备 *v.t* equip

zhuāng bèi 装备 *n.* kit

zhuāng bèi 装备 *v.t* outfit

zhuāng bō li gōng 装玻璃工 *n.* glazier

zhuāng guàn 装罐 *v.* can

zhuāng huò 装货 *n.* shipment

zhuāng jìn 装进 *v.t.* stow

zhuāng mǎn 装满 *v.t* fill

zhuāng pèi gōng 装配工 *n* fitter

zhuāng píng jī 装瓶机 *n* bottler

zhuāng rù bāo lǐ 装入包里 *v.i.* bag

zhuāng rù dài 装入袋 *v.t.* sack

zhuāng rù pén zhōng 装入盆中 *v.t.* pot

zhuāng shàng chuán 装上船 *v.t.* ship

zhuāng shì 装饰 *v.t.* apparel
zhuāng shì 装饰 *v.t.* bedight
zhuāng shì 装饰 *v.t* deck
zhuāng shì 装饰 *v.t* decorate
zhuāng shì 装饰 *v.t.* mould
zhuāng shì 装饰 *v.t.* ornament
zhuāng shì 装饰 *n.*
  ornamentation
zhuāng shì de 装饰的 *a.*
  ornamental
zhuāng shì pǐn 装饰品 *n*
  decoration
zhuāng shì pǐn 装饰品 *n.*
  ornament
zhuāng tián 装填 *v.t.* pad
zhuāng xiāng 装箱 *v.t* encase
zhuāng xié dǐ 装鞋底 *v.t* sole
zhuāng yǐ bō li 装以玻璃 *v.t.*
  glaze
zhuāng yǐ mǎ ān 装以马鞍 *v.t.*
  saddle
zhuāng zài 装载 *v.t.* lade
zhuāng zài 装载 *v.t.* load
zhuāng zài guò zhòng huò wù
  装载过重货物 *v.t.* overload
zhuāng zài kǒu dai lǐ 装在口袋
  里 *v.t.* pocket
zhuāng zhì 装置 *n* device
zhuàng dǎn 壮胆 *v.t.* embolden
zhuàng guān 壮观 *a.*
  spectacular
zhuàng lì 壮丽 *n.* pomp
zhuàng kuàng 状况 *n.* state
zhuàng 撞 *v.t.* bang
zhuàng 撞 *v.i* crash
zhuàng 撞 *v.i.* ram
zhuī 追 *v.t.* chase1
zhuī 锥 *n.* wimble
zhuī bǔ 追捕 *n.* chase2
zhuī bǔ zhě 追补者 *n* follower
zhuī gǎn 追赶 *n.* pursuance
zhuī qiú 追求 *v.t.* pursue
zhuī qiú 追求 *n.* pursuit
zhuī qiú 追求 *v.t.* woo
zhuī shàng 追上 *v.t.* overtake
zhuī sù 追溯 *v.t.* retrace
zhuī yì 追忆 *n.* retrospection
zhuī zōng 追踪 *v.i.* stalk
zhuī zōng 追踪 *v.t.* track

zhǔn bèi 准备 *v.i.* gird
zhǔn bèi 准备 *n.* outfit
zhǔn bèi 准备 *n.* preparation
zhǔn bèi 准备 *v.t.* prepare
zhǔn bèi 准备 *n.* readiness
zhǔn bèi hǎo de 准备好的 *a.*
  ready
zhǔn bèi xìng de 准备性的 *a.*
  preparatory
zhǔn què de 准确的 *a.* accurate
zhǔn què de 准确的 *a* exact
zhǔn què de 准确的 *a.* precise
zhǔn què xìng 准确性 *n.*
  accuracy
zhǔn shí de 准时的 *a.* punctual
zhuō liè de mó fǎng 拙劣的模仿
  n. parody
zhuō liè dì mó fǎng 拙劣地模仿
  v.t. parody
zhuō 捉 *v.t.* capture
zhuō 捉 *n.* capture
zhuō zi 桌子 *n.* table
zhuó yuè de 卓越的 *a.*
  transcendent
zhuó 啄 *v.i.* peck
zhuó hén 啄痕 *n.* peck
zī shì 姿势 *n.* pose
zī shì 姿势 *n.* posture
zī běn zhǔ yì zhě 资本主义者 *n.*
  capitalist
zī chǎn 资产 *n.* asset
zī yuán 资源 *n.* resource
zī yuán fēng fù de 资源丰富的
  a. resourceful
zī jīn 资金 *n.* fund
zī bǔ de 滋补的 *a.* tonic
zī wèi 滋味 *n* relish
zī wèi 滋味 *n.* savour
zī yǎng 滋养 *v.t.* nourish
zī zī xiǎng 嗞嗞响 *v.i.* sizzle
zī zī xiǎng 嗞嗞响 *n.* sizzle
zí nǚ 子女 *n.* offspring
zǐ wǔ xiàn 子午线 *a.* meridian
zǐ dàn 子弹 *n* bullet
zǐ gōng 子宫 *n.* uterus
zǐ gōng 子宫 *n.* womb
zǐ sūn 子孙 *n.* progeny
zǐ xì fān xún 仔细翻寻 *v.i.*
  rummage

zǐ xì fān zhǎo 仔细翻找 *n* rummage

zǐ xì jiǎn chá 仔细检查 *v.t.* scrutinize

zǐ xì jiǎn chá 仔细检查 *n.* scrutiny

zǐ xì kǎo lǜ 仔细考虑 *v.i* deliberate

zǐ mèi 姊妹 *n.* sister

zǐ luó lán 紫罗兰 *n.* violet

zǐ mèi yì bān de 姊妹一般的 *a.* sisterly

zǐ mèi zhī yì 姊妹之谊 *n.* sisterhood

zǐ sè 紫色 *adj.&n.* purple

zì diǎn 字典 *n* dictionary

zì miàn shàng de 字面上的 *a.* literal

zì mǔ 字母 *n.* alphabet

zì mǔ shùn xù 字母顺序 *a.* alphabetical

zì bēi 自卑 *n.* inferiority

zì běi de 自北的 *a.* northerly

zì chēng de 自称的 *a.* would-be

zì cǐ yǐ hòu 自此以后 *adv.* henceforth

zì cóng 自从 *prep.* since

zì dà 自大 *n.* arrogance

zì dà 自大 *n* brag

zì dòng de 自动的 *a.* automatic

zì fā de 自发的 *a.* spontaneous

zì fù 自负 *n* conceit

zì fù 自负 *n.* pretension

zì fù 自负 *n.* vanity

zì fù de 自负的 *a.* vain

zì fù de 自负的 *a.* vainglorious

zì mǎn de 自满的 *adj.* complacent

zì jǐ 自己 *n.* self

zì jǐ de 自己的 *a.* own

zì kuā 自夸 *v.i* boast

zì kuā 自夸 *n* boast

zì liàn 自恋 *n.* narcissism

zì mìng bù fán de 自命不凡的 *a.* pretentious

zì rán dì 自然地 *adv.* naturally

zì rán shén lùn xìn yǎng zhě 自然神论信仰者 *n.* deist

zì shā 自杀 *n.* suicide

zì shā xìng de 自杀性的 *a.* suicidal

zì shēng 自生 *n.* spontaneity

zì sī de 自私的 *a.* selfish

zì wèi de 自卫的 *adv.* defensive

zì wǒ 自我 *n* ego

zì wǒ zhǔ yì 自我主义 *n* egotism

zì xiāng máo dùn de 自相矛盾的 *a.* paradoxical

zì xiāng máo dùn de huà 自相矛盾的话 *n.* paradox

zì xíng chē 自行车 *n.* bicycle

zì yóu 自由 *n.* freedom

zì yóu 自由 *n.* liberty

zì yóu de 自由的 *a.* free

zì yóu mín 自由民 *n.* yeoman

zì yóu zhǔ yì 自由主义 *n.* liberalism

zì yuàn 自愿 *v.t.* volunteer

zì yuàn de 自愿的 *a.* voluntary

zì yuàn dì 自愿地 *adv.* voluntarily

zì zé 自责 *n.* remorse

zì zhì de 自治的 *a* autonomous

zì zhuàn 自传 *n.* autobiography

zì zhuàn 自转 *n.* spin

zōng jiào 宗教 *n.* religion

zōng pài de 宗派的 *a.* sectarian

zōng hé 综合 *n.* synthesis

zōng huáng sè 棕黄色 *n.a.* tan

zōng lú shù 棕榈树 *n.* palm

zōng sè 棕色 *a* brown

zōng sè 棕色 *n* brown

zōng máo 鬃毛 *n.* manes

zóng tǒng 总统 *n.* president

zóng tǒng de 总统的 *a.* presidential

zǒng de 总的 *a.* total

zǒng dū 总督 *n.* viceroy

zǒng jì 总计 *v.i* amount

zǒng jié 总结 *v.t.* sum

zǒng jié 总结 *v.t.* summarize

zǒng jié 总结 *n.* summary

zǒng shì 总是 *adv* always

zǒng shù 总数 *n.* count

zǒng shù 总数 n. gross
zǒng shù 总数 n. sum
zǒng shù 总数 n. total
zòng huǒ zuì 纵火罪 n arson
zòng qíng yú 纵情于 v.t.
   indulge
zòng róng 纵容 n. connivance
zòng róng 纵容 n. indulgence
zòng róng 纵容 v.t. pamper
zòng róng de 纵容的 a.
   indulgent
zǒu láng 走廊 n. corridor
zǒu shī le de 走失了的 a stray
zǒu sī 走私 v.t. smuggle
zǒu sī zhě 走私者 n. smuggler
zū chū 租出 v.t. lease
zū hù 租户 n. tenant
zū jīn 租金 n. rent
zū qī 租期 n. tenancy
zū yòng 租用 n. hire
zū yòng 租用 v.t. rent
zū yuē 租约 n. lease
zú gòu 足够 a. ample
zú gòu 足够 adv enough
zú gòu 足够 v.i. suffice
zú gòu de 足够的 a enough
zú gòu de 足够的 a. sufficient
zú 族 n. tribe
zǔ 组 n. group
zǔ ài 阻碍 v.t. discourage
zǔ ài 阻碍 v.t. encumber
zǔ ài 阻碍 v.t. hinder
zǔ ài de 阻碍的 a. obstructive
zǔ ài shēng zhǎng 阻碍生长 v.t.
   stunt
zǔ ài wù 阻碍物 n. hindrance
zǔ náo 阻挠 v.t. thwart
zǔ sè 阻塞 v.t block
zǔ zhǐ 阻止 v.i bog
zǔ zhǐ 阻止 v.t foil
zǔ zhǐ 阻止 v.t. impede
zǔ zhòu 诅咒 v.t curse
zǔ zhòu 诅咒 v.t. damn
zǔ zhòu 诅咒 n. malediction
zǔ chéng de 组成的 adj.
   constituent
zǔ hé 组合 n combination
zǔ jiàn 组件 n. component
zǔ zhī 组织 n. organization

zǔ zhī 组织 v.t. organize
zǔ xiān 祖先 n. ancestor
zǔ xiān 祖先 n. ancestry
zǔ xiān 祖先 n forefather
zǔ xiān de 祖先的 a. ancestral
zuān kǒng qì 钻孔器 n. auger
zuàn jìn 钻进 n plunge
zuàn shí 钻石 n diamond
zuǐ 嘴 n. mouth
zuì 罪 n. offence
zuì è 罪恶 n. sin
zuì fàn 罪犯 n convict
zuì fàn 罪犯 n criminal
zuì fàn 罪犯 n culprit
zuì fàn 罪犯 n. malefactor
zuì rén 罪人 n. sinner
zuì xíng 罪行 n. misdeed
zuì chū de 最初的 a. initial
zuì dà de 最大的 a. maximum
zuì dà xiàn dù 最大限度 n
   maximum
zuì dà xiàn dù 最大限度 n
   utmost
zuì dī diǎn 最低点 n. nadir
zuì duō 最多 adv. most
zuì duō 最多 n most
zuì gāo de 最高的 a. paramount
zuì gāo de 最高的 a. supreme
zuì gāo dì wèi 最高地位 n.
   supremacy
zuì gāo jí 最高级 n. superlative
zuì gāo quán wēi 最高权威 n.
   majesty
zuì hòu 最后 adv. eventually
zuì hòu 最后 adv. last
zuì hòu 最后 n last
zuì hòu 最后 adv. lastly
zuì hòu 最后 adv. ultimately
zuì hòu de 最后的 a final
zuì hòu de 最后的 a. last1
zuì hòu de bù fen 最厚的部分
   n. thick
zuì hòu tōng dié 最后通牒 n.
   ultimatum
zuì hòu yí gè 最后一个 n.
   omega
zuì huài de 最坏的 a worst
zuì huài de shì qíng 最坏的事情
   n. worst

zuì jìn 最近 *adv.* lately

zuì jìn 最近 *adv.* recently

zuì jìn de 最近的 *a.* proximate

zuì jìn de 最近的 *a.* recent

zuì shàng de 最上的 *a.* superlative

zuì shǎo 最少 *a.* least

zuì shǎo de 最少的 *a.* minimal

zuì shǎo de 最少的 *a* minimum

zuì shǎo xiàn dù 最少限度 *n.* minimum

zuì shì tiáo jiàn 最适条件 *n.* optimum

zuì shì yí de 最适宜的 *a* optimum

zuì xiǎo 最小 *adv.* least

zuì xīn de 最新的 *a.* up-to-date

zuì zhòng yào de 最重要的 *a* foremost

zuì zhòng yào de 最重要的 *a.* primary

zuì zhòng yào de 最重要的 *a* principal

zūn chóng 尊崇 *n.* homage

zūn jìng 尊敬 *n* esteem

zūn jìng 尊敬 *v.t* esteem

zūn jìng 尊敬 *v.t* honour

zūn jìng 尊敬 *v.t.* respect

zūn jìng 尊敬 *v.t.* revere

zūn jìng 尊敬 *n.* reverence

zūn jìng 尊敬 *n.* veneration

zūn jìng de 尊敬的 *a.* reverent

zūn yán 尊严 *n* dignity

zūn zhòng 尊重 *n* deference

zūn zhòng 尊重 *n.* respect

zūn cóng 遵从 *n.* conformity

zūn shǒu 遵守 *v.i.* adhere

zūn shǒu 遵守 *n.* adherence

zuó rì 昨日 *n.* yesterday

zuó tiān 昨天 *adv.* yesterday

zuó wǎn de 昨晚的 *a* overnight

zuǒ 左 *n.* left

zuǒ bian de 左边的 *a.* left

zuǒ pài 左派 *n* leftist

zuǒ lún shǒu qiāng 左轮手枪 *n.* revolver

zuò … de mó xíng 作…的模型 *v.t.* model

zuò chuān suō shì yùn dòng 作穿梭式运动 *v.t.* shuttle

zuò dǎ yóu shī de rén 作打油诗的人 *n.* rhymester

zuò dīng dāng shēng 作叮当声 *v.i.* jingle

zuò è de 作恶的 *a.* maleficent

zuò fèi 作废 *v.t.* invalidate

zuò hū lū shēng 作呼噜声 *v.i.* grunt

zuò jì hao de rén 作记号的人 *n.* marker

zuò mó nǐ biáo yǎn 作摹拟表演 *v.i* mime

zuò pǐn 作品 *n* composition

zuò pǐn 作品 *n* creation

zuò sān fèn 作三份 *n.* triplication

zuò sī guāng chú lǐ 作丝光处理 *v.t.* mercerize

zuò xù 作序 *v.t.* preface

zuò wéi… de kāi tóu 作为…的开头 *v.t.* prelude

zuò zhàn 作战 *v.i.* war

zuò zhě 作者 *n.* author

zuò zhě 作者 *n.* writer

zuò zhěn tou 作枕头 *v.t.* pillow

zuò 坐 *v.i.* sit

zuò wèi 座位 *n.* seat

zuò 做 *prep.* as

zuò 做 *v.t.* commit

zuò 做 *v.t* do

zuò biāo jì yú 做标记于 *v.t* mark

zuò chéng guàn tóu shí pǐn 做成罐头食品 *v.t.* tin

zuò huài shì 做坏事 *v.i.* misbehave

zuò mǎi mai 做买卖 *v.i.* traffic

zuò mèng 做梦 *v.i.* dream

zuò péng you 做朋友 *v.t.* befriend